THE AMERICAN PAST
Conflicting Interpretations of the Great Issues

VOLUME I

THE
AMERICAN PAST

CONFLICTING INTERPRETATIONS
OF THE GREAT ISSUES

S E C O N D
E D I T I O N

VOLUME I

Edited by Sidney Fine & Gerald S. Brown

The Macmillan Company, New York   Collier–Macmillan Limited, London

To Jean and Dorothy

First Printing

Earlier edition, entitled *The American Past,* Volume I, copyright 1961 by
The Macmillan Company.
Library of Congress catalog card number: 65-15184
THE MACMILLAN COMPANY, NEW YORK
COLLIER–MACMILLAN CANADA, LTD., TORONTO, ONTARIO
Printed in the United States of America

PREFACE
TO THE REVISED EDITION

The present edition retains the basic pattern of organization of the first edition, the reception of which by teachers and students alike has been most gratifying to the editors. Approximately one third of the selections in this edition are new. Some of the new selections replace pieces of historical writing used for the same topics in the first edition; others have been paired to form entirely new topics. The new selections, in addition to sharpening the focus of conflict and enhancing the teachability of the work, help to keep *The American Past* abreast of the scholarship in American history that has become available since the appearance of the first edition.

The editors are pleased to express here their gratitude to both teachers and students for their helpful comments on the first edition.

Sidney Fine
Gerald S. Brown

Preface to the First Edition

This book has three main features: it brings into sharp focus the major issues of the American past; it presents conflicting interpretations of these issues; and it draws for its selections upon historical literature which is often relatively inaccessible to the college student. The literature presented here is taken from the professional historical journals, from periodicals of a more general nature, and from monographs and other works. Each of the items selected, in the editors' view, makes a distinct, individual contribution to our knowledge of a controversial historical problem.

For each of the great issues selected, two historians present either directly conflicting interpretations or interpretations which illuminate the whole problem from complementary, but essentially different, approaches or emphases. A glance through the table of contents will show that many of the writers represented here are among the great historians of this century. One of the purposes which the editors had in view in bringing this body of historical writing together was to introduce American college students to good historical writing upon their own past, in a sense, by their own historians, men who, in the overwhelming majority, are still living and still active in the profession. Each historian is represented by a substantial piece of writing within the limits of which he could, so to speak, move around and develop his interpretation in some depth and with that degree of sophistication which characterizes the mature writing of history. The editors have deliberately avoided the snippets and shreds and the mélange of primary and secondary materials which so often typify volumes of this kind. It is hoped that it is history with style and meaning which is presented here.

The seventeen pairs of selections in Volume I, edited by Gerald S. Brown, pertain to the period before 1865; the seventeen pairs of selections in Volume II, edited by Sidney Fine, to the years since Appomattox. The two volumes are designed to supplement the textbook and the lectures in the survey course in American history. Each pair of selections is preceded by a brief introduction which places the two interpretations in their historical and historiographical setting and which points up the nature of the conflict between them. It is expected that the selections will serve to stimulate discussion and thought concerning the principal themes of American history, and will help to give the reader an appreciation of the nature of the historical process, and of the variety and the richness of contemporary historical writing.

S. F.
G. S. B.

Contents

I

The Puritan Leadership: Glacial or Humanitarian?

II

Democracy in Colonial America: Fact or Fiction?

Contents

VI

The Confederation Period:
Federalist (Radical) vs. Nationalist (Conservative)

VII

The Constitution: Economic Determinism or
Eighteenth-Century Political Theory?

VIII

Alexander Hamilton: Realist or Idealist?

Contents

IX

The Causes of the War of 1812:
Manifest Destiny or Maritime Rights?

X

The Ideas of the Monroe Doctrine:
Adamsonian, Jeffersonian, or Monrovian?

XI

The American West As Symbol and Myth:
Poetic Inspiration or Pragmatic Perspective?

Contents

XII

American Negro Slavery:
U. B. Phillips vs. Revisionist Historians

XIII

The Jacksonians and the Bank:
Democrats in Principle or Democrats by Trade?

XIV

John C. Calhoun: Philosopher of Liberty
or Marx of the Master Class?

XV

Manifest Destiny: A Mystique or
an Extension of the Area of Freedom?

Contents

XVI

The Proslavery Argument: Internal Defense or External Aggression?

XVII

The Civil War: Repressible or Irrepressible Conflict?

I

The Puritan Leadership:
Glacial or Humanitarian?

INTRODUCTION

There have been two conflicting interpretations of the place of the Puritan leadership—ministerial and magisterial—in the life of colonial America.

One view running from Charles Francis and Brooks Adams through James Truslow Adams, Vernon L. Parrington, and Thomas J. Wertenbaker saw the Puritan leadership as repressive, intolerant, and imposing a "theologico-glacial" period upon the life of the intellect in Massachusetts from the Cambridge Synod of 1637 to the era of the American Revolution. "As a period," wrote Charles Francis Adams, "it was singularly barren and almost inconceivably somber." [1] Thomas J. Wertenbaker generalizing very broadly wrote, "No truthful historian will withhold from New England the credit due her for her part in the creation and moulding of the nation. But most of the contributions were made after the fall of the Puritan oligarchy, and the men to whom the chief credit is due were not its supporters, but, on the contrary, those who rebelled against it." [2]

Another view of the Puritan leadership attributes to it qualities of a very different nature. Clifford K. Shipton, Samuel Eliot Morison, and Perry Miller, though differing in emphasis, do not interpret the period of the Puritan leadership as a "glacial" period. Morison states emphatically, "Now all my studies of early New England go to prove that there was no 'glacial' period; that interest in literature and scholarship grew rather than diminished during the entire course of the seventeenth century; that the dominant Puritan clergy, far from being indifferent to culture and hostile to science as the Adams school briskly asserted, did everything possible to stimulate, promote, and even produce intellectual activity. Moreover, it was largely the clergy who persuaded a poor and struggling people to set up schools and a college which continued to serve the community in later generations." [3]

The two selections presented below supply examples which illustrate this conflict of interpretation. James Truslow Adams, who in 1921 received the Pulitzer Prize for the book from which the first selection is taken, presents an unsympathetic approach to the problem of the Puritan leadership. Clifford K. Shipton in the second selection, in a paper read before the American Historical Association, directly challenges the main thesis that Adams advances.

---

[1] Charles Francis Adams, *Massachusetts: Its Historians and Its History* (1893), p. 64.

[2] Thomas J. Wertenbaker, *The Puritan Oligarchy* (1947), p. 345.

[3] Samuel Eliot Morison, *The Intellectual Life of Colonial New England* (1956), p. VI.

The New Order

James Truslow Adams

Just a year before the events of that 18th of April,* . . . the Reverend Increase Mather had sailed for England as representative of "many congregations" in the colony, in an effort to secure from King James the restoration of an assembly, confirmation of land-titles, and as many of the old charter privileges as possible. Although he was more than once received in audience by the King, before the Revolution brought the negotiations to an abrupt end, it had been evident for some time that the churches' agent was likely to gain little more than fair words and memories of royal interviews.[1] He had, however, succeeded in making useful friends, one among whom, Sir Henry Ashurst, became associated with him as agent, and another, Lord Wharton, introduced him to the Prince of Orange a month before the coronation, enabling him thus early to present a petition for the restoration of the charter.[2]

Three days after that interview, a circular letter was prepared, to be sent to all the English colonies, ordering officials then in office to continue to administer affairs temporarily until the new government could send different instructions.[3] Word of this was given to Mather by Jephson, a cousin of Wharton and an under-secretary to the King. Mather's alarm, when he heard of it, would seem to indicate that he either had definite information of the uprising planned in Boston, or very strong suspicions of what might occur. Prince William had already been two months in

From James Truslow Adams, *The Founding of New England* (Boston: The Atlantic Monthly Press, 1921), pp. 431–456. Reprinted by permission.

* Editor's note: As part of a policy of colonial consolidation, James II projected a Dominion of New England that would also include New Jersey and New York. These colonies were to be ruled over by a single, strong, royal governor, and the legislatures were to be abolished. Sir Edmund Andros arrived as a governor in December, 1686. The government was not a popular one and "the events of that 18th April," referred to here, are the events that overthrew the Andros regime on April 18, 1689. The news of the invasion of England by Prince William of Orange, which resulted in the overthrow of James II and the victory of Parliament, arrived in Boston just before the overthrow of Andros.

[1] Mather sailed April 7, 1688. *Andros Tracts*, vols. III, pp. 130 ff., and II, pp. 274 ff. As the addresses which he carried with him were unsigned, and as they were merely issued "in the name of many Congregations," it is impossible to say whom he really represented when he sailed.

[2] *Andros Tracts*, vol. III, pp. 146 f.   [3] *Cal. State Pap., Col., 1689–92*, pp. 4, 7.

England, and it is incredible that Mather should not have sent home some word of an event of such overwhelming importance to the colony as the overthrow of the Stuart monarchy. His later censure of the colonists for not having promptly resumed the charter government, instead of temporizing, and his laying the blame for his partial failure in England upon their not having done so, may also suggest the nature of the advice sent by him.[4] He could hardly have expected the new King to determine offhand the form of government for the Dominion of New England, then constituting over one half of the empire in America. An order for a few months' longer continuance of the Andros government, under the circumstances, would not have been a serious matter, unless that government had already been overthrown, or was about to be, by the colonists' acts. However that may be, Mather and Sir William Phips, now also temporarily in London, petitioned against the dispatch of the letter to New England, and succeeded in having orders issued instead for a new governor in place of Andros, and a temporary form of government, to include a popular assembly.[5]

News of the revolution at Boston reached London the last week in June, and soon letters from Randolph and others supplied the English government with the details of what had occurred.[6] Toward the end of July, orders were issued to the provisional government in Boston to send Andros and the other prisoners to England "forthwith," on the first ship bound thither, and that they be treated civilly.[7] The order was not received in Massachusetts until November 24, and then was not complied with.[8] Although two ships were ready to sail in December, an embargo was laid upon the vessels, and it was not until the middle of the next February that the prisoners, after treatment which they considered unnecessarily harsh, were allowed to start.[9] It had probably been felt that their presence in London might interfere with the success of the colony's agents.

The leaders who had planned the Boston revolution had undoubtedly desired the eventual restoration of the old charter, and the return of the Church and themselves into control of the government. It is probable also that the majority of the inhabitants wished for the reëstablishment of charter government, which they looked upon as ensuring themselves against arbitrary acts by England or English officials. The desires of the people as a whole, however, were by no means identical with those of the leaders who formed the temporary government in Boston, or were acting as agents in

---

[4] *Andros Tracts*, vol. II, p. 291. *Cf.*, however, Cotton Mather, *Diary*, vol. I, p. 138 *n.*

[5] *Andros Tracts*, vols. II, p. 274, and III, p. 148; Palfrey, *History*, vol. III, p. 591 *n.*; *Cal. State Pap., Col., 1689–92*, pp. 6, 8, 11.

[6] Sewall, *Diary*, vol. I, pp. 261 *f.*

[7] *Randolph Papers*, vol. IV, pp. 290 *f.*; *Andros Tracts*, vol. III, p. 111. The list of prisoners is in *Cal. State Pap., Col., 1689–92*, p. 109.

[8] *Randolph Papers*, vol. V, p. 23.

[9] *Randolph Papers*, vols. II, pp. 110, 116, 118, 121, v, pp. 20, 26 *ff.*, and vi, pp. 325, 331, 334; *Andros Tracts*, vol. I, p. 174; *Cal. State Pap., Col., 1689–92*, p. 263.

England, virtually all of whom were of the narrowest clerical party. When the fall of the Andros government necessitated the formation of another, those who had taken the lead on the day of its overthrow associated twenty-two others with themselves, and formed a "Council for the safety of the people and conservation of the peace," with Bradstreet and Wait Winthrop in the chief offices.[10] The decision of a convention, held May 8, as to a new government was not considered sufficiently decisive, and another was convened, which included representatives from fifty-four towns. Hutchinson says that "two days were spent in disputes," and that "the people without doors were also much divided in sentiments." Apparently the representatives of forty towns voted in favor of resuming the charter, and those of fourteen against it.[11] A compromise, not only between those for and against the charter, but also between those for and against the expediency of immediate resumption, resulted in the formation of a government composed of those officials who had been chosen in the last election under the old charter. Within a few weeks, Plymouth, which had never had a charter, and Connecticut and Rhode Island, the legal proceedings against which had never been consummated, also quietly resumed their former governments.[12]

Of the points to be considered in granting a new charter for Massachusetts, or the resumption of the old one, those most likely to be discussed by the people—outside of the question of land-titles, as to which the colonists were naturally unanimous—would be the assembly, the governorship, and the franchise. As to the justice and necessity of a representative body for legislation and taxation, there was probably no difference of opinion in the colony. For that matter, . . . there was virtually none in the English government at home, or among its officials in Massachusetts, with the all-important exception of the late, but unlamented, monarch. As to the governor, it was natural that the majority of the people should prefer a chief magistrate elected by themselves rather than one appointed by England, though it is not at all certain that they were right. The old oligarchical government had grossly misused its power, and those who had a keen recollection of what toleration had meant in the days before Andros, and who realized the military danger in the old system of small, disunited, and contentious colonies, can certainly be accused of no lack of "patriotism" in their preference for a royal governor, to serve as a check upon the intolerance and military incapacity of the old régime.

Probably the most disputed point, and the one on which the leaders in control were opposed to the best opinion among the people at large, was that of the franchise. The question was, whether Massachusetts was to remain the private preserve of a persecuting religious sect, or was to be

---

[10] Hutchinson, *History*, vol. I, p. 340.   [11] *Ibid.*, p. 344; *Mather Papers*, pp. 708 *f.*
[12] *Plymouth Colonial Records*, vol. VI, pp. 206 *ff.*; *R. I. Records*, vol. III, p. 266; *Cal. State Pap., Col., 1689–92*, pp. 34, 62; *Conn. Col. Records*, vol. III, pp. 250 *ff.*, 463 *ff.*

the home of a free people. For half a century, the leaders and the old church party had resisted, by every means in their power,—by fraud, trickery, and bloodshed, as well as by legitimate influence,—the granting of a voice in the government to any individual who could not be counted upon to uphold the power and authority of the priesthood and the Church. Little by little, that power and authority had been declining as, on the one hand, the people had grown in intellectual independence, and, on the other, the leaders had shown themselves less and less worthy of their exalted position. But, in England, Mather was exerting every means to fasten the shackles permanently on the colony by insisting upon the old Congregational test for the suffrage. In acting thus, he claimed to be the representative, not of one element, but of the whole people, a majority of whom would have been disfranchised by his success. What the people themselves were thinking was shown by the vote at the town-meeting of Watertown on May 20, 1689, to choose representatives for the convention. After it had been agreed that they should be instructed to vote for the resumption of the charter, until further orders were received from England, it was added, as the only but significant restriction, that the number of freemen "be inlarged further then have been the Custom of this Colony formerly." [13] In this crisis, therefore, . . . it is necessary to distinguish clearly the two separate struggles for freedom—that between the colony as a whole and England, and that between the liberal element among the people and the narrow oligarchical leaders, lay and clerical, of the theocratical party in control.

The weakness of the provisional government, due both to the character of the men composing it, and to the lack of a clear mandate from the people, was evident from the start. When, for example, Dudley was released from prison on account of illness, on a bond for £1000, and confined to his own house, a mob broke into it and carried him back to jail. The keeper refused to retain him without a warrant, and he was again confined, in another house. The mob having discovered this, the excitement became so great, and the control of the government was so slight, that Bradstreet, the Governor, had to write to Dudley, and abjectly beg him to reincarcerate himself voluntarily, as otherwise the authorities could not protect his family.[14] A fortnight later, a writer from Boston stated that there was much division among the people, and that "every man is a Governor." Another wrote, July 31, 1689, that "all is confusion"; and, in October, Elizabeth Usher sent word to her husband that "there is little trade and the ferment is as great as ever." A few days later, Governor Brad-

---

[13] *Watertown Records,* vol. II, p. 37.

[14] *Cal. State Pap., Col., 1689–92,* pp. 111, 120. Bradstreet's letter is cited from Board of Trade Mss., by Kimball, *Joseph Dudley,* pp. 52 f. The *Cal. State Pap.* reference gives the bail as £10,000. I have followed Kimball in stating it at £1000.

street himself was complaining to the Lords of Trade of the people who "are busy to weaken the hands of the Government," and lamenting the Indian depredations and the empty treasury.[15]

Almost the first act of the provisional government had been to draw off and disperse many of the troops left by Andros to guard the eastern province, while the discipline of all was ruined by the dismissing of a number of officers on religious and political grounds.[16] The Indians realized the situation, and, with the arms and ammunition previously supplied to them by the Boston merchants, descended upon the unhappy settlers. The fort at Pemaquid, the great importance of which had always been denied by the colonists because it was urged by Andros, was captured, owing to the carelessness of the small garrison left there, and about twenty houses were destroyed by the savages. At Saco, Oyster River, and other places, houses were burned, and the inhabitants murdered, and all the horrors of Indian warfare once more came thick upon the border. The sudden disintegration of the Dominion, the inability of the separate colonies to act together quickly and harmoniously, and the lack of authority and military ability, left the frontier defenseless. In April, 1689, war had been declared between France and England, and the colonies seemed helpless before the menace of the French and Indians from the north.

A few weeks after Massachusetts had disbanded the forces that Andros had collected, the government attempted to raise more by a draft. The people questioned both its authority to press men, and its ability to pay them, and, for the most part, flatly refused either to volunteer or to be drafted.[17] A large part of Maine and the country eastward was overrun, and in October the inhabitants were reported to be flocking into Boston.[18] In that month, Bradstreet wrote to the Lords of Trade that there had been great depredations in Maine, New Hampshire, and even in Massachusetts, and that the government's efforts to check them had been of no avail, although a joint force had finally been raised by Plymouth, Connecticut, and Massachusetts.[19] Part of this force, wretchedly clothed and poorly supplied, had been sent eastward under Colonel Church, the veteran of Philip's War, but had accomplished little. Indeed, so carelessly was it outfitted and officered, that it was only when unexpectedly forced into action that the unhappy soldiers discovered that the ammunition did not fit their guns.

In January, 1690, the people of Maine sent a petition to England, complaining of lack of protection by Massachusetts, begging for help, and plac-

---

[15] *Cal. State Pap., Col., 1689–92*, pp. 82, 111, 120, 158, 167.

[16] *Andros Tracts*, vol. III, pp. 24 ff. The colony's defense against Andros's charges in this connection is weak and far from truthful. *Ibid.*, pp. 34 ff.

[17] *Cal. State Pap., Col., 1689–92*, pp. 111, 120.

[18] *Ibid.*, p. 158.   [19] *Ibid.*, p. 167.

ing their losses at three hundred lives and £40,000 in goods.[20] The people of Great Island, New Hampshire, likewise wrote to the mother-country, complaining of Massachusetts and of the danger from the French and Indians.[21] In midwinter, came the frightful massacres at Schenectady and Salmon Falls; and even Bradstreet and the Council, on behalf of Massachusetts herself, wrote to the Lords of Trade, begging for arms and ammunition. The request was granted, and stores, including two hundred barrels of powder, were ordered shipped to Boston by the English government, although too late for the purpose that the colonists had had in mind but had not stated.[22] In addition, the English navy was active in providing convoys for all the colonial shipping, including that of New England.[23] Such items in the English records as "the convoys for Virginia, Maryland, Newfoundland and New England will sail on the 31st. October, and that for Africa on the 20th.," or a list of ninety merchant ships, forming only one of the convoyed fleets from America, or the request by Massachusetts for a royal ship-of-war to guard her coastwise commerce, were the best answers to such premature "patriots" as the Reverend Joshua Moody, who was telling the men of Boston that they had no dependence on the Crown, and that the power of England was of no authority over them.[24]

The plan which had been conceived, and for which additional resources were needed, was that of attacking the French, who were the driving force behind the Indian raids, at their headquarters in Canada, instead of carrying on an almost impossible system of defensive tactics along a frontier several hundred miles long. The theory was good; but to put it in practice would require leaders with military ability, and a whole-hearted willingness on the part of the separate colonies to sink their petty jealousies and act together. Unfortunately, both the ability and the spirit of coöperation were lacking.

Massachusetts, indeed, carried out an easy and successful raid upon Acadia, whither Sir William Phips sailed from Nantasket, on April 28, 1690, with five ships and several hundred soldiers.[25] Phips, who is said to have been one of twenty-six children of a Maine backwoodsman, and who in his youth was unable to read or write, had acquired wealth and social position, first, by the not very original method of marrying a rich widow, and, secondly, by the more unusual one of locating a sunken treasure-ship with £300,000 sterling, of which his share was a considerable one. He had already married the widow. When he arrived at Port Royal, in command of the Massachusetts fleet, he had no difficulty in securing the surrender of the fort, as his force outnumbered the garrison ten to one. A succinct diary tells,

---

[20] *Ibid.*, p. 212.   [21] *Ibid.*, pp. 262 *f.*
[22] *Ibid.*, pp. 240, 273, 282 *f.*   [23] *Ibid.*, pp. 322, 575, 577 *f.*, 675.
[24] *Randolph Papers*, vol. VI, p. 295.
[25] The number of men and vessels varies in different accounts. *Cf. Cal. State Pap., Col., 1689–92*, pp. 275 *f.*, 376; Parkman, *Frontenac*, p. 247.

in admirable style, the important events of his short sojourn, it being pertinent to note that the Reverend Joshua Moody was his chaplain. "May, 11. The fort surrendered. May, 12. Went ashore to search for hidden goods. We cut down the cross, rifled the church, pulled down the high altar, and broke their images. May, 13. Kept gathering plunder all day. May, 14. The inhabitants swore allegiance to King William and Queen Mary." [26] All very satisfying, doubtless, to the Reverend Mr. Moody. But, unfortunately, the plunder, about the distribution of which some unpleasant things were later said in Boston, was found to amount to £3000 less than the cost of the expedition.[27]

The easy conquest, however, inspired larger hopes, while the common danger to all the colonies might have been counted upon to induce them to lay aside their particularism, and join in a common effort, if anything could. A meeting of commissioners from Massachusetts, Plymouth, Connecticut, and New York was held at the latter city, and a combined attack on Canada was planned.[28] A land force, made up of troops from Maryland and the four colonies just mentioned, was to march from Albany to capture Montreal, while, simultaneously, a fleet from Boston was to attack Quebec. There seems to have been no realization of the difficulties of carrying out such a complex joint operation, although, to the very letter notifying the English government of the grandiose scheme, had to be added a postscript, to the effect that there were already "great distractions amongst the Forces." Everything went wrong. New York provided only one hundred and fifty of the four hundred men promised. The hundred and sixty sent from Massachusetts were recalled on news of the sacking of Casco. Plymouth sent none, and Connecticut less than her quota; the Indian allies, always uncertain, declined to move, and there were desertions among the whites. The colonies fell out over the appointment of a commander, agreement, but not harmony, finally being attained with the selection of Winthrop.[29] Although the unfortunate force, ill-equipped and badly organized, reached Wood Creek, near the southern end of Lake Champlain, they were unable to advance farther, and, save for a little skirmishing, the whole expedition was a costly failure, demonstrating conclusively that, even in the face of overwhelming danger, the colonies, if left to themselves, were as yet unable to unite in effective action.

Although the naval expedition against Quebec reached its objective, it also was unsuccessful, and was a mixture of farce and tragedy. Phips, who was quite incompetent as the leader of such an undertaking, was put in chief command, and on August 9 sailed from Boston with a force of about twenty-two hundred men, in thirty-two vessels of all sorts, mostly small. For

---

[26] *Cal. State Pap., Col., 1689–92*, pp. 275 f.   [27] *Ibid.*, p. 376.
[28] *N. Y. Col. Docts.*, vol. III, p. 732.
[29] *Ibid.*, vols. IV, p. 194, and III, pp. 727, 752; *Documentary History of New York*, vol. II, p. 266.

some reason, which does not appear, nine weeks were consumed in reaching Quebec, of which the last three were spent within a few days of the city, owing to the lack of a pilot.[30] The failure of the land expedition against Montreal, and Phips's delay in ascending the river, had allowed Frontenac to reach Quebec with reinforcements before the hostile fleet dropped anchor a little below the town. The conqueror of Port Royal first tried the effect of a demand for surrender, and sent a summons "as severe as our four clergymen (who were joined to the Council of War) could make it." [31] Frontenac treated it with contempt, and refused to send more than a verbal reply, except by his cannon.

Phips then called another council of war, and delayed action while seven hundred more reinforcements arrived at the city. The plan finally decided upon was a simultaneous attack by land and water. About twelve hundred men were to be landed, and after crossing a small river, were to ascend to the rear of the city, which they were to attempt to carry by assault, while the fleet bombarded it from the front. The land forces, under Major Walley, were set on shore, where they remained for some days, unable to advance, and suffering greatly from disease, hunger, and exposure. The necessary and expected support which the fleet was to provide them was almost wholly lacking, and neither boats, ammunition, nor food was supplied in proper quantities. On the other hand, Phips, with a total disregard of the land expedition with which he was supposed to be coöperating, fired away all the fleet's scanty store of powder and shot, expending a considerable portion of it in an unsuccessful effort to hit a picture of the Holy Family, which had been hung on the cathedral spire. Nothing having been accomplished by the futile cannonading, except to provide the Quebec gunners with shot for their guns, and the English ammunition being exhausted, the incompetent commander had nothing to do but to order a retreat and return to Boston. The land forces under Walley had behaved well, but in reëmbarking lost all semblance of discipline, took to the boats much like a base-ball crowd to the street cars, and abandoned their cannon.[32] The self-flattering belief of democracy that training of any sort is a waste of time, and that, in military affairs, competent commanders and disciplined troops can be found at any moment in a crisis, had again proved a costly fallacy.

In November, Phips reached Boston with the first of his armada; and other vessels continued to straggle in at intervals until February. Some of them were never heard of at all. As the colony gradually came to a realiza-

---

[30] Walley's Journal, in Hutchinson, *History*, vol. I, p. 477; *Cal. State Pap., Col., 1689–92*, p. 384. Most of the contemporary accounts, French and English, are conveniently brought together by E. Myrand, in *Sir Wm. Phips devant Québec*; Quebec, 1893.

[31] *Cal. State Pap., Col., 1689–92*, p. 384. The summons is in Mather, *Magnalia*, vol. I, p. 186. *Cf.* Parkman, *Frontenac*, p. 279 n.

[32] Parkman, *Frontenac*, p. 287; Walley's Journal, pp. 470 ff.; Phips's own account is in *Cal. State Pap., Col., 1689–92*, p. 45.

tion of the magnitude of the disaster, it was in despair, as it well might be. Few men had fallen in fighting, but, owing to the incompetence and thoughtlessness of the leaders, both civil and military, the mortality had been great. The lack of clothes and food, the cold, smallpox, fever, and exposure had killed men by scores. The loss was estimated as high as a thousand, and certainly ran into many hundreds.[33] Moreover, the government, with an empty treasury, had recklessly financed the expedition by promises to pay, expecting to be reimbursed from the anticipated plunder. There was no plunder, and the colossal failure had cost £50,000.[34] A Boston merchant wrote to a correspondent in London that, since assuming office, the new government had involved the colony to the extent of, possibly, £200,000, and that it was almost "run aground." [35]

Virtually bankrupt, and with the discharged soldiers and other creditors clamoring for their pay, the government took the fiist step on the road to paper money, which was later to cost it dear. The debts were ordered paid with certificates receivable for taxes, ranging in denomination from two shillings to ten pounds.[36] An original issue of £7000 was increased in a few months to £40,000; and owing to the government's lack of credit and stability, the notes fell quickly in value, and were soon at a discount of thirty to fifty per cent.[37] Taxes rose to formerly unheard-of amounts, and the depression both of business and of sentiment became extreme.[38] Cotton Mather was said to be satisfied to attribute all the colony's troubles to the presence of the Episcopalian congregation worshiping in the King's Chapel; and the Governor and Council wrote to England, pointing out that the whole disaster must have been due to God, who had "spit in our faces"—a phrase for a state paper which darts a vivid light, in several directions, among the colony's elect.[39] There were many, however, who were inclined to lay the blame for the growing ruin of all their affairs in less exalted quarters. The government did its best to suppress or refute all criticism, and the press, whose lack of freedom had been so bitterly complained of only a few months before under Andros, was quickly taken in hand again, and a stricter censorship than ever established.[40] Although nothing could be printed except propaganda in favor of the provisional government, the increasing discontent of many in all classes made itself heard, both in the colony and in England.

Despite all that has been written of the town-meeting, and the general

---

[33] *Ibid.*, pp. 376 f., 385, 369, 387.

[34] *Cal. State Pap., Col., 1689–92*, pp. 377, 369; Parkman, *Frontenac*, p. 297; *Andros Tracts*, vol. II, p. 238.

[35] *Cal. State Pap., Col., 1689–92*, p. 377.

[36] A. McF. Davis, *Currency and Banking in the Province of Massachusetts Bay* (New York, 1900), vol. I, pp. 10 ff.

[37] Davis, *Currency*, vol. I, pp. 16 f.; *Cal. State Pap., Col., 1689–92*, p. 377.

[38] *Ibid.*, pp. 385, 387, 399.   [39] *Ibid.*, p. 369; *Andros Tracts*, vol. III, p. 53.

[40] Duniway, *Freedom of the Press*, pp. 67 ff.

impression that the average New Englander was almost solely a political and religious animal, there is little evidence to prove that the ordinary man in that section cared any more about government than the ordinary man in Virginia or Maryland. In fact, at a little later period, the more accurate election returns would seem to indicate that he then cared even less.[41] The small minority that ran the government and the churches was naturally active and vocal. But the fact that four fifths of the people were reasonably content to join no church, and to have no voice in the government, certainly does not argue, in that time and place, any very high degree of political, religious, or intellectual interest as compared with the rest of America. In the blue haze of that incense in honor of the colonial New Englanders, lighted by themselves and tended by their descendants, we are apt, a little absurdly sometimes, to lose sight of coarse fundamentals. . . .

Such very truthful remarks as that already quoted, made by the residents of Cape Ann, when they replied to an early whiff of the incense by saying that their main end had been fish, cannot be too much emphasized. They are as precious as they are rare. Impersonal love of liberty is about as common as uncombined oxygen; and so long as the average man could catch cod, sell whiskey to the Indians, raise crops on land he felt was his own, or stand at his little shop-counter, he did not much care—much as, by way of conversation, he might talk—about the governor in Boston or the king in England. But let him believe that either was threatening his God-given right to accumulate pine-tree shillings, and there would be trouble.

This, the Governor and Council, by their evident inability to handle the situation, were rapidly bringing about. There is nothing unexpected in the cry now beginning to ascend to England, that "we mightily want a government," [42] or unpatriotic in the attitude of those who did not desire the complete restoration of the former conditions. In England, however, that was exactly what the agents, with Mather at their head, were striving for. Their charges against Andros had entirely broken down, as had their hopes of a restoration of the old charter.[43] Attempts to have it restored by Parliamentary action or by a Writ of Error had both failed, and the agents' efforts were thereafter directed to obtaining from the King a new charter, with as favorable terms as possible.[44] It may be pointed out that the agents were not representatives of the colony as a whole, but only of the old church party, and that the terms which would be considered favorable by them would be such as would ensure continued control by the theocratic element.

The echoes of the events in the colony that we have been describing had

---

[41] McKinley, *Suffrage Franchise*, pp. 47, 357. *Cf.*, also, L. G. Tyler, in *William and Mary Quarterly*, vol. xxvi, p. 278.

[42] *Cal. State Pap., Col., 1689–92*, p. 300.

[43] No one would sign even the brief charges submitted, and they were dismissed. *Andros Tracts*, vols. ii, pp. 173 *ff.*, i, pp. 150 *ff.*, and iii, pp. 19 *ff.*

[44] *Andros Tracts*, vols. ii, pp. 15 *ff.*, 75 *ff.*, and iii, pp. 149 *ff.*

been sounding in England with increasing loudness and frequency, in the shape of private letters and formal addresses.[45] Mather, indeed, attempted to minimize all complaints from the colony, from whatever source, and was somewhat reckless in his imputations and disregard of facts. Thirty-four petitioners of Charlestown, including many substantial men, he character- ized as "a few bankrupt Publicans and Vagabonds," "persons brought up and educated in all manner of Debauchery and Depravation," "greedy as Hell." [46] In his effort to prove the great prosperity and importance of New England under the old theocratic government, he grotesquely claimed that, whereas New England had turned a wilderness into a fruitful field, most of the other colonies had "turned a fruitful field into a barren wilderness." The facts were probably far better known to the Lords of Trade than they were to Mather, and these showed that the population of the other colonies outnumbered that of New England more than two to one, while of Eng- land's colonial trade seven eighths was with the "barren wildernesses" of the sugar and tobacco colonies, and only one ninth with New England's "fruitful field." [47] In that very year, of the two hundred and twenty-six ships sailing from England to colonial ports, but seven were bound for New England.[48]

Mather's anonymous but scarcely veiled threats that the colony would revolt, if the old theocracy and its charter privileges were not restored,[49] failed to impress the government, which, however, had been seriously en- deavoring to meet all the legitimate aspirations of the colonists. Mather, who had had several interviews with King William, and had enlisted the sympathy of the Queen,[50] had little difficulty in getting a number of pro- posals altered, when the reasons were pointed out; but the King and gov- ernment were both firm in favor of a governor appointed by England, and a property, not a religious, qualification for the franchise. Mather bitterly opposed both these suggestions, particularly that relating to the suffrage, saying he would sooner part with his life than consent. The ministers of state, however, were growing somewhat tired of the clergyman's representa- tions and misrepresentations, and curtly told him that his consent was

---

[45] *Cf.*, besides the authorities already cited, *Cal. State Pap., Col., 1689–92*, pp. 212, 213 (2), 343, 366, 368, 409.

[46] *Andros Tracts*, vol. II, pp. 230, 240 *ff*. A report to the Board of Trade, in regard to these "vagabond" signers, probably exaggerated on the other side, puts down two as worth £12,000 each, two at £10,000, three at £6000, two at £5000, two at £4000, five at £3000, etc. *Cal. State Pap., Col., 1689–92*, p. 422.

[47] *Andros Tracts*, vol. II, pp. 254 *f*.; *A Century of Population*, p. 9, gives 82,000 in New England and 124,000 in the south, in 1690. To the latter figure must be added those for the island colonies; Beer, *Old Colonial System*, vol. I, pp. 41 *ff*. The trade figures are for 1697.

[48] Beer, *Old Colonial System*. Of the remainder, 103 went to Virginia and Maryland, 71 to Barbadoes, 23 to the Leeward Islands, 20 to Jamaica, one to Bermuda, and one to Pennsylvania.

[49] *Andros Tracts*, vol. II, pp. 245, 248, 269. [50] *Ibid.*, vols. II, pp. 277 *ff*., and III, pp. 156 *ff*.

neither "expected nor desired"; that he was not a plenipotentiary from a sovereign state; and that, if it was true, as he claimed, that Massachusetts would not accept the new charter, then she could "take what would follow," for "his Majesty was resolved to settle the Countrey." [51]

The obvious fact that the colonists were not by any means unanimous in their desire for the old charter, the genuine wish of the English government to provide toleration, the long record of delays and bickerings in the colony's relations with England, and the necessity for a different organization if the Navigation Acts were to be enforced, probably all had their influence in shaping the government's policy. Of still greater immediate import, perhaps, was the military situation. With the prospect of a life-and-death struggle with France, the Franco-British frontier in America became a sphere of the highest military interest and importance; and, aside from previous records or any preconceived ideas on the part of English statesmen, the colonists had, within the past year, shown that, if left to themselves, they were unable properly to safeguard either their own homes or the interests of the Empire.

As a matter of fact, the new charter, as finally granted, was a far better document than the one desired by Mather. What he had tried to get was a constitution for a virtually independent theocratic state, the fundamental law of which should provide for the perpetual retention of political power in the hands of a religious sect. What the English government granted was a charter by which the colony took her natural place, indeed, in an empire without whose protection she was defenseless, but which, at the same time, gave to her citizens a degree of self-government and political freedom which the theocratic group would never have been willing to concede. The substitution of a moderate property qualification for the franchise, in place of any other whatsoever, at once placed the colony abreast of the most liberal political thought of the day; while local self-government was restored in the form of a popular assembly. Regardless of the whims or religious prejudices of any clique in power, and irrespective of his class or creed, any resident of the colony who had been sufficiently industrious or fortunate to acquire a freehold estate worth forty shillings per annum, or real or personal property to the value of forty pounds, could now claim, as a right, a voice in the government of his commonwealth.[52] Thanks to England, the final deathblow had legally been dealt to the theocracy, and the foundation laid for genuine self-government and religious toleration in the colony. Those elements in its future development which we are apt to consider as typically American had, in fact, in the case of Massachusetts, been forced upon her leaders, fighting against them to the last ditch, by an English King who could hardly speak the language of his subjects.

---

[51] *Andros Tracts*, vols. II, p. 281, and III, p. 165.
[52] The charter is printed in *Colonial Society Massachusetts Publications*, vol. II, pp. 7 *ff*.

One important aspect of this change in the franchise must not be overlooked. Under the old religious test, there had been, within the body of enfranchised voters, no social question. All had possessed the vote, without distinction between rich and poor. The struggle for the franchise, therefore, would always have remained a purely religious one between those within and those without the pale of a particular church. With the abandonment of the religious test, and the substitution of a property qualification, the question became a social one, and the way was opened for that struggle for the democratization of the state and society which became the dominant motive in the Revolution of a century later. The colonies could never have united on a question of religion, or even of trade. The basis had to be so wide as to appeal to the most numerous class in every colony; and that appeal could only be social, and was found to lie in the demand for the abolition of privilege and the extension of democracy.

The new charter of 1691 must be regarded as an honest effort to devise such a governmental system as should allow to the colonists the greatest degree of local liberty consistent with the welfare and administrative necessities of the Empire as a whole, in the light of existing political theory. It cannot too often be pointed out that the colonial period *was* a colonial period, and that the relations subsisting between England and the colonies were necessarily those subsisting between a sovereign state and its dependencies. . . .

*　　*　　*

To many in the colony, however, the change from the old charter form to the new seemed a loss of independence. The former governing element felt that their control had been vastly weakened. The church party anticipated that the end of all things might be due when the Congregational church no longer legally controlled the elections. The presence of a governor and other officials appointed by the Crown, the review of legislation, the right of appeal, and other evidences of the colony having become part of a great organization instead of a practically independent, even if insignificant, little collection of towns, was unwelcome to those who had had a false idea of the rôle which, in that time and place, it was possible for them and the colony to play in the world.

On the other hand, there were very substantial advantages under the new régime. Although, owing to an obscure and probably not very reputable intrigue, New Hampshire was given a separate government, the bounds of the new Massachusetts were extended to include Plymouth, Maine, and the eastern country as far as Nova Scotia.[53] Moreover, the colonists had never really possessed anything like the rights which they had claimed and exer-

---

[53] For the form of government established in New Hampshire, which became a royal province, *vide* Fry, *New Hampshire*, pp. 71 *ff.*

cised under the old charter. The whole system of town government, for example, had been extra-legal. The infliction of the death-penalty was illegal, and there was no question that the colonists had exceeded their rights in taxing the non-freemen. Now all the false reasoning and sophistries that the settlers had indulged in, in their efforts to prove the old charter adequate as the basis of a government, were no longer necessary. Massachusetts at last had, what she had never possessed before, a written constitution, which clearly set forth her form of government, and validated, to a very great extent, those institutions which she had cherished.[54] The royal officials, disliked as their presence might be by the irreconcilables, actually and symbolically brought the colony into relations with the larger life of the empire. In her thought, her commerce, and her political relations, New England's largest colony was at last forced out of that position of defiant isolation which her former leaders had chosen for her, and made to participate, so far as her provincial position allowed, in the main currents of the world's activities. The new charter definitely marked the end of one era and the beginning of another.

This change was more than political and economic. It has been evident from the foregoing narrative that the power of the clergy had been felt in every sphere of the colony's life. In the pulpits, in the schools, in the colleges, in the censorship of the press, in the legislature, even in the councils of war and the courts of justice, their influence had been incalculable. The story of the struggle against it, and of its gradual yielding to defeat, as the people more and more made good their right to believe as they would and live their lives as they chose, has occupied many of our pages. The course of development, however, which was to make Massachusetts the leader of liberal thought among the states, was a long one, and, in part, it was but a reaction and a protest against the theological repression of this earlier period.

Although the charter of 1691 had definitely ended the legalized control of the Congregational church, which was still to maintain a privileged position until 1812, the organization desperately struggled to retain its power. The members of the new government, thanks to the efforts of Mather in England, were nearly all of the clerical party. He had, indeed, succeeded in having the more important offices filled with the most fanatical, or the most subservient, of the men in the colony's public life. His son, the Reverend Cotton Mather, when he heard of the list of officials, wrote ecstatically in his diary: "The time for Favour was now come; the sett Time was come! . . . all the Councellors of the Province are of my own Father's Nomination; and my Father-in-law, with several related unto me, and several

---

[54] *Cf.* Greene, *The Provincial Governor,* pp. 92, 179. For a discussion of the charter, *vide* Osgood, *American Colonies,* vol. III, pp. 439 *ff.*

Brethren of my own church, are among them. The Governour of the Province is not my Enemy but one whom I baptized, namely Sir William Phips, and one of my own Flock, and one of my dearest Friends." [55] He might have added that the savagely bigoted Stoughton was made Deputy Governor.

At the very time when this effort was being made still to control the government, in spite of its altered form, events occurred that gave a staggering blow to that unofficial power which the clergy had been accustomed to exert as the acknowledged intellectual leaders of the community. For, in the generation of 1690, the witchcraft frenzy, in which the clergy took a leading part, brought about the same sort of anti-clerical reaction that had been a result of the Quaker persecutions by them in the generation of 1660.

We shall not concern ourselves with the details of the horrible delusion, which, for the last time in New England, caused the blood of innocent victims to be shed as a result of theological beliefs. They may be found amply set forth elsewhere, and concern rather the antiquarian and the psychologist than the historian.[56] For us, the interest lies in their influence upon the intellectual development of the colony, and the growth of its people.

It is quite true that communities in all ages and places have been occasionally subject to being thrown off their mental balance, and during the period of frenzy or panic have committed acts of folly or crime, for which they have subsequently been heartily repentant. But to state a fact is not to explain it; and to find the underlying cause of the psychologic disturbance in northeastern Massachusetts in 1692—during which two hundred persons were accused of being in league with the devil, one hundred and fifty were imprisoned, and twenty-nine put to death,—in such influences as the loss of the charter, or the "harsh aspects of the scenery"—seems to me wholly inadequate, to say the least.[57] The scenery of the native American wild "invited to stern and melancholy musing," as New England's best-known historian phrases it, for about a thousand miles north and south of Mr. Mather's study in Boston, or the Reverend Mr. Parris's cottage in Salem Village, and would seem to be rather dispersed as the cause of a very localized phenomenon.

It is needless to point out that the belief in witchcraft had been widespread throughout the world; but since the days of King James I, there had been, among English people, only isolated cases, save during the years of the Puritan political supremacy in England and the closing days of that

---

[55] Cotton Mather, *Diary*, in *Mass. Hist. Soc. Coll.*, Series VII, vol. vii, p. 148.

[56] *Cf.* C. W. Upham, *History of Witchcraft and Salem Village*, Boston, 1867, 2 vols.; Palfrey, *History*; vol. iv, pp. 96 *ff.*; the works of Cotton Mather and Robert Calef, edited by S. G. Drake and published as *The Witchcraft Delusion in New England*, 3 vols., Roxbury, 1866; I. Mather, *Remarkable Providences*, London, 1890.

[57] Palfrey, *History*, vol. iv, pp. 128 *f.*

same supremacy in Massachusetts.[58] Of the more than seventy cases in England since the Restoration, the great majority had resulted in acquittals, and in two cases only had the unfortunate victims been executed.

We have seen, in an earlier chapter, the extraordinarily large sphere accorded to the devil in Puritan theology, and that theology's virtual repudiation of science by its considering every event in the universe, from the sun's course in heaven to a spider's falling into the porridge, as a direct interposition of the divine will. While Boyle, Newton, and other founders of the new scientific age in England, were tracing the reign of law, the intellectual leaders of New England were engaged in gathering together collections of "remarkable providences," ranging in interest from the sudden death of a Sabbath-breaker to the evident marking for destruction, out of a whole library, of a copy of the book of Common Prayer, by a mouse evidently brought up in the "New England way." Of the moral earnestness of such men there is no question, nor of the abiding stamp which they have left upon the New England consciousness. Happily, much of the good they did has survived, while much of the political and intellectual damage they likewise did, and would have continued to do, had they had their way, has passed.

In 1681, a group of the most eminent of the clergy around Boston determined upon a large coöperative work, to involve the research of many authors, and the labor of some years. It was to be a collection of remarkable providences, of divine judgments, of "thunders as are unusual, strange apparitions, or whatever else shall happen that is prodigious, witchcrafts, diabolical possessions, judgments upon noted sinners," and the like.[59] Each clergyman was to make diligent search among his congregation, and it is obvious what a stimulant such a wholesale inquiry among the people, by the intellectual leaders of the community, would be toward arousing interest, and intensifying the belief, in such matters. A few years later, Increase Mather published his book on the subject, in which he gave numerous cases of witchcraft and possession, and recited the signs by which it might be known. It became the study of the young Cotton Mather, whom in 1686, at the age of twenty-three, we find wrestling in prayer to cast the devils out of New England, and undertaking to track down those leagued with them.[60]

Interest in the subject continued to be stirred up, and in 1688, the criminal nonsense of some children of Boston, and their accusations against a washerwoman, resulted in her being denounced as a witch. Cotton Mather, who had now found the case for which he had been longing, and in which he might do ghostly battle, took the eldest girl home with him. She played upon the clergyman's colossal vanity, and, on evidence which ought not to

---

[58] W. Notestein, *History of Witchcraft in England* (American Historical Association, 1911), pp. 400 *ff.*

[59] I. Mather, *Remarkable Providences*, Preface.   [60] C. Mather, *Diary*, vol. I, p. 114.

have shut up a dog, the unfortunate washerwoman was hanged. Mather now proceeded, by another book and by frenzied sermons, to arouse the fears and superstitions of the crowd. With one of the most noted clergymen in Boston doing all he could to foster it, the belief deepened and spread, and the minds of many, who would not otherwise have given thought to it, were prepared to believe in that "plot of the Devil against New England" which Mather preached.

Early in 1692, some children of Salem feigned the symptoms of which they had heard their elders speak. Two of them belonged to the family of the local clergyman, Mr. Parris, who now entered on the devil-hunt, with a fanaticism which knew no bounds, and an honesty which seems to have been questionable.[61] To his efforts were added those of the Reverend Mr. Noyes. Charge after charge was launched against innocent people, and by the time Phips arrived in the colony as governor, in May, over a hundred persons were already in prison awaiting trial. Vain of his undeserved authority, the appointee and pliant tool of Mather, he immediately appointed an illegal court to try the witchcraft cases, with Stoughton as presiding judge. In the frenzy of superstitious fanaticism which followed, justice, legal evidence, even a verdict of the jury, were set aside, and victim after victim hurried to the gallows, while one, with horrible tortures lasting several days, was pressed to death under heavy weights.[62] The clergy, formally referred to by the Governor and court for advice, while carefully hedging as to certain particulars, urged the court on to "speedy and vigorous prosecution"; and Mather wrote to one of them, extolling "the noble service" of "Encountering the Wicked Spiritts in the high places of our Air, & of detecting & of confounding of their confederates."[63] The Reverend Mr. Burroughs, of Wells, who avowed that "there neither are, nor ever were witches," was condemned; and although the spectators at his hanging were so moved as almost to prevent the sentence from being carried out, Mather, who was witnessing the spectacle from horseback, told the people that the victim was not an ordained clergyman, and that, in any case, the devil often appeared as an Angel of Light.[64]

Finally, the reaction set in, and the sober sense of the community set itself against the ravings and goadings of the more fanatical clergy and church members. The commission of the special court expired with the assembling of the General Court, and was not renewed. Phips, evidently fearing criticism from England, wrote to the Earl of Nottingham, disingenuously laying all the blame for the judicial proceedings on Stoughton,

---

[61] *Vide* the remonstrance against him, in Upham, *Witchcraft*, vol. II, pp. 497 f., and Drake, *Witchcraft Delusion*, vol. II, p. 142.

[62] Sewall, *Diary*, vol. I, p. 364.

[63] Hutchinson, *History*, vol. II, pp. 52 f.; *Mass. Hist. Soc. Coll.*, Series IV, vol. VIII, p. 391.

[64] Sewall, *Diary*, vol. I, p. 363; Drake, *Witchcraft Delusion*, vol. III, pp. 38 f.

and quoted Increase Mather and the other divines.[65] Courageous laymen, like Thomas Brattle and Robert Calef, both merchants, exerted their influence against the delusion; and when Mather tried to start another alarm in Boston, less than a year after the last execution at Salem, public opinion was arrayed solidly against him. In 1700, Calef's book in answer to Mather's "Wonders of the Invisible World" was printed in London and quickly imported into the colony. Though the rage of the Mathers, father and son, was unbounded, their cause had been thoroughly discredited, and their day was past. They belonged, in reality, to the sixteenth century, while Calef, the merchant, defending the cause of intellectual freedom with no weapon but that of common sense, belonged to the eighteenth, the dawn of which was now at hand.

It was the voice of that century to which the people were now to hearken. Thenceforth, happily for itself as well as for America, the church was to be unable to rely either upon political power or upon blind fanaticism to uphold its leadership—a leadership which now, perforce, took on a nobler form. The work of the founders was over. In the extension of their influence throughout the country, wherever we find groups of settlers from the New England states, we find, indeed the church, the common-school, and the town-meeting; but it is a liberalized church, a non-sectarian school, and a town-meeting in which the citizen's vote is not dependent upon the possession of any peculiar theological belief.

It was usual, in an earlier and less critical day, to trace all of New England's greatness, and of her noble contributions to our common American life, to the same little group of leaders, who were supposed to have done all because they did much. Life is not so simple as that, and in the founding of New England, and the development of her liberties, we must find place for English kings and statesmen, for colonial liberals and martyrs, as well as for Pilgrim Father and Puritan Priest.

---

[65] *Cal. State Pap., Col., 1693–96*, p. 30.

A Plea for Puritanism

Clifford K. Shipton

A dozen years ago, James Truslow Adams by a brilliant and convincing essay on New England history popularized the old thesis that a bigoted clergy tyrannized over Massachusetts and her satellite colonies until the people, angered by the persecution of the Quakers and the Salem witches, overthrew the theocracy. Several of our leading historians whose special fields of interest and knowledge lie elsewhere have been deceived by the logic of this thesis and in the common textbooks have given it the sanction of their names.

In the space allotted to me[1] I cannot deal with the entire question, so I shall center my attention on the keystone of the argument—the clergy themselves in what is supposed to have been their lowest period, the years between King Philip's War and the Great Awakening.

The standard argument assumes that the influence which the clergy enjoyed under the old charter was unpopular, and that when the religious requirement for the franchise was removed in 1691, the oppressed masses, to quote Mr. Adams, "made good their right to believe as they would and live their lives as they chose" by using the ballot to overthrow the theocracy.[2] As a matter of fact, after the fall of Andros two popularly elected conventions voted to return to the old Massachusetts charter government; and when the councilors of the new province gathered for the first time, they found that forty-six per cent of their number had sat seven years before in the old court of assistants. That was a smaller turnover than had taken place in the last seven years under the old charter and certainly indicates no desire for a change of leadership. The new general court at once re-enacted the fundamental statutes of the old government, and in 1701 gave the ministers a larger voice in town affairs than they had enjoyed under the so-called theocracy. In like manner New Hampshire, far from rejoicing in the enforced separation from Massachusetts, twice expressed its sorrow at what recent writers have called its "liberation." [3]

From *American Historical Review*, XL (April 1935), 460–467. Reprinted by permission.

[1] The paper was read at a session of the American Historical Association, Dec. 29, 1934.

[2] *The Founding of New England* (Boston, 1922), p. 450. See also Homer C. Hockett, *Political and Social Growth of the United States* (New York, 1933), p. 120; Marcus W. Jernegan, *The American Colonies* (New York, 1929), p. 160; Thomas Jefferson Wertenbaker, *The First Americans* (American Life series, New York, 1927), pp. 108–109.

[3] Jeremy Belknap, *History of New-Hampshire* (Boston, 1792), I, 178.

Mr. Adams assumes that the old charter government was unpopular, assumes that the clerical influence was overthrown by the newly enfranchised masses, and proceeds to the logical conclusion that the clergy made great efforts to restore the old system under which they had enjoyed so much power. By common consent Increase Mather is held to have been the soul of the theocracy, as the old charter is held to have been its foundation. But he and his son Cotton maintained that the new charter, the adoption of which is regarded as marking the end of the rule of the clergy, was a far better document, containing, they said, "New and more Ample Privileges; Without which, the Old would not have been Sufficient." [4] Had the enfranchisement of non-church members had the significance that modern writers give to it, Increase Mather, astute politician that he was, would not have praised the new charter and claimed the glory of having obtained it; he would have proved conclusively that some of his numerous enemies were responsible for it. Indeed for the next fifty years, the clergy united in praising the new charter, while the popular political party did its best to have restored the old one on which the theocracy had rested. The new electorate, far from being indifferent or liberal in matters of religion, insisted that every politician from Elisha Cooke to James Otis assume the cloak of fundamentalism. The house of representatives was the tool with which the religious conservatives tried to dislodge the Leverett-Colman group from the college, and it was the house, not the clergy, which was anxious to force Congregational preachers on Baptist and Quaker towns. Neither the mass of the voters nor any important group of the upper class was anti-clerical. The group of parson-baiting skeptics which Mr. Adams hails as typical of the new age, was a small and uninfluential minority which drops from sight after the exile of Jim Franklin. The failure of the *Courant* and the fact that no attempt was made to revive it, even after the collapse of censorship, shows that its critical stand was unpopular—and unprofitable.

The picture of the Mathers attempting to regain their lost influence by depriving the individual churches of their congregational liberty is another logical reconstruction. The pamphlets of John Wise are well known; but all of the recent writers who praise him as the champion of liberty have followed Mr. Parrington in disdaining to read Increase Mather's writings on the subject. His *Disquisition concerning Ecclesiastical Councils,* to take the best example, shows him to have been much nearer to Wise than to Pemberton, Colman, and the other young ministers who were the real power behind the movement which Wise opposed. One of their chief purposes, as a study of their policies shows, was to strengthen the hands of the ministers and to check the growth of the institution of lay elders, who, being

---

[4] *Andros Tracts* (Prince Society, 1868–1874), III, 155, 169–173; Cotton Mather, *Diary* (Massachusetts Historical Society, *Collections,* ser. 7, vols. VII–VIII), I, 148. The Mathers are the ministers most frequently cited in this paper, not because they were more liberal than their fellows, but because they are the best known and most often maligned.

older men and usually uneducated, bitterly opposed the efforts of the young clergy to introduce the halfway covenant and otherwise ameliorate the religious order.

It is frequently said that the decline in the influence of the New England clergy was due largely to popular resentment against their bigoted persecution of the religious minorities. When we weigh the responsibility for the hanging of the Quakers in early Boston, we should not forget the violence of the mob against them after the ministers and the Puritan magistrates had accepted them, nor should we ignore the popular petitions for the enforcement of the laws.[5] In the years which followed, the clergy with frequency and vigor censured the zeal which had, Cotton Mather said, "sent the mad Quakers unto the gallows instead of bedlam." [6] In the period with which we are dealing, John Callender, a Baptist, seems to have been the only preacher to offer excuses for the early persecutions. Cotton Mather time and again denounced them. In speaking before the general court in 1709 he laid down two fundamental axioms of government which he put in bold-faced type in the printed sermon. One was, "No man may be Persecuted, because he is Conscienciously not of the same Religious Opinion, with those that are uppermost." [7]

By the time of the Great Awakening, Massachusetts had taken the Baptist, Quaker, and Anglican churches into the religious establishment where they had every legal privilege which the Congregationalists enjoyed, including the use of the civil arm to collect their rates, if they wished. This religious system, far more liberal than that prevailing in Virginia to the time of the Revolution, was adopted with the hearty support of the Puritan clergy. In preaching an election sermon, a sort of keynote address for the coming session of the general court which was to consider such legislation, Israel Loring said: "Unity of the Faith is not to be expected, till we get to Heaven. . . . By all Means, let us espouse generous Principles; let us breathe a catholick Spirit; let us be one with every one, that is one with Jesus Christ; whether they be Lutherans, or Calvinists, Episcopalians, or Presbyterians, Congregationalists, or Antipœdobaptists; or whatever other Denomination they may be of." [8]

Loring was a country parson of the old generation, always to be found among the most conservative ministers. From the writings of the younger clergy one could cull scores of pages of praise of religious toleration, but not, at least among the hundreds of sermons I have scanned, one word against it. From the funeral sermons they preached and the obituary notices they contributed to the papers, it is clear that they considered no virtue more laudable or more common among parsons than what they called "a

---

[5] Massachusetts Archives, Ecclesiastical Affairs volumes, *passim*.

[6] Cotton Mather, *Optanda* (Boston, 1692), pp. 42–45.

[7] *Theopolis Americana* (Boston, 1710), p. 29.

[8] *The Duty of an Apostatizing People* (Boston, 1737), p. 67.

liberal and catholic mind in matters of religion." Cotton Mather praised the new charter provisions for a "Righteous and Generous Liberty of Conscience," [9] and when the Boston mob became excited over the manufacture of a popish image in the town, it was he who tried to quiet them by saying that it was only "an ornamental Business." [10] Yet Mr. Parrington asserted that Mather did not have "a grain of liberalism in his make-up." [11]

Between 1680 and 1740 there were 500 Puritan ministers in New England. We have sufficient data regarding 400 of these to enable us to judge of their relations with the laymen who were taxed to pay their salaries. This material shows that practically without exception the parsons were more liberal than the people. Most of them were educated at Harvard College where a "free and Catholick aire" was a boast even under the presidency of Increase Mather,[12] and where Episcopal and Quaker students were welcome a century and a half before Dissenters were admitted to degrees at Oxford and Cambridge. The principle of an Index of Prohibited Books was abhorrent to them. The quotations in their sermons and the inventories of their libraries show that they read the works of Catholic writers from the earliest fathers to Pascal, whom Ebenezer Pemberton publicly praised as "One of the greatest Masters of Thought." [13] They read and corresponded with the liberal Anglican bishops whom George Whitefield and the generality of the Episcopal clergy here expected to be damned for their heresies. They followed with sympathy the Pietist movement in Germany and even dipped into the Deists. It was inevitable that they should be far more liberal than the scantily educated masses. Against the resistance of the lay elders they carried on the work of liberalizing the churches, Cotton Mather using trickery[14] and Ebenezer Pemberton stealth[15] to introduce their reforms. And at every step, including such simple improvements as that of singing by note, they were opposed by obstinate laymen who raised the cry of "popery."

In the field of science they showed the same intellectual eagerness and the same willingness to accept new ideas. They and certain pious laymen founded the *New England Weekly Journal* in order to bring to the provincials the latest in European thought. This orthodox paper with its solid articles on science is much more important in the intellectual history of New England than is the short-lived *Courant*. The clergy adopted the new geology and the new astronomy as soon as these became available, frankly admitting that in such matters the Bible was not to be taken as the last

---

[9] *Andros Tracts*, III, 170.   [10] *Diary*, II, 445.

[11] Vernon Louis Parrington, *The Colonial Mind (Main Currents of American Thought*, New York, 1927), p. 113.

[12] Ebenezer Turell, *Life and Character of the Reverend Benjamin Colman* (Boston, 1749), pp. 136–137.

[13] *The Divine Original* (Boston, 1710), p. 1.

[14] Mass. Hist. Soc., *Coll.*, ser. 4, vol. VIII, p. 401; *Diary*, I, 161–162.

[15] Samuel Sewall, *Diary* (Mass. Hist. Soc., *Coll.*, ser. 5, vols. V–VII), II, 267.

word. Increase Mather once preached a sermon in which he described comets as portents of God's anger. Informed by an English friend that such views had been challenged by Dr. Spencer of Cambridge, he sent for a copy of Spencer's book, and soon after receiving it let it be known in a public sermon that he had been converted to the theory that comets proceeded from natural causes.[16] It was the parson, not the layman, who wrested from the hand of God the meteor and the comet. It was not until the 1740's that a layman, John Winthrop, took the lead in scientific thought in New England.

How can we reconcile all this with Mr. Jernegan's statement that the Salem witchcraft affair was "an effort on the part of the old clerical order to retain their influence and power?" [17] We cannot. Just as religiously inclined scientists from Sir Charles Lyell to Kirtley Mather have pointed to the field of the unknown as a place for God in the modern world, so some seventeenth-century parsons, English and colonial, sought to illustrate the nearness of God by collecting examples of phenomena which could not then be explained by natural causes. Either the great part of phenomena then before men's eyes emanated from God or the Devil, or had no cause at all. The collecting of records of such phenomena is no proof of evil intent. But certain recent writers, assuming that the power of the clergy had been broken by the extension of the franchise in 1691, assuming that the clergy wished to restore the old order, make the ghastly accusation that the clergy fanned "the flames of intolerance and persecution," [18] and sent the poor people of Salem Village to the gallows, a blood sacrifice for a political end. None of the Puritan-baiters has ever produced one word of contemporary evidence in support of this thesis, nor have I found any in the thousands of pages of the writings of the clergy that have passed before my eyes.

When the Salem arrests began, parsons, individually and collectively, privately and publicly, addressed the judges, saying that any persons guilty of witchcraft should be punished, but urging that none of the traditional superstitious witchhunting methods of the European courts be allowed here. They demanded that no evidence be accepted that would not have been allowed in ordinary civil and criminal cases.[19] "In Massachusetts," says Mr. Hockett, "it was the class least interested in religion which first denounced the persecution." [20] Is that true? First, the relatives of the accused raised their voices in protest, then, when the first hangings had taken place, a group of the clergy went over the heads of the court to the governor and council, urging the "need of a very critical and exquisite Caution." [21] The

---

[16] Mass. Hist. Soc., *Coll.*, ser. 4, vol. VIII, pp. 354–355.

[17] *American Colonies*, p. 187.   [18] *Founding*, p. 396.

[19] Mass. Hist. Soc., *Coll.*, ser. 4, vol. VIII, pp. 391–397; Deodat Lawson, *Christ's Fidelity* (London, 1704), pp. 70 *ff.*; Samuel Willard, *Some Miscellany Observations* (Philadelphia, 1692), *passim.*

[20] *Political and Social Growth*, p. 125.

[21] Increase Mather, *Cases of Conscience* (Boston, 1693), appendix.

hangings continued; so on the eve of the opening of the August session of the court, the Cambridge association of ministers unanimously reiterated their condemnation of the type of evidence which was being accepted by the judges.[22] But still the hangings continued, so Increase Mather drew up the statement of the position of the ministers which was printed as *Cases of Conscience,* and, securing the signatures of fourteen leading clergymen, placed it before Governor Phips. Then the governor ended the Salem tragedy.[23]

It was now, according to Mr. Adams, that Cotton Mather "proceeded, by another book and by frenzied sermons, to arouse the fears and superstitions of the crowd . . . doing all that he could to foster it." [24] These sermons are unknown to bibliographers. The book to which Mr. Adams refers is Mather's *Wonders of the Invisible World,* which begins with a denunciation of the water trial and like superstitions, says that all good men were amazed at the Salem proceedings, expresses fear that innocent persons have suffered, and urges a "most Critical Enquiry . . . to find out the Fallacy." [25] In order to find out the Salem fallacy he describes foreign cases which he is sure were witchcraft, but he concludes with a warning in the form of a horrible story of a Stockholm woman recently burned on false testimony. Now Mather was not an ass; that was no way to work up a witch frenzy. Far from trying to promote the hysteria, the Mathers prevented Margaret Rule from making statements which might have led to an indictment against her, and they permitted no case, with one early exception,[26] which they personally handled to come to the scaffold.

No one ever won cheaper canonization than Thomas Brattle and Robert Calef, those "courageous laymen" of Mr. Adams's story.[27] Brattle, who never publicly opposed the proceedings, certainly was not one of the class "least interested in religion," for he was shortly thereafter engaged in founding the Church in Brattle Square, and he supported his private criticism of the Salem court by saying that the clergy almost to a man thought with him.[28] The laymen whom he names as opposing the proceedings were, perhaps with one exception, noted for their orthodox piety. Calef, so far as we know, did not offer even private criticism until the hangings were ended, and did not raise his voice in public for seven years more. If one may judge by library inventories and by contemporary mention, his book was much less influential than that of the Rev. John Hale. It was Hale's book that men of the clerical class some years later proposed to distribute to prevent a pos-

[22] *Ibid.,* p. 32.

[23] Thomas James Holmes, *Increase Mather: a Bibliography of his Works* (Cleveland, 1931), I, 115–138.

[24] *Founding,* p. 454.

[25] Especially "Enchantments Encountered" and pp. 50–51 of text (Boston, 1693).

[26] The case of 1688.   [27] *Founding,* p. 455.

[28] Mass. Hist. Soc., *Coll.,* ser. 1, vol. V, pp. 61–79.

sible outbreak of what one of them called that "execrable . . . nonentity," witchcraft.[29] Far from attempting to revive the frenzy, many of the clergy, including Michael Wigglesworth, spoke harshly of those who had defiled their hands with the blood of the "poor innocents" at Salem.[30] That no civil court should ever again accept such evidence was one of the two axioms of government which Cotton Mather laid down for the guidance of the general court.[31] It was the clergy, individually and collectively, who for the next fifty years kept reminding the legislature that innocent people had suffered at Salem, and that all possible restitution should be made. Had the people blamed them for the Salem tragedy, they would not have kept the subject open.

In short there was no general anticlerical feeling in the Puritan colonies, hence no sudden overthrow of clerical power, and no such efforts to regain it as Mr. Adams describes. Far from being narrow bigots, the ministers were the leaders in every field of intellectual advance in New England in these years. And such difficulties as they experienced were in no small degree due to the fact that they were too liberal, not too conservative, for the mass of the people.

---

[29] *Ibid.*, MSS., Letters and Papers, 1721–1760, 71 J. 135.

[30] *Ibid.*, *Coll.*, ser. 4, vol. VIII, pp. 646–647; for the Essex clergy, see the *New-England Historical and Genealogical Register*, XXXIII, 193.

[31] *Theopolis Americana*, p. 29.

II

Democracy in Colonial America: Fact or Fiction?

INTRODUCTION

Fifty years ago Carl Becker, with rare historical insight, posed a dual question concerning the interpretation of the American Revolution. He declared there were two problems involved: the problem of home rule and the problem of who should rule at home. The first problem concerned imperial relations; the second problem concerned the relations in civil society of Americans in America. The latter formulation has as its fundamental query the relationship of colonial democracy to the American Revolution.

Robert E. Brown, who has intensively studied the structure of society in colonial Massachusetts, has concluded that in that colony a middle-class democracy existed before the Revolution, and that the Revolution had the purpose to preserve a social order and not to change it. He thus asserts that as far as Massachusetts is concerned, the majority ruled at home and further believes that what was true in Massachusetts "was not fundamentally different from the other colonies and states." His recent study, in collaboration with his wife, of colonial Virginia leads to the conclusion: "Except for slavery and British influence, what now passes in this country as middle-class representative democracy was well-entrenched in the Old Dominion long before the American Revolution." (Virginia 1705–1786: Democracy or Aristocracy (1964), p. 308). *The real meaning of the Revolution, in Brown's view, is thus to be sought in the struggle for independence from Britain.*

Merrill Jensen, an authority on the period of the Confederation (1781–1789), takes direct issue with Brown. Even if virtual manhood suffrage is granted to have existed in colonial Massachusetts, Jensen perceives other features of political organization that force him to deny that democracy was there established. He contends that "colonial political society was not democratic in operation despite the elective lower house and the self-government which had been won from Great Britain." The Revolution, therefore, was designed to change a social order and not to preserve it, and Jensen denies that the majority ruled at home.

Middle-Class Democracy and the Revolution in Massachusetts, 1691–1780

Robert E. Brown

PREFACE

For the past fifty years or more a thesis has been current in the teaching and writing of American history, political science, and literature that the society which produced the American Revolution and the federal Constitution was not a democratic society. There are differences of opinion as to just how undemocratic this society was, but in general the point is usually made that even though eighteenth-century America was more democratic than Europe, democracy as we know it did not arrive in this country until the time of Andrew Jackson.

This concept of an undemocratic society is based on two major assumptions: one, that property qualifications for voting eliminated a large portion of the free adult male population from participation in political affairs; the other, that inequitable representation heavily favored the older aristocratic commercial areas along the seacoast at the expense of the more recently settled inland agricultural areas. Hence it followed naturally that colonial political and economic life was dominated by the upper economic classes.

Writers who accept the thesis that colonial society was undemocratic have also generally followed the interpretation that the American Revolution was a "dual" revolution. On one hand, there was the conflict between Great Britain and her American colonies—what might be called the "War for Independence." But accompanying this, and of equal or perhaps greater significance, was a struggle within the colonies over which class would dominate economic and political life. According to this theory, the second phase of the conflict, which might well be designated the "American Revolution" to distinguish it from the "War of Independence," was primarily an effort by the unenfranchised and dissatisfied lower classes to gain economic, political, and social equality with their betters.

From Robert E. Brown, *Middle-Class Democracy and the Revolution in Massachusetts,* 1691–1780, pp. V–VII, 401–408. Copyright 1955 by the American Historical Association, used with permission of Cornell University Press.

Both the "War of Independence" and the "American Revolution" succeeded to a greater or lesser extent in their objectives, according to most writers. The first won political independence for the colonies from Great Britain, although economic independence was not achieved until the War of 1812. The second succeeded by the elimination of colonial ruling classes, or a reduction in their power, and by the elevation of the "common man" to a position of importance in society which he had not hitherto enjoyed. This was reflected in the elimination or diminution of such manifestations of aristocratic domination as property qualifications for voting, inequitable representation, established churches, and entail and primogeniture in the distribution of inheritances. Later, aristocratic upper classes staged a "counterrevolution" by putting over a conservative Constitution on the people, and it was not really until the time of Andrew Jackson that democracy came fully into its own.

In the following pages I have raised some questions about this accepted interpretation as it applies to one colony and state, Massachusetts from 1691 to 1780. Did an upper economic class control economic life in the colony? Were property qualifications for voting sufficiently high to exclude an important number of adult men from participation in politics? Is the "American Revolution" interpretation a valid one, and if not, what part did democracy play in the "War for Independence"? And did the Revolution result in social changes in the state of Massachusetts significant enough to justify the concept of an "internal revolt"?

In the process of gathering material for this work, I have also seen sufficient evidence to suggest the need for reconsideration of assumptions with regard to other colonies as well as to Massachusetts.

Some of the basic ideas in the following pages first made their appearance as a doctoral dissertation at the University of Wisconsin in 1946. Since then, additional research has added much new material, and much rewriting has changed the original organization materially. But most of the general thesis presented in the original dissertation withstood the test of additional research; in fact, much of it was greatly strengthened by new material. Naturally for a work of this scope there are sources which I did not consult, but I reached a point where additional sources were merely adding more weight to points already well documented. . . .

*   *   *

CONCLUSION

In Massachusetts, therefore, we find one of the unique "revolutions" in world history—a revolution to preserve a social order rather than to change it. It was not, as we have often assumed, a dual revolution in which Americans won their independence from the British on one hand, and in which unenfranchised and underprivileged lower classes wrested democratic rights from a privileged local aristocracy on the other.

To understand what happened, we must first have a clear picture of Massachusetts society. Economically speaking, it was a middle-class society in which property was easily acquired and in which a large portion of the people were property-owning farmers. There was undoubtedly more economic democracy for the common man then than there is now. A large permanent labor class was practically nonexistent; men could either acquire land and become farmers or work for themselves as skilled artisans. If we insist that Americans who came to this country brought their accustomed class or caste lines with them, we must do so in the face of all the evidence to the contrary. If there was anything that observers at the time agreed on, it was that American society was almost the exact opposite of European society. There was nothing approaching the spread between the rich and the poor that Europe had at that time or that we have at present; a much larger proportion of society owned property then than now. Yet today, many people, even including many laborers, look on American society as predominantly middle class, though the opportunity for almost universal ownership of property is far less now than it was before the Revolution.

Economic opportunity, or economic democracy, in turn contributed to political democracy. While it is true that property ownership was a prerequisite for province and town voting, it is also true that the amount of property required for the franchise was very small and that the great majority of men could easily meet the requirements. There were probably a few men who could not qualify for voting, but the number could not have been very large. We cannot condone the practice of excluding even those few, but we should try to place the unenfranchised in their proper perspective. It makes a tremendous difference in our understanding of colonial society whether 95 per cent of the men were disfranchised or only 5 per cent. Furthermore, representation was apportioned in such a way that the farmers, not a merchant aristocracy, had complete control of the legislature.

It is not enough to say that the people of Massachusetts perhaps had more democracy than the people of Europe, but that they still did not have what we call democracy today. Neither is it sufficient to say that the germs of democracy were present, or that democracy, as a growing process if not as a reality, could be found in colonial times. When Hutchinson said that anything that looked like a man was a voter and that policy in general was dictated by the lower classes, he was certainly using the term "democracy" as we mean it now. A Hutchinson might deplore the view that government existed for the benefit of the people and that the people were to decide when government had served its proper functions, but this is the democratic idea. He might also deplore the fact that the people not only elected their representatives but also told them how to vote, yet this, too, is democracy.

In many respects, the people of Massachusetts had a government more responsive to the popular will than we have at the present time. There were far more representatives in proportion to population than we now have, and the representatives were more responsible to their constituents for their actions than are legislators at present. If a man votes against his belief to please his constituents so that he can hold his elected position, we cannot demand much more of democracy.

The number of men who could vote in the colony must not be confused with the number who did vote. These are entirely different problems, for the fact that there was much indifference on election day did not mean that many men could not participate. If we are attempting to explain events in terms of class conflict or internal revolution, it is especially important that we do not confuse the unfranchised and the disinterested. It is one thing if a man wants the vote but cannot meet the property requirements; it is another if he has the vote but fails to use it. Neither should we confuse the issue by giving percentages of voters in terms of the entire population, for probably less than 20 per cent of the people in colonial times were adult men.

In addition to economics and politics, there were also other manifestations of democracy in colonial Massachusetts. The system of education was, for its day, undoubtedly the best provided for the common people anywhere, and the correct comparison is with other educational systems at the time, not with our own. Many democratic practices were used in the operation of the Congregational church, and again we should remember that some 98 per cent of the people were Congregationalists. Furthermore, the Congregational church was not established as it was in England. Men who belonged to other churches did not pay taxes to the Congregational church; education and political office were open to those who were not Congregationalists. Perhaps there was not the complete religious freedom—or religious indifference—that we now associate with a liberal society, but there was also little dissatisfaction with religion to contribute to internal conflict. Even the colonial militia was democratic in its organization and in the influence which it exerted on politics.

In brief, Massachusetts did not have a social order before the American Revolution which would breed sharp internal class conflicts. The evidence does not justify an interpretation of the Revolution in Massachusetts as an internal class conflict designed to achieve additional political, economic, and social democracy. Although democracy was important as a factor in the conflict, it was a democracy which had already arrived in the colony long before 1776.

If we turn to British-American relations, however, we do not need to search long to find areas of conflict. The British for many years had developed a mercantilist-imperialist colonial system that had not functioned as expected. The aim of the system, as men at the time frankly admitted, was the ultimate benefit of the mother country. They believed that colonies should be regulated, both economically and politically, to further the well-being of the parent state. British officials were fully aware of the shortcomings in colonial administration, but, until 1760, Britain was not in a favorable position to remedy these defects. British officials were also fully aware of the fact that colonial democracy was one of the chief obstacles to effective enforcement of British colonial policy.

These two ingredients—an effective middle-class democracy and British imperial policies which had been thwarted by this democracy—explain what happened in Massachusetts from 1760 to 1776. In order to make their colonial system effective, the British believed that they had to recover authority over colonial officials. This, in turn, called for a colonial revenue which would be administered by Parliament, especially to pay the salaries of colonial officials and thus remove them from under the dominating influence of colonial assemblies. But of course the assembly of Massachusetts was fully aware of the power which control of the purse conferred and was equally determined to retain this power over British officials.

Throughout the story runs another thread—the threat, or at least what the British considered the threat, of colonial independence. This gave an air of urgency to British measures. There was the frequently expressed fear that time was on the side of the colonists. A rapidly growing population, bolstered by a phenomenal birthrate due to economic opportunity and by immigrants attracted by economic and political democracy, posed the problem to the British of recovering authority before the colonies became too large. When the showdown came with the Tea Act and the Coercive Acts, there was no doubt whatever that the British intended to curtail colonial democracy as a necessary step toward recovery of British authority and the prevention of colonial independence. The result was the very thing the British had tried to prevent—American independence.

Obviously democracy played an important part in the events before 1776, not as a condition to be achieved but as a reality which interfered with British policies. If the British had been successful, there would undoubtedly have been much less democracy in Massachusetts—hence the interpretation that the Revolution was designed to *preserve* a social order rather than to change it. We search in vain for evidence of class conflict that was serious enough to justify revolution; we do not have to look far for copious quantities of proof that colonial society was democratic and that the colonists were attempting to prevent British innovations.

Furthermore, the results of the Revolution more than confirm the interpretation presented here. There is a logic to what happened after the Revolution—or perhaps it would be more accurate to say what did not happen—if we accept the fact that the people of Massachusetts were not conducting an internal revolution. We are not confronted with the contradiction, which most writers fail to resolve, of a social revolution which was presumably successful but which failed to achieve social change. Why would a people, who were supposedly demanding a more democratic government, adopt a constitution which restricted democracy even more than it had been restricted in colonial days? On the other hand, the Massachusetts Constitution of 1780 was a logical consequence of a middle-class society which believed in the protection of property because most men were property owners. The almost complete absence of social revolution in Massachusetts should stand as convincing evidence that internal social revolution was not one of the chief aims of the American Revolution as far as the people of Massachusetts were concerned.

It is not necessary to explain whatever conservatism existed in colonial times in terms of a limited electorate. There is implied in this approach an assumption that universal suffrage will result in increased liberalism, but this is not necessarily so. The elections of 1920, 1924, 1928, and even 1952, when women as well as men had the vote, should convince us that "the people" can and do vote for conservatism. If the people of Massachusetts believed that a man should own property to be a voter or that an official should be a Protestant to be elected to office, they might well vote for both propositions and not be out of character. And since most men in Massachusetts were Protestants and property owners, the fact that both property and religious qualifications found their way into the Constitution of 1780 should not be surprising.

We do not need a "conservative counterrevolution" or a thermidorean reaction to explain either the Massachusetts Constitution of 1780 or the adoption of the federal Constitution in 1788. If there was no "social revolution," there could hardly be a "conservative counterrevolution." Both constitutions must be explained in terms of a middle-class society in which most men could vote.

In recent years it has been frequently said that the British did not intend to tyrannize the colonies by the policies which they adopted. Colonists thought otherwise, however, and judging by the material presented in these chapters, one might suspect that many British policies looked like tyranny to them. Perhaps we of today would also consider as tyranny trials without juries, instructions by the king which were supposed to be law, taxation by a people who were considered foreigners, a declaration by the Parliament of these same "foreign people" that it had the power to legislate in all cases whatsoever, appointed governors who could dissolve assemblies or determine town meetings, and navigation acts regulating colonial trade in British interests. It would be interesting to speculate on the reaction of a modern oleomargarine manufacturer whose suit against the butter interests was to be tried in Wisconsin by a jury of Wisconsin dairy farmers presided over by a judge appointed by the governor of Wisconsin. This hypothetical case might seem exaggerated, but it is not too far removed from the attitude expressed by colonists toward their relations with the British. The fact is that colonists looked on British measures as tyrannical, and if we are going to explain colonial actions, we must consider the colonial point of view.

How should we rate in importance the various factors that entered into this British-American war? That, of course, is difficult to answer, but it is not so difficult to say that many items contributed and that some were probably more important to some individuals than to others.

There is no doubt that economic motives were fundamental. That Americans would oppose a mercantilist system which they considered inimical to their interests should not be surprising. After all, they looked on many British regulations as simply devices by which some segments of the Empire were favored at the expense of other segments. The tax program also had its economic side, for as many men said, a mother country which could collect a stamp tax could also tax a man's land, his cattle, or his home. Undoubtedly, too, the threat of monopoly contained in the Tea Act had its economic influence. In fact, a middle-class society would almost inevitably place great emphasis on property and its economic interests, a fact which is only too apparent in the sources. The importance of economic factors, however, did not lie in their contribution to class conflict as a cause of the American Revolution.

But economic elements were not the only forces making for revolution. Equally significant was the fact that Massachusetts had long been accustomed to democratic government and intended to maintain its accustomed system. Politics inevitably include economics, since economic subjects are some of the most important items in politics, but not all politics is economic. The very fact that people govern their own destinies is important in itself. As one old soldier of the Revolution put it, the British intended to govern the Americans and the Americans did not intend that they should. To a people accustomed to the democracy both of province and town affairs, the danger inherent in British imperial controls was far more than a mere threat. When the common people talked of dying for their liberties or pledging their lives and property for the defense of their liberties, they were not dealing in abstractions; and they would not have talked in this way if their society had been dominated by a merchant aristocracy.

Neither can religious democracy be ignored as a factor in the Revolution. We must remember that the people of Massachusetts were accustomed to a church organization which lived by democratic procedures and opposition to the Church of England. We must not forget, either, that many people at the time considered religion more important than politics. The threat that the British might impose the Church of England on them and enforce conformity was not a threat to be taken lightly. As many of them often said, religious and political freedom were inextricably connected and would rise or fall together. Little wonder, then, that the Congregational clergy supported the Revolution almost to a man.

This study of Massachusetts raises some rather serious questions about our interpretation of colonial society and the Revolution in other colonies. Were the other colonies as undemocratic as we have supposed them to be? Was their economic and social life dominated by a coastal aristocracy of planters in the South and merchants in the North? How was property distributed? Exactly how many men could meet the voting qualifications? Was representation restricted in such a way that conservative areas could dominate the legislature? These are questions for which we need well-documented answers before we interpret the colonial and revolutionary periods with any assurance of accuracy.

Evidence which has turned up in the course of this study suggests that Massachusetts was not fundamentally different from the other colonies and states. If so—and the idea is certainly worth extensive investigation—we might be forced to make some drastic revisions in our interpretation of American history before 1830. Perhaps we will find in America as a whole, as in Massachusetts, that American democracy as we know it goes far deeper than the election of 1828 and that the "common man" in this country had come into his own long before the era of Jacksonian Democracy.

Democracy and the American Revolution

Merrill Jensen

The historian who ventures to talk about democracy in early America is in danger because there are almost as many opinions as there are writers on the subject. The Puritans have been pictured as the founders of American democracy, and it is vigorously denied that they had anything to do with it. Some have seen in Roger Williams the father of American democracy, and others have denied that he was a democrat, whatever his putative

From *Huntington Library Quarterly*, XX (August 1957), 321–341. Reprinted by permission. Delivered at the Conference of Early American History at the Henry E. Huntington Library, February 9, 1957.

progeny may be. The conflict is equally obvious when it comes to the American Revolution, and the problems of solution are far more complex than they are for the seventeenth century. The difficulty is compounded, for all too often men's emotions seem to become involved.

It is sometimes suggested that we avoid the use of the word "democracy" when discussing the seventeenth and eighteenth centuries. It seems to me that this is a flat evasion of the problem, for the Americans of those centuries used the word and they meant something by it. Our task, then, is not to avoid the issue but to try to understand what they meant, and understand what they meant in the context of the times in which they lived. What we must not do is to measure the seventeenth and eighteenth centuries in terms of our own assumptions about what democracy is or should be. This is all the more important since many of us do not seem to be too clear about our assumptions, even for the century in which we live.

A number of years ago I took the position that "in spite of the paradoxes involved one may still maintain that the Revolution was essentially, though relatively, a democratic movement within the thirteen American colonies, and that its significance for the political and constitutional history of the United States lay in its tendency to elevate the political and economic status of the majority of the people." And then, with a somewhat rhetorical flourish which I have sometimes regretted but have not as yet withdrawn, I went on to say that "the Articles of Confederation were the constitutional expression of this movement and the embodiment in governmental form of the philosophy of the Declaration of Independence." [1] One thing can be said for this statement at least: reviewers read it and quoted it, some with raised eyebrows, and some with approval, whether or not they said anything at all about the rest of the book.

During most of the present century historians have assumed that democracy was involved somehow or other in the American Revolution. They have assumed also that there were conditions within the American colonies that were not satisfactory to at least some of the American people. The causes of internal discontent were various, ranging all the way from religious to economic differences. The discontent was of such intensity that in certain colonies it led to explosive outbreaks in the 1760's such as the Regulator movements in the Carolinas, the Paxton Boys' uprising in Pennsylvania, and the tenant farmer revolt in New York, outbreaks that were suppressed by the armed forces of the colonial governments and with the help of British power.

Most historians have agreed also that the individual colonies were con-

---

[1] Merrill Jensen, *The Articles of Confederation: An Interpretation of the Social-Constitutional History of the American Revolution, 1774–1781,* reprint with new foreword (Madison, Wis., 1948), pp. 15, 239.

trolled politically by relatively small groups of men in each of them, allied by family, or economic or political interests, or by some combination of these. The colonial aristocracies owed their position to many things: to their wealth and ability, to their family connections and political allies, and to the British government which appointed them to office. As opposed to Britain, they had won virtual self-government for the colonies by 1763. Yet in every colony they were a minority who managed to maintain internal control through property qualifications for the suffrage, especially effective in the growing towns, and through refusal or failure to grant representation in any way proportional to the population of the rapidly growing frontier areas. Probably more important than either of these was the fact that in most colonies the aristocracies manned the upper houses of the legislatures, the supreme courts, and other important posts—all by royal appointment. Beyond this, their control extended down through the county court system, even in Massachusetts. In short, colonial political society was not democratic in operation despite the elective lower houses and the self-government which had been won from Great Britain.[2]

This is a brief but, I think, fair summary of a widely held point of view concerning the political actualities at the beginning of the revolutionary era.

This view has been challenged recently. A writer on Massachusetts declared that "as far as Massachusetts is concerned, colonial society and the American Revolution must be interpreted in terms something very close to a complete democracy with the exception of British restraints." It was not controlled by a wealthy aristocracy. There was little inequality of representation, and property was so widely held that virtually every adult male could vote.[3] The assumption that Massachusetts was an idyllic democracy, united in the fight against British tyranny, will be somewhat surprising to those who have read the letters of Francis Bernard and the diary of John Adams, not to mention the history of Thomas Hutchinson, and, I suspect, would be even more surprising to those gentlemen as well. Elsewhere, this writer has implied that what was true for Massachusetts was probably true for other colonies and for the United States after the Revolution.[4]

---

[2] *Ibid.*, ch. iii, "The Internal Revolution"; Leonard W. Labaree, *Conservatism in Early American History* (New York, 1948); and Robert J. Taylor, *Western Massachusetts in the Revolution* (Providence, 1954), as examples. For methods of local control see Charles S. Sydnor, *Gentlemen Freeholders: Political Practices in Washington's Virginia* (Chapel Hill, 1952).

[3] Robert E. Brown, "Democracy in Colonial Massachusetts," *New England Quarterly*, XXV (1952), 291–313, and at length in *Middle Class Democracy and the Revolution in Massachusetts, 1691–1780* (Ithaca, N. Y., 1955).

[4] Robert E. Brown, "Economic Democracy Before the Constitution," *American Quarterly*, VII (1955), 257–274.

On the other hand it is asserted that democracy had nothing to do with the Revolution. Such an assertion made in connection with Pennsylvania is a little startling, for ever since C. H. Lincoln's work of more than a half century ago, down to the present, it has been held that there was a democratic movement in Pennsylvania during the revolutionary era. Not so, says a reviewer of the most recent study. He declares that "the attribution of democratic motivations and ideas to eighteenth century colonists is a common fault among many historians of the colonial period. . . ." He argues that the struggle in Pennsylvania before 1776 was one between "radical and conservative variants of whiggism," which he defines as one between "those who held privilege most dear and those who valued property above all." The Pennsylvania Constitution of 1776 itself was not democratic, but a triumph of "colonial radical whiggism." [5]

It is clear that a considerable diversity of opinion prevails. It is also clear that the time has come to set forth certain propositions or generalizations which seem to me to have a measure of validity.

First of all, a definition of democracy is called for. And just to face the issue squarely, I will offer one stated at Newport, Rhode Island, in 1641 when a meeting declared that "the government which this body politic doth attend unto . . . is a democracy or popular government; . . . that is to say: It is in the power of the body of freemen, orderly assembled, or the major part of them, to make or constitute just laws, by which they will be regulated, and to depute from among themselves such ministers as shall see them faithfully executed between man and man." That such an idea was not confined to Newport was shown six years later when the little towns in Rhode Island formed a confederation, the preamble of which states: "It is agreed, by this present assembly thus incorporate, and by this present act declared, that the form of government established in Providence Plantations is democratical; that is to say, a government held by the free and voluntary consent of all, or the greater part of the free inhabitants."

These are simple but, I think, adequate definitions. I will go even further and offer as a theoretical and philosophical foundation for democracy the statement by Roger Williams in the *Bloudy Tenent* of 1644. After describing civil government as an ordinance of God to conserve the civil peace of the people so far as concerns their bodies and goods, he goes on to say: "The sovereign, original, and foundation of civil power lies in the people (whom they must needs mean by the civil power distinct from the government set up). And if so, that a people may erect and establish what form of government seems to them most meet for their civil condition. It is evident that such governments as are by them erected and established

---

[5] Roy N. Lokken, review of Theodore Thayer, *Pennsylvania Politics and the Growth of Democracy, 1740–1776* (Harrisburg, 1953), in *William and Mary Quarterly*, XII (1955), 671.

have no more power, nor for no longer time, than the civil power or people consenting and agreeing shall betrust them with. This is clear not only in reason, but in the experience of all commonweals where the people are not deprived of their natural freedom by the power of tyrants." [6]

The central issue in seventeenth-century New England was not social equality, manhood suffrage, women's rights, or sympathy for the Levellers, or other tests which have been applied. The central issue was the source of authority for the establishment of a government. The English view was that no government could exist in a colony without a grant of power from the crown. The opposite view, held by certain English dissenters in New England, was that a group of people could create a valid government for themselves by means of a covenant, compact, or constitution. The authors of the Mayflower Compact and the Fundamental Orders of Connecticut operated on this assumption, although they did not carry it to the logical conclusion and call it democracy as did the people in Rhode Island. It is the basic assumption of the Declaration of Independence, a portion of which reads much like the words of Roger Williams written 132 years earlier.

The second proposition is that colonial governments on the eve of the Revolution did not function democratically, nor did the men who controlled them believe in democracy. Even if we agree that there was virtually manhood suffrage in Massachusetts, it is difficult, for me at least, to see it as a democracy. In 1760 the government was controlled by a superb political machine headed by Thomas Hutchinson, who with his relatives and political allies occupied nearly every important political office in the colony except the governorship. The Hutchinson oligarchy controlled the superior court, the council, the county courts, and the justices of the peace; with this structure of appointive office spread throughout the colony, it was able to control the house of representatives elected by the towns. For six years after 1760 the popular party in Boston, led by Oxenbridge Thacher and James Otis, suffered one defeat after another at the hands of the Hutchinson machine. The popular leaders in the town of Boston tried everything from slander to mob violence to get control of the government of the colony but it was not until after the Stamp Act crisis that they were able to win a majority of the house of representatives to their side. Even then, men like James Otis did not at first realize that the Stamp Act could be turned to advantage in the fight against the Hutchinson oligarchy.[7] In terms of political support between 1760 and 1765, if Massachusetts had a democratic leader, that man was Thomas Hutchinson, a

---

[6] *English Historical Documents*, IX, *American Colonial Documents to 1775*, ed. Merrill Jensen (London and New York, 1955), pp. 168, 226, 174.

[7] See Ellen E. Brennan, *Plural Office Holding in Massachusetts 1760–1780* (Chapel Hill, 1945), and "James Otis: Recreant and Patriot," *New England Quarterly*, XII (1939), 691–725.

charge to which he would have been the first to issue a horrified denial.

The third proposition is that before 1774 or 1775 the revolutionary movement was not a democratic movement, except by inadvertence. The pamphleteers who wrote on political and constitutional questions, and the town and county meetings and legislatures that resolved endlessly between 1763 and 1774, were concerned with the formulation of constitutional arguments to defend the colonies and their legislatures from interference by parliament.

The colonial theorists wrote much about the British constitution, the rights of Englishmen, and even of the laws of nature, but they accepted the British assumption that colonial governments derived from British charters and commissions. Their essential concern was with the relationship that existed, or ought to exist, between the British government and the colonial governments, and not with the relationship between man as man, and government itself. Such writers showed no interest in domestic problems, and when it was suggested that the arguments against taxation by parliament were equally applicable to the taxation of under-represented areas in the colonies, or to dissenting religious groups, such suggestions were looked upon as being quite out of order.

The same indifference was displayed in the realm of political realities. The ardent leaders of the fight against British policies showed no interest in, or sympathy for, the discontent of back-country farmers or religious groups such as the Baptists. Instead, they temporarily joined with their political enemies to suppress or ignore it. Such sympathy as the discontented got, they got from the British government, or from colonial leaders charged with being tools of the British power.

The fact is that the popular leaders of the revolutionary movement had no program of domestic reform.[8] Instead, their program was a combination of a continuous assault on the local office-holding aristocracies and an ardent attack on British policies; and in the course of time they identified one with the other. It is sometimes difficult to tell with which side of the program the popular leaders were more concerned. In Massachusetts, for instance, before 1765 they were so violent in their attack on Hutchinson that they prevented Massachusetts from joining the other colonies in making formal protests against British legislation.

The fourth proposition is related to the third. It is that although the popular leaders in the colonies showed no interest in internal political and social change, they were still able to build up a political following, particularly in the seacoast towns. They were superb organizers, propa-

---

[8] For example, see Irving Mark, *Agrarian Conflicts in Colonial New York, 1711–1775* (New York, 1940); *The Carolina Background on the Eve of the Revolution*, ed. Richard J. Hooker (Chapel Hill, 1953); and Elisha Douglass, *Rebels and Democrats* (Chapel Hill, 1955).

gandists with a touch of genius, and possessed of an almost demonic energy in their dual fight against the local political aristocracies and British policies. After a few false starts such as that of James Otis, who at first called the Virginia Stamp Act Resolves treason,[9] the popular leaders took an extreme stand on the subject of colonial rights. The political aristocracies might object to British policies, as most of them did, but considering what they owed to British backing, they displayed an understandable caution, a caution that made it impossible for them to pose as patriotic leaders.

The popular leaders were also willing to take extreme measures in practical opposition to British policies, ranging all the way from mob violence to non-importation agreements forced upon unwilling merchants. And with ever more force and violence they accused Americans who did not agree with them or their methods of knuckling under to British tyranny and of readiness to sell the liberties of their country for a little pelf. In the course of this campaign they appealed to the people at large. Men who normally could not or did not take part in political life, particularly in the cities, were invited to mass meetings where the rules of suffrage were ignored and where they could shout approval of resolutions carefully prepared in advance by their leaders. In addition, the mob was a constant factor in political life, particularly in Boston where it was efficiently organized. Mobs were used to nullify the Stamp Act, to harass British soldiers, to hamper the operations of the customs service, and to intimidate office holders.

All these activities on the part of the disfranchised, or the hitherto politically inactive, accustomed men to taking part in public affairs as never before; and it gave them an appetite for more. From the beginning of the crisis in 1774 onward, more and more "new men," which was the politest name their opponents called them, played an ever more active role, both on the level of practical politics and on the level of political theory. They began writing about and talking about what they called "democracy." And this was a frightening experience, not only to the conservative-minded leaders of the colonies, but to many of the popular leaders as well.

For instance, when a New York mass meeting gathered in May 1774 to answer the letter of the Boston Town Meeting asking for a complete stoppage of trade with Britain as an answer to the Boston Port Act, the people talked about far more than letter writing. One alarmed observer wrote: "I beheld my fellow-citizens very accurately counting all their chickens, not only before any of them were hatched, but before above one half of the eggs were laid. In short, they fairly contended about the future forms of our government, whether it should be founded upon aristocratic or democratic principles." The leaders had "gulled" the mob for years, and now,

---

[9] Brennan, "James Otis: Recreant and Patriot," p. 715.

said Gouverneur Morris, the mob was waking up and could no longer be fooled. The only salvation for the aristocracy of New York was peace with Britain at almost any price.[10]

Another witness to the stirrings among the people was John Adams. Unlike Gouverneur Morris, he never wavered in his belief in independence, but at the same time he was constantly concerned with the danger of an internal upheaval. Years later in his "Autobiography," he recalled as vividly as if it had happened the day before an event that took place while he was home in Massachusetts in the fall of 1775. While there he met a man who had sometimes been his client. "He, though a common horse jockey, was sometimes in the right, and I had commonly been successful in his favor in our courts of law. He was always in the law, and had been sued in many actions at almost every court. As soon as he saw me, he came up to me, and his first salutation to me was, 'Oh! Mr. Adams, what great things have you and your colleagues done for us! We can never be grateful enough to you. There are no courts of justice now in this province, and I hope there never will be another.'" Then Adams goes on: "Is this the object for which I have been contending? said I to myself, for I rode along without any answer to this wretch. Are these the sentiments of such people, and how many of them are there in the country? Half the nation for what I know; for half the nation are debtors, if not more, and these have been, in all countries, the sentiments of debtors. If the power of the country should get into such hands, and there is great danger that it will, to what purpose have we sacrificed our time, health, and everything else? Surely we must guard against this spirit and these principles, or we shall repent of all our conduct." [11]

In May of 1776, with the talk of independence filling the air and the Virginia convention planning to draft a constitution, old Landon Carter of Virginia wrote to Washington bewailing the "ambition" that had "seized on so much ignorance all over the colony as it seems to have done; for this present convention abounds with too many of the inexperienced creatures to navigate our bark on this dangerous coast. . . ." As for independence, he said, "I need only tell you of one definition that I heard of Independency: It was expected to be a form of government that, by being independent of the rich men, every man would then be able to do as he pleased. And it was with this expectation they sent the men they did, in hopes they would plan such a form. One of the delegates I heard exclaim against the Patrolling Law, because a poor man was made to pay for keeping a rich

---

[10] Gouverneur Morris to [John] Penn, May 20, 1774, in *English Historical Documents*, IX, 861–863.

[11] John Adams, "Autobiography," *The Works of John Adams*, ed. Charles F. Adams (Boston, 1856), II, 420–421.

man's slaves in order. I shamed the fool so much for it that he slunk away; but he got elected by it." [12]

One could go on endlessly giving examples like these from the hectic days between 1774 and 1776, examples of the fear among leaders of all shades of opinion that the people would get or were getting out of hand. Meanwhile there was an increasing amount of political writing in the newspapers, writing which was pointing in the direction of independence and the creation of new governments in America. More than a year before *Common Sense,* a piece which appeared first in the *Pennsylvania Packet* declared that "the history of kings is nothing but the history of the folly and depravity of human nature." "We read now and then, it is true, of a good king; so we read likewise of a prophet escaping unhurt from a lion's den, and of three men walking in a fiery furnace without having even their garments singed. The order of nature is as much inverted in the first as it was in the last two cases. A good king is a miracle." [13]

By early 1776 the debate over future governments to be adopted was in full swing. Disliking intensely the ideas of government set forth in *Common Sense,* John Adams drafted his *Thoughts on Government.* His plan was modeled on the old government of Massachusetts, with an elective rather than a royal governor, of course, but it certainly contemplated no radical change in the political structure.[14] John Adams was no innovator. He deplored what he called "the rage for innovation" which had appeared in Massachusetts by June of 1776. The projects, said he, are not for repairing the building but for tearing it down. "The projects of county assemblies, town registers, and town probates of wills are founded in narrow notions, sordid stinginess, and profound ignorance, and tend directly to barbarism." [15]

There was equal alarm in the south at demands for change and new governments. Among those who sought to defend the old order was Carter Braxton. In a long address to the Virginia convention he praised the British constitution and declared that it would be "perverting all order to oblige us, by a novel government to give up our laws, our customs, and our manners." The spirit or principles of limited monarchy should be preserved. Yet, he said, we daily see it condemned by the advocates of "popular governments. . . . The systems recommended to the colonies seem to accord with the temper of the times, and are fraught with all the tumult and riot incident to simple democracy. . . ." Braxton declared that democracies would not

---

[12] *American Archives,* ed. Peter Force, 4th ser. (Washington, 1837–1846), VI, 390–391. May 9, 1776.

[13] *English Historical Documents,* IX, 816–817.   [14] *Works of John Adams,* IV, 189–200.

[15] To John Winthrop, Philadelphia, June 23, 1776, in Mass. Hist. Soc. *Collections,* 5th ser. (Boston, 1878), IV, 310. This was in reply to a letter of John Winthrop, written on June 1, in which he reported to Adams on the various schemes afoot in Massachusetts. *Ibid.,* 305–308.

tolerate wealth, and that they could exist only in countries where all the people are poor from necessity. Nowhere in history could he find an example of a successful democracy. What he proposed for Virginia was a three-part government with a house of representatives elected by the voters for three years. The house, in turn, would choose a governor to serve during good behavior and a council of twenty-four to hold their places for life and to act as an upper house of the legislature.[16] Braxton in Virginia, like John Adams in Massachusetts, hoped to make the transition from dependence to independence without any fundamental political change.

But change was in the air, and writer after writer sought to formulate new ideas about government and to offer concrete suggestions for the theoretical foundations and political structures of the new states to be. In 1775, on hearing that congress had given advice to New Hampshire on the establishment of a government, General John Sullivan offered his thoughts to the revolutionary congress of his colony. All government, he wrote, ought to be instituted for the good of the people. There should be no conflicting branches in imitation of the British constitution "so much celebrated by those who understand nothing of it. . . ." The two houses of the legislature and a governor should all be elected by the people. No danger can arise to a state "from giving the people a free and full voice in their own government." The so-called checks upon the licentiousness of the people "are only the children of designing or ambitious men, no such thing being necessary. . . ." [17]

In the middle colonies appeared an address "To the People of North America on the Different Kinds of Government." After defining monarchy, aristocracy, oligarchy, and democracy, the anonymous writer said: "Popular government—sometimes termed democracy, republic, or commonwealth— is the plan of civil society wherein the community at large takes the care of its own welfare, and manages its concerns by representatives elected by the people out of their own body."

"Seeing the happiness of the people is the true end of government; and it appearing by the definition, that the popular form is the only one which has this for its object; it may be worth inquiring into the causes which have prevented its success in the world."

This writer then undertakes to explain the failure of former democracies. First of all, he says that past republics tried democracy too late and contained within them remnants of aristocracies and military cliques which

---

[16] *The Virginia Gazette* (Dixon and Hunter), June 8, 1776. This had been printed earlier in pamphlet form. For similar ideas see the letter of William Hooper, North Carolina delegate to the Continental Congress, to the North Carolina Provincial Congress, October 26, 1776, in *The Colonial Records of North Carolina*, ed. W. L. Saunders, X (1890), 866–869.

[17] John Sullivan to Meshech Weare, Winter Hill [Mass.], December 11, 1775, in *American Archives*, IV, 241–242.

disliked it. A second cause was that men did not have adequate knowledge of representation and that their large and tumultuous assemblies made it possible for unscrupulous men to charge all troubles to the constitution. A third cause of failure has been the political writers who from ignorance or ulterior motives have tried to discredit democracy. "This has been carried to such a length with many, that the mentioning a democracy constantly excites in them the idea of anarchy; and few, except such as have emancipated themselves from the shackles of political bigotry and prejudice, can talk of it with patience, and hearken to anything offered in its defence." Such are the causes of the destruction of former republics, but the Americans have the best opportunity ever open to mankind to form a free government, "the last and best plan that can possibly exist." [18]

In "The Interest of America," another writer says that new governments must soon be created in America and that "the good of the people is the ultimate end of civil government." Therefore, "we should assume that mode of government which is most equitable and adapted to the good of mankind . . . and I think there can be no doubt that a well-regulated democracy is most equitable." The annual or frequent choice of magistrates is most likely to prevent usurpation and tyranny; and most likely to secure the privileges of the people. Legislatures should be unicameral for a plurality of branches leads to endless contention and a waste of time.[19]

In New England, where the revolutionary congresses of Massachusetts and New Hampshire were controlled by leaders along the seacoast, there was a growing discontent among the people of the back-country counties. Out of it came one of the clearest democratic statements of the times: "The People are the Best Governors." The author starts with the premise that "there are many very noisy about liberty, but are aiming at nothing more than personal power and grandeur." "God," he said, "gave mankind freedom by nature, made every man equal to his neighbor, and has virtually enjoined them to govern themselves by their own laws." Representatives in legislatures should have only the power to make laws. They should not have power to elect officials or to elect councils or senates to veto legislation. Only the people have this power. If there must be senates, they should be elected by the people of the state at large and should have only advisory powers. Representation should not be according to taxable property, for "Nature itself abhors such a system of civil government, for it will make an inequality among the people and set up a number of lords over the rest." Representation according to population also has its difficulties. The solution is for each town to have one representative, with more for larger towns if the legislature thinks fit. So far as property qualifications for representatives are concerned, there should be none. "Social virtue and knowl-

---

[18] *American Archives*, V, 180–183. [March 1776.]   [19] *Ibid.*, VI, 840–843. [June 1776.]

edge . . . is the best and only necessary qualification of the person before us." If we have property qualifications "we root our virtue; and what will then become of the genuine principle of freedom?" "Let it not be said in future generations that money was made by the founders of the American states an essential qualification in the rulers of a free people." The writer proposed annual elections of a one-house legislature, of a governor, and of the judges of the superior court. The people in the counties should elect annually all their own officials—judges, sheriffs, and others—as should the inhabitants of the towns. And in all elections "any orderly free male of ordinary capacity" should have the right to vote if he has lived in a town for a year.[20]

From such discussions one may sum up certain of the essential ideas. (1) They agree that the "good" or the "happiness" of the people is the only end of government. (2) They agree that "democracy" is the best form of government to achieve that end. (3) They show a distrust of men when in power—a distrust shared with far more conservative-minded writers of the times.

As to details of government there are variations, but they do agree on fundamentals. (1) The legislatures, whether one or two houses, are to be elected by the people. (2) Public officials, state and local, are to be elected by the people or by their representatives in the legislatures. (3) There should be annual elections. (4) Some argue for manhood suffrage, and one writer even advocated that tax-paying widows should vote. (5) There should be freedom of religion, at least for Protestants; in any case, freedom from taxation to support established churches.

One may well ask: did such theoretical discussions have any meaning in terms of practical politics, or were they idle speculations by anonymous writers without influence? The answer is that they did have meaning. I have already cited the discussion of the principles of government in New York in the spring of 1774, and the litigious jockey in Massachusetts in 1775 who hoped that the courts would remain closed forever. These are not isolated examples. By the end of 1775 all sorts of organized activity was under way, ranging in place from North Carolina to New Hampshire, and from militia groups to churches.

In North Carolina the defeat of the Regulators in 1771 had not ended discontent but merely suppressed it. By September 1775 Mecklenburg County was instructing its delegates in the provincial congress to work for a plan of government providing for equal representation and the right to vote for every freeman who supported the government, either in person or property. Legislation should not be a "divided right"; no man or body of men should be "invested with a negative on the voice of the people duly

---

[20] Reprinted in Frederick Chase, *A History of Dartmouth College and the Town of Hanover, New Hampshire* (Cambridge, 1891), I, Appendix D, 654-663.

collected. . . ." [21] By November 1776, when North Carolina elected a congress to write its first state constitution, Mecklenburg County was even more specific in its instructions. It told its delegates that they were to endeavor to establish a free government under the authority of the people of North Carolina, and that the government was to be a "simple democracy, or as near it as possible." In fixing fundamental principles, the delegates were to "oppose everything that leans to aristocracy or power in the hands of the rich and chief men exercised to the oppression of the poor." [22]

In the middle colonies militia organizations made demands and suggestions. Pennsylvania was in turmoil, with the assembly controlled by the opponents of independence and the revolutionary party working in large measure through a voluntary militia organization called the Associators. In February 1776 a committee of privates from the Philadelphia Associators told the assembly "that it has been the practice of all countries, and is highly reasonable, that all persons . . . who expose their lives in the defense of a country, should be admitted to the enjoyment of all the rights and privileges of a citizen of that country. . . ." All Associators should be given the right to vote.[23]

In June the committee of privates again protested to the legislature. This time they denied the right of the assembly to appoint two brigadier generals for the Associators as recommended by the Continental Congress. The privates declared that since many of them could not vote, they were not represented in the assembly. Furthermore, many counties where the Associators were most numerous did not have proportional representation. And for that matter, since many members of the assembly were members of a religious profession "totally averse to military defense," they could not possibly be called representatives of the Associators.[24]

While such ideas were being expounded in Pennsylvania, some militia in Maryland were proposing a new constitution. There was a growing discontent in Maryland with the revolutionary convention which was opposed to independence, and whose members were appointing one another to military posts. Government by convention should stop, said one writer, and regular government be instituted.[25]

Late in June 1776 deputies from the militia battalions in Anne Arundel County met and proposed a constitution to be submitted to the people of the county. They started out with the declaration that the right to legislate is in "every member of the community," but that for convenience the right

---

[21] Colonial Records of North Carolina, X, 239–242. [Sept. 1775.]

[22] Ibid., 870, a-f. [Nov. 1776.]

[23] Votes and Proceedings of the Assembly, Feb. 23, 1776, in Pennsylvania Archives, 8th ser. [Harrisburg, 1935], VIII, 7406.

[24] Ibid., 7546–47. June 14, 1776.

[25] "An American" in "To the People of Maryland," American Archives, VI, 1094–96.

must be delegated to representatives chosen by the people. The legislature must never form a separate interest from the community at large, and its branches must "be independent of and balance each other, and all dependent on the people." There should be a two-house legislature chosen annually "as annual elections are most friendly to liberty, and the oftener power reverts to the people, the greater will be the security for a faithful discharge of it." All provincial officials, including judges, should be elected annually by joint ballot of the two houses. All county officials should be chosen annually by the people of each county. Nothing is said of property qualifications for either voting or office-holding. So far as taxes are concerned, "the unjust mode of taxation by poll" should be abolished, and all monies raised should be according to a fair and equal assessment of people's estates.[26]

In New Jersey the revolutionary congress, like that in other colonies, was trying to prevent change and was maintaining the land qualification for voting for its members. But the complaints grew so loud that it was forced to yield. One petition in 1776, for instance, declared that "we cannot conceive the wise author of our existence ever designed that a certain quantity of earth on which we tread should be annexed to a man to complete his dignity and fit him for society. Was the sole design of government either the security of land or money, the possession of either or both of these would be the only necessary qualifications for its members. But we apprehend the benign intentions of a well regulated government to extend to the security of much more valuable possessions—the rights and privileges of freemen, for the defense of which every kind of property and even life itself have been liberally expended." [27]

In Massachusetts the Baptists were quick to draw a parallel between the fight for civil liberty against England and their own fight for religious liberty. Baptists were being jailed for refusal to pay taxes to support churches. Their leader, the Reverend Isaac Backus, put Sam Adams squarely on the spot in January 1774. "I fully concur with your grand maxim," wrote Backus, "that it is essential to liberty that representation and taxation go together." Hence, since the representatives in the Massachusetts legislature have only civil qualifications, how can they levy ecclesiastical taxes? "And I am bold in it," Backus goes on, "that taxes laid by the British Parliament upon America are not more contrary to civil freedom, than these taxes are to the very nature of liberty of conscience. . . ." He hopes, he says, that Adams will do something about it so that a large number of peaceable people "may not be forced to carry their complaints before those

---

[26] *Ibid.*, 1092–94. June 26–27, 1776.
[27] Richard P. McCormick, *The History of Voting in New Jersey . . . 1664–1911* (New Brunswick, 1953), pp. 66–68.

who would be glad to hear that the legislature of Massachusetts deny to their fellow servants that liberty which they so earnestly insist upon for themselves. A word to the wise is sufficient." [28]

Samuel Adams was not interested in liberty of conscience, particularly for Baptists, and he did not reply. But Backus pursued him to the first Continental Congress in Philadelphia where a four-hour meeting was held in Carpenter's Hall one night. The Massachusetts delegation met with the Baptists, but with a large audience present, among whom were the Quaker leaders James and Israel Pemberton, and members of congress like Joseph Galloway. The Backus diary gives a picture of Sam and John Adams quite literally squirming as the Baptists cited the facts of religious life in Massachusetts.[29] One can well imagine with what delight Galloway and the Pembertons looked on as the Massachusetts delegation vainly tried to wriggle out of a dilemma produced by the contradiction between their theory and their practice.

The Declaration of Independence was taken seriously by many Americans, or at least they found its basic philosophy useful in battling for change in the new states. Nowhere was this done more neatly than in Grafton County, New Hampshire. The Provincial Congress was in the control of eastern leaders and they refused to grant representation that the western towns thought adequate. In calling elections in the fall of 1776, the Congress grouped various towns together for electing representatives and told them that the men they elected must own real estate worth £200 lawful money. Led by professors at an obscure little college at Hanover, the people of Grafton County went on strike. They refused to hold elections, and town after town met and passed resolutions. The whole procedure of the Congress was unconstitutional. No plan of representation had been adopted since the Declaration of Independence. By the Declaration, said Hanover and two other towns in a joint statement, "we conceive that the powers of government reverted to the people at large, and of course annihilated the political existence of the Assembly which then was. . . ." Six other towns joined together and declared it to be "our humble opinion, that when the declaration of independency took place, the Colonies were absolutely in a state of nature, and the powers of government reverted to the people at large. . . ." Such being the case, the Provincial Congress has no authority to combine towns, each of which is entitled to representation as a corporate entity. And it has no right to limit the choice of representatives to the owners of £200, said the people of Lyme, because "every elector in free states is capable of being elected." [30]

---

[28] To Samuel Adams, Jan. 19, 1774, in Alvah Hovey, *A Memoir of the Life and Times of the Rev. Isaac Backus* (Boston, 1859), pp. 195–197.

[29] *Ibid.*, ch. xv.

[30] *American Archives*, 5th ser. (Washington, 1848–1853), III, 1223–24, and Chase, *History of Dartmouth*, I, 426–433.

It seems clear, to me at least, that by 1776 there were people in America demanding the establishment of democratic state governments, by which they meant legislatures controlled by a majority of the voters, and with none of the checks upon their actions such as had existed in the colonies. At the same time there were many Americans who were determined that there should be no changes except those made inevitable by separation from Great Britain.

The history of the writing of the first state constitutions is to a large extent the history of the conflict between these two ideals of government. The conflict can be exaggerated, of course, for there was considerable agreement on structural details. Most of the state constitutions worked out in written form the structure of government that had existed in the colonies, all the way from governors, two-house legislatures, and judicial systems, to the forms of local government. In terms of structure, little that is revolutionary is to be found. Even the much maligned unicameral legislature of Pennsylvania was only a continuation of what Pennsylvania had had since the beginning of the century.

The significant thing is not the continuity of governmental structure, but the alteration of the balance of power within the structure, and in the political situation resulting from the break away from the supervising power of a central government—that of Great Britain.

The first and most revolutionary change was in the field of basic theory. In May 1776, to help bring about the overthrow of the Pennsylvania assembly, the chief stumbling block in the way of independence, Congress resolved that all governments exercising authority under the crown of Great Britain should be suppressed, and that "all the powers of government [be] exerted under the authority of the people of the colonies. . . ." John Adams described it as "the most important resolution that ever was taken in America." [31] The Declaration of Independence spelled it out in terms of the equality of men, the sovereignty of the people, and the right of a people to change their governments as they pleased.

Second: the Revolution ended the power of a sovereign central government over the colonies. Britain had had the power to appoint and remove governors, members of upper houses of legislatures, judges, and other officials. It had the power to veto colonial legislation, to review cases appealed from colonial supreme courts, and to use armed force. All of this superintending power was wiped out by independence.

Third: the new central government created in America by the Articles of Confederation was, in a negative sense at least, a democratic government. The Congress of the United States had no power over either the states or their citizens. Hence, each state could govern itself as it pleased, and as a

---

[31] *Warren-Adams Letters,* I (Boston, 1917), 245; in Mass. Hist. Soc. *Collections,* Vols. 72, 73.

result of some of the new state constitutions, this often meant by a majority of the voters within a state.

Fourth: in writing the state constitutions, change was inevitable. The hierarchy of appointed legislative, executive, and judicial officials which had served as a check upon the elective legislatures was gone. The elective legislature became the supreme power in every state, and the lower houses, representing people however inadequately, became the dominant branch. The appointive houses of colonial times were replaced by elective senates, which in theory were supposed to represent property. They were expected to, and sometimes did, act as a check upon the lower houses, but their power was far less than that of pre-war councils.

Fifth: the office of governor underwent a real revolution. The governors of the royal colonies had, in theory at least, vast powers, including an absolute veto. In the new constitutions, most Americans united in shearing the office of governor of virtually all power.

Sixth: state supreme courts underwent a similar revolution. Under the state constitutions they were elected by the legislatures or appointed by governors who were elected officials. And woe betide a supreme court that tried to interfere with the actions of a legislature.

What such changes meant in terms of political realities was that a majority of voters within a state, if agreed upon a program and persistent enough, could do what it wanted, unchecked by governors or courts or appeals to a higher power outside the state.

There were other areas in which changes took place, although they were only beginnings. A start was made in the direction of ending the property qualification for voting and office-holding. A few states established what amounted to manhood suffrage, and a few years later even women voted in New Jersey although that was stopped when it appeared that woman suffrage meant only a means of stuffing ballot boxes. A few states took steps in the direction of representation according to population, a process as yet unsolved in the United States. A large step was taken in the direction of disestablishing state churches, but on the whole one still had to be a Protestant, and a Trinitarian at that, to hold office.

In connection with office-holding, there is one eighteenth-century American idea that is worthy of a whole study by itself, and that is the concept of rotation in office. Many Americans were convinced that office-holding bred a lust for power in the holder. Therefore there must be frequent, if not annual, elections; and there must be a limitation on the time one might spend in certain offices. There is probably no more remarkable self-denying ordinance in the history of politics than the provision in the Articles of Confederation that no man could be a member of Congress more than three years out of any six. I have often been accused of wanting to go back to the Articles of Confederation, which is nonsense, but there are times when I do wish that this one provision might be revived in the twentieth century.

What I have done in this paper is to set before you some of the reasons for believing that the American Revolution was a democratic movement, not in origin, but in result. Certainly the political leaders of the eighteenth century thought the results were democratic. Whether they thought the results were good or bad is another story.

III

*The British Empire
Before the American Revolution:
Imperial Theory
or Colonial Practice?*

INTRODUCTION

The essential nature and character of the constitutional relations between the American colonies and the mother country between 1689 and 1763 have provided matter for controversy from conflicting interpretations at the time to conflicting contemporary interpretations. The English view of the matter was well stated in the 1760's by Sir William Blackstone in his celebrated Commentaries on the Laws of England. *He declared that in every form of government ". . . there is and must be . . . a supreme, irresistible, absolute, uncontrolled authority, in which the* jura summi imperii, *or the rights of sovereignty, reside." Samuel Johnson, in his downright manner, concurred: "In sovereignty there are no gradations." This view saw sovereignty as indivisible and held that that sovereignty unquestionably lay in Great Britain and, there, in the Parliament of Great Britain. This was the unitary view of the nature of the British Empire before the American Revolution; this was the imperial theory. It asserted the right of Parliament to legislate for the colonies "in all cases whatsoever."*

A divergent and growing American concept of the nature of the Old Empire was based upon colonial practice over more than half a century and was strongly empirical and pragmatic as contrasted with the legalism and formality of the English view. The American concept held that whatever may have been the case at the foundation of the colonies, the historical experience since 1689 had evolved a different relationship. History denies legalism. The growth in power of the lower Houses of Assembly in all the colonies from a position of subordination to the colonial executive in the late seventeenth century, through a position of equality during the early eighteenth century, to the final achievement of a position of dominance by 1763, was, in fact, what the colonial practice had led to. The relationship between the colonies and the mother country was a federal relationship and not a unitary one. In the period 1763–1776, the direct confrontation of imperial theory and imperial practice took place as high drama and independence resulted.

There have been many schools of historical interpretation of the colonial background of the American Revolution—a Whig patriotic view, an imperial view, a socioeconomic view, and others. (See Edmund S. Morgan, "The American Revolution: Revisions in Need of Revising," William and Mary Quarterly, *Third Series,* XIV *[January 1957], 3–15.) Lawrence Henry Gipson has, for many years, been engaged in the writing of a great multivolume history entitled* The British Empire Before the American Revolution. *He belongs to what has been called the imperial school of historians, viewing the relations between England and America from the cen-*

ter, from the imperial point of view. In the first piece of historical writing below, taken from Gipson's great history, we have what our second author, Jack P. Greene, calls ". . . a classic statement of the imperial argument." Here Gipson gives us a view of the relations between the colonies and the mother country in 1750. Basically the picture Gipson draws shows the relations of mother country and colonies as agreeable and mutually advantageous. He perceives ". . . a quality of dynamism in the civilization of the eighteenth-century British Empire which was lacking in the culture of any other contemporary imperial system. This dynamic quality expressed itself in a challenging of older ideas and older modes of action and doubtless flowed from the degree of freedom enjoyed by people in every English colony. Thinking was not canalized." In the second essay below, Greene gives a different estimate of the constitutional relations existing between England and America, with special emphasis upon the role of the lower Houses of Assembly. He states: "But the lower houses had done more than simply acquire a new status in colonial politics. They had in a sense altered the structure of the constitution of the British Empire itself by asserting colonial authority against imperial authority and extending the constitutions of the colonies far beyond the limitations of the charters, instructions or fixed notions of imperial authorities."

The British Colonial System in 1750

Lawrence Henry Gipson

This volume of the series, as well as the preceding one, has stressed various local and regional aspects of the mid-eighteenth-century British colonial system. It now remains to emphasize some of the more general characteristics of this system.

First of all, the government of the British colonies in 1750 was based upon certain well-established principles—the same principles that later were to be called into question. Unlike the colonies of France, Spain, and Portugal in the New World, which were under the full personal control of the king and his appointed ministers, the British colonies were not subject to the personal rule of George II. It is true that in the seventeenth century

Reprinted from *The British Empire Before The American Revolution* by Lawrence Henry Gipson, by permission of Alfred A. Knopf, Inc. Copyright 1936, 1960 by Alfred A. Knopf, Inc. Vol. III, 275–281.

the kings of England made grants to individuals and to companies of lands in the New World and at the same time issued letters patent to them for establishing governments within these possessions. But by 1750 the royal authority had declined to such a point that the exercise of the old prerogative powers in important matters had either quite ceased or was now very narrowly circumscribed by the combined authority of King, Lords, and Commons in the High Court of Parliament.

Colonials were fully aware of the evolution that had taken place in the constitution of England and of the Empire. For example, when leaders from a number of North American colonies assembled at Albany in a congress in 1754 and proceeded, among other things, to draw up a plan of union to include most of the continental colonies, it was quite clear to them that only by an act of Parliament could this union be achieved—just as the Union of England and Scotland was brought about earlier in the century under Queen Anne only by means of a fundamental statute. They therefore embodied this as a basic feature in the final draft of the Albany Plan of Union.

In other words, in 1750 Parliament alone was held to possess inherent power to determine great matters of state. Therefore, if the King's Great Seal was still the symbol for the authentication of colonial charters and the commissions of the colonial governors, this seal could not be used in derogation of the sovereign powers of the Parliament of Great Britain. This issue had been settled definitively in the days of William III when in 1698 he had sought without success to provide for a reorganization of the East India Company under the Great Seal in opposition to the views of the House of Commons. Furthermore, that the Privy Council was still active and powerful in colonial administration after the Revolution of 1688 was simply due to the fact that Parliament had seen advantages in permitting this body—initially brought into existence by the use of the royal prerogative—to continue to function as the government's chief administrative agency for colonial affairs. That sovereignty within the Empire was centred in Parliament after 1688 can also be illustrated by the comprehensive act of 1696 relating to colonial trade (7 and 8 Wm. III, c. 7), which still remained in the statute books in 1750. This statute provided that any colonial law repugnant to it or to any other law that Parliament should pass in the future was "illegal, null and void."

Parliament did not stop at this point in dealing with colonial matters. It proceeded to legislate in this field and by the middle of the eighteenth century had passed a series of laws that amounted in effect to a code held binding on all the colonies. To illustrate. It forbad the sale of colonial lands to aliens without the consent of the Crown (7 and 8 Wm. III, c. 22) and the export from the colonies of wool, woollen yarn and cloth (10 and 11 Wm. III, c. 10), provided that colonial governors accused of crimes might be tried in England (11 and 12 Wm. III, c. 12), prohibited the destruction

in the colonies of pine trees designated as serviceable for the royal navy
(3 and 4 Anne, c. 10), determined the value of lawful colonial currency in
terms of the Spanish specie circulating in the colonies (6 Anne, c. 30 followed by 9 Anne, c. 17, 8 Geo. I, c. 12, and 2 Geo. II, c. 35), laid down a
rule for the indenture to service of minors living in the colonies (4 Geo. I,
c. 11), established the principle that land in the colonies was liable for the
debts of its owner (5 Geo. II, c. 7), placed restraints on the manufacture of
hats in the colonies and forbad their sale outside of the particular colony
where they were made (5 Geo. II, c. 22), levied high duties on foreign-
produced molasses, rum, and sugar imported into colonies (6 Geo. II, c. 13),
provided a comprehensive rule for the naturalization of foreigners in the
colonies (13 Geo. II, c. 7), extended to the colonies the restraints already
placed on unlawful business enterprises and stock-jobbing in Great Britain
(14 Geo. II, c. 37), and put under severe restrictions both the colonial iron
industry (23 Geo. II, c. 29) and the governments of the New England colonies in the matter of issuing and circulating bills of credit (24 Geo. II, c. 53).

In view of the major issue that developed from 1760 to 1775 between
Great Britain and the continental colonies over the question of what powers
Parliament could exercise in colonial affairs, it is remarkable that at no
time during a period of some sixty years subsequent to the Revolution of
1688 did any colonial assembly or any other authorized representative
group of a colony openly challenge that body's competence and right thus
to legislate. This is especially noteworthy in light of the rather impressive
body of laws listed above covering many important colonial matters, both
internal and external, which were enacted during that period.

While Parliament was the final source of authority throughout the Old
British Empire and while it legislated freely on matters affecting the colonial system, it never saw fit to create by statute any rigid pattern of government to which all colonies should conform. On the contrary, the machinery
of government of each colony in 1750 was based on the circumstances of its
origins and the conditions under which it evolved. Each therefore had a
constitution that was unique, at least in some respects. That of Newfoundland was markedly different from that of Nova Scotia—both of them royal
colonies—and neither had much in common with the constitutions of the
four New England colonies, New Hampshire, Massachusetts Bay, Rhode
Island, and Connecticut, which in turn differed more or less strikingly from
one another. This same point may be made concerning the constitutions of
the Middle Atlantic Seaboard colonies of New York, New Jersey, Pennsylvania, and the Lower Counties on the Delaware. It was true as well of the
constitutions of the Southern colonies of Maryland, Virginia, North Carolina, and South Carolina, and also the Trusteeship of Georgia, then on the
threshold of becoming a royal colony. While the similarities were greater
than the differences in the constitutions of the royal island colonies of the
Bermudas, the Bahamas, the four British Leeward Islands, Barbados, and

Jamaica, the general frame of government of each was shaped in light of existing local conditions and the specific needs of the inhabitants and was distinctive to this extent.

The colonial constitutions were based either on letters patent, as in the case of Massachusetts Bay, Rhode Island, Connecticut, Pennsylvania, Maryland, and Georgia (between 1732 and 1752), or on commissions and instructions issued to the governors of the royal colonies—these also applied to the semi-royal colony of Massachusetts Bay. To the above constitution-forming documents must be added all colonial laws of a fundamental nature passed by a colony that had been approved by the Privy Council, as well as all those parliamentary statutes that limited freedom of action and therefore restricted colonial legislative competence.

During the period under consideration, the powers that the provincial governments could freely exercise were quite broad, except in the cases of Newfoundland and Nova Scotia. This latitude accorded to the local governments helped to make possible the distinctiveness of the British colonial constitutions, something that was true in 1750 even of the four Leeward Islands of Antigua, St. Christopher, Nevis, and Montserrat, despite the fact that they were all under the same royal governor, who was granted only one commission and a single set of general instructions. For each island possessed its own assembly and used its powers within permissible limits to mould the structure of its own government.

Nevertheless, the commissions and instructions of the governors of all royal colonies were made as much alike as possible for the purpose of establishing a constitutional pattern for these colonies. That all of them could not—and therefore did not—conform rigidly to such a pattern is clear. There were, for example, striking differences between the commission and instructions issued, on the one hand, to the Governor of Newfoundland and, on the other, to the Governor of Jamaica; therefore notable variations existed between the constitutions of these two island provinces. But there were also extraordinary similarities. Certain common duties were assigned to all royal Governors as an inseparable part of the responsibilities of their high office.

When one thinks of a constitution as an instrument of government, one has in mind its quality of permanence—in so far as human institutions possess this quality. Since the governor's commission and instructions formed a most vital part of the constitutional framework of every royal colony, they were not altered each time a new governor was appointed. However, as good reasons for change arose, alterations of certain articles often resulted in both the commission and the instructions. To illustrate. In the middle of the eighteenth century the Governor of Newfoundland was empowered to set up courts of oyer and terminer on the island with power to punish offenders capitally, instead of sending persons accused of capital crimes to England for trial as had been the rule. At the time of this change the commission, as well as the general instructions, had to be recast to a certain degree in light of the opinion of the King's legal advisers that such power could be bestowed on a colonial governor only under the Great Seal.

Modifications of less importance in the structure of governmental powers would ordinarily be reflected simply in modifications in the instructions. For example, when William Henry Lyttelton was appointed Governor of South Carolina in 1755 in place of James Glen, nine articles of Glen's instructions were omitted from Lyttelton's as "useless and improper"; three other articles having to do with judicial appeals were also omitted and were replaced by a single article embodying the decision of the Privy Council respecting appeals. Such was the process in the evolution of the constitutions of the royal provinces.

One of the most salient and important features of British colonial government, in contrast to the systems of colonial government of other European powers established in the New World, was the existence in 1750 in every colony excepting Newfoundland and Nova Scotia of a legislature elected by the freemen or freeholders. These assemblies possessed very broad powers of law-making, even in the face of the limitations placed upon them by the mother country. They also had the power of the purse. Far from being awed by the governor, be he royal or proprietary, the provincial assembly was more apt to frustrate or even awe him. Indeed, in no other part of the New World did the inhabitants have such opportunity to shape their own destinies as they had in the English colonies. Likewise, in no other part of the New World was so large a proportion of the people literate, possessed of knowledge of the conditions of other peoples and of a political awareness that reflected their experience in public service. Literally thousands of British colonials were active in such service at the town, parish, or county level in the middle of the eighteenth century. Every assembly contained men trained in the law—in some cases unquestionably more highly trained than the governor himself. These men were also adept in the art of the parliamentary manœuvre designed to bend the governor to the will of the representatives of the people. As a result, the colonial assemblies continued to increase in prestige during the course of the eighteenth century, while the executive authority was proportionately weakened. Therefore, only a governor who had arrived at an understanding with his assembly could expect to have a successful and fruitful administration. At the same time, if he submitted too far to the provincial legislature and in so doing ignored his instructions, he was in danger of recall. His role, except in the two corporate colonies of Connecticut and Rhode Island and in the non-corporate colony of the Lower Counties on the Delaware, was not an easy one.

One of the powers granted to all governors of royal colonies and to those of the proprietaries was a veto on colonial legislation. But the assemblies could bring pressure by refusing to appropriate funds and in other ways, with the result that the governors were frequently torn between two desires: that of maintaining friendly relations with the assemblymen, and that of fulfilling their chief responsibility—supporting the principles that were the foundation of British imperial policy.

Even when a local law had been agreed to by the governor, it was necessary, in every colony except Rhode Island, Connecticut, Maryland, and the Lower Counties on the Delaware, that it be submitted to the Privy Council in England for final approval or disapproval. This might have constituted a serious check, if not a stoppage, to most colonial legislation, especially if it differed from the laws of Great Britain. But this was not the case. While laws were disapproved from time to time, the total that met this fate was insignificant in comparison with the number submitted and permitted to stand. During the entire colonial period before 1775, less than six per cent of all laws sent home as required were disapproved.

Again, although the laws of every colony were subject to final review by the Privy Council on appeal from the highest court in a colony—irrespective of whether or not the colony was under obligation to submit its acts to the approval of the Privy Council—this happened only at rare intervals. Once a law had passed the scrutiny of a governor, it was likely to stand, unless modified subsequently by the originating assembly.

Of all the laws passed which were apt to run counter to a royal governor's instructions, none was more vigorously supported by the local assembly than currency legislation. It was obviously necessary for the colonies to have a medium of exchange for the conduct of business in the absence of English specie, which could not be sent out of the Kingdom by prohibition going back to the days of Edward I. The medium of exchange took the form of so-called bills of credit in most of the northern colonies in the eighteenth century. The debasing of this money and the consequent defrauding of creditors—especially on the part of a colony such as Rhode Island, where inflation reached unprecedented heights by 1750—led the British government finally to take strong measures. These were to culminate in the New England currency act passed in 1751 placing the four colonies under great restraints. However, instructions had previously been sent to the governors of all royal colonies requiring them to refuse to sign any bill that would permit the inhabitants of a colony to liquidate debts incurred in terms of English sterling money by repayment in that colony's depreciated money. In North Carolina and in New Jersey, in particular, this led to bitter controversies between the Governor and the Assembly over legal-tender acts. It may be added that, whereas North Carolina had been guilty of serious abuses in issuing paper money, New Jersey had taken steps to maintain the face value of its currency, so that the people of the colony, not without reason, felt they were being punished for the misdeeds of others. In substance, such problems as those of colonial currency were not to be resolved during the period under consideration.

There was in truth a quality of dynamism in the civilization of the eighteenth-century British Empire which was lacking in the culture of any other contemporary imperial system. This dynamic quality expressed itself in a challenging of older ideas and older modes of action and doubtless flowed from the degree of freedom enjoyed by people in every English colony. Thinking was not canalized. Books were not placed on an index of forbidden reading matter. Non-indentured white people shifted freely from one occupation to another and rose without great difficulty from one class level to a higher one, unhampered by the social restrictions of "status" in the European sense of the term. Although this was not true of people during the period of their indenture as part of a white labouring force, even the indentured servant was free to make his way as he could when he had fulfilled his obligation. People in the British colonies were on the move —and in a hurry.

The means of higher education were expanding as the older institutions of learning—Harvard, William and Mary, and Yale—were joined in the 1740's by the College of Philadelphia and Princeton, to be followed later by King's (Columbia), Brown, Queen's (Rutgers), and Dartmouth.

There was a variety of vocations and also avocations open to colonials of ambition and enterprise, despite the previously mentioned limitations on certain types of activity superimposed upon them by Parliament. It is small wonder, therefore, that the Old British Empire drew to its confines like a magnet thousands of non-English people seeking greater liberty of thought or a better way of life than was possible under existing circumstances either in their ancestral homes in the Old World or in the colonies of other European powers in the New World. By their coming they greatly enriched and slowly modified the seventeenth- and eighteenth-century English New World civilization. Among the contributors to this enrichment and flowering were Welshmen, Ulster Scots, Scottish Highlanders, native Irish, Germans, Swiss, and French Huguenots, together with the offspring of the Dutch, Swedish, and Finnish early settlers in the valleys and estuaries of the Hudson and Delaware rivers.

With all the change in modes of life which took place in this New World environment people were constantly faced with new situations. Yet a quality of stability in the British colonial institutions and a hard core of conservatism in the British-American people led most of them to hold fast to what their own lives and the experiences of their forefathers had persuaded them were good things and to discard other ideas and methods that had not met the test. Thus, the codes of laws, based upon the Old Testament, which had been adopted by the early Puritans in New England and had proved to be unworkable gave way in the eighteenth century not to new, untried, theoretical systems of jurisprudence but to judicial systems adhering ever more closely as time went on to English common and statutory laws. A similar development took place in Pennsylvania, where the Quakers in the seventeenth century had adopted a code of law based on the spirit of the New Testament which, in practice, had not met the needs of the situation. Moreover, the machinery for the administration of justice in the British colonies reflected the constant conservative attitudes of a dynamic American society.

The Role of the Lower Houses of

Assembly in Eighteenth-Century Politics

Jack P. Greene

The rise of the representative assemblies was perhaps the most significant political and constitutional development in the history of Britain's overseas empire before the American Revolution. Crown and proprietary authorities had obviously intended the governor to be the focal point of colonial government with the assemblies merely subordinate bodies called together when necessary to levy taxes and ratify local ordinances proposed by the executive. Consequently, except in the New England charter colonies, where the representative bodies early assumed a leading role, they were dominated by the governors and councils for most of the period down to 1689. But beginning with the Restoration and intensifying their efforts during the years following the Glorious Revolution, the lower houses engaged in a successful quest for power as they set about to restrict the authority of the executive, undermine the system of colonial administration laid dawn by imperial and proprietary authorities, and make themselves paramount in the affairs of their respective colonies.

Historians have been fascinated by this phenomenon. For nearly a century after 1776 they interpreted it as a prelude to the American Revolution. In the 1780's the pro-British historian George Chalmers saw it as the early manifestation of a latent desire for independence, an undutiful reaction to the mild policies of the Mother Country.[1] In the middle of the nine-

---

From *Journal of Southern History*, XXVII (November 1961), 451–474. Copyright 1961 by the Southern Historical Association. Reprinted by permission of the Managing Editor.

[1] George Chalmers, *An Introduction to the History of the Revolt of the American Colo-*

teenth century the American nationalist George Bancroft, although more interested in other aspects of colonial history, looked upon it as the natural expression of American democratic principles, simply another chapter in the progress of mankind.[2] The reaction to these sweeping interpretations set in during the last decades of the nineteenth century, when Charles M. Andrews, Edward Channing, Herbert L. Osgood, and others began to investigate in detail and to study in context developments from the Restoration to the end of the Seven Years' War. Osgood put a whole squadron of Columbia students to work examining colonial political institutions, and they produced a series of institutional studies in which the evolution of the lower houses was a central feature. These studies clarified the story of legislative development in each colony, but this necessarily piecemeal approach, as well as the excessive fragmentation that characterized the more general narratives of Osgood and Channing, tended to emphasize the differences rather than the similarities in the rise of the lower houses and failed to produce a general analysis of the common features of their quest for power.[3] Among later scholars, Leonard W. Labaree in his excellent monograph *Royal Government in America* presented a comprehensive survey of the institutional development of the lower houses in the royal colonies and of the specific issues involved in their struggles with the royal governors but he did not offer any systematic interpretation of the general process and pattern of legislative development.[4] Charles Andrews promised to tackle this problem and provide a synthesis in the later volumes of his magnum opus, *The Colonial Period of American History,* but he died before completing that part of the project.[5]

---

nies (2 vols., Boston, 1845), I, 223–26, and II, 226–28, particularly, for statements of Chalmers' position.

[2] George Bancroft, *History of the United States* (14th ed., 10 vols., Boston, 1854–1875), III, 1–108, 383–98, particularly.

[3] Herbert L. Osgood, *The American Colonies in the Seventeenth Century* (3 vols., New York, 1904–1907) and *The American Colonies in the Eighteenth Century* (4 vols., New York, 1924–1925). For Edward Channing's treatment see *A History of the United States* (6 vols., New York, 1905–1925), II. Representative of the studies of Osgood's students are William R. Shepherd, *History of Proprietary Government in Pennsylvania* (New York, 1896); Newton D. Mereness, *Maryland As a Proprietary Province* (New York, 1901); W. Roy Smith, *South Carolina As a Royal Province, 1719–1776* (New York, 1903); Charles L. Raper, *North Carolina: A Study in English Colonial Government* (New York, 1904); William H. Fry, *New Hampshire As a Royal Province* (New York, 1908); Edwin P. Tanner, *The Province of New Jersey, 1664–1738* (New York, 1908); Edgar J. Fisher, *New Jersey As a Royal Province, 1738–1776* (New York, 1911); and Percy S. Flippin, *The Royal Government in Virginia, 1624–1775* (New York, 1919).

[4] Leonard W. Labaree, *Royal Government in America* (New Haven, 1930), 172–311, particularly. Two other illuminating studies by Labaree's contemporaries are A. B. Keith, *Constitutional History of the First British Empire* (Oxford, 1930), which is legalistic in emphasis, and John F. Burns, *Controversies Between Royal Governors and Their Assemblies in the Northern American Colonies* (Boston, 1923), which fails to tie together in any satisfactory way developments in the four colonies it treats.

[5] Charles M. Andrews, "On the Writing of Colonial History," *William and Mary Quar-*

As a result, some fundamental questions have never been fully answered, and no one has produced a comprehensive synthesis. No one has satisfactorily worked out the basic pattern of the quest; analyzed the reasons for and the significance of its development; explored its underlying assumptions and theoretical foundations; or assessed the consequences of the success of the lower houses, particularly the relationship between their rise to power and the coming of the American Revolution. This essay is intended to suggest some tentative conclusions about these problems, not to present ultimate solutions. My basic research on the lower houses has been in the Southern royal colonies and in Nova Scotia. One of the present purposes is to test the generalizations I have arrived at about the Southern colonies by applying them to what scholars have learned of the legislatures in the other colonies. This procedure has the advantage of providing perspective on the story of Southern developments. At the same time, it may serve as one guidepost for a general synthesis in the future.

Any student of the eighteenth-century political process will sooner or later be struck by the fact that, although each of the lower houses developed independently and differently, their stories were similar. The elimination of individual variants, which tend to cancel out each other, discloses certain basic regularities, a clearly discernible pattern—or what the late Sir Lewis Namier called a morphology—common to all of them. They all moved along like paths in their drives for increased authority, and, although their success on specific issues differed from colony to colony and the rate of their rise varied from time to time, they all ended up at approximately the same destination. They passed successively through certain vaguely defined phases of political development. Through most of the seventeenth century the lower houses were still in a position of subordination, slowly groping for the power to tax and the right to sit separately from the council and to initiate laws. Sometime during the early eighteenth century most of them advanced to a second stage at which they could battle on equal terms with the governors and councils and challenge even the powers in London if necessary. At that point the lower houses began their bid for political supremacy. The violent eruptions that followed usually ended in an accommodation with the governors and councils which paved the way for the ascendancy of the lower houses and saw the virtual eclipse of the colonial executive. By the end of the Seven Years' War, and in some instances considerably earlier, the lower houses had reached the third and final phase of political dominance and were in a position to speak for the colonies in the conflict with the imperial government which ensued after 1763.

---

terly, s. 3, I (January 1944), 29–42. The line of interpretation that Andrews would probably have followed is briefly developed in his brilliant *The Colonial Background of the American Revolution* (New Haven, 1924), 3–65.

By 1763, with the exception of the lower houses in the corporate colonies of Rhode Island and Connecticut, which had virtually complete authority, the Pennsylvania and Massachusetts houses of representatives were probably most powerful. Having succeeded in placing its election on a statutory basis and depriving the Council of direct legislative authority in the Charter of Privileges in 1701, the Pennsylvania House under the astute guidance of David Lloyd secured broad financial and appointive powers during the administrations of Daniel Gookin and Sir William Keith. Building on these foundations, it gained almost complete dominance in the 1730's and 1740's despite the opposition of the governors, whose power and prestige along with that of the Council declined rapidly.[6] The Massachusetts House, having been accorded the unique privilege of sharing in the selection of the Council by the royal charter in 1691, already had a strong tradition of legislative supremacy inherited from a half century of corporate experience. During the first thirty years under the new charter first the benevolent policies of Sir William Phips and William Stoughton and then wartime conditions during the tenures of Joseph Dudley and Samuel Shute enabled the House, led by Elisha Cooke, Jr., to extend its authority greatly. It emerged from the conflicts over the salary question during the 1720's with firm control over finance, and the Crown's abandonment of its demand for a permanent revenue in the early 1730's paved the way for an accommodation with subsequent governors and the eventual dominance of the House under Governor William Shirley after 1740.[7]

The South Carolina Commons and New York House of Assembly were only slightly less powerful. Beginning in the first decade of the eighteenth century, the South Carolina lower house gradually assumed an ironclad control over all aspects of South Carolina government, extending its supervision to the minutest details of local administration after 1730 as a succession of governors, including Francis Nicholson, Robert Johnson, Thomas Broughton, the elder William Bull, and James Glen offered little

---

[6] Developments in Pennsylvania may be traced in Shepherd, *Proprietary Government;* Benjamin Franklin, *An Historical Review of Pennsylvania* (London, 1759); Roy N. Lokken, *David Lloyd: Colonial Lawmaker* (Seattle, 1959); Sister Joan de Lourdes Leonard, *The Organization and Procedure of the Pennsylvania Assembly, 1682–1772* (Philadelphia, 1949); Winifred T. Root, *The Relation of Pennsylvania with the British Government, 1696–1765* (Philadelphia, 1912); and Theodore Thayer, *Pennsylvania Politics and the Growth of Democracy, 1740–1776* (Harrisburg, 1953). On Rhode Island and Connecticut see David S. Lovejoy, *Rhode Island Politics and the American Revolution, 1760–1776* (Providence, 1958), and Oscar Zeichner, *Connecticut's Years of Controversy, 1754–1775* (Chapel Hill, 1949).

[7] Useful studies on Massachusetts are Robert E. Brown, *Middle-Class Democracy and the Revolution in Massachusetts, 1691–1780* (Ithaca, N. Y., 1955); Martin L. Cole, The Rise of the Legislative Assembly in Provincial Massachusetts (unpublished Ph.D. thesis, State University of Iowa, 1939); Thomas Hutchinson, *The History of the Colony and Province of Massachusetts-Bay,* Lawrence S. Mayo, ed. (3 vols., Cambridge, 1936); and Henry R. Spencer, *Constitutional Conflict in Provincial Massachusetts* (Columbus, O., 1905).

determined opposition. The Commons continued to grow in stature after 1750 while the Council's standing declined because of the Crown policy of filling it with placemen from England and the Common's successful attacks upon its authority.[8] The New York House of Assembly began to demand greater authority in reaction to the mismanagement of Edward Hyde, Viscount Cornbury, during the first decade of the eighteenth century. Governor Robert Hunter met the challenge squarely during his ten-year administration beginning in 1710, but he and his successors could not check the rising power of the House. During the seven-year tenure of George Clarke beginning in 1736, the House advanced into the final stage of development. Following Clarke, George Clinton made a vigorous effort to reassert the authority of the executive, but neither he nor any of his successors was able to challenge the power of the House.[9]

The lower houses of North Carolina, New Jersey, and Virginia developed more slowly. The North Carolina lower house was fully capable of protecting its powers and privileges and competing on equal terms with the executive during the last years of proprietary rule and under the early royal governors, George Burrington and Gabriel Johnston. But it was not until Arthur Dobbs' tenure in the 1750's and 1760's that, meeting more regularly, it assumed the upper hand in North Carolina politics under the astute guidance of Speaker Samuel Swann and Treasurers John Starkey and Thomas Barker.[10] In New Jersey the lower house was partially thwarted in its spirited bid for power during the 1740's under the leadership of John Kinsey and Samuel Nevill by the determined opposition of Governor Lewis Morris, and it did not gain superiority until the administrations of Jonathan Belcher, Thomas Pownall, Francis Bernard, and Thomas Boone during the Seven Years' War.[11] Similarly, the Virginia Burgesses vigorously sought to establish its control in the second decade

---

[8] The best published study on South Carolina is Smith, *South Carolina As a Royal Province*. Also useful are David D. Wallace, *The Life of Henry Laurens* (New York, 1915); Jack P. Greene, The Quest for Power of the Lower Houses of Assembly in the Southern Royal Colonies, 1730–1763 (unpublished Ph.D. thesis, Duke University, 1956); and M. Eugene Sirmans, "The South Carolina Royal Council, 1720–1763," *William and Mary Quarterly*, s. 3, XVIII (July 1961), 373–92.

[9] Developments in New York can be followed in Carl L. Becker, *The History of Political Parties in the Province of New York, 1760–1776* (Madison, 1909); Milton M. Klein, "Democracy and Politics in Colonial New York," *New York History*, XL (July 1959), 221–46; Lawrence H. Leder, *Robert Livingston, 1654–1728, and the Politics of Colonial New York* (Chapel Hill, 1961); Beverly McAnear, Politics in Provincial New York, 1689–1761 (unpublished Ph.D. thesis, Stanford University, 1935); Irving Mark, *Agrarian Conflicts in Colonial New York, 1711–1775* (New York, 1940); William Smith, *The History of the Late Province of New York* (2 vols., New York, 1829); and Charles W. Spencer, *Phases of Royal Government in New York, 1691–1719* (Columbus, 1905).

[10] Useful analyses of North Carolina are Raper, *North Carolina*, and Desmond Clarke, *Arthur Dobbs Esquire, 1689–1765* (Chapel Hill, 1957).

[11] New Jersey developments can be traced in Donald L. Kemmerer's excellent study, *Path to Freedom: The Struggle for Self-Government in Colonial New Jersey, 1703–1776* (Princeton, 1940).

of the century under Alexander Spotswood, but not until the administrations of Sir William Gooch and Robert Dinwiddie, when first the expansion of the colony and then the Seven Years' War required more regular sessions, did the Burgesses finally gain the upper hand under the effective leadership of Speaker John Robinson.[12]

Among the lower houses in the older colonies, only the Maryland House of Delegates and the New Hampshire House of Assembly failed to reach the final level of development in the period before 1763. The Maryland body made important advances early in the eighteenth century while under the control of the Crown and aggressively sought to extend its authority in the 1720's under the leadership of the older Daniel Dulany and again in the late 1730's and early 1740's under Dr. Charles Carroll. But the proprietors were usually able to thwart these attempts, and the Delegates failed to pull ahead of the executive despite a concerted effort during the last intercolonial war under the administration of Horatio Sharpe.[13] In New Hampshire, the House had exercised considerable power through the early decades of the eighteenth century, but Governor Benning Wentworth effectively challenged its authority after 1740 and prevented it from attaining the extensive power exercised by its counterparts in other colonies.[14] It should be emphasized, however, that neither the Maryland nor the New Hampshire lower house was in any sense impotent and along with their more youthful equivalent in Georgia gained dominance during the decade of debate with Britain after 1763. Of the lower houses in the continental colonies with pre-1763 political experience, only the Nova Scotia Assembly had not reached the final phase of political dominance by 1776.[15]

The similarities in the process and pattern of legislative development from colony to colony were not entirely accidental. The lower houses faced

---

[12] Among the more useful secondary works on Virginia are Flippin, *Royal Government;* Bernard Bailyn, "Politics and Social Structure in Virginia," in James M. Smith (ed.), *Seventeenth-Century America: Essays on Colonial History* (Chapel Hill, 1959), 90–115; Lucille Blanche Griffith, The Virginia House of Burgesses, 1750–1774 (unpublished Ph.D. thesis, Brown University, 1957); Ray Orvin Hummel, Jr., The Virginia House of Burgesses, 1689–1750 (unpublished Ph.D. thesis, University of Nebraska, 1934); David J. Mays, *Edmund Pendleton, 1721–1803* (2 vols., Cambridge, 1952); Charles S. Sydnor, *Gentlemen Freeholders: Political Practices in Washington's Virginia* (Chapel Hill, 1952); Thomas J. Wertenbaker, *Give Me Liberty: The Struggle for Self-Government in Virginia* (Philadelphia, 1958); and David Alan Williams, Political Alignments in Colonial Virginia, 1698–1750 (unpublished Ph.D. thesis, Northwestern University, 1959).

[13] On Maryland see two excellent studies, Charles A. Barker, *The Background of the Revolution in Maryland* (New Haven, 1940), and Aubrey Land, *The Dulanys of Maryland* (Baltimore, 1955).

[14] New Hampshire developments can be followed in Fry, *New Hampshire,* and Jeremy Belknap, *History of New Hampshire* (3 vols., Boston, 1791–1792).

[15] On Georgia see W. W. Abbot, *The Royal Governors of Georgia, 1754–1775* (Chapel Hill, 1959), and Albert B. Saye, *New Viewpoints in Georgia History* (Atlanta, 1943). John Bartlett Brebner, *The Neutral Yankees of Nova Scotia* (New York, 1937), is the best study of developments in that colony.

like problems and drew upon common traditions and imperial precedents for solutions. They all operated in the same broad imperial context and were affected by common historical forces. Moreover, family, cultural, and commercial ties often extended across colony lines, and newspapers and other printed materials, as well as individuals, often found their way from one colony to another. The result was at least a general awareness of issues and practices in neighboring colonies, and occasionally there was even a conscious borrowing of precedents and traditions. Younger bodies such as the Georgia Commons and Nova Scotia Assembly were particularly indebted to their more mature counterparts in South Carolina and Massachusetts Bay.[16] On the executive side, the similarity in attitudes, assumptions, and policies among the governors can be traced in large measure to the fact that they were all subordinate to the same central authority in London, which pursued a common policy in all the colonies.

Before the Seven Years' War the quest was characterized by a considerable degree of spontaneity, by a lack of awareness that activities of the moment were part of any broad struggle for power. Rather than consciously working out the details of some master plan designed to bring them liberty or self-government, the lower houses moved along from issue to issue and from situation to situation, primarily concerning themselves with the problems at hand and displaying a remarkable capacity for spontaneous action, for seizing any and every opportunity to enlarge their own influence at the executive's expense and for holding tenaciously to powers they had already secured. Conscious of the issues involved in each specific conflict, they were for the most part unaware of and uninterested in the long-range implications of their actions. Virginia Governor Francis Fauquier correctly judged the matter in 1760. "Whoever charges them with acting upon a premeditated concerted plan, don't know them," he wrote of the Virginia burgesses, "for they mean honestly, but are Expedient Mongers in the highest Degree." [17] Still, in retrospect it is obvious that throughout the eighteenth century the lower houses were engaged in a continuous movement to enlarge their sphere of influence. To ignore that continuity would be to miss the meaning of eighteenth-century colonial political development.

One is impressed with the rather prosaic manner in which the lower houses went about the task of extending their authority, with the infrequency of dramatic conflict. They gained much of their power in the course of routine business, quietly and simply extending and consolidating their authority by passing laws and establishing practices, the implications of which escaped both colonial executives and imperial authorities and were not always fully recognized even by the lower houses themselves. In

---

[16] On this point see Abbot, *Royal Governors,* and Brebner, *Neutral Yankees.*

[17] Fauquier to Board of Trade, June 2, 1760, in Colonial Office Papers (Public Record Office, London), Series 5/1330, folios 37–39.

this way they gradually extended their financial authority to include the powers to audit accounts of all public officers, to share in disbursing public funds, and eventually even to appoint officials concerned in collecting and handling local revenues. Precedents thus established soon hardened into fixed principles, "undoubted rights" or "inherent powers," changing the very fabric of their respective constitutions. The notable absence of conflict is perhaps best illustrated by the none too surprising fact that the lower houses made some of their greatest gains under those governors with whom they enjoyed the most harmony, in particular Keith in Pennsylvania, Shirley in Massachusetts, Hunter in New York, and the elder and younger Bull in South Carolina. In Virginia the House of Burgesses made rapid strides during the 1730's and 1740's under the benevolent government of Gooch, who discovered early in his administration that the secret of political success for a Virginia governor was to reach an accord with the plantation gentry.

One should not conclude that the colonies had no exciting legislative-executive conflicts, however. Attempts through the middle decades of the eighteenth century by Clinton to weaken the financial powers of the New York House, Massachusetts Governors Samuel Shute and William Burnet to gain a permanent civil list, Benning Wentworth to extend unilaterally the privilege of representation to new districts in New Hampshire, Johnston to break the extensive power of the Albemarle Counties in the North Carolina lower house, Dinwiddie to establish a fee for issuing land patents without the consent of the Virginia Burgesses, and Boone to reform South Carolina's election laws each provided a storm of controversy that brought local politics to a fever pitch.[18] But such conflicts were the exception and usually arose not out of the lower houses' seeking more authority but from the executives' attempts to restrict powers already won. Impatient of restraint and jealous of their rights and privileges, the lower houses responded forcefully and sometimes violently when executive action threatened to deprive them of those rights. Only a few governors, men of the caliber of Henry Ellis in Georgia and to a lesser extent William Henry Lyttelton in South Carolina and Bernard in New Jersey, had the skill to challenge established rights successfully without raising the wrath of the lower houses. Clumsier tacticians—Pennsylvania's William Denny, New York's Clinton, Virginia's Dinwiddie, North Carolina's Dobbs, South Carolina's Boone, Georgia's John Reynolds—failed when pursuing similar goals.

---

[18] The details of these disputes can be traced in Smith, *History of New York*, II, 68–151; Hutchinson, *History of Massachusetts Bay*, 163–280; Labaree, *Royal Government*, 180–85; Lawrence F. London, "The Representation Controversy in Colonial North Carolina," *North Carolina Historical Review*, XI (October 1934), 255–70; Jack P. Greene (ed.), "The Case of the Pistole Fee," *Virginia Magazine of History and Biography*, LXVI (October 1958), 399–422, and "The Gadsden Election Controversy and the Revolutionary Movement in South Carolina," *Mississippi Valley Historical Review*, XLVI (December 1959), 469–92.

Fundamentally, the quest for power in both the royal and the proprietary colonies was a struggle for political identity, the manifestation of the political ambitions of the leaders of emerging societies within each colony. There is a marked correlation between the appearance of economic and social elites produced by the growth in colonial wealth and population on the one hand and the lower houses' demand for increased authority, dignity, and prestige on the other. In the eighteenth century a group of planters, merchants, and professional men had attained or were rapidly acquiring within the colonies wealth and social position. The lower houses' aggressive drive for power reflects the determination of this new elite to attain through the representative assemblies political influence as well. In another but related sense, the lower houses' efforts represented a movement for autonomy in local affairs, although it is doubtful that many of the members recognized them as such. The lower houses wished to strengthen their authority within the colonies and to reduce to a minimum the amount of supervision, with the uncertainties it involved, that royal or proprietary authorities could exercise. Continuously nourished by the growing desire of American legislators to be masters of their own political fortunes and by the development of a vigorous tradition of legislative superiority in imitation of the imperial House of Commons, this basic principle of local control over local affairs in some cases got part of its impetus from an unsatisfactory experience early in the lower houses' development with a despotic, inefficient, or corrupt governor such as Thomas, Lord Culpeper, or Francis, Lord Howard of Effingham, in Virginia, Lionel Copley in Maryland, Sir Edmund Andros in Massachusetts, Seth Sothell in North Carolina, or the infamous Cornbury in New York and New Jersey. Clearly, the task of defending men's rights and property against the fraud and violence of tyrannical executives fell most appropriately to the representatives of those whose rights and property demanded protection.

But the quest for power involved more than the extension of the authority of the lower houses within the colonies at the expense of the colonial executives. After their initial stage of evolution, the lower houses learned that their real antagonists were not the governors but the proprietors or Crown officials in London. Few governors proved to be a match for the representatives. A governor was almost helpless to prevent a lower house from exercising powers secured under his predecessors, and even the most discerning governor could fall into the trap of assenting to an apparently innocent law that would later prove damaging to the royal or proprietary prerogative. Some governors, for the sake of preserving amicable relations with the representatives or because they thought certain legislation to be in the best interest of a colony, actually conspired with legislative leaders to present the actions of the lower houses in a favorable light in London. Thus, Jonathan Belcher worked with Massachusetts leaders to parry the

74

Crown's demand for a permanent revenue in the 1730's, and Fauquier joined with Speaker John Robinson in Virginia to prevent the separation of the offices of speaker and treasurer during the closing years of the Seven Years' War.

Nor could imperial authorities depend upon the colonial councils to furnish an effective check upon the representatives' advancing influence. Most councilors were drawn from the rising social and economic elites in the colonies. The duality of their role is obvious. Bound by oath to uphold the interests of the Crown or the proprietors, they were also driven by ambition and a variety of local pressures to maintain the status and power of the councils as well as to protect and advance their own individual interests and those of their group within the colonies. These two objectives were not always in harmony, and the councils frequently sided with the lower houses rather than with the governors. With a weakened governor and an unreliable council, the task of restraining the representative assemblies ultimately devolved upon the home government. Probably as much of the struggle for power was played out in Whitehall as in Williamsburg, Charleston, New York, Boston, or Philadelphia.

Behind the struggle between colonial lower houses and the imperial authorities were two divergent, though on the colonial side not wholly articulated, concepts of the constitutions of the colonies and in particular of the status of the lower houses. To the very end of the colonial period, imperial authorities persisted in the views that colonial constitutions were static and that the lower houses were subordinate governmental agencies with only temporary and limited lawmaking powers—in the words of one imperial official, merely "so many Corporations at a distance, invested with an Ability to make Temporary By Laws for themselves, agreeable to their respective Situations and Climates." [19] In working out a political system for the colonies in the later seventeenth century, imperial officials had institutionalized these views in the royal commissions and instructions. Despite the fact that the lower houses were yearly making important changes in their respective constitutions, the Crown never altered either the commissions or instructions to conform with the realities of the colonial political situation and continued to maintain throughout the eighteenth century that they were the most vital part of the constitutional structure of the royal colonies. The Pennsylvania and to a lesser extent the Maryland proprietors were less rigid, although they also insisted upon their theoretical constitutional and political supremacy over the lower houses.

Colonial lower houses had little respect for and even less patience with such a doctrinaire position, and whether or not royal and proprietary instructions were absolutely binding upon the colonies was the leading con-

---

[19] Sir William Keith, A Short Discourse on the Present State of the Colonies in America with Respect to the Interest of Great Britain (1729) in Colonial Office Papers, Series 5/4, folios 170–71.

stitutional issue in the period before 1763. As the political instruments of what was probably the most pragmatic society in the eighteenth-century Western World, colonial legislators would not likely be restrained by dogma divorced from reality. They had no fear of innovations and welcomed the chance to experiment with new forms and ideas. All they asked was that a thing work. When the lower houses found that instructions from imperial authorities did not work in the best interests of the colonies, that they were, in fact, antithetic to the very measures they as legislatures were trying to effect, they openly refused to submit to them. Instructions, they argued, applied only to officials appointed by the Crown.

> Instructions from his majesty, to his governor, or the council, are binding to them, and esteemed as laws or rules; because, if either should disregard them, they might immediately be displaced,

declared a South Carolina writer in 1756 while denying the validity of an instruction that stipulated colonial councils should have equal rights with the lower houses in framing money bills. "But, if instructions should be laws and rules to the people of this province, then there would be no need of assemblies, and all our laws and taxes might be made and levied by an instruction." [20] Clearly, then, instructions might bind governors, but never the elected branch of the legislature.

Even though the lower houses, filled with intensely practical politicians, were concerned largely with practical political considerations, they found it necessary to develop a body of theory with which to oppose unpopular instructions from Britain and to support their claims to greater political power. In those few colonies that had charters, the lower houses relied upon the guarantees in them as their first line of defense, taking the position that the stipulations of the charters were inviolate, despite the fact that some had been invalidated by English courts, and could not be altered by executive order. A more basic premise which was equally applicable to all colonies was that the constituents of the lower houses, as inhabitants of British colonies, were entitled to all the traditional rights of Englishmen. On this foundation the colonial legislatures built their ideological structure. In the early charters the Crown had guaranteed the colonists "all privileges, franchises and liberties of this our kingdom of England . . . any Statute, act, ordinance, or provision to the contrary thereof, notwithstanding." [21] Such guarantees, colonials assumed, merely constituted recognition that their privileges as Englishmen were inherent and unalterable and that it mattered not whether they stayed on the home islands or migrated to the colonies. "His Majesty's Subjects coming over to America,"

---

[20] Charleston *South Carolina Gazette*, May 13, 1756.
[21] For instance, see the provision in the Maryland charter conveniently published in Merrill Jensen (ed.), *English Historical Documents: American Colonial Documents to 1776* (New York, 1955), 88.

the South Carolina Commons argued in 1739 while asserting its exclusive right to formulate tax laws, "have no more forfeited this their most valuable Inheritance than they have withdrawn their Allegiance." No "Royal Order," the Commons declared, could "qualify or any wise alter a fundamental Right from the Shape in which it was handed down to us from our Ancestors." [22]

One of the most important of these rights was the privilege of representation, on which, of course, depended the very existence of the lower houses. Imperial authorities always maintained that the lower houses existed only through the consent of the Crown,[23] but the houses insisted that an elected assembly was a fundamental right of a colony arising out of an Englishman's privilege to be represented and that they did not owe their existence merely to the King's pleasure.

> Our representatives, agreeably to the general sense of their constituents, [wrote New York assemblyman William Smith in the 1750's] are tenacious in their opinion, that the inhabitants of this colony are entitled to all the privileges of Englishmen; that they have a right to participate in the legislative power, and that the session of assemblies here, is wisely substituted instead of a representation in parliament, which, all things considered, would, at this remote distance, be extremely inconvenient and dangerous.[24]

The logical corollary to this argument was that the lower houses were equivalents of the House of Commons and must perforce in their limited spheres be entitled to all the privileges possessed by that body in Great Britain. Hence, in cases where an invocation of fundamental rights was not appropriate, the lower houses frequently defended their actions on the grounds that they were agreeable to the practice of the House of Commons. Thus in 1755 the North Carolina Lower House denied the right of the Council to amend tax bills on the ground that it was "contrary to Custom and Usage of Parliament." [25] Unintentionally, Crown officials encouraged the lower houses to make this analogy by forbidding them in

---

[22] James H. Easterby and Ruth S. Green (eds.), *The Colonial Records of South Carolina: The Journals of the Commons House of Assembly* (8 vols., Columbia, 1951–1961), *1736–1739*, 720 (June 5, 1739).

[23] This view was implicit in most thinking and writing about the colonies by imperial authorities. For the attitude of John Carteret, Lord Granville, an important figure in colonial affairs through the middle decades of the eighteenth century, see Benjamin Franklin to Isaac Norris, March 19, 1759, as quoted by William S. Mason, "Franklin and Galloway: Some Unpublished Letters," American Antiquarian Society, *Proceedings*, n. s., XXXIV (1925), 245–46. Other examples are Jack P. Greene (ed.), "Martin Bladen's Blueprint for a Colonial Union," *William and Mary Quarterly*, s. 3, XVII (October 1960), 516–30, by a prominent member of the Board of Trade, and Archibald Kennedy, *An Essay on the Government of the Colonies* (New York, 1752), 17–18, by an official in the colonies.

[24] Smith, *History of New York*, I, 307.

[25] Journals of the Lower House, January 4–6, 1755, William L. Saunders (ed.), *The Colonial Records of North Carolina* (10 vols., Raleigh, 1886–1890), V, 287.

the instructions to exercise "any power or privilege whatsoever which is not allowed by us to the House of Commons . . . in Great Britain." [26]

Because neither fundamental rights nor imperial precedents could be used to defend practices that were contrary to customs of the mother country or to the British Constitution, the lower houses found it necessary to develop still another argument: that local precedents, habits, traditions, and statutes were important parts of their particular constitutions and could not be abridged by a royal or proprietary order. The assumptions were that the legislatures could alter colonial constitutions by their own actions without the active consent of imperial officials and that once the alterations were confirmed by usage they could not be countermanded by the British government. They did not deny the power of the governor to veto or of the Privy Council to disallow their laws but argued that imperial acquiescence over a long period of time was tantamount to consent and that precedents thus established could not be undone without their approval. The implication was that the American colonists saw their constitutions as living, growing, and constantly changing organisms, a theory which was directly opposite to the imperial view. To be sure, precedent had always been an important element in shaping the British constitution, but Crown officials were unwilling to concede that it was equally so in determining the fundamental law of the colonies. They willingly granted that colonial statutes, once formally approved by the Privy Council, automatically became part of the constitutions of the colonies, but they officially took the position that both royal instructions and commissions, as well as constitutional traditions of the mother country, took precedence over local practice or unconfirmed statutes.[27] This conflict of views persisted throughout the period after 1689, becoming more and more of an issue in the decades immediately preceding the American Revolution.

If imperial authorities would not grant the validity of the theoretical arguments of the lower houses, neither after 1689 did they make any systematic or concerted effort to force a rigid compliance with official policies. Repressive measures, at least before 1763, rarely went beyond the occasional disallowance of an offending statute or the official reprimand of a rambunctious lower house. General lack of interest in the routine business of colonial affairs and failure to recognize the potential seriousness of the situation may in part account for this leniency, but it is also true that official policy under both Walpole and the Pelhams called for a light rein on the colonies on the assumption that contented colonies

[26] Leonard W. Labaree (ed.), *Royal Instructions to British Colonial Governors, 1670–1776* (2 vols., New York, 1935), I, 112–13.

[27] For a classic statement of the imperial argument by a modern scholar see Lawrence H. Gipson, *The British Empire Before the American Revolution* (10 vols., Caldwell, Idaho, and New York, 1936–1961), III (rev.), 275–81.

created fewer problems for the administration. "One would not Strain any point," Charles Delafaye, secretary to the lords justices, cautioned South Carolina's Governor Francis Nicholson in 1722, "where it can be of no Service to our King or Country." "In the Plantations," he added, "the Government should be as Easy and Mild as possible to invite people to Settle under it." [28] Three times between 1734 and 1749 the ministry failed to give enthusiastic support to measures introduced into Parliament to insure the supremacy of instructions over colonial laws.[29] Though the Calverts were somewhat more insistent upon preserving their proprietary prerogatives, in general the proprietors were equally lax as long as there was no encroachment upon their land rights or proprietary dues.

Imperial organs of administration were in fact inadequate to deal effectively with all the problems of the empire. Since no special governmental bodies were created in England to deal exclusively with colonial affairs, they were handled through the regular machinery of government—a maze of boards and officials whose main interests and responsibilities were not the supervision of overseas colonies. The only body sufficiently informed and interested to deal competently with colonial matters was the Board of Trade, and it had little authority, except for the brief period from 1748 to 1761 under the presidency of George Dunk, Earl of Halifax. The most useful device for restraining the lower houses was the Privy Council's right to review colonial laws, but even that was only partly effective, because the mass of colonial statutes annually coming before the Board of Trade made a thorough scrutiny impossible. Under such arrangements no vigorous colonial policy was likely. The combination of imperial lethargy and colonial aggression virtually guaranteed the success of the lower houses' quest for power. An indication of a growing awareness in imperial circles of the seriousness of the situation was Halifax's spirited, if piecemeal, effort to restrain the growth of the lower houses in the early 1750's. Symptomatic of these efforts was the attempt to make Georgia and Nova Scotia model royal colonies at the institution of royal government by writing into the instructions to their governors provisions designed to insure the continued supremacy of the executive and to prevent the lower houses from going the way of their counterparts in the older colonies. However, the outbreak of the Seven Years' War forced Halifax to suspend his activities and prevented any further reformation until the cessation of hostilities.

Indeed, the war saw a drastic acceleration in the lower houses' bid for authority, and its conclusion found them in possession of many of the

---

[28] Delafaye to Nicholson, January 22, 1722, in Papers Concerning the Governorship of South Carolina (Houghton Library, Harvard University, Cambridge, Massachusetts), bMs Am 1455, Item 9.

[29] For a discussion of these measures see Bernhard Knollenberg, *Origin of the American Revolution, 1759–1766* (New York, 1960), 49.

powers held less than a century before by the executive. In the realm of finance they had imposed their authority over every phase of raising and distributing public revenue. They had acquired a large measure of independence by winning control over their compositions and proceedings and obtaining guarantees of basic English Parliamentary privileges. Finally, they had pushed their power even beyond that of the English House of Commons by gaining extensive authority in handling executive affairs, including the right to appoint executive officers and to share in formulating executive policy. These specific gains were symptoms of developments of much greater significance. To begin with, they were symbolic of a fundamental shift of the constitutional center of power in the colonies from the executive to the elected branch of the legislature. With the exception of the Georgia and Nova Scotia bodies, both of which had less than a decade of political experience behind them, the houses had by 1763 succeeded in attaining a new status, raising themselves from dependent lawmaking bodies to the center of political authority in their respective colonies.

But the lower houses had done more than simply acquire a new status in colonial politics. They had in a sense altered the structure of the constitution of the British Empire itself by asserting colonial authority against imperial authority and extending the constitutions of the colonies far beyond the limitations of the charters, instructions, or fixed notions of imperial authorities. The time was ripe for a re-examination and redefinition of the constitutional position of the lower houses. With the rapid economic and territorial expansion of the colonies in the years before 1763 had come a corresponding rise in the responsibilities and prestige of the lower houses and a growing awareness among colonial representatives of their own importance, which had served to strengthen their long-standing, if still imperfectly defined, impression that colonial lower houses were the American counterparts of the British House of Commons. Under the proper stimuli, they would carry this impression to its logical conclusion: that the lower houses enjoyed an equal status under the Crown with Parliament. Here, then, well beyond the embryonic stage, was the theory of colonial equality with the mother country, one of the basic constitutional principles of the American Revolution, waiting to be nourished by the series of crises that beset imperial-colonial relations between 1763 and 1776.

The psychological implications of this new political order were profound. By the 1750's the phenomenal success of the lower houses had generated a soaring self-confidence, a willingness to take on all comers. Called upon to operate on a larger stage during the Seven Years' War, they emerged from that conflict with an increased awareness of their own importance and a growing consciousness of the implications of their activities. Symptomatic of these developments was the spate of bitter controversies that characterized colonial politics during and immediately after the war.

The Gadsden election controversy in South Carolina, the dispute over judicial tenure in New York, and the contests over the pistole fee and the two-penny act in Virginia gave abundant evidence of both the lower houses' stubborn determination to preserve their authority and the failure of Crown officials in London and the colonies to gauge accurately their temper or to accept the fact that they had made important changes in the constitutions of the colonies.

With the shift of power to the lower houses also came the development in each colony of an extraordinarily able group of politicians. The lower houses provided excellent training for the leaders of the rapidly maturing colonial societies, and the recurring controversies prepared them for the problems they would be called upon to meet in the dramatic conflicts after 1763. In the decades before Independence there appeared in the colonial statehouses John and Samuel Adams and James Otis in Massachusetts Bay; William Livingston in New York; Benjamin Franklin and John Dickinson in Pennsylvania; Daniel Dulany the younger in Maryland; Richard Bland, Richard Henry Lee, Thomas Jefferson, and Patrick Henry in Virginia; and Christopher Gadsden and John Rutledge in South Carolina. Along with dozens of others, these men were thoroughly schooled in the political arts and primed to meet any challenge to the power and prestige of the lower houses.

Britain's "new colonial policy" after 1763 provided just such a challenge. It precipitated a constitutional crisis in the empire, creating new tensions and setting in motion forces different from those that had shaped earlier developments. The new policy was based upon concepts both unfamiliar and unwelcome to the colonists such as centralization, uniformity, and orderly development. Yet it was, for the most part, an effort to realize old aspirations. From Edward Randolph in the last decades of the seventeenth century to the Earl of Halifax in the 1750's colonial officials had envisioned a highly centralized empire with a uniform political system in each of the colonies and with the imperial government closely supervising the subordinate governments.[30] But, because they had never made any sustained or systematic attempt to achieve these goals, there had developed during the first half of the eighteenth century a working arrangement permitting the lower houses considerable latitude in shaping colonial constitutions without requiring crown and proprietary officials to give up any of their ideals. That there had been a growing divergence between imperial theory and colonial practice mattered little so long as each re-

---

[30] On this point see Charles M. Andrews, *The Colonial Period of American History* (4 vols., New Haven, 1934–1938), IV, 368–425; Michael Garibaldi Hall, *Edward Randolph and the American Colonies, 1676–1703* (Chapel Hill, 1960); Arthur H. Basye, *Lords Commissioners of Trade and Plantations, 1748–1782* (New Haven, 1925); and Dora Mae Clark, *The Rise of the British Treasury: Colonial Administration in the Eighteenth Century* (New Haven, 1960).

frained from challenging the other. But the new policy threatened to up-set this arrangement by implementing the old ideals long after the con-ditions that produced them had ceased to exist. Aimed at bringing the colonies more closely under imperial control, this policy inevitably sought to curtail the influence of the lower houses, directly challenging many of the powers they had acquired over the previous century. To protect gains they had already made and to make good their pretensions to greater po-litical significance, the lower houses thereafter no longer had merely to deal with weak governors or casual imperial administrators; they now faced an aggressive group of officials bent upon using every means at their disposal, including the legislative authority of Parliament, to gain their ends.

Beginning in 1763 one imperial action after another seemed to threaten the position of the lower houses. Between 1764 and 1766 Parliament's at-tempt to tax the colonists for revenue directly challenged the colonial legislatures' exclusive power to tax, the cornerstone of their authority in America. A variety of other measures, some aimed at particular colonial legislatures and others at general legislative powers and practices, posed serious threats to powers that the lower houses had either long enjoyed or were trying to attain. To meet these challenges, the lower houses had to spell out the implications of the changes they had been making, con-sciously or not, in the structures of their respective governments. That is, for the first time they had to make clear in their own minds and then to verbalize what they conceived their respective constitutions in fact were or should be. In the process, the spokesmen of the lower houses laid bare the wide gulf between imperial theory and colonial practice. During the Stamp Act crisis in 1764–1766 the lower houses claimed the same authority over taxation in the colonies as Parliament had over that matter in Eng-land, and a few of them even asserted an equal right in matters of in-ternal policy.[31] Although justified by the realities of the colonial situa-tion, such a definition of the lower houses' constitutional position within the empire was at marked variance with imperial ideals and only served to increase the determination of the home government to take a stricter tone. This determination was manifested after the repeal of the Stamp Act by Parliament's claim in the Declaratory Act of 1766 to "full power and authority" over the colonies "in all cases whatsoever." [32]

---

[31] See the sweeping claim of the Virginia House of Burgesses to the "Inestimable Right of being governed by such Laws respecting their internal Polity and Taxation as are devised from their own Consent" in objecting to Grenville's proposed stamp duties. Henry R. McIlwaine and John P. Kennedy (eds.), *Journals of the House of Burgesses in Virginia* (13 vols., Richmond, 1905–1913), *1761–1765*, 302–304 (December 18, 1764). The protests of all the lower houses against the Stamp Act are conveniently collected in Edmund S. Mor-gan (ed.), *Prologue to Revolution: Sources and Documents on the Stamp Act Crisis, 1764–1766* (Chapel Hill, 1959), 8–17, 46–69.

[32] Danby Pickering (ed.), *The Statutes at Large from Magna Carta to the End of the*

The pattern over the next decade was on the part of the home government one of increasing resolution to take a firmer tone with the colonies and on the part of American lawmakers a heightened consciousness of the implications of the constitutional issue and a continuously rising level of expectation. In addition to their insistence upon the right of Parliament to raise revenue in the colonies, imperial officials also applied, in a way that was increasingly irksome to American legislators, traditional checks like restrictive instructions, legislative review, and the suspending clause requiring prior approval of the Crown before laws of an "extraordinary nature" could go into effect. Finally Parliament threatened the very existence of the lower houses by a measure suspending the New York Assembly for refusing to comply with the Quartering Act in 1767 and by another altering the substance of the Massachusetts constitution in the Massachusetts Government Act in 1774. In the process of articulating and defending their constitutional position, the lower houses developed aspirations much greater than any they had had in the years before 1763. American representatives became convinced in the decade after 1766 not only that they knew best what to do for their constituents and the colonies and that anything interfering with their freedom to adopt whatever course seemed necessary was an intolerable and unconstitutional restraint but also that the only security for their political fortunes was in the abandonment of their attempts to restrict and define Parliamentary authority in America and instead to deny Parliament's jurisdiction over them entirely by asserting their equality with Parliament under the Crown. Suggested by Richard Bland as early as 1766, such a position was openly advocated by James Wilson and Thomas Jefferson in 1774 and was officially adopted by the First Continental Congress when it claimed for Americans in its declarations and resolves "a free and exclusive power of legislation in their several provincial legislatures, where their right of representation can alone be preserved, in all cases of taxation and internal polity." [33]

Parliament could not accept this claim without giving up the principles it had asserted in the Declaratory Act and, in effect, abandoning the traditional British theory of empire and accepting the colonial constitutional position instead. The First Continental Congress professed that a return to the *status quo* of 1763 would satisfy the colonies, but Parliament in 1774–1776 was unwilling even to go that far, much less to promise them exemption from Parliamentary taxation. Besides, American legislators now aspired to much more and would not have been content with a return to the old inarticulated and undefined pattern of accommodation between imperial theory and colonial practice that had existed through most of

---

Eleventh Parliament of Great Britain, Anno 1761, Continued to 1806 (46 vols., Cambridge, 1762–1807), XXVII, 19–20.

[33] Worthington C. Ford and others (eds.), *Journals of the Continental Congress* (34 vols., Washington, 1904–1937), I, 68–69 (October 14, 1774).

the period between 1689 and 1763. Rigid guarantees of colonial rights and precise definitions of the constitutional relationship between the Mother Country and the colonies and between Parliament and the lower houses on American terms, that is, imperial recognition of the autonomy of the lower houses in local affairs, would have been required to satisfy them.

Between 1689 and 1763 the lower houses' contests with royal governors and imperial officials had brought them political maturity, a considerable measure of control over local affairs, capable leaders, and a rationale to support their pretensions to political power within the colonies and in the Empire. The British challenge after 1763 threatened to render their accomplishments meaningless and drove them to demand equal rights with Parliament and autonomy in local affairs and eventually to declare their independence. At issue was the whole political structure forged by the lower houses over the previous century. In this context the American Revolution becomes in essence a war for political survival, a conflict involving not only individual rights as traditionally emphasized by historians of the event but assembly rights as well.

IV

The Relevance of Mr. Jefferson:
To the America of 1943
(Carl Becker);
To the America of 1961
(Dumas Malone)

INTRODUCTION

Since his death, which occurred with strikingly dramatic symbolism on July 4, 1826, Thomas Jefferson, as a person, as a philosopher, and as a statesman, has exercised a peculiar fascination upon each succeeding generation of Americans. John Adams who, almost unbelievably, also died on July 4, 1826, declared at the very end, "Thomas Jefferson still survives." And Jefferson has survived down to the present as an image for Americans. In this sense, for posterity, Merrill Peterson in his book The Jefferson Image in the American Mind *(1960) has set forth for us what Jefferson has meant to the generations of Americans since his time, whether as a symbol and image to follow or to turn away from, to inspire or to corrupt.*

In the two selections that follow we have estimates of the relevance of Jefferson to Americans separated by almost exactly one generation. It adds much to the excitement of these two estimates to recall that they were written by two of the outstanding, if not, indeed, the most profound and gifted Jefferson scholars America has produced in all the long years since Jefferson's death.

In the first of the essays that follow, Carl Becker, for more than a quarter of a century professor of history at Cornell, asks the question: What is still living in the political philosophy of Thomas Jefferson for an America deeply committed to the total war against the Nazi Reich and the Japanese Empire? Becker finds that, though by no means all of Jefferson's philosophy is relevant to the present, yet in its deepest sense, as wholly opposed to "every form of tyranny over the mind of man" and totally committed to the noble concept of liberty, which he did so much warmly, directly, and allusively to define for Americans, that in this sense, Jefferson is completely relevant. A reading of Jefferson will bring again the national conviction ". . . that 'liberty, equality, fraternity,' and the 'inalienable rights' of man are phrases, glittering or not, that denote realities—the fundamental realities that men will always fight and die for rather than surrender."

Dumas Malone, sometime Thomas Jefferson Professor of History at the University of Virginia, which Jefferson founded, addresses himself, in the second essay that follows, essentially to the same question that Becker posed; only now a generation has passed, and instead of Franklin Roosevelt being in the White House, the young Mr. Kennedy is halfway through his first year in office. Now the Nazi Reich is no longer the enemy but the cold war is deepening, after the confrontation in Vienna in June 1961 of Mr. Kennedy and Mr. Khrushchev, in all its awful threatened consequences. Dumas Malone found in 1961, as Carl Becker had found in 1943, that, after taking account of the great historical chasm separating Jefferson's day from our own, the Jefferson image, in a deep and profoundly moving human way, was still wholly relevant. "He left us no road map, but more than any public man in our history, he pointed us to the star by which our course should be guided."

What Is Still Living in the Political Philosophy of Thomas Jefferson

Carl Becker

I believe . . . that there exists a right independent of force.
Thomas Jefferson

Many nations have traced their history back to some fabled Golden Age, to the beginning of created things, when, as Hesiod said, men lived like gods, free from toil and grief. Our own history can likewise be traced, through its European origins, back to that mythical time. But we commonly think of it as beginning more recently, somewhat abruptly, in the clear light of day, with the settlement at Jamestown, the landing of the Mayflower, and the founding of Massachusetts Bay colony. Men did not then live like gods, or free from toil and grief; but there were among them men of heroic stature, round whom myths have gathered, and whom we delight, with good reason, to honor. The beginning of our history as an independent nation is still more recent, and still more open to critical inspection, in the still brighter light of the eighteenth century; and yet this is for us still more truly the time of our Golden Age and of our ancestors of heroic stature. Among the founders of the American federal republic (to name only the most distinguished) were Washington, Franklin and John Adams, Alexander Hamilton and John Jay, Robert Morris and James Wilson, Richard Henry Lee, James Madison, and Thomas Jefferson. No doubt we are apt to magnify these "Fathers" beyond their just merits. Their just merits are, nevertheless, sufficient, for it would be difficult to find in the history of any other country, or in the history of our own

From the *American Historical Review*, XLVIII (July 1943), 691–706. Reprinted by permission. The Penrose Lecture, delivered before the American Philosophical Society in Philadelphia, April 22, 1943, in connection with the celebration of the two hundredth anniversary of the birth of Thomas Jefferson. Printed by permission of the Society.

country at any other time, within a single generation, as many statesmen in proportion to the population of equal distinction for learning, probity, and political intelligence. And of these ten men none exhibited these qualities to better advantage or more lasting effect than Thomas Jefferson.

Jefferson, like Franklin, attained an international as well as a national eminence. Like Franklin, he was familiar with all of the ideas of his time, contributed something to its accumulated knowledge, and was identified with its most notable activities and events. There was indeed scarcely anything of human interest that was alien to his curious and far-ranging intelligence. Nevertheless, his name is for us inevitably associated with a certain general idea, a certain way of regarding man and the life of man, a certain political philosophy. The word that best denotes that philosophy is democracy. More than any other man we think of Jefferson as having formulated the fundamental principles of American democracy, of what we now like to call the American way of life.

Any significant political philosophy is shaped by three different but closely related influences. The first of these is what Alfred North Whitehead has taught us to call the "climate of opinion"—those fundamental presuppositions which in any age so largely determine what men think about the nature of the universe and what can and cannot happen in it, and about the nature of man and what is essential to the good life. The second influence is more specific: it derives from the particular political and social conflicts of the time, which dispose groups and parties to accept a particular interpretation of current ideas as a theoretical support for their practical activities. The third influence is more specific still: it derives from the mind and temperament of the individual who gives to the political philosophy its ordered literary form. Whatever is original in the philosophy is usually contributed by the individual who gives it this form. Whatever value it has for its own time and place will depend largely on the extent to which it serves to illuminate or resolve the particular political issues of that time and place. But its value for other times and places will depend upon the extent to which the general presuppositions upon which it rests have a universal validity, the extent to which they express some enduring truth about nature and the life of man.

The political philosophy of Thomas Jefferson was not in essentials original with him. It was his only in the sense that he gave to ideas widely accepted at the time and genuinely entertained by him a Jeffersonian form and flavor. Nowhere is this peculiarity of form and flavor more evident than in the famous Declaration of Independence; but Jefferson did not claim that the ideas themselves were in any way novel. Some years later his old friend John Adams, a little irritated (as he was apt to be on slight provocation) by the laudation of Jefferson as the author of the Declaration, protested to Pickering that "there is not an idea in it that was not hackneyed in Congress two years before." [1] To this Jefferson replied that it was not his purpose "to say things which had never been said before, but to place before mankind the common sense of the subject," and to harmonize the "sentiments of the day, whether expressed in conversation, in letters, printed essays, or the elementary books of public right." [2] It was indeed Jefferson's merit, and the high value of the Declaration for his own time, that he expressed in lucid and persuasive form political ideas then widely accepted and thereby provided a reasoned justification for renouncing the authority of the British government. But the Declaration professes to do more than that. In providing the reasons for renouncing the authority of a particular government at a particular time, Jefferson took occasion to formulate the universal principles which, as he thought, could alone justify the authority of any government at any time.

These principles are set forth in a single brief paragraph. We are all familiar with it, having read it or heard it read many times. But it will always, and at no time more than now, bear repeating; and so I will repeat it once more, not exactly as it appears in the Declaration but as Jefferson first wrote it in the original draft.

> We hold these truths to be sacred and undeniable; that all men are created equal and independent; that from that equal creation they derive rights inherent and inalienable, among which are the preservation of life, and liberty, and the pursuit of happiness; that to secure these ends, governments are instituted among men, deriving their just powers from the consent of the governed; that whenever any form of government shall become destructive of these ends, it is the right of the people to alter or to abolish it, and to institute new government, laying it's foundation on such principles and organizing it's powers in such form, as to them shall seem most likely to effect their safety and happiness.

This brief statement contains the substance of Jefferson's political philosophy, which may be reduced to four principles: (1) that the universe and man in it are governed by natural law; (2) that all men are endowed with certain natural and imprescriptible rights; (3) that governments exist to secure these rights; and (4) that all just governments derive their authority from the consent of the governed. These principles, made explicit in our Federal and state constitutions, are still the foundation of the political system which Thomas Jefferson did so much to establish. It is indeed appropriate, therefore, in this memorial year, for us to ask, What is still living in this political philosophy? In order to answer this question, I will break it down into two more specific questions. First, what did Jefferson understand by natural law and natural rights, and what form

---

[1] *The Works of John Adams* (Boston, 1850–56), II, 512.
[2] *The Writings of Thomas Jefferson* (Philadelphia, 1869–71), VII, 304, 407.

of government did he think best suited to secure those rights? And, second, to what extent is his conception of rights and of government still valid for our time?

The doctrine of natural law, as it was understood by Jefferson and his contemporaries, was revolutionary only in the sense that it was a reinterpretation, in secular and liberal terms, of the Christian theory of the origin, nature, and destiny of man. As commonly understood in the eighteenth century, it was perhaps never better defined than by the French writer Volney.

> Natural law is the regular and constant order of facts by which God rules the universe; the order which his wisdom presents to the sense and reason of men, to serve them as an equal and common rule of conduct, and to guide them, without distinction of race or sect, towards perfection and happiness.[3]

For Jefferson, as for Volney, God still existed. But for them God the Father of Christian tradition had become attenuated into God the Creator, or First Cause. Having created the world for a beneficent purpose and on a rational plan, the Creator had withdrawn from the immediate and arbitrary control of human affairs into the dim recesses where absolute being dwells, leaving men to work out their own salvation as best they could. But this they could do very well, because the Creator had revealed his purposes, not in Holy Writ but in the open Book of Nature, which all men, in the light of reason, could read and interpret. "Is it simple," exclaimed Rousseau, "is it natural, that God should have gone in search of Moses to speak to Jean Jacques Rousseau?" To Jefferson, as to Volney, it seemed more natural to suppose that God had revealed his purpose in his works, from which it followed that the whole duty of man was progressively to discover the invariable laws of nature and of nature's God and to bring their ideas, their conduct, and their political and social institutions into harmony with them.

From this conception of natural law Jefferson derived the doctrine that all men are created equal and are endowed with certain natural rights. Many otherwise intelligent men have thought to refute Jefferson by pointing out that all men are in fact not equal. With the same ingenuity and poverty of imagination one could refute St. Augustine's doctrine of the brotherhood of man by pointing out that all men are in fact not brothers. St. Augustine would have said that all men are brothers in the sight of God, and Jefferson's doctrine of equality comes to the same thing. All men are equal in the possession of a common humanity, and if they are in fact not equal and have not in fact the same rights and privileges, the highest morality, both for the individual and for society, is to act on the

---

[3] *Oeuvres de Volney* (2d ed., Paris, 1826), I, 249.

assumption that all men should be accorded, so far as is humanly possible, the same consideration and opportunity. To act on this assumption would be, both for the individual and for society, to do the will of God and to live the good life.

In these respects—in respect to the primary values of life—the natural rights philosophy was essentially at one with the Christian faith; but in respect to the means by which these values might be realized, it differed sharply from current official Christian teaching. It denied that man is naturally prone to evil and error and for that reason incapable, apart from the compulsion of church and state, of arriving at the truth or living the good life. It affirmed, on the contrary, that men are endowed by their Creator with reason, in order that they may progressively discover that which is true, and with conscience, in order that they may be disposed, in the measure of their enlightenment, to follow that which is good. It was perhaps the dominant quality of Jefferson's mind and temperament, as it was of so many of his contemporaries, to have faith in the dignity and worth of the individual man, and it was for this reason that, in respect to the means for achieving the good life, they relied so confidently upon the negative principle of freedom of the individual from social constraint: freedom of opinion, in order that the truth might prevail; freedom of occupation and of enterprise, in order that careers might be open to talent; freedom from arbitrary political authority, in order that no man might be compelled against his will.

These freedoms were precisely what Jefferson meant by "liberty" as one of the natural rights of man, and it was through the fullest enjoyment of these freedoms that the "pursuit of happiness" would be most likely to result in the greatest happiness for the greatest number of men. And so we arrive at the central idea of the natural rights philosophy as to the proper function of government—the happy idea that the best way to secure the natural rights of men is just to leave them as free as possible to enjoy them, and that no form of government can secure these rights so well as the one that governs least. This idea was so engaging that anyone with an unbounded faith in the natural goodness of men and an equal faith in formal logic could push straight on to the conclusion arrived at by Proudhon—the conclusion that "property is theft," that all governments exist to condone it, and that men will never be free and happy until all governments are abolished.

Fortunately, Jefferson had not sufficient faith either in logic or in the native goodness of men to carry him that far. He had more faith in the goodness of men than some of his contemporaries—more, for example, than John Adams, but less than some others—less, for example, than Samuel Adams or Thomas Paine. He had a logical mind, but logic was not for him "a systematic way," as has been said, "of going wrong with confidence" —not, that is, a dialectical device for manipulating empty concepts in the void in vain—but a method of reaching sound conclusions on the basis of knowledge and common sense. History and political experience, rather than abstract political speculation, convinced Jefferson that men had been governed too much, and above all too arbitrarily, by kings claiming divine right, and that among the institutions that obscured the native goodness of men by depriving them of equal rights none was less defensible than a hereditary aristocracy enjoying privileges that were unearned and exacting a deference that was unmerited. It seemed to him self-evident, therefore, that men could govern themselves better than kings and aristocrats, whose powers rested upon the accident of birth, could do it for them. Not that the people could govern themselves in perfection or without difficulty. All forms of government had their evils, and the principal evil of popular government, Jefferson said, was "turbulence"; but "weigh this against the oppressions of monarchy, and it becomes nothing." [4]

Jefferson was thus profoundly convinced that republican government—government by representatives elected by the people—was the best form, because "it is the only form of government that is not eternally at open or secret war with the rights of mankind." [5] But what, in concrete instances, did Jefferson mean by the people, and how was the consent of the governed to be obtained? The people in this sense might mean all the people in the world, or all the people in Virginia, or all the people composing a particular class or sect. Practical statesman that he was, Jefferson took the world, politically speaking, as he found it, divided into groups that by tradition and community of interest regarded themselves, and were commonly regarded, as nations. Such nations might at any time "assume, among the powers of the earth, that equal and independent station to which the laws of nature and of nature's God entitle them." Thus nations as well as individuals had their natural rights—the right of national self-determination. But nations are composed of individuals, and individuals necessarily differ in their interests and opinions; and it seemed to Jefferson self-evident that the only practical way of reconciling these differences was by majority vote. Even a monarchy with all of its trappings, or an aristocracy with all of its privileges, if supported by a majority vote, would be a "just government," because it would rest upon "the consent of the governed."

The right of national self-determination and majority vote—these were fundamental to all of Jefferson's ideas about the particular form of government best suited to any country at any time. Not that majority vote conferred upon the majority of the moment any fundamental right not shared by the minority. It was simply a necessary device imposed upon individuals bound by their nature to live together, and aiming to live

---

[4] *The Writings of Thomas Jefferson,* ed. Paul L. Ford (New York, 1892–99), IV, 362.
[5] *Ibid.,* V, 147.

together with the maximum degree of harmony and good will; and Jefferson justified it by saying that, this law disregarded, "no other remains but that of force, which ends necessarily in military despotism." [6] There is, of course, no more obdurate problem in political philosophy than the problem of the one and the many, the difficulty being to reconcile the desirable liberties of the individual with the necessary powers of society; and Jefferson was no more successful in solving it than other political philosophers have been. His solution, such as it is, is presented in a letter to Dupont de Nemours, some portions of which I venture to quote, because in it Jefferson states categorically, and perhaps better than anywhere else, the principal tenets of his political faith.

> I believe with you that morality, compassion, generosity, are innate elements of the human constitution; that there exists a right independent of force; that the right to property is founded on our natural wants, in the measure with which we are endowed to satisfy these wants, and the right to what we acquire by those means without violating the similar rights of other sensible beings; that no one has a right to obstruct another exercising his faculty innocently for the relief of sensibilities made a part of his nature; that justice is the fundamental law of society; that the majority, oppressing an individual, is guilty of a crime, abuses its strength, and by acting on the law of the strongest breaks up the foundations of society; that action by the citizens in person, in affairs within their reach and competence, and in all others by representatives, chosen immediately, and removable by themselves, constitutes the essence of a republic; that all governments are more or less republican in proportion as this principle enters more or less into their composition; and that government by a republic is capable of extension over a greater surface of country than any other form.[7]

In this passage, as in most of Jefferson's political writings, we can note the disposition to believe that man is naturally good but that men are prone to evil; or, translating it into political terms, that citizens in the mass are to be trusted but that citizens elected to office need to be carefully watched. I have quoted Jefferson as saying that the chief evil of republican government is "turbulence," but he did not really think so. On the contrary, he believed that a little turbulence now and then would do no harm, since it would serve to remind elected officials that their authority was merely a franchise from the people. What Jefferson really believed is that political power is inherently dangerous and that the chief evil of any form of government is to have too much of it. From this it followed that the chief aim in devising a republican government should be to disperse power among magistrates, separate it in respect to function,

---

[6] *Ibid.,* X, 89.   [7] *Ibid.,* X, 24.

and otherwise to limit it by applying the grand negative principle of checks and balances. Jefferson agreed with Thomas Paine that whereas society is the result of our virtues government is the result of our vices and is therefore a necessary evil: necessary, in order to preserve order, protect property, and guarantee contracts; an evil, because inherently prone to magnify its authority and thereby impair the liberties of the individual.

Jefferson's ideal of a democratic society was best realized in a small agricultural community, such as he was familiar with at Monticello, composed of a few men of substance and learning, such as himself and his friend James Madison, and otherwise chiefly of industrious, upstanding yeoman farmers, making altogether a community of good neighbors in which everyone knows who is who and what is being done and who is doing it. The affairs of such a community, being easily within the "reach and competence" of the people, could be easily managed by them with the minimum of officials, exercising the minimum of authority, and attended with the minimum of palaver and ceremonial display. Unfortunately, this ideal community could not live to itself, and in managing the affairs of the larger area it was necessary for the people to act through representatives. This departure from the ideal was the beginning of danger, but there was no help for it except to prepare in good time by electing the representatives for very short terms and limiting their power to very specific matters.

The general principle would then be that the wider the area the less safe it would be to intrust representatives with power; and from this principle it followed that representatives from the counties to the state capital of Virginia could be safely intrusted with more power than could be safely intrusted to representatives from Virginia to Philadelphia. That the states must remain united Jefferson fully realized; but he was convinced that they should retain their sovereign powers, and at first the Articles of Confederation seemed to him very nearly the ideal form for such a union. When experience proved that a "more perfect union" was necessary, he approved of the Constitution of 1787 but insisted, as a safeguard against too much power in the hands of a government far removed from the people, that a bill of rights should be incorporated in the Constitution and that the powers therein granted to the Federal government should be strictly and narrowly interpreted.[8] As it happened, Jefferson's grasp of international political realities was destined to override this principle. He pushed through the purchase of Louisiana, in spite of the fact that in doing so he was exercising an authority which he believed he did not possess.[9] That perverse circumstances should have made Thomas

---

[8] *Ibid.*, V, 41–42, 45, 81.

[9] Jefferson's views are given in a letter to Robert R. Livingston, April 18, 1802 (*ibid.*, VIII, 143), in which he makes the much quoted statement about "marrying ourselves to

Jefferson the man to usurp power from the people is ironical enough, and it troubled his political conscience not a little; but he could console himself with the reflection that he had tried, although in vain, to get an amendment to the Constitution to authorize the act and that in any case his conscience was clear, since he had acted solely for the public good.

Closely associated with Jefferson's fear of the open usurpation of political power was his fear of the secret and more insidious influences by which men become debased and corrupted. Republican government, he was well aware, could not be very successful unless the majority of the citizens were independent, honest, and reasonably intelligent. Intelligence could be sufficiently trained and directed by education—schools for the people and colleges for the leaders. But honesty and independence depended less upon precept than upon the conditions in which men lived. The best conditions were those of country life. "Cultivators of the earth," Jefferson said, "are the most virtuous citizens." Vice, he thought, flourished chiefly in cities and in industrial communities which produce cities. In cities, where most people are unacquainted with each other, unscrupulous men could push their selfish interests under cover of the general indifference; and industrial communities, making so much use of impalpable and evanescent forms of wealth, opened the door to speculation for unearned profit, encouraged greed, and rewarded useless luxury: provided all the conditions, in short, for the rise of a corrupt and politically influential "money power." Jefferson regarded commerce and industry as necessary adjuncts to agriculture, but he had the farmer's settled antipathy to banks. "The exercise, by our own citizens, of so much commerce as may suffice to exchange our superfluities for our wants" he cautiously admitted, "may be advantageous to the whole"; but he was convinced that it would be fatal for us "to become a mere city of London, to carry on the commerce of half the world at the expense of waging eternal war with the other half." Capital invested in agriculture or useful industry was productively employed; but "all the capital employed in paper speculation is barren and useless, producing, like that on a gaming table, no accession to itself." And as for banks, they "are a blot left in all our constitutions, which, if not removed, will end in their destruction." [10] Jefferson was never weary of pointing to England as the most striking example of a country losing its freedom by the unchecked multiplication of such evils, and he was convinced that the United States would suffer the same loss if it did not profit in time by that example.

Such in brief was the political philosophy of Thomas Jefferson—his conception of human rights and of the form of government best suited to

---

the British fleet and nation." The reasons given by Jefferson for uniting with the British fleet and nation are as valid today as they were in 1802.

[10] *Ibid.,* III, 279; X, 28, 34.

secure these rights. What then is still living in this political philosophy? To what extent is his conception of rights still valid for us? To what extent is the form of government recommended by him well adapted for securing the rights, whatever they are, that need to be secured in our time?

Any comprehensive study of Jefferson and his writings is apt, sooner or later, to leave one with the impression that he was more at home in the world of ideas than in the world of men and affairs. He had little of Franklin's zest for life in the rough, little of his genial, tolerant acceptance of men as they are, and none of his talent for being comfortable in crowds, or of hobnobbing on equal terms with persons of every station, from kings to scullions in the kitchen. Jefferson was a democrat by intellectual conviction but by training and temperament a Virginia aristocrat—a man of cultivated tastes and preferences, with an aversion from all that is crude and boisterous, vulgar and passionate, in human intercourse. It may be said that he felt with his mind, as some people think with the heart. John Adams said that Jefferson's writings were characterized by "a peculiar felicity of expression." [11] They were indeed— perhaps a little too much so. In reading Jefferson's writings one feels that it would be a relief to come now and then on a hard, uncompromising, passionate sentence, such as: "As for me, give me liberty or give me death!" What we expect to find is rather: "Manly sentiment bids us die freemen rather than live as slaves." Jefferson's ideas were also characterized by a peculiar felicity, and also perhaps a little too much so. One feels that they come a little too easily to birth and rest a little precariously on the ideal aspirations of good men and not sufficiently on the harsh, brute facts of the world as it is. Jefferson was no visionary, and on occasions, such as the purchase of Louisiana, he exhibited a remarkable grasp of political realities. But it was entirely characteristic of him that, in respect to the Embargo, he should have taken the position that since our rights were in principle equally violated by England and France, they should be impartially defended against both countries, although England alone was in fact able to do us any material injury; equally characteristic that the high aim of his policy was to defend our rights by humane and peaceful methods, and the signal effect of it to inflict more material injury on the United States than on either of the countries by which its rights had been violated. One often feels that if there had been a little more humane sentiment and a good deal more passion in Jefferson's make-up, he would have been an out and out non-resistance pacifist. As it is, he presents us with the anomaly of a revolutionist who hated violence and a President of the United States who was disconcerted by the possession of political power.

If Jefferson was more at home in the world of ideas than in the world of

---

[11] *Works of John Adams,* II, 514.

men and affairs, it follows that, as a political philosopher, he was a better judge of ends than of means. In all that relates to the fundamental values of life, for the individual and for society, in all that relates to the ideal aims which the democratic form of government aims to realize, his understanding was profound. But in respect to the means, the particular institutions by which these values and ideal aims may be realized, he was often at fault, if not for his own time at least for ours; and when he was at fault he was so partly because he conceived of society as more static than it really is and partly because he conceived of American society as something that might remain predominantly agricultural and with relatively simple institutional devices be kept isolated in a relatively arcadian simplicity. But Jefferson's chief limitation as a political philosopher (and in fairness to him it should be remembered that it was the limitation of most political philosophers of his time) was that he was unduly influenced by the idea that the only thing to do with political power, since it is inherently dangerous, is to abate it. He failed to appreciate sufficiently the hard fact that political power always exists in the world and will be used by those who possess it; and as a consequence of this failure he was too much concerned with negative devices designed to obstruct the use of political power for bad ends and not sufficiently concerned with positive devices designed to make use of it for good ends.

This gives us then our general answer. In respect to fundamentals—the nature of human rights and the form of government best suited to secure them—Jefferson's philosophy is still valid for us; in respect to particular political forms and policies, much of it is now outmoded. In elaborating this general answer I can touch only on the main points.

None of Jefferson's ideas is so irrelevant to our needs as that concerning cities and industrial communities, not because there is not much truth in what he has to say about them but because his hope that the United States might remain a predominantly agricultural society was entirely misplaced. During Jefferson's time there was occurring a revolution of which he was unaware, or the significance of which he at all events entirely failed to grasp. I refer, of course, to the Industrial, or more properly the Technological, Revolution, brought about by the discovery of steam power, electricity, and radiation. It was one of the two or three major revolutions in the history of civilization, since by giving men an unprecedented control over material things it transformed, within a brief span of years, the relatively simple agricultural societies of the eighteenth century into societies far more complex and integrated and at the same time far more mobile and swiftly changing than any ever known before—formidable, blank-faced Leviathans that Thomas Jefferson would have regarded as unreal, fantastic, and altogether unsuited to liberty and equality as he understood those terms. That Jefferson did not foresee this momentous revolution is no discredit to him: no one in his time foresaw it more than dimly. But the point is that these are the societies in which we live and in connection with which we have to reconsider the nature of human rights and the institutions best suited to secure them; and it is now clear that Jefferson's favorite doctrine of laissez faire in respect to economic enterprise, and therefore in respect to political policy also, can no longer serve as a guiding principle for securing the rights of men to life, liberty, and the pursuit of happiness.

The doctrine of laissez faire, as it was understood by Jefferson and the social philosophers of the early nineteenth century, rested upon the assumption that if each individual within the nations, and each nation among the nations, was left as free as possible to pursue its own interest, something not themselves, God or Nature, would do whatever else was necessary for righteousness; or, better still, as Professor Carr puts it in his recent book, the assumption that from the unrestrained pursuit of individual self-interest a "harmony of interests" would more or less automatically emerge.[12] In the political realm this meant that the function of government should be confined in principle to the protection of life and property, the guaranteeing of contracts, the preservation of civil order, and the defense of the country against aggression. In the economic realm it meant that the free play of individual initiative, stimulated by the acquisitive instinct, would result in the maximum production of wealth, and that the competitive instinct, functioning through the price system, would result in as equitable a distribution of wealth as the qualities and defects of men permitted. In the international world it meant that the promotion of its own interest and power by each sovereign state would tend to create a balance of power and of interests which would serve, better than any other system, to promote commercial exchanges and cultural relations and to preserve the peace.

It is now sufficiently clear that the doctrine of laissez faire—of letting things go—however well adapted it may have been to the world in which Jefferson lived, is not well adapted to the world in which we live. In a world so highly integrated economically, a world in which the tempo of social change is so accelerated and the technological power at the disposal of corporations and governments is so enormous and can be so easily used for anti-social ends—in such a world the unrestrained pursuit of individual and national self-interest results neither in the maximum production or the equitable distribution of wealth, nor in the promotion of international comity and peace, but in social class conflicts and in total and global wars so ruthless as to threaten the destruction of all interests, individual and national, and even the foundations of civilized living. In such a world the inalienable right to life, liberty, and the pursuit of happiness can be secured, not by letting things go and trusting to God or Nature to see that they go right but in deciding beforehand where they ought to go and doing what is desirable and possible to make them go there. The harmony of in-

---

[12] Edward H. Carr, *The Conditions of Peace* (Toronto, 1942), p. 105.

terests, if there is to be any, must be deliberately and socially designed and deliberatively and co-operatively worked for. To bring this harmony of interests to pass is now the proper function of government; and it will assuredly not be brought to pass by any government that proceeds on the assumption that the best government is the one that governs least.

The history of the United States during a hundred years past confirms this conclusion and thereby refutes Jefferson's idea that the several states should retain their sovereign powers, and that the powers of the Federal government should be strictly and narrowly interpreted. Decade by decade the states have lost their sovereign powers, and the Federal government, by virtue of a liberal interpretation of the Constitution and of amendments to it, has assumed the authority to pass legislation limiting the activities of some individuals in order to secure the rights of others. This expansion of power and enlargement of function has been brought about, in spite of the inertia of traditional ideas and the pressure of interested groups, by the insistent need of regulating the activities of great corporations which, although in theory private enterprises, are in fact public utilities, and thereby possess irresponsible power which they are sometimes unwilling but more often unable to use for the public good. It is in respect to this situation that the engaging word "liberty" emerges in a guise unknown to Jefferson and his contemporaries. In his time the most obvious oppressions, for the majority of men, were the result of arbitrary governmental restrictions on the activities of individuals, so that liberty could be most easily conceived in terms of the emancipation of the individual from governmental constraint. But in our time the development of free economic enterprise has created a situation in which the most obvious oppressions, for the majority of men, arise not from an excess of governmental regulation but from the lack of it, so that in our time liberty can be understood only in terms of more and more intelligently designed supervision of free economic enterprise. Jefferson and his contemporaries, as James Bryce has well said, "mistook the pernicious channels in which selfish propensities had been flowing for those propensities themselves, which were sure to find new channels when the old had been destroyed." [13] The selfish propensities with which we have to deal are the same as those with which Jefferson and his contemporaries had to deal, but since the channels—the particular institutions and customs—through which they flow are different, the remedies have to be different also.

In this respect—in respect to the proper function of government—the political philosophy of Jefferson is now outmoded. But this is after all the more superficial aspect of Jefferson's philosophy, and if we turn to its more fundamental aspects—to the form of government as distinct from its func-

---

[13] *Modern Democracies* (New York, 1921), I, 49.

tion, and to the essential rights to be secured as distinct from the particular institutional forms for securing them—we find that Jefferson's political philosophy is as valid for our time as it was for his.

Jefferson was profoundly convinced that the best form of government was the republican—that is, government by elected representatives—because it was the only form, as he said, that "is not eternally at open or secret war with the rights of mankind." The form of government which Jefferson did so much to establish still exists, essentially unchanged; and today we accept it with even less qualification and divided loyalty than obtained in Jefferson's time. We accept it for many reasons, no doubt—because it has on the whole worked so well, because we have become habituated to it, and because there is in our political tradition no model for any other form. But we also accept it for the same reason that Jefferson accepted it—because we are profoundly convinced that it is the one form of government that is not at war with the rights of mankind, or at all events with those familiar rights and privileges which we regard as in some sense natural, because from long settled habit they seem to us so imprescriptibly American.

Recent events have greatly strengthened this conviction. Twenty years ago we were in a mood to ask whether the representative system of government might not be, if not at open, at least too often at secret, war with the rights of mankind. That was the result of comparing the democratic practice with the democratic ideal, with the inevitable if perhaps salutary effect of magnifying the defects and minimizing the virtues of democratic government as a going concern. But for ten years past now we have been permitted, have indeed been compelled, to reappraise democratic government in the light, not of the ideal, but of the practical alternative as presented for our admiration in Germany and elsewhere. And the result of this reappraisal has been to convince us that the defects of our system of government are, in comparison, trivial, while its virtues are substantial. Indeed the incredible cynicism of Adolf Hitler's way of regarding man and the life of man, made real by the servile and remorseless activities of his bleak-faced, humorless Nazi supporters, has forced men everywhere to re-examine the validity of half-forgotten ideas and to entertain once more half-discarded convictions as to the substance of things not seen. One of these convictions is that "liberty, equality, fraternity," and the "inalienable rights" of man are phrases, glittering or not, that denote realities—the fundamental realities that men will always fight and die for rather than surrender.

In defense of these rights and of our democratic form of government, we are now fighting a desperate war; and in justification of our action we are advancing the same reasons that Jefferson proclaimed—that the democratic form of government is the one best adapted to secure the inalienable rights of man. We may be less sure than Jefferson was that a beneficent intelligence created the world for man's special convenience. We may think that the laws of nature, and especially the laws of human nature, are less easily discovered than he supposed. We may have found it more difficult to define the natural rights of man and to secure them by simple institutional forms than he anticipated. Above all, we may have learned that human reason is not quite so infallible an instrument for arriving at the truth as he supposed it to be and that men are less amenable to rational persuasion. Nevertheless, in essentials Jefferson's political philosophy is our political philosophy; in essentials democracy means for us what it meant for him.

Democracy is for us, as it was for him, primarily a set of values, a way of regarding man and the life of man. It is for us, as it was for him, also a set of concrete institutions through which these values may be realized. We now realize, as he did, but rather better than he did, that the institutional forms are bound to change: they have changed since Jefferson's time, they are changing now, and they will change still further in time to come. But we may believe, as Jefferson did, that the values themselves are enduring; one reason for believing so being the fact that the values we cherish are the same as those which Jefferson proclaimed and the same as those which for more than two thousand years the saints and sages of the world have regarded as the ideal aim and ultimate test of civilized living. If we were to write a Declaration of the modern democratic faith, it might run somewhat as follows:

> We hold these truths to be self-evident: that the individual man has dignity and worth in his own right; that it is better to be governed by persuasion than by force; that fraternal good will is of greater worth than a selfish and contentious spirit; that in the long run all values, both for the individual and for society, are inseparable from the love of truth and the disinterested search for it; that the truth can be discovered only insofar as the mind of man is free; that knowledge and the power it gives should be used for promoting the welfare and happiness of all men rather than for the selfish interests of those individuals and classes whom intelligence and fortune have endowed with a temporary advantage; and that no form of government yet invented is so well adapted to realize these high ends as one that is designed to be a government of the people, by the people, for the people.

To this declaration of the modern democratic faith Thomas Jefferson would subscribe, I feel sure, without qualification. And it is in this sense, the most important sense of all, that his philosophy, and still more the humane and liberal spirit of the man himself, abides with us, as a living force, to clarify our purposes, to strengthen our faith, and to fortify our courage.

The Relevance of Mr. Jefferson

Dumas Malone

I

In almost the last year of his long life, replying to a query about the Declaration of Independence, Thomas Jefferson wrote a letter which is worth recalling. Certain people, especially people who did not care for his politics, had suggested that in fact that famous document was not original. When he was eighty-two years old he made a statement about its objects—that is, his own objects in writing it—which I quote in part:

> Not to find out new principles, or new arguments, never before thought of, not merely to say things which had never been said before; but to place before mankind the common sense of the subject. . . .

The present utterance can hardly be compared to the immortal Declaration, and I do not presume to address it to all mankind, but, without pretense of originality, I hope to set forth the common sense of the matter in dealing with Mr. Jefferson himself. While many true and wonderful things have been said about this inexhaustible man since his death, a considerable number of things have been said that should really be described as nonsense. Perhaps it would be fairer to say of many of these that they are partial truths which have been paraded as whole truths, deriving from the law and gospel. At all events, confusion is confounded when an historic personage is quoted on opposite sides in a contemporary controversy, as Mr. Jefferson repeatedly has been. Instances will quickly come to mind in connection with the presidential campaign of 1960, when it was solemnly announced that he would have voted for both candidates; or in connection with the New Deal, which he is said both to have opposed and favored.

It is not my purpose to declare which side he was on, since I really have no way of knowing. Also, I recognize the likelihood that I should arrive at the pleasant conclusion that he always agreed with me. The proneness of the human mind to rationalize can hardly be exaggerated. In view, however, of the well-authenticated fact that contradictory statements have been

From *Virginia Quarterly Review*, XXXVII, (Summer 1961), 332–349. Reprinted by permission.

made about him ever since his death I am disposed to ask certain questions. What meaning does he really have for *us* in our present situation? Are his words and actions relevant to *our* circumstances, or irrelevant? If he is relevant in certain respects and irrelevant in others, what is the ground of distinction? How is anyone to know? On this confused situation I should like to turn what the late William S. Gilbert called "the hose of common sense." Surely the common sense of the matter is to try to distinguish between those words and actions which related solely or primarily to his own time, and those which have the quality of timelessness. That is, we need to separate what is or may be properly regarded as dateless from what is necessarily dated.

In this connection, I do not need to focus attention on him as a human being. Human nature seems to have changed little in the course of recorded history, and human personality defies barriers of space and time. In spirit we can live intimately with persons from the past whenever their words and deeds are sufficiently recorded for us to know them. We soon forget that their clothes were unlike ours and that they wore their hair quite differrently. We have to allow for changes in manners and morals, and even when they employ our own language we may detect a certain quaintness in their speech. But the common denominator of human nature and individual experience is so large that great personalities can speak to us across the generations, even across the centuries, in language that is understandable since it is the language of life itself.

By precept and example the father of the University of Virginia can still teach anyone who will take the trouble to listen to him and observe him. Many things can we learn from him about the fine art of living. Not the least of these is that once an apostle of equality lived a notably elevated life, an extraordinarily rich, perennially interesting, endlessly generous, and ceaselessly useful life, in a society which he himself had made more democratic. He exemplified excellence, not the dull level of mediocrity; individuality, not unthinking conformity. He dared to build his house upon a mountain and to be himself, surveying the universe in personal independence. As a human being he has real meaning for our time: in his own person he reminds us what man can do with freedom.

Though human nature and human personality seem to be the most constant factors in history except the earth and the waters round it, along with the seasons and the tides, they manifest themselves in widely varying circumstances, of course, and no human being of either the past or the present can be fully understood apart from his particular environment. We should be foolish to assume that Mr. Jefferson would make precisely the same domestic arrangements at Monticello if he were living there now as he made a hundred and fifty years ago; or that, if one of his grandchildren became ill today, he would be as dubious as he was then about the value of medical services; presumably he would not now suggest that doctors may do more harm than good. We can appreciate the realism which enabled him to appraise them so well in his day, but we should be unwise to seek his *specific* advice in the conduct of our personal affairs, medical or otherwise.

Anything that may be said about considering a human being, in his personal life, on the background of his own environment has to be heavily underlined when we speak of him as a public man. We *have* to view statesmen, past and present, in their own settings of time, place, and circumstance. To do otherwise would be to render them a grave injustice. For forty years, with only a few interruptions, Mr. Jefferson was a public official—burgess, delegate, governor, minister to a foreign country, secretary of state, vice president, and president. During all these years he was dealing with current public affairs and day-to-day problems. More than most statesmen, he tried to take the long view and to guide his steps by enduring principles, and if he had not done so better than most men his fame would have been less enduring. Nonetheless, he could not escape the necessity, and no statesman ever can, of adjusting policies to the existing situation. Public affairs are not conducted in a vacuum. It is of the utmost importance, therefore, to seek a fair understanding of the public situation he had to face.

Since he devoted a very large part of his time and labors to foreign relations, and world affairs are of such vital concern to us today, we can profitably take a quick look at the general world situation in his era. Even in his slow-moving age that situation changed, to be sure, but certain of its features were relatively constant during most of his public life. Some of these features were so similar to what we ourselves have faced that his age seems positively familiar. Most of his career was set on a background of general war. The conflict which broke out in Europe when he was secretary of state and lasted, with only slight interruption, considerably beyond his presidency, if not world war in our sense, came nearer being that than any that our planet was to know until the twentieth century. In his day this planet was a less dangerous place than it has been in our era of world war, total war, cold war, and threat of nuclear destruction. Furthermore, because of the slowness of movement and communication, peril was less imminent. There was not the same sense of desperate urgency, and statesmen could be less hurried. That is one thing the statesmen of this day can deeply envy them. Nonetheless, the dangers faced in the two eras were strikingly similar, even if in our time they have been greatly intensified.

His age was one of revolution which touched virtually all parts of the globe that our country was concerned with. Indeed, it was commonly regarded as *the* age of revolution until our generation pre-empted the title. In our day the revolutionary spirit has spread to continents which were still slumbering in his time. It has taken on social and economic forms which were little dreamed of by our forefathers when they proclaimed revolution in the name of political independence, and which were not approached even in revolutionary France. But his time was also one of great political and considerable social convulsion. Thus one can say that, in its international aspects, no other period in American history can so fitly be compared to ours as the age of Washington and Jefferson. I have been particularly struck with what may be called the psychological parallels. Human nature being much the same, personal and social reactions to war and revolution show a great deal of similarity. This is frequently reflected in language: many of the things that were said in manifestos and resolutions, in newspapers and in private letters, sound like utterances of our time if you change the names and places.

There were numerous differences, however, and we can readily recognize the paramount importance of one of them. The position from which Mr. Jefferson and others charged with the national interest and security viewed a warring and revolutionary world was virtually the reverse of the one our leaders now occupy. The potential giant of the West was then only a stripling, a weakling among the Powers, while today our Republic is in all respects gigantic. They had to lead from weakness, where we can lead from strength. The policy which will always be associated with the names of Washington and Jefferson was to keep out of the raging power struggle in so far as possible, regardless of personal predilections one way or the other, regardless of ideology. Thus was born the classic American doctrine of neutrality or non-involvement, which, despite occasional aberrations, endured for generations. It arose from the necessities of national security, and its wisdom at that time cannot be doubted. Everybody knows that the policy has been completely reversed in our century, also because of the necessities of national security.

What does this signify about the bearing of the acts, the policies, the words of Mr. Jefferson on the world problems of our day? Can we really learn anything from him? In my opinion, we can learn much. As an example I will cite the year 1793, when the European war broadened so as to threaten us, when the French Revolution passed into its greatest excesses, when this young Republic entered upon its historic policy of neutrality. To consider the activities of Mr. Jefferson, the Secretary of State, in one of the most momentous years in modern history, observing his incessant labors, his extraordinary patience amid frustrations, his unflagging patriotism, and his basic wisdom, is to share a tremendous experience. Regarding the controversy into which he, a friend of France, was drawn in 1793 with the insolent envoy of the French revolutionary government, one of the greatest of his successors in the office of Secretary of State, John Quincy Adams, said that his papers on that controversy "present the most perfect model of diplomatic discussion and expostulation of modern times." This was American diplomacy at one of its highest points, revealing rare skill and a realistic appraisal of the existing situation which should command the admiration of anyone dealing with international problems in any age.

Yet the policy at which President Washington and Secretary Jefferson arrived has had to be repudiated in our century, when at length we reluctantly assumed the rôle of world leadership which destiny imposed upon us. Conceivably it might have been reversed sooner, to the advantage of mankind, but for the sad human proclivity to learn the wrong lessons from history and miss the right ones. As an exemplar of the skillful and realistic conduct of foreign affairs, which he generally was, Mr. Jefferson is very relevant. So far as specific policies go, however, time has rendered him quite irrelevant. To be sure, some people in our century have sought specific answers to the problems of contemporary foreign policy in the Neutrality Proclamation of 1793, Washington's Farewell Address of 1796, and Jefferson's First Inaugural of 1801. In a world that has been turned upside down, that sort of reliance on sharply dated pronouncements, wonderful as they were when written, hardly seems the common sense of the matter. Indeed, one is inclined to ask, as Elmer Davis used to: "How silly can you be?"

II

Now let us turn from the world situation to the home scene. When we fly on the wings of the spirit back into Mr. Jefferson's America, of course we can recognize many landmarks—the configuration of the coasts, the rivers flowing to the sea, the mountains on the western horizon. We can quickly perceive that he and his contemporaries were persons of like passions and vanities with ourselves. In his day political organization—party organization, for example—was rudimentary from our point of view, but the minds of politicians worked very much as they do right now and they used the same sort of wiles—slogans, name-calling, and various devices designed to show that they were more honest and more patriotic than their rivals. All of this is very familiar and should make us feel at home. But it is difficult for us to realize how few people there were or how scattered, and how slowly they got around. When Jefferson became President the population of New York did not greatly exceed that of present-day Charlottesville. If he could see the national metropolis today he would no doubt regard it as an incredible monstrosity. It took him ten days to come home to Albemarle from Philadelphia; and the post rider from Richmond was so erratic that he sometimes didn't get to Charlottesville with the mail for three weeks, although Mr. Jefferson insisted that the roads were generally passable to a carriage and always, he believed, to a man on horseback. Getting out of one's locality and keeping in touch with the outside world was an exceedingly difficult thing, and it is no wonder that so much government devolved upon the county court in Virginia, or that the town meeting was so important in New England. To a degree which is hard for us to conceive, emphasis *had* to be laid on the locality and the self-reliance of individuals. By our standards that society was amazingly simple, delightfully simple, though by the same standards life was extraordinarily inconvenient and must often have been extremely dull.

The fact is that the series of non-political revolutions which have so profoundly affected the physical conditions of existence and have transformed our economy and society occurred *after* Mr. Jefferson's public career was over. The industrial revolution had begun in Europe by his time, but it did not really get started in this country until the very end of his presidency, and even then our industries were only infants. The successive revolutions in transportation and communication all came later. Fulton's steamboat, the *Clermont,* plied the Hudson in his second term, but it has been aptly said that Jefferson, like Nebuchadnezzar, never saw anything faster than a horse.

It would be rather absurd for me to attempt to describe the various revolutions in science and technology which have followed one upon another with ever-increasing speed. I have had difficulty in adjusting my mind to the ones that have occurred in my own lifetime, finding some of them utterly bewildering. Indeed, I escape from them nearly every day into the age of Mr. Jefferson. The air seems clearer there, and the unhurried pace leaves more time for thought. In the uncrowded country there were no huge factories—scarcely any at all, in fact; there were no immense aggregations of capital and formidable organizations of labor. There were sailing vessels in the harbors and merchants in the ports and inland centers, but nearly all the workers in this farflung country were tillers of the soil. This was no Golden Age of health, comfort, and convenience, but perhaps it may be regarded as a sort of heyday of individualism. Human beings may have been dwarfed by the vastness of the land, though relatively few had traveled over much of it; they were *not* dwarfed by any of the works of man.

Almost exactly one hundred and sixty years ago the raw-boned country gentleman who had been chosen head of this predominantly agricultural republic delivered his first inaugural address in the Senate chamber, the only part of the capitol that was yet finished in the straggling wilderness village that went by the name of Washington. It is said that few in the audience could hear him, he spoke so low; but his speech could be read afterwards in the newspapers, and it proved to be one of the few to which historians recur. Does it have any present bearing on *our* problems?

It was admirably suited to its particular circumstances. One of the important conflicts in the previous campaign had been over the right to oppose, to criticize the existing government—a thing the group in power had sought to prevent by means of the notorious Sedition Act. Historians often say that, whatever else Jefferson's election signified, it vindicated the legitimacy of political opposition. But terrible things had been predicted if this man should be elected; Bibles might be confiscated. Accordingly, he felt impelled to speak words of reassurance, and some of these are still fresh after more than a century and a half. He announced one principle which he called sacred and which may be regarded as timeless, I think, in any self-governing society: "that though the will of the majority is in all cases to prevail, that will, to be rightful, must be reasonable; that the minority possess their equal rights, which equal laws must protect, and to violate which would be oppression." It is a great pity that Abraham Lincoln did not quote those words in *his* first inaugural. They would have been eminently appropriate then, as they would have been on January 20, 1961.

There are other nuggets of abiding wisdom in Mr. Jefferson's address, and there is some deeply moving language. I am most concerned here, however, with what he said in the year 1801 about the way he meant to conduct the government. Since he never wrote anything like a systematic treatise on government but scattered his ideas throughout his profuse writings, the things he said here have been regarded by many as a handy summary of his working political philosophy. Judging from this address, he believed that the federal government should devote itself largely to the conduct of foreign affairs, which were always important in his era. With special reference to domestic matters he summed up federal functions in a passage which has been quoted for more than a century and a half:

> Still one thing more, fellow citizens—a wise and frugal government, which shall restrain men from injuring one another, which shall leave them otherwise free to regulate their own pursuits of industry and improvement, and shall not take from the mouth of labor the bread it has earned. This is the sum of good government. . . .

That is, the federal government, outside the conduct of foreign relations, was to be little more than a policeman and an umpire. It was to grant special privileges to none and secure equal and exact justice for all—an obligation requiring diligence as well as forbearance—but if we take these words at their face value its functions were to be essentially negative. From the vantage point of today, the "sum of good government" as thus described is very small.

Even at that time some intelligent people thought it dangerously small. Midway in his first term his ancient antagonist, Alexander Hamilton, lamented that the Constitution was a "frail and worthless fabric," despite all his own efforts to prop it up. He believed that under Jefferson's interpretation the government could withstand no serious strain; and he had little hope that it would further the economic development of the country in the directions he himself had pointed. Hamilton wanted to stimulate that part of the economic society now described as "business," which by modern standards was then little more than rudimentary. He was particularly interested in banks, the facilitation of trade, the creation of fluid capital; and if anyone deserves to be described as the father of American capitalism surely it is Hamilton. He wanted to use the government, and when in office he did use it, for the development of business. He thought Jefferson uninformed in these matters—indifferent, even hostile to this development. In my opinion, he did not fully understand his great rival; it seems to me that the bitter feeling of the Eastern merchants and emerging financiers of that time toward Jefferson went beyond the point of reason. He certainly knew little about banks and deplored speculation in securities; to him property pre-eminently was real property, that is, land; but he unquestionably knew a great deal about foreign commerce, and he was an economic nationalist in his own way. Nonetheless, I think I can understand why to the Hamiltonians he often seemed an old-fashioned farmer who was blind to the wave of the future. It can be argued that John Marshall did not sufficiently recognize the flexibility of his distant kinsman in the face of actual circumstances. Yet it is not hard to see why the Chief Justice sought to counter the centrifugal tendencies he perceived in the Jeffersonian philosophy by asserting through a long generation the scope of national authority.

How well adjusted the policies of President Jefferson really were to the conditions of his own time is a matter of historical judgment. In his own person he was certainly not negative or lethargic; this incessantly active and extraordinarily dynamic man cannot be rightly regarded as the historical prototype of Calvin Coolidge. Actually, his administration was more economical than Coolidge's, but if anybody should be disposed to think that his main service was that of counting pennies in the Executive Mansion, or that his rôle was primarily that of a caretaker, that person should take a look at the map. There was a large element of luck in the Louisiana Purchase, as well as some theoretical inconsistency on Jefferson's part—or at least this has been alleged; but no one can properly deny to him the credit for doubling the area of his country. The domestic consequences of his actions were to prove momentous. He left to his successor a different country from the one he had begun to govern at the age of fifty-eight; and just as soon as new states began to emerge from this huge domain the Union began to be a different sort of Union. The balance of power within it was bound to shift, and in the long run it shifted decisively against his own Virginia. There was no little irony in the course of later events, but this majestic achievement, this creation of what he happily termed an "empire for liberty," makes it impossible to think of him as the caretaker of an old order, or as one whose main function was to put brakes to the wheels of progress.

One of his undoubted purposes, as expressed in his own words, was to "lead things into the channel of harmony between the governors and governed," and in this he was conspicuously successful. He gave his countrymen what most of them wanted, and I think he gave his country what it then needed most—which was mainly a chance to grow without either aid or interference. The immediate task and the dominant desire was to possess the land. He handed out no subsidies to farmers or anybody else, but to his land-hungry generation he pointed the door of unparalleled opportunity, seeking to maintain approximate equality of opportunity but otherwise largely leaving human nature to take its course. He hoped that the vast preponderance of his countrymen would be self-supporting farmers, whom he regarded as the best citizens and the freest and happiest men on earth. His countrymen liked the idea; indeed, they embroidered it into a legend which long survived the circumstances which gave it birth. It became a myth which invested agricultural problems of later generations with nostalgia.

What present reality is there in his pronouncement of one hundred and sixty years ago about limiting the functions of government? Does this mean today that the federal government ought to be small even though everything else has become gigantic—that the best way to solve our national political and economic problems is to set down a pigmy among the giants? And all this in a time of world crisis to which we can see no end? It would hardly be fair to Mr. Jefferson to claim that he would favor that degree of impotence. This is not to say that he would like all of our huge organizations, or any of them. The processes of consolidation in all departments of life have been greatly accelerated in our time by the series of wars and crises we have gone through. Mr. Jefferson would certainly not rejoice that we have had to adjust all our institutions to the needs of these, and he might not like the way we have done it. Very likely he would approve of Lord Acton's well-known dictum: "Power tends to corrupt; absolute power corrupts absolutely." His entire career reflects his distrust of power as well as his undying concern for freedom, and it is just as true now as it ever was that the price of liberty is eternal vigilance. But when speaking of the threat of tyranny, he kept on talking about kings, who are not much of a menace now. Tyranny changes its face from age to age, and every era has to decide for itself where the greatest and most imminent danger to the freedom of the individual really lies. The contradiction which we face arises from the dreadful circumstance that the very survival of liberty at home and abroad depends on the employment of power such as Mr. Jefferson never dreamed of and which inevitably carries within itself a threat to personal freedom. We can't expect him to resolve this contradiction. He would be bewildered by this strange new world, this wonderful and terrible new world. In his day he was an alert sentinel and generally, though not always, a sagacious guide. But he is well beyond the age of retirement and we can't expect him to chart our course for us.

He himself summed things up sufficiently in one of the most important of his sayings: "The earth belongs always to the living generation." Whatever opinions he may have held at one time or another about specific problems, he held tenaciously to the conviction that the present need not and should not be guided by the dead hand of the past. We can learn greatly from past experience, but we must not ask too much of history. It often provides suggestive analogies, but rarely if ever can we find in it an answer to a specific question, a precise solution for a contemporary problem. It offers us no detailed road map to guide the traffic of today. The common sense of the matter is that the particular policies or methods Mr. Jefferson announced one hundred and sixty years ago are now essentially irrelevant, if not wholly so. The same can be said, of course, of the historic policies of George Washington and Abraham Lincoln. And the saying goes for Queen Elizabeth I, Julius Caesar, Alexander the Great, and Pericles, though the careers of all of them are well worth studying.

III

The undiscriminating use of the past has had unfortunate consequences on Mr. Jefferson's reputation. This incessant builder, who was ceaselessly striving to advance knowledge and improve society, has often been cast in the rôle of perpetual obstructionist. One of the signers of the Declaration of Independence was known as "the great objector"; that was not Mr. Jefferson, though no one more than he insisted on the right of any man to object to anything on the merits of the case. There is an even greater danger than that of judging him unfairly: in stressing what is actually irrelevant, people tend to overlook or disregard acts and words of his which do have the ring of timelessness and are applicable to our age or any other. He left us no road map, but, more than any public man in our history, he pointed us to the star by which our course should be guided. It would be a pity if, while following some ancient and long-abandoned trail, we should fail to see what is shining overhead.

He has left us in no doubt whatever about the way to separate the temporary from the enduring elements in his heritage to posterity. He explicitly stated that he wanted no public offices listed on his tombstone—not even the Presidency of the United States. He knew that his official actions were necessarily dated, that policies could not be expected to last forever. He wanted to be remembered for words and deeds which had the quality of timelessness about them, and there can be no possible doubt that he made a wise selection.

The Declaration of Independence, which he listed first, has a date, to be sure—our most famous date since it marks the birthday of our Republic; and this was identified with him all the more irrevocably when he died fifty years later on July 4, as though by Divine Providence. Part of the document itself is unmistakably dated: historians do not accept all those charges against King George III as eternal truth. But the part of the Declaration we know best and prize most was undoubtedly regarded by its author as timeless and universal. How can you date truths which you regard as eternal and self-evident? By virtue of their birth into the world as human beings, all men are equal—not in status certainly, and surely not in ability, but in rights. The implications of the assertion that everybody is a human being and should be treated as one were not fully perceived by all who approved the historic pronouncement of our national faith, but these words have gone ringing down the generations. They were still vibrant words when we answered the mad ravings of Adolf Hitler and countered the arrogant cruelty of the German Nazis. (At the time many historians must have reflected, as I surely did, that history offers no more striking antithesis than that between Adolf Hitler and Thomas Jefferson.) No ways and means are specified in the great Declaration; these must be determined by every living generation for itself in the light of its own circumstances. But those phrases, which we have heard a hundred times, have in them the perennial freshness of the spring; today as in 1776 they breathe undying faith in human beings. Many people, many high-minded people, find it hard to extend that faith to groups they have long regarded as "lesser breeds without the law"; and it is difficult indeed to uphold the freedom and dignity of all men when so many are unworthy and so many abuse their freedom. But we need not look to our historic Declaration for soothing words, for words that condone complacency or excuse any form of arrogance. We can find there no specific solution for any of our immediate problems, but we can find an eternal summons to proceed upon unfinished tasks.

To this timeless document we can also turn for a sense of values—for an everlasting criterion by which to judge all human institutions. So far as my knowledge and judgment go, history provides none better. Man was not made for government, but government was made for man; and the final criterion of its actions or its inaction is the degree to which it supports the freedom, upholds the dignity, and promotes the happiness of individual human beings. This is our answer to Communism and to any form of totalitarianism, whether of the right or left. Man was not made for organization—business, labor, professional, or any other; these were made for man, and the only proper test of them is what they do for him. We should think of this when we consider these giants of government, of business, of labor which our society has nurtured, and which so often seem to dwarf human beings. Surely the purpose of government should never be to augment power for its own sake, of business to produce profits solely for themselves, of labor to increase wages merely for the sake of wages. What is the product worth in terms of human happiness? When change is not productive of human happiness, surely it is not progress. This is no mere matter of material things, though no one can question their importance. "Man shall not live by bread alone," was said by a greater teacher than Mr. Jefferson. The challenge of our times and of all times is to humanize institutions—*all* institutions.

The Virginia act establishing religious freedom was adopted by the General Assembly on a particular date, but the date is unimportant. Actually, Jefferson drew his bill some years before it was passed, and it is just as fresh in the twentieth century as it was on the day he drew it. Here, even more clearly than in the Declaration, perhaps, can one perceive the essence of his philosophy. Above all things, he was a champion of the freedom of the human spirit, and by this he meant even more than the right to worship God in any way one likes—supremely important as that is. He meant the entire freedom of the mind, the sacred right of any man to his own opinions, whether these be popular or not, whether they be moderate or radical or conservative. There was no mistake in choosing the key quotation for the Jefferson Memorial and in putting it as a motto on a postage stamp. He was eternally hostile to all tyrannies but most of all to tyranny over the human mind. I sometimes wonder if some of the people who take his name on their lips really like this, the most typical of all Jefferson quotations. I doubt if the Communists even begin to comprehend it, but surely it is in his insistence on the freedom of men to think that he becomes most dangerous to the monolithic state and the philosophy of complete conformity.

The University of Virginia, with which he ended his select list of memorable achievements, was chartered on a particular date, and we are not yet warranted in describing it as immortal. But in the Western world universities have been exceedingly long-lived; they flow on like so many streams, and this one may be expected to flow as long as our civilization shall endure. Besides being virtually timeless, any university, to be worthy of its name, must in spirit be universal. In his own lovely county, amid its eternal hills, this lifelong student institutionalized his undying faith in intelligence and knowledge. Nothing that he ever did was more characteristic of this inveterate builder—of this ardent farmer who prized the harvest of the mind beyond all others. If I understand him aright, he would not expect his academic heirs to pay much heed to specific things he once said about courses and regulations, but he would want them to apply to their life and learning the final tests of value. Not only does learning languish in the air of conformity and complacency; not only does it fail if it does not liberate the spirit; learning becomes a sterile thing when it loses its humanity.

Nothing is immutable but "the inherent and inalienable rights of man," he said. "The earth belongs always to the living generation." Times change, needs change, policies and methods change with them. But human beings remain, always. And the star of liberty still shines over Monticello. That star and the people it shines on are what he would most want us to see.

113

V

*The American Revolution as a
Social Movement:
A Glass Half Full
or a Glass Half Empty?*

INTRODUCTION

Until the publication in 1926 of J. Franklin Jameson's The American Revolution Considered as a Social Movement *the norm in American historiography had been to treat the Revolution in terms of military, political, diplomatic, and constitutional history. The permanent value of Jameson's work lies not in the fact that he said the last word upon the social consequences of the Revolution but that he opened up this whole field to further research and evaluation. The work is a minor classic not so much in the sense that it has remained unchallenged but in the sense that it was itself a challenge. It encouraged a whole generation of American historians to broaden its historical inquiries beyond the conventional approaches which had, up until then, characterized the research and writing in American history.*

The challenge was taken up and after the passage of almost 30 years it seemed appropriate to assess Jameson's work in order to determine its continuing validity in the light of the further scholarship that it had evoked. To take and mildly to twist a wise saying, the results demonstrate that every generation is its own historian. The results of this reevaluation of Jameson's work are given in Frederick B. Tolles' reevaluative essay presented here. The main thrust of this essay is to establish that many of the social movements, which Jameson had associated with the fervor and ideology of the Revolution, had, as Bernard Bailyn has written, ". . . been matters of fact before they were matters of theory and revolutionary doctrine." The large revisionist scholarship upon which Tolles' article is based tends to make of the American Revolution, in the sphere of social change, a much less dramatic and satisfying American experience than Jameson had taught us to believe it was.

Bernard Bailyn, in an important recent study reprinted below, adds a new and striking dimension to our conceptual realization of the American Revolution. He accepts that in social "experience and behavior," there is continuity between the colonial and revolutionary periods, but that in the realm of "habits of mind and belief" there was a great change, for now the advancing social reforms took on the coloration of legitimacy. There was continuity with the past, but the sense of deviation and impropriety was gone. In a particularly happy passage Bailyn writes: "The glass was half full, not half empty . . . ," and further on he concludes, "This completion, this rationalization, this symbolization, this lifting into consciousness and endowing with high moral purpose inchoate, confusing elements of social and political change—this was the American Revolution."

The American Revolution Considered as
a Social Movement: A Re-Evaluation

Frederick B. Tolles

Sometimes a single essay, a monograph, or a series of lectures makes historiographical history. It was so in 1893 when Frederick Jackson Turner read his paper on "The Significance of the Frontier in American History." It was so again in 1913 when Charles A. Beard published his *Economic Interpretation of the Constitution*. And it was so in 1925 when J. Franklin Jameson delivered his four lectures at Princeton on "The American Revolution Considered as a Social Movement."

At first glance the comparison with Turner and Beard may seem strained. We are accustomed to think of Jameson as a scholar's scholar, a kind of indispensable historical midwife—curator and editor of manuscripts, director of other men's research, editor of the *American Historical Review*—not as a path-breaker, an innovator. But this is to do him less than justice. *The American Revolution Considered as a Social Movement* stands as a landmark in recent American historiography, a slender but unmistakable signpost, pointing a new direction for historical research and interpretation. Before Jameson, the American Revolution had been a chapter in political, diplomatic, and military history, a story of Faneuil Hall and Lexington, Independence Hall and Valley Forge, Versailles and Yorktown. After Jameson, it became something different, something greater —a seismic disturbance in American society, a sudden quickening in the American mind.

The American Revolution, like the French, Jameson believed, was accompanied by social and cultural changes of profound significance.

> The stream of revolution, once started, could not be confined within narrow banks, but spread abroad upon the land. Many economic desires, many social aspirations were set free by the political struggle, many aspects of colonial society profoundly altered by the forces thus let loose. The relations of social classes to each other, the institution

From the *American Historical Review*, LX (October 1954), 1–12. Reprinted by permission. Read at the meeting of the Pacific Coast Branch of the American Historical Association, held at the University of California at Davis, December 28–30, 1953.

of slavery, the system of landholding, the course of business, the forms and spirit of the intellectual and religious life, all felt the transforming hand of revolution, all emerged from under it in shapes advanced many degrees nearer to those we know.[1]

No more than Turner's or Beard's was Jameson's notion wholly new. Just a year earlier, in his massive volume on *The American States during and after the Revolution,* Allan Nevins had devoted fifty pages to the task of demonstrating in impressive detail that "a social and intellectual revolution" occurred between Lexington and Yorktown.[2] Nearly twenty years before, Carl Becker had described the Revolution as a twofold contest: for home-rule on the one hand, for "the democratization of American politics and society" on the other.[3] As far back as 1787, Benjamin Rush had perceived that the American revolution was bigger than the American war, that the real revolution was in "the principles, morals, and manners of our citizens," and that, far from being over, that revolution had only begun.[4]

Jameson's view of the Revolution was not new, but no one hitherto had marshaled the evidence so compactly, conveyed it so lucidly, or argued from it so persuasively. Perceptive historians immediately greeted his little volume as a gem of historical writing—"a truly notable book," Charles A. Beard called it, ". . . cut with a diamond point to a finish, studded with novel illustrative materials, gleaming with new illumination, serenely engaging in style, and sparingly garnished with genial humor." [5]

The influence of this little book with the long title has grown steadily. A year after its publication, the Beards summarized its thesis in their widely read *Rise of American Civilization.*[6] Jameson's emphasis on social factors harmonized perfectly with the intellectual and political climate of the 1930's. In 1940, after the author's death, a second edition appeared, and in 1950 a third—an unusual tribute to a set of academic lectures. With the passage of a quarter-century, the book has achieved the standing of a minor classic.[7] One will find hardly a textbook that does not paraphrase or

---

[1] *The American Revolution Considered as a Social Movement* (Princeton, 1926), p. 11.

[2] New York, 1924, chap. x.

[3] *The History of Political Parties in the Province of New York* (Madison, Wis., 1909), p. 5.

[4] *American Museum,* I (1787), 9. Jameson quoted part of this well-known passage but ascribed it, for some reason, to "a writer in South Carolina." *American Revolution.* p. 29.

[5] *New Republic,* XLVII (Aug. 11, 1926), 344. In the *American Historical Review* discussion of the book was relegated to the "Minor Notices," perhaps because of its brevity, more likely because of the modesty of the managing editor—J. Franklin Jameson. The reviewer, Allan Nevins, called its scholarship "impeccable," its style "polished," its outlook "broad and thoughtful." XXXII (1926–27), 167–68.

[6] New York, 1927, I, 291–96.

[7] In a recent poll, in which 103 historians were asked to name the ten best historical works published between 1920 and 1935, Jameson's *American Revolution* got twenty-six votes. The pollster, analyzing the returns, observed that a brief book stood at a disad-

quote Jameson's words, borrow his illustrations, cite him in its bibliography. The notion of the Revolution as a social upheaval has achieved the final seal of acceptance: it has been taken over by the historical novelists—by such writers as Kenneth Roberts and Howard Fast, to name two rather unlikely bedfellows.

Jameson, one suspects, had no idea he was writing a classic. His aim was simply to challenge American historians by opening new windows on the Revolutionary era, suggesting new directions for future research, throwing out tentative hypotheses for others to test. Over the past quarter-century historians have risen to his challenge with a flood of articles, monographs, academic dissertations, and full-dress histories bearing on one or another of his propositions. But the average textbook-writer, one is tempted to believe, has not got beyond Jameson. The time has come to go back and ask how Jameson's original thesis stands up in the light of all this detailed research; what modifications, if any, must be made; what further extensions, if any, are possible.

Jameson disposed his arguments under four rubrics—the status of persons, the land, industry and commerce, thought and feeling. If we recognize, as he did, that such divisions are purely arbitrary, we may adopt his procedure.

American society, he suggested, was measurably democratized during the Revolution. The upper stratum, the old colonial aristocracy, was largely liquidated—by banishment, voluntary exile, or impoverishment. New groups rose to the surface to take their places. "In most states the strength of the revolutionary party lay most largely in the plain people," and the social changes which they brought about naturally tended "in the direction of levelling democracy." Broadening of the suffrage elevated "whole classes of people . . . in their social status," and the revolutionary philosophy of liberty wrought improvements in the condition of the most debased class in America—the Negro slaves.[8]

Recent studies of individual states and regions seem to suggest that Jameson was too sweeping when he equated colonial aristocrats with Loyalists and implied that this group was erased from American society. In eastern Massachusetts it was perhaps true that "a majority of the old aristocracy" emigrated.[9] But in the central and western part of the state the oldest, most respected families chose the Whig side and remained to

---

vantage in the poll but offered the comment, for whatever it might be worth, that Jameson's book showed "the best vote-getting record per word." John Walton Caughey, "Historians' Choice: Results of a Poll on Recently Published American History and Biography," *Mississippi Valley Historical Review*, XXXIX (September, 1952), 293, 299. W. Stull Holt's figures on the number of copies sold—only 1,356 in the quarter-century since first publication—suggest that the book may deserve the name of classic in a Pickwickian sense—a work that everyone knows about but few read. "Who Reads the Best Histories?" *Ibid.*, XL (1954), 617.

[8] Jameson, pp. 25, 26.   [9] *Ibid.*, p. 22.

perpetuate their local rule in the days of the early Republic.[10] In New Hampshire, except around Portsmouth, society had never been highly stratified, and the Tory emigration bore away few outstanding individuals.[11] In Connecticut, where "the native aristocracy of culture, wealth, religion, and politics" tended to be loyal to the crown, at least half of the Tories never left the state. Others were welcomed back even before the war was over. Within six months of the peace treaty, New Haven was openly extending an invitation to former Loyalists to return, and President Ezra Stiles of Yale College was grumbling about efforts "silently to bring the Tories into an Equality and Supremacy among the Whigs." [12] In New York and Philadelphia, many prominent merchants—perhaps the majority —were Loyalists, or at least "neutralists," and they stayed on in such numbers as to give a definite tone to postwar society, politics, and business in these important centers.[13] In Maryland, the "internal" Revolution turns out to have been a struggle between one group of aristocrats—planters, merchants, lawyers—and another; the "plain people" took little part in the conflict and the resultant social shifts were minimal.[14] In Virginia, of course, most of the "F.F.V.'s" were Whigs, and their control of politics was to continue through the days of the "Virginia dynasty." [15] In the North Carolina back country it was the "plain people"—the old Regulators—who were most stubbornly Loyalist.[16] Clearly Jameson's generalizations about the fate of the old aristocracy must be qualified.[17]

---

[10] In the inland counties, finds Lee N. Newcomer, "no internal upheaval" accompanied the Revolution. *The Embattled Farmers: A Massachusetts Countryside in the American Revolution* (New York, 1953), pp. 86–87. Nor do the Tories of this region "fit readily into any definite categories or groups." In Ashfield, for instance, the Baptists, whom historians are accustomed to lump among the Whigs, tended to remain loyal because they had found royal authority friendly in their fight against the "standing order." *Ibid.,* p. 59.

[11] Richard F. Upton, *Revolutionary New Hampshire* (Hanover, N. H., 1936), p. 130.

[12] Oscar Zeichner, "The Rehabilitation of Loyalists in Connecticut," *New England Quarterly*, XI (1938), 308–30. Stiles's comment is found in his *Literary Diary*, ed. F. B. Dexter (New York, 1901), III, 111.

[13] "The return of former Loyalists to participation in the life and politics of [New York City] was comparatively rapid," concludes Sidney I. Pomerantz, *New York: An American City, 1783–1803* (New York, 1938), p. 90. The early relaxation of the Pennsylvania test laws, originally designed to exclude Loyalists from voting and holding office, undoubtedly hastened the conservative triumph in that state. Robert L. Brunhouse, *The Counter-Revolution in Pennsylvania, 1776–1790* (Harrisburg, 1942), pp. 179–80.

[14] Philip A. Crowl, *Maryland during and after the Revolution* (Baltimore, 1943), chap. I.

[15] See Charles S. Sydnor, *Gentlemen Freeholders: Political Practices in Washington's Virginia* (Chapel Hill, 1952), chap. I.

[16] Robert O. DeMond, *The Loyalists in North Carolina during the Revolution* (Durham, N. C., 1940), pp. 34–50.

[17] For a recent summary of the postwar status of Loyalists see Merrill Jensen, *The New Nation: A History of the United States during the Confederation, 1781–1789* (New York, 1950), pp. 265–81. For a more subtle social analysis of the Tory group than Jameson was able to give in his limited space see Evarts B. Greene, *The Revolutionary Generation* (New York, 1943), pp. 211–30.

What about the new democracy of the Revolutionary period? Unquestionably a sense of dignity and importance came to the common man—the small farmer, the town artisan—as a result of his revolutionary activities and the limited extension of the suffrage. But before we can say with assurance how democratic the new society was, we must answer the prior question: how undemocratic was the old? No one will dispute the fact that provincial society was stratified, that class distinctions existed, that political and social equality were hardly dreamed of. A recent brilliant study of electoral practices in colonial Massachusetts raises, however, some questions. By means of ingenious statistical methods and samplings of contemporary opinion, the author of this study has shown rather convincingly that, in the Bay Colony at least, practically all adult males had the vote. Massachusetts society before 1776, he concludes, was "very close to a complete democracy." And he hints of further revisions to come. "As for the 'internal revolution' in other colonies," he says, "—perhaps we should take another look. There is more than a hint in the records that what applies to Massachusetts applies without too much change to other colonies as well." [18]

Though the Negro slave received some indirect benefits from the Revolution, the indentured servant, Jameson found, received none. Nor has subsequent research uncovered any important evidence that he overlooked.[19] While he was dwelling on the negative side, Jameson might have mentioned another large dependent class that gained nothing in status as a result of the Revolution. Even before independence was declared, that doughty feminist Abigail Adams was writing to her husband in Congress: "By the way, in the new code of laws which I suppose it will be necessary for you to make, I desire you would remember the ladies and be more generous and favorable to them than your ancestors." Her husband wrote back, as much in earnest as in jest: "Depend on it, we know better than to repeal our masculine systems." [20] It was to be nearly three quarters of a century before the Declaration of Independence would be revised by a group of determined ladies at Seneca Falls to read: "All men and women are created equal." Both negative and positive evidence, then, suggests that the Revolution made less difference in the status of persons in America than Jameson believed.

---

[18] Robert E. Brown, "Democracy in Colonial Massachusetts," *New England Quarterly*, XXV (1952), 291–313.

[19] William Miller, "The Effects of the American Revolution on Indentured Servitude," *Pennsylvania History*, VII (1940), 131–41; Samuel McKee, Jr., *Labor in Colonial New York* (New York, 1935), pp. 175–78.

[20] Charles Francis Adams, ed., *Familiar Letters of John Adams and His Wife Abigail Adams during the Revolution* (New York, 1876), pp. 149, 155. Mary Beard points out that the legal subjection of women to men was actually buttressed after the Revolution by the steadily growing weight of Blackstone's authority in the United States. *Woman as Force in History* (New York, 1946), chaps. v, vi. See also Elizabeth Cometti, "Women in the American Revolution," *New England Quarterly*, XX (1947), 329–46.

The doctrine that underlies Jameson's second lecture is, quite explicitly, economic determinism: "political democracy," he says flatly, "came to the United States as a result of economic democracy." The movement for manhood suffrage which reached its fruition in Jacksonian America, he maintains, was rooted in a peculiarly American type of land tenure—the system of small holdings or what he chooses to call "peasant proprietorship." This system the Revolution fixed upon the nation when it swept away the royal restrictions, the archaic manorial laws and usages which had encumbered the land throughout the colonial period. There was, he makes clear, "no violent outbreak," no bloody massacre of landlords as in France a decade later. Still, "in a quiet, sober, Anglo-Saxon way a great change was effected in the land-system of America between the years 1775 and 1795." [21] Specifically, the changes were of three sorts: the discontinuance of quitrents and of the king's right to mast-trees, the abolition of primogeniture and entail, the confiscation and distribution of the Tory estates.

The importance of the quitrents and the king's "broad arrow" was probably more symbolic than real. Jameson himself admitted this: payment of quitrents, he pointed out, was "largely evaded"; the law giving the king's surveyors the right to reserve the tallest, straightest pine trees for the Royal Navy "was not rigorously enforced." [22] Still, no historian will deny the importance of an emotion-laden symbol, and Jameson insists, quite rightly, that the quitrent and the king's "broad arrow" were symbols of an obsolete and alien feudalism, that until they were done away with, private property was not private property.

There is high authority, of course, for attaching great significance to the abolition of primogeniture and entail in Virginia—the authority of Thomas Jefferson. But these gestures too, it now appears, were more important in the realm of symbol than of economic reality. In point of fact, neither primogeniture nor entail operated to any important degree in Virginia. Recent research has shown that most estates in the Old Dominion were not entailed but could be freely alienated. And primogeniture was mandatory only if the property-owner died intestate. Most Virginia planters were careful to make wills. By their wills they often distributed their property among all their sons, and sometimes even their daughters. So Jefferson, in the words of his most authoritative biographer, "did not destroy the country gentry as a group with the blows of his mighty ax, and there is insufficient reason to believe that he wanted to." What he did was merely to "remove legal vestiges of Old World aristocracy." The sweeping conclusion reached by a recent student of this problem in Virginia may well apply to other colonies: "No radical change of custom in devising estates resulted from the abolition of primogeniture and entail." [23]

---

[21] Jameson, pp. 41, 42, 48–49. [22] *Ibid.*, pp. 50, 51.
[23] Dumas Malone, *Jefferson the Virginian* (Boston, 1948), pp. 252–57; Clarence R. Keim,

On the confiscation of Loyalist lands much has been written of late years. The evidence has not been canvassed for all the states, but a definite conclusion seems to be emerging: that considerably less diffusion and democratization of landownership resulted from the breakup of these estates and their disposition in small parcels than Jameson supposed.

The most intensive study has been centered on the southern counties of New York, where the DeLanceys, the Bayards, the Philipses held sway in colonial times over their vast baronies. When the revolutionary New York government seized the estates and sold them off, some of the land, to be sure, went to former tenants and other landless individuals. But the bulk of it was bought up by wealthy patriots and merely augmented the domains of rival families like the Livingstons, Schuylers, and Roosevelts. "While it is true," concludes the author of this study, "that the disposal of the loyalist estates effected a greater diffusion of ownership, it is questionable whether it went far toward a radical redistribution of landed wealth and a new social and economic order." [24]

The same thing seems to have been true in Maryland, where wealthy Whig planters and speculators bought up a large proportion of the desirable Tory lands in Baltimore and Frederick counties. Nor is the story greatly different in western Massachusetts or New Hampshire. The South Carolina confiscation law, in the opinion of a contemporary, was actually "so framed that a man who wants land has no chance to get any," for the state required security which only the wealthy landowner could provide.[25]

The case of North Carolina is instructive. The authority on the Loyalists of that state, noting that the confiscated lands were sold in plots averaging two hundred acres, concludes with Jameson that the confiscations "tended to make the Revolution economic and social as well as political." [26] From his own evidence, however, one could draw the equally justified inference that many a wealthy patriot took advantage of the bargain prices to increase his holdings and consequently his social status. The largest Tory estate was that of the great speculator Henry McCulloh—some 40,000 acres. Of the ninety purchasers of McCulloh's lands thirty-four bought more than one tract. Some acquired as many as ten or fifteen, thereby creating

---

"Influence of Primogeniture and Entail in the Development of Virginia," University of Chicago, *Abstracts of Theses, Humanistic Series*, V (1928), 289–92.

[24] Harry B. Yoshpe, *The Disposition of Loyalist Estates in the Southern District of the State of New York* (New York, 1939), p. 60. Thomas C. Cochran earlier arrived at a similar conclusion in his *New York in the Confederation* (New York, 1932), p. 64. E. Wilder Spaulding, on the contrary, emphasizes the democratizing effects of the confiscations (*New York in the Critical Period* [New York, 1932], p. 70), and feels that Yoshpe's evidence really supports this thesis (see his review of Yoshpe in the *American Historical Review*, XLV [1939–40], 899–900).

[25] Crowl, chap. II; Newcomer, p. 151; Upton, p. 172; Aedanus Burke to Arthur Middleton, July 6, 1782, *South Carolina Historical and Genealogical Magazine*, XXVI (1925), 203.

[26] DeMond, p. 180.

estates as large as 5,000 acres. Robert Raiford purchased parcels from five different Tories and put together an estate of more than a thousand acres. The 3,600-acre estate of Thomas Hooper passed almost intact to John McKinsey. Before a final generalization can be made about the social effects of the confiscations in North Carolina, we need to know more about the previous economic status of the purchasers.[27]

The largest estate to be confiscated in America, as Jameson pointed out, was that of the Penn family. By the Divesting Act of 1779 the Pennsylvania legislature assumed control of twenty-one and a half million acres—all the ungranted lands which by royal charter had belonged to the proprietors. But this proprietary land, from which the Penns had never received any income, was comparable, surely, to the ungranted crown lands which fell into the hands of the other commonwealths. Much more significant is the fact that the private manors, the "proprietary tenths," of the Penns, amounting to more than 500,000 acres, together with the quitrents on them, were specifically "confirmed, ratified and established for ever" in the hands of the Penn family—and this by the most "radical" of all the revolutionary legislatures! [28]

Clearly, there are two ways of reading the evidence concerning the confiscation and sale of Loyalist lands. Jameson, who was arguing a thesis, chose to stress the "democratizing" effects. But there were other social consequences of an opposite tendency—the aggrandizement of certain individuals and families already well entrenched, the opportunities opened for speculation—and we shall not understand all the social results of this great sequestration of lands until we assess these as well.

In particular, until someone has studied the social effects of land speculation in the Revolutionary and post-Revolutionary era as Professor Paul W. Gates has done for a later period, we shall not know whether the operations of the speculators hastened or delayed settlement, encouraged or hindered the system of small holdings. Meanwhile, we may note that Professor Abernethy considers the Virginia land office act of 1779 (drafted, incidentally, by Thomas Jefferson) "a colossal mistake," a blow to economic democracy, and a retarding influence on settlement because it played into the hands of speculators and thus *prevented* the diffusion of land in small holdings. By this act, he says, "democracy was defeated in Virginia at the moment when it might have had its birth." [29]

Land speculation was, of course, a form of business enterprise. And business enterprise, it is now clear, took a sharp spurt as a direct result

---

[27] The list of real estate confiscated and sold is printed by DeMond in an appendix (pp. 240–50).

[28] *The Acts of the General Assembly of the Commonwealth of Pennsylvania* (Philadelphia, 1782), p. 260.

[29] Cf. Gates, "The Role of the Land Speculator in Western Development," *Pennsylvania Magazine of History and Biography*, LXVI (1942), 314–33; Thomas P. Abernethy, *Western Lands and the American Revolution* (New York, 1937), p. 228.

of Revolutionary conditions. That Jameson should have perceived and stressed this in 1925 is sufficiently remarkable. His chapter on "Industry and Commerce" undoubtedly opened the eyes of many American historians to the economic facts which, as everyone now recognizes, are as crucial in the history of a war as the political, diplomatic, and military facts.

Some of the new economic paths which the Revolution opened, turned out to be blind alleys. Postwar interest in the improvement of agriculture, reflected in the sudden popularity of farmers' societies, proved to be short-lived and relatively ineffectual.[30] In some regions the wartime growth of manufacturing, which Jameson noted, was choked off by the postwar flood of cheap British goods, which he neglected to mention.[31]

But in other ways enterprise burgeoned and flourished under wartime and postwar conditions. Opportunities for quick gains in privateering and profiteering, the opening of new markets, the expansion of the credit system, the injection of new supplies of specie into the economy as a result of foreign borrowing, the rise of new business groups around men like Jeremiah Wadsworth, William Duer, Robert Morris, the very idea (a new one for Americans) of large-scale business association—all these were constructive economic forces generated by the Revolution.[32] Especially important were the rise of banking and the spread of incorporation. In the words of one economic historian, the Bank of North America, which opened in Philadelphia in 1782, "was identified with the American Revolutionary 'settlement,'—as the Bank of England was with that of the 'Glorious Revolution.'"

The same scholar gives us some revealing statistics on the chartering of business corporations: "In contrast with the half-dozen American business charters granted in the entire colonial period, eleven were issued in the United States between 1781 and 1785, twenty-two between 1786 and 1790, and 114 between 1791 and 1795." [33] Economic facts of this order have led one writer to treat the American Revolution as "the triumph of American mercantile capitalism." [34] Whether or not one wishes to adopt this view, it is clear, as Jameson dimly perceived, that the Revolution loosed potent new forces in the American economy. How these forces were related to the social and political democracy which Jameson saw as products of the Revolution remains to be studied.

When he turned from the hard facts of economic history to the impalpa-

---

[30] Jameson implies (pp. 79–80) that French influence was chiefly responsible for this sudden burst of interest in scientific farming. Actually, the major inspiration came from England. See Frederick B. Tolles, "George Logan and the Agricultural Revolution," *Proceedings of the American Philosophical Society,* XCV (1951), 590.

[31] Jensen holds, however, that there was no real collapse in manufacturing, only a temporary recession. *The New Nation,* pp. 219–27.

[32] Robert A. East, *Business Enterprise in the American Revolutionary Era* (New York, 1938), chap. II.

[33] *Ibid.,* pp. 285, 288.

[34] Louis Hacker, *The Triumph of American Capitalism* (New York, 1940), chap. XIII.

ble realm of "thought and feeling," Jameson was less at home. Yet even here he opened vistas which a generation of intellectual and cultural historians have explored with profit. The greater part of his final lecture is concerned with the effect of independence on the churches—with disestablishment and the separation of church and state, with the reorganization of the churches on a national basis, with the wartime decline of religious life and the postwar spread of liberal theologies. Subsequent research has added little to Jameson's account of these matters, except to fill in details.[35] What Jameson did—and it was no trifling achievement—was to bring American church history within the purview of American historians—to take, as it were, the first steps toward giving this neglected orphan child a home and a standing within the family of historical disciplines.

Certain of his insights, naturally, have proved more fruitful than others. His *obiter dictum* to the effect that military men can never again play the part in public life that they played after the Revolution falls strangely on our ears, who have known the proconsulate of MacArthur, the foreign ministry of Marshall, the Presidency of Eisenhower. Curiously, Jameson found little evidence of educational advance in the Revolutionary era, except for the founding of new colleges. Had he taken a broader view of education, he might have recognized a number of important developments directly or indirectly related to wartime experience: the improvement of medicine (including dentistry) and of medical education;[36] the emergence of civil engineering from military engineering; the founding of Judge Tapping Reeve's "law school" at Litchfield, Connecticut, in 1784; the diffusion of scientific knowledge through the revived activity of the American Philosophical Society and the founding of the American Academy of Arts and Sciences; the popularity of pamphleteering as a form of mass education; and—not least important—the informal education, the widening of horizons, that resulted from wartime mobility, from the fact that, for the first time, many Americans rubbed elbows—and minds—not only with Europeans but with other Americans.[37] The school of intellectual

---

[35] Here Jameson had the benefit of E. F. Humphrey's solidly documented, probably little-read monograph on *Nationalism and Religion in America* (Boston, 1924). One added comment which he might have made—for it would have fitted his emphasis on French influences—was that the French alliance and the hope of enlisting Canadian support brought some improvement in the legal status of Roman Catholics and a more tolerant attitude toward them. See Evarts B. Greene, *Religion and the State: The Making and Testing of an American Tradition* (New York, 1941), pp. 76–78; Sister M. Augustana Ray, *American Opinion of Roman Catholicism in the Eighteenth Century* (New York, 1936), p. 348.

[36] Fielding H. Garrison says flatly: "The War of Independence was the making of medicine in this country." *An Introduction to the History of Medicine* (4th ed.; Philadelphia, 1929), p. 376.

[37] Dixon Ryan Fox ("Culture in Knapsacks," in *Ideas in Motion* [New York, 1935] pp. 37–76) emphasizes contacts with foreigners and foreign ideas; Evarts B. Greene

and cultural historians which has sprung up in the last quarter century has made much of the "intellectual democracy" and the "cultural nationalism" which Jameson vaguely perceived as concomitants, in the realm of "thought and feeling," of the American Revolution.[38]

The danger here as elsewhere is that the historian, misled by his enthusiasm for the concept of "revolution," will posit too abrupt a set of changes, will pay too little attention to the evidences of historical continuity. Jameson himself did not altogether avoid this pitfall. For example, he wrote that "Joel Barlow's *Vision of Columbus,* or President Stiles's celebrated election sermon on *The United States Elevated to Glory and Honor,* could not possibly have been written twenty years earlier." [39] If he meant by this that the idea of the United States as an independent nation was not entertained in the 1760's, the statement is obviously correct, though hardly startling. If he meant that before 1775 no American felt or expressed love for the land, pride in its people, confidence in its future, he was just as obviously wrong. For one finds strong feelings of American patriotism in a pre-Revolutionary poem like Freneau and Brackenridge's "The Rising Glory of America," written in 1771, in the sermons of Samuel Davies and Jonathan Mayhew in the 1750's, even in Judge Samuel Sewall's proud paean to his beloved Plum Island, Crane Pond, and Turkey Hill as far back as the last decade of the seventeenth century.[40] Indeed the points at which the supports to Jameson's thesis seem weakest—where for example he argues for sharper changes in the political and social status of individuals than can be justified on the evidence—are precisely those points at which he overlooked or underestimated dynamic forces already present in the society of late colonial America.

Still, a historian who fashions so useful a conceptual tool, who popularizes so fruitful a hypothesis, who enlarges so notably our understanding of a significant era in American history, can be forgiven a few oversights, a few overstatements. Basically, the "Jameson thesis" is still sound, and, what is more important, still vital and suggestive, capable of still further life, still greater usefulness. Jameson, after all, did much more than give us a new approach to the American Revolution. He formulated and cogently applied to a particular period an important general thesis—"the

("Some Educational Values of the American Revolution," *Proceedings of the American Philosophical Society,* LXVIII [1929], 185–94) stresses the association of Americans with men from other states.

[38] See Merle Curti, *The Growth of American Thought* (New York, 1943), chap. VI.

[39] P. 120.

[40] See the excellent chapter "Of Loyalties and of the British American Nation" in Max Savelle, *Seeds of Liberty: The Genesis of the American Mind* (New York, 1948), pp. 553–82; also Merle Curti, *The Roots of American Loyalty* (New York, 1946), chap. I. For the Sewall passage, which appeared in his *Phaenomena quaedam Apocalyptica ad Aspectum Novi Orbis configurata* (1697), see Perry Miller, *The New England Mind: From Colony to Province* (Cambridge, Mass., 1953), pp. 189–90.

thesis that all the varied activities of men in the same country and period have intimate relations with each other, and that one cannot obtain a satisfactory view of any one of them by considering it apart from the others." [41] For this he deserves homage as one of the founders of American social and cultural history.

---

[41] Jameson, p. 158.

Political Experience and Enlightenment Ideas in Eighteenth-Century America

Bernard Bailyn

The political and social ideas of the European Enlightenment have had a peculiar importance in American history. More universally accepted in eighteenth-century America than in Europe, they were more completely and more permanently embodied in the formal arrangements of state and society; and, less controverted, less subject to criticism and dispute, they have lived on more vigorously into later periods, more continuous and more intact. The peculiar force of these ideas in America resulted from many causes. But originally, and basically, it resulted from the circumstances of the prerevolutionary period and from the bearing of these ideas on the political experience of the American colonists.

What this bearing was—the nature of the relationship between Enlightenment ideas and early American political experience—is a matter of particular interest at the present time because it is centrally involved in what amounts to a fundamental revision of early American history now under way. By implication if not direct evidence and argument, a number of recent writings have undermined much of the structure of historical thought by which, for a generation or more, we have understood our eighteenth-century origins, and in particular have placed new and insup-

From *American Historical Review*, LXVII (January 1962), 339–351. Reprinted by permission. Mr. Bailyn, professor at Harvard University, presented this paper in a briefer form to the XIth International Congress of Historical Sciences, Stockholm, 1960. As printed here, it was read at the Massachusetts Historical Society, January 12, 1961.

portable pressures on its central assumption concerning the political significance of Enlightenment thought. Yet the need for rather extensive rebuilding has not been felt, in part because the architecture has not commonly been seen as a whole—as a unit, that is, of mutually dependent parts related to a central premise—in part because the damage has been piecemeal and uncoordinated: here a beam destroyed, there a stone dislodged, the inner supports only slowly weakened and the balance only gradually thrown off. The edifice still stands, mainly, it seems, by habit and by the force of inertia. A brief consideration of the whole, consequently, a survey from a position far enough above the details to see the outlines of the over-all architecture, and an attempt, however tentative, to sketch a line—a principle—of reconstruction would seem to be in order.

A basic, organizing assumption of the group of ideas that dominated the earlier interpretation of eighteenth-century American history is the belief that previous to the Revolution the political experience of the colonial Americans had been roughly analogous to that of the English. Control of public authority had been firmly held by a native aristocracy—merchants and landlords in the North, planters in the South—allied, commonly, with British officialdom. By restricting representation in the provincial assemblies, limiting the franchise, and invoking the restrictive power of the English state, this aristocracy had dominated the governmental machinery of the mainland colonies. Their political control, together with legal devices such as primogeniture and entail, had allowed them to dominate the economy as well. Not only were they successful in engrossing landed estates and mercantile fortunes, but they were for the most part able also to fight off the clamor of yeoman debtors for cheap paper currency, and of depressed tenants for freehold property. But the control of this colonial counterpart of a traditional aristocracy, with its Old World ideas of privilege and hierarchy, orthodoxy in religious establishment, and economic inequality, was progressively threatened by the growing strength of a native, frontier-bred democracy that expressed itself most forcefully in the lower houses of the "rising" provincial assemblies. A conflict between the two groups and ways of life was building up, and it broke out in fury after 1765.

The outbreak of the Revolution, the argument runs, fundamentally altered the old regime. The Revolution destroyed the power of this traditional aristocracy, for the movement of opposition to parliamentary taxation, 1760–1776, originally controlled by conservative elements, had been taken over by extremists nourished on Enlightenment radicalism, and the once dominant conservative groups had gradually been alienated. The break with England over the question of home rule was part of a general struggle, as Carl Becker put it, over who shall rule at home. Independence gave control to the radicals, who, imposing their advanced doctrines on a traditional society, transformed a rebellious secession into a social revolution. They created a new regime, a reformed society, based on enlightened political and social theory.

But that is not the end of the story; the sequel is important. The success of the enlightened radicals during the early years of the Revolution was notable; but, the argument continues, it was not wholly unqualified. The remnants of the earlier aristocracy, though defeated, had not been eliminated: they were able to reassert themselves in the postwar years. In the 1780's they gradually regained power until, in what amounted to a counterrevolution, they impressed their views indelibly on history in the new federal Constitution, in the revocation of some of the more enthusiastic actions of the earlier revolutionary period, and in the Hamiltonian program for the new government. This was not, of course, merely the old regime resurrected. In a new age whose institutions and ideals had been born of revolutionary radicalism, the old conservative elements made adjustments and concessions by which to survive and periodically to flourish as a force in American life.

The importance of this formulation derived not merely from its usefulness in interpreting eighteenth-century history. It provided a key also for understanding the entire course of American politics. By its light, politics in America, from the very beginning, could be seen to have been a dialectical process in which an aristocracy of wealth and power struggled with the People, who, ordinarily ill-organized and inarticulate, rose upon provocation armed with powerful institutional and ideological weapons, to reform a periodically corrupt and oppressive polity.

In all of this the underlying assumption is the belief that Enlightenment thought—the reforming ideas of advanced thinkers in eighteenth-century England and on the Continent—had been the effective lever by which native American radicals had turned a dispute on imperial relations into a sweeping reformation of public institutions and thereby laid the basis for American democracy.

For some time now, and particularly during the last decade, this interpretation has been fundamentally weakened by the work of many scholars working from different approaches and on different problems. Almost every important point has been challenged in one way or another.[1] All argu-

---

[1] Recent revisionist writings on eighteenth-century America are voluminous. The main points of reinterpretation will be found in the following books and articles, to which specific reference is made in the paragraphs that follow: Robert E. Brown, *Middle-Class Democracy and the Revolution in Massachusetts, 1691–1780* (Ithaca, N. Y., 1955); E. James Ferguson, "Currency Finance: An Interpretation of Colonial Monetary Practices," *William and Mary Quarterly*, X (Apr. 1953), 153–80; Theodore Thayer, "The Land Bank System in the American Colonies," *Journal of Economic History*, XIII (Spring 1953), 145–59; Bray Hammond, *Banks and Politics in America from the Revolution to the Civil War* (Princeton, N. J., 1957); George A. Billias, *The Massachusetts Land Bankers of 1740* (Orono, Me., 1959); Milton M. Klein, "Democracy and Politics in Colonial New York," *New York History*, XL (July 1959), 221–46; Oscar and Mary F. Handlin, "Radicals and Conservatives in Massachusetts after Independence," *New England Quarterly*, XVII

ments concerning politics during the prerevolutionary years have been affected by an exhausted demonstration for one colony, which might well be duplicated for others, that the franchise, far from having been restricted in behalf of a borough-mongering aristocracy, was widely available for popular use. Indeed, it was more widespread than the desire to use it— a fact which in itself calls into question a whole range of traditional arguments and assumptions. Similarly, the Populist terms in which economic elements of prerevolutionary history have most often been discussed may no longer be used with the same confidence. For it has been shown that paper money, long believed to have been the inflationary instrument of a depressed and desperate debtor yeomanry, was in general a fiscally sound and successful means—whether issued directly by the governments or through land banks—not only of providing a medium of exchange but also of creating sources of credit necessary for the growth of an underdeveloped economy and a stable system of public finance for otherwise resourceless governments. Merchants and creditors commonly supported the issuance of paper, and many of the debtors who did so turn out to have been substantial property owners.

Equally, the key writings extending the interpretation into the revolutionary years have come under question. The first and still classic monograph detailing the inner social struggle of the decade before 1776—Carl Becker's *History of Political Parties in the Province of New York, 1760–1776* (1909)—has been subjected to sharp criticism on points of validation and consistency. And, because Becker's book, like other studies of the movement toward revolution, rests upon a belief in the continuity of "radical" and "conservative" groupings, it has been weakened by an analysis proving such terminology to be deceptive in that it fails to define consistently identifiable groups of people. Similarly, the "class" characteristic of the merchant group in the northern colonies, a presupposition of important studies of the merchants in the revolutionary movement, has been questioned, and along with it the belief that there was an economic or occupational basis for positions taken on the revolutionary controversy. More important, a recent survey of the writings following up J. F. Jameson's classic essay, *The American Revolution Considered as a Social Movement*

(Sept. 1944), 343–55; Bernard Bailyn, "The Blount Papers: Notes on the Merchant 'Class' in the Revolutionary Period," *William and Mary Quarterly*, XI (Jan. 1954), 98–104; Frederick B. Tolles, "The American Revolution Considered as a Social Movement: A Re-Evaluation," *American Historical Review*, LX (Oct. 1954), 1–12; Robert E. Brown, *Charles Beard and the Constitution: A Critical Analysis of "An Economic Interpretation of the Constitution"* (Princeton, N. J., 1956); Forrest McDonald, *We the People: The Economic Origins of the Constitution* (Chicago, 1958); Daniel J. Boorstin, *The Genius of American Politics* (Chicago, 1953), and *The Americans: The Colonial Experience* (New York, 1958). References to other writings and other viewpoints will be found in Edmund S. Morgan, "The American Revolution: Revisions in Need of Revising," *William and Mary Quarterly*, XIV (Jan. 1957), 3–15; and Richard B. Morris, "The Confederation Period and the American Historian," *ibid.*, XIII (Apr. 1956), 139–56.

(1926), has shown how little has been written in the last twenty-five years to substantiate that famous statement of the Revolution as a movement of social reform. Most dramatic of all has been the demolition of Charles Beard's *Economic Interpretation of the Constitution* (1913), which stood solidly for over forty years as the central pillar of the counterrevolution argument: the idea, that is, that the Constitution was a "conservative" document, the polar opposite of the "radical" Articles of Confederation, embodying the interests and desires of public creditors and other moneyed conservatives, and marking the Thermidorian conclusion to the enlightened radicalism of the early revolutionary years.

Finally, there are arguments of another sort, assertions to the effect that not only did Enlightenment ideas not provoke native American radicals to undertake serious reform during the Revolution, but that ideas have never played an important role in American public life, in the eighteenth century or after, and that the political "genius" of the American people during the Revolution as later, has lain in their brute pragmatism, their successful resistance to the "distant example and teachings of the European Enlightenment," the maunderings of "garret-spawned European illuminati."

Thus from several directions at once have come evidence and arguments that cloud if they do not totally obscure the picture of eighteenth-century American history composed by a generation of scholars. These recent critical writings are of course of unequal weight and validity; but few of them are totally unsubstantiated, almost all of them have some point and substance, and taken together they are sufficient to raise serious doubts about the organization of thought within which we have become accustomed to view the eighteenth century. A full reconsideration of the problems raised by these findings and ideas would of course be out of the question here even if sufficient facts were now available. But one might make at least an approach to the task and a first approximation to some answers to the problems by isolating the central premise concerning the relationship between Enlightenment ideas and political experience and reconsidering it in view of the evidence that is now available.

Considering the material at hand, old and new, that bears on this question, one discovers an apparent paradox. There appear to be two primary and contradictory sets of facts. The first and more obvious is the undeniable evidence of the seriousness with which colonial and revolutionary leaders took ideas, and the deliberateness of their efforts during the Revolution to reshape institutions in their pattern. The more we know about these American provincials the clearer it is that among them were remarkably well-informed students of contemporary social and political theory. There never was a dark age that destroyed the cultural contacts between Europe and America. The sources of transmission had been numerous in the seventeenth century; they increased in the eighteenth. There were not only the impersonal agencies of newspapers, books, and pamphlets, but also continuous personal contact through travel and correspondence. Above all, there were Pan-Atlantic, mainly Anglo-American, interest groups that occasioned a continuous flow of fresh information and ideas between Europe and the mainland colonies in America. Of these, the most important were the English dissenters and their numerous codenominationalists in America. Located perforce on the left of the English political spectrum, acutely alive to ideas of reform that might increase their security in England, they were, for the almost endemically nonconformist colonies, a rich source of political and social theory. It was largely through nonconformist connections, as Caroline Robbins' recent book, *The Eighteenth-Century Commonwealthman* (1959), suggests, that the commonwealth radicalism of seventeenth-century England continued to flow to the colonies, blending, ultimately, with other strains of thought to form a common body of advanced theory.

In every colony and in every legislature there were people who knew Locke and Beccaria, Montesquieu and Voltaire; but perhaps more important, there was in every village of every colony someone who knew such transmitters of English nonconformist thought as Watts, Neal, and Burgh; later Priestley and Price—lesser writers, no doubt, but staunch opponents of traditional authority, and they spoke in a familiar idiom. In the bitterly contentious pamphlet literature of mid-eighteenth-century American politics, the most frequently cited authority on matters of principle and theory was not Locke or Montesquieu but *Cato's Letters,* a series of radically libertarian essays written in London in 1720–1723 by two supporters of the dissenting interest, John Trenchard and Thomas Gordon. Through such writers, as well as through the major authors, leading colonists kept contact with a powerful tradition of enlightened thought.

This body of doctrine fell naturally into play in the controversy over the power of the imperial government. For the revolutionary leaders it supplied a common vocabulary and a common pattern of thought, and, when the time came, common principles of political reform. That reform was sought and seriously if unevenly undertaken, there can be no doubt. Institutions were remodeled, laws altered, practices questioned all in accordance with advanced doctrine on the nature of liberty and of the institutions needed to achieve it. The Americans were acutely aware of being innovators, of bringing mankind a long step forward. They believed that they had so far succeeded in their effort to reshape circumstances to conform to enlightened ideas and ideals that they had introduced a new era in human affairs. And they were supported in this by the opinion of informed thinkers in Europe. The contemporary image of the American Revolution at home and abroad was complex; but no one doubted that

133

a revolution that threatened the existing order and portended new social and political arrangements had been made, and made in the name of reason.

Thus, throughout the eighteenth century there were prominent, politically active Americans who were well aware of the development of European thinking, took ideas seriously, and during the Revolution deliberately used them in an effort to reform the institutional basis of society. This much seems obvious. But, paradoxically, and less obviously, it is equally true that many, indeed most, of what these leaders considered to be their greatest achievements during the Revolution—reforms that made America seem to half the world like the veritable heavenly city of the eighteenth-century philosophers—had been matters of fact before they were matters of theory and revolutionary doctrine.

No reform in the entire Revolution appeared of greater importance to Jefferson than the Virginia acts abolishing primogeniture and entail. This action, he later wrote, was part of "a system by which every fibre would be eradicated of antient or future aristocracy; and a foundation laid for a government truly republican." But primogeniture and entail had never taken deep roots in America, not even in tidewater Virginia. Where land was cheap and easily available such legal restrictions proved to be encumbrances profiting few. Often they tended to threaten rather than secure the survival of the family, as Jefferson himself realized when in 1774 he petitioned the Assembly to break an entail on his wife's estate on the very practical, untheoretical, and common ground that to do so would be "greatly to their [the petitioners'] Interest and that of their Families." The legal abolition of primogeniture and entail during and after the Revolution was of little material consequence. Their demise had been effectively decreed years before by the circumstances of life in a wilderness environment.

Similarly, the disestablishment of religion—a major goal of revolutionary reform—was carried out, to the extent that it was, in circumstances so favorable to it that one wonders not how it was done but why it was not done more thoroughly. There is no more eloquent, moving testimony to revolutionary idealism than the Virginia Act for Establishing Religious Freedom: it is the essence of Enlightenment faith. But what did it, and the disestablishment legislation that had preceded it, reform? What had the establishment of religion meant in prerevolutionary Virginia? The Church of England was the state church, but dissent was tolerated well beyond the limits of the English Acts of Toleration. The law required nonconformist organizations to be licensed by the government, but dissenters were not barred from their own worship nor penalized for failure to attend the Anglican communion, and they were commonly exempted from parish taxes. Nonconformity excluded no one from voting and only the very few Catholics from enjoying public office. And when the itineracy

of revivalist preachers led the establishment to contemplate more restrictive measures, the Baptists and Presbyterians advanced to the point
of arguing publicly, and pragmatically, that the toleration they had so
far enjoyed was an encumbrance, and that the only proper solution was
total liberty: in effect, disestablishment.

Virginia was if anything more conservative than most colonies. The
legal establishment of the Church of England was in fact no more rigorous
in South Carolina and Georgia: it was considerably weaker in North
Carolina. It hardly existed at all in the middle colonies (there was of
course no vestige of it in Pennsylvania), and where it did, as in four counties of New York, it was either ignored or had become embattled by
violent opposition well before the Revolution. And in Massachusetts and
Connecticut, where the establishment, being nonconformist according to
English law, was legally tenuous to begin with, tolerance in worship and
relief from church taxation had been extended to the major dissenting
groups early in the century, resulting well before the Revolution in what
was, in effect if not in law, a multiple establishment. And this had been
further weakened by the splintering effect of the Great Awakening. Almost everywhere the Church of England, the established church of the
highest state authority, was embattled and defensive—driven to rely more
and more on its missionary arm, the Society for the Propagation of the
Gospel, to sustain it against the cohorts of dissent.

None of this had resulted from Enlightenment theory. It had been
created by the mundane exigencies of the situation: by the distance that
separated Americans from ecclesiastical centers in England and the Continent; by the never-ending need to encourage immigration to the colonies;
by the variety, the mere numbers, of religious groups, each by itself a
minority, forced to live together; and by the weakness of the coercive
powers of the state, its inability to control the social forces within it.

Even more gradual and less contested had been the process by which
government in the colonies had become government by the consent of
the governed. What has been proved about the franchise in early Massachusetts—that it was open for practically the entire free adult male population—can be proved to a lesser or greater extent for all the colonies. But
the extraordinary breadth of the franchise in the American colonies had
not resulted from popular demands: there had been no cries for universal
manhood suffrage, nor were there popular theories claiming, or even
justifying, general participation in politics. Nowhere in eighteenth-century America was there "democracy"—middle-class or otherwise—as we
use the term. The main reason for the wide franchise was that the traditional English laws limiting suffrage to freeholders of certain competences
proved in the colonies, where freehold property was almost universal, to
be not restrictive but widely permissive.

Representation would seem to be different, since before the Revolution

complaints had been voiced against the inequity of its apportioning, especially in the Pennsylvania and North Carolina assemblies. But these complaints were based on an assumption that would have seemed natural and
reasonable almost nowhere else in the Western world: the assumption that
representation in governing assemblages was a proper and rightful attribute
of people as such—of regular units of population, or of populated land
—rather than the privilege of particular groups, institutions, or regions.
Complaints there were, bitter ones. But they were complaints claiming injury and deprivation, not abstract ideals or unfamiliar desires. They assumed from common experience the normalcy of regular and systematic
representation. And how should it have been otherwise? The colonial assemblies had not, like ancient parliaments, grown to satisfy a monarch's
need for the support of particular groups or individuals or to protect the
interests of a social order, and they had not developed insensibly from
precedent to precedent. They had been created at a stroke, and they were
in their composition necessarily regular and systematic. Nor did the process,
the character, of representation as it was known in the colonies derive
from theory. For colonial Americans, representation had none of the
symbolic and little of the purely deliberative qualities which, as a result
of the revolutionary debates and of Burke's speeches, would become celebrated as "virtual." To the colonists it was direct and actual: it was, most
often, a kind of agency, a delegation of powers, to individuals commonly
required to be residents of their constituencies and, often, bound by instructions from them—with the result that eighteenth-century American
legislatures frequently resembled, in spirit if not otherwise, those "ancient
assemblies" of New York, composed, the contemporary historian William
Smith wrote, "of plain, illiterate husbandmen, whose views seldom extended farther than to the regulation of highways, the destruction of
wolves, wild cats, and foxes, and the advancement of the other little
interests of the particular counties which they were chosen to represent."
There was no theoretical basis for such direct and actual representation.
It had been created and was continuously reinforced by the pressure of
local politics in the colonies and by the political circumstances in England,
to which the colonists had found it necessary to send closely instructed,
paid representatives—agents, so called—from the very beginning.

But franchise and representation are mere mechanisms of government
by consent. At its heart lies freedom from executive power, from the independent action of state authority, and the concentration of power in representative bodies and elected officials. The greatest achievement of the
Revolution was of course the repudiation of just such state authority and
the transfer of power to popular legislatures. No one will deny that this
action was taken in accordance with the highest principles of Enlightenment theory. But the way had been paved by fifty years of grinding factionalism in colonial politics. In the details of prerevolutionary American poli-

tics, in the complicated maneuverings of provincial politicians seeking the benefits of government, in the patterns of local patronage and the forms of factional groupings, there lies a history of progressive alienation from the state which resulted, at least by the 1750's, in what Professor Robert Palmer has lucidly described as a revolutionary situation: a condition

> . . . in which confidence in the justice or reasonableness of existing authority is undermined; where old loyalties fade, obligations are felt as impositions, law seems arbitrary, and respect for superiors is felt as a form of humiliation; where existing sources of prestige seem undeserved . . . and government is sensed as distant, apart from the governed and not really "representing" them.

Such a situation had developed in mid-eighteenth-century America, not from theories of government or Enlightenment ideas but from the factional opposition that had grown up against a succession of legally powerful, but often cynically self-seeking, inept, and above all politically weak officers of state.

Surrounding all of these circumstances and in various ways controlling them is the fact that that great goal of the European revolutions of the late eighteenth century, equality of status before the law—the abolition of legal privilege—had been reached almost everywhere in the American colonies at least by the early years of the eighteenth century. Analogies between the upper strata of colonial society and the European aristocracies are misleading. Social stratification existed, of course; but the differences between aristocracies in eighteenth-century Europe and in America are more important than the similarities. So far was legal privilege, or even distinction, absent in the colonies that where it existed it was an open sore of festering discontent, leading not merely, as in the case of the Penn family's hereditary claims to tax exemption, to formal protests, but, as in the case of the powers enjoyed by the Hudson River land magnates, to violent opposition as well. More important, the colonial aristocracy, such as it was, had no formal, institutional role in government. No public office or function was legally a prerogative of birth. As there were no social orders in the eyes of the law, so there were no governmental bodies to represent them. The only claim that has been made to the contrary is that, in effect, the governors' Councils constituted political institutions in the service of the aristocracy. But this claim—of dubious value in any case because of the steadily declining political importance of the Councils in the eighteenth century— cannot be substantiated. It is true that certain families tended to dominate the Councils, but they had less legal claim to places in those bodies than certain royal officials who, though hardly members of an American aristocracy, sat on the Councils by virtue of their office. Councilors could be and were removed by simple political maneuver. Council seats were filled either by appointment or election: when appointive, they were vulnerable to political pressure in England; when elective, to the vagaries of public opinion at home. Thus on the one hand it took William Byrd II three years of maneuvering in London to get himself appointed to the seat on the Virginia Council vacated by his father's death in 1704, and on the other, when in 1766 the Hutchinson faction's control of the Massachusetts Council proved unpopular, it was simply removed wholesale by being voted out of office at the next election. As there were no special privileges, no peculiar group possessions, manners, or attitudes to distinguish councilors from other affluent Americans, so there were no separate political interests expressed in the Councils as such. Councilors joined as directly as others in the factional disputes of the time, associating with groups of all sorts, from minute and transient American opposition parties to massive English-centered political syndicates. A century before the Revolution and not as the result of antiaristocratic ideas, the colonial aristocracy had become a vaguely defined, fluid group whose power—in no way guaranteed, buttressed, or even recognized in law—was competitively maintained and dependent on continuous, popular support.

Other examples could be given. Were written constitutions felt to be particular guarantees of liberty in enlightened states? Americans had known them in the form of colonial charters and governors' instructions for a century before the Revolution; and after 1763, seeking a basis for their claims against the constitutionality of specific acts of Parliament, they had been driven, out of sheer logical necessity and not out of principle, to generalize that experience. But the point is perhaps clear enough. Major attributes of enlightened polities had developed naturally, spontaneously, early in the history of the American colonies, and they existed as simple matters of social and political fact on the eve of the Revolution.

But if all this is true, what did the Revolution accomplish? Of what real significance were the ideals and ideas? What was the bearing of Enlightenment thought on the political experience of eighteenth-century Americans?

Perhaps this much may be said. What had evolved spontaneously from the demands of place and time was not self-justifying, nor was it universally welcomed. New developments, however gradual, were suspect by some, resisted in part, and confined in their effects. If it was true that the establishment of religion was everywhere weak in the colonies and that in some places it was even difficult to know what was orthodoxy and what was not, it was nevertheless also true that faith in the idea of orthodoxy persisted and with it belief in the propriety of a privileged state religion. If, as a matter of fact, the spread of freehold tenure qualified large populations for voting, it did not create new reasons for using that power nor make the victims of its use content with what, in terms of the dominant ideal of balance in the state, seemed a disproportionate influence of "the democracy." If many colonists came naturally to assume that representation should be direct and actual, growing with the population and bearing some relation to its distribution, crown officials did not, and they had the weight of precedent and theory as well as of authority with them and hence justification for resistance. If state authority was seen increasingly as alien and hostile and was forced to fight for survival within an abrasive, kaleidoscopic factionalism, the traditional idea nevertheless persisted that the common good was somehow defined by the state and that political parties or factions—organized opposition to established government—were seditious. A traditional aristocracy did not in fact exist; but the assumption that superiority was indivisible, that social eminence and political influence had a natural affinity to each other, did. The colonists instinctively conceded to the claims of the well-born and rich to exercise public office, and in this sense politics remained aristocratic. Behavior had changed—had had to change—with the circumstances of everyday life; but habits of mind and the sense of rightness lagged behind. Many felt the changes to be *away from,* not *toward,* something: that they represented deviance; that they lacked, in a word, legitimacy.

This divergence between habits of mind and belief on the one hand and experience and behavior on the other was ended at the Revolution. A rebellion that destroyed the traditional sources of public authority called forth the full range of advanced ideas. Long-settled attitudes were jolted and loosened. The grounds of legitimacy suddenly shifted. What had happened was seen to have been good and proper, steps in the right direction. The glass was half full, not half empty; and to complete the work of fate and nature, further thought must be taken, theories tested, ideas applied. Precisely because so many social and institutional reforms had already taken place in America, the revolutionary movement there, more than elsewhere, was a matter of doctrine, ideas, and comprehension.

And so it remained. Social change and social conflict of course took place during the revolutionary years; but the essential developments of the period lay elsewhere, in the effort to think through and to apply under the most favorable, permissive, circumstances enlightened ideas of government and society. The problems were many, often unexpected and difficult; some were only gradually perceived. Social and personal privilege, for example, could easily be eliminated—it hardly existed; but what of the impersonal privileges of corporate bodies? Legal orders and ranks within society could be outlawed without creating the slightest tremor, and executive power with equal ease subordinated to the legislative: but how was balance within a polity to be achieved? What were the elements to be balanced and how were they to be separated? It was not even necessary formally to abolish the interest of state as a symbol and determinant of the common good; it was simply dissolved: but what was left to keep clashing factions from tearing a government apart? The problems were pressing, and the efforts to solve them mark the stages of revolutionary history.

In behalf of Enlightenment liberalism the revolutionary leaders undertook to complete, formalize, systematize, and symbolize what previously had been only partially realized, confused, and disputed matters of fact. Enlightenment ideas were not instruments of a particular social group, nor did they destroy a social order. They did not create new social and political forces in America. They released those that had long existed, and vastly increased their power. This completion, this rationalization, this symbolization, this lifting into consciousness and endowing with high moral purpose inchoate, confused elements of social and political change —this was the American Revolution.

VI

The Confederation Period:
Federalist (Radical) vs.
Nationalist (Conservative)

INTRODUCTION

There are two conflicting interpretations of the historical meaning of the Confederation Period (1781–1789). One view emerges from a particular approach to the revolutionary background. This approach to the problem sees the basic issues of the 1760's as a struggle between radicals and conservatives for the control of the colonial governments, though the two united, somewhat uneasily, in the struggle for American liberty against British oppression. According to this view the Declaration of Independence was a radical victory with the conservatives either opposed or reluctant. The struggle over the Articles of Confederation was a struggle between federalist (states rights advocates) and nationalists, and the adoption of the Articles, with their emphasis upon states rights, was a victory for the federalists. The whole of the history of the United States under the Articles was a further conflict between federalists, most of whom "believed, as a result of their experience with Great Britain before 1776 and of their reading of history, that the states could be best governed without the intervention of a powerful central government"—and the nationalists who "declared that national honor and prestige could be maintained only by a powerful central government." Further, these two groupings differed from each other in that the federalists emphasized the beneficent operation of government by legislative authority, and the nationalists emphasized government by the executive and judicial branches. The adoption of the federal constitution (1787–1788), according to this interpretation, is the culminating victory for the nationalist cause. Professor Merrill Jensen is the outstanding advocate of this interpretation; his views are represented below in two selections from his book The New Nation *(1950).*

The Jensen interpretation has been challenged in recent years and largely upon the basis that it is too simplistic; that it sets up fixed categories and imposes these categories upon the historical reality. The new view contends that the historical reality of the Confederation Period was much more complex and diffuse; that individuals in the main did not remain fixed in their categories of federalist (radical) or nationalist (conservative). They crossed these lines on different issues, and this makes a uniform interpretation unreal and unhistorical, because it forces rigidity upon a differentiated historical development. An example of this type of critique of Jensen is supplied below in the article by Professor Richard Morris, "The Confederation and the American Historian." A problem in semantics arises in using Jensen and Morris as conflicting interpretations. For Jensen, federalist (radical) and nationalist (conservative) are the opposites; for Morris, antifederalist (radical) and federalist (conservative) are the opposites, though Morris does not accept these strict categories.

The Confederation Period:

Perspectives and Significance*

Merrill Jensen

THE CONFEDERATION PERIOD IN AMERICAN HISTORY

This book is an account of the first years of the new nation that was born of the American Revolution. Like every other segment of time, the history of the United States from 1781 to 1789 was an integral part of the past in which it was rooted and of the future into which it was growing. It was a time when men believed they could shape the future of the new nation, and since it was also a time in which they disagreed as to what that future should be, they discussed great issues with a forthrightness and realism seldom equalled in political debates. The history of the Confederation is therefore one of great inherent importance for the study of human society if for no other reason than that during it men debated publicly and even violently the question of whether or not people could govern themselves.

Aside from its inherent importance, the history of the Confederation has been of enormous significance to one generation of Americans after another in the years since then. Repeatedly Americans have turned to that history in the course of innumerable social and political struggles. They have done so because it was during those years that the Articles of Confederation were replaced by the Constitution of 1787. In order to explain their Constitution, Americans have appealed to the history of the period out of which it came. In the course of such appeals, sometimes honestly for light and guidance and sometimes only for support of partisan arguments, Americans have usually found what they sought. As a result the "history" has been obscured in a haze of ideas, quotations, and assumptions torn bodily from the context of fact that alone gives them meaning. Again and again political opponents have asserted that the founding fathers stood for this or that, while

---

* The over-all title for the selections from this work was supplied by the editor.

Reprinted from *The New Nation; A History of the United States During the Confederation Period, 1781-1789* by Merrill Jensen, by permission of Alfred A. Knopf, Inc. Copyright 1950 by Alfred A. Knopf, Inc. Pp. vii–xiv; 422–428.

their writings have stood idly and helplessly in volumes on shelves or have lain buried in yellowed manuscripts and newspapers.

Since the founding fathers themselves disagreed as to the nature of the history of the period and as to the best kind of government for the new nation, it is possible to find arguments to support almost any interpretation one chooses. It is not surprising therefore that conflicting interpretations have filled thousands of pages and that all this effort has never produced any final answers and probably never will, for men have ever interpreted the two constitutions of the United States in terms of their hopes, interests, and beliefs rather than in terms of knowable facts.

The conflict of interpretation has been continuous ever since the first debates over the Articles of Confederation in the summer of 1776. Men then differed as to the kind of government which should be created for the new nation. They continued to debate the issue during the 1780's. The members of the Convention of 1787 differed as to the need for and the amount of constitutional change. When the Constitution was submitted to the public in October 1787 the controversy rose to new heights. Men talked in public meetings and wrote private letters and public essays in an effort to explain, justify, or denounce what the Convention had done. They disagreed as to what had happened since the war. Some said there had been chaos; others said there had been peace and prosperity. Some said there would be chaos without the new Constitution; others that there would be chaos if it were adopted.

Once it was adopted Thomas Jefferson and Alexander Hamilton, with two opposed ideals of what the United States should be, laid down two classic and contradictory opinions of the nature of the Constitution. These two basic interpretations may be simply stated. Jefferson held that the central government was sharply limited by the letter of the Constitution; that in effect the states retained their sovereign powers except where they were specifically delegated. Hamilton argued in effect that the central government was a national government which could not be restrained by a strict interpretation of the Constitution or by ideas of state sovereignty. These rival interpretations did not originate with Hamilton and Jefferson, for they had been the very core of constitutional debate ever since the Declaration of Independence, and even before it, for that matter.

Jefferson and his followers used the states rights idea to oppose the plans of the Federalists when they passed the Alien and Sedition Acts in 1798. But when Jefferson became president and purchased Louisiana, he justified his actions by constitutional theories that even Hamilton hardly dared use. Meanwhile Jefferson's opponents seized upon his earlier theories in a vain attempt to block the expansion of the United States. They did so again during the War of 1812 when the Federalists of New England became out-and-out exponents of "states rights" and threatened secession because they were opposed to the war.

In the decades before the Civil War, Daniel Webster and John C. Calhoun carried on the dispute, each having changed sides since his youthful years in politics. Webster, who had been a states rights spokesman during the War of 1812, became the high priest of nationalism, while Calhoun, a leading nationalist in 1812, became the high priest of the states rights idea which he elaborated to defend the slave-owning aristocracy of the South.

The Civil War itself was the bloody climax of a social conflict in which the ultimate nature of the Constitution was argued again and again in seeking support for and arguments against antagonistic programs. But even the Civil War did not finally settle the constitutional issue. The stresses and strains that came with the rise of industrial and finance capitalism produced demands for social and regulatory legislation. The passage of such legislation by the states involved the interpretation of the nature of the Constitution, for business interests regulated by state governments denied their authority and appealed to the national courts. Those courts soon denied the power of regulation to state legislatures. Then, when regulatory laws were passed by the national government, the regulated interests evolved a "states rights" theory that limited the power of the central government, and the national courts once more agreed.

Throughout American history the courts have drawn boundary lines between state and national authority. The pose of judicial impartiality and finality assumed by the courts cannot hide the fact that they have shifted those boundary lines with the shifting winds of politics, and always with sufficient precedents, if not with adequate grace. As a result they had created by 1900 a legal and constitutional no man's land in which all sorts of activity could be carried on without effective regulation by either state or national governments.

The crash of American economy in 1929 once more posed in imperative terms the problem of the nature of the Constitution. How should it, how could it deal with the potentiality of chaos inherent in unemployment, starvation, and bankruptcy, and ultimately, the loss of faith in the utility of the economic and political foundation of the society itself.

As the national government began to act where, plainly, state and local governments had failed to or were unable to act, the question of constitutionality was raised. For a time the courts once more listened to and heeded states rights constitutional theories which were expounded by opponents of the New Deal. New Deal lawyers, in turn, adopted as weapons John Marshall's nationalistic interpretations of the Constitution for ends which Marshall himself would have fought to the death. President Roosevelt, in his fight on the Supreme Court, declared that the Constitution was not a lawyer's document; yet some of the ablest lawyers who ever lived in America wrote it. New Deal publicists wrote tracts in the guise of history to prove that there had been a "national sovereignty" in the United States from the beginning of the Revolution. Therefore, they argued, the courts could not stop the New Deal from doing what needed doing by following a strict interpretation of the Constitution. Both the New Dealers and the Republicans insisted that they were the sole heirs of the legacy of Thomas Jefferson, while Alexander Hamilton went into an eclipse from which he has not yet emerged.

The most recent appeal to the history of the Confederation Period has come from those who support some form of world government. Adequate arguments for such a government can be found in twentieth-century experience, but, like most men, its backers turn to history for analogies and lessons.

When the League of Nations was set up at the end of the First World War men turned to American history after the American Revolution as a parallel experience. At that time books were written to show the "chaos" of the Confederation Period and the happy solution that came with the Constitution of 1787. Among them was a book by a great authority on international law with the title *James Madison's Notes of Debates in the Federal Convention of 1787 and their Relation to a More Perfect Society of Nations.* The book was widely distributed by the Carnegie Endowment for International Peace. This and other books like it had little relation to the realities of world politics in the 1920's and 1930's, but despite this supporters of the United Nations and of various plans of world government have again turned to the history of the American states after the American Revolution.

The most notable appeal has been that of Clarence Streit. In his book *Union Now* he analyzes the history of our past as he sees it. He calls the Articles of Confederation a "league of friendship." He says, paraphrasing John Fiske, that by 1786 there was universal depression, trade had wellnigh stopped, and political quackery with cheap and dirty remedies had full control of the field. Trade disputes promised to end in war between states. Territorial disputes led to bloodshed. War with Spain threatened. The "league" could not coerce its members. Secession was threatened by some states. Congress had no money and could borrow none. Courts were broken up by armed mobs. When Shays's Rebellion came, state sovereignty was so strong that Massachusetts would not allow "league" troops to enter the state, even to guard the "league's" own arsenal. Streit goes on to say that the idea of turning a league into a union was not even seriously proposed until the Convention opened in May 1787. And then, he says, within two years the freedom-loving American democracies decided to try out this invention for themselves. Streit goes on to argue that it would be just as easy to secure union of the democracies now as it was for the American democracies to achieve a union then. Some things made it difficult then; some make it so now. Some made it easy then; some make it easy now.

Many men have followed in Streit's footsteps. His book was first published in 1939. In 1940 Federal Union Incorporated published a pamphlet called

It Must be done Again; the Case for World Federal Union . . . illustrated by excerpts from John Fiske's Critical Period, etc.

In the February issue of 1945, the *Reader's Digest* published an article called "Our Post War Problems of 1787" which was still another summary of John Fiske's *The Critical Period of American History*. In May 1945, the *Saturday Review of Literature* had an editorial called "Where do we go From Here?" They urged John Fiske's *Critical Period* as timely reading for the constitutional convention of the United Nations then meeting in San Francisco. The *Review* argued that American experience in the eighteenth century was analogous, despite those who pointed to the disparities. It declared that the crucial lesson offered by American experience was that unified government is not created by similarities, but by differences. But the *Review* was willing, for the sake of argument, to agree that even if the American colonies (it called them that instead of states) offer no valid parallel, even then the basic question is how to control differences. The answer, said the *Review*, is that the historical fact remains that "only government has been able to control war."

One more example will suffice, not only to show how the proponents of world government continue to use what they call "history," but to show how they too swing with the tide. On 12 March 1948 Federal Union took a full page in the *New York Times* to advertise this proposition in a headline: "By Hamilton's 'Stroke of Genius' Plan . . . we can stop Stalin Now . . . and avert Freedom's suicide." Hamilton's plan was "boiled down" to the following statement: "Unite democracies by federal union and have the Union not only replace their currencies with its currency but assume each democracy's public debt." The advertisement goes on to give the traditional story of how Hamilton saved public credit, saved money, cut government expenses, and so on. Thus a litter of ideas, fathered by hope and ignorance, are set before the public as historical fact.

Even if it can be granted that most appeals to the history of the Confederation have been sincere, let it also be said that they have seldom been infused with any knowledge of the period or its problems. The result has been the drawing of lessons the past does not have to teach. This is a luxury too expensive in an age when men have discovered how to unhinge the very force that holds matter itself together but have advanced very little beyond cave men in their notions of how to live peacefully with one another.

Yet it is little wonder that such false lessons have been drawn in the twentieth century because most of them have come from John Fiske's *The Critical Period of American History*, a book of vast influence but of no value as either history or example. Fiske, a philosopher and popular lecturer, wrote the book "without fear and without research," to use the words of Charles A. Beard. As long ago as 1905, Andrew C. McLaughlin, an impeccably conservative historian of the Constitution who wrote a far better book on the same period, said that Fiske's book was "altogether without scientific standing, because it is little more than a remarkably skilful adaptation of a very few secondary authorities showing almost no evidence of first hand acquaintance with the sources."

The story told by Fiske and repeated by publicists and scholars who have not worked in the field—and some who have, for that matter—is based on the assumption that this was *the* "critical period" of American history during which unselfish patriots rescued the new nation from impending anarchy, if not from chaos itself. The picture is one of stagnation, ineptitude, bankruptcy, corruption, and disintegration. Such a picture is at worst false and at best grossly distorted. It is therefore important to attempt a history which makes an effort to examine the sources, which is concerned with the nature of political and economic problems rather than with proving that one side or another in the innumerable political battles of the period was "right" or "wrong." Nothing is to be gained by following a "chaos and patriots to the rescue" interpretation. We have too long ignored the fact that thoroughly patriotic Americans during the 1780's did not believe there was chaos and emphatically denied that their supposed rescuers were patriotic. The point is that there were patriots on both sides of the issue, but that they differed as to desirable goals for the new nation. At the same time, of course, there were men as narrow and selfish on both sides as their political enemies said they were.

If one approaches the history of the Confederation in this way, if one tries to see it as men who lived in it saw it and to write of it in their terms, one may achieve some semblance of reality. It is not the task of the historian to defend or attack the various groups of men whose conflicts were the essence of the period, but to set forth what they believed and what they tried to achieve. This can be illustrated no better than in the definition of terms. Throughout this book the words "federalist" and "nationalist" are used to describe two opposed bodies of opinion as to the best kind of central government for the United States. In so doing I have followed the members of the Convention of 1787. Those men believed that the Articles of Confederation provided for a "federal" government and the majority of them wanted to replace it with a "national" government. The fact that the men who wanted a national government called themselves Federalists after their work was submitted to the public is relevant to the history of politics after 1787, not to the discussion of the nature of the central government prior to and during the Convention of 1787.

Whatever the confusion since then, there was none at the time. Gouverneur Morris stated the issue concisely in the Convention when he "explained the distinction between a federal and a national, supreme government; the former being a mere compact resting on the good faith of the parties; the latter having a complete and compulsive operation." This explanation was in answer to those members of the Convention who wanted to know what Edmund Randolph meant in his opening speech when he spoke of the "defects of the federal system, the necessity of transforming it into a national efficient government. . . ."

The issue was not, as has been argued from time to time, whether there was a "nation" before the adoption of the Constitution of 1787. That was not the question at all during the 1780's. There was a new nation, as the men of the time agreed: they disagreed as to whether the new nation should have a federal or a national government. They did so from the outset of the Revolution and men have continued to do so ever since. The Constitution of 1787 was, as Madison said, both national and federal. And while this fact has led to innumerable conflicts of interpretation, it has also been a source of strength; for as one political group after another has gotten control of the central government it has been able to shape the Constitution to its needs and desires. Thus with the single exception of the Civil War, peaceful change has always been possible, and as long as Americans are willing to accept the decisions of ballot boxes, legislatures, and courts, the Constitution will continue to change with changing needs and pressures. . . .

THE SIGNIFICANCE OF THE CONFEDERATION PERIOD

The foregoing pages indicate that the Confederation Period was one of great significance, but not of the kind that tradition has led us to believe. The "critical period" idea was the result of an uncritical acceptance of the arguments of the victorious party in a long political battle, of a failure to face the fact that partisan propaganda is not history but only historical evidence. What emerges instead is a much more complex and important story in which several themes are interwoven. It was a period of what we would call post-war demobilization, of sudden economic change, dislocation, and expansion, and fundamental conflict over the nature of the Constitution of the United States. Each of these themes is so interwoven with the others that any separation is arbitrary but, taken separately or together, they are better keys to an understanding of the period than the traditional one.

At the end of the war Americans faced innumerable problems arising from it. What should be done with war veterans? Should the Loyalists return to their homes? What should be our relations with foreign friends and foes? Should commerce be free or should there be discrimination, and if so, against whom and for whose benefit? How would peace affect the economy? How should the war debt be paid? What kind of taxes should be levied to pay it, and who should pay them? When the war-boom collapsed, why did it? What should the state or central governments, or both, do about it? Should government encourage one form of economic enterprise over another or should it keep hands off? What about discontented groups: should government ignore them, cater to them, or forcibly suppress those who might revolt?

Such questions or others like them have probably been asked after every great war in history. They were asked, debated, and given various solutions during the 1780's. The significance of those debates and solutions has often been misunderstood. This is no better illustrated than in the case of the national debt during the 1780's which is usually discussed only in terms of depreciation and nonpayment of interest. Actually much more was involved than this. The debt was fantastically low compared with the national debt of today—about twelve dollars per capita as compared with seventeen hundred—and the nation had vast untouched natural resources with which to pay it. Multitudes of accounts had to be reduced to simple forms so that they could be paid, and this the Confederation government managed to do. But even more important than the economics of the national debt was its politics: should it be paid by the states or the central government? A fundamental assumption of every political leader was that the political agency which paid the debt would hold the balance of power in the new nation. Hence, the supporters of a strong central government insisted that the national debt must be paid by Congress while their opponents insisted that it should be divided among the states and paid by them. The latter group was on the way to victory by the end of the 1780's, for they were supported by clamoring creditors. The result was that one state after another assumed portions of the national debt owing to its citizens. Thus the traditional story is so out of context as to be virtually meaningless. This is true of other traditions as well. Most of the ports of the world were open, not closed, to American citizens. Reciprocity and equal treatment of all United States citizens was the rule in the tonnage and tariff acts of the states, not trade barriers.

To say that many of the pessimistic traditions are false is not to say that all Americans were peaceful and satisfied. The holders of national and state debts wanted bigger payments than they got. The merchants wanted more government aid than was given them. The farmers, hit by high taxes and rigid collection of both taxes and private debts, demanded relief in the form of lower taxes and government loans from state legislatures. Such demands kept state politics in an uproar during the 1780's. However, the often violent expression of such discontents in politics should not blind us to the fact that the period was one of extraordinary economic growth. Merchants owned more ships at the end of the 1780's than they had at the beginning of the Revolution, and they carried a greater share of American produce. By 1790 the export of agricultural produce was double what it had been before the war. American cities grew rapidly, with the result that housing was scarce and building booms produced a labor shortage. Tens of thousands of farmers spread outwards to the frontiers. There can be no question but that freedom from the British Empire resulted in a surge of activity in all phases of American life. Of course not all the problems of the new nation were solved by 1789—all have not yet been solved—but there is no evidence of stagnation and decay in the 1780's. Instead the story is one of a newly free people who seized upon every means to improve and enrich themselves in a nation which they believed had a golden destiny.

Politically the dominating fact of the Confederation Period was the struggle between two groups of leaders to shape the character of the state and central governments. The revolutionary constitutions of the states placed final power in the legislatures and made the executive and judicial branches subservient to them. The members of the colonial aristocracy who became Patriots, and new men who gained economic power during the Revolution deplored this fact, but they were unable to alter the state constitutions during the 1780's. Meanwhile they tried persistently to strengthen the central government. These men were the nationalists of the 1780's.

On the other hand the men who were the true federalists believed that the greatest gain of the Revolution was the independence of the several states and the creation of a central government subservient to them. The leaders of this group from the Declaration of Independence to the Convention of 1787 were Samuel Adams, Patrick Henry, Richard Henry Lee, George Clinton, James Warren, Samuel Bryan, George Bryan, Elbridge Gerry, George Mason and a host of less well known but no less important men in each of the states. Most of these men believed, as a result of their experience with Great Britain before 1776 and of their reading of history, that the states could be best governed without the intervention of a powerful central government. Some of them had programs of political and social reform; others had none at all. Some had a vision of democracy; others had no desire except to control their states for whatever satisfactions such control might offer. Some were in fact as narrow and provincial as their opponents said they were. However, the best of them agreed that the central government needed more power, but they wanted that power given so as not to alter the basic character of the Articles of Confederation. Here is where they were in fundamental disagreement with the nationalists who wanted to remove the central government from the control of the state legislatures.

The nationalist leaders from the Declaration of Independence to the Philadelphia convention were men like Robert Morris, John Jay, Gouverneur Morris, James Wilson, Alexander Hamilton, Henry Knox, James Duane, George Washington, James Madison, and many lesser men. Most of these men were by temperament or economic interest believers in executive and judicial rather than legislative control of state and central governments, in the rigorous collection of taxes, and, as creditors, in strict payment of public and private debts. They declared that national honor and prestige could be maintained only by a powerful central government. Naturally, not all men who used such language used it sincerely, for some were as selfish and greedy as their opponents said they were. The nationalists frankly disliked the political heritage of the Revolution. They deplored

151

the fact there was no check upon the actions of majorities in state legislatures; that there was no central government to which minorities could appeal from the decisions of such majorities, as they had done before the
Revolution.

There were men who veered from side to side, but their number is relatively small and their veering is of little significance as compared with the
fact that from the outset of the Revolution there were two consistently opposed bodies of opinion as to the nature of the central government. There
was, of course, a wide variation of belief among adherents of both points
of view. There were extremists who wanted no central government at all
and others who wanted to wipe out the states entirely. There were some
who wanted a monarchy and others who would have welcomed dictatorship. But such extremists are not representative of the two great bodies of
men whose conflict was the essence of the years both before and after 1789.

While the federalist leaders gradually moved to a position where they
were willing to add specific powers to the Articles of Confederation, the
nationalist leaders campaigned steadily for the kind of government they
wanted. During the war they argued that it could not be won without creating a powerful central government. After the war they insisted that such
a government was necessary to do justice to public creditors, solve the
problems of post-war trade, bring about recovery from depression, and win
the respect of the world for the new nation. Meanwhile their experience
with majorities in state legislatures merely intensified their desire. They
became desperate as state after state in 1785 and 1786 adopted some form
of paper money that could be loaned on farm mortgages and be used to
pay taxes, and in some cases private debts as well. When they were able to
hold off such demands and farmers revolted, as in Massachusetts, they were
thoroughly frightened.

They looked upon such events as evidence of the horrors of unchecked
democracy and they said so in poetry, private letters, newspaper essays, and
public speeches. The problem, they said, was to find some refuge from democracy. They worked hard to control state legislatures and they were often
successful, but such control was uncertain at best, for annual elections
meant a constant threat of overturn and the threat was realized repeatedly.

We may not call it democracy, but they did. Edmund Randolph put their
case bluntly in his opening speech in the Convention of 1787. He said, "our
chief danger arises from the democratic parts of our constitutions . . . None
of the [state] constitutions have provided a sufficient check against the democracy. The feeble senate of Virginia is a phantom. Maryland has a more
powerful senate, but the late distractions in that state, have discovered that
it is not powerful enough. The check established in the constitutions of
New York and Massachusetts is yet a stronger barrier against democracy,
but they all seem insufficient." Outside the Convention General Knox was

saying that a "mad democracy sweeps away every moral trait from the human character" and that the Convention would "clip the wings of a mad democracy." James Madison in the *Federalist Papers* argued that the new Constitution should be adopted because a "republican" form of government was better than a "democracy."

The debate was white-hot and was carried on with utter frankness. It was white-hot because for a moment in history self-government by majorities within particular political boundaries was possible. Those majorities could do what they wanted, and some of them knew what they wanted. Democracy was no vague ideal, but a concrete program: it meant definite things in politics, economics, and religion. Whatever side of the controversy we take, whether we think the majorities in state legislatures governed badly or well—the fact to face is that men of the 1780's believed that the issue was democracy as a way of government for the United States of those days.

They faced the issue squarely. They thought hard and realistically about the problems of government. They understood that society is complex and that the truth about it is multifold rather than simple. James Madison summed it up as well as it has ever been done. There are, he said, many passions and interests in society and these will ever clash for control of government and will ever interpret their own desires as the good of the whole. Men like Madison and John Adams believed, as Madison said, that the "great desideratum which has not yet been found for Republican governments seems to be some disinterested and dispassionate umpire in disputes between different passions and interests in the state." In the tenth number of *The Federalist,* after citing various origins of political parties, Madison said that "the most durable source of factions [parties] has been the various and unequal distribution of property. Those who hold and those who are without property have ever formed distinct interests in society. Those who are creditors and those who are debtors, fall under a like discrimination. A landed interest, a manufacturing interest, a mercantile interest, a monied interest, with many lesser interests, grow up of necessity in civilized nations, and divide them into different classes, actuated by different sentiments and views. The regulation of these various and interfering interests forms the principal task of modern legislation, and involves the spirit of party and faction in the necessary and ordinary operations of the government."

The constitutional debate of the 1780's was thus carried on by men with a realistic appreciation of the social forces lying behind constitutional forms and theories, by men who were aware of the relationship between economic and political power. This realistic approach was lost sight of in the nineteenth century by romantic democrats who believed that once every man had the right to vote the problems of society could be solved. It was lost sight of too by those who came to believe in an oversimplified economic interpretation of history. In a sense they were as romantic as the democrats, for they assumed a rationality in the historic process that is not always supported by the evidence.

If the history of the Confederation has anything to offer us it is the realistic approach to politics so widely held by the political leaders of the time, however much they might differ as to forms of government and desirable goals for the new nation. Throughout the Confederation men with rival goals pushed two programs simultaneously. The federalists tried to strengthen the Articles of Confederation; the nationalists tried to create a new constitution by means of a convention, and thus avoid the method of change prescribed by the Articles of Confederation. The movement to strengthen the Articles failed on the verge of success; the movement to call a convention succeeded on the verge of failure. The failure of one movement and the success of the other, however we may interpret them, is one of the dramatic stories in the history of politics.

The Confederation Period and the

American Historian

Richard B. Morris

Plautus tells us that "one eyewitness is worth ten hearsays," but I am not sure that he would have left us this counsel if he had lived during the Confederation period of American history. In this era the eyewitnesses themselves failed to see eye to eye. In fact, the two opposing views of the post-Revolutionary years which are held by historians of the twentieth century can be traced directly to the Founding Fathers. The first we might call the Washington-Madison-Hamilton approach, accepted by most historians of the post-Revolutionary generation, and developed by George Bancroft, John Fiske, John B. McMaster, and with some reservations by Andrew C. McLaughlin. The other is the approach of certain Antifederalist leaders, an approach adopted by Henry B. Dawson, by J. Allen Smith, by the early Charles A. Beard, and by the more recent Merrill Jensen.

If one could read the minds of the majority of the Founding Fathers in

From *William and Mary Quarterly*, XIII (April 1956), 139–156. Reprinted by permission.

1787—and an abundant and ever-increasing quantity of first-hand documentation makes this a less formidable effort than it seems on its face—he might be very much surprised indeed that any issue should have arisen in historiography about the years of the Confederation. The majority of the Founders saw a clear drift toward anarchy culminating in a crisis. Constantly needled by such correspondents as Henry Knox and David Humphreys, Washington's alarm at the weaknesses of the Confederacy was deepened as the disorders in Massachusetts in the fall of 1786 seemed to portend a crisis for the nation. "I predict the worst consequences from a half-starved, limping government, always moving upon crutches and tottering at every step," he wrote. On August 1, 1786, he asserted: "I do not conceive we can long exist as a nation without having lodged somewhere a power which will pervade the whole Union in as energetic a manner as the authority of the State governments extends over the several states." On October 22 he wrote David Humphreys: "But for God's sake tell me what is the cause of all these commotions? . . . I am mortified beyond expression that in the moment of our acknowledged independence we should by our conduct verify the predictions of our transatlantic foe, and render ourselves ridiculous and contemptible in the eyes of all Europe." Nine days later he wrote Henry Lee, "To be more exposed in the eyes of the world, and more contemptible than we already are, is hardly possible." [1] On November 5 he told James Madison, "We are fast verging to anarchy and confusion!" [2]

Others than the New England Federalists, who were closest to Shays' Rebellion and understandably perturbed, shared Washington's views about the state of the nation. Henry Lee declared: "We are all in dire apprehension that a beginning of anarchy with all its calamitys has approached, and have no means to stop the dreadful work." [3] In December of 1786 Madison wrote Jefferson of "dangerous defects" in the Confederation. [4] During the fall of 1786 John Jay kept writing Jefferson that "the inefficacy of our Government becomes daily more and more apparent," and intimated that the Shaysites had more "extensive" objectives than the immediate redress of grievances. [5] Edmund Randolph, who oscillated between Federalism and Antifederalism, wrote Washington in March of 1787, "Every day brings forth some new crisis"; and he expressed doubt whether Congress could survive beyond the current year. [6] No one at the Constitutional Convention

---

[1] *The Writings of George Washington from the Original Manuscript Sources, 1745–1799*, ed. J. C. Fitzpatrick (Washington, 1931–44), XXVIII, 502; XXIX, 27, 34.

[2] *Ibid.*, XXIX, 51.

[3] Henry Lee to George Washington, Oct. 17, 1786, *Letters of Members of the Continental Congress*, ed. E. C. Burnett (Washington, 1921–33), VIII, 486.

[4] *The Papers of Thomas Jefferson*, ed. Julian P. Boyd (Princeton, 1950–), X, 574.

[5] *Ibid.*, p. 489.

[6] *The Writings of George Washington* . . . , ed. Jared Sparks (Boston, 1834–37), IX, 243 n.

was more explicit than Randolph in spelling out the defects of the government, which he considered "totally inadequate to the peace, safety, and security of the Confederation" and which he repeatedly denounced for its "imbecility." [7]

For the classic contemporary view of the alarming weaknesses of the Confederation we must turn to *The Federalist*. Therein Hamilton, a consistent viewer-with-alarm during this period, attacks the Confederation government as inefficient, asserts that the country had "reached almost the last stage of national humiliation," speaks disparagingly of "the present shadow of a federal government," views the Confederacy as dying, and urges ratification of the Constitution to prevent anarchy, civil war, and "perhaps the military despotism of a victorious demagogue." [8] It would be easy to pile up assertions in similar vein from the pens of Knox and the two Morrises.

These Federalist worthies were in general agreement that the weaknesses of the Confederation could be attributed to financial muddling by the states; to English dumping; to the loss of the British West Indian market; to paper money; to stay laws; to state tariffs; but, above all, to a lack of coercive power by a central authority. Observers in charge of foreign affairs, notably Jay and John Adams, felt that this was the most critical spot in the American system of government. "I may reason till I die to no purpose," declared Adams in June 1785. "It is unanimity in America which will produce a fair treaty of commerce." [9]

In eloquence, prestige, and even in numbers among the leadership the Federalist view of conditions had impressive support, but it was far from universally held. George Clinton, the bête noire of the nationalist leaders, was quoted as intimating that the calling of a Constitutional Convention was "calculated to impress the people with an idea of evils which do not exist." [10] At the Convention, Gunning Bedford of Delaware expressed a complacent view of the government of the Confederacy, and at the Pennsylvania ratifying convention Antifederalists under the leadership of William Findley, Robert Whitehill, and John Smilie asserted that the people along with the legislature had been frightened into consenting to a state convention by unfounded talk of impending anarchy.

Thus there was a division of opinion in 1787 about conditions in the Confederation, and there never has ceased to be down to the present day. More recent writers who look at the Confederation through Antifederalist spectacles are buoyed up by the fact that Franklin and Jefferson were not as disturbed about conditions as other contemporaries. Yet Jefferson, as he

---

[7] *Records of the Federal Convention of 1787*, ed. Max Farrand (New Haven, 1911–37), I, 19, 24, 25.

[8] See especially *Federalist* 1, 15, 16, and 85.

[9] Adams to Jay, June 26, 1785, *Works of John Adams*, ed. C. F. Adams (Boston, 1850–56), VIII, 276.

[10] *Advertiser*, New York, July 21, 1787.

was passing through Boston on his way to France, found "the conviction growing strongly that nothing could preserve the confederacy unless the bond of union, their common council, should be strengthened." [11] It is perhaps especially significant that when Franklin, Jefferson, and Robert R. Livingston expressed in writing a more roseate view of conditions than other Founding Fathers, they were making these observations to foreigners —to Frenchmen or to Englishmen. They were seeking to reassure friends and well-wishers of America abroad that this country was not headed for a collapse. Such assertions must be discounted as skillful propaganda. In France, for example, Jefferson reassured Démeunier that the United States was in no danger of bankruptcy and that, with certain minor exceptions, "the Confederation is a wonderfully perfect instrument." [12] Similarly, when Franklin wrote to M. Le Veillard on March 6, 1786, that "America never was in higher prosperity," [13] commodity prices had steadily dropped— they were to decline thirty per cent between 1785 and 1789; farm wages were shrinking and were to fall to a low of forty cents a day by 1787; mortgage foreclosures and judgments for debts in central and western Massachusetts had reached an all-time high; and in the Valley of Virginia, as Freeman Hart has pointed out, executions more than doubled between 1784 and 1788.[14] In fact, the only economic index that showed an upturn was that for foreign trade, for in commerce the worst of the depression set in a bit earlier than in other lines and showed a more complete recovery by 1788. Again, when Livingston wrote Lafayette in April 1787 that com- modity prices and wages were higher than before the war, he was evading the real issue of how far they had dropped since the coming of the peace.[15]

This double standard of correspondence—one line for Americans, the other for foreign well-wishers—is revealed in the writings of that arch- pessimist, George Washington. It is true that he was somewhat more candid with his old friend Lafayette, whom he wrote on August 15, 1786, that he chose to remain silent on domestic affairs "since I could not disguise or palliate, where I might think them erroneous." [16] Yet two weeks earlier he had written two letters which are very nearly contradictory to each other. On August 1 he wrote the Chevalier de la Luzerne a reassuring letter to

---

[11] Jefferson to Madison, July 1, 1784, *Jefferson Papers*, VII, 356.

[12] *Jefferson Papers*, X, 14 ff.

[13] *Complete Works of Benjamin Franklin*, ed. John Bigelow (New York, 1887–88), IX, 300–301.

[14] Freeman H. Hart, *The Valley of Virginia in the American Revolution* (Chapel Hill, 1942), pp. 123–125. For evidence from the court records of sharply mounting in- debtedness in central and western Massachusetts, see R. B. Morris, "Insurrection in Massachusetts," in *America in Crisis*, ed. Daniel Aaron (New York, 1952), p. 24. On the steady upsurge of insolvency in Connecticut during the entire Confederation period, see *Public Records of the State of Connecticut (1776–1796)*, eds. C. J. Hoadly and L. W. Labaree (Hartford, 1894–1951), VII, xv, xvi.

[15] R. R. Livingston Papers, Bancroft Transcripts, New York Public Library.

[16] Washington, *Writings*, ed. Fitzpatrick, XXVIII, 521.

counteract reports of the American situation circulating in Europe. "In short," he concluded his picture of domestic America, "the foundation of a great empire is laid, and I please myself with a persuasion, that Providence will not leave its work imperfect." On the same day, however, he wrote John Jay, then Secretary for Foreign Affairs, expressing the doubt that the nation could exist much longer unless stronger powers were lodged with the central government.[17]

Even the younger generation, men who could scarcely be accused of strong Federalist attachments, accepted the Federalist view of the glaring weaknesses of the Confederation. Consider, for example, Andrew Jackson, who was admitted to practice law the year the Constitutional Convention met in Philadelphia. In his Proclamation against Nullification Jackson declared in 1832: "But the defects of the Confederation need not be detailed. Under its operation we could scarcely be called a nation. We had neither prosperity at home nor consideration abroad. This state of things could not be endured, and our present happy Constitution was formed, but formed in vain if this fatal doctrine prevails." [18]

Jackson's view of the Confederation period was the view of the nationalist commentators on the Constitution and of the nationalist historians. It was expounded by James Wilson and Nathaniel Chipman, by Nathan Dane, and most notably by Joseph Story and George Ticknor Curtis, who gave formal expression to the views of Daniel Webster. In his *History of the Origin, Formation, and Adoption of the Constitution,* first published in 1854, Curtis begins by declaring: "The Constitution of the United States was the means by which republican liberty was saved from the consequences of impending anarchy. . . ." Paraphrasing the Founding Fathers, Curtis saw the Confederation as "a great shadow without the substance of a government. . . ." He saw the whole period as replete with "dangers and difficulties," full of "suffering and peril." [19]

Curtis' view of the Confederation interlude was fully shared by the nationalist historians writing in the generation or two following the adoption of the Constitution. Most distinguished of this group, George Bancroft— whose literary career spans the period from the Age of Jackson to the Age of Chester A. Arthur—put off writing about the post-Revolutionary era until the closing years of his life. His *History of the Formation of the Constitution of the United States of America* was not published until 1882. As might be expected, Bancroft viewed the period from a nationalist or continental point of view. He stressed the "helplessness" of Congress, whose

---

[17] *Ibid.*, pp. 501, 502.

[18] *Compilation of the Messages and Papers of the Presidents, 1789–1902,* ed. J. D. Richardson (Washington, 1903), II, 643.

[19] George Ticknor Curtis, *History of the Origin, Formation, and Adoption of the Constitution of the United States . . .* (New York, 1854), I, xi, 233, 234, 330.

"perpetual failures" he considered "inherent and incurable." To Bancroft "no ray of hope remained" but from the convention summoned at Annapolis.[20] Nevertheless, he treats the Massachusetts debtors with sympathy and understanding, approves of Bowdoin's lenity toward the Shaysites, and reviews the economic decline which set in at the start of the period in sober language, in sharp contrast with the more intemperate treatment of the insurrection by his contemporary Richard Hildreth, who had surveyed the period many years earlier.[21]

Perhaps the historian who coined the term "critical period" to describe the Confederation interlude was William Henry Trescot. In his rather temperate and fair-minded *Diplomatic History of the Administrations of Washington and Adams,* published in 1857, he asserted: "Indeed, it would be more correct to say, that the most critical period of the country's history embraced the time between the peace of 1783 and the adoption of the constitution in 1788." [22] This point of view was adopted by Frothingham, by Schouler, and by von Holst. The last-named spoke of "the contemptible impotence of congress. . . ." This was strong language, but Washington had used it before him.[23]

The classic exposition of the Federalist approach is found in John Fiske's *The Critical Period of American History, 1783–1789*. His title has fastened upon an epoch in American history a popular nomenclature that dies hard. The first edition appeared in 1888, not too long after the appearance of Bancroft's *Last Revision*. The title and theme of the book were suggested by the fact of Tom Paine's stopping the publication of the "Crisis," on hearing the news of the treaty of peace in 1783. Now, Paine said, "the times that tried men's souls are over." Fiske does not agree with Paine. The next five years, he contends, were to be the most critical time of all. Fiske used the term "critical" first to settle the question whether there was to be a national government or a group of small city-states. Secondly, he used the term to describe what he regarded to be the utter incompetence of the states and the federal government to deal with the problem of postwar

[20] George Bancroft, *History of the Formation of the Constitution of the United States of America* (New York, 1885), I, 262–266.

[21] *Ibid.*, pp. 274–275; Richard Hildreth, *The History of the United States of America* (New York, 1848–51), III, 472–477.

[22] William Henry Trescot, *The Diplomatic History of the Administrations of Washington and Adams: 1789–1801* (Boston, 1857), p. 9. Long before Trescot, however, Richard Henry Lee, a leading Antifederalist, wrote, Oct. 8, 1787: "I know our situation is critical, and it behoves us to make the best of it." "Letters of the Federal Farmer," Letter I, in *Pamphlets on the Constitution of the United States*, ed. P. L. Ford (Brooklyn, 1888), p. 280.

[23] Richard Frothingham, *The Rise of the Republic of the United States* (Boston, 1910. First published in 1872), pp. 583 ff.; James Schouler, *History of the United States of America under the Constitution* (revised ed., New York, 1894), I, 13 ff.; H. von Holst, *The Constitutional and Political History of the United States,* trans. John J. Lalor and Alfred B. Mason (Chicago, 1889–92), I, 37.

reconstruction. To Fiske the drift "toward anarchy" was only checked by the eleventh-hour ratification of the federal Constitution.[24]

It has become the fashion of latter-day historians to criticize Fiske's scholarship. McLaughlin concedes that "there are not many errors in fact in the book," but insists that "as an authority the work is altogether without scientific standing, because it is little more than a remarkably skilful adaptation of a very few secondary authorities, showing almost no evidence of first-hand acquaintance with the sources." [25] Yet McLaughlin himself shows surprisingly little acquaintance with the sources when he describes economic conditions in the Confederation and gives the reader a string of generalizations entirely unsupported by statistical evidence or other business documentation. But the issue is not whether Fiske used first-hand sources, but whether he produced a valid synthesis. As one who has conducted graduate seminars for some time, I am not unaware of the fact that a good many people saturate themselves in the primary sources but are utterly unable to interpret them intelligently. Whether or not William Macdonald's appraisal of Fiske's book as "the best comprehensive account of the period" [26] still stands today, John Fiske's approach to the era had an enormous impact both upon the public and upon fellow historians. John Bach McMaster adopts it without reservations. In his *History of the People of the United States* he refers to the "disaffected," meaning the Shaysites, "associating for evil purposes," as opposed to "the better-minded," equally active in forming societies "for good purposes." [27] His treatment might well have been written by George R. Minot, clerk of the Massachusetts lower house, whose contemporary account of Shays' Rebellion betrays the fears of the conservative element as to the broader implications of the insurrection.[28] McMaster excoriates Clinton and New York for particularist tendencies. Save for Rhode Island, no state behaved worse than New York, McMaster contends.[29]

Other writers, while generally accepting the nationalist synthesis of the period, have approached the Confederation years in a somewhat more objective spirit than did Fiske and most of his predecessors. In the editor's introduction to Andrew C. McLaughlin's volume in the old *American Nation* series, Albert Bushnell Hart expresses doubt whether Fiske's "critical

---

[24] John Fiske, *The Critical Period of American History, 1783–1789* (Boston and New York, 1888), pp. 55–57, and Chap. IV, *passim*.

[25] Andrew C. McLaughlin, *The Confederation and the Constitution, 1783–1789*, in *The American Nation: A History*, ed. Albert Bushnell Hart, X (New York and London, 1905), 319–320.

[26] William Macdonald, in *The Literature of American History: A Bibliographical Guide . . .* , ed. J. N. Larned (Boston, 1902), p. 156.

[27] John Bach McMaster, *A History of the People of the United States, From the Revolution to the Civil War* (New York, 1883–1913), I, 313.

[28] *History of the Insurrection in Massachusetts in 1786 . . .* (Worcester, 1788).

[29] *History*, I, 369–370.

period" was "really a time of such danger of national dissolution as people then and since have supposed." He views the McLaughlin volume as showing "a more orderly, logical, and inevitable march of events than has commonly been described." [30] McLaughlin sees little or no justification for the constant lament about poverty in this period. "Some tribulation there was," he concedes, "but that the country was forlorn, destitute, and poverty-stricken is far from the truth." He sees indications of an upturn in trade by 1786. However, on the constitutional and diplomatic aspects of the period there is little difference between McLaughlin and Fiske. Referring to the humiliating relations with the Barbary states, McLaughlin asserts: "All this, like everything else one touches during the dismal period, discloses the helplessness of the confederacy." Toward the Shaysites he is far less sympathetic than Bancroft. "The vicious, the restless, the ignorant, the foolish—and there were plenty of each class—were coming together to test the strength of the newly established government of Massachusetts." The result, as he sees it, was "nothing short of civil war," but its virtue was that it disclosed the dangers, helped to bring about a reaction, discredited extreme democratic tendencies, and thereby aided the men who sought to inject vigor into the union. [31] Thus, those who were led by the editor of the series to believe that they were going to read a revisionist book were to find that it was essentially conventional in interpretation. Similarly, Edward Channing, in his *History of the United States,* published some years after McLaughlin, stresses the "helplessness" of the existing government and its failure to win respect either at home or abroad, but finds evidence of a business upthrust before the new Constitution went into operation. [32]

The Antifederalist or pro-democratic interpretation (and I need hardly say that the two terms are not necessarily equated) was perhaps first, among nineteenth-century historians, expounded by Henry B. Dawson, a learned military historian of the American Revolution, who also devoted himself to studying the role of the masses in that war, and had a penchant for picking controversial issues which he fought with relish and passion. In an article in the *Historical Magazine* in 1871, Dawson attempted to refute John Lothrop Motley, who, in a celebrated letter to the London *Times* written during the Civil War, had asserted that the Confederation was a period of "chaos," in which the absence of law, order, and security for life and property was "as absolute as could be well conceived in a civilized land." These were reckless and false accusations, Dawson charged. He traced their origin to distinguished men of the Confederation period who had spread them "for selfish or partisan motives." He accused these leaders

---

[30] McLaughlin, *The Confederation and the Constitution,* p. xv.
[31] *Ibid.,* pp. 71, 107, 156, 161.
[32] Edward Channing, *A History of the United States* (New York, 1916–26), III, 491, 414–415, 426–427.

of having "nullified the established law of the Confederacy and violently and corruptly substituted for it what they styled the Constitution of the United States." Dawson had made extreme and curiously unbalanced charges but failed to substantiate them. The significance of the attack, however, lies far less in the kind of evidence adduced than in its formulation of the notion that the Federalists conspired to falsify the true conditions of the period in a deliberate effort to create panic and undermine the government of the Confederation. Oddly enough, the criminal statistics Dawson cites for New York State not only are inconclusive regarding lawlessness, but point directly opposite to what Dawson believed. They indicate that in New York City and County there were almost twice as many indictments between 1784 and 1789 as there were for the first five years under the new federal government.[33] Concerning law and order, Dawson may very well have been on the right track, but somewhere along the path he lost the scent.

Despite the intemperate character of his attack, Dawson had touched off certain doubts as to the reportorial objectivity both of the Founding Fathers and of later historians. These were again raised in 1907, when J. Allen Smith, in his *The Spirit of American Government*, attacked on a second front, contending that the Constitution was the result of a counterrevolution. To him the Declaration of Independence spelled sweeping changes in the American form of government, changes manifest in an omnipotent legislature and the overthrow of the system of checks and balances which had been derived from the English constitution, with its characteristic blending of monarchical, aristocratic, and democratic elements. To Smith the chief feature of the Articles of Confederation was the entire absence of checks and balances, the vesting of all power in a single legislative body, unchecked by a distinct executive or judiciary. The fact that the power which was vested in the continental legislature was ineffectual did not disturb him. His main point, though, was that such democratic changes had been wrought by radical forces and that the conservatives, once they had a chance to assess the situation, set about, in more or less conspiratorial fashion, to redress the balance. The Constitutional Convention was called, according to Smith, not only to impart vigor to the government but to institute an elaborate system of constitutional checks. The adoption of this system he calls a "triumph of a skillfully directed reactionary movement." [34] The idea that the adoption of the Constitution was the result of a struggle among interest groups was pressed by Arthur F. Bentley in *The Process of Government* (1908), in language which stemmed from Madison's *Federalist*

[33] Henry B. Dawson, "The Motley Letter," *Historical Magazine*, 2nd Ser., IX (Mar., 1871), 157 ff.

[34] J. Allen Smith, *The Spirit of American Government: A Study of the Constitution, Its Origin, Influence, and Relation to Democracy* (Chautauqua, 1911), p. 37.

10, and in a more naked form by A. M. Simons' *Social Forces in American History* (1911).

The most significant amplification of the Smith-Bentley-Simons approach came in 1913 from the pen of Charles A. Beard. In his *An Economic Interpretation of the Constitution of the United States* Beard concedes that "interpretative schools seem always to originate in social antagonism," but he prefers the road which explains proximate or remote causes and relations to the so-called "impartial" history which surveys outward events and classifies and orders phenomena.[35] Beard was profoundly influenced by the Turnerian school, which substituted for the states'-rights interpretation of our history a recognition of social and economic areas, independent of state lines, which acted as units in political history. For the period of the Confederation the most important Turnerian contribution was Orin G. Libby's *Geographical Distribution of the Vote of the Thirteen States on the Federal Constitution,* an original and searching study published as far back as 1894. Beard found that nationalism cut across state lines, that it was created by a welding of economic interests of creditors, holders of personality—especially public securities—, manufacturers, shippers, commercial groups, and speculators in western lands. While this majestic formula helped explain why people were Federalists, it has failed dismally in explaining differences between Federalists and Antifederalists. Recent studies by Robert Thomas of the property interests of members of the ratifying convention in Virginia have failed to turn up any significant differences between the two parties either in the kind and quantity of their property-holdings or in their relative status as creditors or debtors. On the other hand, Jackson T. Main asserts that the Virginians who favored greater centralization were found in pro-creditor areas, the Northern Neck and much of the Tidewater, while the opposition came from the debtor Piedmont. After 1785, Main contends, the Shenandoah Valley counties, which had previously voted with the Piedmont on most issues, now supported a grant to Congress of power over commerce. But the picture is at best hardly clean-cut or conclusive.[36]

Beard suggested that general social conditions were prosperous and that the defects of the Articles did not justify the "loud complaints" of the advocates of change. In short, Beard found that the "critical period" was really not so critical after all, but, drawing upon Dawson's article, "a phantom of the imagination produced by some undoubted evils which could

---

[35] Charles A. Beard, *An Economic Interpretation of the Constitution of the United States* (New York, 1949), pp. 3–4.

[36] Robert E. Thomas, "The Virginia Convention of 1788: A Criticism of Beard's *An Economic Interpretation of the Constitution,*" *Journal of Southern History,* XIX (1953), 63–72. Jackson T. Main, "Sections and Politics in Virginia, 1781–1787," *William and Mary Quarterly,* 3rd Ser., XII (1955), 96–112.

have been remedied without a political revolution." [37] Save for a quotation from Franklin, Beard fails to document this crucial generalization.

Lest anyone should carry away with him the view that Beard opposed the Constitution, as did J. Allen Smith, it might be well to point out that in his *Supreme Court and the Constitution,* published the previous year, he praised the Constitution and furnished historical precedents for judicial review. In later years he drew further and further away from any monolithic economic interpretation of the period. Although his *Rise of American Civilization* adhered to the approach of his *Economic Interpretation,* as did Parrington's treatment in *Main Currents in American Thought,* Beard by 1935 completely repudiated economic determinism. In *The Republic* (1943) he considered the adoption of the Constitution as the alternative to military dictatorship. In his *Basic History of the United States* (1944) he defended checks and balances as curbs on despotic powers, whereas in his earlier *Rise of American Civilization* he insists that checks and balances dissolved "the energy of the democratic majority." [38] In *The Enduring Federalist,* published in 1948, he refers to the Congress of the Confederation as "a kind of debating society," and describes conditions in the Confederation period in language which would have gratified Fiske and perhaps shocked Bancroft.[39] In short, by the end of his career, Beard, the confirmed nationalist and isolationist, had moved a long way from the Beard of pre-World War I days.

But it is the unreconstructed Beard who still captures the imagination of our younger scholars. Today the chief disciple of J. Allen Smith and the early Beard is Merrill Jensen. In two significant books, *The Articles of Confederation,* published in 1940, and a more amplified treatment of the same problem, *The New Nation,* which appeared in 1950, Professor Jensen expounds learnedly and at length the argument that the Federalist party was organized to destroy the kind of democratic government and economic practice made possible by the Articles of Confederation.[40] Jensen sees the Articles as a constitutional expression of the philosophy of the Declaration of Independence, the Constitution as a betrayal of those principles. To Jensen the Articles were designed to prevent the central government from infringing upon the rights of the states, whereas the Constitution was designed to check both the states and the democracy that found expression within state bounds. As Jensen sees it, the Confederation government failed, not because it was inadequate, but because the radicals

---

[37] Beard, *An Economic Interpretation of the Constitution,* pp. 47–48.

[38] Charles A. Beard and Mary R. Beard, *The Rise of American Civilization* (New York, 1930. First published in 1927), I, 326.

[39] Beard, *The Enduring Federalist* (New York, 1948), pp. 27–30.

[40] *The Articles of Confederation: An Interpretation of The Social-Constitutional History of the American Revolution, 1774–1781* (University of Wisconsin, 1940. Second printing with additional foreword, 1948). *The New Nation: A History of the United States During the Confederation, 1781–1789* (New York, 1950).

failed to maintain the organization they had created to bring about the American Revolution. He speaks of the radicals as having won *"their* war," but the fact remains that it was as much the war of the conservatives; probably a good deal more so.

Mr. Jensen finds conspiracy and betrayal at various levels. He suggests that the conservatives might well have betrayed the diplomatic objectives of the Revolution were it not for the integrity of Jay and Adams. He deplores the fact that radical leaders of the Thomas Burke-Richard Henry Lee-Sam Adams vintage quit the field and left it to what General Horatio Gates, scarcely an objective or disinterested patriot, called "the rapacious graspers of power and profit." Gates was one grasper of power who just missed the brass ring. Mr. Jensen sees this revolutionary group outnumbered by 1781, and worn down by defeat. Then from 1781 to 1783 the government revolved around Robert Morris and his satellites, for all practical purposes a dictatorship in Mr. Jensen's eyes. But when we look more closely at these counterrevolutionaries, the sharp line between radicals and conservatives seems to fade away. Who was more radical than Alexander McDougall in Sons-of-Liberty days? Yet it was he who headed a delegation of officers to Congress in the winter of 1783. Perhaps Hamilton was not far wrong when he defended the Morris faction as not only "the most liberal," but as "the men who think continentally." The issue does not seem to have been one between radicals and conservatives, but between extreme particularists of the Clinton stripe and continental nationalists of varying shades and degrees.

Mr. Jensen is most effective in recounting the constructive steps taken in the Confederation period to repair federal and state finances. He points out that the Confederation actually managed to reduce the principal of its debt, and praises the states for their role in paying the national debt. Mr. Jensen points to the rapid amortization of state debts as evidence of the ability of the states to put their financial houses in order without much help from a central government. There is no doubt whatsoever that the states had now largely assumed the debt-funding function that the federal government had proven incapable of shouldering. Dr. E. J. Ferguson's studies of the assumption of the federal debts by the states reveal the considerable progress that was made in that direction in the Confederation period.[41] But, in terms of more recent ideas of economic planning, it would now seem that states like Massachusetts made the mistake of a too rapid amortization of the state debt, thereby initiating a sharp deflationary thrust. Even a conservative like Governor Bowdoin urged in 1786 a more gradual plan of amortization than that which the property-conscious legislature had enacted.

---

[41] E. J. Ferguson, "State Assumption of Federal Debt During the Confederation," *Mississippi Valley Historical Review*, XXXVIII (1951), 403.

In short, the Beard-Jensen approach has served to present the Confederation period in a more constructive light, to give greater recognition to signs of economic expansion in the period and to the stabilizing role of the states, particularly in financial matters. As Allan Nevins has pointed out, when the new federal government went into effect, in no state was the debt appallingly high, and in some it was already low.[42] Mr. Jensen is doubtless correct in arguing that in most states the forces of law and order never lost the upper hand. In New York that arch-Antifederalist George Clinton personally led the troops of the state against the insurrectionary Shays. In most cases—and Maryland is an excellent example—the disgruntled elements confined their efforts to obtaining relief in a legal manner through legislative action.

In truth, the real difference between the nationalist and Antifederalist schools of historiography turns neither on the extent of the depression nor on the amount of anarchy in the "critical period," but springs from a deep divergence in interpreting the American Revolution and the issues for which it was fought. Mr. Jensen sees the radical party in the Revolution as comprising the town masses and the frontier groups. As he views it, the radicals fought for an internal revolution; those conservatives who reluctantly supported the war merely wanted independence from England. In fact, this school of historiography depicts the American Revolution as essentially a civil war among the Whigs. In this version there seems to be little or no room for Tories, for redcoats, or for Hessians. This formula fails to explain why New York City and Philadelphia were hotbeds of Loyalism, why the regulators of Carolina and the levelers of upstate New York were Tories, or why debtors and creditors, hard-money men and paper-money men, suffrage expansionists and suffrage restrictionists were arrayed on the same side. It fails to explain the prominent role of the Whig conservative elite in bringing about the Revolution or to lay the foundation for understanding why in so many areas the radicalism of the leadership was that of the Gironde, not the Mountain.[43]

In the last analysis the view that the course of the Confederation period was determined by a counterrevolutionary movement, which, through the

[42] Allan Nevins, *The American States During and After the American Revolution* (New York, 1927), p. 541.

[43] For examples from New England, see Lee N. Newcomer, *The Embattled Farmers: A Massachusetts Countryside in the American Revolution* (New York, 1953); Oscar Zeichner, *Connecticut's Years of Controversy, 1750–1776* (Chapel Hill, 1949). Robert E. Brown, *Middle-Class Democracy and the Revolution in Massachusetts, 1691–1780* (Ithaca, N. Y., 1955), demonstrates that in Massachusetts the property qualification for voting did not bar the majority of adult males from taking part in elections. He opposes the view of an "internal revolution" on the ground that democracy was already established. It is unlikely, however, that a re-examination of the nature and extent of the franchise and other so-called democratic indices in most of the remaining twelve states will support his concluding speculation that the "common man . . . had come into his own long before the era of Jacksonian Democracy."

instrumentality of the Constitutional Convention, nipped democracy in the bud, hinges upon one's ideas about the American Revolution. Unless one is ready to accept the thesis that the group that started the war were libertarians and democrats and were supplanted by a conservative authoritarian party, one cannot give uncritical adherence to the Smith-Beard-Jensen approach to the Confederation period. The facts simply will not support the argument that the democratic forces originally seized control of the movement in the states. Even in the short run, these forces were unsuccessful in every state save Pennsylvania and Georgia. In New Jersey, then as now hospitable to democracy, the Constitution, as Mr. McCormick has demonstrated,[44] was welcomed by all classes because it promised needed financial relief. In that state a western conservative coalition brought about deflationary policies, but not until the very end of the period under review. But the counterrevolution, if the halting of the leftward swing of the pendulum deserves that appellation, was gradual and mild. States like Delaware and Maryland, as John A. Munroe[45] and Philip Crowl[46] have shown us, did not have a counterrevolution, because there never was the kind of democratic upthrust that characterized the early Revolutionary years in Pennsylvania.

The failure of the so-called democratic forces, as Elisha P. Douglass has recently restated for us,[47] is a tribute to the vigorous Revolutionary leadership of the Whig conservative forces and their awareness of the fundamental issues at stake. It was the Whig conservatives, not the regulators in North Carolina or the back-country insurgents in Massachusetts, who took the lead in the movement toward independence. Only where the Whig elite seemed timorous and unwilling to move from protest to revolution did the democratic and back-country forces have any chance of seizing power. That was the case in Pennsylvania, where the conservatives had abdicated their political leadership, and to a lesser degree in Georgia, where the story still remains to be spelled out and where the democratic victory was by no means as clear-cut as in Pennsylvania.

The Burke-Bryan-Lee-Clinton forces that comprised the so-called "democratic" party in the Revolutionary years—just what did they stand for? What kind of democracy did they want? The touchstone of their democracy seems to have been an advocacy of a unicameral legislature, a popularly elected judiciary, and a weak executive—and very little else. In some respects the Whig conservatives held more advanced views than did the radicals. Judged by present-day standards the majoritarians were not always liberal. Back-country enthusiasts of the Great Awakening, they

---

[44] Richard P. McCormick, *Experiment in Independence: New Jersey in the Critical Period, 1781–1789* (New Brunswick, 1950).

[45] *Federalist Delaware, 1775–1815* (New Brunswick, 1954).

[46] *Maryland During and After the Revolution* (Baltimore, 1942).

[47] *Rebels and Democrats* (Chapel Hill, 1955).

were by no means as ready to tolerate non-Protestant religious beliefs as were the deistically-minded Whig leaders. In fact, some of the most revealing evidence presented by Mr. Douglass is that which indicates that left-wing Protestants of Pietist or evangelical inclinations were fundamentalists in outlook and often basically conservative on political issues. It was they who tried to curb the political rights of non-Protestants, and in Pennsylvania it was the so-called radicals who enacted a law restricting freedom of expression. No, the majoritarians did not always act in democratic ways, nor did they seem always willing to abide by the will of the majority. Witness the shocking abuse of power by the radicals in Pennsylvania who established the state constitution by fiat and did not dare submit it to the people. In fact, they went so far as to require the people to take an oath to support the constitution as a prerequisite to exercising the franchise.

Much has been made of the distrust of the masses held by the Whig conservatives, of the views of men like Jay that "the mass of men are neither wise nor good." But many of the Antifederalists shared similar views. Take Samuel Chase, who, as Philip Crowl has shown us, was instrumental in framing Maryland's ultraconservative constitution, and is alleged to have been unstinting in his praise of the aristocratic features of that document, particularly of the electoral college for choosing senators. His desertion to the Antifederalist camp is perhaps best explained by his financial reverses, but he did not linger in it too long. In the federal Convention the Antifederalist John F. Mercer had opposed allowing the people to participate, declaring, "The people cannot know and judge of the characters of Candidates. The worst possible choice will be made." [48] Elbridge Gerry, who refused to sign the Constitution, asserted that "the evils we experience flow from the excess of democracy" and expressed concern at "the danger of the levilling [sic] spirit." [49] In New York the bulwark of Antifederalism was the landowner, with his rural isolation, his dread of the federal impost, and his jealousy of sharing political power. True, he was supported in his opposition to the Constitution by tenants and small farmers, but the Antifederalist leaders of that state had little faith in the people. At the New York Convention George Clinton criticized the people for their fickleness, their tendency "to vibrate from one extreme to another." It was this very disposition, Clinton confessed, against which he wished to guard.[50]

The Antifederalists were not poured out of one democratic mold,[51] any

---

[48] *Records of the Federal Convention of 1787,* ed. Max Farrand (New Haven, 1911–37) II, 205.

[49] *Ibid.,* I, 48.

[50] *Debates in the Several State Conventions on the Adoption of the Federal Constitution, . . . Together with the Journal of the Federal Convention . . . ,* ed. Jonathan Elliot (Philadelphia, 1881), II, 359.

[51] The reader is referred to the provocative article by Cecelia M. Kenyon, "Men of Little Faith: The Anti-Federalists on the Nature of Representative Government," *William and Mary Quarterly,* 3rd Ser., XII (1955), 3–43.

more than the Federalists represented a unitary point of view about how to strengthen the central government. As Robert East has demonstrated,[52] there was a wide breach between the Bowdoin-Adams kind of federalism in Massachusetts and the Cabot-Pickering stripe of particularism, with its strong sectional and anti-Southern overtones. There was an even wider gulf between the democratic nationalism of Franklin and the authoritarian nationalism of Hamilton.

On the pro-democratic side of the Federalist ledger must be credited the position of the Whig conservatives in support of certain basic human rights which they conceived as fundamental and not subject to change at the caprice of majority rule. Fortunately for the evolution of American democracy, the principles of the conservative revolutionaries and their so-called democratic opponents were largely complementary to each other. Although almost everywhere the radicals were defeated in their efforts to seize the machinery of Revolution, the liberative effects of the war proved a deterrent to the kind of social revolution which would have enshrined class hatreds and ensured violent reaction.[53]

Yes, the American Whigs were divided in the years of the Revolution on almost all issues except that of political independence from Great Britain. Since diverse and even divergent interests forged the Whig alliance, it was only to be expected that the victory of the patriots would settle no single social or economic issue except freedom from British mercantilist controls, hardly an unmixed blessing in the years of the Confederation. Despite the efforts of J. Franklin Jameson to consider the American Revolution as a social movement, the fact is that the great internal social reforms lay ahead. As Harrison Gray Otis once wrote to a friend of Revolutionary days: "You and I did not imagine when the first war with Britain was over that the revolution was just begun." [54] Similar sentiments were expressed by Dr. Benjamin Rush on an earlier occasion. In his "Address to the People of the United States on the Defects of the Confederation" Rush declared: "The American war is over; but this is far from being the case with the American Revolution." [55]

Indeed, the imposition of a vitalized federalism and the tightening of the bonds of union precipitated a greater revolution in American life than did separation from England. To those who view the adoption of a system of republican federalism as constituting a more thoroughgoing

---

[52] "The Massachusetts Conservatives in the Critical Period," in *The Era of the American Revolution*, ed. R. B. Morris (New York, 1939), pp. 349–391.

[53] "Was there ever a revolution brought about, especially so important as this, without great internal tumults and violent convulsions!" Sam Adams asked rhetorically. *The Writings of Samuel Adams*, ed. H. A. Cushing (New York, 1904–08), III, 304.

[54] Samuel Eliot Morison, *The Life and Letters of Harrison Gray Otis* (Boston and New York, 1913), I, 49.

[55] Reprinted in H. Niles, *Principles and Acts of the Revolution in America* (Baltimore, 1822), p. 402.

break with the political system of the past than did that earlier severing of the tenuous bonds of empire—and there is impressive evidence in the Confederation interlude of our history to substantiate this interpretation— the Federalists, not the Antifederalists, were the real radicals of their day.

VII

The Constitution: Economic Determinism or Eighteenth-Century Political Theory?

INTRODUCTION

Each generation of Americans interprets the Constitution in the light of its own problems in an effort to bring the force of the Constitution to bear upon the "felt needs of mankind." Both majorities and minorities have sought protection within the Constitution's hospitable bounds. In the years before the Civil War the great constitutional issues related to the nature of the federal union, the relations of the states to the federal government, the powers and relative positions of the three branches of the government, and the protection of sectional minorities under the federal form of government. The emphasis was upon a legalistic, political science, and political theory point of view.

In the years following the Civil War, with the emergence of a new industrial order, with the businessman, the banker, and the railroad magnate emerging to an ever more dominant place and the corporate form of business enterprise everywhere gaining ground, the old traditional interpretations were no longer relevant. To the new ruling groups associated with the new industrial order, as Douglass Adair has pointed out, ". . . the greatest glory of the American system established by the Constitution was its political and economic conservatism." It was Hamilton with his supposed businessman's philosophy of government and respect for property who was the hero among the founding fathers and not the agrarian James Madison. Emerging out of the hard times of the 1890's and growing in strength down to the First World War, the Progressive Movement came to develop an interpretative faculty respecting American life and American institutions that sought to use the new tools of the social sciences. The Supreme Court in Muller vs. Oregon (1908) began to accept the findings of social workers and social scientists as relevant material to consider in the decisions of the Court.

This was the characteristic intellectual climate in which Charles A. Beard came to maturity, and this "younger Beard" published in the year 1913 his epoch-making An Economic Interpretation of the Constitution, *from which two excerpts setting forth the fundamentals of interpretation follow. Beard's main thesis, that economic motives and interests dominated "the founding fathers" in their drawing up of the new federal constitution in 1787, led scholars, in the main, during the twenties and thirties to subscribe to an economic interpretation of history. Beard declared in the most forthright manner that his inquiry "is based upon the political science of James Madison, the father of the Constitution and later President of the Union he had done so much to create." He then went on to quote from Madison's* Federalist No. 10 *and concluded: "Here we have a masterly statement of the theory of economic determinism in politics."*

Beard's thesis has been, since the end of the Second World War, subjected to sweeping criticism by R. E. Brown, Forrest McDonald, Cecelia Kenyon, Douglass Adair, and others. Adair, in particular, is highly critical of Beard's use of Madison's Tenth Federalist *as the major documentary source for his theory that economic determinism, primarily, motivated the founding fathers. Adair declares: "In the process of studying the evolution of Madison's ideas it will become apparent that it is highly anachronistic to tag his theory "anti-democratic" in the nineteenth- or twentieth-century meaning of the term. Madison's* Tenth Federalist *is eighteenth-century political theory directed to an eighteenth-century problem; and it is one of the great creative achievements of that intellectual movement that later ages have christened "Jefferson democracy." ("The Tenth Federalist Revisited,"* William and Mary Quarterly, *VIII (January 1951), 67.) The second piece below is a most persuasive exposition of Madison's political theory and its relation to the formation of our federal constitution.*

An Economic Interpretation of the Constitution of the United States

Charles A. Beard

This volume was first issued in 1913 during the tumult of discussion that accompanied the advent of the Progressive party, the split in Republican ranks, and the conflict over the popular election of United States Senators, workmen's compensation, and other social legislation. At that time Theodore Roosevelt had raised fundamental questions under the head of "the New Nationalism" and proposed to make the Federal Government adequate to the exigencies created by railways, the consolidation of industries, the closure of free land on the frontier, and the new position of labor in American economy. In the course of developing his conceptions, Mr. Roosevelt drew into consideration the place of the judiciary in the American system. While expressing high regard for that branch of government, he proposed to place limitations on its authority. He contended that "by the abuse of the power to declare laws unconstitutional the courts have be-

From *An Economic Interpretation of the Constitution of the United States* (New York: The Macmillan Company, 1936), pp. v–xiv, 1–18. Reprinted by permission.

come a law-making instead of a law-enforcing agency." As a check upon judicial proclivities, he proposed a scheme for "the recall of judicial decisions." This project he justified by the assertion that "when a court decides a constitutional question, when it decides what the people as a whole can or cannot do, the people should have the right to recall that decision when they think it wrong." Owing to such declarations, and to the counter-declarations, the "climate of opinion" was profoundly disturbed when *An Economic Interpretation of the Constitution* originally appeared.

Yet in no sense was the volume a work of the occasion, written with reference to immediate controversies. Doubtless I was, in common with all other students, influenced more or less by "the spirit of the times," but I had in mind no thought of forwarding the interests of the Progressive party or of its conservative critics and opponents. I had taken up the study of the Constitution many years before the publication of my work, while a profound calm rested on the sea of constitutional opinion. In that study I had occasion to read voluminous writings by the Fathers, and I was struck by the emphasis which so many of them placed upon economic interests as forces in politics and in the formulation of laws and constitutions. In particular I was impressed by the philosophy of politics set forth by James Madison in Number X of the *Federalist* (below, page 193), which seemed to furnish a clue to practical operations connected with the formation of the Constitution—operations in which Madison himself took a leading part.

Madison's view of the Constitution seemed in flat contradiction to most of the theorizing about the Constitution to which I had been accustomed in colleges, universities, and legal circles. It is true, older historians, such as Hildreth, had pointed out that there had been a sharp struggle over the formation and adoption of the Constitution, and that in the struggle an alignment of economic interests had taken place. It is true that Chief Justice Marshall, in his life of George Washington, had sketched the economic conflict out of which the Constitution sprang. But during the closing years of the nineteenth century this realistic view of the Constitution had been largely submerged in abstract discussions of states' rights and national sovereignty and in formal, logical, and discriminative analyses of judicial opinions. It was admitted, of course, that there had been a bitter conflict over the formation and adoption of the Constitution; but the struggle was usually explained, if explained at all, by reference to the fact that some men cherished states' rights and others favored a strong central government. At the time I began my inquiries the generally prevailing view was that expressed recently by Professor Theodore Clarke Smith: "Former historians had described the struggle over the formation and adoption of the document as a contest between sections ending in a victory of straight-thinking national-minded men over narrower and more local opponents." How some men got to be "national-minded" and "straight-thinking," and others became narrow and local in their ideas did not disturb the thought of scholars who presided over historical writing at the turn of the nineteenth century. Nor were those scholars at much pains to explain whether the term "section," which they freely used, meant a segment of physical geography or a set of social and economic arrangements within a geographic area, conditioned by physical circumstances.

One thing, however, my masters taught me, and that was to go behind the pages of history written by my contemporaries and read "the sources." In applying this method, I read the letters, papers, and documents pertaining to the Constitution written by the men who took part in framing and adopting it. And to my surprise I found that many Fathers of the Republic regarded the conflict over the Constitution as springing essentially out of conflicts of economic interests, which had a certain geographical or sectional distribution. This discovery, coming at a time when such conceptions of history were neglected by writers on history, gave me "the shock of my life." And since this aspect of the Constitution had been so long disregarded, I sought to redress the balance by emphasis, "naturally" perhaps. At all events I called my volume "an economic interpretation of the Constitution." I did not call it "the" economic interpretation, or "the only" interpretation possible to thought. Nor did I pretend that it was "the history" of the formation and adoption of the Constitution. The reader was warned in advance of the theory and the emphasis. No attempt was made to take him off his guard by some plausible formula of completeness and comprehensiveness. I simply sought to bring back into the mental picture of the Constitution those realistic features of economic conflict, stress, and strain, which my masters had, for some reason, left out of it, or thrust far into the background as incidental rather than fundamental.

When my book appeared, it was roundly condemned by conservative Republicans, including ex-President Taft, and praised, with about the same amount of discrimination, by Progressives and others on the left wing. Perhaps no other book on the Constitution has been more severely criticized, and so little read. Perhaps no other book on the subject has been used to justify opinions and projects so utterly beyond its necessary implications. It was employed by a socialist writer to support a plea for an entirely new constitution and by a conservative judge of the United States Supreme Court to justify an attack on a new piece of "social legislation." Some members of the New York Bar Association became so alarmed by the book that they formed a committee and summoned me to appear before it; and, when I declined on the ground that I was not engaged in legal politics or political politics, they treated my reply as a kind of contempt of court. Few took the position occupied by Justice Oliver Wendell Holmes, who once remarked to me that he had not got excited about the book, like some of his colleagues, but had supposed that it was intended to throw light on the nature of the Constitution, and, in his opinion, did so in fact.

Among my historical colleagues the reception accorded the volume varied. Professor William A. Dunning wrote me that he regarded it as "the pure milk of the word," although it would "make the heathen rage." Professor Albert Bushnell Hart declared that it was little short of indecent. Others sought to classify it by calling it "Marxian." Even as late as the year 1934, Professor Theodore Clarke Smith, in an address before the American Historical Association, expressed this view of the volume, in making it illustrative of a type of historical writing, which is "doctrinaire" and "excludes anything like impartiality." He said: "This is the view that American history, like all history, can and must be explained in economic terms. . . . This idea has its origin, of course, in the Marxian theories." [1] Having made this assertion, Professor Smith turned his scholarly battery upon *An Economic Interpretation of the Constitution.*

Now as a matter of fact there is no reason why an economic interpretation of the Constitution should be more partisan than any other interpretation. It may be employed, to be sure, to condemn one interest in the conflict or another interest, but no such use of it is imposed upon an author by the nature of the interpretation. Indeed an economic analysis may be coldly neutral, and in the pages of this volume no words of condemnation are pronounced upon the men enlisted upon either side of the great controversy which accompanied the formation and adoption of the Constitution. Are the security holders who sought to collect principal and interest through the formation of a stronger government to be treated as guilty of impropriety or praised? That is a question to which the following inquiry is not addressed. An answer to that question belongs to moralists and philosophers, not to students of history as such. If partiality is taken in the customary and accepted sense, it means "leaning to one party or another." Impartiality means the opposite. Then this volume is, strictly speaking, impartial. It supports the conclusion that in the main the men who favored the Constitution were affiliated with certain types of property and economic interest, and that the men who opposed it were affiliated with other types. It does not say that the former were "straight-thinking" and that the latter were "narrow." It applies no moralistic epithets to either party.

On the other hand Professor Smith's statement about the conflict over the Constitution is his *interpretation* of the nature of things, in that it makes the conflict over the Constitution purely psychological in character, unless some economic content is to be given to the term "section." In any event it assumes that straight-thinking and national-mindedness are entities, particularities, or forces, apparently independent of all earthly considerations coming under the head of "economic." It does not say how these

---

[1] *American Historical Review,* April, 1935, p. 447.

entities, particularities, or forces got into American heads. It does not show whether they were imported into the colonies from Europe or sprang up after the colonial epoch closed. It arbitrarily excludes the possibilities that their existence may have been conditioned if not determined by economic interests and activities. It is firm in its exclusion of other interpretations and conceptions. Whoever does not believe that the struggle over the Constitution was a simple contest between the straight-thinking men and narrower and local men of the respective sections is to be cast into outer darkness as "Marxian" or lacking in "impartiality." Is that not a doctrinaire position?

Not only is Professor Smith's position exclusive. It is highly partial. The men who favored the Constitution were "straight-thinking" men. Those who opposed it were "narrower" men. These words certainly may be taken to mean that advocates of the Constitution were wiser men, men of a higher type of mind, than the "narrower" men who opposed it. In a strict sense, of course, straight-thinking may be interpreted as thinking logically. In that case no praise or partiality is necessarily involved. A trained burglar who applies his science to cracking a safe may be more logical than an impulsive night watchman who sacrifices his life in the performance of duty. But in common academic acceptance a logical man is supposed to be superior to the intuitional and emotional man.

Nor is there exactness in such an antithesis as "straight-thinking" and narrowness. Narrowness does not, of necessity, mean lack of straight-thinking. Straight-thinking may be done in a narrow field of thought as well as in a large domain. But there is a true opposition in national-mindedness and local-mindedness, and the student of economic history merely inquires whether the antithesis does not correspond in the main to an economic antagonism. He may accept Professor Smith's psychological antithesis and go beyond it to inquire into its origins. But in so doing he need not ascribe any superior quality of intellect to the one party or the other. To ascribe qualities of mind—high or low—to either party is partiality, dogmatic and doctrinaire partiality. It arbitrarily introduces virtues of intellectual superiority and inferiority into an examination of matters of fact.

In the minds of some, the term "Marxian," imported into the discussion by Professor Smith, means an epithet; and in the minds of others, praise. With neither of these views have I the least concern. For myself I can say that I have never believed that "all history" can or must be "explained" in economic terms, or any other terms. He who really "explains" history must have the attributes ascribed by the theologians to God. It can be "explained," no doubt, to the satisfaction of certain mentalities at certain times, but such explanations are not universally accepted and approved. I confess to have hoped in my youth to find "the causes of things," but I never thought that I had found them. Yet it has seemed to me, and does now, that in the great transformations in society, such as was brought about by the formation and adoption of the Constitution, economic "forces" are primordial or fundamental, and come nearer "explaining" events than any other "forces." Where the configurations and pressures of economic interests are brought into an immediate relation to the event or series of events under consideration, an economic interpretation is effected. Yet, as I said in 1913, on page 195, "It may be that some larger world process is working through each series of historical events; but ultimate causes lie beyond our horizon." If anywhere I have said or written that "all history" can "be explained" in economic terms, I was then suffering from an aberration of the mind.

Nor can I accept as a historical fact Professor Smith's assertion that the economic interpretation of history or my volume on the Constitution had its origin in "Marxian theories." As I point out in Chapter I of my *Economic Basis of Politics,* the germinal idea of class and group conflicts in history appeared in the writings of Aristotle, long before the Christian era, and was known to great writers on politics during the middle ages and modern times. It was expounded by James Madison, in Number X of the *Federalist,* written in defense of the Constitution of the United States, long before Karl Marx was born. Marx seized upon the idea, applied it with rigor, and based predictions upon it, but he did not originate it. Fathers of the American Constitution were well aware of the idea, operated on the hypothesis that it had at least a considerable validity, and expressed it in numerous writings. Whether conflicting economic interests bulk large in contemporary debates over protective tariffs, foreign trade, transportation, industry, commerce, labor, agriculture, and the nature of the Constitution itself, each of our contemporaries may decide on the basis of his experience and knowledge.

Yet at the time this volume was written, I was, in common with all students who professed even a modest competence in modern history, conversant with the theories and writings of Marx. Having read extensively among the writings of the Fathers of the Constitution of the United States and studied Aristotle, Machiavelli, Locke, and other political philosophers, I became all the more interested in Marx when I discovered in his works the ideas which had been cogently expressed by outstanding thinkers and statesmen in the preceding centuries. That interest was deepened when I learned from an inquiry into his student life that he himself had been acquainted with the works of Aristotle, Montesquieu, and other writers of the positive bent before he began to work out his own historical hypothesis. By those who use his name to rally political parties or to frighten Daughters of the American Revolution, students of history concerned with the origins of theories need not be disturbed.

For the reason that this volume was not written for any particular political occasion but designed to illuminate all occasions in which discussion of the Constitution appears, I venture to re-issue it in its original form.

It does not "explain" the Constitution. It does not exclude other explanations deemed more satisfactory to the explainers. Whatever its short-comings, the volume does, however, present some indubitable facts pertaining to that great document which will be useful to students of the Constitution and to practitioners engaged in interpreting it. The Constitution was of human origin, immediately at least, and it is now discussed and applied by human beings who find themselves engaged in certain callings, occupations, professions, and interests. . . .

HISTORICAL INTERPRETATION IN THE UNITED STATES

Broadly speaking, three schools of interpretation have dominated American historical research and generalization. The first of these, which may be justly associated with the name of Bancroft, explains the larger achievements in our national life by reference to the peculiar moral endowments of a people acting under divine guidance; or perhaps it would be more correct to say, it sees in the course of our development the working out of a higher will than that of man. There is to be observed in the history of the struggle for the Constitution, to use Bancroft's words, "the movement of the divine power which gives unity to the universe, and order and connection to events." [2]

Notwithstanding such statements, scattered through Bancroft's pages, it is impossible to describe in a single phrase the ideal that controlled his principles of historical construction, because he was so often swayed by his deference to the susceptibilities of the social class from which he sprang and by the exigencies of the public life in which he played a by no means inconspicuous part. Even telling the whole truth did not lie upon his conscience, for, speaking on the question of the number of Americans who were descendants from transported felons and indented servants, he said that "Having a hand full, he opened his little finger." [3]

Nevertheless, Bancroft constantly recurs in his writings to that "higher power" which is operating in human affairs, although he avoids citing specific events which may be attributed to it. It appears to him to be the whole course of history, rather than any event or set of events, which justifies his theory. "However great," he says, "may be the number of those who persuade themselves that there is in man nothing superior to himself, history interposes with evidence that tyranny and wrong lead inevitably to decay; that freedom and right, however hard may be the struggle, always prove resistless. Through this assurance ancient nations learn to renew their youth; the rising generation is incited to take a generous part in the grand drama of time; and old age, staying itself upon sweet Hope as its companion and cherisher, not bating a jot of courage, nor seeing

[2] *The History of the Constitution of the United States* (1882 ed.), Vol. II, p. 284.
[3] American Historical Review, Vol. II, p. 13.

cause to argue against the hand or the will of a higher power, stands waiting in the tranquil conviction that the path of humanity is still fresh with the dews of morning, that the Redeemer of the nations liveth." [4]

The second school of historical interpretation, which in the order of time followed that of Bancroft, may be called the Teutonic, because it ascribes the wonderful achievements of the English-speaking peoples to the peculiar political genius of the Germanic race. Without distinctly repudiating the doctrine of the "higher power" in history, it finds the secret to the "free" institutional development of the Anglo-Saxon world in innate racial qualities.

The thesis of this school is, in brief, as follows. The Teutonic peoples were originally endowed with singular political talents and aptitudes; Teutonic tribes invaded England and destroyed the last vestiges of the older Roman and British culture; they then set an example to the world in the development of "free" government. Descendants of this specially gifted race settled America and fashioned their institutions after old English models. The full fruition of their political genius was reached in the creation of the Federal Constitution.

For more than a generation the Teutonic theory of our institutions deeply influenced historical research in the United States; but it was exhausted in the study of local government rather than of great epochs; and it produced no monument of erudition comparable to Stubbs' *Constitutional History of England*. Whatever may be said of this school, which has its historical explanation and justification,[5] it served one exceedingly useful purpose: it was scrupulously careful in the documentation of its preconceptions and thus cultivated a more critical spirit than that which characterized the older historians.[6]

The third school of historical research is not to be characterized by any phrase. It is marked rather by an absence of hypotheses. Its representatives, seeing the many pitfalls which beset the way of earlier writers, have resolutely turned aside from "interpretation" in the larger sense, and concerned themselves with critical editions of the documents and with the "impartial" presentation of related facts. This tendency in American scholarship has been fruitful in its results, for it has produced more care in the use of historical sources and has given us many excellent and accurate surveys of outward events which are indispensable to the student who would inquire more deeply into underlying causes.[7]

---

[4] Bancroft, *op. cit.*, Vol. I, p. 6.

[5] It has been left to a Russian to explain to Englishmen the origin of Teutonism in historical writing. See the introduction to Vinogradoff, *Villainage in England*. W. J. Ashley, in his preface to the translation of Fustel de Coulanges, *Origin of Property in Land*, throws some light on the problem, but does not attempt a systematic study.

[6] Note the painstaking documentation for the first chapters in Stubbs' great work.

[7] What Morley has said of Macaulay is true of many eminent American historical writers: "A popular author must, in a thoroughgoing way, take the accepted maxims

Such historical writing, however, bears somewhat the same relation to scientific history which systematic botany bears to ecology; that is, it classifies and orders phenomena, but does not explain their proximate or remote causes and relations. The predominance of such a historical ideal in the United States and elsewhere is not altogether inexplicable; for interpretative schools seem always to originate in social antagonisms.[8] The monarchy, in its rise and development, was never correctly understood as long as it was regarded by all as a mystery which must not be waded into, as James I put it, by ordinary mortals. Without the old régime there would have been no Turgot and Voltaire; Metternich and Joseph de Maistre came after the Revolution.

But the origin of different schools of interpretation in controverises and the prevalence of many mere preconceptions bolstered with a show of learning should not lead us to reject without examination any new hypothesis, such as the theory of economic determinism, on the general assumption of Pascal "that the will, the imagination, the disorders of the body, the thousand concealed infirmities of the intelligence conspire to reduce our discovery of justice and truth to a process of haphazard, in which we more often miss than hit the mark." Such a doctrine of pessimism would make of equal value for the student who would understand, for instance, such an important matter as the origin of the state, Mr. Edward Jenk's severely scientific *History of Politics* and Dr. Nathaniel Johnston's *The Excellency of Monarchical Government, especially the English Monarchy, wherein is largely treated of the Several Benefits of Kingly Government and the Inconvenience of Commonwealths. . . . Likewise the Duty of Subjects and the Mischief of Faction, Sedition, and Rebellion,* published in 1686.

It is not without significance, however, that almost the only work in economic interpretation which has been done in the United States seems to have been inspired at the University of Wisconsin by Professor Turner, now of Harvard. Under the direction of this original scholar and thinker, the influence of the material circumstances of the frontier on American politics was first clearly pointed out. Under his direction also the most important single contribution to the interpretation of the movement for

---

for granted. He must suppress any whimsical fancy for applying the Socratic elenchus; or any other engine of criticism, scepticism, or verification to those sentiments or current precepts or morals which may in truth be very equivocal and may be much neglected in practice, but which the public opinion of his time requires to be treated in theory and in literature as if they had been cherished and held *semper, ubique, et ab omnibus."* *Miscellanies,* Vol. I, p. 272.

[8] For instance, intimate connections can be shown between the vogue of Darwinism and the competitive ideals of the mid-Victorian middle-class in England. Darwin got one of his leading ideas, the struggle for existence, from Malthus, who originated it as a club to destroy the social reformers, Godwin, Condorcet, and others, and then gave it a serious scientific guise as an afterthought.

the federal Constitution was made: O. G. Libby's *Geographical Distribution of the Vote of the Thirteen States on the Federal Constitution.*

In a preface to this work, Professor Turner remarks that the study was designed to contribute "to an understanding of the relations between the political history of the United States, and the physiographic, social, and economic conditions underlying this history. . . . It is believed that many phases of our political history have been obscured by the attention paid to state boundaries and to the sectional lines of North and South. At the same time the economic interpretation of our history has been neglected. In the study of the persistence of the struggle for state particularism in American constitutional history, it was inevitable that writers should make prominent the state as a political factor. But, from the point of view of the rise and growth of sectionalism and nationalism, it is much more important to note the existence of great social and economic areas, independent of state lines, which have acted as units in political history, and which have changed their political attitude as they changed their economic organization and divided into new groups." [9]

Although the hypothesis that economic elements are the chief factors in the development of political institutions has thus been used in one or two serious works, and has been more or less discussed as a philosophic theory,[10] it has not been applied to the study of American history at large—certainly not with that infinite detailed analysis which it requires. Nor has it received at the hands of professed historians that attention which its significance warrants. On the contrary, there has been a tendency to treat it with scant courtesy and to dismiss it with a sharpness bordering on contempt.[11] Such summary judgment is, of course, wholly unwarranted and premature; for as Dr. William Cunningham remarks, the validity of no hypothesis can be determined until it has been worked to its utmost limits. It is easier to write a bulky volume from statutes, congressional debates,[12] memoirs, and diplomatic notes than it is to ascertain the geographical distribution and political significance of any important group of economic factors. The theory of economic determinism has not been tried out in American history, and until it is tried out, it cannot be found wanting.

---

[9] See also the valuable and suggestive writings on American history by Professor W. E. Dodd, of Chicago University; W. A. Schaper, "Sectionalism in South Carolina," *American Historical Association Report* (1900), Vol. I; A. Bentley, *The Process of Government;* C. H. Ambler, *Sectionalism in Virginia.* There are three works by socialist writers that deserve study: Simons, *Social Forces in American History;* Gustavus Myers, *History of Great American Fortunes* and *History of the Supreme Court.*

[10] See Seligman, *The Economic Interpretation of History.*

[11] Vincent, in his treatise on *Historical Research* (1911), dismisses the economic theory without critical examination.

[12] The *Congressional Record* requires more care in use than any other great source of information on American politics.

Sadly as the economic factors have been ignored in historical studies, the neglect has been all the more pronounced in the field of private and public law. The reason for this is apparent. The aim of instruction in these subjects is intensely practical; there are few research professorships in law; and the "case" system of teaching discourages attempts at generalization and surveys.[13] Not even the elementary work has been done. There has been no generous effort to describe the merely superficial aspects of the development of private law in the United States. There has been no concerted attempt to bring together and make available to students the raw materials of such a history. Most of the current views on the history of our law are derived from occasional disquisitions of judges which are all too frequently shot through with curious errors of fact and conception.

Nor has England advanced far beyond us in the critical interpretation of legal evolution—its explanation in terms of, or in relation to, the shifting economic processes and methods in which the law is tangled. It is true that English scholars have produced admirable histories of the law in its outward aspects, such as the monumental work of Pollock and Maitland; and they have made marvellous collections of raw materials, like the publications of the Selden Society. But apart from scattered and brilliant suggestions thrown off occasionally by Maitland [14] in passing, no interpretation has been ventured, and no effort has been made to connect legal phases with economic changes.

In the absence of a critical analysis of legal evolution, all sorts of vague abstractions dominate most of the thinking that is done in the field of law. The characteristic view of the subject taken by American commentators and lawyers immersed in practical affairs is perhaps summed up as finely by Carter as by any writer. "In free, popular states," he says, "the law springs from and is made by the people; and as the process of building it up consists in applying, from time to time, to human actions the popular ideal or standard of justice, justice is only interest consulted in the work. . . . The law of England and America has been a pure develop-

---

[13] Attention should be drawn, however, to the good work which is being done in the translation of several European legal studies, the "Modern Legal Philosophy Series," under the editorial direction of the Association of American Law Schools. Perhaps the most hopeful sign of the times is the growth of interest in comparative jurisprudence. See Borchard, "Jurisprudence in Germany," Columbia Law Review, April, 1912.

[14] For examples of Maitland's suggestiveness, see the English Historical Review, Vol. IX, p. 439, for a side light on the effect of money economy on the manor and consequently on feudal law. See also the closing pages of his Constitutional History of England, where he makes constitutional law in large part the history of the law of real property. "If we are to learn anything about the constitution, it is necessary first and foremost that we should learn a good deal about the land law. We can make no progress whatever in the history of parliament without speaking of tenure; indeed our whole constitutional law seems at times to be but an appendix to the law of real property" (p. 538). Maitland's entire marvellous chapter on "The Definition of Constitutional Law" deserves the most careful study and reflection. He was entirely emancipated from bondage to systematists (p. 539).

ment proceeding from a constant endeavor to apply to the civil conduct of men the ever advancing standard of justice."[15] In other words, law is made out of some abstract stuff known as "justice." What set the standard in the beginning and why does it advance?

The devotion to deductions from "principles" exemplified in particular cases, which is such a distinguishing sign of American legal thinking, has the same effect upon correct analysis which the adherence to abstract terms had upon the advancement of learning—as pointed out by Bacon. The absence of any consideration of the social and economic elements determining the thought of the thinkers themselves is all the more marked when contrasted with the penetration shown by European savants like Jhering, Menger, and Stammler. Indeed, almost the only indication of a possible economic interpretation to be found in current American jurisprudence is implicit in the writings of a few scholars, like Professor Roscoe Pound and Professor Goodnow,[16] and in occasional opinions rendered by Mr. Justice Holmes of the Supreme Court of the United States.[17]

What has here been said about our private law may be more than repeated about our constitutional history and law. This subject, though it has long held an honorable position in the American scheme of learning, has not yet received the analytical study which its intrinsic importance merits. In the past, it has often been taught in the law schools by retired judges who treated it as a branch of natural and moral philosophy or by practical lawyers who took care for the instant need of things. Our great commentaries, Kent, Story, Miller, are never penetrating; they are generally confined to statements of fact; and designed to inculcate the spirit of reverence rather than of understanding. And of constitutional histories, strictly speaking, we have none, except the surveys of superficial aspects by Curtis and Bancroft.

In fact, the juristic theory of the origin and nature of the Constitution is marked by the same lack of analysis of determining forces which characterized older historical writing in general. It may be stated in the following manner: The Constitution proceeds from the whole people; the

[15] J. G. Carter, *The Proposed Codification of Our Common Law* (1884), pp. 6–8.

[16] Of the newer literature on law, see the following articles by Professor Roscoe Pound: "Do we need a Philosophy of Law?" Columbia Law Review, Vol. V, p. 339; "Need of a Sociological Jurisprudence," Green Bag, Vol. XIX, p. 607; "Mechanical Jurisprudence," Columbia Law Review, Vol. VIII, p. 605; "Law in Books and Law in Action," American Law Review, Vol. XLIV, p. 12; Professor Munroe Smith, "Jurisprudence" (in the Columbia University Lectures in Arts and Sciences); Goodnow, *Social Reform and the Constitution.*

[17] Consider, for example, the following remarks by this eminent Justice in his dissenting opinion in the New York Bakery case: "This case is decided upon an economic theory which a large part of the country does not entertain. . . . The Fourteenth Amendment does not enact Mr. Herbert Spencer's *Social Statics.* . . . General propositions do not decide concrete cases. The decision will depend on a judgment or intuition more subtle than any articulate major premise." 198 U. S. 75.

people are the original source of all political authority exercised under it; it is founded on broad general principles of liberty and government entertained, for some reason, by the whole people and having no reference to the interest or advantage of any particular group or class. "By calm meditation and friendly councils," says Bancroft, "they [the people] had prepared a Constitution which, in the union of freedom with strength and order, excelled every one known before. . . . In the happy morning of their existence as one of the powers of the world, they had chosen justice for their guide; and while they proceeded on their way with a well-founded confidence and joy, all the friends of mankind invoked success on their endeavor as the only hope for renovating the life of the civilized world." [18]

With less exaltation, Chief Justice Marshall states the theory, in his opinion in the case of McCulloch v. Maryland: "The government proceeds directly from the people; is 'ordained and established' in the name of the people; and is declared to be ordained 'in order to form a more perfect union, to establish justice, insure domestic tranquillity, and secure the blessings of liberty' to themselves and to their posterity. The assent of the states, in their sovereign capacity, is implied in calling a convention, and thus submitting that instrument to the people. But the people were at perfect liberty to accept or reject it; and their act was final. . . . The government of the Union, then (whatever may be the influence of this fact on the case) is emphatically and truly a government of the people. In form and in substance it emanates from them. Its powers are granted by them, and are to be exercised directly on them, and for their benefit. . . . It is the government of all; its powers are delegated by all; it represents all, and acts for all." [19]

In the juristic view, the Constitution is not only the work of the whole people, but it also bears in it no traces of the party conflict from which it emerged. Take, for example, any of the traditional legal definitions of the Constitution; Miller's will suffice: "A constitution, in the American sense of the word, is any instrument by which the fundamental powers of the government are established, limited, and defined, and by which these powers are distributed among the several departments for their more safe and useful exercise, for the benefit of the body politic. . . . It is not, however, the origin of private rights, nor the foundation of laws. It is not the cause, but the consequence of personal and political freedom. It declares those natural and fundamental rights of individuals, for the security and common enjoyment of which governments are established." [20]

---

[18] *Op. cit.*, Vol. II, p. 367.

[19] 4 Wheaton, p. 316. No doubt the learned Justice was here more concerned with discrediting the doctrine of state's rights than with establishing the popular basis of our government.

[20] S. F. Miller, *Lectures on the Constitution* (1891), p. 71.

Nowhere in the commentaries is there any evidence of the fact that the rules of our fundamental law are designed to protect any class in its rights, or secure the property of one group against the assaults of another. "The Constitution," declares Bancroft, "establishes nothing that interferes with equality and individuality. It knows nothing of differences by descent, or opinions, of favored classes, or legalized religion, or the political power of property. It leaves the individual along-side of the individual. . . . As the sea is made up of drops, American society is composed of separate, free, and constantly moving atoms, ever in reciprocal action . . . so that the institutions and laws of the country rise out of the masses of individual thought, which, like the waters of the ocean, are rolling evermore." [21]

In turning from the vague phraseology of Bancroft to an economic interpretation of constitutional history, it is necessary to realize at the outset that law is not an abstract thing, a printed page, a volume of statutes, a statement by a judge. So far as it becomes of any consequence to the observer it must take on a real form; it must govern actions; it must determine positive relations between men; it must prescribe processes and juxtapositions.[22] A statute may be on the books for an age, but unless, under its provisions, a determinate arrangement of human relations is brought about or maintained, it exists only in the imagination. Separated from the social and economic fabric by which it is, in part, conditioned and which, in turn, it helps to condition, it has no reality.

Now, most of the law (except the elemental law of community defence) is concerned with the property relations of men, which reduced to their simple terms mean the processes by which the ownership of concrete forms of property is determined or passes from one person to another. As society becomes more settled and industrial in character, mere defence against violence (a very considerable portion of which originates in forcible attempts to change the ownership of property) becomes of relatively less importance; and property relations increase in complexity and subtlety.

But it may be said that constitutional law is a peculiar branch of the law; that it is not concerned primarily with property or with property relations, but with organs of government, the suffrage, administration. The superficiality of this view becomes apparent at a second glance. Inasmuch as the primary object of a government, beyond the mere repression of physical violence, is the making of the rules which determine the property relations of members of society, the dominant classes whose rights are thus to be determined must perforce obtain from the government such rules as are consonant with the larger interests necessary to the continuance of their economic processes, or they must themselves control the organs of government. In a stable despotism the former takes place; under any other

---

[21] *Op. cit.*, Vol. II, p. 324.   [22] See A. Bentley, *The Process of Government.*

system of government, where political power is shared by any portion of the population, the methods and nature of this control become the problem of prime importance—in fact, the fundamental problem in constitutional law. The social structure by which one type of legislation is secured and another prevented—that is, the constitution—is a secondary or derivative feature arising from the nature of the economic groups seeking positive action and negative restraint.

In what has just been said there is nothing new to scholars who have given any attention to European writings on jurisprudence. It is based in the first instance on the doctrine advanced by Jhering that law does not "grow," but is, in fact, "made"—adapted to precise interests which may be objectively determined. It was not original with Jhering. Long before he worked out the concept in his epoch-making book, *Der Zweck im Recht,* Lassalle had set it forth in his elaborate *Das System der erworbenen Rechte,* and long before Lassalle had thought it through, our own Madison had formulated it, after the most wide-reaching researches in history and politics.[23]

In fact, the inquiry which follows is based upon the political science of James Madison, the father of the Constitution and later President of the Union he had done so much to create. This political science runs through all of his really serious writings and is formulated in its most precise fashion in *The Federalist*[24] as follows: "The diversity in the faculties of men, from which the rights of property originate, is not less an insuperable obstacle to a uniformity of interests. The protection of these faculties is the first object of government. From the protection of different and unequal faculties of acquiring property, the possession of different degrees and kinds of property immediately results; and from the influence of these on the sentiments and views of the respective proprietors, ensues a division of society into different interests and parties. . . . The most common and durable source of factions has been the various and unequal distribution of property. Those who hold and those who are without property have ever formed distinct interests in society. Those who are creditors, and those who are debtors, fall under a like discrimination. A landed interest, a manufacturing interest, a mercantile interest, a moneyed interest, with many lesser interests, grow up of necessity in civilized nations and divide them into different classes, actuated by different sentiments and views. The regulations of these various and interfering interests forms the principal task of modern legislation, and involves the spirit of party and faction in the necessary and ordinary operations of the government."

Here we have a masterly statement of the theory of economic determin-

---

[23] And before Madison's century, Harrington had perceived its significance. H. A. L. Fisher, *Republican Tradition in Europe,* p. 51.

[24] Number 10.

ism in politics.[25] Different degrees and kinds of property inevitably exist in modern society; party doctrines and "principles" originate in the sentiments and views which the possession of various kinds of property creates in the minds of the possessors; class and group divisions based on property lie at the basis of modern government; and politics and constitutional law are inevitably a reflex of these contending interests. Those who are inclined to repudiate the hypothesis of economic determinism as a European importation must, therefore, revise their views, on learning that one of the earliest, and certainly one of the clearest, statements of it came from a profound student of politics who sat in the Convention that framed our fundamental law.

The requirements for an economic interpretation of the formation and adoption of the Constitution may be stated in a hypothetical proposition which, although it cannot be verified absolutely from ascertainable data, will at once illustrate the problem and furnish a guide to research and generalization.

It will be admitted without controversy that the Constitution was the creation of a certain number of men, and it was opposed by a certain number of men. Now, if it were possible to have an economic biography of all those connected with its framing and adoption,—perhaps about 160,000 men altogether,—the materials for scientific analysis and classification would be available. Such an economic biography would include a list of the real and personal property owned by all of these men and their families: lands and houses, with incumbrances, money at interest, slaves, capital invested in shipping and manufacturing, and in state and continental securities.

Suppose it could be shown from the classification of the men who supported and opposed the Constitution that there was no line of property division at all; that is, that men owning substantially the same amounts of the same kinds of property were equally divided on the matter of adoption or rejection—it would then become apparent that the Constitution had no ascertainable relation to economic groups or classes, but was the product of some abstract causes remote from the chief business of life—gaining a livelihood.

---

[25] The theory of the economic interpretation of history as stated by Professor Seligman seems as nearly axiomatic as any proposition in social science can be: "The existence of man depends upon his ability to sustain himself; the economic life is therefore the fundamental condition of all life. Since human life, however, is the life of man in society, individual existence moves within the framework of the social structure and is modified by it. What the conditions of maintenance are to the individual, the similar relations of production and consumption are to the community. To economic causes, therefore, must be traced in the last instance those transformations in the structure of society which themselves condition the relations of social classes and the various manifestations of social life." *The Economic Interpretation of History,* p. 3.

Suppose, on the other hand, that substantially all of the merchants, money lenders, security holders, manufacturers, shippers, capitalists, and financiers and their professional associates are to be found on one side in support of the Constitution and that substantially all or the major portion of the opposition came from the non-slaveholding farmers and the debtors —would it not be pretty conclusively demonstrated that our fundamental law was not the product of an abstraction known as "the whole people," but of a group of economic interests which must have expected beneficial results from its adoption? Obviously all the facts here desired cannot be discovered, but the data presented in the following chapters bear out the latter hypothesis, and thus a reasonable presumption in favor of the theory is created.

Of course, it may be shown (and perhaps can be shown) that the farmers and debtors who opposed the Constitution were, in fact, benefited by the general improvement which resulted from its adoption. It may likewise be shown, to take an extreme case, that the English nation derived immense advantages from the Norman Conquest and the orderly administrative processes which were introduced, as it undoubtedly did; nevertheless, it does not follow that the vague thing known as "the advancement of general welfare" or some abstraction known as "justice" was the immediate, guiding purpose of the leaders in either of these great historic changes. The point is, that the direct, impelling motive in both cases was the economic advantages which the beneficiaries expected would accrue to themselves first, from their action. Further than this, economic interpretation cannot go. It may be that some larger world-process is working through each series of historical events; but ultimate causes lie beyond our horizon.

"That Politics May Be Reduced to a Science": David Hume, James Madison, and the Tenth *Federalist*

Douglass Adair

In June 1783, the war for American independence being ended, General Washington addressed his once-famous circular letter to the state governors with the hopeful prophecy that if the Union of the States could be preserved, the future of the Republic would be both glorious and happy. "The foundation of our Empire was not laid in the gloomy age of Ignorance and Superstition," Washington pointed out, "but at an Epocha when the rights of mankind were better understood and more clearly defined, than at any former period; the researches of the human mind after social happiness, have been carried to a great extent, the treasures of knowledge, acquired by the labours of Philosophers, Sages, and Legislators, through a long succession of years, are laid open for our use, and their collected wisdom may be happily applied in the Establishment of our forms of Government . . . At this auspicious period, the United States came into existence as a Nation, and if their Citizens should not be completely free and happy, the fault will be intirely their own."

The optimism of General Washington's statement is manifest; the reasons he advances for this optimism, however, seem to modern Americans a century and a half later both odd and naive, if not slightly un-American. For Washington here argues in favor of "the Progress of the Human Mind." Knowledge gradually acquired through "researches of the human mind" about the nature of man and government—knowledge which "the gloomy age of Ignorance and Superstition" did not have—gives Americans in 1783 the power to new-model their forms of government according to the precepts of wisdom and reason. The "Philosopher" as Sage and Legislator, General Washington hopes, will preside over the creation and reform of American political institutions.

From *Huntington Library Quarterly*, XX (August 1957), 343–360. Reprinted by permission. Delivered at the Conference of Early American History at the Henry E. Huntington Library, February 9, 1957.

"Philosopher" as written here by Washington was a word with hopeful and good connotations. But this was 1783. In 1789 the French Revolution began; by 1792 "philosophy" was being equated with the guillotine, atheism, the reign of terror. Thereafter "philosopher" would be a smear-word, connoting a fuzzy-minded and dangerous social theorist—one of those impractical Utopians whose foolish attempts to reform society according to a rational plan created the anarchy and social disaster of the Terror. Before his death in 1799 Washington himself came to distrust and fear the political activities of philosophers. And in time it would become fashionable among both French conservatives and among all patriotic Americans to stress the sinister new implications of the word "philosophy" added after 1789 and to credit the French philosophers with transforming the French Revolution into a "bad" revolution in contrast to the "good" non-philosophical American Revolution. But this ethical transformation of the word still lay in the future in 1783. Then "philosophy" and "philosopher" were still terms evoking optimism and hopes of the high tide of Enlightenment on both sides of the Atlantic.

Dr. Johnson in his *Dictionary* helps us understand why Washington had such high regard for philosophy as our war for independence ended. "Philosophy," according to the lexicographer, was "knowledge natural or moral"; it was "hypothesis or system upon which natural effects are explained." "To philosophize," or "play the philosopher," was "to search into nature; to enquire into the causes of effects." The synonym of "Philosophy" in 1783 then was "Science"; the synonym of "Philosopher" would be our modern word (not coined until 1840) "Scientist," "a man deep in knowledge, either moral or natural."

Bacon, Newton, and Locke were the famed trinity of representative great philosophers for Americans and all educated inhabitants of Western Europe in 1783. Francis Bacon, the earliest prophet of philosophy as a program for the advancement of learning, had preached that "Knowledge is Power" and that Truth discovered by Reason through observation and free inquiry is as certain and as readily adapted to promote the happiness of human life, as Truth communicated to mankind through God's direct revelation. Isaac Newton, "the first luminary in this bright constellation," had demonstrated that Reason indeed could discover the laws of physical Nature and of Nature's God, while John Locke's researches into psychology and human understanding had definitely channeled inquiry toward the discovery of the immutable and universal laws of Human Nature. By the middle of the eighteenth century a multitude of researchers in all the countries of Europe were seeking, in Newtonian style, to advance the bounds of knowledge in politics, economics, law, and sociology. By the middle of the century the French judge and *philosophe* Montesquieu had produced a compendium of the behavioral sciences, cutting across all these fields in his famous study of *The Spirit of the Laws.*

However, Washington's assurance that already scientific knowledge about government had accumulated to such an extent that it could be immediately applied to the uses of "Legislators," pointed less toward France than toward Scotland. There, especially in the Scottish universities, had been developed the chief centers of eighteenth-century social science research and publication in all the world. The names of Francis Hutcheson, David Hume, Adam Smith, Thomas Reid, Lord Kames, Adam Ferguson, the most prominent of the Scottish philosophers, were internationally famous. In America the treatises of these Scots, dealing with history, ethics, politics, economics, psychology, and jurisprudence in terms of "system upon which natural effects are explained," had become the standard textbooks of the colleges of the late colonial period. At Princeton, at William and Mary, at Pennsylvania, at Yale, at King's, and at Harvard, the young men who rode off to war in 1776 had been trained in the texts of Scottish social science.

The Scottish system, as it had been gradually elaborated in the works of a whole generation of researchers, rested on one basic assumption, had developed its own special method, and kept to a consistent aim. The assumption was "that there is a great uniformity among the actions of men, in all nations and ages, and that human nature remains still the same, in its principles and operations. The same motives always produce the same actions; the same events follow from the same causes. . . . Would you know the sentiments, inclinations, and course of life of the Greeks and Romans? Study well the temper and actions of the French and English . . ."—thus David Hume, presenting the basis of a science of human behavior. The method of eighteenth-century social science followed from this primary assumption—it was historical-comparative synthesis. Again Hume: "Mankind are so much the same, in all times and places, that history informs us of nothing new or strange in this particular. Its chief use is only to discover the constant and universal principles of human nature, by showing men in all varieties and situations, and furnishing us with materials from which we may form our observations and become acquainted with the regular springs of human action and behavior." [1] Finally, the aim of studying man's

---

[1] David Hume, "Of Liberty and Necessity," in *An Enquiry Concerning Human Understanding* (London, 1748). An examination of the social theory of the Scottish school is to be found in Gladys Bryson, *Man and Society: The Scottish Inquiry of the Eighteenth Century* (Princeton, 1945). Miss Bryson seems unaware both of the position held by Scottish social science in the curriculum of the American colleges after 1750— Princeton, for example, where nine members of the Constitutional Convention of 1787 graduated, was a provincial carbon-copy, under President Witherspoon, of Edinburgh— and of its influence on the revolutionary generation. For a brilliant analysis of Francis Hutcheson's ideas and his part in setting the tone and direction of Scottish research, as well as the trans-Atlantic flow of ideas between Scotland and the American colonies in the eighteenth century, with a persuasive explanation of why the Scots specialized in social science formulations that were peculiarly congenial to the American revolutionary elite, see Caroline Robbins, "When It Is That Colonies May Turn Independent," *William and Mary Quarterly*, 3d ser., Vol. XI (April, 1954), pp. 214–251.

behavior in its comparative-historical manifestations was for the purpose of prediction—philosophy would aid the legislator in making correct policy decisions. Comparative-historical studies of man in society would allow the discovery of the constant and universal principle of human nature, which, in turn, would allow at least some safe predictions about the effects of legislation "almost as general and certain . . . as any which the mathematical sciences will afford us." "Politics" (and again the words are Hume's) to some degree "may be reduced to a science."

By thus translating the abstract generalizations about "philosophy" in Washington's letter of 1783 into the concrete and particular type of philosophy to which he referred, the issue is brought into new focus more congenial to our modern understanding. On reviewing the specific body of philosophical theory and writing with which Washington and his American contemporaries were familiar, we immediately remember that "the collected wisdom" of at least some of the Scottish academic philosophers was applied to American legislation during the nineteenth century. It is obvious, for example, that the "scientific predictions," based on historical analysis, contained in Professor Adam Smith's *An Inquiry into the Nature and Causes of the Wealth of Nations* (London, 1776), concerning the role of free enterprise and economic productivity, was of prime significance in shaping the relations of the state with the American business community, especially after 1828. Washington's expectations of 1783 were thus accurate in the long-run view.[2]

It is the purpose of this paper, however, to show that Washington's immediate expectations of the creative role of "philosophy" in American politics were also accurate in the period in which he wrote. It is thus the larger inference of the following essay that "philosophy," or "the science of politics" (as defined above), was integral to the whole discussion of the necessity for a *more* perfect Union that resulted in the creation of the American Constitution of 1787.

It can be shown, though not in this short paper, that the use of history in the debates both in the Philadelphia Convention and in the state ratifying conventions is not mere rhetorical-historical window-dressing, concealing substantially greedy motives of class and property. The speakers were making a genuinely "scientific" attempt to discover the "constant and universal principles" of any republican government in regard to liberty, justice, and stability.

In this perspective the three hundred pages of comparative-historical research in John Adams's *Defence of the Constitutions of the United States*

---

[2] The theoretical and prophetic nature of Adam Smith's classic when it was published in 1776 is today largely ignored by both scholars and spokesmen for the modern American business community. In 1776, however, Smith could only theorize from scattered historical precedents as to how a projective free enterprise system might work, because nowhere in his mercantilist world was a free enterprise system of the sort he described on paper actually operating.

(1787), and the five-hour closely argued historical analysis in Alexander Hamilton's Convention Speech of June 18, 1787, were both "scientific" efforts to relate the current difficulties of the thirteen American republics to the universal tendencies of republicanism in all nations and in all ages. History, scientifically considered, thus helped *define* both the nature of the crisis of 1787 for these leaders and their audience, and also determined in large part the "reforms" that, it could be predicted, would end the crisis. To both Adams and Hamilton history proved (so they believed) that sooner or later the American people would have to return to a system of mixed or limited monarchy—so great was the size of the country, so diverse were the interests to be reconciled that no other system could be adequate in securing both liberty and justice. In like manner Patrick Henry's prediction, June 9, 1788, in the Virginia Ratifying Convention, "that one government [i.e., the proposed constitution] cannot reign over so extensive a country as this is, without absolute despotism" was grounded upon a "political axiom" scientifically confirmed, so he believed, by history.

The most creative and philosophical disciple of the Scottish school of science and politics in the Philadelphia Convention was James Madison. His effectiveness as an advocate of a new constitution, and of the particular constitution that was drawn up in Philadelphia in 1787, was certainly based in large part on his personal experience in public life and his personal knowledge of the conditions of America in 1787. But Madison's greatness as a statesman rests in part on his ability quite deliberately to set his limited personal experience in the context of the experience of men in other ages and times, thus giving extra reaches of insight to his political formulations.

His most amazing political prophecy, formally published in the tenth *Federalist,* was that the size of the United States and its variety of interests could be made a guarantee of stability and justice under the new constitution. When Madison made this prophecy the accepted opinion among all sophisticated politicians was exactly the opposite. It is the purpose of the following detailed analysis to show Madison, the scholar-statesman, evolving his novel theory, and not only using the behavioral science techniques of the eighteenth century, but turning to the writings of David Hume himself for some of the suggestions concerning an extended republic.

It was David Hume's speculations on the "Idea of a Perfect Commonwealth," first published in 1752, that most stimulated James Madison's thought on factions.[3] In this essay Hume disclaimed any attempt to substi-

---

[3] David Hume, *Essays, Moral, Political, and Literary* (London, 1875). Madison apparently used the 1758 edition, which was the most complete printed during the Scot's lifetime, and which gathered up into two volumes what he conceived of as the final revised version of his thoughts on the topics treated. Earlier versions of certain of the essays had been printed in 1742, 1748, 1752; there are numerous modern editions of the 1758 printing. All page references to Hume in this article are to the 1875 edition.

tute a political Utopia for "the common botched and inaccurate governments" which seemed to serve imperfect men so well. Nevertheless, he
argued, the idea of a perfect commonwealth "is surely the most worthy
curiosity of any the wit of man can possibly devise. And who knows, if this
controversy were fixed by the universal consent of the wise and learned,
but, in some future age, an opportunity might be afforded of reducing the
theory to practice, either by a dissolution of some old government, or by
the combination of men to form a new one, in some distant part of the
world." At the very end of Hume's essay was a discussion that could not
help being of interest to Madison. For here the Scot casually demolished the
Montesquieu small-republic theory; and it was this part of his essay, contained in a single page, that was to serve Madison in new-modeling a
"botched" Confederation "in a distant part of the world." (I, 480–481, 492.)

Hume concluded his "Idea of a Perfect Commonwealth" with some observations on "the falsehood of the common opinion, that no large state,
such as France or Great Britain, could ever be modelled into a commonwealth, but that such a form of government can only take place in a city
or small territory." The opposite seemed to be true, decided Hume.
"Though it is more difficult to form a republican government in an extensive country than in a city; there is more facility, when once it is formed,
of preserving it steady and uniform, without tumult and faction."

The formidable problem of first unifying the outlying and various segments of a big area had thrown Montesquieu and like-minded theorists off
the track, Hume believed. "It is not easy, for the distant parts of a large
state to combine in any plan of free government; but they easily conspire
in the esteem and reverence for a single person, who, by means of this
popular favour, may seize the power, and forcing the more obstinate to
submit, may establish a monarchical government." (I, 492.) Historically,
therefore, it is the great leader who has been the symbol and engine of
unity in empire building. His characteristic ability to evoke loyalty has
made him in the past a mechanism both of solidarity and of exploitation.
His leadership enables diverse peoples to work for a common end, but because of the power temptations inherent in his strategic position he usually
ends as an absolute monarch.

And yet, Hume argued, this last step is not a rigid social law as Montesquieu would have it. There was always the possibility that some modern
leader with the wisdom and ancient virtue of a Solon or of a Lycurgus
would suppress his personal ambition and found a free state in a large territory "to secure the peace, happiness, and liberty of future generations."
("Of Parties in General," I, 127.) In 1776—the year Hume died—a provincial notable named George Washington was starting on the career that was
to justify Hume's penetrating analysis of the unifying role of the great man
in a large and variegated empire. Hume would have exulted at the discovery that his deductive leap into the future with a scientific prediction

was correct: all great men who consolidated empires did not necessarily desire crowns.

Having disposed of the reason why monarchies had usually been set up in big empires and why it still was a matter of free will rather than necessity, Hume then turned to the problem of the easily founded, and unstable, small republic. In contrast to the large state, "a city readily concurs in the same notions of government, the natural equality of property favours liberty,[4] and the nearness of habitation enables the citizens mutually to assist each other. Even under absolute princes, the subordinate government of cities is commonly republican. . . . But these same circumstances, which facilitate the erection of commonwealths in cities, render their constitution more frail and uncertain. Democracies are turbulent. For however the people may be separated or divided into small parties, either in their votes or elections; their near habitation in a city will always make the force of popular tides and currents very sensible. Aristocracies are better adapted for peace and order, and accordingly were most admired by ancient writers; but they are jealous and oppressive." (I, 492.) Here, of course, was the ancient dilemma that Madison knew so well, re-stated by Hume. In the city where wealth and poverty existed in close proximity, the poor, if given the vote, might very well try to use the power of the government to expropriate the opulent. While the rich, ever a self-conscious minority in a republican state, were constantly driven by fear of danger, even when no danger existed in fact, to take aggressive and oppressive measures to head off the slightest threat to their power, position, and property.

It was Hume's next two sentences that must have electrified Madison as he read them: "In a large government, which is modelled with masterly skill, there is compass and room enough to refine the democracy, from the lower people, who may be admitted into the first elections or first concoction of the commonwealth, to the higher magistrates, who direct all the movements. At the same time, the parts are so distant and remote, that it is very difficult, either by intrigue, prejudice, or passion, to hurry them into any measures against the public interest." (I, 492.) Hume's analysis here had turned the small-territory republic theory upside down: *if* a free state could once be established in a large area, it would be stable and safe from the effects of faction. Madison had found the answer to Montesquieu. He had also found in embryonic form his own theory of the extended federal republic.

---

[4] Hume seems to be referring to the development in cities of a specialized product, trade, or industrial skill, that gives the small area an equal interest in a specific type of economic activity. All the inhabitants of Sheffield from the lowly artisan to the wealthiest manufacturer had an interest in the iron industry; every dweller in Liverpool had a stake in the prosperity of the slave trade. It was this regional unity of occupation that Hume was speaking of, not equality of income from the occupation, as is shown by the latter part of his analysis.

Madison could not but feel that the "political aphorisms" which David Hume scattered so lavishly in his essays were worthy of his careful study. He re-examined the sketch of Hume's perfect commonwealth: "a form of government, to which," Hume claimed, "I cannot in theory discover any considerable objection." Hume suggested that Great Britain and Ireland— "or any territory of equal extent"—be divided into a hundred counties, and that each county in turn be divided into one hundred parishes, making in all ten thousand minor districts in the state. The twenty-pound freeholders and five-hundred-pound householders in each parish were to elect annually a representative for the parish. The hundred parish representatives in each county would then elect out of themselves one "senator" and ten county "magistrates." There would thus be in "the whole commonwealth, 100 senators, 1100 [sic] county magistrates, and 10,000 . . . representatives." Hume would then have vested in the senators the executive power: "the power of peace and war, of giving orders to generals, admirals, and ambassadors, and, in short all the prerogatives of a British King, except his negative." (I, 482–483.) The county magistrates were to have the legislative power; but they were never to assemble as a single legislative body. They were to convene in their own counties, and each county was to have one vote; and although they could initiate legislation, Hume expected the senators normally to make policy. The ten thousand parish representatives were to have the right to a referendum when the other two orders in the state disagreed.

It was all very complicated and cumbersome, but Hume thought that it would allow a government to be based on the consent of the "people" and at the same time obviate the danger of factions. He stated the "political aphorism" which explained his complex system.

> The lower sort of people and small proprietors are good judges enough of one not very distant from them in rank or habitation; and therefore, in their parochial meetings, will probably chuse the best, or nearly the best representative: But they are wholly unfit for county-meetings, and for electing into the higher offices of the republic. Their ignorance gives the grandees an opportunity of deceiving them.[5]

This carefully graded hierarchy of officials therefore carried the system of indirect elections to a logical conclusion.

Madison quite easily traced out the origin of Hume's scheme. He found

---

[5] *Essays*, I, 487. Hume elaborated his system in great detail, working out a judiciary system, the methods of organizing and controlling the militia, etc. The Scot incidentally acknowledged that his thought and theories on the subject owed much to James Harrington's *Oceana* (London, 1656), "the only valuable model of a [perfect] commonwealth that has yet been offered to the public." For Hume thought that Sir Thomas More's *Utopia* and Plato's *Republic* with all other utopian blueprints were worthless. "All plans of government, which suppose great reformation in the manners of mankind," he noted, "are plainly imaginary." *Ibid.*, 481.

it in the essay entitled "Of the First Principles of Government." Hume had been led to his idea of fragmentizing election districts by his reading of Roman history and his contemplation of the historically verified evils incident to the direct participation of every citizen in democratical governments. The Scotsman had little use for "a pure republic," that is to say, a direct democracy. "For though the people, collected in a body like the Roman tribes, be quite unfit for government, yet when dispersed in small bodies, they are more susceptible both of reason and order; the force of popular currents and tides is, in a great measure, broken; and the public interest may be pursued with some method and constancy." (I, 113.) Hence, Hume's careful attempts to keep the citizens with the suffrage operating in thousands of artificially created electoral districts. And as Madison thought over Hume's theoretic system, he must suddenly have seen that in this instance the troublesome corporate aggressiveness of the thirteen American states could be used to good purpose. There already existed in the United States local governing units to break the force of popular currents. There was no need to invent an artificial system of counties in America. The states themselves could serve as the chief pillars and supports of a new constitution in a large-area commonwealth.

Here in Hume's *Essays* lay the germ for Madison's theory of the extended republic. It is interesting to see how he took these scattered and incomplete fragments and built them into an intellectual and theoretical structure of his own. Madison's first full statement of this hypothesis appeared in his "Notes on the Confederacy" written in April 1787, eight months before the final version of it was published as the tenth *Federalist*.[6] Starting with the proposition that "in republican Government, the majority, however composed, ultimately give the law," Madison then asks what is to restrain an interested majority from unjust violations of the minority's rights? Three motives might be claimed to meliorate the selfishness of the majority: first, "prudent regard for their own good, as involved in the general . . . good"; second, "respect for character"; and finally, religious scruples.[7] After examining each in its turn Madison concludes that they are but a frail bulwark against a ruthless party.

In his discussion of the insufficiency of "respect for character" as a curb on faction, Madison again leans heavily upon Hume. The Scot had stated paradoxically that it is "a just *political* maxim *that every man must be supposed a knave:* Though at the same time, it appears somewhat strange, that a maxim should be true in *politics,* which is false in *fact* . . . men

---

[6] *Federalist*, X, appeared in *The New York Packet*, Friday, Nov. 23, 1787. There are thus three versions of Madison's theoretic formulation of how a properly organized republic in a large area, incorporating within its jurisdiction a multiplicity of interests, will sterilize the class conflict of the rich versus the poor: (1) the "Notes" of Apr. 1787; (2) speeches in the convention during June 1787; and (3) the final polished and elaborated form, in the *Federalist*, Nov. 1787.

[7] James Madison, *Letters and Other Writings*, 4 vols. (Philadelphia, 1867), I, 325–326.

are generally more honest in their private than in their public capacity, and will go greater lengths to serve a party, than when their own private interest is alone concerned. Honour is a great check upon mankind: But where a considerable body of men act together, this check is, in a great measure, removed; since a man is sure to be approved of by his own party . . . and he soon learns to despise the clamours of adversaries." [8] This argument, confirmed by his own experience, seemed to Madison too just and pointed not to use, so under "Respect for character" he set down: "However strong this motive may be in individuals, it is considered as very insufficient to restrain them from injustice. In a multitude its efficacy is diminished in proportion to the number which is to share the praise or the blame. Besides, as it has reference to public opinion, which, within a particular society, is the opinion of the majority, the standard is fixed by those whose conduct is to be measured by it." [9] The young Virginian readily found a concrete example in Rhode Island, where honor had proved to be no check on factious behavior. In a letter to Jefferson explaining the theory of the new constitution, Madison was to repeat his category of inefficacious motives,[10] but in formally presenting his theory to the world in the letters of Publius he deliberately excluded it.[11] There was a certain disadvantage in making derogatory remarks to a majority that must be persuaded to adopt your arguments.

In April 1787, however, when Madison was writing down his first thoughts on the advantage of an extended government, he had still not completely thought through and integrated Hume's system of indirect elections with his own ideas. The Virginian, nevertheless, had not dismissed the subject from his thoughts. He had taken a subsidiary element of Hume's "Perfect Commonwealth" argument and developed it as the primary factor in his own theorem; but he was also to include Hume's major technique of indirect election as a minor device in the constitution he proposed for the new American state. As the last paragraph of "Notes on the Confederacy" there appears a long sentence that on its surface has little organic relation to Madison's preceding two-page discussion of how "an extensive Republic meliorates the administration of a small Republic."

---

[8] "Of the Independency of Parliament," *Essays*, I, 118–119.   [9] *Letters*, I, 326.

[10] *Ibid.*, p. 352. To Thomas Jefferson, Oct. 24, 1787.

[11] In Madison's earliest presentation of his thesis certain other elements indicating his debt to Hume appear that have vanished in the *Federalist*. In the "Notes on the Confederacy" the phrase "notorious factions and oppressions which take place in corporate towns" (*Letters*, I, 327) recalls the original starting point of Hume's analysis in the "Perfect Commonwealth." Also the phraseology of the sentence: "The society becomes broken into a greater variety of interests . . . which check each other . . ." (*ibid.*), varied in the letter to Jefferson to: "In a large society, the people are broken into so many interests" (*ibid.*, 352), is probably a parallel of Hume's "The force of popular currents and tides is, in a great measure, broken." ("First Principles of Governments," *Essays*, I, 113.)

An auxiliary desideratum for the melioration of the Republican form is such a process of elections as will most certainly extract from the mass of the society the purest and noblest characters which it contains; such as will at once feel most strongly the proper motives to pursue the end of their appointment, and be most capable to devise the proper means of attaining it.[12]

This final sentence, with its abrupt departure in thought, would be hard to explain were it not for the juxtaposition in Hume of the material on large area and indirect election.

When Madison presented his thesis to the electorate in the tenth *Federalist* as justification for a more perfect union, Hume's *Essays* were to offer one final service. Hume had written a scientific analysis on "Parties in General" as well as on the "Parties of Great Britain." In the first of these essays he took the position independently arrived at by Madison concerning the great variety of factions likely to agitate a republican state. The Virginian, with his characteristic scholarly thoroughness, therefore turned to Hume again when it came time to parade his arguments in full dress. Hume had made his major contribution to Madison's political philosophy before the Philadelphia Convention. Now he was to help in the final polishing and elaboration of the theory for purposes of public persuasion in print.

Madison had no capacity for slavish imitation; but a borrowed word, a sentence lifted almost in its entirety from the other's essay, and above all, the exactly parallel march of ideas in Hume's "Parties" and Madison's *Federalist,* X, show how congenial he found the Scot's way of thinking, and how invaluable Hume was in the final crystallizing of Madison's own convictions. "Men have such a propensity to divide into personal factions," wrote Hume, "that the smallest appearance of real difference will produce them." (I, 128.) And the Virginian takes up the thread to spin his more elaborate web: "So strong is this propensity of mankind to fall into mutual animosities, that where no substantial occasion presents itself, the most frivolous and fanciful distinctions have been sufficient to kindle their unfriendly passions and excite their most violent conflicts." [13] Hume, in his parallel passage, presents copious examples. He cites the rivalry of the blues and the greens at Constantinople, and recalls the feud between two tribes in Rome, the Pollia and the Papiria, that lasted three hundred years after everyone had forgotten the original cause of the quarrel. "If mankind had not a strong propensity to such divisions, the indifference of the rest of the community must have suppressed this foolish animosity [of the two tribes], that had not any aliment of new benefits and injuries. . . ."

[12] *Letters,* I, 328.
[13] *The Federalist,* ed. Max Beloff (Oxford and New York, 1948), No. X, p. 43. Hereafter page references to the *Federalist* will be to this edition.

(I, 128–129.) The fine Latinity of the word "aliment" [14] apparently caught in some crevice of Madison's mind, soon to reappear in his statement, "Liberty is to faction what air is to fire, an aliment, without which it instantly expires." [15] So far as his writings show, he never used the word again; but in this year of 1787 his head was full of such words and ideas culled from David Hume.

When one examines these two papers in which Hume and Madison summed up the eighteenth century's most profound thought on party, it becomes increasingly clear that the young American used the earlier work in preparing a survey on faction through the ages to introduce his own discussion of faction in America. Hume's work was admirably adapted to this purpose. It was philosophical and scientific in the best tradition of the Enlightenment. The facile damnation of faction had been a commonplace in English politics for a hundred years, as Whig and Tory vociferously sought to fasten the label on each other. But the Scot, very little interested as a partisan and very much so as a social scientist, treated the subject therefore in psychological, intellectual, and socio-economic terms. Throughout all history, he discovered, mankind has been divided into factions based either on personal loyalty to some leader or upon some "sentiment or interest" common to the group as a unit. This latter type he called a "Real" as distinguished from the "Personal" faction. Finally he subdivided the "real factions" into parties based on "interest," upon "principle," or upon "affection." Hume spent well over five pages dissecting these three types; but Madison, while determined to be inclusive, had not the space to go into such minute analysis. Besides, he was more intent now on developing the cure than on describing the malady. He therefore consolidated Hume's two-page treatment of "personal" factions, and his long discussion of parties

---

[14] L. *alimentum*, fr. *alere* to nourish. Food; nutriment; hence, sustenance, means of support.—SYN. see PABULUM. This word is not a common one in 18th century political literature. Outside of *The Federalist* and Hume's essay I have run across it only in Bacon's works. To the man of the 18th century even the cognate forms "alimentary" (canal), and "alimony," so familiar to us in common speech, were still highly technical terms of medicine and law.

[15] *Federalist*, p. 42. Compare Hume's remarks: "In despotic governments, indeed, factions often do not appear; but they are not the less real; or rather, they are more real and more pernicious, upon that very account. The distinct orders of men, nobles and people, soldiers and merchants, have all a distinct interest; but the more powerful oppresses the weaker with impunity and without resistance; which begets a seeming tranquility in such governments." (I, 130.) Also see Hume's comparison of faction to "weeds . . . which grow most plentifully in the richest soil; and though absolute governments be not wholly free from them, it must be confessed, that they rise more easily, and propagate themselves faster in free governments, where they always infect the legislature itself, which alone could be able, by the steady application of rewards and punishments, to eradicate them" (I, 127–128); and notice Madison's "The regulation of these various and interfering interests forms the principal task of modern legislation, and involves the spirit of party and faction in the necessary and ordinary operations of the government." (*Federalist*, p. 43.)

based on "principle and affection" into a single sentence. The tenth *Federalist* reads: "A zeal for different opinions concerning religion, concerning government, and many other points, as well of speculation as of practice;[16] an attachment to different leaders ambitiously contending for pre-eminence and power;[17] or to persons of other descriptions whose fortunes have been interesting to the human passions,[18] have, in turn, divided mankind into parties, inflamed them with mutual animosity, and rendered them much more disposed to vex and oppress each other than to cooperate for their common good." [19] It is hard to conceive of a more perfect example of the concentration of idea and meaning than Madison achieved in this famous sentence.

It is noteworthy that while James Madison compressed the greater part of Hume's essay on factions into a single sentence, he greatly expanded the quick sketch of the faction from "interest" buried in the middle of the

---

[16] This clause of Madison's refers to Hume's "parties from *principle,* especially abstract speculative principle," in the discussion of which he includes "different political principles" and "principles of priestly government . . . which has . . . been the poison of human society, and the source of the most inveterate factions." Hume, in keeping with his reputation as the great sceptic, feels that while the congregations of persecuting sects must be called "factions of principle," the priests, who are "the prime movers" in religious parties, are factions out of "interest." The word "speculation" that appears in Madison is rendered twice as "speculative" in Hume. (I, 130–132.)

[17] Here is Hume's "Personal" faction, "founded on personal friendship or animosity among such as compose the contending parties." Hume instances the Colonesi and Orsini of modern Rome, the Neri and Bianchi of Florence, the rivalry between the Pollia and Papiria of ancient Rome, and the confused mass of shifting alliances that marked the struggle between Guelfs and Ghibellines. (I, 128–129.)

[18] This phrase, which is quite obscure in the context, making a separate category of a type of party apparently just covered under "contending leaders," refers to the loyal bitter-end Jacobites of 18th-century England. These sentimental irreconcilables of the Squire Western ilk made up Hume's "party from *affection.*" Hume explains: "By parties from affection, I understand those which are founded on the different attachments of men towards particular families and persons, whom they desire to rule over them. These factions are often very violent [Hume was writing only three years before Bonnie Prince Charlie and the clans had frightened all England in '45]; though, I must own, it may seem unaccountable, that men should attach themselves so strongly to persons, with whom they are no wise acquainted, whom perhaps they never saw, and from whom they never received, nor can ever hope for any favour." (I, 133.)

The fact that Madison includes this category in his paper satisfies me that, when he came to write the tenth *Federalist* for publication, he referred directly to Hume's volume as he reworked his introduction into its final polished form. One can account for the other similarities in the discussion of faction as a result of Madison's careful reading of Hume's works and his ·retentive memory. But the inclusion of this "party from affection" in the Virginian's final scheme where its ambiguity indeed detracts from the force of the argument, puts a strain on the belief that it resulted from memory alone. This odd fourth classification, which on its face is redundant, probably was included because Hume's book was open on the table beside him, and because James Madison would leave no historical stone unturned in his effort to make a definitive scientific summary.

[19] *Federalist*, X, pp. 42–43.

philosopher's analysis. This reference, in Madison's hands, became the climax of his treatment and is the basis of his reputation in some circles as the progenitor of the theory of economic determinism. Hume had written that factions from interest "are the most reasonable, and the most excusable. When two orders of men, such as the nobles and people, have a distinct authority in a government, not very accurately balanced and modelled, they naturally follow a distinct interest; nor can we reasonably expect a different conduct, considering that degree of selfishness implanted in human nature. It requires great skill in a legislator to prevent such parties; and many philosophers are of opinion, that this secret, like the *grand elixir,* or *perpetual motion,* may amuse men in theory, but can never possibly be reduced to practice." (I, 130.) With this uncomfortable thought Hume dismissed the subject of economic factions as he fell into the congenial task of sticking sharp intellectual pins into priestly parties and bigots who fought over abstract political principles.

Madison, on the contrary, was not satisfied with this cursory treatment. He had his own ideas about the importance of economic forces. All that Hume had to say of personal parties, of parties of principle, and of parties of attachment, was but a prologue to the Virginian's discussion of "the various and unequal distribution of property," throughout recorded history. "Those who hold, and those who are without property, have ever formed distinct interests in society. Those who are creditors, and those who are debtors, fall under a like discrimination. A landed interest, a manufacturing interest, a mercantile interest, a moneyed interest, with many lesser interests, grow up of necessity in civilized nations, and divide them into different classes actuated by different sentiments and views." [20] Here was the pivot of Madison's analysis. Here in this multiplicity of economic factions was "the grand elixir" that transformed the ancient doctrine of the rich against the poor into a situation that a skillful American legislator might model into equilibrium. Compound various economic interests of a large territory with a federal system of thirteen semi-sovereign political units, establish a scheme of indirect elections which will functionally bind the extensive area into a unit while "refining" the voice of the people, and you will have a stable republican state.

This was the glad news that James Madison carried to Philadelphia. This was the theory which he claimed had made obsolete the necessity for the "mixed government" advocated by Hamilton and Adams. This was the message he gave to the world in the first *Federalist* paper he composed. His own scientific reading of history, ancient and modern, his experience with religious factions in Virginia, and above all his knowledge of the scientific axiom regarding man and society in the works of David Hume, ablest

---

[20] *Federalist,* X, p. 43.

British philosopher of his age, had served him and his country well. "Of all men, that distinguish themselves by memorable achievements, the first place of honour seems due to Legislators and founders of states, who transmit a system of laws and institutions to secure the peace, happiness, and liberty of future generations." (I, 127.)

VIII

Alexander Hamilton: Realist or Idealist?

INTRODUCTION

"Every day proves to me more and more, that this American world was not made for me." So Hamilton wrote to Gouverneur Morris in February 1802. Two and one half years later he was dead by the pistol of Aaron Burr.

In the century and a half since Hamilton's death, his reputation in "this American world" has gone through a cyclical rise and fall. To the men of his own generation, whether political friend or foe, his name and reputation were formidable and imposing; as Jefferson said, he was "a host unto himself." In the age of Jackson, with the emergence of populistic democracy, Hamilton and the ideas he stood for fell into eclipse. In the period from the end of the Civil War to the turn of the century, characterized by the triumph of industrial America and the protective tariff, the Hamiltonian tradition supplied a congenial rhetoric, though applied to an industrial order whose leaders Hamilton would have found quite out of his taste. "I hate money-making men," he once cryptically observed.

The whole climate of opinion of the early twentieth century, marked by the rise of the Progressive Movement, was antipathetic to the legacy of Hamilton's ideas. "A very great man, but not a great American," was the verdict of Woodrow Wilson. In the years between the great wars of this century, Hamilton was variously estimated by Hoover Republicans and Roosevelt New Dealers, the former approving Hamilton and the latter disapproving him. In our own day, with the triumph of a big superintending national government and the effort to implement a "realistic foreign policy," the tradition he stood for has come to seem a reinvigorated orthodoxy. His bicentenary celebrated in 1957—two years too late—gave stimulus to a substantial addition to Hamiltonian scholarship in the works of Broadus Mitchell, Louis Hacker, Leonard White, Hans Morgenthau, and others, to mention a few. A great project to edit and publish his writings has been set on foot under the general editorship of Harold C. Syrett.

The new scholarship has been generally favorable to Hamilton, but there have been dissentient voices, and his place has not been fixed even for our generation. He is an enigmatic political and social philosopher despite the apparent clarity of his clean, strong prose style.

The selections presented here are illustrative, though certainly not exhaustive, of the diversity of contemporary interpretation. Saul K. Padover's representation and estimation of Hamilton may be characterized as traditional and eclectic; Cecelia M. Kenyon's interpretation of Hamilton as "the Rousseau of the Right," as an idealist rather than a realist in his views of politics and society, is brilliantly novel and conflicts in a most marked degree with the Padover interpretation.

The Controversial Mr. Hamilton

Saul K. Padover

I

Of all the outstanding Founding Fathers, Alexander Hamilton is the one who has never been fully enshrined as a hero acceptable to all his countrymen. There are few if any divisions of opinion in regard to Washington or Franklin or Jefferson; these are widely accepted, although with varying degrees of admiration. But not so Hamilton. Admired for generations by conservatives (who perhaps did not always understand him), he has been consistently assaulted by liberals.

As late as 1948, nearly a century and a half after Hamilton's death, a distinguished historian found it necessary to complain that the name of Hamilton "still arouses choking emotions in the bosoms of all 'right thinkers' who confine their knowledge and thinking to the Anti-Federalist tradition." [1] In brief, as he was during his short and stormy life, so Hamilton has remained after a tragic death—a figure of paradox and controversy.

Much of the difficulty lies in Hamilton's character. There was something turbulent and explosive about him. Contemporaries were struck by his restlessness and lack of personal serenity. He gave the impression of a man who could not curb his feelings—or his tongue. "My heart," he once said to General Henry Knox, "has always been the master of my judgment." He could be sweet-tempered to some people and unbearably arrogant to others. On occasion he could be gentle and diplomatic, but more often he was ruthless and aggressive. The consistent pattern of Hamilton's character was one of outer unquietness and inner disharmony.

His life, although not, as we shall see, his basic ideas, reflected this internal imbalance. Deeply attached to his wife and family, he was, nevertheless, capable of an unsavory amorous adventure (which he admitted publicly). Scrupulously honest himself, he winked at the peculations of friends. Under lasting obligation to Washington, he made insulting and slighting remarks about the General. A bitter enemy of the "visionary" and "chimerical" Jefferson, he nevertheless helped him decisively in the election to the

From pp. 1–23 *The Mind of Alexander Hamilton,* arranged by Saul K. Padover. Copyright 1958 by Saul K. Padover. Reprinted with the permission of Harper & Row, Publishers, Incorporated.

[1] Charles A. Beard, *The Enduring Federalist,* 1948, p. 10.

Presidency in 1801. A humble-born British colonial, he openly sang the praises of Britain's aristocracy. A lifelong believer in monarchy as the best form of government, he fought magnificently for the adoption of the Federal Constitution. Filled with contempt for democracy, he gave the American Republic loyal and invaluable support. Rejecting dueling as unchristian, he permitted himself to be drawn into a duel that killed him. This by no means exhausts the list of paradoxes.

The judgment of contemporaries—especially political opponents—reflects awareness of Hamilton's inconsistencies, as well as, of course, his great gifts. Jefferson's final evaluation of his enemy, written fourteen years after Hamilton's death, has the merit of fairness. "Hamilton," he wrote (in 1818), "was, indeed, a singular character. Of acute understanding, disinterested, honest, and honorable in all private transactions, amiable in society, and duly valuing virtue in private life, yet so bewitched and perverted by the British example, as to be under thorough conviction that corruption was essential to the government of a nation."

James Madison, a milder critic, after paying tribute to Hamilton's "intellectual powers of the first order," made a similar point. "If," Madison said of his collaborator on *The Federalist*, "his theory of government deviated from the republican standard he had the candor to avow it, and the greater merit of cooperating faithfully in maturing and supporting a system which was not his choice." And John Quincy Adams, whose father was one of Hamilton's pet aversions (and vice versa), summarized the paradoxical character of John Adams' enemy in the following terms:

> [Hamilton's] talents were of the highest order, his ambition transcendent, and his disposition to intrigue irrepressible. His consciousness of talent was greater than its reality. . . . His valor was deliberate and undaunted; his experience in war not inconsiderable; the powers and resources of his mind extraordinary; his eloquence, both of speaking and writing, in the very first style of excellence; he had within him to a great degree that which subdues the minds of other men, perhaps the first of all qualities for the commander of an army. But he was of that class of characters which cannot bear a rival—haughty, overbearing, jealous, bitter and violent in his personal enmities, and little scrupulous of the means which he used against those who stood in the way of his ambition.

II

Hamilton's background helps to an understanding of his character. Psychologically, his birth and parentage must have left an ineradicable scar on his life. For, like William the Conqueror, Leonardo da Vinci, Erasmus, and many another famous man, Alexander Hamilton was born illegitimate.

There has been much confusion about Hamilton's early dates and parentage. Recent researchers, however, especially in the Danish State Archives at Copenhagen, have helped to clear up some obscure points. We now know, for example, that Hamilton was two years older than he claimed or perhaps knew. His mother died on February 19, 1768, and in that year the court, when it settled her small estate, noted that she had a son, Alexander, who was "thirteen years of age." If he was thirteen in 1768, then the year of his birth was 1755 instead of 1757, which is usually given in the history books. This year's celebration of Hamilton's 200th anniversary is thus two years late.

There is some obscurity about the early period of his life. What is indisputable is that he was born in Nevis, the smallest (sixty square miles) of the Leeward Islands in the British West Indies. Beyond that, the record is not full. His mother was Rachel Faucette, variously spelled as Faucitt, Fawcette, Fawcet, Fotzet; she was the daughter of an impecunious island family. Sometime about 1745, when Rachel was around sixteen, she married an older man named John Michael Levine—or Lawein or Leweine or Lavine or Lavien—said to be a Danish Jew. The marriage to Levine, who had a small plantation in nearby St. Croix, lasted about five years; after giving birth to a son, Peter, Mrs. Levine, at the age of around twenty-one, left her husband.

Sometime after abandoning her husband, Rachel Levine set up household with an itinerant Scotsman named James Hamilton, about whom not much is known, except that he was a drifter and a failure. Although without benefit of clergy, the ménage seemed to have been respectable and continued for a few years. Then James Hamilton, after having sired Alexander and one older boy, somehow drifted away, out of the family's life. On February 25, 1759, about four years after Alexander's birth, John Michael Levine sued his wife Rachel for divorce in the court of St. Croix. Levine charged that she had "absented herself from him for nine years and gone elsewhere, where she has begotten several illegitimate children." Rachel Levine—legally she was never Mrs. Hamilton—thus accused of desertion and adultery, did not contest the suit and, on June 25, 1759, the court granted the divorce but, under Danish law, denied Rachel the right to remarry. Alexander, therefore, could not be made legitimate.

After the death of his mother, the thirteen-year-old Alexander was for a while supported by relatives. Then he entered the counting house of a local businessman named Nicholas Cruger, and by the time he was fifteen was in charge of the establishment. But Alexander was too proud and ambitious to be satisfied with a clerkship in a colonial shop. At the age of fourteen he wrote to his intimate young friend, Edward Stevens:

> To confess my weakness, Ned, my ambition is prevalent, so that I contemn the grovelling condition of a clerk or the like, to which my fortune, etc., condemns me, and would willingly risk my life, though not my character, to exalt my station. I am confident, Ned, that my

youth excludes me from any hopes of immediate preferment; nor do
I desire it; but I mean to prepare the way for futurity.

In this youthful letter we see the germs of the later Hamilton—pride,
ambition, desire for place and prestige, iron determination to achieve his
goals. While clerking, he read incessantly, taught himself the indispensable
art of disciplined writing, and learned to speak French fluently. *"Il parle
et écrit parfaitement bien la langue,"* a French traveler, the Marquis de
Chastellux, said of him after he met him in the United States. This knowledge of French not only marked him as an educated gentleman, but was to
be useful to Hamilton when he had to deal with Lafayette and other French
officers when he was aide to General Washington, whose knowledge of that
tongue was close to zero.

Soon young Hamilton was ready to break out of the narrow confines of
his insular world. Sometime in September or October, 1772, he sailed from
St. Croix to Boston, whence he went to New York. Apart from a little
money given to him by his aunts on the island, his most precious material
possessions were letters of introduction to influential Americans. Among
the most important of them was one from his teacher Hugh Knox, a Pres-
byterian clergyman who had studied at Princeton, to William Livingston,
member of a prominent New Jersey family, later governor of his state and
a delegate, as was Hamilton, to the Constitutional Convention in 1787.

Hamilton was seventeen when he came to America, a frail boy of small
stature, reddish-haired and blue-eyed. He was full of fire, precocious, energetic, and burning with desire to make his name and place in this new
world. After a year at boarding school in New Jersey, he entered King's
College (now Columbia University) in New York. King's was not much of
a college in those days. It had a total faculty of three, one of whom, Myles
Cooper, was the president; another, Samuel Clossy, taught in the medical
school; and the third, John Vardill, taught nearly everything, including
rhetoric, philosophy, theology, disputation, and what is today known as
economics and sociology or their equivalents. The underlying ideas of the
curriculum at King's College, as was also the case in the rest of America, were
natural law and Old Testament ethics. These were given as "self-evident
truths." Central to this universe was the enshrinement of property and its
institutions as virtually sacred to man in civilized society. There is no reason to assume that Hamilton, then or later, questioned for a moment the
immutability of those principles.

Hamilton did not require much intellectual guidance or help at King's
College. He was, to say the least, as quick, as perceptive, as articulate as any
of his elders at the college. A mind of immense discipline and retentive
power, he read voraciously and with a concentration that was oblivious to
everything except the world of hard facts and logical construction. His
brain stored everything away in an orderly fashion, ready for use when
the time came; thus in later years the busy Hamilton's utterances and writ-

ings impressed people by their scholarship. He sharpened his mind to become an instrument of marvelous precision. He learned to express his thoughts in a lean and muscular style, without subtlety or adornment. In his type of mental structure there was no room for originality or the exploration of new avenues of thought or for questioning of major premises. Hamilton acquired his basic ideas early in life and he never changed them. Blunt, tough, and practical, he had no understanding for dreamers, visionaries, or imprecise idealists.

At nineteen, after a year at King's College, Hamilton was ready for a life of action. This was the year 1774, when the colonies were on the threshold of the great crisis that was to lead to war and, ultimately, independence. Young Hamilton entered upon the historic scene in an America that was in a state of agitation and uncertainty. Although antagonized by British imperial policy, the leading men in the colonies did not yet quite know what course to pursue. Few as yet thought of complete independence from Great Britain; but at bottom they no longer felt themselves to be Englishmen. They were something new, something they did not yet altogether understand. There was no American nation—only undercurrents of nationalism. But the crisis was rapidly evolving and, as Hamilton soon found out, men had to take sides. The young man from the island of Nevis promptly joined what is known as the "popular cause," that is, the side that challenged the absolute authority of the British crown over the colonies and that was ready, if necessary, to cut the umbilical cord with the mother country.

Hamilton began to contribute political articles to Holt's *New York Journal, or General Advertiser* in 1774. At the end of the year, when he was not yet twenty, he published his first important work, a major contribution to the literature of the American Revolution. This consisted of two pamphlets, *A Full Vindication of the Measures of the Congress from the Calumnies of their Enemies* (14,000 words) and *The Farmer Refuted* (35,000 words). Following the fashion of the times, they were written anonymously as answers to widely read articles by Samuel Seabury, who, under the pen name of "A Westchester Farmer," eloquently defended the British colonial system. Hamilton's polemics against Seabury were so brilliantly conceived and maturely reasoned that contemporaries, when they learned the name of the author, could not believe that they had before them the work of a stripling just out of college.

III

When hostilities broke out between the colonies and Great Britain, Hamilton enlisted and became a captain of artillery. He attracted the attention of Nathanael Greene, one of the ablest generals of the Revolutionary War, who in turn introduced him to George Washington, who was having trouble with incompetent adjutants. As usual, Hamilton made a great impression and in March, 1777, the commander in chief of the American Revolutionary forces appointed him aide-de-camp with the rank of lieutenant colonel. Of General Washington's seven aides-de-camp, Hamilton was by far the best equipped—he wrote many of the General's important military papers and letters—and certainly the one most appreciated by the commander. Despite his icy reserve and aloofness, General Washington referred affectionately to the youthful Colonel Hamilton as "my boy."

It is a commentary on Hamilton's personality that he did not, then or ever, reciprocate Washington's affection and admiration. Indeed, Hamilton was one of the few contemporaries and collaborators of the General who was unimpressed by his true greatness. Hamilton never showed any understanding of the paramount quality that made Washington so impressive a figure, namely, the General's towering character, a mixture of unshakable strength, balance, dignity, and fairness. Hamilton, the insecurely born, seems to have had an instinctive dislike of Washington, the big man who so easily loomed as a father image to so many people. "Our dispositions," Hamilton frankly admitted, "are the opposites of each other." The two were in sharp contrast. The tall General was slow-minded, deliberate, shy, inarticulate in speech, modest, and without any sparkle; the little colonel was quick-witted, intellectually arrogant, self-assured, and brilliant. Washington was apparently unaware that his young aide-de-camp harbored anything but friendly feelings toward him; he continued to respect and admire the younger man throughout his life.

After about four years as aide-de-camp, Colonel Hamilton broke with Washington. The decision to do so was not sudden; it had been in his mind for some time. Hamilton had long been fretting at what he considered his position as an underling. In view of his insatiable ambition, it is also possible that he was jealous and resentful of Washington's high military position and reputation. As a matter of fact, Hamilton, who fancied himself fit to command armies, secretly disparaged Washington's military abilities and his knowledge of the art of war. The twenty-six-year-old colonel, thirsting for martial glory which he could not attain so long as he was chained to a desk at headquarters, soon found an opportunity abruptly to leave "the General's family," as he put it. The story, as related by Hamilton to his father-in-law, General Philip Schuyler (whose daughter Elizabeth he married on December 14, 1780), is self-revealing.

One day in February, 1781, at headquarters in New Windsor, as Washington passed Hamilton on the stairs, the General said that he wanted to see him. Hamilton replied he would do so immediately, as soon as he had delivered something to his fellow adjutant, Colonel Tench Tilghman. On his way to Washington's room, Hamilton was stopped by General Lafayette and the two young officer friends had a brief conversation. Suddenly General Washington appeared at the head of the stairs and spoke up angrily:

"Colonel Hamilton, you have kept me waiting at the head of the stairs these ten minutes. I must tell you, sir, you treat me with disrespect."

Hamilton, sure that his conversation with Lafayette had lasted only about two minutes, snapped back: "I am not conscious of it, sir; but since you have thought it necessary to tell me so, we part."

"Very well, Sir," said Washington, "if it be your choice."

An hour later, Colonel Tilghman came with a conciliatory message from General Washington, assuring Hamilton of his "great confidence" in him and explaining that the regrettable incident "could not have happened but in a moment of passion." Would Colonel Hamilton forget the whole thing and return to his duties? Hamilton adamantly refused. He would not only not resume his post but also would not see the General. He was through, he said.

"Perhaps," he explained to his father-in-law, "you may think I was precipitate in rejecting the overture made by the General. . . . I assure you, my dear Sir, it was not the effect of resentment; it was the deliberate result of maxims I had long formed for the government of my own conduct." He went on to say that he disliked the General and that for the last three years he neither felt nor professed any friendship for him. He considered Washington merely a connection that might be useful. "He was an Egis," Hamilton was to say cold-bloodedly after Washington's death in 1799, "very essential to me."

> I always disliked the office of aide-de-camp [Hamilton continued his explanation] as having in it a kind of personal dependence. I refused to serve in this capacity with two major-generals at an early period of the war. Infected, however, with the enthusiasm of the time, an idea of the General's character, *which experience taught me to be unfounded,* overcame my scruples, and induced me to accept his invitation to enter into his family. It was not long before I discovered he was neither remarkable for delicacy nor good temper. . . . I was always determined, if there should ever happen a breach between us, never to consent to an accommodation.

Hamilton's petulance and antipathy found no responsive echo in George Washington. Although the younger man never showed the General any warmth or affection, Washington continued to be unfailingly generous toward Hamilton. Three-quarters of a year after the breach between them, in the autumn of 1781, Hamilton, yearning for a chance to distinguish himself on the field of battle before the war was over, asked General Washington to permit him to lead a small storming party during the siege of Yorktown. The General gave him his chance—and Hamilton had his brief moment of military glory, which he felt he needed for the record. After the Revolutionary War, when Hamilton was rising rapidly as a prominent lawyer and politician in New York, he asked Washington in Mount Vernon to scotch a rumor spread by his enemies that he, Hamilton, had "palmed" himself off on Washington as aide-de-camp and had been dismissed from his service. Washington promptly gave him his clearance, saying, "I do . . . explicitly declare that both charges are entirely unfounded" and that "quitting was altogether . . . your own choice."

As President, he appointed the youthful Hamilton to the second highest position in his Cabinet and gave him stanch support throughout a stormy administration. When the time came for Washington to retire from public life, it was to Hamilton that he turned, in 1796, for help in the drafting of the Farewell Address. And in 1798, when war with France seemed imminent and the country was mobilizing for it, George Washington used his immense influence to have President John Adams appoint Hamilton major general and second in command, a post the latter hungrily coveted and clamored for, thereby by-passing and antagonizing older and more experienced officers. Yes, as Hamilton wrote to the widowed Martha Washington early in 1800, her husband had always been useful to him.

IV

But the usefulness worked both ways. Just as Washington had been essential to Hamilton's career, so Hamilton was to the early history of the United States. What greatness there was in Hamilton came out in the years of the formation of the Constitution and the first Washington administration. It was the period when the American national structure was built, and Hamilton was beyond doubt one of its indispensable architects. Here, paradoxically enough, his foreign birth played a not inconsiderable role, for it gave him the kind of perspective most native Americans still lacked. For the leading men of the day did not yet think of themselves as citizens of America. They were, rather, Virginians, Pennsylvanians, New Yorkers, Carolinians, and so forth; their loyalties and roots were in their native states. It was therefore with some difficulty that they could identify with a political unit larger than the state; when they finally moved from the native state to the union of states, they did so slowly, reluctantly, and with many grave reservations.

Not so Hamilton. He had no native roots in America. He was not emotionally attached to any single state. He could not, indeed, understand how anybody could have strong attachments to a comparatively small political entity such as Rhode Island or Delaware or New Jersey or, for that matter, New York. To his logical mind, it made no sense to continue the existence of separate and independent states when, instead, they could combine and transform themselves into a powerful "American empire," as he liked to call it. He saw the vision of such a union from the beginning. As a young staff officer during the Revolution, he had firsthand experience with the shocking incompetence that prevailed under the loose government of the Congress. His sense of order was outraged by the political weakness, the local intrigues, the disunity, the parochial patriotism of the Confederation. Referring to the self-oriented states, he wrote early in the Revolutionary War: "This pernicious mistake must be corrected."

And so he became one of the prime agents in the movement for an effective federal union. He had two main objectives. The first was the creation of a united nation, which, he frankly hoped, would eliminate the individual states. The second was the establishment of a centralized government with power to defend property and to maintain order in the face of potentially turbulent radical forces. Both of these goals were more difficult of achievement than would appear to a twentieth-century observer. For Hamilton was aware, and painfully aware, that public opinion in general was against a strong national union and that the Revolutionary War had unleashed popular forces that were outspokenly hostile to any rule by the rich and the aristocratic.

The delegates to the Constitutional Convention, which sat in Philadelphia from May to September, 1787, consisted mostly of the well-to-do; they shared Hamilton's awareness of the prevailing anti-authoritarian temper of the American people, which they all dreaded. Like Hamilton, the majority of them—only thirty-nine of the fifty-five chosen delegates attended the sessions more or less regularly—were conservative in their economics and politics. With exceptions, they distrusted the people, as did Hamilton, who was more blunt and candid than most.

A fellow delegate, William Pierce of Georgia, has left the following sketch of Hamilton at the Convention:

> Colo. Hamilton is deservedly celebrated for his talents. He is . . . a finished Scholar. To a clear and strong judgment he unites the ornaments of fancy. . . . He is rather a convincing Speaker, than a blazing Orator. Colo. Hamilton requires time to think—he enquires into every part of his subject with the searchings of phylosophy, and when he comes forward he comes highly charged with interesting matter, there is no skimming over the surface of a subject with him, he must sink to the bottom to see what foundation it rests on. . . . His eloquence is not so diffusive as to trifle with the senses, but he rambles just enough to strike and keep up the attention. He is . . . of small stature, and lean. His manners are tinctured with stiffness, and sometimes with a degree of vanity that is highly disagreeable.

During the first weeks of the convention, Hamilton was mostly a silent member. He listened to various proposals, including those that provided for a mere patching up of the Articles of Confederation, instead of a new Constitution. He was increasingly depressed as the delegates, still state-oriented, at first refused to face boldly the central problem that confronted them, namely, the creation of a strong national union with a totally new Constitution.

Hamilton finally lost patience with what he thought was mere shilly-shallying and one day he rose and delivered a major speech in which he cut across all those currents of doubt and bluntly focused attention on the political realities as he saw them. James Madison, in his journal of the Convention, thus briefly summarized Hamilton's long and brilliant speech:

> This view of the subject almost led him [Hamilton] to despair that a republican government could be established over so great an extent [of American territory]. He was sensible, at the same time, that it would be unwise to propose one of any other form. In his private opinion, he had no scruple in declaring . . . that the British Government was the best in the world; and that he doubted much whether any thing short of it would do in America. He hoped gentlemen of different opinions would bear with him in this, and begged them to recollect the change of opinion on this subject which had taken place, and was still going on. It was once thought that the power of Congress was amply sufficient to secure the ends of their institution. The error was now seen by everyone. The members most tenacious of republicanism . . . were as loud as any in declaiming against the vices of democracy. This progress of the public mind led him to anticipate the time when others . . . would join in the praise bestowed by Mr. Necker on the British Constitution, namely, that it is the only government in the world, "which unites public strength with individual security."

Much of Hamilton's reputation as a "reactionary" derives from this particular speech at the Convention. In the course of it, and secure in the feeling that he was protected by the secrecy that covered the proceedings and debates, he uttered many sentiments which, while familiar doctrine to his upper-class contemporaries, are shocking to democratic American ears today. It was in the Constitutional Convention that Hamilton used the expression: "Take mankind in general, they are vicious." He also remarked: "The voice of the people has been said to be the voice of God; and, however generally this maxim has been quoted and believed, it is not true to fact. The people are turbulent and changing; they seldom judge or determine right."

These are, indeed, extreme statements, uttered in the heat of oratory. As Martin Van Buren comments in his *Autobiography,* Hamilton, "absorbed in the egotism and . . . vanity which have been the lot of great orators in all ages," blindly threw himself "headlong upon the Convention and recklessly proclaimed sentiments at variance with . . . what experience has since shown to be the riveted feeling of the American people." Standing by themselves, Hamilton's utterances in the Convention would condemn him as a hopelessly narrow politician, unworthy of consideration as a leader of men in a republic. But in proper context they merely underline a well-reasoned and consistently held political philosophy, although one that was voiced without tact and without regard for general public opinion.

One may reject Hamilton's view of mankind and his theory of political society as too Hobbesian and needlessly myopic; but one must grant him that he did have a clearly defined philosophy which had the merit of candor and which he had the courage to proclaim and defend. In a negative way, Hamilton may perhaps be given some credit for the fact that his outspoken antidemocratic views, by irritating contemporaries who believed in democracy, provoked them to a truly vigorous and searching defense of their democratic faith. This can certainly be said of Jefferson, who was not infrequently angered by Hamilton's candidly and repeatedly uttered contempt for democracy, which he labeled a "poison." Jefferson could barely control his aversion when he heard Hamilton, at his own dinner table (as he relates in his diary, April, 1791), proclaim that the British monarchical-aristocratic system, precisely *because it was corrupt,* was the "most perfect government which ever existed."

How did so superlatively intelligent a man as Hamilton justify such a view? He did so on the basis of what he conceived to be psychology. His political philosophy, which also shaped his economic principles and policies, was based on a firmly held view of human nature. Indeed, it is not possible to understand his political beliefs without a knowledge of his psychological assumptions. For central to Hamilton's thought was the conception of man as a corrupt and selfish animal, motivated by the worst passions, such as greed and selfishness. "The passions . . . of avarice, ambition, interest," he told his fellow delegates at the Constitutional Convention, ". . . govern most individuals, and all public bodies." Not a tactful observation under the circumstances, but a truly Hamiltonian one!

Here, of course, is the crucial idea on which Hamilton parted company with democrats, then and forever. For underlying the democratic belief is confidence in the virtue and potentialities of the average human being, as well as, according to the Jeffersonians, in his perfectibility, through education and other means. Without such an assumption about human nature, democracy, or any other polity that calls for even a limited amount of self-government, becomes impossible and, in fact, a contradiction in terms. For how can the corrupt and the selfish be expected to rule, with any prospect of success or stability, over others who are no less corrupt and selfish? For that matter, how can *any* government endure if *all* people are morally rotten? Did not an assumption of total human depravity lead to the pigsty type of government?

As Jefferson, probably thinking of Hamilton and his followers, put it in his First Inaugural Address: "Sometimes it is said that man cannot be trusted with the government of himself. Can he, then, be trusted with the government of others? Or have we found angels in the forms of kings to govern him? Let history answer this question."

Hamilton, it must be said, was consistent and logical in his views on government. Since human passions were a fact of nature and could not be altered, he proposed that they be recognized as such and harnessed for useful political ends. It was, he said, "a principle of human nature" that political institutions must be founded on "men's interests." He could, therefore, see no other way to build a successful government except through an appeal to what he called "avarice and ambition."

> Political writers [he argued] . . . have established it as a maxim, that, in contriving any system of government, and fixing the several checks and controls of the constitution, *every man ought to be supposed a knave;* and to have no other end, in all his actions, but private interest. By this *interest we must govern him;* and, by means of it, make him co-operate to public good, notwithstanding his insatiable avarice and ambition. Without this, we shall in vain boast of the advantages of any constitution.

Although his generalizations about human nature and behavior applied to all men, Hamilton, nevertheless, made a distinction between the few and the many, between the "rich and well born" and the mass of the people. The many, he said, were "turbulent and uncontrollable," driven by nothing but blind passion, and hence too imprudent to be entrusted with governmental power. The few, on the other hand, while also motivated by greed and selfishness, had enough sense and education to judge matters and, in consequence, could be depended upon to realize that their own best interests lay in using political power responsibly. It was not that he had any special affection for or illusion about the wealthy—"I hate money making men," he once blurted out in a letter to an intimate friend —but that he thought they were a safer depository of power than the equally base and selfish common people. Having no illusions about what motivated the greedy upper classes, Hamilton suggested that their loyalty to the new government be won through special privileges and economic advantages—through what he called "a dispensation of . . . regular honors and emoluments."

More than that. He proposed that the rich be given "a distinct, permanent share in the government," to serve as an unalterable check on whatever democratic institutions might develop in the future. To keep the "imprudence of democracy" in leash, he advocated the establishment of a permanent Senate and an Executive for life. Both were to be chosen indirectly, through electors or governors in the states (if there must be individual states), from the ranks of the economically superior individuals in the community.

Would not such a lifelong Executive be a monarch to all intents and purposes? That, countered Hamilton, was a matter of definition; if, he argued, you choose an Executive for, say, seven years, what have you? You have a seven-year monarch, but still a monarch, or whatever you care to call him. So what difference did it make, particularly if he be an excellent man and on his good behavior?

Again, was not a Senate chosen for life too dangerous? If human nature was as depraved and avaricious as Hamilton said it was, how could a handful of senators be safely entrusted with unrestrained power? Not so, said Hamilton. Precisely because they were assured of lifelong positions, special privileges, and conspicuous honors, the senators would have no motive for corruption or temptation for radical changes. In other words, give this elite everything and it would have no reason to ask for anything more. This was likewise true of the lifelong Executive. Assure his position for ever and remunerate him richly, and he will give you loyal service. Such, Hamilton pointed out, had been the experience of Great Britain, with its marvelous system of Lords and hereditary crown. As he told his fellow delegates at the Convention (June 18, 1787):

> The British . . . House of Lords is a most noble institution. Having nothing to hope for by a change, and a sufficient interest by means of their property, in being faithful to the national interest, they form a permanent barrier against every pernicious innovation, whether . . . on the part of the crown or Commons. No temporary Senate will have firmness enough to answer the purpose. . . .
>
> As to the Executive . . . no good one could be established on republican principles. . . . The English model was the only good one on this subject. The hereditary interest of the King was so interwoven with that of the nation, and his personal emoluments so great, that he was placed above the danger of being corrupted.

But would the American people tolerate a class government? Public opinion, Hamilton admitted, was hostile to anything resembling hereditary rule or domination by the wealthy. He felt, however, that once the people realized that it was to their advantage to have an elite in office, their hostility would melt away. Furthermore, he said, the mass of the people would not be completely powerless or totally disfranchised, since there was a general feeling—which he shared, although with reluctance—that, as a sop to the people, at least the lower legislative chamber should be popularly elected. The House of Representatives, with its periodic and frequent elections, would thus give the common people a certain amount of control over their rulers. So what reason would the masses have to complain?

A popularly chosen lower chamber, Hamilton knew, raised two important questions. One was that the congressmen elected by the people might be dangerous and irresponsible democrats. The other was that the House of Representatives might not truly represent the various classes in the country and hence would lead to discontent. Hamilton argued that the chances were that, even in the democratic lower chamber, the representatives would come from the ranks of the well-to-do and the educated. Would such upper-class individuals truly be able to represent, and hence satisfy, the less privileged people? Yes, said Hamilton. Only the rich and the educated, he was convinced, could know what was good for the others and, therefore, could best represent them for their common interest. This is the way he stated his argument in *The Federalist* (No. 35):

> The representative body . . . will be composed of landholders, merchants, and men of the learned professions. But where is the danger that the interests and feelings of the different classes of citizens will not be understood or attended to by these three descriptions of men? Will not the landholder know and feel whatever will promote or insure the interest of landed property? And will he not, from his own interest in that species of property, be sufficiently prone to resist every attempt to prejudice or encumber it? Will not the merchant understand and be disposed to cultivate, as far as may be proper, the interests of the mechanic and manufacturing arts, to which his commerce is so nearly allied? Will not the man of the learned profession, who will feel a neutrality to rivalships between the different branches of industry, be likely to prove an impartial arbiter between them, ready to promote either, so far as it shall appear to him conducive to the general interests of the society?

Who, Hamilton asked, was in a better position to understand the problems and feelings of the people as a whole than the individual who has had a chance to travel and to study? The impecunious and the uneducated did not, of necessity, possess an enlarged view and hence could not be expected to be as good a representative as the one who had opportunities to widen his intellectual and political horizon.

> Is the man [Hamilton asked rhetorically] whose situation leads to extensive inquiry and information less likely to be a competent judge of their [national problems] nature, extent, and foundation than one whose observation does not travel beyond the circle of his neighbors and acquaintances? Is it not natural that a man who is a candidate for the favor of the people, and who is dependent on the suffrages of his fellow-citizens for the continuance of his public honors, should take care to inform himself of their dispositions and inclinations, and should be willing to allow them their proper degree of influence upon his conduct? This dependence, and the necessity of being bound . . . by the laws to which he gives his assent, are the true, and they are the strong chords of sympathy between the representative and the constituent.

These Hamiltonian ideas, forming in their sum a kind of aristocratic republicanism, were not, in the last analysis, acceptable to the Constitutional Convention. While the majority of the delegates agreed with much of what Hamilton said and believed, virtually all of them being members of the well-to-do and professional classes, they yet sensed that public opinion would reject a government from which the common people would be, as Hamilton desired, to a large extent excluded. And, as Hamilton's Federalists were to discover to their sorrow a decade later, the "rich and well born" were too few in numbers to impose their will permanently on the sprawling, restless, energetic, independent, rapidly growing population of farmers, frontiersmen, and workers.

Unlike Hamilton, the delegates to the Constitutional Convention were mostly native-born, with roots and relations in their home communities; hence they were able almost instinctively to understand, without necessarily sharing, the outlooks and feelings of their neighbors. The delegates knew that there were limits to American tolerance and patience, and that the Hamiltonian proposals for the creation of what in effect would have amounted to a permanent ruling class went beyond anything that a fiercely individualistic people would tolerate. The Convention, moreover, contained a small group of what today would be called liberals—among them such personalities as Benjamin Franklin, James Wilson, and, to a lesser degree, James Madison—who warned their colleagues not to push things to an extreme. As Franklin once dryly reminded the delegates, it was the common people who had fought and died in the Revolutionary War. If they were good enough to fight for independence, were they not also good enough to have a voice in their own government?

Fortunately for all concerned, Hamilton was not present during some of the most crucial debates at the Convention. For about two months, during July and August, he was absent from Philadelphia. Sensing that he could not sway the delegates, he had left the Convention in a mood of near despair. "I own to you, Sir," he wrote to the Convention's presiding officer, General Washington, on his way back to New York, "that I am seriously and deeply distressed at the aspect of counsels which prevailed when I left Philadelphia. I fear that we shall let slip the golden opportunity of rescuing the American empire from disunion, anarchy, and misery."

In his absence, however, the delegates abated their antidemocratic position and, despite serious doubts, agreed to a number of compromises which, in their total, added up to the granting of a considerable share of potential power to the people. This was not to Hamilton's liking; in his eyes, the Constitution's democratic features—the periodic election of the President and the senators, for example—made it fundamentally defective. He found it so when he returned to Philadelphia, as the Constitution was ready for signing in September. But, as a practical man, the delegate from New York signed it.

> General Hamilton [his friend Gouverneur Morris recalled years after Hamilton signed the Constitution] hated republican government, because he confounded it with democratical government, and he detested the latter, because he believed it must end in despotism, and be, in the meantime, destructive to public morality. . . . His study of ancient

history impressed on his mind a conviction that democracy ending in tyranny is, while it lasts, a cruel and oppressive domination.

Why, then, did Hamilton sign a Constitution that called for the creation of a republican government for which he had the deepest distrust? He did so because, first, it was better than nothing, and, second, because the upper classes might yet be able to shape it to their own ends. He hoped that in some future crisis, war, for example, this "frail and worthless fabric," as he later called the Constitution, might be transformed into a powerful instrument that would help the ruling elements of the country curb the centrifugal and democratic forces then at large in America.

V

At this point, in September, 1787, when the Constitution was made public and was submitted to the states for ratification, began Hamilton's great services to the United States. In a short span of some eight years, from 1787 to 1795, his contributions to America were to be of paramount importance. In that period of time, he was pre-eminent in the fight for the adoption of the Constitution, wrote the majority of the *Federalist* papers in its defense, and, finally, as the first Secretary of the Treasury, laid the durable foundations of the fiscal and economic policies of the United States. Although he lived for nearly another decade after his resignation from President Washington's Cabinet in January, 1795, his great work was over by the time he was forty.

The Constitution, so patiently and painfully hammered out in Philadelphia during a period of sixteen weeks, met with a storm of opposition throughout the country as soon as it was made public. Just as Hamilton did not like it because it was too democratic, so the American people in general objected to it because it was not democratic enough. It was this widespread popular hostility to the Constitution that contributed to the nerving and steeling of Hamilton's will in its defense; for clearly an instrument so detested by the masses must after all have something good in it.

Hamilton threw himself into the championship of the Constitution with characteristic energy and unmatched brilliance. A proper appreciation of his achievements in that crucial struggle, however, calls for an understanding of the main currents of opinion that swirled and eddied around the controverted document.

Three major streams of opinion can be discerned. They may be described, for the sake of simplicity, as conservative, popular, and liberal. The first gave the Constitution wholehearted support. The second was hostile. The third had reservations.

The conservative viewpoint, the position taken by Hamilton's rich and well-born, ranged from total approval because it was a perfect instrument to endorsement because it was the best under the circumstances. The whole position was perhaps best summarized by George Washington, when he said: "The Constitution . . . is not free from imperfections, but there are as few radical defects in it as could well be expected."

Popular opinion showed opposition to the Constitution on two main grounds. First, by providing for a central government, it threatened the independence of the individual states, which were regarded as bulwarks of personal liberty; second, the proposed new federal system appeared to be an instrument of the rich for the oppression of the poor, particularly since the latter were not represented at the Convention. Patrick Henry was the most eloquent exponent of this viewpoint. In his violent, and nearly successful, attack on the Constitution in the Virginia Ratification Convention, Henry described it as "extremely pernicious, impolitic and dangerous." Others argued that the Constitution would "take away all we have—all our property"; that it contained "no proper restriction of power"; that it was "founded on the principles of monarchy"; and that it was "like a mad horse" that would run away with its rider. As one opponent said in the New York State Constitutional Convention, anybody who trusted this newfangled Constitution was like a man getting on a horse without a bridle; he would "justly be deemed a mad man, and deserve to have his neck broken."

Finally, there was the liberal opposition. This group, while granting that the Constitution contained a number of good features, objected to the absence of a Bill of Rights. The Constitution, the liberals said, provided safeguards for the protection of property but not for liberty—an oversight which, by the way, aroused the most hostility and which in the end forced its defenders to promise a Bill of Rights at the first opportunity. The liberal viewpoint was most articulately voiced by Jefferson, who, in a famous letter to his friend James Madison (December 20, 1787), wrote:

> I like much the general idea of framing a government, which should go on of itself. . . . I like the organization of the government into legislative, judiciary and executive. I like the power given the legislature to levy taxes. . . . I approve the greater House being chosen by the people directly. . . . I am captivated by the compromise of the opposite claims of the great and little States. . . . There are other good things. . . .
>
> I will now tell you what I do not like. First, the omission of a Bill of Rights, providing clearly, and without the aid of sophism, for freedom of religion, freedom of the press, protection against standing armies, restriction of monopolies, the eternal and unremitting force of the habeas corpus laws, and trials by jury. . . . To say . . . that a Bill of Rights was not necessary, because all is reserved in the case of the general government which is not given . . . is surely a *gratis dictum.* . . . It would have been much more just and wise to have concluded the other way . . . and to have established general right instead of general wrong. Let me add that a Bill of Rights is what the

people are entitled to against every government on earth . . . and what no just government should refuse, or rest on inferences.

Hamilton was acutely aware of all these voices of approval, hostility, and criticism; and in one of the great tours de force in the history of political thought, he faced them head on. He lost no time in plunging into the national debate on the subject. About two weeks after the Constitution was signed in Philadelphia, he published, in the New York *Independent Journal* of October 2, 1787, the first of the famous articles in its defense. The series continued, in the *Journal* and in other New York publications, until April, 1788, in which year all the articles, including those written by Hamilton's collaborators, John Jay and James Madison, were published in book form under the title of *The Federalist*.

Of the eighty-five *Federalist* papers, Hamilton wrote fifty-one by himself and three in collaboration with Madison. The authorship of twelve is uncertain; they were written either by Hamilton or by Madison. In any case, the bulk of the contributions were Hamilton's.[2]

This is not the place to laud the virtues of *The Federalist*. The work has been sufficiently and rightly praised by many others in the past. Written in the heat of the campaign for the ratification of the Constitution, and designed as a polemic against its critics, *The Federalist* has, nevertheless, become not only an American classic but also a major contribution to the world's literature of political science. In its searching and far-ranging analysis of the principles of free government, as well as of the mechanics of republicanism in general, *The Federalist* has probably no equal in any language. "It is," Chancellor James Kent said of it in his *Commentaries on American Law* (Vol. I, 1826), "equally admirable in the depth of its wisdom, the comprehensiveness of its views, the sagacity of its reflections, and the fearlessness, patriotism, candor, simplicity, and elegance, with which its truths are uttered and recommended."

Considering Hamilton's deep-rooted prejudices against democracy and republicanism, it is ironic to reflect that in *The Federalist* he wrote what is probably still the best and most powerfully reasoned defense of the institution of free government. His *Federalist* essays show unusual moderation and a profound grasp of republicanism, if not democracy, the latter of which, he argued, was embodied in the Constitution since, in the last analysis, it derived its power from the people. In pleading that the Constitution be given a chance, Hamilton showed that he was capable of rising above personal bias to statesmanlike heights.

Hamilton threw himself into the battle for the Constitution not because

---

[2] *By Hamilton:* Nos. 1, 6–9, 11–13, 15–17, 21–36, 59–61, 65–85; *by Hamilton and Madison:* Nos. 18–20; *by Hamilton or Madison:* Nos. 49–58, 62–63.

Of the rest of the nineteen papers, Madison wrote fourteen (Nos. 10, 14, 37–48), and Jay five (Nos. 2–5, 64).

he loved republicanism but because he hated anarchy. He was revolted by the prevailing disunity and by the, to him, senseless pretensions to independence on the part of the thirteen individual states. Rejection of the Constitution, he was convinced, would not lead to a better one at some future date, but to chaos and possibly military dictatorship. Thus the great opportunity to create a free and powerful nation, which was, he said, America's destiny, would be forever lost. In his final plea for the adoption of the Constitution, Hamilton, citing David Hume on the desirability of moderation in political affairs, wrote in the concluding paragraph of the last (No. 85) *Federalist* paper:

> These judicious reflections contain a lesson of moderation to all the sincere lovers of the Union, and ought to put them upon their guard against hazarding anarchy, civil war, a perpetual alienation of the States from each other, and perhaps the military despotism of a victorious demagogue. . . . It may be in me a defect of political fortitude, but I acknowledge that I cannot entertain an equal tranquillity with those who affect to treat the dangers of a longer continuance in our present situation as imaginary. A nation without a national government, is, in my view, an awful spectacle. The establishment of a Constitution, in time of profound peace, by the voluntary consent of a whole people, is a prodigy, to the completion of which I look forward with trembling anxiety. . . . I dread the more the consequences of new attempts, because I know that powerful individuals, in this and in other States, are enemies to a general national government in every possible shape.

While the *Federalist* papers were coming out, friends of the Constitution, perhaps strengthened and inspired by Hamilton's writings, won ratification victories in seven states. Delaware, Pennsylvania, and New Jersey ratified in December, 1787; Georgia and Connecticut, in January, 1788; Massachusetts and Maryland, in February and April. Two more states were needed to make up the nine required to put the Constitution into effect. Of the remaining six states, some, like the Carolinas, had too small a population to be politically potent, and others, like Rhode Island, were hostile to the Constitution; the latter, indeed, did not ratify until long after the Federal Government was established. Everything, therefore, now depended upon the two most populous and influential States, Virginia and New York. Rejection of the Constitution there would have been a disaster.

For a while it did look as if both pivotal states, where the Ratification Conventions met in June, 1788, would turn down the Constitution; and Hamilton, who kept in contact with Madison in Virginia, was filled with anxiety at the outcome of the contest. After a sharp struggle, on June 25, thanks largely to the eloquence of Madison and the prestige of Washington, the Constitution squeezed through the Virginia Convention by the narrow vote of 89 to 79. Now it was up to New York—and to Alexander Hamilton.

The situation in New York State was bad, and Hamilton girded himself for what was, beyond a doubt, the most important battle of his political career. For New York opinion was inimical to the Constitution, and the state's Ratification Convention, which met at Poughkeepsie, reflected this hostility. "The anti-Federal party," Hamilton informed Madison in a mood of unhappiness and pessimism, "have a majority of two thirds in the Convention, and . . . about four sevenths in the community." Of the sixty-five delegates, only nineteen were known to be willing to vote for the Constitution; forty-six were opposed to it. Dreading that nonadoption would lead to "disunion and chaos," Hamilton took on the seemingly hopeless task of winning over the hostile delegates. For seven days, between June 20 and June 28, he poured himself out in a torrent of oratory, logic, and political analysis so formidable that his audience was dazzled and overcome. It was not a vain effort. In the end, nearly a dozen reluctant delegates were won over by Hamilton's forensic performance—just enough to give victory to the Constitution. The final vote—by far the slimmest of all the states—stood 30 for and 27 against. It was mainly the triumph of one lone individual, a young man of only thirty-three, who was truly, in Jefferson's words, "a host unto himself."

Thus the Constitution went into effect, and on April 30 in the following year George Washington was inaugurated first President of the new union. For the post of Secretary of the Treasury, which turned out to be the most crucial position in the Cabinet, the President selected his former aide-de-camp, the brilliant Alexander Hamilton. It was in some ways a strange appointment, for Hamilton, whose reputation was primarily that of a lawyer-politician and orator, had no special experience in finance or economics. As it turned out, he needed no previous experience. A careful student of Adam Smith, he grasped the whole economic picture with his usual acuteness, and by applying his disciplined mind and energies to unaccustomed problems, he arrived at clearly defined conclusions and decisive recommendations.

For more than five years, from September, 1789, to January, 1795, Hamilton served as Secretary of the Treasury, and in that critical period he laid the foundations of fiscal and economic policies that have remained substantially the same ever since. Only George Washington himself excelled him in the durability of his achievements as the early builder of the Republic.

Alexander Hamilton: Rousseau of the Right

Cecelia M. Kenyon

The thesis of this paper is suggested in the title. It is that Hamilton's political thought was characterized by a heavy emphasis on a concept central to Rousseau's theory, the general will or the public good; that for Hamilton, as for Rousseau, this public good was morally and politically prior to private, individual ends, with which it was occasionally if not frequently in conflict; that the content of this public good as Hamilton visualized it was alien to the prevailing will of the majority of Americans in the early years of the Republic; that Hamilton was never able to reconcile his political ideal with his announced view of political reality; and that, as a result, his political theory is confused, contradictory, and basically unrealistic.

It is no light matter to charge Alexander Hamilton with a lack of realism. His writings are filled with references to what has been called the "dark side of humanity"; none of his contemporaries excelled him in constant emphasis on self-interest as man's dominant political motive, or in warnings against the evil passions of man's nature. Every undergraduate knows that Hamilton had a "pessimistic" conception of human nature. Every undergraduate knows, too, that the new government established under the Constitution desperately needed its finances put in order, and that Hamilton accomplished this. How, then, can such a man be called unrealistic? My argument is that Hamilton was not able to accept with equanimity the political facts of life as he saw them, or to relate them successfully to the political ideals he pursued. There remained within his thought an unresolved tension between what he believed man was, and what he believed man ought to be. Such a tension is not of course unusual, but the distance between the *is* and the *ought* in Hamilton's ideas was extreme.

This tension can best be examined by comparing the Hamilton of the

Reprinted from *Political Science Quarterly*, Volume LXXIII, No. 2, June 1958, pp. 161–178. Reprinted by permission.

Federal Convention with the Hamilton of the Federalist party. They are the same man, but not quite the same thinker.

In his speech of June 18, 1787, Hamilton presented his plan of a political system proper for America. He wanted to do two things: to transfer the attachment of the people from the governments of their separate states to that of the Union; and to construct that government in such a way that it would not be wrecked by the turbulence of democracy and the imprudence of the people.

In the first part of the speech Hamilton analyzed those "great and essential principles necessary for the support of government," [1] and found that all of them then operated in favor of the states rather than of the Union. These principles of political obedience were several—interest, love of power, habit, force, influence. In order to make them support the nation rather than the separate states, Hamilton advocated an almost complete transfer of sovereignty from the latter governments to the former. This proposal is significant because of its apparent assumption that those very passions by which the people were so strongly attached to their state governments might remain sufficiently quiescent to permit the reduction of the states to the position of administrative provinces. It was the most drastic proposal of Hamilton's career and suggests his affinity with the classical tradition of the Legislator as well as his propensity—usually restrained—for Draconian measures.

In the second part of the speech Hamilton defended that part of his plan which provided for a senate and an executive elected for life. These were to serve as checks on the people's will, which would be represented in a popularly elected lower house with limited tenure. The reports of Madison and Yates differ somewhat, and for that reason I shall quote both versions of the crucial passage, beginning with that of Madison.

> In every community where industry is encouraged, there will be a division of it into the few and the many. Hence, separate interests will arise. There will be debtors and creditors, etc. Give all power to the many, they will oppress the few. Give all power to the few, they will oppress the many. Both, therefore, ought to have the power, that each may defend itself against the other. To the want of this check we owe our paper-money instalment laws, etc. To the proper adjustment of it the British owe the excellence of their constitution. Their House of Lords is a most noble institution. Having nothing to hope for by a change, and a sufficient interest, by means of their property, in being faithful to the national interest, they form a permanent barrier against every pernicious innovation whether attempted on the part of the Crown or of the Commons. No temporary Senate will have firmness enough to answer the purpose.[2]

---

[1] Max Farrand, *Records of the Federal Convention* (New Haven, 1911), vol. I, p. 365.
[2] Farrand, *Records,* vol. I, p. 371.

> All communities divide themselves into the few and the many. The
> first are the rich and well-born, the other the mass of the people. The
> voice of the people has been said to be the voice of God; and however
> generally this maxim has been quoted and believed, it is not true in
> fact. The people are turbulent and changing; they seldom judge or
> determine right. Give, therefore, to the first class a distinct, permanent
> share in the government. They will check the unsteadiness of the
> second, and, as they cannot receive any advantage by a change, they
> therefore will ever maintain good government. Can a democratic As-
> sembly, who annually revolve in the mass of the people, be supposed
> steadily to pursue the public good? Nothing but a permanent body can
> check the imprudence of democracy. Their turbulence and uncontrol-
> ling disposition requires checks.[3]

I believe these statements constitute the cornerstone of Hamilton's theory.
They were made in the course of debates not intended for publication,
and in defense of a system which Hamilton should have known had little
chance of being adopted. Here Hamilton was his own advocate, not as in
The Federalist, advocate of a system which he believed to be less than
second best. These statements, therefore, require careful explication.

There is, to begin with, the familiar division of men into the few and
the many, or the rich and the well-born, and the mass of the people.
There is the further assumption that the interests of these two classes
will be different, that they will be in conflict with each other at least part
of the time, that the political behavior of each class will be motivated by
its interests, and that each class will oppress the other if it gets the chance
and has the power to do so. Hamilton does not want this last to happen:
"Both, therefore, ought to have the power, that each may defend itself
against the other." It was not, then, a class government that Hamilton
sought, at least not in the sense of one that had as its end the direct and
deliberate promotion of class interests.

Thus far, there is no real difficulty in interpreting Hamilton. But the
remainder of the passage, whether as reported by Madison or Yates, is less
clear because it is, or appears to be, elliptical. In the second part of the
passage, Hamilton suggests that the few will be more reliable in the cause
of good government than the many. They, then, should have a share in
the governing process, not only to protect their class interests, but in
order to secure the national interest. Why will the few be the better
guardians of this interest than the many? There seem to be two reasons,
though neither is fully expounded.

In both the Madison and Yates versions, Hamilton expresses hostility to
change and implies, if he does not explicitly state, that change is inimical
to the "national interest" (Madison) or "good government" (Yates). This
attitude is accompanied by the assertion that the upper class will be op-

---

[3] *Ibid.,* p. 382. *Cf.* Hamilton's notes prepared for the speech, pp. 387–388.

posed to change. Therefore, the upper class will be the safer guardian of the public interest, not because its members are fundamentally more virtuous than "the people," but because on this particular issue—of change—their separate, class interest coincides with the public interest. It is also suggested (in the Madison but not in the Yates version) that the property of the Lords keeps that body faithful to the national interest in Britain.

This is a curious and revealing passage. Consider first the attitude toward change. It seems inconsistent with most of Hamilton's own career, for who among his contemporaries was more constantly in the vanguard of reform than he? He was an ardent Revolutionist; he was wholeheartedly in support of the movement for a new Constitution; his proposals as Secretary of the Treasury envisioned a deliberate effort to effect profound changes in the nature of American society; and the very speech in which he expressed this hostility to change was the speech in which he was recommending changes in the existing system far too drastic for his colleagues to accept. In comparison, the fluctuating policies followed by some of the states between 1776 and 1787, and which were so deplored by Hamilton and the other delegates, were the merest piddling. Hamilton was not alone in his quest for stability, but the attitude expressed in this speech, coupled with his own ardent support of sweeping changes, does call for a bit of explaining.

Again, I think, it reveals Hamilton as the modern prototype of the Legislator: take whatever measures are necessary to establish good Laws, and then guard against the undermining forces of future change. It is an attitude which cannot be reconciled with the theory of conservatism expounded by Burke three years later, for not only does it call for radical reconstruction, but it is hostile to the gradual, piecemeal process of adaptation which Burke accepted as characteristic of the natural life of society.

Consider next the assumption implicit in the relationship Hamilton posited between the national interest, the interest of the upper classes, good government, and an inclination or disinclination toward change. He assumes, first, that change is not compatible with good government. He assumes, second, that the upper classes will not be inclined toward change. These two assumptions are explicit. There is a third assumption which is implicit: good government is that which favors or protects the interests of these classes, but not the interests of the many—for it is they who are most likely to advocate change. It is therefore difficult to escape the conclusion that no matter how pure and patriotic Hamilton was in intent, he nevertheless tended to associate good government and the national interest with the interest of the rich, the well-born, and the few.

The exact nature of this relationship is difficult to pin down. The national interest is apparently regarded as both different from and separate from that of the many, and different from though not always separate from that of the few. It is, in short, distinct. It is the Hamiltonian counterpart of the Rousseauan general will, that will of the community toward its corporate good, something quite distinct from the will of all, which is the sum of individual and group private, self-interested wills. For Hamilton, this national interest was the primary end of government.

What we are concerned with here, then, is the fundamental question in any political theory: the end of government. It is a question which was not much discussed during the debate over ratification, and its answer was assumed and accepted rather than reached by any genuinely searching analysis even during the Revolutionary debate. This answer was more or less ready-made, and packaged in the doctrine of natural law and natural rights. Now this doctrine is ambivalent in its implications with respect to individuals and social unity. If the emphasis is on natural *law*, as it was during the medieval period, the doctrine tends in the direction of harmony and consensus. But if the emphasis is on *rights*, and especially if happiness is included among the rights, then the doctrine tends toward individualism. It cannot do otherwise, and it was no mere whim which led Rousseau to reject natural rights doctrine as the basis for his state.

Some political thinkers in America in the eighteenth century realized the ethical implications of their accepted doctrine quite fully, and others did not. Jefferson was among those who did. His poetic passages on the virtues of agrarianism really boil down to a belief that this way of life was the one in which men could most easily fulfill their self-interest without being driven to do so by means which corrupted their integrity or injured their fellows. If Jefferson had an "optimistic" view of human nature, it was because his expectations and hopes were limited not only by a recognition of egoism but by an acceptance of it as ethically legitimate.

Tom Paine, though fully committed to the doctrine of natural rights as a justification for freedom, was not aware of and was not committed to its egoistic ethical implications. Thus his apologia for unicameralism:

> My idea of a single legislature was always founded on a hope, that whatever personal parties might be in the state, they would all unite and agree in the general principles of good government—that these party differences would be dropped at the threshold of the state house, and that the public good, or the good of the whole, would be the governing principle of the legislature within it.
>
> Party dispute, taken on this ground, would only be, who should have the honor of making the laws; not what the laws should be.[4]

Implicit in this lost hope is the Rousseauan concept of the ideal citizen, he who distinguishes between his private interest and the public good, suppresses the former, and votes wholeheartedly for the latter.

It is my belief that this was also Hamilton's ideal, that he never aban-

---

[4] Philip S. Foner (ed.), *The Complete Writings of Thomas Paine* (New York, 1945), from *Dissertations on Government*, vol. 2, p. 409.

doned it as the standard for judging political behavior, even though he fully realized that it was not in accord with the facts of human nature. This standard, essentially a non-liberal standard, was the springboard of his bitter attacks on the reason and virtue of the people. Thus I would argue that the real difference between Hamilton's and Jefferson's conceptions of human nature and their respective estimates of the people's capacity for self-government lay not in what either believed man actually to be, but in what each thought man ought to be and do. As far as politics was concerned, Jefferson thought man should pursue his happiness; Hamilton thought he should seek the national interest. One called for egoistic behavior, the other for altruistic. It was Hamilton who was the greater idealist, Jefferson the greater realist.

Yet Hamilton strove mightily for realism. His method was ambitious, arrogant, and in the great tradition of Plato, Machiavelli and Rousseau. It was the method of the Legislator. The following passages indicate the spirit of Hamilton's belief that man's nature could and should be molded for his own good as well as for that of the state.

> Take mankind in general, they are vicious, their passions may be operated upon. . . . Take mankind as they are, and what are they governed by? Their passions. There may be in every government a few choice spirits, who may act from more worthy motives. One great error is that we suppose mankind more honest than they are. Our prevailing passions are ambition and interest; and *it will ever be the duty of a wise government to avail itself of the passions, in order to make them subservient to the public good; for these ever induce us to action.*[5]
>
> The true politician . . . takes human nature (and human society its aggregate) as he finds it, a compound of good and ill qualities, of good and ill tendencies. . . .
>
> With this view of human nature he will not attempt to warp or disturb from its natural direction, he will not attempt to promote its happiness by means to which it is not suited . . . but he will seek to promote his action according to the bias of his nature, to lead him to the development of his energies according to the scope of his passions, and erecting the social organization on this basis he will favor all those institutions and plans which tend to make men happy according to their natural bent, which multiply the sources of individual enjoyment and increase of national resources and strength.[6]

This is the spirit of the Legislator, though, to be sure, infinitely less ruthless than that of Plato or Rousseau. It implies wisdom on the one hand, malleability on the other, and an essentially manipulative relationship be-

---

[5] Farrand, *Records*, vol. I, pp. 388–389 (as reported by Yates). Emphasis added.

[6] Richard B. Morris (ed.), *Alexander Hamilton and the Founding of the Nation* (New York, 1957). Quotation from "Defence of the Funding System," dated 1795–1798 in a hand other than Hamilton's, pp. 313–314.

tween the two. In modern times this sort of thing goes by the name of social engineering. Before and during the eighteenth century, it was usually associated with some form of benevolent despotism. Hamilton's problem, like Rousseau's, was to adapt it to republican government. The difficulty for each was the same: the people had the power but not the wisdom, while the leaders had the wisdom but not the power. How, then, could the people be made to follow wisdom? Rousseau's answer was simple: let the Legislator claim for his plans the authority of the gods.

Hamilton's answer was not so simple. *The Federalist Papers* were an appeal to reason, to self-interest, and to patriotism. Most of his other publicist ventures were similar. In spite of all his diatribes about the weakness of man's reason and the dominance of man's passions, Hamilton never abandoned hope that the better side of man's nature might be reached and might respond. Even the misguided *Caesar Letters*,* if indeed they were his, represented an appeal to the people's reason. This was the idealist in Hamilton, relatively pure and certainly indestructible.

His financial program both reveals and represents the other major facet in his answer to the problem of the Legislator. It reflects Hamilton the blundering realist. It is sometimes said that, having failed to secure a permanent share in the structure of government for the upper classes, Hamilton sought to secure their attachment to the new government through his financial program. I believe this is correct. It was a long-term policy and it is succinctly stated in a sentence chosen by Professor Morris to head one of the selections in his excellent anthology. "The only plan that can preserve the currency is one that will make it the *immediate* interest of the moneyed men to cooperate with government in its support." [7] The emphasis on the word *immediate* was Hamilton's. Nearly a decade passed after this was written before he became Secretary of the Treasury, and during that period his fiscal theories were elaborated and matured. But the basic principle remained the same: the private interest of the moneyed class must be made the ally of the national interest. Selfish interest must be made to support the public good. And how? By having the moneyed class's bread buttered by the government. There would, then, be no conflict between its interest and the general welfare. So far, so good. By catering to its self-interest, one class is led to do what is right. This is a fine exercise in political realism.

---

* Two letters appearing in the New York *Daily Advertiser* on October 1 and 15, 1787 over the signature of Caesar constitute the Caesar Letters. They were attributed by Paul Leicester Ford to Hamilton and have often been used to show that Hamilton distrusted the people and that his most desired form of government was a dictatorship or a monarchy. Recent scholarship throws strong doubt on Hamilton's authorship of the Caesar Letters. See J. E. Cooke, "Alexander Hamilton's Authorship of the 'Caesar' Letters." *William and Mary Quarterly*, XVII (January 1960), 78–85. *Editor's note.*

[7] *Op. cit.*, pp. 335 and 339. From a letter "To a Member of Congress." See Morris' notes for date (probably 1779 or 1780) and addressee.

But what of the other class, the "many" of the June 18th speech in the Convention? In that speech Hamilton implied, though he did not explicitly state, that the interests of the two classes, the few and the many, would be in conflict with each other. Logically, then, any policy which served the interests of the few would injure or at least jeopardize the interests of the many. It is true that Hamilton believed that his fiscal policies would serve the national interest, and it is also true that he believed they would ultimately serve the self-interest of the many. But he *did* emphasize the necessity of attaching the *immediate* interest of the moneyed class to the government, and he had stated, in *The Federalist*, that men in general were much more likely to act in accordance with what they believed to be their immediate interests than their long-run interests.[8] Logically, therefore, he ought to have expected widespread opposition to the policies he advocated as Secretary of the Treasury, and equally logically he ought to have accepted such opposition with equanimity.

That he did not is well known. His letters and papers of the 1790's are filled with blasts against Jefferson, blasts against the people, blasts against factionalism, and laments about the lack of patriotism in everyone except himself and a few kindred Federalists. Hamilton was genuinely shocked, and he should really not have been. For consider what he had done. In his Convention speech he had posited the existence of two classes, with probably conflicting interests. In the Convention and elsewhere—innumerable times—he had argued that men are dominated by self-interest. He had occasionally, though not consistently, suggested that the upper classes were more likely to be patriotic than the mass of the people.[9] Nevertheless, he had sought the support of this group, not by appealing to their patriotism, altruism, or even long-run interest, but by appealing deliberately to their *immediate* self-interest. It was to them that he held out the carrot. And it was the other class, the many, the mass of the people, upon whom he now called for patriotism, and/or appreciation of long-run self-interest. It was from this class that he now expected and demanded the greater exercise of both reason and virtue. In so doing, he was not logical, he was not realistic, and he led his party straight down the road to extinction.

There were times during the late 1790's and early 1800's when he half-realized what he had done and cast about for practical solutions. In 1799 he advocated road-building as a method of courting the people's good will. It was a measure "universally popular." He also advocated the institution of a society with funds for the encouragement of agriculture and the arts. Such a program, he wrote, would "speak powerfully to the feelings and

---

[8] Number 6. In the Modern Library edition at p. 30.

[9] H. C. Lodge (ed.), *The Works of Alexander Hamilton* (New York, 1885), vol. VII, p. 241. In the eighth number of his "Examination of Jefferson's Message to Congress of December 7, 1801," Hamilton wrote that the safety of the Republic depended, among other things, "on that love of country which will almost invariably be found to be closely connected with birth, education, and family."

interests of those classes of men to whom the benefits derived from the government have been heretofore the least manifest." [10]

Before commenting on this proposal, I should like to place beside it a passage from another attempt by Hamilton to explain his party's failure to win popular support.

> Nothing is more fallacious than to expect to produce any valuable or permanent result in political projects by relying merely on the reason of men. Men are rather reasoning than reasonable animals, for the most part governed by the impulse of passion. This is a truth well understood by our adversaries, who have practised upon it with no small benefit to their cause; for at the very moment they are eulogizing the reason of men, and professing to appeal only to that faculty, they are courting the strongest and most active passion of the human heart, vanity! It is no less true, that the Federalists seem not to have attended to the fact sufficiently; and that they erred in relying so much on the rectitude and utility of their measures as to have neglected the cultivation of popular favor, by fair and justifiable expedients.[11]

These comments reveal the very deep conflict in Hamilton's thought. In the later one (1802), Hamilton saw his party's error in having relied "so much on the rectitude and utility of their measures, as to have neglected the cultivation of popular favor, by fair and justifiable expedients." In the earlier letter, Hamilton admitted that the benefits of the new government had thus far not been "manifest" to certain classes—in the context, the many. In both letters, the two Hamiltons show through: the idealist, sure of the rightness of his policies and regretful that the people were neither rational nor virtuous enough to accept them on their merits; the realist, ever ready to seek support by the enlistment of man's worse (but never worst) nature. He had deliberately done the latter to win the moneyed class over to his side in the early 1790's. Now, at the end of the decade, he proposed to do the same thing for the majority. But it was a classic case of too little, too late. He had, in effect, made a partnership between the national interest and a special class interest. I am not sure whether he intended this partnership to be permanent and exclusive. He did intend it to be universally benevolent; its fruits were meant to trickle down and be enjoyed by everyone. Yet there remains that implicit assumption of the June 18th speech: a desire for change is more likely to exist among the many than the few, because good government will leave the interests of the many unsatisfied. There is an ambivalence in Hamilton's theory which I find it impossible to resolve.

My primary interest is not to decide whether he was or was not a class theorist, however. His political ideas are significant and rewarding because

---

[10] Lodge, *Works,* vol. VIII, pp. 518–519. From a letter to Jonathan Dayton, 1799.

[11] *Ibid.,* p. 597. From a letter to James A. Bayard, April 1802.

they reflect and illumine a difficult stage in the evolution of liberal democratic thought.

As I have suggested earlier, Hamilton's basic difference from Jefferson, and I think from most Americans of the era, was his rejection of the ethical egoism implicit in natural rights doctrine. This difference ought not to be exaggerated. No American of the age was an advocate of unrestrained self-interest, and the concept of a general interest which may be separate from and in conflict with private interests was generally present. It was at the root of the Revolutionary generation's distrust of faction. Nor, on the other hand, did Hamilton advocate or desire an absolute subjection of the individual to the state. It was rather that Hamilton, like Paine, was more extreme in his condemnation of egoism and in fact represented an older view of the proper end of government.

This older view was pre-individualistic, pre-modern. It was the medieval view that government existed for the good of society, and its end therefore was the common good. One of the things that distinguishes modern theory from medieval is the greater difficulty modern theorists face in defining this concept, the common good. There are a number of reasons for this; among them are the greater unity of medieval society by virtue of Christianity, and the relative rôles of legislative and customary law in the governing process. The point is that the existence of a common good was assumed in the earlier period, and its content was easier to define. But introduce into the political system the concept of ethical individualism combined with the practice of legislative determination of policy, and the difficulty of defining the common good is obvious—by hindsight. It was not obvious in the sixteenth century, or the seventeenth. It became increasingly obvious to Americans in the first three quarters of the eighteenth century because they were virtually self-governing communities and met the problem in the everyday conduct of their affairs. Madison's Tenth *Federalist* was the culmination of a long and painful process of thought on this subject. Madison, and I think he was here accurately reflecting the dominant opinion of his contemporaries, seems to hover ambivalently between two conceptions: (1) that of an ever elusive public good somehow distinct from the clashing of selfish and private interests; (2) that of the public good as a reconciliation or compromise of these same interests.

Hamilton clung more closely to the former view. One of the reasons may have been his late arrival as a practitioner of republicanism. In this respect he was very like Tom Paine, and I think a comparison of their lives from the time of their arrival in this country will show their fundamental kinship, though one was politically of the Right, the other of the Left. Each devoted himself without reserve to the service of his country. For each of them this entailed a sacrifice of the private interests common to most men —property, or at least greater property for both, and for Hamilton, the welfare of his family. For him, the sacrifice in the end was extreme. Among the documents he wrote before the duel there is one which concludes with a sentence profoundly symbolic of his entire life. After recounting his abhorrence of the practice on religious and ethical grounds, his unwillingness to give grief to his wife and children, his feeling of responsibility to his creditors, his intention of reserving fire on the first and perhaps even the second shot, Hamilton concluded: "The ability to be in future useful, whether in resisting mischief or in effecting good, in those crises of our public affairs which seem likely to happen, would probably be inseparable from a conformity with public prejudice in this particular." [12] He was indeed a patriot.

At every step of his career (except possibly the row with Washington), Hamilton—and Paine—put country first, self second. In a sense this was not sacrifice but fulfillment of their deepest desires. But in so far as it was fulfillment, it marked them off from other men. Each was in essence a political being, intensely so; each realized his nature, his self-interest, in devoting himself to the public good. The personality of each reinforced his conception of this public good as something better than and different from a mere reconciliation of individual and group interests. Neither ever ceased to regard his standard of political behavior as the standard proper for every man. For Paine, this meant an ever recurring optimism punctuated with bitter disillusion. For Hamilton, it meant a steady and self-nourishing pessimism. Both were idealists, and both shared the same ideal: a Rousseauistic community in which men were citizens first and individuals second. Hamilton knew his ideal was incapable of realization, and he sought a substitute which might still achieve the same goal—a government that governed in the national interest. The substitute was an alliance of upper-class interests with the national interests.

Jefferson and Madison opposed him partly because of the nature of the alliance, partly because the content of his conception of the public good was too nationalistic for their tastes. I do not think either he or they ever fully realized the more theoretical, and I think more fundamental, difference between them. The difference was subtle but profound. Jefferson and Madison were committed to the ethical individualism implicit in natural rights theory: the end of the government as the protection of life, liberty, and the pursuit of happiness. This doctrine recognizes the political legitimacy of egoism. Hamilton was only partly committed to the doctrine. The basic difference between him and most of his contemporaries was that his conception of the public good was the older, corporate one, and theirs was the newer one in which the corporate element, though still present, had given ground to individualism.

The tension between these two concepts, a corporate and an individualistic public good, can be observed throughout the Revolutionary period. It

---

[12] Morris, *op. cit.,* p. 608.

underlay the colonial opposition to the British theory of virtual representation; it was central to the debates in the Federal Convention, and it was a major element in the ratification controversy. During the latter, James Winthrop seemed to be speaking directly to Hamilton when he wrote, "It is vain to tell us that we ought to overlook local interests. It is only by protecting local concerns that the interest of the whole is preserved." [13] This was the spirit of the future of American politics: local interests, sectional interests, class interests, group interests, individual interests. The conflict, compromise, or sometimes reconciliation of these interests was to be the main determinant of public policy, not the Hamiltonian ideal of a transcendent national interest, not the Rousseauan ideal of an overriding general will.

Here lay the heart of Hamilton's dilemma. As a genuine patriot of his adopted country, he was loyally committed to the practice of republican government. His grave doubts about the success of the experiment stemmed from his rejection of ethical individualism coupled with his acceptance of egoism as a fact of political life. The real trouble was that his end was incompatible with the means which, as a patriot, he had to accept. Logically, he should have ended up with some sort of philosopher-king theory, and he did have leanings in that direction. Since he was not a closet-philosopher, this way out of the dilemma was closed. There was really no way out. The way he chose, an alliance of one special interest group with what he conceived to be the national interest, simply stimulated opposition to the latter because he *had* linked it to the former. So he intensified in both groups the selfishness which was his enemy, and encouraged the growth of factions which he so deplored. That he was regarded by his contemporary opponents as a representative of class interests is perhaps regrettable, but their misunderstanding of him and his motives was no greater than his misunderstanding of them and theirs. They were wrong in believing him to be an oligarch, but they were right in believing that his political ideals were opposed to theirs. His were corporate, theirs individualistic. His end was not logically anti-republican, but, in the context of public opinion at the time, it was bound to make him doubtful that it could be achieved under republicanism. It was unlikely that the people, left to themselves, would faithfully pursue the national interest. They needed a Legislator. Hamilton volunteered for the job.

In this aspect of his thought—means rather than ends—I would again argue that Hamilton's ideas were subtly but profoundly different from those of most of his contemporaries. They all talked a lot about man's passions and emphasized the necessity of taking these into account when constructing a constitution. I think Hamilton had a much more ambitious opinion concerning the extent to which these passions could be actively

---

[13] From the *Agrippa Letters,* in P. L. Ford (ed.), *Essays on the Constitution of the United States* (Brooklyn, 1892), p. 17.

used—manipulated—by politicians. Consider the benevolent passage quoted above in which he outlined the principles a wise politician must follow if he would lead the people toward the achievement of their happiness and the national interest. Consider his injunction that "it will ever be the duty of a wise government to avail itself of the passions, in order to make them subservient to the public good. . . ." Consider his proposal in the Convention to transfer sovereignty from the state governments to the national government in order to transfer the people's passions from the former to the latter. And consider his tendency during the 1790's to regard the people as dupes who had been led astray by designing politicians. All this adds up to a fairly consistent picture. The people are clay in the hands of the potter, but the potter may be either wise and virtuous, or shrewd and vicious. The former will give them what they ought to have, the latter will pretend to give them what they think they want.

As a Legislator, Hamilton was initially successful. The conditions which existed during and shortly after the inauguration of the new government were congenial for the exercise of his special talents. Afterwards, his effectiveness as politician and statesman declined with remarkable rapidity. Both his ends and his means were alien to the ideals and the experience of the people he sought to lead. Their ideals were liberal and individualistic, and their practice of self-government had rendered them impervious to the benevolent molding Hamilton had in mind to impose upon them. They would govern themselves. It was inevitable that he should be rejected.

Though his corporate idealism and manipulative methods be rejected, the central problem for which he offered them as solutions cannot be ignored. That problem is basic: how, in a nation governed by the people, is agreement on the public good to be obtained and put into effect? In this process, what is and should be the relationship between wisdom and public opinion, between private interest and national interest? These were fundamental questions when Hamilton grappled with them, and they still are. We have not yet worked out a satisfactory theory that will tell us precisely when the individual is ethically obligated to sacrifice his interests or when he may legitimately refuse to do so. Hamilton's plea for altruism in politics is relevant and salutary. The pursuit of selfish individual or group interests unrestrained by any sense of the general welfare may produce such bitter and divisive competition as to destroy the unity and consensus which sustain individual freedom as well as national strength.

Yet the Hamiltonian ideal, of each citizen placing the national interest before his own, is not without its dangers. It places an indefinite limitation on the exercise of individual freedom. There must be limits, of course, but this limit is an abstraction, and abstractions, when reified, are powerful forces to set against the solitary right and will of the individual. The national interest, with some exceptions such as sheer survival, will always be an elusive concept, its substance difficult to determine. Therefore there are practical reasons for refusing to concede it a permanently and categorically preferred position in all contests with individual, separate interests.

These practical reasons are merely corollaries of the main one. The main one is the ethical priority of the individual and his welfare as the proper and ultimate end of government. To this end, the national interest is logically and ethically secondary; to this end, the national interest must stand in the relationship of means. At least it must if one still accepts the Declaration of Independence as a statement of the purposes of American government. Hamilton mistook the means for the end, and tipped the scale too far in the direction of the national interest. In so doing he gave it ethical priority over the demands of the individual.

Such a priority seems to necessitate resort to manipulative techniques in order to induce the individual to forego what he conceives to be his own interest. Thus Plato resorted to the persuasion of the myth of the metals, Rousseau to the authority of the gods. In his idealistic moods, Hamilton appealed to reason; in his self-consciously realistic moods, he attempted a calculated alliance between the national interest and selfish class interests. This was bound not only to accentuate conflict between factions, but to obscure the national interest itself. Hamilton's idealism was thus vitiated by a would-be realistic policy which was both shrewd and obtuse at the same time.

The fault lay in the man himself. Hamilton's idealism was genuine and profound. It was also touched with arrogance. His penchant for what he regarded as realism was a fundamental trait of his character; he liked to think of himself as a skillful maneuverer of men's emotions. Thus his realism was likewise touched with arrogance. It may be that this dual arrogance was subjectively justified—Hamilton *was* a superior individual. But in the politics of republican government, such arrogance may operate to blind its possessor to that which he must see and understand if he is to achieve a successful blend of idealism and realism. That is the nature of man, or, more specifically, the motivation and behavior of the voter. It was Hamilton's fortune to serve his country well for a brief and crucial period in its history; it was his fate to be rejected by the countrymen whose ideals he did not share, and whose politics he did not understand.

The Causes of
The War of 1812:
Manifest Destiny or
Maritime Rights?

INTRODUCTION

Broadly speaking, there are two schools of American historical writing on the question of the causes of the War of 1812. One school emphasizes the thesis that war resulted from the maritime grievances of America against Britain chiefly in two respects: the British practice of impressment, which often resulted in the impressment of American seamen into the Royal Navy, and British invasion of what Americans regarded as their lawful rights of neutral trade in time of war. This is the oldest school of historical interpretation, and it is associated with the tradition set by Henry Adams in his great history of the United States during the administrations of Jefferson and Madison.

The other main school of historical interpretation emphasizes American grievances and American ambitions with respect to the West. According to this view, the chief American grievance was the widespread belief that the British in Canada stood behind and encouraged the Indian tribes in their menacing attitude toward the advancing American frontier; and the chief American ambition was actuated by the insatiable land hunger of both the northwestern and southwestern frontiers, which sought expansion toward Canada and the Floridas. Historians in this tradition were much influenced by the writings of Frederick Jackson Turner, with his emphasis upon the frontier influence in American history, and see the War of 1812 as an early manifestation of what later came to be known as "Manifest Destiny."

Julius W. Pratt in his Expansionists of 1812 *(1925), from which a selection is presented below, is probably the classic expositor of this latter view; and, though he recognizes that other factors operated, he still asserts that he "feels safe in saying that without the peculiar grievances and ambitions of the West there would have been no war." A. L. Burt in his* The United States, Great Britain, and British North America from the Revolution to the Establishment of Peace After the War of 1812 *(1940), from which our second selection is taken, says flatly, "This conclusion, I have been driven to reject." His emphasis is in the earlier Adams tradition, with the main focus upon maritime and commercial grievances.*

The Expansionists of 1812

Julius W. Pratt

INTRODUCTION

That the United States went to war with Great Britain in 1812 at the insistence of western and southern men, and over the opposition of the Northeast, is a fact about which there has never been any doubt. There was a paradox here which apparently gave little concern to the older historians. If the real grievances which caused the war were interference by Great Britain with American commerce and the rights of American sailors, why was war to redress those grievances opposed by the maritime section of the nation and urged by the inland section, which they scarcely affected? The old answers, that New England was Anglophile, and that the West and South had developed a more aggressive and martial spirit, which felt the humiliation if not the pecuniary loss occasioned by the British measures, were in a measure true, but hardly sufficient. For some years past, historians have been turning to new explanations.

In this field, as in almost every other in American history, it is easy to see the profound influence of Professor F. J. Turner. Before the publication in 1893 of his essay, "The Significance of the Frontier in American History," [1] the frontier had been regarded as little more than a picturesque phase in the national development. Since that event, the frontier—the "West"—has come to be recognized as the source of many aspects of American character and the determining factor in many American policies.[2] It was natural, therefore, that students of the War of 1812 should come to view the West—particularly the Northwest—with more careful scrutiny. The result of such examination has been the placing of new emphasis upon the western demand for the annexation of Canada, which is seen to have arisen in large part from the conviction that the British were in league

[1] Conveniently reprinted with other essays in Turner, F. J., *The Frontier in American History*, New York, 1920.

[2] A recent illustration is seen in Adams, J. T., *Revolutionary New England* (1923), in which the growth of the revolutionary spirit from 1700 to 1775 is credited largely to the frontier influence.

with the northwestern Indians and that only by destroying that alliance could the Northwest continue its career of expansion.[3]

The war found its sponsors, however, not only in the Northwest but along the whole frontier from New Hampshire round about to Georgia. For the states south of Kentucky, there was little to be gained by the conquest of Canada, and, since the divergence of interests between North and South was already evident, there was reason for southern states to fear the political effect of a large addition to northern territory. Why, then, did the Southwest support the war? The answer to this question has been suggested,[4] but has never been worked out with anything approaching completeness. The examination made in the course of this study reveals an ardent expansionist sentiment already at work along the whole southern and southwestern border, varying in scope from the relatively modest proposal for the annexation of the Floridas to the more visionary idea of seizing all the Spanish possessions on the continent of North America. The link between the designs of the Southwest and those of the Northwest was the existence of the alliance between Great Britain and Spain. It was widely assumed that war with Great Britain would mean war with Spain, and that thus expansion at the north and at the south would proceed *pari passu*.

The purposes of the present study have been: to examine the development in the Northwest of the demand for the conquest and annexation of Canada; to trace the rise in the South and Southwest of the plan to annex the Floridas and possibly Mexico; to discover the relations of these two proposals to each other and to the question of war with Great Britain; to determine the position of the executive branch of the United States government (especially of Madison and his Secretary of State, Monroe) toward the plans for expansion, north and south; and finally, to determine the causes for the failure, all along the line, of the expansionist hopes with which the war began.

The principal conclusions arrived at may be summarized as follows

I. The belief that the United States would one day annex Canada had a continuous existence from the early days of the War of Independence to the War of 1812. From 1783 to about 1810 such annexation was thought of only as a matter for an indefinite future, the nation during those years having neither the strength, nor any sufficient motive, for taking Canada by force. The rise of Tecumseh, backed, as was universally believed, by the British, produced an urgent demand in the Northwest that the British be

---

[3] In addition to the works cited at close of chap. i, see Johnson, *Jefferson and His Colleagues*, chap. x; Anderson, "The Insurgents of 1811," *A. H. A. Reports,* 1911, Vol. I, 165–176.

[4] Adams, *United States*, VI, 123; Bassett, *Life of Andrew Jackson*, I, 77; Channing, *History of the United States*, IV, 456.

expelled from Canada. This demand was a factor of primary importance in bringing on the war.

II. The South was almost unanimous in its demand for the Floridas, for agrarian, commercial, and strategic reasons, and in the spring of 1812 appeared to be in a fair way to accomplish its purpose. In the Southwest, at the same time, there was a lively interest in Mexico and a widely prevalent opinion that it was ready to fall into American hands.

III. Even within the Republican party, there was already a distinct sectional rift between North and South, and neither section was anxious to see the other increase its territory and population. But if both could gain at the same time, and in something like equal proportion, such objections would be obviated on both sides. There is good evidence that, before the declaration of war, northern and southern Republicans came to a definite understanding that the acquisition of Canada on the north was to be balanced by the annexation of the Floridas on the south. Thus the war began with a double-barrelled scheme of territorial aggrandizement.

IV. Both Madison and Monroe, especially the latter as Secretary of State, were wholly in sympathy with the proposal for annexing Florida. The invasion of East Florida by General Mathews in March and April, 1812, was effected with the full knowledge of the administration. Special circumstances forced the government to repudiate Mathews, but the territory he had taken from the Spanish was held for over a year, until Congress had twice refused to sanction the occupation. At the same time, Monroe's official correspondence shows that he never really desired or expected the annexation of Canada.

V. It appears that in the all round failure of the expansionist plans, sectional feeling played a larger part than is commonly supposed. The sectional bargain with which the war had begun broke down. Opposition from northern Republicans combined with Federalists forced the abandonment of East Florida. On the other hand, it is evident that in the utter failure of the efforts to take Canada, not only want of skill and preparation, but also a lack of enthusiasm on the part of the administration and of certain southern men in Congress played a part.

VI. Finally, in the expansionist program with which the war opened, we have the first general appearance of the idea which later received the name of "Manifest Destiny." Although enthusiasts like Jefferson had dreamed years before of a nation destined to embrace the continent, the date usually given for the dawn of "Manifest Destiny" is about 1830.[5] Yet both in the Congressional debates of 1812 and in the contemporary press, particularly that of the Southwest, we find the idea repeatedly expressed. "Where is it written in the book of fate," asked the editor of the Nashville *Clarion*

---

[5] Adams, E. D., *The Power of Ideals in American History,* chap. iii.

(April 28, 1812), "that the American republic shall not stretch her limits from the Capes of the Chesapeake to Nootka sound, from the isthmus of Panama to Hudson bay?"

Two explanations are due, with respect to the scope and proportions of this study. First, it makes no effort to give a full account of the causes of the War of 1812, but deals with one set of causes only. The exclusion from all but briefest mention of the maritime grievances against Great Britain is with no wish to belittle them. Without them, it is safe to say, there would have been no war, just as the writer feels safe in saying that without the peculiar grievances and ambitions of the West there would have been no war. One set of causes was perhaps as essential as the other.

Second, the writer has thought best to give some account of those military operations during the war which bore a direct relation to the plans for territorial expansion. The campaigns of 1812 and 1813 on the Canadian border are given in the barest outline, while the operations in East Florida, though on a smaller scale, receive a more detailed treatment. For this apparent lack of proportion the justification is that the details of the northern campaigns are well known and can be read in a dozen careful accounts, whereas no full account of the East Florida operations has ever been published.

War of 1812: Causes, from 1809

A. L. Burt

According to a thesis which has been widely accepted in recent years, we cannot understand why there was a War of 1812 unless we look inland. This thesis[1] may be summarized as follows. The quarrel over neutral rights

From *The United States, Great Britain, and British North America from the Revolution to the Establishment of Peace After the War of 1812* (New Haven: Yale University Press, 1940), pp. 305–316. Reprinted by permission of the Carnegie Endowment for International Peace.

[1] Julius W. Pratt, *Expansionists of 1812,* an interesting book in which the author tries to explain the paradox, "which apparently gave little concern to the older historians," of the United States' going to war to uphold maritime rights despite the stout opposition of maritime New England. He carefully explains in his preface that his work "makes no effort to give a full account of the causes of the War of 1812, but deals with one set of causes only. The exclusion from all but briefest mention of the maritime grievances against Great Britain is with no wish to belittle them." Ignoring this caution, many readers have leaped to the conclusion, which he never intended to suggest and does not, that

on the sea brought the United States to the verge of war with Britain but did not do more than that, for the maritime constituencies voted against war. The force that induced the last fatal step was largely, though not wholly, an urge to conquer Canada. This urge was chiefly inspired by the determination to uproot the British-Indian evil but was also compounded of the old jealousy of the British fur trade and a new lust for territorial expansion that anticipated "Manifest Destiny"; and it found abundant "righteous pretexts" in the maritime quarrel. "By the end of the spring of 1812, the whole frontier country from New Hampshire to Kentucky was insisting that the British must be expelled from Canada." [2] But the people of the Northwest might have clamored in vain for war if they had not found fortuitous allies in the people of the South, who were likewise impatient to take Florida from Spain, the weak ally of Britain. This combination, which promised to preserve the balance between North and South by adding territory and population to both, brought on the war. This explanation is supported by the much quoted words of John Randolph delivered in the House on December 16, 1811.

> Sir, if you go to war it will not be for the protection of, or defence of your maritime rights. Gentlemen from the North have been taken up to some high mountain and shown all the kingdoms of the earth; and Canada seems tempting in their sight. That rich vein of Gennesee land, which [sic] is said to be even better on the other side of the lake than on this. Agrarian cupidity, not maritime right urges the war. Ever since the report of the Committee on Foreign Relations came into the House, we have heard but one word—like the whip-poor-will, but one eternal monotonous tone—Canada! Canada! Canada! Not a syllable about Halifax, which unquestionably should be our great object in a war for maritime security.[3]

Confirmation has also been found in the division of Congress on the war issue, "most of the navigating interests voting nay, and the interior, particularly the whole frontier in a great crescent from Vermont to Louisiana, voting aye," with "only a small majority for war." [4]

There is more than one *non sequitur* in this argument. Does the voting of the maritime constituencies prove that neutral rights alone could not

---

the traditional causes were of relatively minor importance and that the real causes of the war are to be found in the West. He admits, however, that he "feels safe in saying that without the peculiar grievances and ambitions of the West there would have been no war." This conclusion, I have been driven to reject. But at the same time I would like to pay tribute to the author for having made an important contribution to the history of Manifest Destiny.

[2] *Ibid.*, p. 58.

[3] *A.C.*, Twelfth Congress, Vol. I, col. 533.

[4] S. F. Bemis, *A Diplomatic History of the United States*, pp. 156–157. Louisiana, however, did not vote. The final vote in the House was 79 to 49, and in the Senate, 19 to 13. One of the names in the last list is omitted from the report in the *A.C.*, Twelfth Congress, Vol. I, col. 297.

have produced the war? Their votes were divided, . . . and the division would have been more equal if it had truly reflected the opinions of the people. Nor should it be forgotten that this was the part of the country that stood to suffer most in a trial of strength with British sea power. Much more serious is another consideration which we have already seen. The American government had to champion the maritime interests not only in spite of their opposition but also because of their opposition. The commercial and shipping elements had been betraying the national honor. They would have sold neutral rights and the country's independence for selfish profit and sectional welfare.

The southern pressure for war is also misconstrued. Why should Americans want war with Britain in order to seize Florida? Part had already been taken without it, and the obstacle that seemed to stand in the way of getting the rest was the possibility of British intervention. Britain ruled the waves, and the waves nearly surrounded Florida. Moreover the administration's schemes for acquiring this weakly held Spanish possession were well under way long before the "War Hawks" flocked to the Twelfth Congress. The one reason why the South should welcome war with Britain to aid in getting Florida was to buy off sectional opposition within the United States by letting the North have its *quid pro quo* in Canada;[5] but, as already suggested, this meant running the obvious danger of the mean's defeating the end. The reports of the debates in the *Annals of Congress* contain no suggestion of Florida's being a motive for war; but they do reveal another material motive which has attracted too little attention. It was a strong one.

The planters were being badly pinched. "Our cotton is reduced to seven cents, and our tobacco to nothing," cried old Robert Wright of Maryland in the House. He denied Randolph's assertion "that our own restrictive system has undone us," pointing out that restrictions on the export of these articles had ceased and if they had been the cause the effect should have ceased too. "The price of cotton depends on the demand for the manufactures of that article; the English-made cottons depend on the continental markets, from which the British manufactures are excluded. The price of tobacco never was materially varied by the consumption in England, but depended on the foreign demand from Great Britain, which, by their exclusion from the continent, is almost entirely arrested." The retaliatory system of the two great belligerents, he said, had ruined the market for these American staples, and since Napoleon had revoked his decrees the blame now rested on the British orders-in-council.[6] Wright put his finger on the sore spot of the South. This was the one section of the country that was vitally dependent upon the markets controlled by Na-

---

[5] This motive was suggested in a speech by Grundy, a Virginian who had moved to Tennessee. *Ibid.*, col. 427.

[6] *Ibid.*, cols. 470–471.

poleon. It was not a commercial region; but its very life was tied up with commerce. Here was a further reason for championing the maritime interests in their own despite. Maritime New England would have deserted the planter South; and the rural North would have done the same thing, for it was attracted by the fabulous price of wheat in England and the market for provisions created by the Peninsular War.

The voting of the frontier constituencies from Kentucky to New Hampshire also calls for more careful analysis. . . . The unanimity was broken in Vermont and more particularly in New York. But if there had been no such break, the attitude of the members from the interior would be quite understandable without any reference to Canada. Practically all the members of Congress, no matter what part of the country they represented or how they voted in the end, admitted that the United States had just grounds for declaring war on Britain. This being so, it stands to reason that those who came from the interior were least inhibited by the fear of consequences.[7] Their electors had little direct interest in the sea-borne commerce which would be disrupted; they had no settlements which might be bombarded by British naval guns; and, if we except inhabitants of New York and Vermont, they were about as secure from a British military attack. This immunity was the common contemporary explanation of the pronounced bellicose attitude of the interior. It was also said that the western members saw in a war a lever to raise the price of hemp and of other produce which their people wished to sell but could not.

Though the Indian menace, which was played up by the Republican press, haunted the minds of some members of Congress, there is a good reason for doubting if it had any appreciable influence in bringing on the war with Britain. The seat of the native strife lay off in a remote corner. Relatively few whites lived anywhere near it, and they had no representatives in Congress. There it was openly said that Americans had stirred up the hornets' nest, and the aggressive character of Harrison's advance on Tippecanoe was so obvious that it was difficult to deny. A close study of all the debates from the opening of the session until the declaration of war shows that very few members, and they only very occasionally, pointed to the red peril or accused Britain of instigating it. If the old nightmare turned any vote from peace to war, there is no evidence for it in the *Annals of Congress*. In the President's historic message of June 1, 1812, recommending a declaration of war, Britain is charged most positively with "a series of acts, hostile to the United States as an independent and neutral nation," and after the enumeration of these acts, which are a catalogue of the maritime grievances, a short paragraph insinuating that there was some connection between the hostility of the savages and their

---

[7] "When a man rises in this House, you may almost tell how ardent he will be, by knowing how far distant he lives from the sea." Stow of New York, on Jan. 6, 1812, *ibid.*, col. 677.

intercourse with the British is inserted as a sort of afterthought. This is the only reference to the Indian troubles and it makes no definite charge.[8] Apparently the administration did not consider the native hostilities to be a cause of war any more than did the majority in Congress.

The conquest of Canada was frequently mentioned in the debates, but the suggestion that it was desirable for its own sake was made so rarely that a reader of the debates might miss it if he did not look for it. Randolph's words which have been quoted above should not be taken at their face value. This Virginian stood out from among his fellow members of the House as the most persistent opponent of war. He denounced it eloquently, at great length, and often. If he really believed that the effective cause of the pressure for war was agrarian cupidity, rather than maritime grievances, we might expect to find that he directed his invective at this dishonorable motive again and again. But he did not. His words which have been so aptly used to support this thesis constitute only a short passage in a long speech delivered six months before the war, and there is hardly an echo of them in the records of his many other speeches during these six months. In the reports of what was said by all the other speakers who opposed war, there is equally little to support the startling charge he flung at the warmongers in December, 1811. Evidently it was not considered to have much point.

This conclusion is confirmed by a careful reading of Foster's[*] letters. They reveal him not only as most interested in whatever was going on but also as one of the best-informed men in the country, and they do not even suggest that an urge for the conquest of Canada was a cause of war. At the very end, during the secret session in which Congress passed the act declaring war, the idea did creep into one of his dispatches. He wrote that Harper of New Hampshire, a member of the committee on foreign relations, was reported as saying that "it would be advisable to go to war for Canada alone" and "he would be for never laying down arms until Canada should be taken." [9] The British minister's only comment was, "It is supposed that this was a manoeuvre by which to get rid of the question of war altogether, as it would be impossible ever to get the House to agree to so great an absurdity." [10] He was perfectly familiar with the talk of an attack on Canada, but he saw war coming as a consequence of what had happened at sea and not because of what was expected to happen on land.

This concept of the war dominated the discussion in Congress, and it

---

[8] *Ibid.*, cols. 1624–1671.

[*] Editor's note: Augustus John Foster, British minister in Washington. In March 1811, he replaced the very unpopular Francis J. Jackson, a Tory and quite unsuited by temperament for the American scene.

[9] This is not reported in the *Annals of Congress*.

[10] Foster to Castlereagh, No. 43, June 9, 1812, *F.O.* 5, Vol. LXXXVI.

was not the product of the "War Hawks." Erskine* had described it before their party was hatched.[11] It was simple, logical, and honorable. Britain had injured the United States on the high seas, where she was invincible. To challenge her there would be to court defeat. Britain had a thousand warships; the United States had not a single ship-of-the-line and only a half dozen frigates. A swarm of American privateers might prey upon British commerce, but a few heavy vessels of the Royal Navy might bombard American cities and even capture American ports. The only way to make Britain submit was to strike her where she was vulnerable—in the provinces adjoining on the north. Quebec might be too hard a nut to crack, but the United States could easily overrun the two Canadas right down to that fortress, and Quebec without the country back of it would be of little value to Britain. The small attention paid to Halifax is explained by the plain fact that it was beyond the American reach. The prevailing thought was that the United States was potentially supreme on land, as Britain was actually supreme on the sea. Each country had its own element, though only one had used it; and Britain would cease from her oppression at sea rather than lose her share of the land. If the worst came to the worst and, as one senator pointed out, Britain should get possession of New York and New Orleans, they could be recovered by an exchange of conquests.[12] The conquest of Canada was anticipated as the seizure of a hostage rather than as the capture of a prize.

Why, then, did the war not come in 1811, shortly after Foster's arrival, when according to Mahan† the breach was assured? Why the delay of a year? The answer is threefold. For one thing, the government in Washington was gravely worried by the possibility that American honor might also require a declaration of war against Napoleon.[13] He seemed determined to ruin American trade with the whole continent of Europe; his minions confiscated American ships and cargoes, they were still burning them at sea, and they even impressed American sailors. Repeated representations in Paris brought no redress nor any promise of it. The President's temper grew very bad as he saw more and more clearly that the Emperor had been making sport of him and his people. Monroe was furious. In defiance of notorious evidence to the contrary, he tried again and again to persuade Foster that the Berlin and Milan decrees were repealed; and then he turned to Serurier‡ and used this evidence to prove the opposite. The outrageous behavior of France was aired in Congress,

---

* Editor's note: David Montague Erskine had preceded Jackson as British Minister in Washington. He is principally notable for having negotiated a treaty (1809) with Madison that was favorable to America but was repudiated by Canning.

[11] Supra, p. 267. [12] A.C., Twelfth Congress, Vol. I, col. 41.

† Editor's note: Alfred Thayer Mahan, officer of the United States Navy in the late nineteenth and early twentieth centuries, was an outstanding authority on naval history.

[13] See Madison to Jefferson, May 25, 1812, in Madison, VIII, 190–192.

‡ Editor's note: Count de Serurier was French Minister in Washington.

where it found scarcely an apologist. Members who advocated war with Britain commonly admitted that hostilities against France would likewise be justified. In his opening message and again in his war message of seven months later, Madison referred to the American grievances against France. It is quite conceivable that, if the French Empire had been as vulnerable as the British, the United States might have made war on Napoleon too.

In the second place, the administration cherished a dying hope that Britain would yet surrender her orders-in-council and thereby open the door for an accommodation of other difficulties, particularly impressment. The discovery of Foster's impotence, which followed almost immediately upon his arrival, was a hard blow, but it did not kill this hope, for Monroe told him in the summer of 1811 that the United States would soon send a minister to London. The appointment was put off until it could be submitted to the Senate for confirmation, and when Congress met he confessed that the appointment had to be abandoned because the Senate would not give its consent.[14] Still the hope was not dead.

The third reason for the delay in declaring war was that the country was absolutely unprepared to wage it, thanks to the sublime faith of Jefferson and Madison in the efficacy of commercial restrictions. Before the United States could begin to fight, an army had to be found and before an army could be found, special legislation had to be passed. This required time, and then more time was needed because it was difficult to find the men and the money. As it was, the declaration came long before the country was ready for it.[15]

Though the President opened Congress with a request for war preparations, he had not yet given himself over to despair. Preparations for war are sometimes the only way to avoid it, and he seems to have believed that London might repent when it heard the rattling of the saber in Washington. The faint hope lingered through the winter and on into the spring, showing signs of life at the approach of every dispatch vessel from England. The end came on May 27 or 28. On those days Foster had several interviews with Madison and Monroe, and to them he communicated a long note he had just received from the British Foreign Secretary.[16] Its categorical insistence on the maintenance of the orders-in-council, supported by new proof that the Napoleonic decrees were still the law, at last convinced Madison that further discussion with the British government was impossible.[17] Thereupon he drafted the war message which he submitted to Congress on June 1.

Reviewing the hostile conduct of Britain only since the renewal of

---

[14] Foster to Castlereagh, No. 24, Nov. 12, No. 25, Nov. 21, 1811, *F.O.* 5, Vol. LXXVII.
[15] Madison, VIII, 242.
[16] Castlereagh to Foster, No. 8, April 10, 1812, *F.O.* 5, Vol. LXXXIII.
[17] Madison, IX, 272–273.

Anglo-French hostilities in 1803, the President made four definite charges. The first was impressments. The second was that British cruisers violated the peace of American coasts, hovering over and harassing entering and departing commerce. The third was the employment of "pretended Blockades" to plunder American commerce. The fourth was "the sweeping system" of the orders-in-council. He said nothing of the *Chesapeake*, for that account had been settled. Nor did he mention the contentious Rule of 1756,* for this question had been liquidated by conquest. There were no French colonies left, and therefore there was no enemy colonial trade. Nor did he refer to the contract with France, for France had patently failed to live up to it.

Henry Adams has accused Madison of "inverting the order of complaints previously alleged," and he says that "this was the first time that the Government had alleged impressment as its chief grievance." [18] But it is just as reasonable to conclude from a study of this document that the discussion of the orders-in-council was intended to be a climax of the indictment. In fact, there appears to have been no intended relation between the order of the charges and Madison's view of their relative gravity. He was proceeding chronologically. It should also be pointed out that he had long since committed himself officially on the importance of the impressment issue. When he was Secretary of State his instructions to Monroe made it the crux of the negotiations in London, and as soon as he learned that Monroe was completing a treaty without requiring Britain to abandon impressments from American vessels on the high seas he notified him that the United States must reject the treaty for this very reason. There had been no subsequent negotiation over the question simply because it seemed so hopeless. The blood it caused to be spilled while the two countries were nominally at peace is grim testimony of its fundamental importance.

The bill declaring war was passed by the House of Representatives on June 4, the Senate passed it in an amended form on the seventeenth, it was returned with the approval of the House on the eighteenth, and the President signed it immediately. On the following day Foster proposed a suspension of hostilities until the declaration of war reached England, and he offered to hurry home with any proposition the American government might wish to make. He met with a refusal.[19] When taking his formal leave on the twenty-third, he asked if a repeal of the orders-in-council would restore peace, and he again urged a suspension of hostilities "until further intelligence should be received from Great Britain." Once more he met with a rebuff. He was told that the repeal would have to be accom-

---

* Editor's note: An Admiralty rule, originally laid down in 1756, but which, during the Napoleonic Wars, was restrictive of American trade with the French West Indies.

[18] Adams, VI, 222.

[19] Foster to Castlereagh, No. 47, June 20, 1812, *F.O.* 5, Vol. LXXXVI.

panied by a promise to negotiate on impressments in order to halt the war, and that there was no prospect of repeal.[20] But on that very day, over in London, the orders-in-council were repealed—conditionally.

To explain this surprising reversal of British policy, it is necessary to go back a little. The orders-in-council had stirred opposition in England from the very beginning, and a rising tide of public opinion blamed them for the growing distress of the country. To allay the discontent, the government clothed its oft-repeated promise in an official form on April 21, 1812. This was a new order-in-council repealing its objectionable predecessors. It was to come into force immediately the Berlin and Milan decrees were unconditionally revoked by some authentic act of the French government, publicly promulgated. Armed with this document, the American minister in Paris, Joel Barlow, presented a stiff note on May 1 to the Duke of Bassano, Cadore's successor. It demanded the publication of an authentic act declaring the decrees had ceased to apply to the United States in November, 1810. Barlow later had "a pretty sharp conversation" with Bassano. Then came an astounding climax. The Frenchman produced a decree exactly fitting the American requirement. From the date it bore, April 28, 1811, it was more than a year old. How it could have been kept secret all this time is still a mystery. When asked if it had been published, Bassano had to admit that it had not; but he blandly asserted that it had been communicated to Jonathan Russell, then American *chargé* in Paris and since transferred to London, and also to Serurier with orders to give it to the American government. Both men denied they had ever received it, and it appears to have been spurious. However that may be, Barlow secured what he had demanded and he sent it posthaste to Russell, who immediately presented it to Castlereagh with a request for corresponding British action. This was on May 20, when no action was possible. Britain was without a government. Only a few days before, a lunatic had assassinated the Prime Minister, Spencer Percival. In the middle of June, almost as soon as the ministry was reconstituted under Lord Liverpool, he announced the provisional repeal of the orders-in-council. Some days were consumed in working out the provisions, and then the requisite order was passed on the twenty-third. The pressure which had produced the order of April 21 had also forced the government to give up its prerequisite of a complete restoration of neutral rights as they existed prior to the Berlin Decree.

Three days later, Foster's suggestion bore fruit in Washington. On June 26, Monroe wrote to Russell informing him of the declaration of war and at the same time authorizing him to arrange an armistice immediately, "if the orders-in-council are repealed, and no illegal blockades are substituted for them, and orders are given to discontinue the impressment of

---

[20] Minute of Interview, June 23, 1812, enclosed in Foster to Castlereagh, No. 49, June 24, 1812, *ibid.*

seamen from our vessels, and to restore those already impressed." As an inducement for Britain to yield on impressments, he was instructed that he might "give assurance that a law will be passed (to be reciprocal) to prohibit the employment of British seamen in the public or commercial service of the United States." [21]

Neither of the two doves of peace which were simultaneously sent forth from opposite sides of the Atlantic could find a resting place. The nature of the British repeal, it is important to note, was not absolute. It was to apply to American vessels and cargoes, being American property, from August 1, and was to operate retrospectively to such vessels and cargoes seized since May 20 as had not already been condemned. But there was to be no repeal at all unless the government of the United States revoked the legislation prohibiting British intercourse as soon as possible after the communication of this order; and even after American compliance nothing in this order was to be understood as precluding a revival of the orders-in-council "if circumstances shall so require." [22] When inspected in Washington, the offer was quickly rejected. It wiped out an unknown number of American claims arising since May 20 and all claims of a previous origin. More serious was another objection. The very act which offered to withdraw the intolerable offense stipulated the right to repeat it at any time. This, said Monroe, the government of the United States "cannot admit." The outbreak of war had also raised an insuperable obstacle to American compliance, for the restoration of intercourse would have meant the admission of British fighting vessels[23] along with British commercial bottoms into American ports. The repeal was therefore null and void. The American government felt little or no regret when repelling this British effort at conciliation. There was consolation in the thought that, if any satisfactory arrangement was possible, Russell was already procuring it in London.

Of the three conditions in the American proposal for an armistice, one was already met. In communicating the repeal order, Castlereagh had informed Russell that it was to be interpreted as extinguishing the blockade of 1806 and that there was no intention of reviving it or any other blockade.[24] But Russell realized that the repeal of the orders-in-council, having been adopted in ignorance of the declaration of war, could not be effective under the new circumstances; and therefore he demanded a reënactment which would make it effective. Castlereagh refused. The British government had acted in good faith and expected the American government to do the same. One may be tempted to condemn this lack of imagination, or obtrusion of national pride, but it appears probable that the British gov-

---

[21] *A.S.P.F.R.*, III, 585.

[22] *Ibid.*, p. 433.

[23] This could have been avoided only by legislation excluding French vessels of the same description.

[24] *Ibid.*, p. 434.

ernment would have accommodated the American government on this point had it not been for the third condition posed by Russell. That touched a vital British interest, and on that Castlereagh was adamant. "You," he said to the American *chargé,* "are not aware of the great sensibility and jealousy of the people of England on this subject; and no administration could expect to remain in power that should consent to renounce the right of impressment, or to suspend the practice, without the certainty of an arrangement which should obviously be calculated most unequivocally to secure its object. Whether such an arrangement can be devised is extremely doubtful, but it is very certain that you have no sufficient powers for its accomplishment." [25] The impressment issue was the rock that wrecked the last hope of peace.

Years afterwards Madison wrote, "Had the repeal of the orders been substituted for the declaration that they would not be repealed, or had they been repealed but a few weeks sooner, our declaration of war as proceeding from that cause would have been stayed, and negotiations on the subject of impressments, the other great cause, would have been pursued with fresh vigor & hopes, under the auspices of success in the case of the orders in council." [26] He did not venture to say that peace would have been preserved, for he was wiser than the later dogmatists who have confidently asserted that there would have been no War of 1812 if there had been an Atlantic cable in 1812. That will always be a debatable question.

---

[25] *Ibid.,* p. 594.

[26] Madison, IX, 273, where the word "improvements" appears instead of "impressments." This is an obvious typographical error.

X

The Ideas of the Monroe Doctrine: Adamsonian, Jeffersonian, or Monrovian

INTRODUCTION

Not until 1852 was Monroe Doctrine *used to describe the foreign policy principles of Monroe's annual message to the Congress of December 2, 1823. Characteristic of the flexible and evolutionary nature of the Doctrine, it had already begun to be amended, interpreted, and given special focus before the world knew it as the Monroe Doctrine. Successive generations of Americans have read into the Doctrine what they needed to read in order to meet the exigencies of American foreign policy. It has been a doctrine of independence, a doctrine of intervention, a doctrine of imperialism, and a doctrine of isolationism.*

A statement of American foreign policy of such profound importance as the one made by Monroe in 1823 has naturally drawn the full interest of Americans respecting all phases of its background, formulation, and adaptation to the changing needs of American foreign policy in the nineteenth and twentieth centuries. Dexter Perkins is the recognized authority on the whole scope of the Doctrine's history, but it was Worthington C. Ford, as far back as 1902, who raised in its modern form, the question of who was primarily responsible for the leading grand ideas of the document.

Samuel Flagg Bemis, distinguished historian of American diplomacy, in the selection from his biography of John Quincy Adams that is used here, fixes upon the subject of his biography the major responsibility and credit for the formulation of the doctrine, though he certainly does not deny that others than Adams, and indeed the processes of history themselves, have done much to shape the basic ideas. It is interesting to note that Bemis, writing in the late forties, followed the Ford interpretation and that he dedicated his book to that eminent scholar.

Bemis postulated "three principal dicta" of the Monroe Doctrine. They were: "Non-Colonization," "Abstention," and "Hands Off." He claims for Adams unique responsibility and unique credit for the "Non-Colonization" principle. "Abstention," he argues, was a generalized and diffuse attitude toward withdrawal from the Old World, shared by all the founding fathers and warmly supported by Adams. Bemis states: "Hands Off, the really most important principle of the Monroe Doctrine, was a principle that he had sponsored in the Cabinet deliberations, but it did not stand out in his mind [23 years later] as much as the Non-Colonization principle. Hands Off was really a corollary of Non-Colonization."

A. P. Whitaker, scholar and writer upon the relations of the United States and Latin America, in the second selection below, takes a different measure of Adams' part in the development of the great ideas of the Monroe Doctrine, and, in consequence, a different measure, too, of the parts of Jefferson and Monroe. Whitaker uses a different organization in his analysis of the ideas of the Doctrine. He refers to the "first part" and the "second part" of the document, separated in Monroe's original message by some 3,000 words on other matters. In general, however, Whitaker's "first part" is Bemis' "Non-Colonization," and his "second part," comprehending the idea of the two spheres, the idea of the American system, and the warning to Europe, corresponds with Bemis' "Abstention" and "Hands Off." Whitaker does not differ from Bemis in ascribing to Adams the credit and responsibility for "Non-Colonization," but he has a different estimate of Adams' contribution to the "second part" of the document. Here ". . . Adams rendered some valuable assistance as draftsman; but its chief architects were Jefferson and Monroe, and it reflects their greater sympathy for Latin America and their more dynamic republicanism."

The Monroe Doctrine:

Background and Statement*

Samuel Flagg Bemis

JOHN QUINCY ADAMS AND THE BACKGROUND OF THE MONROE DOCTRINE (1792–1823)

We shall assume distinctly the principle that the American continents are no longer subjects for *any* new European colonial establishments.

> *John Quincy Adams to Baron Von Tuyll,*
> *Russian Minister, July 17, 1823*

The Monroe Doctrine, as the celebrated message of President Monroe to the Congress on December 2, 1823 came to be called in later years,[1] and as we shall call it by prolepsis, consisted of three principal dicta. They were:

---

* The over-all title for this section was supplied by the editor.

Reprinted from *John Quincy Adams and the Foundations of American Foreign Policy* by Samuel Flagg Bemis, by permission of Alfred A. Knopf, Inc. Copyright 1945 by Samuel Flagg Bemis. Pp. 363–394. Occasional passages reprinted in Chapters XV, XVII, XVIII, and XIX from *The Latin American Policy of the United States*, copyright 1943 by Samuel Flagg Bemis, with permission of Harcourt, Brace & World, Inc.

[1] The phrase "Monroe Doctrine" was not coined until 1852. Dexter Perkins: *The Monroe Doctrine, 1826–1867* (Baltimore, 1933), p. 223.

(1) The Non-Colonization Principle applied to South America as well as North America, in "the rights and interests of the United States." On this point the message said: "the American Continents, by the free and independent condition which they have assumed and maintain, are henceforth not to be considered as subjects for future colonization by any European power."

(2) The principle of Abstention from the wars of the European powers in matters relating to themselves, as being in another political system than that of this Hemisphere: "It is only when our rights are invaded, or seriously menaced, that we resent injuries, or make preparations for our defense."

(3) Consequently, the dictum of Hands Off the independent states of the New World: "We could not view any interposition for the purpose of oppressing them, or controuling in any other manner, their destiny, by any European power, in any other light, than as the manifestation of an unfriendly disposition towards the United States."

Before describing the circumstances under which President Monroe pronounced the message, it is worth while to recall the part which John Quincy Adams already had played in articulating these principles.[2] Rather than consider the three postulates in the sequence in which they lie in the message, it will be better to take them in their historical order: (1) Abstention, (2) Non-Colonization, (3) Hands Off the New World. Adams had long since been intimately associated with the maxim of Abstention. It will soon be evident that he was the sole author of the Non-Colonization Principle. His connection with the precept Hands Off may be postponed to a later and more lengthy portion of this chapter and to the following one. We may now bring together some of his contributions to the Monroe Doctrine before the famous presidential pronouncement of 1823.

1

The dictum of Abstention was common to all the Fathers of American independence, including John Adams. In its classic exposition it was Washingtonian, although Alexander Hamilton was responsible for its phraseology. From the beginning John Quincy Adams had thought like

---

[2] No later student can touch the subject of this and the following chapter without a word of gratitude to Worthington Chauncey Ford for his pioneer documentary studies. The first was "Some Original Documents on the Genesis of the Monroe Doctrine," MHS *Proc.*, 2d Series, XV (1902), 373–436, separately published under the title of *John Quincy Adams, His Connection with the Monroe Doctrine (1823)* (Cambridge, 1902). It is to this separate print, a copy of which the late author presented to me in 1925, that I make my page references. A subsequent article, based on the documents printed in the first contribution, appeared in the *AHR*, VII (No. 4, July 1902), 676–96, and VIII (No. 1, October 1902), 28–52.

Washington on foreign affairs. His advocacy of Abstention had originally commended him to the serious attention of the first President. In the letters of "Marcellus" in 1794 he had said: "It is our duty to remain, the peaceful and silent, though sorrowful spectators of the European scene." The famous warning of the Farewell Address against entanglement in the ordinary vicissitudes and the ordinary combinations of European wars and politics bears traces of the ideas and phraseology of John Quincy Adams's early diplomatic dispatches from the Netherlands. As early as 1796 he had discerned and labeled "the American System"[3] of polity, as opposed to the European System—two separate systems, two spheres. Years later, as Secretary of State, he had sensed in the South American revolutions the same temptation that had beset his fellow countrymen in the time of the French Revolution: to rush into a foreign conflict to save somebody else's liberty—and perhaps to lose their own. In explaining to Onís why the United States declined the mediation offer of Great Britain in 1818 he said: "It has hitherto been the policy both of Europe and of the United States, to keep aloof from the general federative system of each other."[4] "America," he declared on the Fourth of July 1821, "is the well-wisher to the freedom and independence of all. She is the champion and vindicator only of her own." In his instructions to Richard Anderson, first American Minister to Colombia, he repeated the words of "Marcellus." The United States would continue to be "tranquil but deeply attentive spectators" of the war between the new republics of Latin America and Spain. In the Monroe Doctrine the words would be "anxious and interested spectators," in favor of the liberty and happiness of fellow men on the other side of the Atlantic.

If the United States, according to John Quincy Adams, were not going to take the side of republican liberty in another people's struggle, whether in Europe or in America, it certainly would not take the side of absolutism and tyranny anywhere on the globe. Ever since 1818 Alexander I of Russia had been urging the Republic of the West to join the Holy Alliance and thus associate it with the collective mediation of legitimist Europe between

---

[3] Above, Ch. III, last page.

[4] "The European states are combined together, and connected with one another by a multitude of important interests and relations with which the United States have no concern, with which they have always manifested the determination not to interfere, and of which, no communication being made to them by the Governments of Europe, they have not information competent to enable them to estimate their extent and bearings. The United States, in justice to themselves, in justice to that harmony which they earnestly desire to cultivate with all the powers of Europe, in justice to that fundamental system of policy which forbids them from entering the labyrinth of European politics, must decline soliciting or acceding to the interference of any other Government of Europe for the settlement of their differences with Spain." JQA to Luis de Onís, March 12, 1818. *ASPFR,* IV, 478. This is the state paper that Jefferson praised so highly.

Spain and her revolted colonies.[5] In his well-known instructions of 1820 to Henry Middleton, Minister to Russia, the Secretary of State explained for the benefit of Czar Alexander I why the President must decline a Russian invitation to membership in the "League of Peace." On this occasion he repeated the "great rule of conduct" of Washington's Farewell Address: "The political system of the United States is also[6] extra-European. To stand in firm and cautious independence of all entanglement in the European system, has been a cardinal point of their policy under every administration of their government from the peace of 1783 to this day. . . . It may be observed that for the repose of Europe, as well as of America, the European and American political systems should be kept as separate and distinct from each other as possible."[7] This is little more than he already had personally explained to the Czar in St. Petersburg back in 1809.

It was not Adams's idea alone. By 1820 the "doctrine of the two spheres," as publicists of the twentieth century call Adams's expressions of 1796, was widely current in American thought. It distilled and crystallized the diplomatic experience of American independence. It was orthodox to all the Fathers, particularly to Thomas Jefferson and John Adams.

John Quincy Adams's American System did not yet embrace the whole Hemisphere. "As to an American System," he exclaimed to President Monroe in 1820 regarding the use of that phrase by the Abbé Correa, "we have it; we constitute the whole of it; there is no community of interests or of principles between North and South America. Mr. Torres and Bolivar and O'Higgins talk about an American system as much as the Abbé Correa, but there is no basis for any such system."[8]

---

[5] "Correspondence of the Russian Ministers in Washington, 1818–1825," *AHR*, XVIII (Nos. 2 and 3, January, April 1913), 309–45, 537–62. Dexter Perkins has described the relationship of "Russia and the Spanish Colonies, 1817–1818," in *ibid.*, XXVIII (No. 4, July 1923), 656–73. See also William Spence Robertson: "Russia and the Emancipation of Spanish America, 1816–1826," *HAHR*, XXI (No. 2, May 1941), 196–221.

[6] I.e., like that of Persia and Turkey, whom Adams mentioned as having the most to dread from "the overshadowing and encroaching powers" of the Holy Alliance.

[7] JQA to Henry Middleton, Department of State, July 5, 1820. *Writings*, VII, 49–50. "I have read with much satisfaction your project of instructions to Mr. Middleton, for the discharge of his duties, in his mission to Russia. The objects to which you call his attention, are judiciously pointed out, and discussed. . . ." James Monroe to JQA, Highland, July 28, 1820. Adams MSS.

[8] Monroe had been telling Adams that the Abbé Correa had been upon a visit to Jefferson, "to whom he talked so much about an American system, in which his Government [Portugal] and ours should be united, and, by concert with the European powers, should agree to keep the coasts of this hemisphere clear of pirates, on condition that they should sweep the seas of the Eastern Hemisphere clear of Barbary pirates. . . ." *Memoirs*, V, 176. September 19, 1820. "The idea [Correa's] has something imposing in it," Monroe had written to Adams on August 11, 1820, "but I am inclined to think, that the effect, would be, to connect us with Portugal, in some degree, against the revolutionary colonies." Adams MSS.

2

The dictum of Non-Colonization was Adamsonian. John Quincy Adams had long since believed that the United States was destined by God and nature peaceably to become a nation coextensive with the North American Continent.[9] Through the first half-century of American independence his continental instincts had nourished an opposition to all colonial dominion first in North America, then in South America. "Our natural dominion of North America" was the phrase he had used when explaining the departure of the *Ontario* to receive the surrender of Fort George at Astoria. In the treaties of 1818 with England and of 1819 with Spain he had successfully asserted that natural dominion.

Adams smarted under the invectives of the British press and English spokesmen against American expansion through the empty Continent. When the Cabinet was discussing the propriety of occupying Texas as well as Florida should Spain refuse to ratify the Transcontinental Treaty, Crawford had quoted William Lowndes, South Carolina's highly respected Congressman, just returned from a European trip, to the effect that in both England and France people seemed profoundly impressed with the idea that Americans were an ambitious and encroaching people. Similar remarks that Alexander H. Everett picked up when passing through London on his way to his post at The Hague had stirred John Quincy Adams's ire.[10] The way to stop such talk, he felt, was to convince the world that it was inevitable that the United States should peaceably take over all of North America: "any effort on our part to reason the world out of a belief that we are ambitious will have no other effect than to convince them that we add to our ambition hypocrisy." [11]

---

[9] Above, Ch. IX.

[10] "The Ministerial papers attack the unprincipled ambition of the United States, which they say will never be satisfied until it has invaded one whole American Continent." A. H. Everett to JQA, private, London, April 19, 1819. Received June 17. Adams MSS.

[11] "Nothing that we can say or do would remove this impression [Adams told his colleagues in the Cabinet] until the world shall be familiarized with the idea of considering our proper dominion to be the continent of North America. . . . Spain has possessions upon our southern and Great Britain upon our northern border. It is impossible that centuries shall elapse without finding them annexed to the United States; not that any spirit of encroachment or ambition on our part renders it necessary, but because it is a physical, moral, and political absurdity that such fragments of territory, with sovereigns at fifteen hundred [*sic*] miles beyond the sea, worthless and burdensome to their owners, should exist permanently contiguous to a great powerful and rapidly-growing nation. Most of the Spanish territory which had been in our neighborhood has already become our own by the most unexceptionable of all acquisitions—fair purchase for a valuable consideration. This renders it still more unavoidable that the remainder of the continent should ultimately be ours. But it is very lately that we have distinctly seen this ourselves; very lately that we have avowed the pretension of extending to the South Sea; and until Europe shall find it a settled geographical element that the United States and North America are identical, any effort on our part to reason the world out of a belief that we

So far this expression was for the privity only of Monroe's official closet. The pretensions of Britain and Russia to the North West Coast of America (to be considered more particularly in later chapters) gave the Secretary of State occasions for presenting the Non-Colonization Principle first to the British Minister in Washington, and next to the Russian Minister.

"We certainly did suppose that the British Government had come to the conclusion," he said to Stratford Canning, in an oft-quoted conversation, January 26, 1821, concerning the Columbia River, "that there would be neither policy nor profit in caviling with us about territory on this North American Continent."

"And in this," Canning asked, "you include our northern provinces on this Continent."

"No," Adams admitted grudgingly. "There the boundary is marked, and we have no disposition to encroach upon it. Keep what is yours, but leave the rest of the Continent to us." [12]

That John Quincy Adams did not expect Great Britain to keep the rest of the Continent very long is evident from his significant Fourth-of-July address of 1821, when he affirmed the theory of noncolonization as a principle of anti-imperialism. In a remarkable exegesis of that discourse to his friend Edward Everett he explained that he had meant to point out that, from the moral and physical nature of man, *"colonial establishments cannot fulfil the great objects of governments in the just purposes of civil society."* The address anticipated a vital question in the national policy of the United States: "whether we too shall annex to our federative government a great system of colonial establishments." It pointed to another principle: "that such establishments are incompatible with the essential character of our institutions." It led to a startling conclusion: "that great colonial establishments are engines of wrong, and that in the progress of social improvement it will be the duty of the human family to abolish them, as they are now endeavoring to abolish the slave trade." [13]

Adams came back to the Non-Colonization Principle again in November 1822 in another conversation with the British Minister, this time on restriction of trade with the British West Indies. "The whole system of modern colonization," he declared to Stratford Canning, "is an abuse of government and it is time that it should come to an end." [14]

The Secretary embodied the principle in a draft of instructions (June 1823) for the guidance of Middleton in St. Petersburg: the United States would contest the right of Russia to any territorial establishments on the

---

are ambitious will have no other effect than to convince them that we add to our ambition hypocrisy." *Memoirs*, IV, 438–9. November 16, 1819. Dexter Perkins's classic dissertation: *The Monroe Doctrine, 1823–1826* (Cambridge, 1927) has brought together in a notable chaper Adams's evolving expressions of the Non-Colonization Principle.

[12] *Memoirs*, V, 252. January 26, 1821.

[13] *Writings*, VII, 197–207. January 31, 1822.

[14] *Memoirs*, VI, 104. November 26, 1822.

Continent of North America. This categorical statement worried the President. After discussing the matter in Cabinet, Monroe decided to recognize the Russian claims north of 55° N.L.[15] But in an interview with von Tuyll on July 17, 1823 Adams managed to say what the President would not let him put into the instructions to Middleton: "I told him specially that we should contest the right of Russia to *any* territorial establishment on this continent, and that we should assume distinctly the principle that the American continents are no longer subjects for any new European colonial establishments." [16]

Adams had summoned forth the Non-Colonization Principle out of his own intuition. He expressed it gratuitously to both the British and the Russian Ministers. Once more before Monroe's famous message of December 2, 1823 he reiterated the idea for the benefit of the British Government. That was when he was drawing up instructions for the guidance of Richard Rush in parallel negotiations by the United States and Great Britain protesting Russian pretensions on the North West Coast. The independence of the South American states and of Mexico, he then stated, had extinguished the exclusive rights of Spain to any part of the Coast, such as she might have claimed at the time of the Nootka Sound Convention of 1790. "A necessary consequence of this state of things will be that the American Continents henceforth will no longer be subjects of *colonization*." [17]

Thus all his life John Quincy Adams had been a spokesman of Abstention. And all students of the question have agreed that he was sole author of Non-Colonization. But what of the third dictum—Hands Off the New World, America for the Americans? To understand the provenience of this dogma and Adams's relation to it, we must return again to Europe, to the predicaments of British and of American diplomacy in the face of the Holy Alliance.

3

British policy after the overthrow of Napoleon embraced supremacy on the seas behind a balance of power concerted in the Quadruple Alliance (Austria, Great Britain, Prussia, Russia) to maintain the peace of Europe against another eruption of revolutionary France. Britain's continental allies under the leadership of Alexander I would fain have used the Quadruple Alliance for another purpose: to repress revolution wherever it might raise its head against a legitimist divine-right ruler. To that end the Czar had proclaimed in 1815, under lofty Christian principles, the

---

[15] *Memoirs*, VI, 157–8. July 27, 1823.
[16] *Memoirs*, VI, 163. July 17, 1823.
[17] JQA to Richard Rush, Department of State, July 22, 1823. *Writings of Monroe*, VI, 356–7.

Holy Alliance. It was signed originally by himself, the King of Prussia, the Emperor of Austria, and all the legitimist monarchs of Europe except the Sultan of Turkey, the Pope, and the Prince Regent of Great Britain. The British Regent could not condemn revolution too directly because his dynasty owed its throne to the Revolution of 1688. Therefore the Regent had to content himself with a personal letter to the Czar applauding the principles of the Holy Alliance without binding his own Government, which was responsible only to Parliament.

For the first few years following the peace settlement of 1815—that is, until after the Conference of Aix-la-Chapelle—Lord Castlereagh had been able to hold the Quadruple Alliance to its strict purpose as interpreted by his Government; but in 1820 the continental allies got out of British control. At the Conference of Troppau-Laibach (1820–1) the Holy Allies, despite the dissent of Great Britain, gave a mandate to Austria to put down republican revolution in Naples and in Piedmont lest it spread to their own realms. At Verona in 1822 they again overrode British opposition and approved French military intervention in Spain to tear up the new constitution there and restore the absolute authority of Ferdinand VII. They even announced that if Great Britain, ally of Spain since the first Peninsular War, should interfere to assist the Spanish constitutionalists, they would come to the aid of France.

Castlereagh had failed in his task of holding the Quadruple Alliance to the compass of British policy. Overburdened by the immense responsibilities and labors of his office, his reason faltered and he made away with his own life on the eve of the Conference of Verona.

Castlereagh's tragic death opened the office of Foreign Affairs to his rival George Canning. Canning was son of an impoverished London barrister of ancient English lineage and Mary Anne Costello, reigning London beauty and in her later years a popular actress. He was the pride of Eton, Oxford, and the Inner Temple. In his youth he had been a liberal Whig, the friend of Burke, Fox, and Sheridan, but the excesses of the French Revolution drove him, like Burke, into the paths of Toryism, and he became Pitt's Undersecretary of Foreign Affairs, 1796–1801 (succeeding George Hammond), and Treasurer of the Navy, 1801–6. When Pitt died he momentarily went out of office. Then he married a rich bride, sister of the Duke of Portland, and came into the Government of his brother-in-law as Secretary for Foreign Affairs, 1807–9. It was Canning who planned the seizure of the Danish fleet after the Treaty of Tilsit, the coup that broke up Napoleon's formidable plans for a northern confederation against England. During his first tenure of the Foreign Office appeared the belligerent orders in council of November 1807, calculated to destroy competing American commerce.

When Castlereagh as Secretary for War diverted English forces originally planned for the Peninsula to stem the French at Flushing, Canning resented the move and intrigued secretly to unseat his colleague, the while preserving outwardly friendly relations with him in the Cabinet. As soon as Castlereagh awoke to the invidious situation, he challenged Canning to a duel. The Ministers fired two rounds at close pistol range. It is a wonder they did not shoot each other dead. Their first shots went nervously wild. Happily Canning's second glanced harmless off a metal button of his opponent's coat, and Castlereagh's next try gave Canning a slight flesh wound in the thigh. The famous encounter ended Canning's first ministerial career; he could scarcely serve in the Cabinet as long as his rival held any office therein.

The two Tory diplomatists, the greatest England ever had, pursued, each in his own way, Britain's interests in holding the balance of power in Europe. Castlereagh, a strong and serene statesman, adroit and tactful in personal diplomacy, strove to keep the balance by grouping the powers lest any one, notably Russia, get out of hand and become preponderant. Canning, a witty litterateur—too much wit, thought John Quincy Adams,[18] for a Secretary of State—and brilliant parliamentarian, did not believe much in the efficacy of the European concert. He sought to maintain the balance in Britain's favor by building up wherever possible irresistible situations with which to oppose and to outweigh his adversaries. One such situation he found ready to hand in Latin America.

When Canning reappeared in the Foreign Office, 1822–7, it was difficult to oppose the Holy Alliance on the Continent of Europe. Wellington's army of the Napoleonic wars no longer existed. The fleet was powerless to stop a continental force from crossing the Pyrenees. Moreover, the King, the Duke of Wellington, and influential Tory leaders sympathized with the French intervention as long as it limited itself to the suppression of revolution and did not extend its force to collide with British interests beyond the boundaries of Spain.

With the Quadruple Alliance in ruins in Europe and the political front divided at home, Canning went as far as he could when he stated in the House of Commons that he hoped the Spanish constitutionalists would win out: "Indifference we can never feel towards the affairs of Spain: and I earnestly hope and trust that she may come triumphantly out of the struggle." [19]

As hostilities broke out south of the Pyrenees, the new Foreign Minister communicated to the French Government, through a dispatch (March 31, 1823) to Sir Charles Stuart, the Ambassador at Paris, a formal warning implying that war would follow if France should establish a permanent military occupation of Spain, or should appropriate any portion of the Spanish colonies, or should violate the territorial integrity of Portugal.

Canning concluded his dispatch to Stuart, published in England within five days after its signature, with these words:

---

[18] *Memoirs*, III, 337.   [19] Temperley: *Canning*, p. 85.

> With respect to the Provinces in America which have thrown off their allegiance to the Crown of Spain. . . . Spain has long been apprized of His Majesty's opinions upon this subject. Disclaiming in the most solemn manner any intention of appropriating to himself the smallest portion of the late Spanish possessions in America, His Majesty is satisfied that no attempt will be made by France to bring under her dominion any of those possessions, either by conquest or by cession from Spain.[20]

France had invaded Spain with the mandate of the Holy Alliance. The Quadruple Alliance was dead. How could the unbalance of Europe now be compensated?[21] Where else could Canning rally an opposition to French intervention in the affairs of Latin America, first step perhaps in a revival of a French colonial empire and of French sea power?

There was left only one direction in which to turn. That was across the Atlantic. In the House of Commons on April 16, 1823 Canning made a speech defending British neutrality and specifically opposing repeal of the Foreign Enlistments Act. He went out of his way to extol as a model the American principles of neutrality in the War of the French Revolution.[22] A week later he gave a dinner to the diplomatic corps to celebrate the King's birthday. When it came the turn of the American Minister to raise his glass, Richard Rush gave the toast: "To the success of neutrals!" Canning applauded conspicuously and made further flattering references to Jefferson and American neutrality.[23]

Responding to Lord Castlereagh's general policy of appeasement and repose, Anglo-American relations had been ameliorating steadily, notably in regard to the territorial questions on the Continent of North America. The focus of rivalry had now shifted from the Great Lakes and the Northwest to the Caribbean and Cuba. That island had become as essential to the protection of Florida as previously Florida had been to the safety of Louisiana. The integrity of both Florida and Louisiana—that is to say, the security of the westward-advancing Continental Republic—now depended on who possessed Cuba. While the Holy Alliance sponsored the French occupation of Spain and British diplomacy deployed to resist any further intervention of France to restore Spanish sovereignty in the New World, John Quincy Adams had his eyes fixed on England as well as on France. Like his father in his time, he knew that France could not break through British sea power to reach the Western Hemisphere. What worried him was that the Spanish constitutionalists might cede Cuba and perhaps Porto Rico to

---

[20] Webster: *Britain and the Independence of Latin America*, II, 111–12.

[21] "Canning had to win diplomatic prestige over Spanish America as a set-off to his diplomatic defeat in Europe." Temperley: *Canning*, p. 103.

[22] *Speeches of George Canning*, R. Thierry, editor, V (London, 1886), 24–52.

[23] Richard Rush to James Monroe, April 24, 1823. Cited by Whitaker: *U. S. and Independence of Latin America*, pp. 435–7.

England as the price of a new Anglo-Spanish alliance in another Peninsular War.

Cuba was of vital interest to the United States, and it was clearly desirable that it should continue for the time being in Spanish hands. Presidents Jefferson, Madison, and Monroe had never been so sympathetic to revolutionary strivings in that island as they had been toward insurrection in the Spanish provinces of the mainland. When an agent, Don Barnabé Sanchez, tried to get the authorities in Washington to encourage a revolution in Havana for the independence of Cuba and its admission into the American Union as a new state, Monroe's Government would not see him or have anything to do with him.[24] The members of the Administration feared that a premature uprising in the Pearl of the Antilles—before the slavery question was settled in the United States[25]—might disturb what Madison had once referred to as the "manifest course of events," and what John Quincy Adams now called "the law of political gravitation" [26]—that is, ultimate annexation to the United States. "The Cuban question," Adams noted after a Cabinet meeting of September 30, 1822, was of "deeper importance and greater magnitude than had occurred since the establishment of our Independence." [27]

There were at least two contingencies in which Europe's new war might become America's war, Adams believed: a maritime war resulting in the impressment of American seamen, or a war threatening the transfer of neighboring Spanish territory, like Cuba or Porto Rico, in such a way as to endanger the security of the Union. It was such a possibility that led him to apply the No-Transfer Principle of 1811 to the island of Cuba in the summer of 1823 as French armies occupied Spain.[28]

Cuba was also of vital interest to Britain. "It may be questioned," noted George Canning in a Cabinet Memorandum, "whether any blow, that could be struck by any power in any part of the world, would have a more sensible effect on the interests of this country or the reputation of its government." The British Government did not want to see the island transferred to France or the United States any more than the United States cared to have it transferred to Great Britain or France. American possession of Cuba would jeopardize the Jamaica trade and ruin Britain's position and

---

[24] Copies of correspondence between Peter S. Duponceau and General John Mason. September 1822. Adams MSS.

[25] "Were the population of the island of one blood and color, there could be no doubt or hesitation with regard to the course they [the United States] would pursue, as dictated by their interests and their rights." *Writings*, VII, 375.

[26] *Writings*, VII, 373.   [27] *Memoirs*, VI, 72–3.

[28] Instructions from JQA to Hugh Nelson, the new Minister going out to Spain. Department of State, April 28, 1823. *Writings*, VII, 369–422. See particularly pp. 379–81 of the *Writings*. Whitaker, op. cit., p. 400, has pointed out from JQA's *Memoirs*, VI, 138, that Adams did not believe it was within the competency of the United States to "prevent by war the British from obtaining possession of Cuba, if they attempted to take it."

interests in the whole Caribbean.[29] Canning directed his cousin Stratford, Minister in Washington, to inquire into the "designs" of the United States upon that Spanish colony, without putting any categorical questions to Mr. Adams.[30]

During the diplomatic crisis that preceded the French invasion of Spain, Canning proclaimed the intention to land naval forces in Cuba if necessary in order to pursue pirates preying on British shipping. For the benefit of Monroe's Government he directed Stratford to read (but not to give a copy) to John Quincy Adams the instructions of December 1 to Sir Charles Stuart, British Ambassador in Paris, disavowing any thought of taking advantage of such a "trespass" on Cuban soil for the purpose of appropriating any part of Spanish America, and "giving full credit" to the King of France for being actuated by similar principles.[31] Such assurance was not a full pledge to the United States, but it was helpful.

It was at this juncture that President Monroe suggested to his Cabinet the proposing to Great Britain of a mutual self-denial not to take Cuba. The Secretary of War as well as the Secretary of State immediately objected. Nothing could be gained by it, thought Calhoun. It would involve a proposal to Spain also, said Adams, and would plunge the United States into the "whirlpool" of European politics.[32]

Reassurance soon came in from London after Stratford Canning had reported the absence of any American intention to occupy Cuba.[33] The Prime Minister, Lord Liverpool, assured Richard Rush that the British Government, although it would tolerate no change in the island's sovereignty, had no intention to take over Cuba itself.[34] In this way a sort of gentleman's agreement sprang up between Monroe and Canning in 1823 that it would be best to let Cuba rest in the quiet possession of Spain. Monroe relied on Great Britain to bring France into the informal understanding.[35]

Thus another great issue in Anglo-American relations seemed quieted, the issue of intervention in the New World, notably in Cuba.[36]

---

[29] Webster: *Britain and the Independence of Latin America*, II, 393–4.

[30] George Canning to Stratford Canning, No. 7, Secret, Foreign Office, October 11, 1822 (draft). PRO, F.O., 5, Vol. CLXV.

[31] George Canning to Sir Charles Stuart, No. 15, December 3, 1822. Webster, op. cit., II, 110.

[32] *Memoirs*, VI, 138. March 17, 1823.

[33] Stratford Canning to George Canning, No. 3, Washington, January 1, 1823 (received February 6, 1823), No. 10 (Secret), January 11, 1823 (received February 14, 1823), and No. 17, February 4, 1823 (received March 10, 1823). PRO, F.O. 5, Vol. CLXXV.

[34] Richard Rush to JQA, No. 298, London, March 10, 1823. Received April 6. DS, *Despatches from U. S. Ministers to Great Britain*, XVIII.

[35] JQA to W. E. Channing, Quincy, July 31, August 11, 1837. *N. E. Quarterly*, V (No. 3, July 1932), 594–600.

[36] Stratford Canning to George Canning, No. 56, Confidential, Washington, June 6, 1823. Webster, op. cit., II, 495–6.

4

Now that the two powers had come to see eye to eye on the Holy Alliance and the danger of European intervention in the Western Hemisphere, the opposing attitudes of the United States and Great Britain as to the *independence* of the new states of Latin America remained the only difference of policy in this part of the world. And it was reasonable to expect that the question of independence must soon settle itself.

There were, however, several other long-standing Anglo-American issues of more than regional significance. The Monroe Administration had been striving in vain ever since its inauguration to settle them with Lord Castlereagh: impressment, suppression of the African slave trade, the Freedom of the Seas, and colonial trade, not to mention still unsettled boundary controversies in the northeast and the northwest. It had long been the thought of Monroe and Adams that if these differences could first be settled the way would be open for a concert of policy in regard to Latin America. Now it looked as though the process might be reversed, that a concert of policy toward Latin America might open the way for settlement of the historic controversies between the United States and Great Britain. The disappearance of issues in regard to the former Spanish Empire—above all, the confirmed neutrality of Great Britain in the Spanish-American conflict as well as in the Franco-Spanish hostilities in the Peninsula—promised to make neutral rights and interests as significant to Great Britain as her old belligerent pretensions had been during the last cycle of wars. At least so Adams professed to believe. If this were true, might it not be possible to resolve the vexatious issues that had separated the two Governments since the Napoleonic conflict? With the President's approbation, he began to draw up instructions to Richard Rush in London for another general negotiation with Great Britain to resolve for all time the old disputes that had caused the War of 1812.[37] Parallel to this would be a negotiation with Russia, by Henry Middleton in St. Petersburg, on the question of neutral rights, freedom of commerce on the North West Coast, and boundaries. These two negotiations will be the subject of later chapters. Here we must observe the more immediate significance of Anglo-American affairs for Latin America.

Stratford Canning noted the new and happier spirit in official Washington. "The course which you have taken in the great politics of Europe," he wrote privately to his cousin George, "has had the effect of making the English almost popular in the United States. The improved tone of public feeling is very perceptible, and even Adams has caught a something of the soft infection. The communication of your correspondence with France has also had its effect. On the whole, I question whether for a long time there has been so favorable an opportunity—as far as general disposition and

---

[37] JQA to R. Rush, Department of State, July 22, July 28 (No. 71), 1823. *Writings of Monroe*, VI, 356–61.

good will are concerned—to bring the two countries nearer together. France for the moment is quite out of fashion. It may possibly be worth your while to give this a turn in your thoughts." [38]

John Quincy Adams broached his plans to the British Minister. "Britain has separated herself from the councils and measures of the alliance," he observed to Stratford. "She avows the principles which are emphatically those of the United States, and she disapproves the principles of the alliance, which this country abhors. This coincidence of principles, connected with the great changes in affairs of the world, passing before us, seems to me a suitable occasion for the United States and Great Britain to compare their ideas and purposes together, with a view to the accommodation of great interests upon which they have hitherto differed."

Stratford Canning preferred to think that this might be a proposal for an alliance, but Adams insisted that it had been always the policy of the United States to hold aloof from the European System of politics. What he was talking about, he said, was an agreement on neutral rights, impressment, the slave trade, and commerce with the British colonies[39]—the settlement of the already historic Anglo-American issues.

With affairs in this satisfying position, Adams, in tranquil spirit, set forth in mid-August 1823 for his annual vacation with his aged father in Quincy.

5

In London, George Canning chose to interpret the soft American infection as a disposition not so much to define and strengthen neutral rights as to oppose European intervention in Latin America, particularly any threatened French occupation of the island of Cuba. An opportunity to exploit the new feeling presented itself when Rush casually asked about affairs on the Continent. "Should France ultimately effect her purpose of overthrowing the constitutional government in Spain," he remarked, "there is, at least, the consolation left that Great Britain would not allow her to go farther and stop the progress of emancipation in the colonies."

In this transient remark George Canning, prompted by Stratford's suggestions from Washington, was quick to see an opening.

"What do you think your Government would say to going hand in hand with England in such a policy?" he asked Rush. "Not that any concert of *action* under it would become necessary, because I fully believe that the simple fact of our two countries being known to hold the same opinions would, by its moral effect, put down the intention on the part of France, if she entertains it. I base this belief upon the large share of the maritime

---

[38] May 8, 1823. Perkins, op. cit., p. 60, citing PRO, F.O., 352, Vol. VIII, and Stratford Canning Papers. See also Stratford Canning to George Canning, No. 56, Washington, June 6, 1823. Webster, op. cit., II, 495.

[39] *Memoirs*, VI, 151–5. June 20, 1823.

power of the world which Great Britain and the United States share between them, and the consequent influence which the knowledge of their common policy, on a question involving such important maritime interests, present and future, could not fail to produce everywhere."

"I am unable to say in what manner my Government would look upon such a suggestion . . ." Rush replied, "but I will communicate it in the same informal manner in which you have thrown it before me." Then he added, acutely: "I can hardly do this to full advantage unless you will at the same time enlighten me as to the precise situation in which England stands in relation to those new communities, and especially on the material point of acknowledging their independence."

Canning answered that Great Britain would not object to an accommodation between Spain and the colonies which might even secure to Spain commercial advantages not extended to other nations. Great Britain would not offer her mediation again but would not interfere to prevent a compromise.

"Is Great Britain at this moment taking any steps," Rush asked more specifically, "or contemplating any, which have reference to the recognition of these new communities, that being the point on which the United States would naturally feel most interest?"

"None whatever, as yet," admitted Canning, "but she is on the eve of taking one of a preparatory nature, which will leave her at large to recognize or not, according to the position of events at a future period." [40]

This was the first of several conversations between the two diplomatists in August and September 1823 during which Canning proposed in writing that the United States and Great Britain issue a joint declaration of policy in regard to the Spanish-American question as follows:

1. We conceive the recovery of the colonies by Spain to be hopeless.

2. We conceive the question of the recognition of them, as independent states, to be one of time and circumstances.

3. We are, however, by no means disposed to throw any impediment in the way of an arrangement between them and the mother country by amicable negotiations.

4. We aim not at the possession of any portion of them ourselves.

5. We could not see any portion of them transferred to any other power with indifference.[41]

---

[40] Richard Rush: *Memoranda of a Residence at the Court of London* (Philadelphia, 1845), II, 10–13. W. C. Ford printed Rush's correspondence on Canning's overture, together with documents from the Adams papers, hitherto unprinted, in his articles, op. cit. See also the documentary history of the origin of the Monroe Doctrine in S. M. Hamilton's edition of *Writings of Monroe*, VI, 319–444. Manning, III, Nos. 790, 791, 797, printed some important dispatches from Rush, and letters from him to Canning, not previously published. I have put the conversation into direct discourse observing its literal content if not its entire phraseology, which varies slightly but not materially in Rush's different versions.

[41] Canning to Rush, Private and Confidential, Foreign Office, August 20, 1823. Moore: *Digest of International Law*, VI, 389.

That is to say, Canning sought to implement by an Anglo-American concert the policy of Britain laid down publicly in the instructions to Stuart of the previous March 31.

The British Foreign Minister asked Rush if he had powers to sign a convention, or at least an exchange of notes, on this subject. In repeated conversations until September 26 he urged the desirability of such a joint pronouncement. He stated that he had just received "notice" that as soon as the French occupation of Spain was completed a conference of the Allies would be proposed to discuss the affairs of South America.

Richard Rush had no explicit powers to join in such a statement. But he was willing to risk his career for the independence of the New World.[42] If the step would benefit his own Government, well and good, he would sign; if he proved to be wrong, his Government could disavow him.[43] But first Canning must recognize the independence of the new republics.

The British Foreign Minister was now courting the United States more and more ardently.[44] Through Rush he had sent to President Monroe and to John Quincy Adams prints, corrected in his own hand, of his speech of April 16, 1823 against repeal of the Foreign Enlistment Act: "If I wished for a guide in a system of neutrality, I should take that laid down by America in the presidency of Washington and the secretaryship of Jefferson." [45]

Canning's flatteries did not stop with this compliment. In Liverpool an obscure American diplomat, happening to be in that port at the time of a visit of the Foreign Minister there, was surprised to find himself the object of unusual attentions. Christopher Hughes, John Quincy Adams's old friend from Ghent days, now chargé d'affaires at Stockholm and voluminous private correspondent on European politics, arrived in Liverpool in mid-August 1823 en route to London and St. Petersburg with instructions to Rush and Middleton. The Mayor of the city invited him to a special dinner for the British statesman, and the Steam Boat Company sent tickets for an "aquatic excursion" for the visiting notables. The captain even stopped the boat to take on Hughes after the excursion had been under way for two hours. On board, Canning overwhelmed him with special courtesies and

---

[42] J. H. Powell: *Richard Rush, Republican Diplomat, 1780–1859* (Philadelphia, 1942), p. 160. This biography adds a few new interesting details to previous accounts of the Rush-Canning conversations, but informs us that the great mass of Rush's papers, now owned by descendants, is still not available to historical scholars. Whitaker, op. cit., however, used the material relating to the immediate background of the Monroe Doctrine.

[43] Rush to JQA, London, August 28, 1823. Manning, III, 1483.

[44] "We were not prepared to acknowledge [Latin-American independence] immediately; and of course we would not stipulate against Spain. Our flirtation therefore went off; but it left a tenderness behind it. It was in the midst of this flirtation that I made the speech at Liverpool. . . ." George Canning to Bagot, Private and Confidential, January 22, 1824. Josceline Bagot: *George Canning and His Friends* (London, 1909), II, 215–18.

[45] *Speeches of George Canning*, V, 50. Rush to JQA, London, July 13, 1823, transmitting copies of the speech, with Canning's personal covering note. Adams MSS.

kindness. When they went on shore he took the astonished diplomat's arm and made a great object of showing him the town, as if to demonstrate how warm his feelings were for Britain's great friends and customers. It was, Hughes thought, as if to make up for all Britain's former offenses to the Yankees.

In seductive confidence Canning informed Hughes that the court of St. Petersburg had retracted all the extravagant old claims and pretensions to the control and command of the North Pacific Ocean.[46] "The only question," he said, "to *settle,* is how moderately *we* shall let them down, or let them off; or what shall be the nature of the atonement we shall consent to receive for their folly. . . . I conceive your interests are in common with ours in these questions with Russia." [47]

The climax came at the banquet when Canning proposed the health of the overwhelmed chargé. Great Britain and the United States, he said, had already forgotten their former dissensions: "The force of blood again prevails, and the daughter and the mother stand together against the world." [48]

Turning Christopher Hughes over to the hospitality of the Duke of Buckingham,[49] George Canning hastened back to London and conferred with his cousin Stratford, just returned from Washington.[50] Then he renewed his American suit. He pleaded long and passionately with Rush to take the plunge into the vortex of European politics without Britain's first recognizing Latin-American independence.

"If you continue to be unable to assent to my past proposals," said the British Minister, "my duties and station as the organ of this Government may oblige me to call upon you in another way. If a Congress be assembled upon the affairs of Spanish America, I shall ask that you, as the representative of the United States at this court, be invited to attend. If you are not invited, I shall reserve to myself the option of determining whether or not Great Britain shall send a representative to it. Hence you see the complication of the whole subject; hence you see how essential it is, in the opinion of Great Britain, that the United States should not be left out of view, if Europe is determined to take cognizance of the subject."

---

[46] See below, Ch. XXV.

[47] Christopher Hughes to JQA, private, Liverpool, August 27, 1823. Italics inserted. Adams MSS.

[48] *Speeches of George Canning,* VI, 414. "He did not know then," says a most distinguished historian of British diplomacy, "that the daughter and the mother, though they were both to stand against the world, were to stand against it in separation." Temperley: *Canning,* p. 2.

[49] Christopher Hughes to JQA, private, Brussels, October 28, 1826, describes how "somehow or other" the Duke of Buckingham "took me into great favor, in the year 1823, as I passed through England." Adams MSS. Canning gave Hughes a letter to Charles Bagot, now British Ambassador to Russia: "I hope he will be as acceptable an accident to you in your Metropolis as he has been to me in mine." "He is not yet recovered from his delight and astonishment of all that befell him at Liverpool," Bagot wrote to Canning on October 29, 1823. J. Bagot: *Canning and His Friends,* II, 199, 200.

[50] J. Bagot: *Canning and His Friends,* II, 200.

Rush was impressed, but not convinced. "You can cure the complication at once," he responded. "Let Great Britain immediately and unequivocally acknowledge the independence of the new states. This will put an end to all difficulty. The moment is auspicious, everything invites to the measure, justice, expediency, humanity; the repose of the world, the cause of national independence, the prosperity and happiness of both hemispheres. Let Britain but adopt this measure—so just in itself, so recommended by the point of time before us—the cause of all Spanish American triumphs. The European Congress may meet afterward, if it sees fit!" [51]

A parallel or even joint recognition of independence is what Monroe's Administration had been suggesting to London ever since 1818 in order to detach Britain from the designs of her continental allies. Castlereagh had consistently avoided the proposal. To accept it was almost equivalent to underwriting the Latin-American policy of the United States. Now Canning, his successor, was almost proposing to do that very thing. But he was unwilling to substitute immediate recognition for point 2 of his proposed joint pronouncement. Even if he wished to do so, it was doubtful whether he could have brought around his Tory colleagues, Lord Liverpool and the Duke of Wellington, to immediate recognition of independence of the new republics. He still insisted on leaving this vital question to "time and circumstances," the most noncommittal formula a diplomat could devise. Rush therefore said that he must wait for instructions.

Suddenly Canning cooled off. He ceased to press his startling proposal upon Rush, except to ask that it be kept absolutely confidential. The American Minister became suspicious. He began to doubt the wisdom of signing the joint pronouncement even after prior British recognition of Latin-American independence. Great Britain, he concluded, was more interested in balancing and holding down European power than in protecting the liberties of Latin America. "It is France that must not be aggrandized, not South America that must be made free." [52] He wondered whether the final complete occupation of Spain had led Canning to secure some fresh explanation from France, which would explain the sudden and full pause of his conversations. "I do not know, and most likely never shall know if events so fall out that Great Britain no longer finds it necessary to seek the aid of the United States in furtherance of her schemes of counteraction as against France and Russia." [53]

Rush had guessed the riddle of Canning's sudden silence. The Foreign Minister, uncertain whether Rush could secure the consent of his Government to the British proposal as it stood, did not wait for the correspondence to cross and recross the ocean. Hastily he turned to the French Ambassador in London, the Prince de Polignac. He notified him in effect that Great

---

[51] Richard Rush to JQA, London, September 19, 1823. Manning, III, 1490.
[52] Rush to JQA, No. 336, October 10, 1823, received November 19. Ford, op. cit., 59–60.
[53] Ibid.

Britain would not allow France to take advantage of the situation in Spain in order to appropriate any part of Spanish possessions in America, or to act against the "Colonies" by force of arms. Specifically, he required the French Ambassador to pledge formally, in the Polignac Memorandum of October 9, 1823:

> That his Government believed it to be utterly hopeless to reduce Spanish-America to the state of its former relation to Spain.
>
> That France disclaimed, on her part, any intention or desire to avail herself of the present state of the Colonies, or of the present situation of France toward Spain, to appropriate to herself any part of the Spanish Possessions in America. . . .
>
> That she abjured, in any case, any design of acting against the colonies by force of arms.[54]

It was this lone British showdown,[55] the Polignac Memorandum, imposed by the controlling force of the royal navy, that cut short any ambitious adventure that France alone might have developed amid the ruins of Spanish America.

Canning did not inform Rush of the Polignac Memorandum until November 24, eight days before the delivery of President Monroe's famous message to Congress, and did not read to Rush the above-quoted part of the document until December 13, eleven days after President Monroe had had his say in Washington.

In the Polignac Memorandum France had by no means renounced the idea of a European conference to settle the status of the former Spanish colonies. In November 1823 Ferdinand VII requested such a gathering. Canning worked ingeniously to frustrate it. The continental Allies themselves were divided as to the wisdom of a meeting. Had there been a conference it is not likely that it would have sanctioned any reconquest of Latin America. But the conflicting interests of the European powers were not fully understood in Washington in the autumn of 1823 any more than people on this side of the Atlantic knew about the Polignac Memorandum. People feared something ominous out of Europe. John Quincy Adams with his rich background of European politics came closest to divining the real situation. And, of course, he had before him Canning's instruction of March 31 to Sir Charles Stuart, which told the world that Britain would not allow France to intervene in Spanish America.

It is time to turn to the deliberations that took place in Monroe's Cabinet when news arrived of Canning's extraordinary proposals to Rush. Out of

---

[54] Perkins: *Monroe Doctrine, 1823–1826*, p. 118, citing *British and Foreign State Papers*, 1823–4, XI (London, 1843), 49–54. The officially published version (March 1824) was only a summary of the conversations. Temperley published the whole record for the first time in *The Cambridge History of British Foreign Policy* (London, 1922–3), II, 633–7, and gives an analytic summary of the full conversations in his *Canning*, pp. 115–17.

[55] Technically it was not an ultimatum.

them came Adams's formulation of the third dictum of the Monroe Doctrine

PRESIDENT MONROE'S MESSAGE OF DECEMBER 2, 1823
(NOVEMBER–DECEMBER, 1823)

"A combined system of policy."
John Quincy Adams's
recommendation to the Cabinet,
November 7, 1823

The President had Rush's dispatches[56] on his desk when John Quincy Adams called at the White House the afternoon of his return from Massachusetts, October 11, 1823. Calhoun was there at the moment. Presently the Attorney General, William Wirt, came in. Some preliminary discussion took place.[57] Monroe thought the subject demanded the highest consideration. But he did not deem it necessary to postpone a visit to his home in Loudon County, Virginia, which he had planned to take as soon as the Secretary of State got back to Washington. He requested Adams to have copies of the documents sent to him in the country.[58]

1

Amid the cooler breezes of Oak Hill, President Monroe pondered Canning's unprecedented propositions and their significance for American foreign policy at the close of the Age of Emancipation. He was inclined to meet the proposals of the British Government. A successful intervention by the Holy Alliance in South America now might mean an attack soon afterward on the United States. Would it not be best to make sure that Great Britain would be on our side in such a danger? But second thought raised disturbing questions. After all, was this an occasion for departing

---

[56] These were Rush's No. 323 of August 19, and No. 326 of August 28, 1823, enclosing Canning's written proposals for the joint pronouncement. They were received October 9, 1823. *Writings of Monroe*, VI, 361–72.

[57] "Some discussion concerning despatches received from R. Rush with a confidential correspondence between G. Canning and him relating to S. America." Diary, October 11, 1823. The private *Memoirs* contain no entry from September 11 to November 7, 1823. JQA's Journal or Diary is blank from October 11 to November 7. But he kept a line-a-day minute book, for reference in writing up his main Diary. From January 25, 1823 to October 31, 1826 he kept a Short Diary of four or five lines a day, in which he made summary entries when pressure of occupations prevented him from writing up the arrears of his Journal. JQA's Minute Book and Short Diary reveal that the President left on October 12 for a visit to his home in Loudon County, Virginia, and returned on November 5; that on the morning of November 5 he discussed Rush's dispatches with Adams; that Monroe held a Cabinet meeting on November 7 to consider Canning's proposals, and the answer to be made to Tuyll's note; but contain no further details concerning these matters.

[58] Monroe to JQA, Washington, October 11, 1823. Adams MSS.

from the sound and long-established maxim, laid down by George Washington and pursued by Thomas Jefferson, of abstention from the ordinary vicissitudes of European politics and the ordinary combinations and collisions of European friendships or enmities? Or was this an ordinary vicissitude? Was it a purely European question? Was it not an American question too?

In this moment for grave consideration President Monroe turned to his two fellow Republican ex-Presidents, Thomas Jefferson and James Madison. For nearly half a century he had contended at their side harmoniously and faithfully for the nation's interests as they had seen them.[59] Perhaps it was only natural that he should seek counsel from them rather than from another surviving ex-President and father of American Independence, John Adams, the one-time Federalist. Anyway, the diplomatist son of the sage of Quincy would be on hand in Washington.

The two Virginia ex-Presidents strengthened the disposition of their fellow statesman at Oak Hill to go along with Canning. Neither Jefferson nor Madison insisted on a prior recognition by Great Britain of the independence of the new republics of Latin America. Jefferson considered the question the most momentous since the independence of the United States. He thought that the proposed concert with Great Britain would introduce and establish the American System, "of keeping out of our land all *foreign powers,* of never permitting those of Europe to interfere with the affairs of our nations." If a war resulted it would be our war as well as Europe's war, with Great Britain on our side.

Jefferson had long coveted Cuba. He did not lose that island from sight as he pondered Canning's fourth proposition: "That we aim not at the possession of any portion of them [the Spanish colonies] for ourselves." Under the circumstances of 1823 he concluded that such a self-denial would be worth the price of making it, particularly because it would bind England against taking the island from Spain; it would not necessarily prevent the annexation of a free and independent Cuba some day to the United States.[60]

Madison, too, was entirely in favor of accepting Canning's proposal of an Anglo-American manifesto. He suggested a step further: that the two powers join in condemning French intervention in Spain, and in a declaration on behalf of the revolted Greeks in southeastern Europe. "There ought not to be any backwardness therefore, I think, in meeting her [Great Britain] in the way she has proposed. . . . Our co-operation is due to ourselves and to the world: and whilst it must ensure success in the event of an

---

[59] James Monroe to Thomas Jefferson, Oak Hill, October 17, 1823. *Writings of Monroe,* VI, 323–4. The President did not reveal to the Secretary of State his correspondence with Jefferson and Madison until November 15, after he had returned to the White House. Ford, *AHR,* VIII (No. 1, 1902), 29.

[60] Jefferson to Monroe, Monticello, October 24, 1823. *Writings of Jefferson,* Memorial Edition, XV, 477–80.

appeal to force, it doubles the chance of success without that appeal. . . . With the British power and navy combined with our own we have nothing to fear from the rest of the nations and in *the great struggle of the Epoch between liberty and despotism,* we owe it to ourselves to sustain the former in this hemisphere at least." [61]

2

With the opinions of Jefferson and Madison in his portfolio, corroborating his own reaction to Canning's propositions, James Monroe returned to Washington on November 4, 1823. Meanwhile surprising new developments had arisen from what was esteemed to be a significant communication from the Russian Minister at Washington.

A "crisis" was heading up in American foreign policy. A formal note from Baron von Tuyll, delivered to Adams October 16, had announced that the Czar, in conformance with the principles of his allies, would not receive any agents whatsoever from any of the rebel governments in America. It suggestively expressed satisfaction that the United States, in recognizing the independence of those Governments, at least had proclaimed its intention *to continue neutral.*[62] Was this not at least an intimation that, if the United States should swerve from neutrality and espouse the cause of the new states, the Czar of Russia, spokesman of the Holy Alliance, would support the authority of old Spain, and of France behind Spain?

In the first Cabinet meeting after his return to Washington the President brought up both Canning's overtures to Rush and Tuyll's note to the Secretary of State. Perhaps the one might be used to offset the other.

Calhoun promptly proposed giving discretionary powers to Rush to join "if necessary" in a declaration with Canning against the interference of the Holy Allies even if it should pledge the United States never to take Cuba or the province of Texas.

"The power of Great Britain being greater than ours to *seize* upon them," declared the Secretary of War, "we should get the advantage of obtaining from her the same declaration we should make ourselves."

John Quincy Adams did not want to bind the United States categorically against its Manifest Destiny. "I do not think the two cases parallel," he said. "We have no intention of seizing either Texas or Cuba. But the inhabitants of either or both of them may exercise their primitive rights, and solicit a union with us. They will certainly do no such thing to Great Britain. . . . Without entering now into the enquiry of the expediency of our annexing Texas or Cuba to our Union, we should at least keep

---

[61] James Madison to James Monroe, Montpelier, October 30, November 1, 1823. *Writings of Monroe,* VI, 394–5. Italics inserted.

[62] Von Tuyll to JQA, Washington, October 4/16, 1823. Ford, op. cit., 32.

ourselves free to act as emergencies arise and not tie ourselves down to any principle which might immediately afterwards be brought to bear against ourselves."

"I incline to the same opinion," said Samuel L. Southard, the new Secretary of the Navy. That was about all he did say during the long discussions that followed. He continued to incline toward Adams's views.

"I am averse to any course which would have the appearance of taking a position subordinate to that of Great Britain," affirmed the President. "I suggest sending a special Minister to *protest* against the interposition of the Holy Alliance."

That idea fell rather flat on everybody present.

"Whether we ought in any event to attend a Congress of the Allies on this subject, if invited," observed Adams, "is a question for separate consideration."

"We ought in no case to attend," said Calhoun.

They all assented to Adams's suggestion that since the United States had recognized the independence of the Latin-American states, there could be no object in attending any European congress to consider their fate.

Adams then launched out on the subject of the recent Russian communication.

"It affords," he stated, "a very suitable and convenient opportunity for us to take our stand against the Holy Alliance and at the same time to decline the overture of Great Britain. It would be more candid, as well as more dignified, to avow our principles explicitly to Russia and France, than to come in as a cock-boat in the wake of the British man-of-war."

All acquiesced readily enough in these sentiments. The Secretary of State then read them the draft of a reply to Tuyll, which they approved, together with what he would be prepared to say to the Russian Minister in oral conference.

John Quincy Adams felt that the occasion required a systematic exposition of policy.

"The answer to be given to Baron Tuyll," he observed to the President after the meeting broke up, "the instructions to Mr. Rush relative to the proposals of Mr. Canning, those to Mr. Middleton at St. Petersburg, and those to the Minister who must be sent to France, *must all be parts of a combined system of policy and adapted to each other.*"

Monroe agreed.[63]

A week later Adams delivered the American note to the Russian Minister, after the President had revised and simplified it in wording rather than content. It was a most moderate and amicable missive. In carefully courteous language it explained why the United States, acting in its sovereign capacity upon principles different from Russia's, had recognized the

---

[63] *Memoirs,* VI, 177–80. November 7, 1823. Italics inserted.

independence of the Latin-American republics and received their agents. And what of neutrality? In conferences meanwhile the Secretary had expressed to Tuyll the President's hope that Russia on her part would also continue to observe the same neutrality.[64] If not, then the United States might have to change its own neutral policy.

The President was still unsettled in his mind what to say to Great Britain. As French troops speedily overran Spain he became more and more alarmed. Calhoun seemed to have convinced him that after the fall of Cádiz the Holy Alliance with no more than ten thousand men would restore all Mexico and all South America to Spanish dominion.

"Perfectly moonstruck," was Adams's opinion of the Secretary of War.

"I won't deny," he said in Cabinet on the 15th of November, "that they may make a temporary impression for three, four, or five years, but I no more believe that the Holy Allies will restore the Spanish dominion upon the American continent than that the Chimborazo will sink beneath the ocean." Otherwise it had been a mistake for the United States to have recognized the independence of the new republics, much more so now to involve itself in their fate.[65]

More news from Rush,[66] that Canning had unexplainably ceased to refer to his earlier proposals, temporarily lightened the President's anxiety. "Canning has changed his purpose," Monroe told Adams. "Probably some inducement has been presented him, after the French triumph in Spain, to quiet his apprehensions." [67]

Such indeed was the case, although Monroe could not have guessed that the "inducement" was the Polignac Memorandum.

The relief was only momentary. That very afternoon (November 17, 1823) the mild-mannered and kindly Baron von Tuyll dropped another bombshell into the now thoroughly agitated village capital on the Potomac. Faithful to instructions from his Government, he handed in a second note. It was in the form of extracts from recent circular instructions of Count Nesselrode to be read to the Secretary of State and copies furnished if desired. The most significant feature of these documents was a long description, for the edification of the various governments, of Russia's policy—an "Io Triumphe," said Adams, "over the fallen cause of revolution." In exultant tones it reviewed the success of the interventions already sponsored by the Holy Alliance for the "liberation" of Naples, Piedmont, and Spain. Nesselrode ended by affirming the Emperor's policy in general to be that of guaranteeing the tranquillity *of all the states of which the civilized world is composed.*[68]

---

[64] For the drafts of JQA's note of November 15, 1823 to Tuyll, and Adams's account for the President of his conferences with the Russian Minister, see Ford, op. cit.

[65] *Memoirs*, VI, 185–6. November 15, 1823.

[66] Rush's dispatches No. 334 of October 2 and No. 336 of October 10.

[67] *Memoirs*, VI, 188. November 17, 1823.

[68] For the Russian note, see Ford, op. cit., pp. 34–7.

"Does this mean the supremacy of Spain over the revolted colonies?" Adams asked the Minister, at the request of the President, as soon as they had read the documents.

"Yes," answered Tuyll.

At the next Cabinet meeting the President appeared extraordinarily dejected. The Secretary of War added to the gloom.

"This confirms me in the view I have taken of the designs of the Holy Allies upon South America," said Calhoun.

"I am quite confirmed in mine," Adams opposed cheerfully enough.[69] The Secretary of State had definite ideas about dealing with the latest Russian piece.

"My purpose," he told the Cabinet three days later, "would be in a moderate and conciliatory manner, but with a firm and determined spirit, to declare our dissent from the principles avowed in those communications; to assert those upon which our own Government is founded, and, while disclaiming all intention of attempting to propagate them by force, and *all interference with the political affairs of Europe, to declare our expectation and hope that the European powers will equally abstain from the attempt to spread their principles in the American hemisphere, or to subjugate by force any part of these continents to their will.*"[70]

The President approved of this idea. He had always been sympathetic to the freedom of the whole New World. The third dictum of the Monroe Doctrine was crystallizing.

John Quincy Adams had already said Hands Off to Europe, including Great Britain, so far as further colonization was concerned. Now he was proposing to say Hands Off as to conquest of any part of the New World, or intervention in its political affairs. He was advancing from Non-Colonization to Non-Intervention. But he had no idea of evoking a public pronouncement, of proclaiming a national "doctrine" beyond his own Non-Colonization Principle. He had already drafted a statement on that for the President's annual message to Congress. It was the basic principle. It would be enough to tell the world at this time.

It had been Adams's expectation that the systematic exposition of American foreign policy called forth by Canning's proposal and Tuyll's notes would be expressed only in diplomatic correspondence. The replies could be written with an eye to spreading them before the public to justify the American position. If the crisis were weathered successfully it would not be necessary to publish anything. If trouble with Europe followed, Congress could call for the documents. Monroe agreed, he told the Cabinet, with the *purpose* of the Secretary of State. He then took up some notes that he had made for his annual message to Congress on the State of the Union. As he read them, it became apparent that he had decided

---

[69] *Memoirs*, VI, 190. November 18, 1823.
[70] *Memoirs*, VI, 194. November 21, 1823. Italics inserted.

to set forth the combined system of American foreign policy, not in a series of diplomatic notes but in a significant statement to Congress and to the world.

The proposed message opened with a tone of deep solemnity and high alarm. Imminent and formidable dangers menaced the country. They called for most vigorous energies and closest union. After this introduction Monroe followed with occasional variations the draft that Adams had sketched out for him a week previously on subjects relating to the Department of State. He stressed the Non-Colonization Principle as applied to Russia and Great Britain earlier in the year. He touched on boundary controversies with Great Britain, on the North West Coast, on the slave trade, on the proposed abolition of private warfare on the seas, on the new Ministers being sent to Buenos Aires and Chile. Then the President passed beyond the content of Adams's draft.[71] He began to mention the recent events in Spain and Portugal. Pointedly he reproved France for her invasion of Spain and for the principles avowed by the King of France to justify it. The proposed message also contained a broad acknowledgment of the revolted Greeks as an independent nation, and a recommendation to Congress of an appropriation for sending a Minister to them.

Calhoun approved it all.

John Quincy Adams objected.

"I wish you would reconsider the whole subject," he told the President, "before you take this course. The tone of the introduction will take the nation by surprise and greatly alarm them . . . like a clap of thunder." [72]

What Adams objected to most was the summons to arms against all Europe, and over objects exclusively European—Greece and Spain—the sudden departure from the policy of George Washington. To champion the cause of conquered Spanish republicans, whom even Britain had been unable to support, would be to charge a windmill whirling in the gales and cross-currents of the Old World. To uphold the cause of the revolted Greeks, so dear to Adams's classical friends in Cambridge,[73] would have been to take sides with the monarchs of Europe against the Turks of Asia to settle the insoluble Eastern Question. Already Count Nesselrode had

---

[71] The draft and Monroe's summary notes on "Mr. Adams's sketch" are in the Monroe Papers in the New York Public Library.

[72] *Memoirs*, VI, 195.

[73] Professor Edward Everett of Harvard suggested the sending out of a commission, like the fact-finding commission to South America in 1817–18, to inquire into the progress of the Greek revolution. "If such a course should be adopted, I wish you would persuade the President to make me Secretary of the Commission." Edward Everett to JQA, Cambridge, October 30, 1823. Adams MSS.

"It is supposed to be the purpose of some gentlemen to get Professor Everett appointed U. S. Commissioner to Greece. If he is a Republican he is totally unknown as such. . . . An appointment of Mr. E. in *your Dept.* wd. naturally be attributed *to you,* and would have a tendency to make the Republicans of N. E. rise up in arms against you." P. P. F. DeGrand to JQA, Boston, January 10, 1824. Adams MSS.

been trying to get an American fleet into the Mediterranean as a naval demonstration against the Turks while the Czar made ready to declare war on them from the north. Already Monroe had decided not to make even a commercial treaty with Russia lest it lead to political involvements in the Balkan region.[74] Was there any more reason to get mixed up in the Near East on account of Greece?

Adams unswervingly opposed any European entanglement whether with friend or foe. "Europe has been in convulsions for more than thirty years," he reminded his colleagues. "Every nation almost of which it is composed [has been] alternately invading and invaded. Empires, kingdoms, and principalities, have been overthrown, revolutionized, and counter-revolutionized, and we had looked on safe in our distance beyond an intervening ocean, and avowing a total forbearance to interfere in any of the combinations of European politics. This message . . . would have an air of open defiance to all Europe, and I should not be surprised if the first answer to it from Spain and France, and even Russia, should be to break off diplomatic intercourse with us. I don't expect the quiet which we have enjoyed for six or seven years to last much longer. The aspect of things is portentous; but if we must come to an issue with Europe, let us keep it off as long as possible. Let us use all possible means to carry the opinion of the nation with us, and the opinion of the world."

"There is not the tranquility that you spoke of," Calhoun objected. "There is great anxiety in the thinking part of the nation. There is a general expectation that the Holy Alliance will employ force against South America. It would be proper for the President to sound the alarm to the nation." [75]

The President took the matter under further consideration.

The next day Adams worked on Monroe alone. Anxiously he urged him to abstain from anything in the message that the Allies could make a pretext for construing as an aggression against them.

"The ground I wish to take," he maintained, "is that of earnest remonstrance against the interference of European powers by force in South America, but to disclaim all interference on our part in Europe; to make an American cause, and adhere inflexibility to that." [76]

In the end Adams had his way. Monroe revised his position to conform with the policy that the Secretary of State had recommended for the emergency. But it was the President himself who decided to give forth that policy to the world in a message to Congress. Behind the public message would be the unprinted diplomatic correspondence of John Quincy Adams with Great Britain and Russia,[77] to be published only when necessary.

---

[74] *Memoirs*, V, 429–31. [75] *Memoirs*, VI, 195–6. November 21, 1823.
[76] *Memoirs*, VI, 198. November 22, 1823. [77] *Memoirs*, VI, 199. November 25, 1823.

Adams now drafted and presented to the Cabinet some observations on the communications received from the Baron von Tuyll. It corresponded to the relevant parts of the President's message as now redrafted to meet the Secretary of State's ideas. Adams added the No-Transfer Principle. He intended the document to be a firm and spirited but withal conciliatory answer to the communications recently received from the Russian Minister. At the same time it would reflect the unequivocal answer to be made separately to Canning's proposals.

"It is meant also," Adams told the Cabinet, "to be eventually an exposition of the principles of this Government, and a brief development of its political system as henceforth to be maintained: essentially republican—maintaining its own independence, and respecting that of others; essentially pacific—studiously avoiding all involvement in the combinations of European politics, cultivating peace and friendship with the most absolute monarchies, highly appreciating and anxiously desiring to retain that of the Emperor Alexander, but declaring that, having recognized that of the South American States, we could not see with indifference any attempt by European powers by forcible interposition either to restore the Spanish dominion on the American Continents or to introduce monarchical principles into those countries, or to transfer any portion of the ancient or present American possessions of Spain to any other European power." [78]

Now the whole matter was determined. The "Gentlemen of the Administration" had agreed on what to say to Canning, through Rush. They had decided how to reply to Tuyll. They had fixed the principles to be stated in the President's message. John Quincy Adams's views by the force of their reason had prevailed over everybody: over President Monroe, over ex-Presidents Jefferson and Madison, over all his colleagues in the Cabinet, Calhoun, Wirt, and Southard. [79] At this moment, when Monroe was making ready to draft his final message, a last most realistic question came up.

After all, asked Wirt, would the United States go to war if the Holy Alliance should act in direct hostility against South America? [80] He did not favor taking any such position without a supporting resolution of Congress.

This most pertinent question gave pause to them all. Adams, too, would have preferred to have Congress surely behind the President. But the Eighteenth Congress had not assembled. The message was to greet the two houses upon their convening. In a time of profound peace no resolution could be expected unless all the confidential papers could be put before Congress to show the danger. To send them in would be premature. Both Canning and Tuyll had insisted on the wholly confidential nature of

---

[78] *Memoirs*, VI, 199. November 24, 1823.
[79] Crawford, Secretary of War, was not present for the deliberations, because of illness.
[80] *Memoirs*, VI, 202–5. November 25, 1823.

their exchanges with the United States. Wirt had won a point. The message as finally worded avoided any unequivocal threat of war.

Here is what President James Monroe said to the Congress of the United States, December 2, 1823, on the relations between the Old World and the New. It is copied from the Senate files, *verbatim et literatim:*

> At the proposal of the Russian Imperial Government, made through the Minister of the Emperor, residing here, a full power and instructions have been transmitted to the Minister of the United States at St. Petersburg, to arrange by amicable negotiation, the respective rights and interests of the two Nations on the North West Coast of this Continent. A similar proposal has been made by His Imperial Majesty, to the Government of Great Britain, which has likewise been acceded to. The Government of the United States has been desirous by this friendly proceeding, of manifesting the great value which they have invariably attached to the friendship of the Emperor, and their solicitude to cultivate the best understanding with his Government. In the discussions to which this interest has given rise, and in the arrangements by which they may terminate, the occasion has been judged proper, for asserting as a principle in which the rights and interests of the United States are involved, that the American Continents, by the free and independent condition which they have assumed and maintain, are henceforth not to be considered as subjects for future colonization by any European Power. . . .

So far the President was using what John Quincy Adams had drafted for the message. There followed about three thousand words dealing mostly with domestic affairs. Then Monroe resumed the subject of foreign relations, turning to the policy recently formulated in the Cabinet as a result of Canning's proposals. It is worth while to note how widely the Non-Colonization Principle was separated, in the body of the message, from the other dicta on foreign policy.

> It was stated at the commencement of the last session [continued the message] that a great effort was then making in Spain and Portugal, to improve the condition of the people of those countries; and that it appeared to be conducted with extraordinary moderation. It need scarcely be remarked, that the result has been, so far, very different from what was then anticipated. Of events in that quarter of the Globe, with which we have so much intercourse, and from which we derive our origin, we have always been anxious and interested spectators. The Citizens of the United States cherish sentiments the most friendly, in favor of the liberty and happiness of their fellowmen on that side of the Atlantic. In the wars of the European powers, in matters relating to themselves, we have never taken any part, nor does it comport with our policy, so to do. It is only when our rights are invaded, or seriously menaced, that we resent injuries, or make preparation for our

defense. With the movements in this Hemisphere we are of necessity more immediately connected, and by causes which must be obvious to all enlightened and impartial observers. The political system of the allied powers, is essentially different in this respect from that of America. This difference proceeds from that, which exists in their respective Governments, and to the defence of our own, which has been atchieved [sic] by the loss of so much blood and treasure, and matured by the wisdom of their most enlightened citizens, and under which we have enjoyed unexampled felicity, this whole nation is devoted. We owe it therefore to candor, and to the amicable relations existing between the United States and those powers, to declare that we should consider any attempt on their part to extend their system to any portions of this Hemisphere, as dangerous to our peace and safety. With the existing Colonies or dependencies of any European power, we have not interfered, and shall not interfere. But with the Governments who have declared their Independence, and maintained it, and whose Independence we have, on great consideration, and on just principles, acknowledged, we could not view any interposition for the purpose of oppressing them, or controuling in any other manner, their destiny, by any European power, in any other light, than as the manifestation of an unfriendly disposition towards the United States. In the war between those new governments and Spain, we declared our neutrality, at the time of their recognition, and to this we have adhered, and shall continue to adhere, provided no change shall occur, which in the judgment of the competent authorities of this Government, shall make a corresponding change, on the part of the United States, indispensable to their security.

The late events in Spain and Portugal, show that Europe is still unsettled. Of this important fact, no stronger proof can be adduced, than that the allied powers should have thought it proper, on any principle satisfactory to themselves, to have interposed by force, in the internal concerns of Spain. To what extent, such interposition may be carried, on the same principle, is a question, in which all Independent powers, whose Governments differ from theirs, are interested; even those most remote, and surely none more so than the United States. Our policy in regard to Europe, which was adopted at an early stage of the wars which have so long agitated that quarter of the Globe, nevertheless remains the same, which is, not to interfere in the internal concerns of any of its powers; to consider the Government de facto; as the legitimate [sic] for us; to cultivate friendly relations with it, and to preserve those relations by a frank, firm and manly policy, meeting in all instances, the just claims of every power; submitting to injuries from none. But, in regard to those continents, circumstances are eminently and conspicuously different. It is impossible that the allied powers, should extend their political systems, to any portion of either continent, without endangering our peace and happiness, nor can anyone believe, that our Southern Brethren, if left to themselves, would adopt it of their own accord. It is equally impossible therefore, that we should behold such interposition in any form with indifference. If we look to the comparative strength and resources of Spain and those new Governments, and their distance from each other, it must be obvious that she can never subdue them. It is still the true policy of the United States, to leave the parties to themselves, in the hope, that other powers will pursue the same course.

3

Looking ahead to John Quincy Adams's Presidency and to his choice of Secretary of State it is proper at this place to notice Henry Clay's comment on the message the day of its delivery, and to say something of Adams's own appraisal of the manifesto and its principles.

Adams called on Clay that evening to make arrangement for the presence of a delegation of the House of Representatives at the obsequies of the Prussian chargé, Frederick Greuhm. Clay mentioned the message. "It seems to be the work of several hands," he twitted good-naturedly. "The War and Navy Departments make a magnificent figure in it, as well as the Post Office."

"There is an account of a full Treasury," Adams reminded his Kentucky rival, "and much concerning foreign affairs, which is the business of the Department of State."

"Yes," acknowledged Clay. "I think the part relating to foreign affairs is the best part of the Message. The Government had weakened itself and the tone of the country by withholding so long the acknowledgment of South American Independence. Even a war for it against all Europe, including even England, would have been advantageous to us."

"A war for South American independence may be inevitable," conceded Adams, "and under certain circumstances might be expedient, but I view war in a different light from you—as necessarily placing high interests of different portions of the Union in conflict with each other, and thereby endangering the Union itself."

"Not a successful war," said Clay, "but a successful war, to be sure, creates a military influence and power, which I consider the greatest danger of war." [81]

Both men were conscious rivals for the succession to the Presidency. Time and circumstances—and James Monroe—had settled the Latin-American policy of the United States. Both Adams and Clay now had other things to think about. With Andrew Jackson in the offing, they might some day be able to agree on a fancied danger of military power and influence to the Republic.

As John Quincy Adams's mind turned toward the next presidential election, as it did more and more frequently, he never thought of taking po-

---

[81] *Memoirs,* VI, 224. December 2, 1823.

litical credit for the Monroe Doctrine. In "John Quincy Adams Loquitur," the memorandum in his handwriting in which he summed up the diplomatic achievements which might commend him to the suffrage of his fellow countrymen, he said nothing of the part that he had played in the formulation of the message of December 2, 1823. He did not fail to note the Treaty of 1818 with Great Britain, made under his instructions. He took credit for the Spanish treaty and the transcontinental boundary. He included among his accomplishments the Commercial Treaty of 1822 with France, the Russian arbitration of the slave question with Great Britain, the unratified treaty of 1824 with Great Britain for the abolition of the slave trade, the Russian Boundary Treaty of 1824. But not a word about the Monroe Doctrine. Not until 1846, when the principles of President Monroe were beginning to enjoy a classic renown, and were being applied to Texas, California, and Oregon,[82] did he acknowledge, with pride, his responsibility for any of them, and then only for the Non-Colonization Principle. Clearly in his mind that was the most noteworthy feature of President Monroe's message. Abstention dated back to George Washington's Farewell Address. Hands Off, the really most important principle of the Monroe Doctrine, was a principle that he had sponsored in the Cabinet deliberations, but it did not stand out in his mind as much as the Non-Colonization Principle. Hands Off was really a corollary of Non-Colonization.

---

[82] *Memoirs*, XII, 218.

How Monroe's Message Was Written

A. P. Whitaker

I

The starting-point of the momentous cabinet discussions of November 15–26 was Monroe's submission to his advisers of the replies that he had received from Jefferson and Madison in regard to Canning's proposal. The latter, which was the first major theme of these discussions, and the disturbing communications from Russia, which also played a prominent part

---

From *The United States and the Independence of Latin America* (Baltimore: The Johns Hopkins Press, 1941), pp. 464–491. Reprinted by permission.

in them, were answered in detail in notes addressed to the British and Russian governments; but the administration's decisions in these cases, as well as on all the other important questions considered at this time, were summed up in the Monroe Doctrine.[1] Consequently the formulation of that pronouncement will serve as the focus for the following account of the great debate on foreign policy that took place in these cabinet meetings.

The chronological narrative is so familiar that it need not be repeated here, and the following account of it, in this chapter and the next, will be presented in the form of answers to certain important questions which have attracted much attention from historians but about which something still remains to be said.

The first of these questions relates to the authorship of the Doctrine. As the reader will recall, the Doctrine consists of two distinct parts, which were presented separately in the message. In the first part, Monroe asserted the non-colonization principle: "the American continents, by the free and independent condition which they have assumed and maintain, are henceforth not to be considered as subjects for future colonization by any European powers." The second part contains the doctrine of the two spheres and the warning to Europe to keep within its own sphere.

> In the wars of the European powers in matters relating to themselves [said Monroe], we have never taken any part, nor does it comport with our policy so to do. . . . With the movements in this hemisphere we are, of necessity, more immediately connected. . . . The political system of the allied powers is essentially different in this respect from that of America. This difference proceeds from that which exists in their respective governments. . . . We owe it, therefore, to candor, and to the amicable relations existing between the United States and those powers, to declare that we should consider any attempt on their part to extend their system to any portion of this hemisphere as dangerous to their peace and safety. With the existing colonies or dependencies of any European power we have not interfered and shall not interfere. But with the Governments who have declared their independence and maintained it, and whose independence we have, on great consideration and on just principles, acknowledged, we could not view any interposition for the purpose of oppressing them, or controlling in any other manner their destiny, by any European power, in any other light than as the manifestation of an unfriendly disposition toward the United States. . . . It is impossible that the allied powers should extend their political system to any portion of either continent without endangering our peace and happiness; nor can anyone believe that our southern brethren, if left to themselves, would adopt it of their own

---

[1] Perkins, *Monroe Doctrine*, p. 74, has already pointed out that "All these matters taken together engaged the attention of the Cabinet during the momentous sessions of November, 1823. All of them have a direct relation to the enunciation of the Monroe Doctrine."

accord. It is equally impossible, therefore, that we should behold such interposition, in any form, with indifference.[2]

Our main concern is with the second part of the message, which related directly to Latin America and asserted a new policy. The first part related directly to the Northwest coast and was designed to check the advance of Russia in that region; and the non-colonization principle contained in it, while novel from the point of view of international law, had already been asserted as a part of the administration's foreign policy several months earlier.[3] Yet it should be noted that this part of the message, too, was related to the larger situation that produced the doctrine of the two spheres and the warning to Europe. For the first formal, written assertion of the non-colonization principle was contained in the instructions to Rush (July 1823) for his general negotiation with Great Britain; and in the message the principle was justified partly on the ground that "the American continents"—that is, not merely the United States, but the new states to the south as well—had established their independence.

II

The complex question of the authorship of the Monroe Doctrine has long been debated by historians and other interested persons. Many different answers to it have been given; but in the past generation careful study has narrowed the debatable ground so greatly that only a few of them need to be considered here.

Some historians, especially Latin Americans, have sought to trace the leading ideas of the Doctrine to earlier sources in Latin America.[4] The similarities are striking and they have an interesting place in the history

---

[2] The text of the Doctrine can be consulted together with the rest of the message in Richardson, *Messages and Papers of the Presidents*, II, 209, 217–219, and separately in Manning, *Dip. Cor.*, I, 216–218.

[3] Perkins, *op. cit.*, p. 3, 11–12, 19–26.

[4] Thus, J. M. Yepes, *Le Panaméricanisme au point de vue historique, juridique et politique* (Paris, 1936), p. 26–27, writes: ". . . On est en droit d'affirmer . . . que le président Monroe puisa largement les idées essentielles et le texte même de son message dans les notes que le premier diplomate d'une république latino-américaine auprès des Etats-Unis, M. Manuel Torres, ministre de Colombie, lui addressa pour lui suggérer l'attitude que Monroe se décida finalement à prendre. Ceci est un point historique suffissament éclairci aujourd'hui sur lequel il est inutile de revenir ici. L'origine latino-américain de la doctrine de Monroe ne fait point de doute pour ceux qui ont étudié l'histoire diplomatique américaine avec un esprit vraiment critique." The case for Torres is set forth in detail and interestingly, but not (to my mind) at all convincingly, in Nicolás García Samudio, *Capitulos de historia diplomática*, p. 77–86. Perkins, *op. cit.*, p. 97–98, considers and rejects the claim for Latin American authorship of the Doctrine as set forth in Charles Lyon Chandler, *Inter-American Acquaintances*, and F. J. Urrutia, *Páginas de la historia diplomática*.

of ideas; but their significance for the present question is doubtful, since the same ideas can be traced to earlier sources in the United States as well and no one has shown the process by which any specifically Latin American idea found its way into the Monroe Doctrine. Probably the most that can be said is that the intensive propaganda conducted in the United States from 1815 to 1823 by Latin American agents (such as Manuel Torres) and by American citizens who were in close touch with Latin America (such as David Porter) did a great deal to popularize some of the ideas that were subsequently gathered up in the Monroe Doctrine.

By hammering away at the ideas of continental solidarity and the great potential value of Latin American trade to the United States, and by their strenuous efforts to break down the Black Legend and build up in its place a belief in the civic virtue and political aptitude of the Latin American people and their devotion to republicanism, these propagandists helped create the climate of opinion that in turn produced the Monroe Doctrine. They doubtless made an impression upon Monroe himself. Throughout this period he gave much thought to the probable effect of the acts and declarations of the United States on public opinion in Latin America. It is not likely that he lost sight of this consideration in framing the most important pronouncement of his whole administration;[5] and for a knowledge of what would make a favorable impression in Latin America he was to a considerable extent dependent upon its propagandists in the United States. Of direct Latin American influence in the formulation of the Doctrine, however, there is no satisfactory evidence.

There was a time when many commentators on the problem before us simplified it by ascribing the Doctrine to a single author, such as John Quincy Adams or (strange as it may seem) George Canning. Only in recent years has the weight of opinion shifted strongly in the direction of the man whose name the Doctrine bears.

The time is long past, if it ever existed, when Canning's claim required serious consideration. As Perkins has observed with commendable restraint, the case for him is "pitifully weak." [6] Nevertheless, the feeling still persists in some quarters that Canning deserves part of the credit (or, to put it another way, must bear part of the responsibility) for the Monroe Doctrine. The feeling finds support in a recent work by a leading British historian, Professor C. K. Webster, who notes with apparent disapproval that "American historians have tended to depreciate the influence of Canning on the Monroe Doctrine." He admits that Canning "disagreed pro-

---

[5] That he did not lose sight of it at that time is indicated by the letter that he wrote Jefferson in December 1823, in which, referring to his recent message, he said: "Had we moved in England, it is probable that it would have been inferr'd that we acted under her influence, and at her instigation, and thus have lost credit with our Southern neighbors, as with the allied powers" (quoted in Perkins, *op. cit.*, p. 75).

[6] *Ibid.*, p. 97.

foundly" with most of the sentiments expressed in it; but, he asserts, Canning provided "the occasion and opportunity for expounding those very sentiments" and "had he not made his offer to Rush, it seems very unlikely that any declaration about America would have been made in the form of Monroe's message." [7]

Even if we agree to Webster's statement of the case, it is not easy to see how he has helped it very much. Employing the same process of reasoning and even the same phraseology, one could say that Daniel Webster's famous "reply to Hayne" was influenced by the latter in the same way that Monroe's message was influenced by Canning. Hayne disagreed profoundly with the sentiments expressed in Webster's reply; but he provided the occasion and opportunity for expounding those very sentiments, and had he not made the speech against which Webster's reply was directed, it seems very unlikely that any declaration about the American Union would have been made in the form of Webster's reply.

But must we agree that no declaration about America would have been made in the form of Monroe's message if Canning had not made his offer to Rush? This is mere conjecture—a might-not-have-been that is entitled to the same respect as the might-have-beens of history of which the exponents of the art are generally skeptical. In this case, skepticism is strengthened when we analyze the two assumptions on which the conjecture seems to rest, namely, that Canning's proposal led to Monroe's declaration because it preceded it, and that Monroe was indebted to Canning for the idea of making a declaration of Spanish American policy.

The first assumption is open to two objections: first, that it involves one of the most obvious of logical fallacies, the *post hoc* fallacy, and second, that the form of Monroe's declaration, which was unilateral, was essentially different from the form of the declaration proposed by Canning, which was joint. As for the second assumption, one may counter by asking whether it is seriously maintained that Canning's proposal suggested to Monroe for the first time the idea of making a declaration of policy in regard to Spanish America and of using a message to Congress as the vehicle for that purpose. The fact is that every president of the United States from Washington to Monroe had made public declarations of foreign policy, and Monroe himself had frequently used his messages to Congress as vehicles for the discussion of his Latin American policy. Moreover, we know that as early as June 1823, two months before Canning first broached his proposal to Rush, Monroe was already considering the advisability of taking a bolder stand in favor of Spanish American independence.[8] He did not say that this new boldness would be expressed in the form of a message; but knowing his penchant for frank and manly declarations and

---

[7] Webster, *Britain*, I, 45.
[8] Monroe, *Writings*, VI, 309–310, Monroe to Jefferson, June 2, 1823.

Adams's for trumpet blasts, and the caution of both men in deeds, we may be confident that bold action was less likely than a bold pronouncement.

The main reason for Monroe's pronouncement of December 2, 1823, lay not in Canning's proposal but in the increasing gravity of the situation in regard to Latin America. This increased throughout November as the time for the submission of the message to Congress approached, and made it ever more desirable for the President to incorporate in his message, as a warning to possible aggressor nations, a statement of the policy of the United States in regard to Spanish America. Consequently, Professor Webster's assumption seems no more reasonable than the contrary assumption that the idea of making a declaration of policy by the perfectly familiar vehicle of a message to Congress would have occurred to Monroe, and would have been adopted by him, at some time in the uneasy month of November, even if he had never received Canning's proposal of a joint declaration.

The point to be emphasized, however, is that when Monroe made his declaration, it was fundamentally different in content as well as in form from the declaration proposed by Canning. Since even Professor Webster, who believes that Canning somehow influenced the Doctrine, admits that he "disagreed profoundly" with most of the sentiments expressed in it,[9] we need not labor the point. It is enough to say that the sentiments in it which most offended him were its republicanism (he was a militant monarchist) and the idea of an American system headed by the United States and separate and different from, and possibly antagonistic to, the European system of which England was a part.

If any of the credit or responsibility for the Monroe Doctrine belongs to Canning, it is remarkable how little pleasure he took in his handiwork. Indeed, from the very beginning he waged relentless war on the basic principle of the Doctrine, the American system, resisting the new order that the Doctrine purported to establish in America with as much vigor and tenacity as the United States has shown, in our own time, in resisting the new order that Japan has undertaken to establish under its "Monroe Doctrine" for Asia. As Professor Webster himself has written,

> Henceforward his [Canning's] policy in Latin America was to undermine by every possible means the position of the United States. During the next three years, with great energy and skill, he used every opportunity to destroy the contention that the New States [of Latin America] had in any way special relations to the United States rather than to Britain. Jealousy of France continued, but it was never allowed to interfere with the other object of countering the blow which Adams had struck.[10]

---

[9] Webster, *Britain*, I, 45.   [10] *Ibid.*, I, 50.

III

The "blow" in question was, of course, the Monroe Doctrine. Was it Adams who struck it? Was he the real author of the Monroe Doctrine? The case for him once seemed overwhelmingly strong, and it still requires respectful consideration; but in recent years the careful studies of Professor Dexter Perkins and other scholars have considerably reduced the extent of his claim. That he was the principal author of the first of the two parts of the doctrine (the part containing the non-colonization principle) is universally admitted,[11] and the question therefore relates only to the second part, which contains the doctrine of the two spheres and the warning to Europe. Early in the present century the question seemed to be resolved in Adams's favor by W. C. Ford's well known articles,[12] which brought to light important new evidence and subjected it to a microscopic scrutiny. In 1927, however, Perkins reopened the investigation, discovered that Ford's microscope had been somewhat out of focus, and reported that "a reasonable view" must "incline the balance, which has been so heavily tipped in favor of the New Englander, back toward Monroe." Specifically, he found that it was Monroe, not Adams, who decided that the South American question should be discussed in the message and who "penned the words in which that question was discussed" and "assumed responsibility for the policy enunciated"; as for Adams's contribution, he found only that "in the clear line which the message draws between the Old World and the New the President, in large part at least, probably followed Adams's views." After presenting this impressive bill of specifications in favor of Monroe, Perkins weakened its effect somewhat by the negative conclusion that "it is not necessary to assume" that Monroe "played a subordinate rôle, that he was dictated to by a stronger and more dominant personality [i.e., Adams's personality]." [13]

---

[11] Even T. R. Schellenberg in the article cited below, note 14, in which Adams's claims are considered with a minimum of sympathy, admits that "for this [non-colonization] principle Adams is unquestionably responsible" (*loc. cit.*, p. 2). Perkins, *op. cit.*, p. 8, writes that the development of this principle "was due almost exclusively" to Adams.

[12] Mr. Ford published two articles on the subject: (1) "Some Documents on the Origins of the Monroe Doctrine," *Mass. Hist. Soc. Proceedings*, 2 Series, XV (1902), 373–476, a poorly constructed article which was nevertheless very valuable at the time because of the many documents published in it for the first time; and (2) an article in two parts in *Am. Hist. Rev.*, VII (1902), 676–696, and VIII (1902), 28–52. While Mr. Ford deserves great credit for his fruitful spade work, the use that he made of the new materials left a great deal to be desired. For example, on the Rush-Canning negotiation of 1823 see Chap. 15, note 11. He subsequently surrendered approximately half of the ground claimed in these articles, for in his article on Monroe in the *Dictionary of American Biography* he wrote that the credit for the message was equally divided between Adams and Monroe.

[13] Perkins, *op. cit.*, p. 102–103. An earlier critique of Ford's articles, James Schouler, "The Authorship of the Monroe Doctrine," Am. Hist. Assn. *Report* (1905), I, 125–131, contains a brief but very effective statement of the case for Monroe. As Schouler pointed out, Stanislaus M. Hamilton had recently published (1902) an exhaustive and valuable

Dissatisfied with Perkins's conclusions, which seemed to him still too heavily weighted in Adams's favor, Mr. T. R. Schellenberg in 1934 carried the war into the enemy's country in an article[14] in which he sought to deprive Adams of credit for the idea of the American system as presented in the message. His reasons are, briefly, that Adams had certain basic ideas about Latin America that were irreconcilable with those on which the doctrine of the two spheres was founded—for example, that he had no faith in the republicanism of the Latin American people and did not believe that there was any real community of interest between the United States and Latin America; and that while he spoke with approval of an "American system," the system he had in mind was one which was *exclusively national* in character" and "limited strictly to the *direct interests* of the United States." [15]

Schellenberg was not, however, seeking to abase Adams merely in order to exalt Monroe; and the main contention of his article is that, for the doctrine of the two spheres and even for much of the very phraseology in which it was incorporated in his famous message, Monroe was indebted to Jefferson, who in turn was indebted for it to no less a person than our old friend the French publicist Abbé de Pradt.[16]

There is a good deal of truth in what Schellenberg says, but it can be accepted only with some important reservations. In the first place, he leaves the reader with the impression that Abbé de Pradt was the real author of the doctrine of the two spheres and the American system,[17] which is the most characteristic part of the Monroe Doctrine. As a matter of fact, de Pradt himself got the doctrine from a French newspaper, the *Moniteur Universel* of November 24, 1818, which in turn got it from an

---

"note" on "The Genesis of the Monroe Doctrine" in his edition of Monroe's correspondence (Monroe, *Writings*, VI, 346–444). The "note" consists almost entirely of documents, many of which had just been published earlier in the same year by Ford (see the preceding note). One of the best contributions prior to the publication of Perkins's book was made by Samuel Eliot Morison in his article, "Les origines de la doctrine de Monroe," *Revue des sciences politiques*, XLVII (1924), 52–84, which continued to tip the scales too heavily in favor of Adams, but otherwise gave an exceptionally well balanced account of the subject and is still very useful.

[14] T. R. Schellenberg, "Jeffersonian Origins of the Monroe Doctrine," *Hispanic Am. Hist. Rev.*, XIV (1934), 1–31.

[15] *Ibid.*, p. 25.

[16] "The paragraph [in Monroe's message] which contained the statement of the doctrine of two spheres bore the imprint of Jefferson's letter [of Oct. 24, 1823, to Monroe], just as this letter bore that of the Abbé de Pradt's remarkable prediction of an American system in his *L'Europe après le Congrès d'Aix la Chapelle* . . . [published in 1819]" (*ibid.*, p. 30–31). Schellenberg's detailed discussion of de Pradt's book and its influence on Jefferson is in *ibid.*, p. 3–8.

[17] Although Schellenberg concludes that "Jefferson, then, more than any other individual, was responsible for the basic doctrine of Monroe's message of 1823," this statement is preceded by the sentence quoted in the preceding note, which (together with the discussion on p. 3–8) leaves the impression that Jefferson was indebted to de Pradt for this idea.

unsigned editorial published in an American newspaper, the *City of Washington Gazette* of October 12 of the same year.[18] Since Schellenberg maintains that the Abbé's phraseology influenced Jefferson and found its way into the Monroe Doctrine through Jefferson's letter of October 24, 1823, to Monroe, the editorial from which the Abbé's idea came is worth quoting. It first mentions the apparent failure of Gallatin's recent efforts to negotiate commercial treaties with France and Holland, and continues:

> No one in the least acquainted with the political reputation of Mr. Gallatin will attribute any share of his failure to a want of diplomatic skill on his part: it more likely grows out of the peculiarity of his instructions from his own government, or the present conceit of the Holy Alliance on their ability to abridge the commercial prosperity of America, thinking this the most favorable opportunity for accomplishing it. If our cabinet understands its true interest, in the advantages offered our commerce with the republics of South America, it will no longer permit its ministers to be knocking at the door of an European sovereign to seek a commercial treaty, and be dismissed empty handed. This, if anything can, will convince us of the necessity of adopting a policy purely American. . . .[19]

Here we find clearly expressed the basic ideas of the doctrine of the two spheres: antagonism to the Holy Alliance, the community of interest between the United States and "South America," and a "purely American" policy oriented away from Europe and towards South America. These ideas were not new when the *City of Washington Gazette* advocated them in 1818. The *Moniteur Universel* and de Pradt could have found them as clearly stated and often better expressed in other American publications of the period.[20] Why they took them from this particular newspaper is a question we do not need to answer. The important point is that the under-

---

[18] Schellenberg himself states this fact in a footnote (*ibid.,* p. 5–6, note 12), but fails to consider its significance either there or in the text of his article.

[19] *City of Washington Gazette,* Oct. 12, 1818, p. 2, editorial column headed "The Gazette" and dated Oct. 12, 1818. The editor of this newspaper was Jonathan Elliot. See the article on Elliot in DAB, and Adams, *Memoirs,* VI, 56–57. In 1817 and 1818 the *Gazette* was almost as friendly to Spanish America and critical of the administration's policy as was Duane's *Aurora.*

[20] Notably in H. M. Brackenridge's pamphlet *South America,* published at Washington in 1817, which is discussed in detail in chap. 6. The idea of the American system embraced two distinct though related principles: first, the severance of America from the European system, and second, cooperation among the states of America. Brackenridge's pamphlet expressed both ideas. There was, of course, a wide difference of opinion as to the degree of cooperation that was desirable or practicable. Some of the opinions on the subject in 1815 and 1816 are discussed in chap. 6. See further in Lockey, *Pan Americanism: Its Beginnings,* p. 263–302. Anticipations of the idea of severance are discussed in Daniel Coit Gilman, *James Monroe* (Boston, 1888), p. 162–170, and J. F. Rippy and Angie Debo, "The Historical Background of the American Policy of Isolation," *Smith College Studies in History,* IX (1924), 75–165. Two valuable articles on the history of American isolationism by Albert K. Weinberg are cited in chap. 12, note 35. Dr. Weinberg has in progress a comprehensive study of the subject.

lying ideas of the doctrine of the two spheres were familiar in the United States before de Pradt borrowed them from a Washington newspaper and still longer before he sent them back to the United States restated in the form in which Jefferson seems to have passed them on to Monroe.

Why Jefferson, who was no mean phrase-maker himself, should have borrowed a French publicist's formulation of a thoroughly American idea, is another question that we do not need to answer. It was certainly not the novelty of the thought that attracted the man who, as far back as 1808, had declared that it was the object of the United States and Spanish America to exclude all European influence from this hemisphere; and there is plenty of evidence that the idea had again been uppermost in his mind in more recent years before he read the book in which de Pradt discussed it. It was likewise familiar to Monroe long before he received Jefferson's letter of October 24, 1823, and was indeed a commonplace of political discussion in both North and South America.[21]

IV

Adams, too, was familiar with the idea of the American system; but, unlike Jefferson and Monroe and, of course, Clay, he had no great enthusiasm for it in the broader, hemispheric sense of the term. Nevertheless, it would not be safe to say that he still regarded it in 1823 with the same impatient scorn of earlier years. In the past two years, as we have had occasion to note,[22] he had come to take a somewhat more sympathetic and hopeful view of Spanish America and this doubtless disposed him more favorably towards the American system. To be sure, his new attitude could hardly be called enthusiastic and he seemed quite ready to revert to the older one. Thus, when Calhoun, who was "moonstruck" (according to Adams) by the surrender of Cadiz to the French, expressed the fear that the Holy Alliance with a mere ten thousand men could restore all Mexico and South America to Spain, Adams's comment was that "if the South Americans were really in a state to be so easily subdued, it would be but a more forcible motive for us to beware of involving ourselves in their fate"; and a few days later he raised the question "whether we had not, after all, been overhasty in acknowledging the South American independence." [23]

Another member of the cabinet, Attorney General William Wirt, was, however, the only one who offered direct opposition in these discussions to the warning to Europe and the closely allied doctrine of the two spheres.

---

[21] As pointed out in earlier chapters, the idea was publicized in the United States by Clay in 1820 and 1821 and was the main inspiration of the mission of the Colombian envoy Mosquera to Buenos Aires in 1822. In 1821 and 1822 it was also a favorite theme of the Colombian envoy in the United States, Manuel Torres (see above, note 4). See also Perkins, *op. cit.*, p. 98–100.

[22] See above, chaps. 12 and 14.

[23] Adams, *Memoirs*, VI, 186 (Nov. 15), and 197 (Nov. 22).

The main reason for his opposition was that "he did not think this country would support the government in a war for the independence of South America." [24] Though Adams did not support Wirt,[25] he did draw him out on the subject in the final meeting of November 26;[26] and when Wirt had finished, Adams, while dissenting,[27] said that he considered Wirt's objections "of the deepest moment" and that he "trusted the President would give them full consideration before coming to his definitive decision." [28] Adams had already confided to his diary the preceding day, after Wirt first raised this question and discussed it briefly, that "it is, and has been, to me, a fearful question," and "the only really important question." [29]

It is easy to understand why Adams regarded this as a fearful question: it is by no means easy to understand how he brought himself to support a message which, as Wirt declared and as Adams himself conceded, might involve the United States in a war for the independence of South America.[30] The difficulty lies in the fact that in this respect the message ran counter to the fundamental policy, the "principle of *duty* . . . which ought forever to govern the Councils of the Union," to which Adams had given the most solemn public expression in his Independence Day address of 1821.[31]

---

[24] *Ibid.*, VI, 205 (Nov. 26). Wirt had already raised this question at the meeting the day before (*ibid.*, VI, 202).

[25] Adams states, however, that it was he himself who first raised the question: ". . . Mr. Wirt made a question far more important, and which I had made at a much earlier stage of these deliberations. It was, whether we shall be warranted in taking so broadly the ground of resistance to the interposition of the Holy Alliance by force to restore the Spanish dominion in South America" (*ibid.*, VI, 202, Nov. 25).

[26] Adams said that the note to Russia, the message, etc., were only various parts of the same question, "and the only really important question to be determined, as it appeared to me, was that yesterday made by Mr. Wirt, and which had been incidentally discussed before, namely, whether we ought at all to take this attitude as regards South America; whether we get any advantage by committing ourselves to a course of opposition against the Holy Alliance" (*ibid.*, VI, 204–205).

[27] Adams said, "If they [Wirt's objections] prevailed, neither the paragraph in the message nor my draft would be proper. . . . I did believe, however, that both would be proper and necessary" (*ibid.*, VI, 207). In introducing the question at this meeting, Adams had already said, "My own mind, indeed, is made up that we ought thus far to take this stand; but I thought it deserved great deliberation, and ought not to be taken without a full and serious estimate of the consequences."

[28] *Ibid.*, VI, 207.   [29] *Ibid.*, VI, 202.

[30] It is important to stress this point because certain passages in Adams's *Memoirs* expressing his disbelief in the Holy Allies' intention of attacking the United States might be misconstrued to mean that he did not believe there was any real danger of war at all. The fact is that in the crucial final discussion of Nov. 26 Adams's position was based on the premise, first, that the danger of an attack by the Allies on Spanish America was real, and second, that Monroe's message would (to the extent of the President's power) commit the United States to war with the Allies if that attack were made (see chap. 17, note 32). It is only in the light of this fact that we can understand why he attached so much importance to the "fearful question" posed by Wirt at this time and anticipated by himself in an earlier session.

[31] See above, chap. 12.

That speech was a blast against Lexington as well as Edinburgh—against Henry Clay, who had ventured to suggest that the United States aid the independence cause in Spanish America, as well as against the *Edinburgh Review,* which wished to enlist the United States in a struggle for liberty in Europe; and Adams had said that his principle forbade the interference of the United States in any foreign war, "even wars for freedom," because such wars had an inevitable tendency "to change the very foundations of our own government from *liberty* to *power.*"

How, then, did Adams bring himself to support in 1823 a course that he had denounced so solemnly and so unreservedly in 1821? This question would be difficult to answer even if we knew that we had all the extant evidence before us. In fact, the only important evidence we have is contained in Adams's published diary, and we can be reasonably certain that additional evidence, possibly of great importance, is contained in his correspondence for this period, the bulk of which is preserved with the family papers, has never been published,[32] and is closed to all students.

Admitting that in view of this difficulty only a tentative answer can be given to the question, we may nevertheless venture to suggest what seems the most probable answer. This is that Adams first convinced himself that the war in which the message of 1823 might involve the United States was not the kind of war against which he had spoken in his address of 1821; and that, although the conviction was not complete, he then resolved whatever doubt lingered in his mind by a process with which we are already familiar, that is, by telling himself that it was his duty to submit his judgment to that of the head of the administration, President Monroe.

The first point is illustrated by his reluctance to come to grips with the question, to admit that there was any real danger of war by act of Europe; and as late as November 25 he declared that he "thought the Holy Alliance would not ultimately invade South America." [33] The point is also illustrated by Adams's determination to regard the hypothetical war as a war not for freedom abroad but in defence of the national interests of the United States. To be sure, he tacitly assented to Wirt's view that the war would aid the independence movement in Spanish America; but when Wirt's strong statement brought the discussion to a sharp focus on this "fearful question," Adams made it perfectly plain that, in his own mind, aid to Spanish America would be merely incidental and that the main purpose of any war he was prepared to support would be to defend the United States itself. If, he said, the Holy Allies should attack and conquer

---

[32] Ford's edition of Adams's letters (*Writings, cit. supra*) stops abruptly and most tantalizingly with June 1823, on the very threshold of this critical period in the development of American foreign policy. The Adams family papers are on deposit with the Massachusetts Historical Society. They were used by W. C. Ford in preparing the articles cited above, note 12, but are now closed to all students.

[33] Adams, *Memoirs,* VI, 201.

Spanish America, it was "not in human absurdity" to imagine that they would do so to re-establish the old Spanish colonial system: their purpose would be to partition the former colonies among themselves. England would take Cuba; Russia, California; France, Mexico; and, he added, Gallatin, who had recently returned from Paris, had told him only a few days earlier that France was even threatening to recover Louisiana where she had a strong party in her favor.[34]

"The danger, therefore," he concluded, "was brought to our own doors, and I thought we could not too soon take our stand to repel it." [35] This was his main reason for deciding against Wirt and in favor of Monroe on this "fearful question." His only reason which related to Spanish America at large was based not on his desire to promote the independence of that region but to prevent Britain from adding it to her already overgrown empire. If the Holy Allies should attack Spanish America and the United States should remain aloof from the contest, Britain would probably resist them single-handed and, through her overwhelming naval superiority, would probably defeat them; and in that case, he said,

> as the independence of the South Americans would only be protected by the guarantee of Great Britain, it would throw them completely into her arms, and in the result make them her colonies instead of those of Spain.[36]

In this danger Adams found an additional reason for acting "promptly and decisively," that is, for supporting the threat of war that Monroe had proposed to make. Yet even now Adams did not accept either for himself or for the cabinet as a whole the responsibility of making the final decision. As we have already seen, he accompanied this statement of his reasons for supporting the pronouncement with the admission that he considered Wirt's objections to it as "of the deepest moment" and with the advice to Monroe to "give them full consideration before coming to his definitive decision." [37]

The phrase "before coming to his definitive decision" deserves special emphasis, for the cabinet meeting in which Adams used it was the last of this momentous series of meetings in which the Monroe Doctrine was discussed before it was communicated to Congress; and yet, although the Secretary of State and (so far as the evidence shows) all the other members of the cabinet, except Wirt, had approved of the passages bearing on the "fearful question," it was Adams's view that the question had not yet been decided and that the decision rested with Monroe alone. Whatever

[34] Hyde de Neuville, writing to the Duke de Richelieu in January 1817, suggested that in case of war with the United States, France might reopen the Louisiana question and employ the French element in Louisiana in attacking the United States. He made some uncomplimentary remarks about these creoles but said that at least they were loyal to France and might be useful in such a crisis. See Hyde de Neuville, *Mémoires et souvenirs,* II, 267–268.

[35] Adams, *Memoirs,* VI, 207–208.   [36] *Ibid.,* VI, 208.   [37] *Ibid.,* VI, 207.

Monroe's decision might be, Adams would be able to accept it with a clear conscience, for, as he had said in August of this year and repeated in another connection at this very time,[38] he acquiesced cheerfully in the decisions of his chief even when they conflicted sharply with his own.

Thus it was, apparently, that Adams reconciled the conflict between the foreign policy that he advocated in 1821 and the one to which he gave his adherence in 1823. The question has been discussed at length because it involves not only the views of one of the leading American secretaries of state and the most important pronouncement in the history of American foreign policy but also a conflict of principle that has run through the whole history of the United States—a conflict which, at the risk of oversimplification, may be called one between isolationists on the one hand and interventionists on the other. As Adams said when he discussed this conflict in 1821, it had already appeared in Washington's administration over the issue of aiding republican France and was now being pressed by Clay in relation to Spanish America; and in our own time it has reappeared on two conspicuous occasions—in connection with the Wilsonian effort to make the world safe for democracy, and in the present world crisis.

The interest of the phase of this conflict that developed in 1823 lies partly in the fact that most of the pros and cons of the question as it has been debated subsequently were stated, or at least suggested, on that occasion. It lies partly also in the fact that Adams followed a course which has subsequently been followed by many of his countrymen, for he first committed himself on theoretical grounds to a policy of non-intervention, and then, when faced by a crisis which demanded action, abandoned the policy without confessing the abandonment and, perhaps, without even being clearly conscious of it. At any rate, it is difficult to read his challenge to Lexington and Edinburgh of 1821, and his subsequent commentaries on it, without concluding that in November 1823 he went a long way towards capitulating to Lexington; but a careful reading of his diary for that month fails to reveal anything more than a vague hint, implicit in his anxious comments on the objections raised by Wirt, that he realized what he was doing.

V

These considerations make it easier for us to answer the question whether Adams contributed anything at all to the second part of the Monroe

---

[38] See above, chap. 14. It was probably this spirit, and not impatience, that inspired the well known passage in Adams's diary for Nov. 13, 1823: "We [Monroe and Adams] discussed the proposals of Canning, and I told him if he would decide either to accept or decline them, I would draft a dispatch conformable to either decision for his consideration" (*Memoirs*, VI, 185).

Doctrine. As we have seen, the researches of Perkins and Schellenberg have reduced this to the question whether Adams contributed materially to drawing a clear line between the Old World and the New, and thus clarifying the idea of the American system. Before we answer this question, we must first recall the form in which Monroe presented this part of the Doctrine to his cabinet.

In this first draft, Monroe embodied ideas drawn from the replies of both Jefferson and Madison to his inquiry regarding Canning's proposal. From Jefferson's reply he took the idea of an American system separate and distinct from the European system; but with a catholicity of republican zeal that does more credit to his heart than his head, he borrowed from Madison's reply the conflicting idea of undertaking to sustain liberty in Spain and Greece as well as in Spanish America. In both replies he found support for his own predisposition to accept Canning's proposal. It was his intention to couple a joint declaration along the lines proposed by Canning with a unilateral statement of policy in his forthcoming message to Congress; and the idea of inserting such a statement in his message was almost certainly his own[39] and he was not indebted for it to Jefferson or Madison any more than he was to Adams.

Adams began his contribution at this point. His prudence recoiled from the suggestion that the United States should undertake to sustain liberty in Spain and Greece, for, he said, this would make the message "a summons to arms against all Europe, and for objects of policy exclusively European," whereas our true policy was "to meet, and not to make" an issue with the Holy Allies.[40] Yet the suggestion held a strong attraction for his chief, and unless Adams was prepared for an open break with him, he must make some concession on his own part in return for the sacrifice he was asking Monroe to make.

It was under these circumstances that Adams undertook his vigorous advocacy of a policy based on the idea of the American system—a system for which he had never before shown comparable enthusiasm. Even now he had no great enthusiasm for it, in the hemispheric sense in which it was understood by Jefferson and Monroe, and he justified his support of it on essentially nationalist grounds and mainly as a means of reducing the scope of Monroe's declaration. This was accomplished by eliminating the ideological principle contained in the passages relating to Spain and Greece, suggested by Madison, and by basing the declaration squarely upon the geographical concept of the American system, suggested by Jefferson.

There was thus nothing original in Adams's contribution, since he was in effect merely supporting Jefferson against Madison in the cabinet discussions of this question; but it was important, for he was an effective advocate and unquestionably did much to convince Monroe that, on both

[39] Perkins, *op. cit.*, p. 74–75.   [40] Adams, *Memoirs*, VI, 195.

logical and practical grounds, a choice must be made between the two and that the preference should be given to Jefferson.

The question of Adams's influence on the decision regarding Canning's proposal requires clarification, as does the nature of the decision itself. There has been a tendency to exaggerate Adams's influence in this matter. Even his severest critic, Schellenberg, credits him with having "effectively prevented a bilateral declaration of policy." [41] Perkins properly notes that "the idea of association with a European power was not . . . entirely repudiated" at this time. But he goes on to say that Adams himself "whose vigorous mind and will had much to do with the decision that was taken, favored cooperation on the basis of Canning's acknowledgment of colonial independence," and he also remarks that, in the instructions to Rush of November 30, "the question of at once accepting the British overtures was virtually decided in the negative." [42]

In order to understand what Monroe and his cabinet actually decided and what share Adams had in the decision, the following facts should be kept in mind. First, the decision was made in the knowledge that Canning had in effect abandoned his proposal. This knowledge was derived from Rush's despatch of October 10, 1823, which was received by Adams on November 16, at the beginning of this momentous series of Cabinet meetings.[43] It is therefore inaccurate to say that Monroe and his advisers rejected Canning's proposal, for they would have stultified themselves by accepting a proposal in which, as Rush's despatch made unmistakably clear to them, Canning had lost interest completely. (2) In this situation, the only alternative immediately open to Monroe and his advisers was to make a unilateral declaration or none at all. The decision in favor of making a unilateral declaration in the forthcoming message was unquestionably Monroe's, not Adams's. (3) The question then remained whether subsequently the United States should attempt to revive the project of cooperation with England, despite Canning's sudden coldness towards it, and, if so, on what terms. Adams's influence in the decision of this question was negligible compared with that of Rush and Monroe. It was Rush who first recommended the principles finally adopted by his government, namely, that cooperation with the British government in this crisis was desirable and that it should be effected on the basis of British recognition of Spanish American independence.[44] It was Monroe who kept the door open to cooperation with England by overruling Adams's effort to make prior recognition a sine qua non.[45]

In summing up what has been said about the authorship of the Monroe

---

[41] Schellenberg, *loc. cit.*, p. 17. [42] Perkins, *op. cit.*, p. 93–94.

[43] This despatch is cited below in chap. 17, note 5, and is discussed at length in that chapter.

[44] For a more detailed discussion of this important point, see below, chap. 17.

[45] Perkins, *op. cit.*, p. 93.

Doctrine, it should be repeated that this consisted of two distinct parts. The first part, containing the non-colonization principle, presents a relatively simple problem. It merely repeated in public, and with special reference to Russia, what had already been said in private, and with special reference to Great Britain, in the instructions to Rush of July 1823. At every stage the influence of Adams appears to have been decisive. It was he who drafted both the instructions to Rush and also the first part of the message and who recommended the discussion of the subject in the message. His recommendation was accepted, and his very phraseology was followed almost without change. For all practical purposes, then, he was the author of the first part of the message.

The problem presented by the second part is more difficult, for it was the work of several hands. The value of each contribution cannot be fixed precisely, but some approximations may be ventured. First, it should be noted that Richard Rush's contribution was more important than has been generally recognized. Though he did not urge the unilateral declaration that was finally made, he gave information and advice which pointed in that direction, as will appear more fully in the following chapter.

Adams's share in establishing the policy was less important than his share in formulating the unilateral declaration that constituted the leading feature of it. When all the evidence has been balanced and due allowance has been made for his lack of originality and his mental reservations, the fact remains that, by his insistence that the administration should "make an American cause, and adhere inflexibly to that," he was largely responsible, as Perkins has said, for "the clear line which the message draws between the Old World and the New." If the original ideas of Jefferson, Madison, and Monroe himself had prevailed, the line would have been less clear. But this is the limit of Adams's contribution. Whatever its ultimate value in clarifying ideas on American policy, its immediate practical value would seem to have been rather small, for it is difficult to see how the Cabinet could have adopted the alternative policy of a joint declaration in the face of Rush's plain statement that Canning was no longer interested in making it.

Moreover, if Adams's original idea had prevailed, the second part of the Monroe Doctrine would not have been stated at all. The message would have contained only the first part, the assertion of the non-colonization principle, which, while it was novel if not bizarre from the point of view of international law, was a far less important statement of policy than the second part of the Doctrine, both at the moment of its publication and subsequently. In drawing up the plans for this part, which contains the doctrine of the two spheres, the idea of the American system, and the warning to Europe, Adams rendered some valuable assistance as draftsman; but its chief architects were Jefferson and Monroe, and it reflects their greater sympathy for Latin America and their more dynamic republicanism.

XI

*The American West as
Symbol and Myth:
Poetic Inspiration or
Pragmatic Perspective?*

INTRODUCTION

In 1950 Henry Nash Smith published his seminal study Virgin Land: The American West as Symbol and Myth. *Smith brought to his study of the American West the conceptual tools of symbol and myth that had never, heretofore, been employed as a methodology in the manner Smith employed them. Not only was the methodology new and exciting but its realization in Smith's writing, eloquent and imaginative, marked the publication of his book as an event in American historiography.*

Smith defined his terms: "The terms 'myth' and 'symbol' occur so often in the following pages that the reader deserves some warning about them. I use the words to designate larger or smaller units of the same kind of thing, normally an intellectual construction that fuses concept and emotion into an image. The myths and symbols with which I deal have the further characteristic of being collective representations rather than the work of a single mind. I do not mean to raise the question whether such products of the imagination accurately reflect empirical fact. [See Barry Marks, "The Concept of Myth in Virgin Land," American Quarterly, V (Spring 1955), 71–76.] *They exist on a different plane. But as I have tried to show, they sometimes exert a decided influence on practical affairs." (Virgin Land, Preface, p. v.) The materials upon which Smith based his study were primarily literary materials. This thematic treatment of myth and symbol from a chapter of his book, "The Agricultural West in Literature," is the first essay reprinted below.*

Rush Welter, though he acknowledges his debt to Smith's insights and judges Virgin Land *to be the main work in the field, is yet critical of the realities of the myths and symbols that Smith evokes as giving any whole image of the West as Americans conceived it. He states that ". . . the predominantly literary antithesis that Henry Nash Smith has traced in* Virgin Land *may not have influenced the American people as much as their novels and some of their congressional rhetoric may suggest." [See Rush Welter, "The Frontier West as Image of American Society: Conservative Attitude Before the Civil War,"* Mississippi Valley Historical Review, XLVI (1960), 594.]*

In the second piece of writing reprinted below, Welter develops his criticism still further: "The themes that Smith and others trace are too nearly poetic in their inspiration, too nearly conventional in their application, to be trustworthy guides to the pragmatic perspective with which most Americans contemplated their lives. Above all, they are too restricted to account for various images of the West as a country that real people might inhabit; and they do not always differentiate the West that was to be occupied and farmed and ultimately to be industrialized from the majestic natural phe-

nomenon that still surrounds Westerns on television and in movies." Welter concludes that between 1776 and 1860 Americans came to view the West as ". . . an almost limitless extension of the social and economic and political values they associated with their country at large."

The Agricultural West in Literature

Henry Nash Smith

I. COOPER AND THE STAGES OF SOCIETY

The Wild West beyond the frontier lent itself readily to interpretation in a literature developing the themes of natural nobility and physical adventure, but the agricultural West, as we have already remarked, proved quite intractable as literary material. The myth of the garden and the ideal figure of the Western yeoman were poetic ideas, as Tocqueville rightly called them, but they could not be brought to fictional expression. The difficulty lay in the class status of the Western farmer. The Declaration of Independence had proclaimed that all men were created equal, and American political institutions had reflected a general acceptance of the proposition in the widespread removal of property qualifications for the franchise as early as the 1820's and 1830's. But there was a lag of half a century between the triumph of the idea of equality in politics and its embodiment in imaginative literature.

The early literary characters in the pattern of Leatherstocking did not really bear upon the problem because they were outside society. In his capacity as Indian fighter and hunter the Western hero could be celebrated without regard to class lines. But we have noted how slowly the Western hunter gained sufficient social standing to be allowed to marry the heroine. This fictional emancipation of the Wild Westerner was not clearly worked out before the late 1870's.

The yeoman had an even harder struggle to achieve full status in literature. Cooper, for all his delight in Leatherstocking and his theoretical approval of political equality, stoutly resisted the tendency to break down distinctions between social classes. Indeed, as he became aroused over the "Anti-Rent War" in upstate New York he concluded that even in the political sphere the cult of the yeoman had been carried too far. He declared in 1848 that politicians eager for votes had made the small farmer into an idol before which they fell down in worship. "We can see citizens in these yeomen," continued the crusty novelist, "but not princes, who are to be especially favored by laws made to take from others to bestow on them." [1] The cult seemed to him a phase of the "bastard democracy" that was coming into favor, a movement to seek for the sovereign people in the gutters, "forgetting that the landlord has just as much right to protection as the tenant, the master as the servant, the rich as the poor, the gentleman as the blackguard." [2] In his Littlepage trilogy, Cooper had roundly denounced the tenants in the Hudson Valley who had resorted to violence in protest against a system of tenures that made it difficult for small farmers to acquire title to land. The ideal of the yeoman society was obviously incompatible with Cooper's aristocratic ideal of a society dominated by great landed proprietors.

Few writers of Cooper's generation were as frank as he in stating their conservative social bias. Perhaps they were not even conscious of it. But it was evidently at work as a force inhibiting the use of the small farmer as a character in fiction. James K. Paulding is a case in point. More than a decade after he had celebrated the career of Basil in *The Backwoodsman* he turned again to the agricultural West in his novel *Westward Ho!* published in 1832. Although the novelist acknowledges Flint's *Recollections of the Last Ten Years* as his source of information about the Mississippi Valley,[3] he builds his plot around a group of plantation gentry who migrate from Virginia to Kentucky; the only character really belonging to the West is the old hunter Ambrose Bushfield, a composite of Leatherstocking and Daniel Boone.[4] The story contains no characters representing the yeoman class.

The expatriate sculptor Thomas Buchanan Read's determined effort to depict an Arcadian West in his long blank verse narrative *The New Pastoral* (1855) shows even more clearly how difficult it was to devise a literary interpretation of the movement of the agricultural frontier into the Mississippi Valley. Read has an ample store of the clichés of agrarian theory. With his oaten pipe, he announces, he plans to celebrate the sweetly contended middle state between the hut and the palace, "The simple life of nature, fresh from God!" He will write of the great mass of Western farmers who labor that the structure of society may be sustained, for these folk are morally superior to the idle rich in their purple and fine linen.[5] But

---

[1] *The Oak Openings; or, The Bee-Hunter*, 2 vols. (New York, 1848), I, 154.

[2] *Ibid.*, I, 113. [3] *Westward Ho! A Tale*, 2 vols. (New York, 1832), I, 4.

[4] Bushfield had been a companion of Boone (*ibid.*, I, 70); he was a loyal retainer of Colonel Dangerfield (I, 71); he felt crowded by the advance of settlement (I, 179–181); he wished to be able to fell a tree near his house for fuel (I, 184); and finally he fled to a remote military post on the Missouri River (II, 193).

[5] *The New Pastoral* (Philadelphia, 1855), p. vi.

how can this claim be made good? Read follows a group of emigrants from rural Pennsylvania overland to Pittsburgh, down the Ohio to Cincinnati, and on into the Indiana forest. As they carve their homes from the wilderness civilization sweeps onward, and soon a golden harvest waves where once dark forests stood. But the poet is hard pressed for incident. He turns in desperation to a wilder West by describing a buffalo hunt and the lassoing of wild horses, and presents an elaborate metrical version of the standard vision of the Mississippi Valley in the future with its cheerful farms, quiet herds, cities, steamboats, a Pacific railway, and a great metropolis on the Lakes.

> Onward still
> The giant movement goes with rapid pace,
> And civilization spreads its arms abroad;
> While the cleared forest-lands look gladly up,
> And nod their harvest plumes.[6]

Of the actual process of agricultural settlement we have little except an account of the malaria among the farmers. Two of the patriarchs of the colony at last give up and make their way back to Pennsylvania—"Too stern the battle for such souls as theirs." [7] The whole performance is remarkably tame, despite Read's ingratiating fluency. As in the case of Paulding's *The Backwoodsman,* the trouble lies not in the poet so much as in an unfortunate lack of congruence between the materials and the literary mode he has chosen. His conventionally bland manner can not convey the coarse and salty reality of his subject, and he is evidently convinced only in theory of the dignity of his characters.

Mrs. Caroline A. Soule's *Little Alice,* to mention only one further effort at a mild and cheerful interpretation of agricultural settlement in the West, is likewise a failure. The author states in her preface that the novel is the fruit of "four years of actual pioneer life in the valley of the Upper Des Moines, of emigrant life in a cabin on the prairie." [8] She is perfectly convinced that frontier farmers are noble and that the process of advancing the agricultural frontier yields vast consequences for the good of mankind. The guests at a wedding, for example, are bathed in an aura of primitive sentiment:

> Fifty sturdy pioneers, clad in clean homespun, stood about in various attitudes, their frank open faces radiant with light from their honest hearts. Upon the mossy logs, sat as many noble women, their coarse garments betokening thrift and neatness, while their pleasant faces told of their sympathy with the fair girl whose bridal they had come to witness.[9]

---

[6] *Ibid.,* p. 208.   [7] *Ibid.,* pp. 215–217, 225, 233–234, 237.
[8] *Little Alice; or, The Pet of the Settlement. A Story of Prairie Land* (Boston, 1863), p. iii.
[9] *Ibid.,* p. 143.

Mrs. Soule asserts that in the earliest period of settlement, hardship and danger promote the spirit of mutual aid to such an extent that "the brotherhood of men is recognized as an actual as well as an ideal thing." [10] Fifteen years later the community shows many evidences of change,

> but thank heaven, only a bright, beautiful change, which has brought hundreds of struggling, debt-ridden, homeless and hungry men and women from the crowded cities of older States, and given them peace and plenty, houses and lands, while they in grateful return have "made the wilderness and the solitary place glad for them; and the desert to rejoice, and blossom as the rose." [11]

Yet the story that is intended to exhibit the process is as unconvincing as Read's poem. The hero and heroine are recent arrivals from New England, formerly wealthy and very genteel. Uncle Billy, an "old and experienced hunter" speaking a strong dialect, is a benign Leatherstocking whose frontier skills are employed in the fashion prescribed by Wild Western convention.[12] Mrs. Soule also provides a female counterpart of Uncle Billy in the charitable but uneducated Grandma Symmes.[13] These characters represent the Western flavor of the book; but they are distinctly subordinate, just as Leatherstocking was subordinate to Cooper's gentry. The scheme of values in the novel is organized about the superiority of the hero and heroine, whose merits have nothing to do with the West or with agriculture. For all her four years on the prairie, Mrs. Soule can not find the literary means to embody the affirmation of the agrarian ideal that her theory calls for.

These early efforts to deal with the agricultural West in literature prove that the frontier farmer could not be made into an acceptable hero. His sedentary and laborious calling stripped him of the exotic glamor that could be exploited in hunters and scouts of the Wild West. At the same time his low social status made it impossible to elaborate his gentility. Whatever the orators might say in glittering abstractions about the virtues of the yeoman, the novelists found themselves unable to control the emotions aroused by the Western farmer's degraded rank in the class system. Since class feeling about the yeoman is the crux of the literary problem presented by the agricultural West, we are obliged to look as closely as possible into prevalent notions concerning the place of the West and its people in American society.

Such an inquiry leads back once again to the contrast between civilization and savagery that lay at the root of the distinction between the Wild West and the domesticated or agricultural West. The frontier of agricultural settlement was universally recognized as the line separating civilization from savagery; but the structure of civilized society within the frontier was conceived according to two contrasting schools of thought. The agrarian tradition that stemmed from Jefferson held up as its ideal simple agricultural

---

[10] *Ibid.*, p. 56. [11] *Ibid.*, p. 236. [12] *Ibid.*, pp. 18, 67, 28. [13] *Ibid.*, p. 45.

communities in which an approximate equality of wealth prevailed, and in which social stratification was accordingly kept to a minimum. But the equalitarian overtones of this ideal were by no means acceptable to the country as a whole. The concept of a classless society appealed only to a radical minority, and was constantly in danger of being obliterated by the much older and deeper belief in social stratification. The situation could hardly have been otherwise. Equalitarianism, especially social and economic equalitarianism, was a recent and perhaps transient notion deriving in large part from French radical thought of the eighteenth century. The ideal of social subordination, of a hierarchy of classes, of a status system, had the weight of centuries behind it. Still more important for the imaginative interpretation of American life was the fact that the assumptions underlying the class structure of English society permeated the genre of the sentimental novel, which was built about the genteel hero and heroine. There was no coherent literary tradition embodying equalitarian assumptions.

The belief in the Western farmer's social inferiority was further strengthened by certain ideas derived from the New England theocratic tradition. From this standpoint, all emigrants were actually or potentially criminal because of their flight from an orderly municipal life into frontier areas that were remote from centers of control. The attitude had developed naturally out of the Puritan devotion to social order maintained by church and state as coöperating agencies. A sermon preached before a Boston congregation by the Reverend Thomas Barnard in 1758 states the theocratic case against the backwoodsman quite clearly. Religion, he said, will flourish most where the arts of peace are cultivated, "especially Industry, among those born for Labour." For a quiet steady life in an orderly community keeps alive a regard for whatever is virtuous and pious, facilitates attendance upon public worship, tends to implant clear notions of justice and a regard for property, and leads men toward a proper submission to their civil rulers. On the other hand, when people wander into the wilderness and settle far apart from one another, the result is "Savageness of Temper, Ignorance, Want of the Means of Religion; (which will attend a solitary State and distant Neighborhood)." Worse still, when a plenty of free land allows men to support themselves "by the spontaneous Products of Nature with Little Labour; Experience has shewn, that Habits of Idleness and Intemperance have been contracted, much to the public Damage." [14]

This general view is so familiar it hardly needs elaborate illustration, but a few later comments may be mentioned to indicate the persistence of the Eastern belief in frontier depravity. The most famous among such statements is that of the Reverend Timothy Dwight, President of Yale, who wrote a characterization of the *"foresters, or Pioneers"* of Vermont on the basis of his travels in the state in 1798 and 1806. Such men, in the opinion

---

[14] *A Sermon Preached in Boston, New-England, before the Society for Encouraging Industry, and Employing the Poor, September 20, 1758* (Boston, 1758), pp. 10–11, 13.

of the noted divine, had proved too idle, talkative, passionate, and shiftless to acquire either property or reputation in stable communities, and therefore wished to escape the restraints of law, religion, morality, and government. Unable to adjust themselves to the social state, "they become at length discouraged: and under the pressure of poverty, the fear of a gaol, and the consciousness of public contempt, leave their native places, and betake themselves to the wilderness." [15] Dwight distinguishes between such dissolute foresters and the virtuous farmers who establish orderly communities after the first pioneers have moved on, but he implies that most settlers in the farther West are of the depraved class which he has described in Vermont.

> The class of men, who have been the principal subject of these remarks [he asserts], have already straggled onward from New-England, as well as from other parts of the Union, to Louisiana. In a political view, their emigration is of very serious utility to the ancient inhabitants. . . . The institutions, and habits, of New-England, more I suspect than those of any other country, have prevented, or kept down, this noxious disposition; but they cannot entirely prevent either its existence, or its effects. In mercy, therefore, to the sober, industrious, and well-disposed, inhabitants, Providence has opened in the vast Western wilderness a retreat, sufficiently alluring to draw them away from the land of their nativity. We have many troubles even now: but we should have many more, if this body of foresters had remained at home.[16]

These characteristics of life in new settlements continued to be especially clear to New Englanders who had enjoyed the advantages of theological training. The tradition was so explicit that even the young and relatively radical Unitarian minister James Freeman Clarke, who had been exposed to Transcendentalism and had gone out to Louisville with vaguely evangelistic aims, struggled in vain against it. In a review of Mann Butler's *History of the Commonwealth of Kentucky* and James Hall's *Sketches of History, Life, and Manners, in the West,* Clarke allowed the West a "genius deep, rich, strong, various, and full of promise," but he was alarmed at the fact that this genius was unbridled, undirected, and ungoverned. Western mothers encouraged their children to fight, women favored duelling, grave judges gambled, and vice ate into the heart of social virtue. The West needed religious restraint, it needed moral principle, it needed greater respect for law and a disposition to follow duty as pointed out to it by wise guidance—presumably from New England.[17]

The covert class bias characteristic of this attitude appears even more clearly in a review of Caroline M. Kirkland's *Forest Life* by Cornelius C. Felton, of Harvard, in 1842. A population was growing up in the West,

---

[15] *Travels; in New-England and New-York,* 4 vols. (New Haven, 1821–1822), II, 459.
[16] *Ibid.,* II, 461–462.   [17] *North American Review,* XLIII, 27–28 (July, 1836).

according to the reviewer, "with none of the restraints which fetter the characters of the working classes in other countries." No feudal feeling of loyalty tempered the natural overflow of passion or restrained the full growth of individual humors. Each man in the West considered himself a sovereign by indefeasible right, and had no idea anyone else was his better in any respect.[18]

To the theocratic suspicion of the Western farmer as a rebellious fugitive from society must be added the unfavorable view of him derived from the idea of civilization and progress. The conception of civilization, like the word itself, had first gained currency in the middle decades of the eighteenth century in the writings of Turgot and Rousseau.[19] Its most persuasive formulation came in the 1790's with Condorcet's *Esquisse d'un tableau historique des progrès de l'esprit humain,* which was immediately translated into English and had two editions in the United States before 1825.[20] The most influential aspect of Condorcet's theory of civilization was the notion that all human societies pass through the same series of social stages in the course of their evolution upward from barbarism toward the goal of universal enlightenment. He divided the history of the human race into ten epochs, the first nine stretching from the dawn of existence to the foundation of the French Republic, the tenth embracing the glorious future opened up for mankind by the triumph of Reason. The most important of these epochs for social theory were the earliest, which comprised the union of autonomous families who subsisted mainly by hunting, into "hordes"; the domestication of animals, inaugurating the pastoral stage of society; and the transition from a pastoral to an agricultural stage. Other writers developed the idea that civilization actually began when a given society adopted an agricultural way of life.[21]

Although in Europe the successive stages of society were naturally thought of as succeeding one another in time, so that primitive conditions could be studied only through historical and archeological research, the situation in America was quite different. When the theory of civilization became current in this country many observers were struck by its applicability

---

[18] *Ibid.,* LV, 511 (October, 1842).

[19] The origins of the conception and its currency in the United States are traced in Charles A. and Mary Beard, *The Rise of American Civilization,* Volume IV: *The American Spirit: A Study of the Idea of Civilization in the United States* (New York, 1942).

[20] Philadelphia, 1796, and Baltimore, 1802.

[21] This point, for example, was frequently made by missionaries working with Western Indians (*Twenty-Sixth Annual Report of the American Board of Commissioners for Foreign Missions,* Boston, 1835, p. 99; *Twenty-Seventh Annual Report,* Boston, 1836, pp. 95–96). William Tooke, an English traveler in Asia cited by William Darby (*View of the United States,* Philadelphia, 1828, p. 321), had asserted that the transition from a migratory pastoral life to agriculture "determines the boundary between civilized and barbarous nations" (*View of the Russian Empire during the Reign of Catherine the Second,* 3 vols., London, 1799, III, 230). Volney made the same point with regard to the Bedouins of Arabia (*Travels through Egypt and Syria,* Eng. trans., 2 vols., New York, 1798, I, 231).

to the actual state of affairs in the West. The comment was frequently made that in America one could examine side by side the social stages that were believed to have followed one another in time in the long history of the Old World. William Darby, for example, wrote in his *Emigrant's Guide* in 1818 that a journey from New Orleans westward to the Sabine showed man in every stage of his progress, from the most civilized to the most savage. New Orleans represented the summit of cultivation, refinement, and luxury. The plantations of the lower Mississippi likewise offered "all that art, aided by wealth, can produce." In Attacapas and Opelousas parishes the glare of luxury vanished, and in its stead the traveler encountered substantial, independent farmers living in rough though comfortable houses. In the western parts of Opelousas parish could be found pastoral hunters who recalled to the imagination the primitive ages of history. Still farther west, along the Sabine, the way of life of the scattered inhabitants suggested "the utmost verge of inhabited earth, and the earliest dawn of human improvement." [22]

In 1824 the *Port Folio* of Philadelphia quoted a remark to this same effect made by the British traveler Adam Hodgson after a journey from west to east across the United States. "I have seen the roving hunter acquiring the habit of the herdsman," said Hodgson; "the pastoral state merging into the agricultural, and the agricultural into the manufacturing and commercial." [23] Jefferson himself, whom Hodgson had visited at Monticello,[24] a short time later expounded the theory at length.

> Let a philosophic observer [he wrote] commence a journey from the savages of the Rocky Mountains, eastwardly towards our sea-coast. These he would observe in the earliest stage of association living under no law but that of nature, [subsisting] and covering themselves with the flesh and skins of wild beasts. He would next find those on our frontiers in the pastoral state, raising domestic animals, to supply the defects of hunting. Then succeed our own semi-barbarous citizens, the pioneers of the advance of civilization, and so in his progress he would meet the gradual shades of improving man until he would reach his, as yet, most improved state in our seaport towns. This, in fact, is equivalent to a survey, in time, of the progress of man from the infancy of creation to the present day.[25]

One or two examples from imaginative literature will be enough to indicate how widespread the theory was. In his *Francis Berrian,* published serially in 1825–1826, Timothy Flint causes the hero to remark that when he traveled westward from Natchitoches into Texas he "had occasion to

[22] *The Emigrant's Guide to the Western and Southwestern States and Territories* (New York, 1818), pp. 61–62.
[23] *Port Folio,* Fourth [Fifth] Series, XVII, 214 (March, 1824).
[24] Adam Hodgson, *Letters from North America,* 2 vols. (London, 1824), I, 318–319.
[25] *Writings,* ed. H. A. Washington, VII, 377–378 (Monticello, September 6, 1824).

experiment the truth of the remark, that in travelling towards the frontier, the decreasing scale of civilization and improvement exhibits an accurate illustration of inverted history." Berrian felt that he had traveled down six centuries in as many days. The half-savage settlers on the remote frontier, who lived as much by hunting as by agriculture, were "the intermediate race between savage and civilized man." [26] A final illustration may be taken from Cooper's *The Prairie* (1827):

> The gradations of society, from that state which is called refined to that which approaches as near barbarity as connexion with an intelligent people will readily allow, are to be traced from the bosom of the states, where wealth, luxury and the arts are beginning to seat themselves, to those distant and ever-receding borders which mark the skirts and announce the approach of the nation, as moving mists precede the signs of the day.[27]

This theoretical statement introduces the character of Ishmael Bush, a Kentucky backwoodsman who represents Cooper's deepest penetration into the problem of the agricultural frontier, and well deserves to stand as the counterpart of Leatherstocking, the Child of the Forest. Whereas Leatherstocking has a natural virtue and an exotic splendor derived from his communion with untouched nature, Bush and his sons are at war with nature. They are the very axemen from whom Leatherstocking has fled halfway across the continent. Cooper is so eager to make this symbolic point that he has Bush's sons chop down a grove of trees conjured up for the purpose in the midst of the treeless great plains.[28] Although Leatherstocking and Bush figure in the same novel, they belong to entirely distinct conceptual systems. The line that divides them is the agricultural frontier. Leatherstocking, living beyond the frontier and following the vocation of a hunter and trapper, is not a member of society at all. Bush, the husbandman, belongs to society; his "connexion with an intelligent people" is his participation in the Social Compact to which Leatherstocking is not a party.

But if Bush has a place in the scheme of civilization that flowers at the top into Cooper's gentry, he represents the lowest of its stages, at a great remove from the level of refinement.[29] He is a wanderer—Cooper's readers would not have missed the biblical allusion in his name; and he also arouses suspicion as a propertyless member of the lowest social class. He is just such a backwoodsman as Barnard and Dwight had described. He is clad in "the coarsest vestments of a husbandman," but wears "a singular and wild display of prodigal and ill-judged ornaments" that bespeak a

---

[26] *Francis Berrian; or, The Mexican Patriot*, 2 vols. (Boston, 1826), I, 39.
[27] *The Prairie* (Philadelphia, 1827), I, 88. [28] *Ibid.*, I, 26, 103.
[29] Cooper calls the Bush group "semi-barbarous" (*ibid.*, I, 165), which was Jefferson's word for American settlers just within the frontier, immediately above the pastoral Indians in the scale of social stages.

half-barbaric taste. The lower part of his face is "coarse, extended, and vacant," while the upper part is "low, receding, and mean." His manner is characterized by apathy and indolence, although it is evident that he has great muscular strength. He is, in short, half animal, as Cooper insists in a simile: ". . . he suffered his huge frame, to descend the gentle declivity, in the same sluggish manner that an over fatted beast would have yielded to the downward pressure." [30] The novelist makes Bush the accomplice of his brother-in-law Abiram White, slave-stealer by trade, who has abducted the heroine Inez de Certavallos and is keeping her prisoner in one of the wagons of Bush's train. And we learn that Bush has shot a deputy sheriff who tried to evict him and fifty other squatters from a tract of land back in Kentucky.[31] This act of rebellion seems somehow vastly more sinister than Leatherstocking's defiance of the law in *The Pioneers,* which was motivated by feudal loyalty to his patron Major Effingham.

All these traits of Bush are in perfect accord with conservative theory. Yet the character has an interest for Cooper that defies theory. The idea of Bush's barbarism, along with its connotations of mere criminality, carries a suggestion of moral sublimity. It is related to the moral beauty of Leatherstocking as the somber and tormented landscapes of Salvator Rosa seemed to Cooper and his contemporaries to be related to the mild and smiling landscapes of their other favorite Claude Lorrain. In exploring this esthetic aspect of Bush, Cooper was able to view him for the moment, so to speak, purely, without judging him by the criterion of refinement or the theory of social stages, and in consequence was led to write one of the best sequences in all the Leatherstocking series. Near the end of the story, Ishmael as patriarch of his tribe sets about administering justice for the murder of his son Asa. A dim acquaintance with the Scriptures has left in his mind the barbaric notion that an eye for an eye is the law of God. When the murderer is revealed to be his wife's brother Abiram, the law of God comes into conflict with primitive clan loyalty, but Ishmael and his wife consult the Scriptures and come to the conclusion that Abiram must die. If Leatherstocking is notable for his intuitive ability to distinguish right from wrong, Ishmael too has his terrifying sense of justice. Abiram's craven pleas for one more hour of life suggest the grim expedient of binding his arms, tying a noose about his neck, and leaving him upon a narrow ledge from which as his strength fails he must in the end cast himself. That night, in a setting of wind and drifting clouds intended to suggest Salvator's style, Ishmael and his wife return to the place of execution, cut down the swinging body, and bury it.[32] The same sense of justice had earlier led Bush, after ponderous meditation, to release Inez of his own volition.[33]

---

[30] *Ibid.,* I, 16–17, 20. At I, 166 Ishmael is again compared to "a well-fed and fattened ox," and is said to be a member of "a race who lived chiefly for the indulgence of the natural wants. . . ."

[31] *Ibid.,* I, 78.   [32] *Ibid.,* II, 237–248.   [33] *Ibid.,* I, 222.

Cooper's perception of values in Ishmael Bush's character that sprang from the conditions of life in a primitively agricultural West, yet could not be accounted for by reference to the ideas of civilization and refinement, pointed the way toward a more adequate literary treatment of the agricultural frontier. But the idea of civilization was so deeply rooted in American thought that it could not be cast aside overnight. Writers who sought to deal with the agricultural West therefore continued for decades to waver between a direct response to their materials and the attitude of reserve or disapproval of Western coarseness dictated by the prevalent social theory. Cooper himself found the problem persistently challenging, although he did not advance very far toward solving it. In *Home as Found*, published in 1838, he returned to the Cooperstown whose early history he had chronicled in *The Pioneers* fifteen years before. He did not try again to draw a Western character on the scale of Ishmael Bush, but he did undertake an elaborate theoretical analysis of what happens in the wake of agricultural settlement in the wilderness.

The goal toward which all such communities evolve is in his opinion clear enough: it is the establishment of a secure class of gentry whose ownership of land confers on them the wealth and the leisure that are indispensable to the flowering of the higher graces of human nature. This social ideal obviously depends upon what Cooper calls a "division into castes," and can not be realized under the conditions of rough equality that prevail in the earliest stages of settlement. It is true that he has a rather unexpected Arcadian dream of the adventurous first years, when for a time "life has much of the reckless gaiety, careless association, and buoyant merriment of childhood." But this is a transient phase. Only when gradations of social station, based on differences in inherited wealth, have become clearly marked, does the society reach its final and ordered stability.[34]

Cooper, a consistent and explicit conservative in social theory despite his carefully limited endorsement of political democracy, was quite willing to acknowledge that refinement and gentility were conceivable only in members of an upper class with enough wealth to guarantee its leisure, and a sufficiently secure social status to give it poise and assurance. The form of the sentimental novel suggested exactly these assumptions. But other novelists who tried to deal with the agricultural West felt themselves under some compulsion to extend the application of the sounding platitudes of democracy and equality from politics to social and economic life. They therefore faced a continual struggle to reconcile their almost instinctive regard for refinement with their democratic theories and their desire to find some values in the unrefined West.

The conflict would not be resolved so long as they clung to the theory

---

[34] *Home as Found*, 2 vols. (Philadelphia, 1838), I, 180–183.

of civilization with its fixed series of social stages. For the West could have only one place in such a scheme: it was primitive and therefore unrefined. This was indeed its defining characteristic. In proportion as the West lost its primitive character it became indistinguishable from the East and there was no basis for a characteristic Western literature. Writers who were attracted by Western materials had an obscure awareness that the unprecedented adventure of agricultural settlement in the Mississippi Valley was somehow worthy of imaginative interpretation. The theory of progress and civilization, on the other hand, could take no account of novelty except as an increase of enlightenment in the most advanced societies. Abstract and rationalistic as it was, it implied that only the most advanced stage of social development produced characters worthy of admiration. The theory offered little ground for finding a value in America as contrasted with Europe, or in the American West as contrasted with the American East. From Cooper's day to that of Hamlin Garland, writers about the West had to struggle against the notion that their characters had no claim upon the attention of sophisticated readers, except through their alarming or at best their picturesque lack of refinement.

II. FROM CAROLINE KIRKLAND TO HAMLIN GARLAND

Literary historians have long been accustomed to find Joseph Kirkland and Hamlin Garland important because they contributed "the bitterness of the frontier" to the development of realism in fiction.[35] It is more relevant here to ask a different question about these men. What were their origins? From what literary background did they proceed? Since there are no absolute beginnings or endings in the history of literature, Kirkland and Garland can be considered the culmination of one development just as profitably as they can be considered the pioneers of another. To see in them nothing except a prophetic mood of disillusionment is to oversimplify a rich and suggestive chapter in the history of American thought. Whatever their shortcomings as artists, they signalize a slow but far-reaching change in literary attitudes toward the Western farmer. In the early nineteenth century, as we have seen, the farmer could be depicted in fiction only as a member of a low social class. By 1890 he could be presented as a human being, unfortunate perhaps, but possessed of dignity even in his tribulations. The purpose of the present chapter is to trace this process through the work of representative writers who dealt with the agricultural West during the half century between the last of the Leatherstocking novels and *Main Travelled Roads*.[36]

---

[35] Vernon L. Parrington, *The Beginnings of Critical Realism in America (Main Currents in American Thought*, Volume, III, 1930), reprint ed. (New York, n. d.), p. 288.

[36] Ludwig Lewisohn's comment greatly overstates the case, but suggests the importance of this development for American literature: "It took genuine courage, genuine inde-

The earliest of these was Mrs. Caroline M. Kirkland. A native of New York, she spent five years in southern Michigan during the late 1830's and early 1840's while her husband took a fling at land speculation and town building. On the basis of this exposure to the West Mrs. Kirkland wrote three books: *A New Home—Who'll Follow?* (1839), *Forest Life* (1842), and *Western Clearings* (1845), besides minor sketches and stories dealing with the same materials. Her books were widely read, and deserved to be, for they have the merits of clear observation and lively reporting. They are also a valuable repository of upper-class Eastern attitudes toward the raw West.

As a grand-daughter of Samuel Stansbury, the Loyalist poet of the Revolutionary period, Mrs. Kirkland had an assured social standing that made it impossible for her to identify herself with the free-and-easy outlook and customs of the Michigan frontier.[37] Instead, she conceived of herself as a traveler who happened to have made an unusually long sojourn in the wilderness "beyond the confines of civilization." [38] Her first book is cast in the form of letters to cultivated friends back home. She realizes these sophisticated readers will hardly be able to believe that Western backwoodsmen "are partakers with themselves of a common nature." [39] The Western indifference to class lines arouses in her by turns a lively amusement and something not far from indignation. She is greatly annoyed with people who pretend to believe in the principle of social equality. To carry out such doctrines in practice would, she assures us, "imply nothing short of a lingering mental martyrdom to the cultivated and the refined." [40]

Yet she responds almost in spite of herself to the generosity and kindness of the pioneer farmers. She says she always returns from her little excursions about the countryside with an increased liking for the people.

> There is after all [she explains] so much kindness, simplicity and trust-fulness—one catches so many glimpses of the lovelier aspect of our common nature—that much that is uncouth is forgotten, and much that is offensive is pardoned. One sees the rougher sort of people in their best light, and learns to own the "tie of brotherhood." [41]

To her second volume of sketches she prefixed six Spenserian stanzas in praise of Sympathy, "Nature's blest decree," which she had learned from

---

pendence of mind to give literary treatment to the rude peasantry that peopled the Mississippi Valley. And it is from the treatment of this peasantry that our modern literature takes its rise. . . . The germs of our period of national expression are to be found in those few writers like Edward Eggleston and E. W. Howe who, whether consenting to it or resisting it, made the collective life of the American people the substance of serious literature" (*The Story of American Literature*, New York, 1932, p. 276).

[37] The fullest account of Mrs. Kirkland's life and work is Langley Carleton Keyes, "Caroline M. Kirkland. A Pioneer in American Realism," Unpublished Doctor's Dissertation, Harvard University, 1935. The social position of the Stansburys is discussed on p. 96.

[38] *A New Home—Who'll Follow? or Glimpses of Western Life*, by Mrs. Mary Clavers (pseud.) (first published 1839; 4th ed., New York, 1850), p. 3.

[39] *Ibid.*, pp. 7, 8.   [40] *Forest Life*, 2 vols. (New York, 1842), I, 122.   [41] *Ibid.*, I, 209.

the Wizard of the North. The master had taught her that the backwoods-man was human after all:

> The power that stirred the universal heart
>   Dwells in the forest, in the common air—
> In cottage lone, as in th' o'er burdened mart—
> For Nature's painter learned from Nature all his art.[42]

If the reader will compare this sentimental theory of the nobility of humble Western farmers—reminiscent of Timothy Flint's preface to *George Mason*—with the kittenish remark which opens Mrs. Kirkland's first volume ("I intend to be 'decidedly low' ")[43] he will recognize how instructive a confusion of attitudes her writing exhibits.

The contradictions between her high-flown theory and her instinctive revulsion from the crudities of backwoods Michigan are reflected in her vain struggle to find a satisfactory literary form. The structure of her books is extremely simple. She writes as if she were keeping a travel diary in which, as a cultivated outsider, she makes notes concerning the natives of a strange land. The form is that which comes naturally to the first ex-plorers of a new area. Hundreds of such narratives had been written about the West by travelers with no literary pretensions. But Mrs. Kirkland uses the strategy of writing in the first person to keep her sensibility constantly before the reader and to emphasize her detachment from her surroundings. She takes it for granted that her readers share with her a higher social status than that of the natives and underlines the assumption by plentiful literary allusions and quotations, plus a sprinkling of French and Italian phrases that authenticate her implied claim to rank as a bluestocking cast among unlettered country folk.

But she can not be permanently content with so simple a literary form and tries valiantly to devise something more complicated. In her three volumes are interpolated perhaps a dozen pieces of fiction that she tries to endow with a plot. The experiments range from the brief autobiography put into the mouth of the admirable Mrs. Danforth in *A New Home*[44] to the more ambitious efforts which Mrs. Kirkland was encouraged to make by the success of her first book. *Forest Life* contains, for example, the tale of how the worthy young backwoodsman Seymour won the hand of Caroline Hay, daughter of the greatest landowner in the country,[45] and an account of an English couple named Sibthorpe which ends up in the epistolary mode of the previous century.[46] Several of the sketches in *Western Clearings* threaten to become plotted narratives, such as the story of the shiftless Silas Ashburn who is still not base enough to resort to illegal violence against a man he considers an enemy,[47] or "Ambuscades," which relates how the

---

[42] *Ibid.*, I, 7.   [43] *A New Home*, p. 9.   [44] *Ibid.*, pp. 29–31.
[45] *Forest Life*, I, 237–250, II, [3]–45.   [46] *Ibid.*, II, 46–146.
[47] *Western Clearings* (New York, 1845), pp. 66–86.

enthusiastic huntsman Tom Oliver forgot to hunt and became a hard-working farmer through love of Emma Levering.[48]

Despite the variety of these experiments in fiction, it cannot be said that Mrs. Kirkland succeeded in finding an adequate form for her Western materials. She could not discover any dependable plot structure except a love story, and her lovers develop toward the stereotypes of the sentimental tradition. In proportion as they are worked into a plot they lose any Western characteristics they may have had at the outset. There is no progress toward overcoming the lack of coherence between materials and form that constituted her literary problem. She demonstrated that the agricultural West offered interesting and even challenging themes for fiction but she could not find a satisfactory method for dealing with them.

During the next two decades the obvious strategy of writing a conventional love story against a Western background was adopted by a number of women novelists, including Mrs. Metta V. Victor, her sister Mrs. Frances Fuller Barritt, and Mrs. Caroline A. Soule, who has been mentioned before. Mrs. Victor's *Alice Wilde, the Raftsman's Daughter. A Forest Romance,* issued in 1860 as Number 4 of Beadle's Dime Novels, conducts the elegant and cultivated Philip More of New York to a remote region of the West. Although the sophisticated Virginia, likewise of New York, cannot understand why he wishes to throw himself away upon "a rude and uncultivated community," [49] Philip falls in love with Alice, daughter of the raftsman David Wilde. The father speaks a strong dialect but the daughter's speech is correct; her rusticity is indicated mainly by the fact that she dresses in the style of twenty years before.[50] After the hero has declared his love, Alice is sent to a seminary at Centre City for a little polishing. Mrs. Victor's conception of the problem she is dealing with is indicated in Alice's exclamation to her fiancé: ". . . you had pride, prejudice, rank, fashion, every thing to struggle against in choosing me." [51] That the triumph of love over these obstacles was widely approved is indicated by the enormous sale of the novel—250,000 copies in the United States, besides an immense run in England.[52]

In *The Backwoods Bride. A Romance of Squatter Life*[53] Mrs. Victor seized upon a conflict growing more directly out of agricultural settlement on the frontier. The elegant and cultivated Harry Gardiner has bought a large tract of government land in Michigan in the 1840's. When he comes out to take possession he finds that numerous squatters have settled on it, including Enos Carter, father of the beautiful seventeen-year-old Susan.[54] Although Mr. Gardiner has bought the land as a speculation, his noble nature leads him to offer to sell to the squatters at the price he gave for

---

[48] *Ibid.,* pp. 118–143.   [49] *Alice Wilde,* p. 72.   [50] *Ibid.,* p. 20.   [51] *Ibid.,* pp. 77, 81.
[52] Advertisement on p. [30] of Edward S. Ellis, *The Frontier Angel,* New and Old Friends, No. 7 (New York, 1873).
[53] Beadle's Dime Novels, No. 10 (1860).   [54] *Ibid.,* pp. [9], 11, 14.

it. But the squatters, perhaps under the influence of George Henry Evans, are convinced that "in the new country men are entitled to all they could cultivate. . . ." [55] Enos Carter states their position eloquently:

> God made this earth to be free to all; and whoever takes wild land, and clears it, and cultivates it, makes it his own—he's a right to it. What right have these men that never did a day's work in their lives, coming along and takin' the bread out of our mouths? [56]

Mrs. Victor allows this very real conflict to develop to the point where a mob, including Enos, tries to break into Gardiner's hotel room to lynch him, whereupon the young hero kills one of the mob with a pistol.[57] But the author is not willing to follow through the issue she has stated, and takes refuge in a reconciliation which leaves Gardiner the squatters' candidate for Congress.[58] He can marry Susan without too great violation of the proprieties because her father was once better off and she retains some gentility from her childhood in rural New York.

Mrs. Victor returns to the problem of the social status of Western farmers in *Uncle Ezekiel and his Exploits on Two Continents,* but this time the roles of hero and heroine are reversed. Edith Lancaster, daughter of an upper-class Englishman, is brought through great exertions of the author to an Illinois prairie. Amos Potter, son of a squatter, does not have his father's backwoods dialect but is still too humble in status to satisfy Edith's father, who takes her to his London mansion.[59] There she pines for her Western lover until the eccentric Uncle Ezekiel, a character in the humorous Down East tradition, manages to reunite the young people and reconcile the father to the match.[60]

Mrs. Barritt, in her *East and West; or, The Beauty of Willard's Mill,* simplifies the problem at the expense of probability by creating an Iowa heroine of impeccable gentility. Although Minnie Willard, the miller's daughter, is unsophisticated in comparison with the urbane Constance, her highbred visiting cousin from New York, the country girl has the elegant accomplishments of writing verses and sketching in charcoal.[61] Fletcher Harris, an artist sent on tour by an Eastern magazine, falls in love with Minnie and draws a picture entitled "The Fawn of the Prairie" that celebrates a lyric moment described in one of Minnie's poems.[62] Yet before this marriage can take place Minnie must be sent to New York to become cultivated by looking at pictures and hearing music.[63] The heroine of Mrs. Barritt's *The Land Claim. A Tale of the Upper Missouri* is established as genteel by being made the daughter of an Englishwoman of noble

---

[55] *Ibid.,* p. 17. [56] *Ibid.,* p. 19. [57] *Ibid.,* p. 23. [58] *Ibid.,* p. 98.
[59] Beadle's Dime Novels, No. 16 (1861), p. 103. [60] *Ibid.,* pp. 103, 119–120.
[61] Beadle's Dime Novels, No. 35 (1862), pp. 9, 41. [62] *Ibid.,* pp. 58–59.
[63] *Ibid.,* pp. 84–85.

family who eloped with the gardener and came to America; in the end the heroine is restored to her grandfather, Sir Deming.[64] It will be recalled that Margaret Belden, heroine of Mrs. Soule's *Little Alice,* could be presented as refined despite her backwoods setting because she had been reared in an affluent New England home.

Each of these authors cleaves to the theory of social stages which places the West below the East in a sequence to which both belong. The West has no meaning in itself because the only value recognized by the theory of civilization is the refinement which is believed to increase steadily as one moves from primitive simplicity and coarseness toward the complexity and polish of urban life. The values that are occasionally found in the West are anomalous instances of conformity to a standard that is actually foreign to the region. This principle is exemplified in the Western heroines, who seem to be worthy of admiration only in proportion as they have escaped from the crudity and vulgarity of their surroundings, either by virtue of birth elsewhere, or through the possession of an implausible innate refinement. The occasional half-hearted tendency to contrast Western freshness with Eastern oversophistication will be recognized as a remnant of the dying theory of cultural primitivism. It is quite inconsistent with the cult of refinement that furnished the intellectual framework for sentimental fiction.

The first step toward solving the literary problem of the agricultural West was to find some means of escape from the assumption that the East was the standard of value and that Westerners were of inferior social status. If novelists were to deal with the West on its own terms, they would have to adopt some criterion besides that of refinement and would have to rid themselves of their unconscious devotion to class distinctions. In practice this meant getting rid of the theory of social stages.

The stories and sketches of Alice Cary of Ohio, published during the 1850's, are the earliest body of writing in which the relation of the West to the East has ceased to be the major problem. It is significant that Miss Cary was the first native of the Ohio Valley who attempted to interpret the region in fiction. With all its shortcomings, her work supports Edward Eggleston's statement that she was the founder of the tradition of honest interpretation of the West.[65] Transmitted through Eggleston to Hamlin Garland, her repudiation of the conventional way of looking at sectional relationships was destined to have important literary consequences. Her indifference toward the East appears to have sharpened her eye for detail and to have helped her achieve moments of direct reporting that still seem sharp and fresh. But her writing suffers from defects that fully account for the neglect into which it has fallen. She is seldom free of conventional

---

[64] Beadle's Dime Novels, No. 39 (1862) , pp. 9, 95.
[65] *The Hoosier School-Master. A Novel* (New York, 1871), p. [5].

sentiment and often verges toward a familiar kind of religiosity. The schoolmaster in the sketch "Two Visits," [66] whose hands evince his gentle origin if indeed his glossy black curls, pale complexion, great melancholy eyes, and fondness for Coleridge were not more than sufficient indications, is pure claptrap. Like Emmeline Grangerford in *Huckleberry Finn,* he shows his gentility by sketching; and like her, he prefers funerary subjects. His masterpiece is a drawing of the grave of his first love, with himself kneeling by it.[67]

Furthermore, Miss Cary's literary method impedes the full development of her characters. She takes over Mrs. Kirkland's habit of writing in the first person and is seldom able to get herself out of the picture. She cannot refrain from occasional reminders that she too is a lady who knows her Spenser and Milton, and is qualified to make judgments concerning refinement or the lack of it in people and houses. In abandoning the intellectual framework offered by the theory of social stages, she was not able to construct any coherent theory to take its place. She asserts that "the independent yeoman, with his simple rusticity and healthful habits, is the happiest man in the world," but this judgment is supported by the condescending line from Gray which she quotes immediately afterward: "When ignorance is bliss, 'tis folly to be wise." [68] She believes that her Western farm and village characters are the "humbler classes" and that she is writing the simple annals of the poor, in contrast with other lady authors who "have apparently been familiar only with wealth and splendor, and such joys or sorrows as come gracefully to mingle with the refinements of luxury and art . . ."

> In our country [she continues], though all men are not "created equal," such is the influence of the sentiment of liberty and political equality, that
>
> > All thoughts, all passions, all delights,
> > Whatever stirs this mortal frame,
>
> may with as much probability be supposed to affect conduct and expectation in the log cabin as in the marble mansion; and to illustrate this truth, to dispel that erroneous belief of the necessary baseness of the "common people" which the great masters in literature have in all ages labored to create, is a purpose and an object in our nationality to which the finest and highest genius may wisely be devoted; but which may be effected in a degree by writings as unpretending as these reminiscences of what occurred in and about the little village where I from childhood watched the pulsations of the surrounding hearts.[69]

---

[66] *Clovernook or Recollections of Our Neighborhood in the West. Second Series* (first published 1853; New York, 1884), pp. 109–145.

[67] *Ibid.,* p. 143.   [68] *Ibid.,* p. 25.

[69] *Ibid.,* pp. 363–364. The Preface to the First Series of Clovernook sketches (New York, 1851, reprint, 1852), pp. v–vi, makes the same point about the failure of city dwellers to

This is perhaps a little more explicit than Flint's and Mrs. Kirkland's statements of similar ideas, and Miss Cary came nearer than they did to realizing her program in fiction. But her sketches are still not consistently organized about her thesis. They reveal an interesting but in the end annoying instability of attitude in the author.

The sketch which contains the touching portrait of the schoolmaster, for example, begins as a contrast between the overaustere household of the prosperous Knights and the charming household of the poorer Lytles. But before she is done, Miss Cary manages to insert the death and funeral of little Henry Hathaway, the courtship and marriage of Hetty Knight, and the death of Kitty Lytle, presumably from heartbreak. The author is not sure where her interest lies or what she is trying to do. To mention only one other example, the sketch "Charlotte Ryan" deals with the daughter of the "last" family in the neighborhood who, brought up in poverty, goes for a visit with relatives near Cincinnati, encounters true elegance for the first time, suffers for her rusticity in the presence of the splendid Mr. Sully Dinsmore, is taken to some vague but glittering greater city by other friends, becomes herself the cynosure of all eyes at the ball, and snubs Mr. Dinsmore in return for his cruelty to her back in Ohio. But Charlotte is no happier in her silks than she had been in her homespun.[70]

Miss Cary's most ambitious effort to deal with the countryside about Cincinnati in fiction is *Married, Not Mated,* published in 1856. This confused work seems to have grown out of an autobiographical reminiscence; one of the young ladies introduced in Part II carries the remainder of the narrative in the first person. The nearest approach to a thread of plot is the story of how the headstrong Annette Furniss of Cincinnati determines to escape from domestic monotony by marrying Henry Graham, a young farmer who supplies the family with butter. Annette is a selfish creature and is really in love with Henry's unpleasant brother Stafford. The marriage therefore fails and Henry dies. By calling her hero a farmer Miss Cary seems to promise a study of rural Western character. There is a faint suggestion that Henry Graham's language and dress need to be refined by the power of love, but he is never made to speak dialect and his character is so profoundly genteel that one cannot take him seriously as a Westerner. He reads poetry, for example, in a secluded grove, and leaves a strip of willows standing along a brook because they improve the landscape. The actual work of the farm is carried on offstage by hired hands. The only labor Henry performs is the sentimental task of tending the grave of Annette's sister Nellie.[71]

---

sympathize with poor and humble farm people. Although Miss Cary does not consider all Westerners socially inferior (Cincinnati, for example, has an upper class), she is vividly conscious of class differences between urban and rural populations.

[70] *Clovernook* (Second Series), pp. 245–280.

[71] *Married, Not Mated; or, How They Lived at Woodside and Throckmorton Hall* (New York, 1856), pp. 67, 97, 266, 270.

The latter half of the novel wanders off into a tedious character sketch of the pompous Mr. Peter Throckmorton and a desperately comic study of the cures undertaken in his behalf by a series of amateur and professional physicians. And there are other grotesque things in the book. It is nevertheless oddly interesting, in part because Miss Cary stumbles almost accidentally into a remarkable technical experiment by telling the story of Henry and Annette from several points of view, in part because she manages to render directly observed depths of squalor and neurosis, but most of all because of the character of Raphe Muggins. Raphe appears first as an adolescent backwoods waif serving the Graham household as maid of all work; later she is married and rearing a vigorous family. She and her husband are of the folk and there is no doubt in the author's mind that they belong to a social class distinct from that of the Grahams. Yet Raphe is made much more real than any other character in the story. Miss Cary not only reproduces her robust speech at length, but admires her shrewd and healthy insight into the tortured lives of the Grahams, and uses Raphe's successful marriage as a foil for the introspective complications of the principal characters. The author's unpatronizing affection for this very ungenteel Western woman all but breaks down the literary convention that consigns the character to an inferior status.[72]

Despite Miss Cary's occasional triumphs, Edward Eggleston's work marks a distinct advance toward the discovery of literary values in the agricultural West. It is true that he was no more able than Miss Cary to get beyond the accepted dogma that a novel is a love story; all his heroes and heroines exhibit a stereotyped variety of sentimental virtue. It is also true that his novels contain traces of the old *a priori* doctrine of Western inferiority. One of the principal themes of *The Hoosier School-Master,* for example, is the desire of Bud Means to "git out of this low-lived Flat Crick way of livin'" by putting in "his best licks for Jesus Christ." [73] Eggleston remarks with approval that Patty Lumsden, heroine of *The Circuit-Rider,* was saved by her pride "from possible assimilation with the vulgarity about her." [74] The character Nancy Kirtley in *Roxy,* studied in considerable detail, is intended as a representation of "that curious poor-whitey race which is called 'tarheel' in the northern Carolina, 'sand-hiller' in the southern, 'corn-cracker' in Kentucky, 'yahoo' in Mississippi and in California 'pike.'" These backwoodsmen, like most of the Means family in *The Hoosier School-Master,* resemble Ishmael Bush in *The Prairie.* They are coarse, illiterate, lawless—in a word, "half-barbarous." Eggleston, like Cooper, is interested in the type, and his conclusions deserve quotation:

---

[72] Miss Cary's other fictional efforts (*Hager. A Story of To-Day,* [New York, 1852; "second edition," 1852]; *The Bishop's Son. A Novel* [New York, 1867]) show no change in the rather confused pattern of her attitudes toward Western farmers.

[73] *Hoosier School-Master,* pp. 122, 125.

[74] *The Circuit Rider: A Tale of the Heroic Age* (New York, 1874), p. [173].

They never continue in one stay, but are the half gypsies of America, seeking by shiftless removals from one region to another to better their wretched fortunes, or, more likely to gratify a restless love of change and adventure. They are the Hoosiers of the dark regions of Indiana and the Egyptians of southern Illinois. Always in a half-barbarous state, it is among them that lynchings most prevail. Their love of excitement drives them into a daring life and often into crime. From them came the Kentucky frontiersmen, the Texan rangers, the Murrell highway-men, the Arkansas regulators and anti-regulators, the ancient keel-boatmen, the more modern flat-boatmen and raftsmen and roustabouts, and this race furnishes, perhaps, more than its share of the "road agents" that infest the territories. Brave men and generous men are often found among them; but they are never able to rise above Daniel Boones and Simon Kentons.[75]

After Mark Bonamy has been led into sin by Nancy, he has a momentary impulse to give up all his past life and go with her to Texas, where he may live out his degradation with no reproach from any moral censor. Among the fugitive criminals and bankrupts there he may hope to become a leader and thus make some sort of a life for himself.

This Nance was a lawless creature—a splendid savage, full of ferocity. Something of the sentiment of Tennyson's "Locksley Hall" was in him. He would commit moral suicide instead of physical,—release the ani-mal part of his nature from allegiance to what was better; and, since he had failed in civilized life, he might try his desperate luck as a savage. It was easier to sink the present Bonamy in the wild elements of the South-western frontier, than to blow out his brains or drown himself.[76]

Evidently, Eggleston is willing to go as far as any New England clergy-man in painting the lawless savagery of the remote frontier. And though he considers Indiana more civilized than Texas, vestiges of a dark earlier barbarism linger even there. After all, Nancy belongs to Indiana as much as Mark does. In the West of his fiction Eggleston finds petty political cor-ruption, dishonest manipulation of the preëmption law, and a sordid devo-tion to profit at any cost.[77] He notes that the greatest wealth of postfrontier communities has come not from hard work but from land speculation.[78] Whiskey Jim, the sympathetic Minnesota stage driver in *The Mystery of Metropolisville*, remarks that the West isn't the country of ideas, but of corner lots. "I tell you," he exclaims, "here it's nothin' but per-cent." [79]

It is rather odd that, holding such conventional views of Western de-pravity and "materialism," Eggleston should nevertheless have been so

---

[75] *Roxy* (New York, 1878), p. 183.   [76] *Ibid.*, p. 343.
[77] *Hoosier School-Master*, p. 163; *The Mystery of Metropolisville* (New York, 1873), p. 93.
[78] *Hoosier School-Master*, p. 29.   [79] *Mystery of Metropolisville*, p. 21.

thoroughly convinced that the region deserved literary treatment. In the preface to *The Hoosier School-Master* he remarks:

> It used to be a matter of no little jealousy with us, I remember, that the manners, customs, thoughts, and feelings of New England country people filled so large a place in books, while our life, not less interesting, not less romantic, and certainly not less filled with humorous and grotesque material, had no place in literature. It was as though we were shut out of good society. And, with the single exception of Alice Cary, perhaps, our Western writers did not dare speak of the West otherwise than as the unreal world to which Cooper's lively imagination had given birth.[80]

But this does not take us very far, and it is certainly not an adequate analysis of Eggleston's attitude toward his Hoosiers. A year later he prefaced *The End of the World* with a quotation from Principal John C. Shairp's lecture on Wordsworth that relates how the poet found "pith of sense and solidity of judgment," as well as the essential feelings and passions of mankind, in greater simplicity and strength among humble country folk.[81] But this too fails to get at Eggleston's own attitude. For one thing, Wordsworth's theory would imply that the Kirtleys (and with them, Western poor whites as a class), as primitive children of nature, are even more admirable than the Mark Bonamys and the Ralph Hartsooks who have acquired a certain degree of literacy and cultivation. Eggleston's acceptance of the theory of progressive refinement through successively higher social stages prevented him from accepting the implications of Wordsworth's attitude. The conception of nature as a source of spiritual value could have little meaning for him. If his intense although undogmatic piety had allowed him to entertain the idea, he would still have found it in conflict with the deterministic notions he had taken over from Taine and Darwin.[82]

Since Eggleston's statement of his intentions is so meager we must make our own inferences from his work. It has been often remarked that before he began *The Hoosier School-Master* he had written a brief notice of a translation of Taine's *Philosophy of Art in the Netherlands* for *The Independent*.[83] The debt cannot have been great, but there are a few indications in the novels that Taine had given him at least an inkling of a pure pictorial feeling for common and familiar scenes, without overtones of

---

[80] *Hoosier School-Master*, p. [5].

[81] *The End of the World. A Love Story* (New York, 1872), p. 8.

[82] Eggleston remarks of Nancy Kirtley that she had only "something which a sanguine evolutionist might hope would develop into a conscience, by some chance, in many generations" (*Roxy*, p. [346]). His interest in and eventual acceptance of Darwin's position is discussed by his biographer William P. Randel (*Edward Eggleston, Author of The Hoosier School-Master* [New York, 1946], pp. 11, 218). In *The Faith Doctor* Eggleston referred to Darwin as "the intellect that has dominated our age" (Randel, *Eggleston*, p. 196). He publicly accepted Darwin in 1887 (*ibid.*, p. 218).

[83] Randel, *Eggleston*, p. 123.

moral or social evaluation. Chapter VI of *Roxy* is entitled "A Genre Piece." It relates how the young minister Whittaker spent an evening with Roxy and her father the shoemaker, and began to fall in love with her. Eggleston apparently wishes to call attention to the visual image of these figures grouped in a kitchen. A clearer example of the novelist's exploitation of pure visual interest is a passage in *The Circuit Rider* which describes Patty Lumsden spinning. Our sculptors, Eggleston remarks, ought to realize that in "mythology and heroics" Americans can never be anything but copyists. If they would turn to our own primitive life they would find admirable subjects like the girl spinning—an activity that reveals as no other can the grace of the female figure. Eggleston adds that the kitchen of the Lumsden home would make a genre subject good enough for the old Dutch masters.[84]

It is refreshing to find even so slight a hint that crude Western materials could be viewed disinterestedly, without the apparatus of theory that had so often beclouded the vision of observers like Mrs. Kirkland. But so long as the achievement was limited to the plane of visual perception, it could not have very far-reaching consequences for literary attitude and method. The borrowing of effects from painting had long been an established convention in writing about the West. Many authors, for example, had invoked the paintings of wild Salvator Rosa to convey their response to Western landscapes felt to be picturesque and sublime.[85] Merely to turn from Salvator to Dutch masters of "realism" was not a startling advance in literary practice. What was requisite was an extension of the technique of disinterested observation to the sphere of ethics, to the psychological interior of the characters as contrasted with their outer appearance or the houses they lived in.[86]

Taine did not help Eggleston very far along this road. The novelist's religiosity and recurrent retreats into sentimentalism lend a strongly archaic air to his work. Yet he did make a beginning. The aspect of his fiction that proved most valuable to the writers who came after him and is most interesting nowadays is his sincere feeling for the "folk"—for the characteristic traits of human beings in a specific geographical and social setting. This is the germ at once of what has been called his "realism" and of the interest in social history that eventually led him to abandon fiction altogether.

The notion that the lore and the mores of the backwoodsman might be

---

[84] *The Circuit Rider*, pp. 55–56.

[85] Some instances: George W. Kendall, *Narrative of the Texan Santa Fe Expedition*, 2 vols. (New York, 1844), I, 216–217; Francis Parkman, *The California and Oregon Trail: Being Sketches of Prairie and Rocky Mountain Life* (New York, 1849), p. 187; Thomas B. Thorpe, *Spirit of the Times*, X, [361] (1840).

[86] If the term "realism" has any use in the vocabulary of literary criticism—and until a Professor Lovejoy discriminates the half-dozen or more current senses of the word it will probably continue to confuse more things than it clarifies—it might well be made to designate precisely these aspects of Dutch pictorial method transferred to the sphere of psychological analysis.

interesting without reference to his function as a standard-bearer of progress and civilization, or his alarming and exciting barbarism, or his embodiment of a natural goodness, was quite late in appearing. Although travelers had reported a few snatches of the songs of French Canadian *voyageurs* and an occasional tall tale from the Far West, especially from the 1830's onward, apparently the first indications of an interest in the folklore of the agricultural West are contained in Alice Cary's work. Since her attitude toward these materials is at once complicated and highly suggestive for the future, it deserves more than a passing glance.

In describing her visit to the household of the grim Mrs. Knight, Miss Cary tells how Sally and Jane Ann, left alone for a few moments with their guest, entertain her by reciting riddles: "Four stiff-standers, four down-hangers, two crook-abouts, two look-abouts, and a whisk-about"; "Through a riddle and through a reel, Through an ancient spinning wheel . . ."; "Long legs, short thighs, Little head, and no eyes"; and "Round as an apple, deep as a cup, And all the king's oxen can't draw it up." They have begun a counting-out rime ("Oneary, oreary, kittery Kay . . .") when their mother comes in and angrily sends them away as if they had been misbehaving. The problem here is of course to define Miss Cary's own attitude toward the charming bits of folklore she has recorded. "Mrs. Knight," she remarks, "had been mortified when she found her daughters indulging in the jargon I have reported, and so imprisoned them, as I have described; but if she had accustomed herself to spend some portion of the day devoted to scolding the children, in their cultivation, few punishments of any kind would have been required. If they had known anything sensible, they would probably not have been repeating the nonsense which seemed to please them so." Miss Cary offered to bring over "some prettily illustrated stories . . . which might please her little girls. . . ." [87]

The riddles and counting-out rime are, then, jargon and nonsense, which should be replaced in the children's minds by systematic cultivation through proper children's books—perhaps the Peter Parley series. Yet Miss Cary is interested enough in the rimes to set them down, as apparently no one before her had done. Furthermore, she considers it deplorable that Mrs. Knight refuses to allow her older girls to attend play-parties where the games depend on folk songs:

> Many a time [she writes] had the young women gone to bed with aching hearts to hear in dreams the music of—
>
> > We are marching forward to Quebec
> > And the drums are loudly beating,
> > America has gained the day
> > And the British are retreating.

---

[87] *Clovernook* (Second Series), pp. 116–117, 121–122.

The wars are o'er and we'll turn back
And never more be parted;
So open the ring and choose another in
That you think will prove true-hearted.[88]

Despite her lapse into a conventionally obtuse attitude concerning the children's rimes, Miss Cary was at least vaguely aware that the nonliterary culture of the Western folk embodied some value.[89]

Eggleston likewise describes a game involving choice of a true-love to the accompaniment of chanted verses ("Oats, peas, beans, and barley grow . . .") of which he reports three stanzas.[90] He perceives that this material raises a literary issue of some consequence, although he does not succeed very well in stating the case for the use of it. People who enjoy society novels, he declares, will consider "these boisterous, unrefined sports" a far from promising beginning for a story. Readers find it easy to imagine heroism, generosity, and courage in people who dance on velvet carpets, but difficult to ascribe similar merits to crude backwoodsmen. This hardly seems a satisfactory statement of the issue. What he is feeling for is a value in the mores of the folk comparable to the pictorial values he could perceive in his backwoods interiors. But he argues instead somewhat irrelevantly that people crude enough to play rowdy kissing games may nevertheless be quite heroic: "the great heroes, the world's demigods, grew in just such rough social states as that of Ohio in the early part of this century." And this leads to a little homily for the benefit of sophisticated readers:

> There is nothing more important for an over-refined generation than to understand that it has not a monopoly of the great qualities of humanity, and that it must not only tolerate rude folk, but sometimes admire in them traits that have grown scarce as refinement has increased. So that I may not shrink from telling that one kissing-play took the place of another until the excitement and merriment reached a pitch which would be thought not consonant with propriety by the society that loves round-dances with *roués*, and "the German" untranslated—though, for that matter, there are people old-fashioned enough to think that refined deviltry is not much better than rude freedom, after all.[91]

---

[88] *Ibid.*, pp. 119–120.

[89] In "Mrs. Wetherbe's Quilting Party" the play-party is a functional part of the plot. The "plays" include the nonmusical "Hunting the Key" as well as "rude rhymes, sung as accompaniments to the playing." Three specimens of the rimes are quoted: "O Sister Phoebe," "Uncle Johnny's sick a-bed," and a four-line stanza announcing, "My love and I will go, / And my love and I will go, / And we'll settle on the banks / Of the pleasant O-h-*i*-ó" (*ibid.*, pp. 50–51).

[90] *The Circuit Rider*, p. 22.

[91] *Ibid.*, p. 21. Volney, among others, had long before compared American Indians to "the nation so much extolled of ancient Greece and Italy"—intending of course to belittle the Greeks and Romans (*A View of the Soil and Climate of the United States of America*, [1803], trans. Charles Brockden Brown [Philadelphia, 1804], p. 410). The theory

While it is far from clear that the same New Yorkers enjoyed reading German with Margaret Fuller and dancing round-dances, the mere fact that Eggleston can conceive of overrefinement liberates him partially from the inadequate literary theories of the 1870's. At least he has realized that folk rimes and games are more than jargon and nonsense, since they represent a tradition "that has existed in England from immemorial time."[92] If the culture of the folk attested a continuity of social evolution reaching far back into the past, it acquired a new dignity. It had a historical dimension that could never be accounted for by the abstract and schematic and even antihistorical theory of uniform progress through fixed social stages. This way of looking at illiteracy and barbarism offered a valid means of escape from the theory of civilization and refinement, and suggested how Western farmers could be rescued from their degraded social status.

The gradual emergence of a new conception of the Western folk in Eggleston and his successors can be traced clearly in the changing attitudes toward language, which after all was the most intimate, the most flexible, the most characteristic and suggestive of all the aspects of folk culture. What were literary interpreters of the agricultural West to do with vernacular speech?

We are familiar with the role of dialect in the tradition of Cooper, and indeed in sentimental fiction generally, as a simple and unambiguous badge of status. No "straight" character could be allowed to speak dialect, and every character who used dialect was instantly recognizable as having a low social rank. In books of more or less direct reporting, like Mrs. Kirkland's, the upper-class observer regales his presumably upper-class readers by rendering the outlandish speech of the natives as a foil for his own elegant rhetoric. Similarly, the heroes and heroines of fiction who come into the West from outside are distinguished from the natives by their correct and elevated diction. If a Westerner is to be made into a hero, like Cooper's Ben Boden the bee hunter in *The Oak Openings,* the author must take pains to tidy up the character's speech. The first notable departure from this simple set of literary conventions is in the work of Miss Cary, where indifference to the contrast between East and West lessens her interest in speech as a badge of social and sectional status. Although she makes a few experiments in transcribing the Western vernacular, she is capable of reporting the speech of characters living in abject poverty, in a remote rural area, without self-conscious attention to dialect at all, using an easy, colloquial style for people of quite various classes.[93]

---

that the American West exhibited all the stages of social development lent itself easily to the discovery of a "heroic" age at some point in the Mississippi Valley.

[92] *The Circuit Rider,* p. 22.

[93] Mrs. Wetherbe, in "Mrs. Wetherbe's Quilting Party," whom Miss Cary admires, is given a marked dialect (*Clovernook,* Second Series, pp. 18–19, etc.), but the poverty-

But if it was a necessary first step to cease exploiting dialect as a badge of status, the achievement was merely negative. The effort to discover positive values in the culture of the folk would obviously suggest some affirmative use of the vernacular. The analogy of Dutch genre painting would imply a pure esthetic concern with dialect, a delight in the object for its own sake without insisting on its meaning as a badge of status or (what amounted to the same thing) as an index of refinement or the lack of it. There is evidence that the germ of Eggleston's first novel, *The Hoosier School-Master,* was precisely such an interest in the folk speech of southern Indiana. The novelist's biographer has found a list of "Hoosierisms" jotted down by Eggleston in February, 1863, eight years before the novel was published.[94] Eggleston was corresponding with James Russell Lowell about this list of dialect terms in January, 1870, and the Harvard professor's enthusiasm doubtless did much to convince him that his linguistic interest was reputable from a scholarly and literary standpoint.[95] Years later, in an issue of *The Critic* honoring Lowell's seventieth birthday, Eggleston wrote that Lowell had been his master more than anyone else. "His magnanimous appreciation of the first lines I ever printed on the subject of American dialect and his cordial encouragement and wise advice gave me heart to go on. . . ." [96] The indebtedness had been acknowledged long before in the preface to *The Hoosier School-Master* by a reference to the "admirable and erudite preface to the Biglow Papers."

> To Mr. Lowell [Eggleston asserted] belongs the distinction of being the only one of our most eminent authors and the only one of our most eminent scholars who has given careful attention to American dialects. But while I have not ventured to discuss the provincialisms of the Indiana backwoods, I have been careful to preserve the true *usus loquendi* of each locution, and I trust my little story may afford material for some one better qualified than I to criticise the dialect.[97]

The attitude of a linguist cannot be compared with that of a genre painter, but they have in common the fact that neither is primarily concerned with ethical judgments of his materials.

If *The Hoosier School-Master* was indeed the leader of the procession of American dialect novels, as Eggleston later asserted,[98] the fact may arouse mixed emotions in modern readers. For much of the dialect writing produced by the local color school in the two decades following the appearance of Eggleston's novel is both unskilful and patronizing. "In all use of dialect," remarked George Philip Krapp, "there is probably present some

---

stricken family in "Ward Henderson" do not speak in dialect (*ibid.,* pp. 346–360). The strongly sentimental atmosphere of this story has perhaps exerted a refining influence on the language of the characters.

[94] Randel, *Eggleston,* p. 79.   [95] *Ibid.,* p. 105.
[96] *Ibid.,* p. 187. It is not clear what publication Eggleston had in mind.
[97] *Hoosier School-Master,* p. 6.   [98] Randel, *Eggleston,* p. 126.

sense of amused superiority on the part of the conventional speaker as he views the forms of the dialect speech. . . ." [99] The generalization certainly applies to run-of-the-mill local color writing, which depends for too many of its effects upon the supposed quaintness of the illiterate natives of various American regions. But despite this danger in the literary use of dialect, it opened up pathways of advance in two directions. On the one hand, the perception that the speech of Western backwoodsmen exemplified the historian's principle that "all which is partakes of that which was" [100] saved it from being considered merely crude, coarse, and unrefined. The discovery added a dignity to the uneducated folk which they could never have acquired within the framework of the theory of progress and civilization. In *Roxy* Eggleston causes the Swiss-American girl Twonnet (Antoinette) to defend the use of "right" for "very" by pointing out to the young minister Whittaker, a graduate of Yale, that "right" occurs in this sense in the Bible; indeed, she even goes on to make the revolutionary suggestion that Yale itself, students and faculty, has its own local dialect.[101] This was a novel way of conceiving the differences between Eastern and Western speech.

The other line of literary development opened up by the growing respect for Western dialect is merely hinted at in Eggleston's work. This is the creation of an American literary prose formed on the vernacular. Whitman had been a pioneer in this respect, but Eggleston found Whitman merely "coarse." [102] And he had little more respect for Mark Twain, whose *Huckleberry Finn* was the first masterpiece of vernacular prose.[103] Yet Eggleston was moving with the current. His style has far fewer literary flourishes than that of Mrs. Kirkland, and on at least one occasion, when his own use of a provincialism (the word "hover" as a transitive verb to describe the action of a hen brooding her chicks) was pointed out to him by a proofreader, he let it stand, merely adding a note to the effect that the word was so used "at least in half the country." [104] Later in his career he became even more fully aware of the potential richness of folk speech as a literary medium. In 1888, commenting on James Whitcomb Riley's language, he wrote very shrewdly: "As dialect it is perfectly sound Hoosier but a little thin. He has known it more among villagers than among rustics. He has known it at a later period than I did, and the tremendous—almost

[99] *The English Language in America*, 2 vols. (New York, 1925), I, 229.
[100] Edward Eggleston, "Folk-Speech in America," *Century Magazine*, XLVIII, 870 (October, 1894).
[101] *Roxy*, pp. 426–427.
[102] Eggleston remarks that if the Backwoods Philosopher in *The End of the World* had known Whitman's work, he would have assigned the poet to the "Inferno" section of his library along with Swinburne, *Don Juan*, and "some French novels" (p. 44).
[103] Eggleston wrote to his wife in 1888, after meeting Mark Twain, that he was "only a good clown after all" (Randel, *Eggleston*, p. 184).
[104] *The End of the World*, p. 37 and note.

unequalled vigor of the public school system in Indiana must have washed the color out of the dialect a good deal." [105]

Eggleston's scientific interest in the speech of Western farmers was carried even farther by Joseph Kirkland in *Zury, the Meanest Man in Spring County* (1887) and *The McVeys* (1888).[106] The plots of these novels are dominated by Anne Sparrow, a New England school teacher who brings an unexampled cultivation and refinement to rural Illinois, but the character of the avaricious Zury Prouder is well observed in the period before he is regenerated by Anne's virtue, and the speech of the countryside is reported with care and skill. Kirkland's ear for what people actually said was keener than that of any other writer who has dealt with the agricultural West, except Sinclair Lewis. In addition to accurate phonetic notations, he made the discovery that in conversation people often use an elliptical syntax and altogether omit various kinds of unemphatic words.

But Zury is more than a dialect. He gives the impression of having been created through the accumulation of tall tales about stinginess just as the legendary Davy Crockett was created through accumulation of tales about coon-hunting, fighting, and drinking whiskey. Kirkland says he is repeating stories told by a man who once worked for Zury and later delighted his comrades in the Union army with them; some of the yarns, he adds, have already found their way into print.[107] The political speech which Zury makes with the assistance of Anne is a masterpiece of vernacular prose filled with shrewd anecdotes, like those of Lincoln, which Kirkland greatly admired.[108] If the novelist's simultaneous devotion to folklore and to female gentility led him to consummate one of the strangest matings in all literature by marrying Zury to Anne Sparrow—a transaction as odd as would have been the marriage of Davy Crockett to Miss Alcott's Jo March —he was nevertheless aware that the folk elements in Zury held a new and vital kind of literary interest. Kirkland makes the point explicitly. Anne's daughter Margaret edits the "Third Page" of the *Springville Bugle,* a section given over to book reviews, anecdotes, pointed paragraphs, and editorials. She and her cultivated friend Dr. Strafford notice that whenever Zury has spent an evening with them her writing is much improved. "How is it, Margaret?" asks Strafford. "How does he help us so much?"

> "Well [she replies, evidently speaking for the author], as nearly as I can make out, it is the *tone* he gives our thoughts. If I read too much,

---

[105] Randel, *Eggleston*, p. 184.

[106] Kirkland told Hamlin Garland he was trying to improve on Eggleston, although he did not specify in what respect (*Roadside Meetings* [New York, 1930], p. 111).

[107] *Zury: The Meanest Man in Spring County. A Novel of Western Life* (Boston, 1887), pp. 80–81. I have not been able to trace this allusion.

[108] *Ibid.*, pp. 348–356. Kirkland explains in a note that one of the illustrations in the speech—based on feeding a calf—is derived from a stump speech of "Representative Horr, of Michigan" (p. 352 *n.*).

the T. P. grows eastern and literary. If I leave it to you, it is scientific and political; but when Mr. Prouder is the inspiration, it is frontierish, quaint, common-sensical, shrewd, strong, gay, and—I don't know what all." [109]

Despite the soft spot in the vicinity of the word "quaint," this is not a bad statement of the qualities that Eggleston and Kirkland were beginning to discover in their Western folk.

But neither the rendering of dialect nor the use of folklore proved after all to be the decisive factor in the complex literary evolution preceding the appearance of Hamlin Garland's *Main Travelled Roads* in 1891. It is true that when Garland was writing his memoirs toward the end of his long life he began his account of this movement by discussing the earliest uses of the "New World's vernacular"—in a few of Leatherstocking's speeches, in the *Biglow Papers,* and in Whittier, Bret Harte, and John Hay.[110] But he passes at once to a discussion of E. W. Howe. This transition is remarkable because Howe was not interested in reporting dialect. The Western farm people of his stories have a colorless diction that tends toward conventional rhetoric, rather than the carefully constructed dialect of Eggleston's or Kirkland's characters. Garland refers to Howe's "strong, idiomatic Western prose," [111] but this is not the same thing as dialect and Garland does not probe further into the interesting problem of an American vernacular literary prose as contrasted with the reported speech of characters held distinct from the narrator.

The letter to Howe which Garland wrote in July, 1886, congratulating him on his novel *Moonlight Boy,* is a valuable document for the study of the various trends and currents that were at work in this important decade. It touches upon a number of attitudes and literary procedures that Garland endorsed, and develops a literary credo of some dimensions. Howe is for Garland one of the representative names standing for "local scene and character painting," the only one who represents the prairie West. He has depicted "homely, prosaic people in their restricted lives," not viewing them from a distance as picturesque, but writing "as from among them." [112] The pattern of the travel narrative, as in Mrs. Kirkland's sketches, has disappeared along with the status system that elevated Easterners above Westerners. In Howe's first and best book, *The Story of a Country Town* (1883), the narrator who speaks in the first person is a young man looking back upon his own bleak childhood in the prairie West.

But the most important trait of Howe's work is the constant note of sadness and disillusionment that bespeaks the fading of the dream of an agrarian utopia. *The Story of a Country Town* is a sardonic commentary

---

[109] *The McVeys: An Episode* (Boston, 1888), p. 339. [110] *Roadside Meetings*, pp. 90–94.
[111] *Ibid.,* p. 95. [112] *Ibid.,* pp. 94–95.

on the theme of going West to grow up with the country. Through an eccentric character named Lytle Biggs, who sometimes speaks for the author, Howe attacks the cult of the yeoman as explicitly as Cooper had attacked it, although from a somewhat different standpoint. The notions that there is a peculiar merit in agricultural labor and that farmers are more virtuous than other men, Biggs declares to be falsehoods circulated by politicians for their own advantage.[113] Howe's West offers neither color to the observer from without nor consolations to the people themselves. It is a world of grim, savage religion, of silent endurance, of families held together by no tenderness, of communities whose only amusement is malicious gossip. Howe's farmers seem on the whole to be prosperous enough, but some not easily analyzed bitterness has poisoned the springs of human feeling. The Reverend John Westlock, father of the narrator, a stern minister and a successful farmer, runs away with a woman he does not love after years of a strange silent battle with himself. Jo Erring, the narrator's closest friend, is destroyed by insane jealousy. The symbol that dominates the opening and the close of the novel is a great bell in the steeple of Fairview church which is used to announce deaths in the community, and is also tolled by the winds "as if the ghosts from the grave lot had crawled up there, and were counting the number to be buried the coming year. . . ." [114]

Garland described this book as "a singularly gloomy, real yet unreal, narrative written in the tone of weary and hopeless age." [115] It is at this point that Howe differs most clearly from Joseph Kirkland, who considered the novel too melodramatic and told Garland that Howe's country town "never had any existence outside of his tired brain." [116] Yet the description of Zury's childhood in Kirkland's own novel is dark and bitter, as is the characterization of the half-insane Hobbs in *The McVeys*, with its end in the ghastly lynching scene; and both Mrs. Kirkland (in her shocked description of the death of a girl from an attempted abortion)[117] and Miss Cary (in her sketch of the newsboy Ward Henderson)[118] had included ominous shadows in their pictures of the West. These shadows had no doubt been somewhat blurred, but in devoting himself to a prolonged exploration of the dark recesses of his own childhood, Howe was merely developing hints in the works of his predecessors. The self-castigating Westlock is only a degree more neurotic than Mrs. Knight in Miss Cary's sketch, and both characters are thwarted by a grim and colorless environment.

Although Howe's extreme conservatism made him unsympathetic with the efforts of Western farmers to organize themselves for political action in

---

[113] *The Story of a Country Town* (Boston, 1883), pp. 239–240.   [114] *Ibid.*, p. 3.
[115] *Roadside Meetings*, p. 94.   [116] *Ibid.*, p. 111.   [117] *A New Home*, pp. 173–176.
[118] *Clovernook* (Second Series), pp. 346–360.

the Farmers' Alliance,[119] the stories collected in *Main Travelled Roads* owe more to Howe's melancholy than to Kirkland's rather cold fidelity to linguistic fact or his use of a tall-tale tradition. Garland did practice faithfully the lesson of exact description, and despite his lack of a good ear for language he worked hard at transcribing the actual speech of his characters. But the method was with him only a means of bringing home to his readers the farmers' sufferings. Many years later he wrote that his point of view when he came back in 1887 to his old homes in Iowa and South Dakota "was plainly that of one who, having escaped from this sad life, was now a pitying onlooker." "That my old neighbors were in a mood of depression," he continued, "was evident. Things were going badly with them. Wheat was very low in price and dairying had brought new problems and new drudgery into their lives. Six years had made little improvement in farm conditions." [120] The visit coincided with the collapse of the great Western boom. Garland's success as a portrayer of hardship and suffering on Northwestern farms was due in part to the fact that his personal experience happened to parallel the shock which the entire West received in the later 1880's from the combined effects of low prices in the international wheat market, grasshoppers, drought, the terrible blizzards of the winter of 1886–1887, and the juggling of freight rates that led to the Interstate Commerce Act in 1887.

In Garland, Howe's undefined sadness, which had no acknowledged connection with economic distress, came into focus about the creed of Henry George's Single Taxers. "There was nothing humorous about the lives of these toilers," he wrote of his trip West in 1887. "On the contrary, I regarded them as victims of an unjust land system. An immense pity took possession of me. I perceived their helplessness. They were like flies in a pool of tar." [121] In the Preface to *Jason Edwards*, a novel written for Benjamin Flower's *Arena* in 1891 and dedicated to the Farmers' Alliance, Garland states his interpretation of what had happened in the agricultural West:

> For more than a half century the outlet toward the free lands of the West has been the escape-valve of social discontent in the great cities of America. Whenever the conditions of his native place pressed too hard upon him, the artisan or the farmer has turned his face toward the prairies and forests of the West. . . . Thus long before the days of '49, the West had become the Golden West, the land of wealth and freedom and happiness. All of the associations called up by the spoken word, the West, were fabulous, mythic, hopeful.[122]

---

[119] Lytle Biggs is an unscrupulous man who organizes chapters of the Alliance to make money for himself. He cynically tells the farmers how industrious, honest, and oppressed they are in order to win their favor (*Story of a Country Town*, p. 240). The character of Biggs is not sympathetic but here he seems to be voicing Howe's own views.

[120] *Roadside Meetings*, p. 113.   [121] *Idem*.

[122] *Jason Edwards, An Average Man* (Boston, 1892), p. [v].

But the hopeful myth had been destroyed. With an element of exaggeration that can certainly be forgiven a novelist if it appeared also in the historian Frederick Jackson Turner, Garland declared, "Free land is gone. The last acre of available farmland has now passed into private or corporate hands." [123] His story is an apologue on the closing of the safety valve. Jason Edwards, a Boston mechanic, takes his family to the Western prairies in search of the free land promised by advertising circulars, only to find that all land within thirty miles of a railroad has been taken up by speculators. After five years of desperate struggle to pay interest and get title to his farm, Edwards is prostrated by a hailstorm that destroys his wheat just before harvest. The family return to Massachusetts in defeat under the protection of Alice Edwards's fiancé, a Boston newspaperman. The evil forces oppressing the farmer are represented by Judge S. H. Balser, land agent, who falsifies the evidences of a boom in order to market his lands, and sits back collecting his interest while Edwards and other farmers grind themselves to illness and despair in their fields.[124] Reeves, the fiancé, points the moral of the tale: "So this is the reality of the dream! This is the 'homestead in the Golden West, embowered in trees, beside the purling brook!' A shanty on a barren plain, hot and lone as a desert. My God!" [125]

In view of actual conditions in the West, the ideal of the yeoman society could be considered nothing but a device of propaganda manipulated by cynical speculators. Yet Garland continued to hope that the ideal might be realized. He endorsed the single-tax program because he saw in it a means to this end. Ida Wilbur, the radical lecturer who voices many of Garland's ideas in *A Spoil of Office,* announces to the hero Bradley Talcott:

> I believe in thickly settled farming communities, communities where every man has a small, highly cultivated farm. That's what I've been advocating and prophesying, but I now begin to see that our system of ownership in land is directly against this security, and directly against thickly-settled farming communities. The big land owners are swallowing up the small farmers, and turning them into renters or laborers.[126]

The social theories which shaped Garland's early stories are evident enough. Land monopolists had blighted the promise of the West; the single tax would eliminate the speculator and allow the yeoman ideal to be realized. But Garland was seldom able to integrate his theories with the materials he had gathered by personal experience and observation. The radical ideas occur as concepts. They are seldom realized imaginatively—perhaps never fully except in "Under the Lion's Paw," which exhibits a shrewd landowner exploiting a tenant.[127] Garland's strength lay rather in a simple humanitarian sympathy that was entirely congruous with the sentimental

---

[123] *Ibid.,* p. [vi].   [124] *Ibid.,* pp. 103, 111.   [125] *Ibid.,* p. 142.
[126] *A Spoil of Office. A Story of the Modern West* (Boston, 1892), p. 152.
[127] *Main-Travelled Roads. Six Mississippi Valley Stories* (Boston, 1891), pp. 217–240.

tradition. His description of an imaginary painting on the wall of Howard McLane's apartment in "Up the Coulé" expresses an emotion deeper than his conscious doctrines. The picture is "a sombre landscape by a master greater than Millet, a melancholy subject, treated with pitiless fidelity." It evidently has a portentous meaning for him:

> A farm in the valley! Over the mountain swept jagged, gray, angry, sprawling clouds, sending a freezing, thin drizzle of rain, as they passed, upon a man following a plough. The horses had a sullen and weary look, and their manes and tails streamed sidewise in the blast. The ploughman clad in a ragged gray coat, with uncouth, muddy boots upon his feet, walked with his head inclined toward the sleet, to shield his face from the cold and sting of it. The soil rolled away black and sticky and with a dull sheen upon it. Near by, a boy with tears on his cheeks was watching cattle, a dog seated near, his back to the gale.[128]

This plowman is neither the yeoman of agrarian tradition, nor a picturesque rural swain, nor a half-barbarian like Ishmael Bush, nor an amusingly unrefined backwoodsman, nor even a victim of a perverted land system. His most direct relation is to nature, and even though this relation is one of conflict, it confers on him a certain dignity and tends to enlarge his stature by making him a representative of suffering humanity, of man in general. Garland's early stories are not a literary achievement of the first or even of the second rank, but they mark the end of a long evolution in attitudes. It had at last become possible to deal with the Western farmer in literature as a human being instead of seeing him through a veil of literary convention, class prejudice, or social theory.

---

[128] *Ibid.*, pp. 96–97.

The Frontier West As Image of American Society, 1776–1860

Rush Welter

After three decades of controversy, American historians find themselves still embroiled in a bitter and often fruitless quarrel over the significance of the frontier in American history. Presumably, the critics of Turner's frontier hypothesis will ultimately win their campaigns to discredit his interpretation, for it is vulnerable both as an intellectual system and as a doctrine appropriate to an earlier and simpler world than the chaos in which we now live. Yet the very tenacity of Turner's hold on his defenders, together with the narrowness with which some of his critics have attacked his doctrines, suggests that a complete victory for Turner's opponents would deprive us of a valuable perspective on our past. Under the circumstances it seems appropriate to attempt a somewhat different evaluation of the Americans' frontier experience, to seek to remove it equally from the realm of too-generous sentiment and from that of literal-minded historiography.

The purpose determines the method and scope of this essay. Instead of insisting that the frontier be understood institutionally, as an economic or a political or a social influence on American life, we may choose to evaluate it in terms of its influence on American thought. This paper is a beginning, a preliminary exploration of the possibilities. Its purpose is not to argue the Turner thesis, but to illuminate it. Its data will be, not evidence that Turner was or was not an accurate historian, but attitudes expressed by American writers before he was born.

Other scholars have already explored some of the same ground. Chief among them is Henry Nash Smith, whose *Virgin Land* marked a new departure in frontier scholarship, and whose methods of studying imaginative literature and sub-literature have worked a near-revolution in American cultural history, not to mention other fields of endeavor.[1] Yet it is probably

From *Pacific Northwest Quarterly*, LII (January 1961), 1–6. Reprinted by permission. Rush Welter, an Easterner born and bred, is professor of the history of American civilization at Bennington College. This paper is a slightly revised version of one read at the Mississippi Valley Historical Association meeting in Louisville in April, 1960. It is part of a larger inquiry into American social values generally before the Civil War.

[1] Henry Nash Smith, *Virgin Land: The American West as Symbol and Myth* (Cambridge, Mass., 1950).

fair to say that in employing the techniques of literary analysis Smith and his followers have sometimes obscured as well as illuminated American thought. That is, they have demonstrated beyond all question that literary stereotypes influenced American writing and hence American thinking about the West; but they have tended to ignore other perspectives in which Americans saw the region.

For example, *Virgin Land* shows us how literary conventions stemming at least from the 18th century helped to shape the West in American eyes, making it seem variously a vast commercial empire, an ambiguous naturalistic refuge, or a perpetual agrarian utopia. Other studies, focused instead on religious imagery, have emphasized the extent to which the same region also appeared to give reality to the Biblical garden or the Biblical wilderness, and so to present Americans with a unique challenge and a unique opportunity to work out their religious destiny on a new stage.[2] But it is at least arguable that Americans saw the West in other terms as well, less arbitrary and less exaggerated.

The themes that Smith and others trace are too nearly poetic in their inspiration, too nearly conventional in their application, to be trustworthy guides to the pragmatic perspectives with which most Americans ordinarily contemplated their lives. Above all, they are too restricted to account for various images of the West as a country that real people might inhabit; and they do not always differentiate the West that was to be occupied and farmed and ultimately to be industrialized from the majestic natural phenomenon that still surrounds the Westerns on television and in the movies.

I suggest, instead, that between 1776 and 1860, far from being bound by literary or religious conventions in their views of the West, Americans came to see in it an almost limitless extension of the social and economic and political values they associated with their country at large. This proposition invites extended empirical inquiry, but there is already evidence enough to suggest that it is worth developing here in outline form. Indeed, the most difficult problem may be to formulate its terms clearly and accurately, for if they are formulated effectively, everyone should be able to test them in his own reading of primary sources.

To begin, we should restrict our inquiry so far as possible to an examination of what eastern writers made of the West. Thanks in large part to eastern condescension, which Smith among others documents, Westerners and western spokesmen often felt the need to describe their section and its prospects in exaggerated and overoptimistic terms. But while their views were undoubtedly significant expressions of American opinion, they also have the defect—for our purposes here—not only of special pleading, but also of irrelevancy. It can hardly be surprising that Westerners should have

---

[2] See particularly George H. Williams, "The Wilderness and Paradise in the History of the Church," *Church History*, XXVIII (1959), 3–24.

advocated the claims of their region to recognition and national approbation. It is both significant and surprising, however, that Easterners should so often have agreed with them. If we are to look anywhere for evidence that the West held special meanings for Americans before the Civil War, we can well afford to focus on eastern sources.

Within the range of eastern opinion, in turn, it is most striking that eastern conservatives—men representing unmistakable orthodoxy in religion or politics or social theory—should have seen the West in a favorable light. I have already urged, in a recent issue of the *Mississippi Valley Historical Review,* that after a notorious early reluctance to accept the West on any terms whatsoever, these conservatives came close to adopting it as their own.[3] That essay is concerned, among other things, with why their views shifted; the important point here is that they did.

Meanwhile, of course, more tolerant Easterners had long since identified the western frontier with the persistence and expansion of valued American institutions. This identification was evident in the writings of both Benjamin Franklin and Thomas Jefferson, who believed that a vast reserve of unsettled land would perpetuate our liberal institutions by protecting us against the growth of cities and the effects of poverty; but the image of the West soon transcended their pastoral and republican dream.

On the one hand, it took shape in the doctrines of manifest destiny: as early as 1819 Representative George F. Strother of Virginia protested against potential limitations on western settlement in the name of civilization, progress, religion, and all the social virtues.[4] On the other hand, it also entered profoundly into the doctrines of Jacksonian democracy. Indeed, Albert K. Weinberg's study, *Manifest Destiny,* suggests indirectly that the two phenomena—manifest destiny and Jacksonian democracy—were closely related through their common western orientation; and while other studies show that the relationship was by no means exact, it is hardly possible to ignore the extent to which each drew on western prospects and resources.[5]

Nevertheless, the categories of manifest destiny and Jacksonian democracy do not exhaust the perspectives in which Americans held the frontier West. For one thing, they do not take sufficient account of the distinctly utilitarian values eastern commentators placed upon the region. These were evident in an essay on the public domain that appeared in the *American Quarterly Review* for December, 1829.

> When we consider the unexampled rapidity with which the western
> states have acquired population and importance, we are surprised, not

---

[3] Rush Welter, "The Frontier West as Image of American Society: Conservative Attitudes before the Civil War," *Mississippi Valley Historical Review,* XLVI (1960), 593–614.

[4] As quoted by Albert K. Weinberg, *Manifest Destiny: A Study of Nationalist Expansionism in American History* (Gloucester, Mass., 1958), 80.

[5] *Ibid.,* 116–117.

only at that fact, but at the inadequate ideas which have heretofore prevailed as to the magnitude and resources of that country. We are a travelling and a calculating people, and it seems strange that those who visited the western wilds in early times, should not have foreseen the events which have since transpired. That they did make golden reports we are aware; but contrary to all experience, those reports have fallen short of the truth, and all that has been dreamt and prophesied in relation to this region, by its most sanguine admirers, has been more than realized.[6]

Moreover, it illustrated these remarks, not by reference to a land of milk and honey, nor even to a yeoman's paradise, but by remarking on the growth of Lexington, Kentucky, and on the flourishing state of the West generally.

The same article also serves to point up another significant characteristic of the eastern perspective on the West: any practical estimate of the area focused of necessity on its habitable, usable regions. The proposition is self-evident, but perhaps it needs to be stated in order to counterbalance the emphasis that has been placed upon literary valuations of the West. Indeed, if we may trust the impressions of a European observer, Easterners saw in the West nothing but regions that would one day be like their own. According to Alexis de Tocqueville,

> In Europe people talk a great deal of the wilds of America, but the Americans themselves never think about them; they are insensible to the wonders of inanimate nature and they may be said not to perceive the mighty forests that surround them till they fall beneath the hatchet. Their eyes are fixed upon another sight: the American people views its own march across these wilds, draining swamps, turning the course of rivers, peopling solitudes, and subduing nature. This magnificent image of themselves does not meet the gaze of the Americans at intervals only; it may be said to haunt every one of them in his least as well as in his most important actions and to be always flitting before his mind.[7]

Even so, to refer to the eastern perspective on the West as if it were reducible solely to utilitarian terms is to miss important characteristics of the frontier image. We must acknowledge that even the most practical writers often endowed the region with certain imaginary attributes, and that it is impossible to understand the place it occupied in American thought without recognizing this fact. Let us see, then, what relatively prosaic eastern imaginations did with the plastic image of the West.

It is already evident that eastern commentators often looked forward to an uncomplicated horizontal extension of eastern political institutions into

---

[6] *American Quarterly Review,* VI (1829), 263.
[7] Alexis de Tocqueville, *Democracy in America,* ed. Phillips Bradley (New York, 1945), II, 74.

the frontier areas. The doughty Jacksonian journalist, Francis Grund, spelled out this concept in 1837:

> Every new colony of settlers contains within itself a nucleus of republican institutions, and revives, in a measure, the history of the first settlers. Its relation to the Atlantic states is similar to the situation of the early colonies with regard to the mother country, and contains the elements of freedom.[8]

Of course, Grund's conservative contemporaries were more apprehensive than he over the actual or the potential consequences of westward migration; but despite differences of emphasis, spokesmen for different points of view generally agreed that the West was a promising arena for most of the advantageous institutions of the East.

By the same token, the westward extension of political institutions also connoted, for many eastern spokesmen, a simultaneous reduplication of the economic opportunities that had already opened up in the East. Grund suggested as much; so did the *Democratic Review* when, in October, 1847, it sponsored territorial expansion at the expense of Mexico:

> Occupation of territory by the people is the great movement of the age, and until every acre of the North American continent is occupied by citizens of the United States, the foundation of the future empire will not have been laid. . . . That which constitutes the strength of the Union, the wealth and independence of its people, is the boundless expanse of territory laid open to their possession; and the more rapidly it is overrun by needy settlers, the greater is the security, that it will be equally and extensively distributed, and the more impossible it becomes for any section or clique to exercise "control over them," or to encroach upon the rights they enjoy under our constitution.[9]

As this passage suggests, most of the commentators who invoked the economic possibilities of the West focused their attention on its agricultural opportunities. They did not entirely limit their hopes to agriculture, as the writers I have already cited and the contemporary guidebooks attest.[10] But it is true that the agricultural West achieved special importance in eastern thought because of the safety-valve doctrine. As Carter Goodrich and Sol Davison pointed out twenty-six years ago, both those who feared the effect of free lands and those who saw benefits in them agreed that western lands would maintain high wages for eastern workingmen. (They also suggested that only partisans of other solutions to contemporary social and

---

[8] Francis J. Grund, *The Americans, in their Moral, Social, and Political Relations* (Boston, 1837), 208.

[9] "New Territory versus No Territory," *The United States Magazine, and Democratic Review,* XXI (1847), 291–92.

[10] See, for example, Samuel R. Brown, *The Western Gazetteer; or Emigrant's Directory* (Auburn, N. Y., 1817), and [Robert Baird], *View of the Valley of the Mississippi; or the Emigrant's and Traveller's Guide to the West* (Philadelphia, 1832).

industrial problems, for example Matthew Carey, were likely to quarrel with the basic premise.)[11] Whether agricultural or not, however, the West seemed to offer apparently unlimited opportunities to Easterners to pursue their own well-being; it seemed made to order for American democrats and American entrepreneurs.

As the safety-valve doctrine particularly implies, moreover, the relatively accurate and relatively neutral appreciation of the West as an underpopulated and underexploited region was easily metamorphosed into a more optimistic and more exaggerated image. Not only did the newness of the region connote opportunities that could not be duplicated in the more settled areas of the country, as eastern writers often suggested, but its vast extent augured an almost endless succession of similar opportunities, guaranteeing the distant future as well as supporting present hopes. It also held out much the same kind of promise for our social and political institutions, a promise that is reflected in Francis Grund's remark that

> The western states, from their peculiar position, are supposed to develope all the resources and peculiarities of democratic governments, without being driven to excesses by the opposition of contrary principles. Their number too augments the intensity of republican life by increasing the number of rallying points, without which the principle of liberty would be too much weakened by expansion.[12]

This was the sort of hope that ultimately influenced the passage of the Homestead Act; but the Homestead Act only documents a broader phenomenon, the constant identification of American prosperity and national well-being in the future with the continued existence of a frontier West.

The image of a West that would perpetually sustain and strengthen established social and political institutions also supported an imaginative identification between the West and the whole nation's character and destiny. The doctrines of manifest destiny undoubtedly played a large part in establishing this wider identification, but they do not satisfactorily define it. For the fundamental meaning of manifest destiny lay in the ways in which it committed Americans to further territorial expansion, whereas what we are concerned with here is their perspectives on territory they had already begun to occupy. The view I am pursuing was better represented by de Tocqueville's report on the Americans' self-image, or by the English review of 1821 that Turner quotes in "Middle Western Pioneer Democracy": "Others appeal to history: an American appeals to prophecy; and with Malthus in one hand and a map of the back country in the other, he boldly defies us to a comparison with America as she is to be." [13]

---

[11] Carter Goodrich and Sol Davison, "The Wage-Earner in the Westward Movement, I," *Political Science Quarterly*, L (1935), 169–74.

[12] Grund, *The Americans*, 209.

[13] Frederick Jackson Turner, *The Frontier in American History* (New York, 1920), 345.

Nor are we compelled to rely upon foreign observers for evidence of this American proclivity. It was implicit, for example, in Representative Orin Fowler's apostrophe to the American character in 1852. During the debate on the Homestead Bill, the Massachusetts Whig exclaimed:

> What indomitable enterprise marks the character of our people! What immense forests have disappeared, and given place to cultivated towns, thriving villages, and wealthy cities! Agriculture, and manufactures, and commerce, and schools, and public buildings, and houses of public worship; all these testify to our matchless enterprise. The rapidity of our progress throws all Eastern countries into the shade. We build steamboats for the Sultan of Turkey, and railroads for the Autocrat of Russia; and our enterprise extends to the icebergs of the poles— to India, China, and Japan.[14]

Even more pointedly, during the 1840's the *Democratic Review* paid tribute to the West because it promised to create a truly American civilization, untrammeled by European influences; while more conservative sources had long since proclaimed, more ambiguously but no less insistently, that its development would decide the fate of the nation.[15]

The corollary of these present satisfactions and future hopes was a belief that in some sense the West had already made unique contributions to American life. Representative Fowler's paean of praise verges on making this assertion; other commentators were more nearly explicit. In particular, they portrayed the West as the breeding ground of a new sort of man, whose qualities would one day influence the whole United States. The tendency was already at work in the *American Quarterly Review* for June, 1829, when, in a review of Timothy Flint's *Condensed Geography and History of the Western States,* it pointed out that "The pioneers are a people peculiar to our country," and went on to describe the backwoodsmen sympathetically yet factually as brave, hardy, indolent, honest, generous, improvident, independent, sagacious, "and capable, when excited, of powerful bodily exertions." [16] The same tendency was even more apparent in the writings of James H. Lanman, the Connecticut businessman who spent several years in Michigan during the late 1830's, and who reported in *Hunt's Merchant's Magazine* in 1840 that

> The people of the west are generous, though crude, unmindful from habit of the luxuries of life, endowed with great boldness and originality of mind, from the circumstances under which they are placed. They are, from the various elements of which they are composed, in a state

---

[14] 32nd Cong., 1st Sess., *Congressional Globe* (March 31, 1852), Appendix, 396.
[15] "The Poetry of the West," *Democratic Review,* IX (1841), 24–25; and see Welter, *loc. cit.*
[16] *American Quarterly Review,* V (1829), 356.

of amalgamation, and from this amalgamation a new and valuable form of American character will spring up.[17]

But the most striking statement of this sort came from the prominent Baptist missionary, J. M. Peck, who developed in the columns of the *Christian Review* for January, 1851, what reads like a primitive version of the Turner thesis. The American people, Peck said, made up of "Puritans" and "Cavaliers," and of Germans, French, Irish, Scots-Irish, and Welsh, are mingling in the West and being molded by their experience there into a new civilization. They characteristically display "great energy, and the spirit of enterprise," intense patriotism, "strong social feelings," "high-toned republicanism, or strong democratic tendencies," a zeal for education, a universal spirit of improvement, and (thanks to itinerant evangelists and the impact of religious revivals) an "increasing influence of pure Christianity." "The feelings of honor, the abhorrence of falsehood, and entire frankness of Western Character," Peck concluded, "only need to be animated by deep, ardent, and intelligent piety to make us what we ought to be." [18]

Neither Lanman nor Peck was a wholly reliable spokesman for eastern attitudes, the former because he remained a western booster even after he had returned to the East, the latter because as a western missionary he obviously portrayed the region in heightened terms. But the critical fact here is not the extent to which these men may have been swayed by their western experience; it is, rather, the way in which they chose to communicate that experience to eastern readers. Moved by western prospects, they virtually identified the United States with its frontier heritage. The West was their country because they were Americans.

At the same time, contemporary critics of these western images often lent them unintended force. For example, Orestes Brownson took issue with the safety-valve doctrine; but in doing so—as a radical social commentator dissenting from contemporary opinion—he only confirmed its authority.[19] Similarly, Horace Bushnell bitterly attacked westward emigration from Connecticut, but in such terms as to minimize his most trenchant criticisms. He told the Hartford County Agricultural Society in 1846:

> If you will sacrifice everything here above the range of raw physical necessity, and consent to become a barbarian as regards all the refinements of life, you will see how it is that the emigrant is able to get a start and why he is supposed to do it so much more easily at the West.

---

[17] James H. Lanman, "The Progress of the Northwest," *The Merchant's Magazine and Commercial Review*, III (1840), 39.

[18] J. M. Peck, "Elements of Western Character," *Christian Review*, XVI (1851), 89–90, 93–94, 95.

[19] *Boston Quarterly Review*, III (1840), 372.

> . . . The first generation can hardly be said to live. They let go life,
> throw it away, for the benefits of the generation to come after them.[20]

Who in America was likely to see only the hardships and to ignore the promise that even Bushnell's words held out?

Finally, southern spokesmen went out of their way during the 1850's to challenge the images of homestead and democracy that spokesmen for the North had attached to the West; but (as Henry Nash Smith has suggested) their attack on these values only demonstrated the futility of their own imagination, their inability to substitute their own projection of a plantation West for the more characteristic northern image of a fee-simple empire.[21] Before the Civil War, those who challenged the frontier West as an image of American society did battle with most of their countrymen.

Dissenters and advocates together support the proposition, therefore, that on many levels and in many ways the frontier West both dramatized and lent independent meaning to a wide range of prevalent social attitudes. Before 1860 a good many Americans, eastern as well as western, believed that the West was a unique possession of the American republic and a unique influence on its past, its present, and its future. They saw in it not simply a struggle between nature and civilization, not merely an agrarian haven, but a model and a vision of themselves.

Indeed, with someone like the Reverend J. M. Peck in mind, it is not too much to suggest that these ante-bellum commentators on the West adumbrated most of the elements of Turner's frontier hypothesis well before its author was born. For that matter, some of Turner's critics have argued that various elements of the frontier thesis were not completely novel, but they have not pursued their discovery far enough to make it fruitful. I suggest that, far from undermining Turner's place in our historiography, these elements point the way toward a fuller appreciation of his work. If Turner somehow gathered together in his writings many of the perspectives in which Americans of fifty or seventy-five years before him had seen the West, the fact may be a tribute as well as a criticism. For Turner was—as he set out to be—an American poet as well as a historian: what he wrote captured historic images that others lost sight of.

Furthermore, placing Turner's work in this broader perspective also has the effect of diminishing some of the criticisms that have been leveled against his intelligence. It is true, for instance, that Turner did not successfully distinguish between the frontier as a line, the frontier as a section, and the frontier as a process; but the confusion was part of our tradition, and

---

[20] As quoted by Clarence H. Danhof, "Economic Validity of the Safety Valve Doctrine," *Journal of Economic History*, I, *Supplement* (December, 1941), 101, n. 17.

[21] Smith, *Virgin Land,* Chaps. 13 and 15.

he did not create it. It is also true that he was vague and hortatory, rather than precise and empirical, in his descriptions of the relationship the West bore to the rest of the United States; but again the attitude and the confusion it encouraged did not originate with him. Finally, it is true that Turner was guilty of thinking in terms of closed space and that in various ways the categories of his frontier theory have limited public debate on crucial political issues. But here, too, it is neither accurate nor relevant to charge him with the whole responsibility for the defects of American social thought. Indeed, if we acknowledge that his thinking embodied traditional valuations of the frontier, we should not find it surprising that he portrayed the crisis of the 1890's in terms of the frontier's disappearance. The frontier was what Americans imagined as well as what they experienced.

I do not mean to argue that Turner was always an adequate historian of the United States, nor to excuse his shortcomings by labeling him a poet wherever it is inconvenient to defend him as a scholar. But I do suggest that those who have criticized Turner for being derivative and confused have often missed the logical implication of their arguments: his images of the frontier West embodied a wide range of historic American attitudes. If we were to concentrate on sorting out these attitudes, to use Turner's work as a kind of retrospective guidebook to ideas as well as events, we might make great strides in understanding the way Americans thought well before his time.

XII

American Negro Slavery:
U. B. Phillips vs.
Revisionist Historians

INTRODUCTION

American Negro slavery, in reality as an existing institution in America before the Civil War and in retrospect since the War, has been a subject upon which Americans have deeply, passionately, and even irrationally disagreed. The disagreement arose prominently to the surface of American public life at the drawing up of the Declaration of Independence, in the debates of the Constitutional Convention in Philadelphia, at the time of the Missouri Compromise, in the Age of Jackson with the rise of abolitionism, as an aspect of American expansion in the 1840's (to get bigger pens to cram with slaves), in the Compromise of 1850, and finally, and in crescendo, it dominated the whole of American politics (and much else) in the decade before the Civil War. It has left its legacy in race relations from Reconstruction days down to the contemporary scene.

And it is not enough to enumerate the great points of public, national controversy as has been done here. Slavery was a smoldering, ever-present provocation between the sections and between individuals in private life, a provocation that mounted in its intensity as slavery became, during the first half of the nineteenth century, more and more a uniquely American institution in the Western world. This gave rise, in the years before the Civil War, to one of the great classic debates on slavery resulting in the extreme positions of the proslavery arguments of George Fitzhugh and the abolitionism of William Lloyd Garrison. More or less, Americans have been arguing, researching, and agonizing the question ever since, and though the canon of scholarship on American Negro slavery is impressive, revisionism still goes forward. The emotional character of the subject has now sunk somewhat into the background, and one of the great difficulties in arriving at a judgment results from the fact that slaves rarely wrote letters or kept diaries.

Ulrich Bonnell Phillips (1877–1934), chiefly in two books, American Negro Slavery *(1918) and* Life and Labor in the Old South *(1929), presented an interpretation of American Negro slavery that had wide acceptance and is spread abroad in the pages of textbook and monographic literature dating from his generation to our own. Phillips' views gave, without approving slavery, a generally favorable and romantic view of the old plantation system. Richard Hofstadter, in an article critical of the selective nature of the sources Phillips used, yet declared: "So thorough was his work that, granted the same purpose, the same materials, and the same methods his treatment . . . is unlikely to be altered in fundamental respects." (Richard Hofstadter, "U. B. Phillips and the Plantation Legend,"* Journal of Negro History *XXIX (April 1944), 124). The first selection below is an example of Phillips' treatment of the characteristic topic of plantation labor.*

During the last three decades there has appeared a great deal of historical literature critical and revisionist of Phillips. (See Kenneth M. Stampp, "The Historian and Southern Negro Slavery," American Historical Review, LVII, (April 1952), 613–624). In the second essay presented below, Ruben F. Kugler questions not only Phillips' selection of sources but the use he made of those he selected, concluding that: "In general, it appears that Phillips did not comply with his own standards of scientific historical method described at the beginning of this article."

Plantation Labor

U. B. Phillips

While produced only in America, the plantation slave was a product of old-world forces. His nature was an African's profoundly modified but hardly transformed by the requirements of European civilization. The wrench from Africa and the subjection to the new discipline while uprooting his ancient language and customs had little more effect upon his temperament than upon his complexion. Ceasing to be Foulah, Coromantee, Ebo or Angola, he became instead the American negro. The Caucasion was also changed by the contact in a far from negligible degree; but the negro's conversion was much the more thorough, partly because the process in his case was coercive, partly because his genius was imitative.

The planters had a saying, always of course with an implicit reservation as to limits, that a negro was what a white man made him. The molding, however, was accomplished more by groups than by individuals. The purposes and policies of the masters were fairly uniform, and in consequence the negroes, though with many variants, became largely standardized into the predominant plantation type. The traits which prevailed were an eagerness for society, music and merriment, a fondness for display whether of person, dress, vocabulary or emotion, a not flagrant sensuality, a receptiveness toward any religion whose exercises were exhilarating, a proneness to superstition, a courteous acceptance of subordination, an avidity for praise, a readiness for loyalty of a feudal sort, and last but not least, a healthy human repugnance toward overwork. "It don't do no good to hurry," was a negro saying, " 'caze you're liable to run by mo'n you overtake." Likewise

From *American Negro Slavery* (New York: Appleton-Century, 1929, copyright 1918), pp. 291–308. Reprinted by permission.

painstaking was reckoned painful; and tomorrow was always waiting for today's work, while today was ready for tomorrow's share of play. On the other hand it was a satisfaction to work sturdily for a hard boss, and so be able to say in an interchange of amenities: "Go long, half-priced nigger! You wouldn't fotch fifty dollars, an' I'm wuth a thousand!" [1]

Contrasts were abundant. John B. Lamar, on the one hand, wrote: "My man Ned the carpenter is idle or nearly so at the plantation. He is fixing gates and, like the idle groom in Pickwick, trying to fool himself into the belief that he is doing something. . . . He is an eye servant. If I was with him I could have the work done soon and cheap; but I am afraid to trust him off where there is no one he fears." [2] On the other hand, M. W. Philips inscribed a page of his plantation diary as follows:[3]

Sunday
July 10, 1853
Peyton is no more
Aged 42
Though he was a bad man in many respects
yet he was a most excellent field
hand, always at his
post.
On this place for 21 years.
Except the measles and its sequence, the
injury rec'd by the mule last. Nov'r and its sequence,
he has not lost 15 days' work, I verily believe, in the
remaining 19 years. I wish we could hope for his
eternal state.

Should anyone in the twentieth century wish to see the old-fashioned prime negro at his best, let him take a Mississippi steamboat and watch the roustabouts at work—those chaffing and chattering, singing and swinging, lusty and willing freight handlers, whom a river captain plying out of New Orleans has called the noblest black men that God ever made.[4] Ready at every touching of the shore day and night, resting and sleeping only between landings, they carry their loads almost at running speed, and when returning for fresh burdens they "coonjine" by flinging their feet in semi-circles at every step, or cutting other capers in rhythm to show their fellows and the gallery that the strain of the cotton bales, the grain sacks, the oil barrels and the timbers merely loosen their muscles and lighten their spirits.

Such an exhibit would have been the despair of the average ante-bellum planter, for instead of choosing among hundreds of applicants and rejecting

---

[1] *Daily Tropic* (New Orleans), May 18, 1846.   [2] *Plantation and Frontier,* II, 38.

[3] Mississippi Historical Society *Publications,* X, 444.

[4] Captain L. V. Cooley, *Address Before the Tulane Society of Economics, New Orleans, April 11th, 1911, on River Transportation and Its Relation to New Orleans, Past, Present and Future.* [New Orleans, 1911.]

or discharging those who fell short of a high standard, he had to make shift with such laborers as the slave traders chanced to bring or as his women chanced to rear. His common problem was to get such income and comfort as he might from a parcel of the general run; and the creation of roustabout energy among them would require such vigor and such iron resolution on his own part as was forthcoming in extremely few cases.

Theoretically the master might be expected perhaps to expend the minimum possible to keep his slaves in strength, to discard the weaklings and the aged, to drive his gang early and late, to scourge the laggards hourly, to secure the whole with fetters by day and with bolts by night, and to keep them in perpetual terror of his wrath. But Olmsted, who seems to have gone South with the thought of finding some such theory in application, wrote: "I saw much more of what I had not anticipated and less of what I had in the slave states than, with a somewhat extended travelling experience, in any other country I ever visited";[5] and Nehemiah Adams, who went from Boston to Georgia prepared to weep with the slaves who wept, found himself laughing with the laughing ones instead.[6]

The theory of rigid coercion and complete exploitation was as strange to the bulk of the planters as the doctrine and practice of moderation was to those who viewed the régime from afar and with the mind's eye. A planter in explaining his mildness might well have said it was due to his being neither a knave nor a fool. He refrained from the use of fetters not so much because they would have hampered the slaves in their work as because the general use of them never crossed his mind. And since chains and bolts were out of the question, the whole system of control must be moderate; slaves must be impelled as little as possible by fear, and as much as might be by loyalty, pride and the prospect of reward.

Here and there a planter applied this policy in an exceptional degree. A certain Z. Kingsley followed it with marked success even when his whole force was of fresh Africans. In a pamphlet of the late eighteen-twenties he told of his method as follows: "About twenty-five years ago I settled a plantation on St. John's River in Florida with about fifty new negroes, many of whom I brought from the Coast myself. They were mostly fine young men and women, and nearly in equal numbers. I never interfered in their connubial concerns nor domestic affairs, but let them regulate these after their own manner. I taught them nothing but what was useful, and what I thought would add to their physical and moral happiness. I encouraged as much as possible dancing, merriment and dress, for which Saturday afternoon and night and Sunday morning were dedicated. [Part of their leisure] was usually employed in hoeing their corn and getting a supply of fish for the week. Both men and women were very industrious. Many of them made

---

[5] Olmsted, *Seaboard Slave States*, p. 179.

[6] Nehemiah Adams, *A Southside View of Slavery, or Three Months in the South in 1854* (Boston, 1854), chap. 2.

twenty bushels of corn to sell, and they vied with each other in dress and dancing. . . . They were perfectly honest and obedient, and appeared perfectly happy, having no fear but that of offending me; and I hardly ever had to apply other correction than shaming them. If I exceeded this, the punishment was quite light, for they hardly ever failed in doing their work well. My object was to excite their ambition and attachment by kindness, not to depress their spirits by fear and punishment. . . . Perfect confidence, friendship and good understanding reigned between us." During the War of 1812 most of these negroes were killed or carried off in a Seminole raid. When peace returned and Kingsley attempted to restore his Eden with a mixture of African and American negroes, a serpent entered in the guise of a negro preacher who taught the sinfulness of dancing, fishing on Sunday and eating the catfish which had no scales. In consequence the slaves "became poor, ragged, hungry and disconsolate. To steal from me was only to do justice—to take what belonged to them, because I kept them in unjust bondage." They came to believe "that all pastime or pleasure in this iniquitous world was sinful; that this was only a place of sorrow and repentance, and the sooner they were out of it the better; that they would then go to a good country where they would experience no want of anything, and have no work nor cruel taskmaster, for that God was merciful and would pardon any sin they committed; only it was necessary to pray and ask forgiveness, and have prayer meetings and contribute what they could to the church, etc. . . . Finally myself and the overseer became completely divested of all authority over the negroes. . . . Severity had no effect; it only made it worse." [7]

This experience left Kingsley undaunted in his belief that liberalism and profit-sharing were the soundest basis for the plantation régime. To support this contention further he cited an experiment by a South Carolinian who established four or five plantations in a group on Broad River, with a slave foreman on each and a single overseer with very limited functions over the whole. The cotton crop was the master's, while the hogs, corn and other produce belonged to the slaves for their sustenance and the sale of any surplus. The output proved large, "and the owner had no further trouble nor expense than furnishing the ordinary clothing and paying the overseer's wages, so that he could fairly be called free, seeing that he could realize his annual income wherever he chose to reside, without paying the customary homage to servitude of personal attendance on the operation of his slaves." In Kingsley's opinion the system "answered extremely well, and offers to us a strong case in favor of exciting ambition by cultivating utility, local attachment and moral improvement among the slaves." [8]

---

[7] [Z. Kingsley] *A Treatise on the Patriarchal System of Society as it exists . . . under the Name of Slavery.* By an inhabitant of Florida. Fourth edition (1834), pp. 21, 22. (Copy in the Library of Congress.)

[8] [Z. Kingsley] *Treatise,* p. 22.

The most thoroughgoing application on record of self-government by slaves is probably that of the brothers Joseph and Jefferson Davis on their plantations, Hurricane and Brierfield, in Warren County, Mississippi. There the slaves were not only encouraged to earn money for themselves in every way they might, but the discipline of the plantations was vested in courts composed wholly of slaves, proceeding formally and imposing penalties to be inflicted by slave constables except when the master intervened with his power of pardon. The régime was maintained for a number of years in full effect until in 1862 when the district was invaded by Federal troops.[9]

These several instances were of course exceptional, and they merely tend to counterbalance the examples of systematic severity at the other extreme. In general, though compulsion was always available in last resort, the relation of planter and slave was largely shaped by a sense of propriety, proportion and cooperation.

As to food, clothing and shelter, a few concrete items will reinforce the indications . . . that crude comfort was the rule. Bartram the naturalist observed in 1776 that a Georgia slaveholder with whom he stopped sold no dairy products from his forty cows in milk. The proprietor explained this by saying: "I have a considerable family of black people who though they are slaves must be fed and cared for. Those I have were either chosen for their good qualities or born in the family; and I find from long experience and observation that the better they are fed, clothed and treated, the more service and profit we may expect to derive from their labour. In short, I find my stock produces no more milk, or any article of food or nourishment, than what is expended to the best advantage amongst my family and slaves." At another place Bartram noted the arrival at a plantation of horse loads of wild pigeons taken by torchlight from their roosts in a neighboring swamp.[10]

On Charles Cotesworth Pinckney's two plantations on the South Carolina coast, as appears from his diary of 1818, a detail of four slaves was shifted from the field work each week for a useful holiday in angling for the huge drumfish which abounded in those waters; and their catches augmented the fare of the white and black families alike.[11] Game and fish, however, were extras. The staple meat was bacon, which combined the virtues of easy production, ready curing and constant savoriness. On Fowler's "Prairie" plantation, where the field hands numbered a little less than half a hundred, the pork harvest throughout the eighteen-fifties, except for a single year of hog cholera, yielded from eleven to twenty-three hundred pounds; and

---

[9] W. L. Fleming, "Jefferson Davis, the Negroes and the Negro Problem," in the *Sewanee Review* (October, 1908).

[10] William Bartram, *Travels* (London, 1792), pp. 307–310, 467, 468.

[11] *Plantation and Frontier*, I, 203–208.

when the yield was less than the normal, northwestern bacon or barreled pork made up the deficit.[12]

In the matter of clothing, James Habersham sent an order to London in 1764 on behalf of himself and two neighbors for 120 men's jackets and breeches and 80 women's gowns to be made in assorted sizes from strong and heavy cloth. The purpose was to clothe their slaves "a little better than common" and to save the trouble of making the garments at home.[13] In January, 1835, the overseer of one of the Telfair plantations reported that the woolen weaving had nearly supplied the full needs of the place at the rate of six or six and a half yards for each adult and proportionately for the children.[14] In 1847, in preparation for winter, Charles Manigault wrote from Paris to his overseer: "I wish you to count noses among the negroes and see how many jackets and trousers you want for the men at Gowrie, . . . and then write to Messrs. Matthiessen and Co. of Charleston to send them to you, together with the same quantity of twilled red flannel shirts, and a large woolen Scotch cap for each man and youth on the place. . . . Send back anything which is not first rate. You will get from Messrs. Habersham and Son the twilled wool and cotton, called by some 'Hazzard's cloth,' for all the women and children, and get two or three dozen handkerchiefs so as to give each woman and girl one. . . . The shoes you will procure as usual from Mr. Habersham by sending down the measures in time." [15] Finally, the register of A. L. Alexander's plantation in the Georgia Piedmont contains record of the distributions from 1851 to 1864 on a steady schedule. Every spring each man drew two cotton shirts and two pair of homespun woolen trousers, each woman a frock and chemises, and each child clothing or cloth in proportion; and every fall the men drew shirts, trousers and coats, the women shifts, petticoats, frocks and sacks, the children again on a similar scale, and the several families blankets as needed.[16]

As for housing, the vestiges of the old slave quarters, some of which have stood abandoned for half a century, denote in many cases a sounder construction and greater comfort than most of the negroes in freedom have since been able to command.

With physical comforts provided, the birth-rate would take care of itself. The pickaninnies were winsome, and their parents, free of expense and anxiety for their sustenance, could hardly have more of them than they wanted. A Virginian told Olmsted, "he never heard of babies coming so fast as they did on his plantation; it was perfectly surprising";[17] and in Georgia, Howell Cobb's negroes increased "like rabbits." [18] In Mississippi M. W. Philips' woman Amy had borne eleven children when at the age of thirty

---

[12] MS. records in the possession of W. H. Stovall, Stovall, Miss.

[13] *Plantation and Frontier*, I, 293, 294.   [14] *Ibid.*, 192, 193.

[15] MS. copy in Manigault's letter book.

[16] MS. in the possession of Mrs. J. F. Minis, Savannah, Ga.

[17] Olmsted, *Seaboard Slave States*, p. 57.   [18] *Plantation and Frontier*, I, 179.

she was married by her master to a new husband, and had eight more thereafter, including a set of triplets.[19] But the culminating instance is the following as reported by a newspaper at Lynchburg, Virginia: "VERY REMARKABLE. There is now living in the vicinity of Campbell a negro woman belonging to a gentleman by the name of Todd; this woman is in her forty-second year and has had forty-one children and at this time is pregnant with her forty-second child, and possibly with her forty-third, as she has frequently had doublets." [20] Had childbearing been regulated in the interest of the masters, Todd's woman would have had less than forty-one and Amy less than her nineteen, for such excesses impaired the vitality of the children. Most of Amy's, for example, died a few hours or days after birth.

A normal record is that of Fowler's plantation, the "Prairie." Virtually all of the adult slaves were paired as husbands and wives except Caroline who in twenty years bore ten children. Her husband was presumably the slave of some other master. Tom and Milly had nine children in eighteen years; Harry and Jainy had seven in twenty-two years; Fanny had five in seventeen years with Ben as the father of all but the first born; Louisa likewise had five in nineteen years with Bob as the father of all but the first; and Hector and Mary had five in seven years. On the other hand, two old couples and one in their thirties had had no children, while eight young pairs had from one to four each.[21] A lighter schedule was recorded on a Louisiana plantation called Bayou Cotonier, belonging to E. Tanneret, a Creole. The slaves listed in 1859 as being fifteen years old and upwards comprised thirty-six males and thirty-seven females. The "livre des naissances" showed fifty-six births between 1833 and 1859, distributed among twenty-three women, two of whom were still in their teens when the record ended. Rhodé bore six children between her seventeenth and thirty-fourth years; Henriette bore six between twenty-one and forty; Esther six between twenty-one and thirty-six; Fanny, four between twenty-five and thirty-two; Annette, four between thirty-three and forty; and the rest bore from one to three children each, including Celestine who had her first baby when fifteen and her second two years after. None of the matings or paternities appear in the record, though the christenings and the slave godparents are registered.[22]

The death rate was a subject of more active solicitude. This may be illustrated from the journal for 1859–1860 of the Magnolia plantation, forty miles below New Orleans. Along with its record of rations to 138 hands, and of the occasional births, deaths, runaways and recaptures, and of the purchase of a man slave for $2300, it contains the following summary under date of October 4, 1860: "We have had during the past eighteen months

---

[19] Mississippi Historical Society *Publications*, X, 439, 443, 447, 480.
[20] *Louisiana Gazette* (New Orleans), June 11, 1822, quoting the Lynchburg *Press*.
[21] MS. in the possession of W. H. Stovall, Stovall, Miss.
[22] MS. in the Howard Memorial Library, New Orleans.

over 150 cases of measles and numerous cases of whooping cough, and then the diphtheria, all of which we have gone through with but little loss save in the whooping cough when we lost some twelve children." This entry was in the spirit of rejoicing at escape from disasters. But on December 18 there were two items of another tone. One of these was entered by an overseer named Kellett: "[I] shot the negro boy Frank for attempting to cut at me and three boys with his cane knife with intent to kill." The other, in a different handwriting, recorded tersely: "J. A. Randall commenst buisnass this mornung. J. Kellett discharged this morning." The owner could not afford to keep an overseer who killed negroes even though it might be in self defence.[23]

Of epidemics, yellow fever was of minor concern as regards the slaves, for negroes were largely immune to it; but cholera sometimes threatened to exterminate the slaves and bankrupt their masters. After a visitation of this in and about New Orleans in 1832, John McDonogh wrote to a friend: "All that you have seen of yellow fever was nothing in comparison. It is supposed that five or six thousand souls, black and white, were carried off in fourteen days." [24] The pecuniary loss in Louisiana from slave deaths in that epidemic was estimated at four million dollars.[25] Two years afterward it raged in the Savannah neighborhood. On Mr. Wightman's plantation, ten miles above the city, there were in the first week of September fifty-three cases and eighteen deaths. The overseer then checked the spread by isolating the afflicted ones in the church, the barn and the mill. The neighboring planters awaited only the first appearance of the disease on their places to abandon their crops and hurry their slaves to lodges in the wilderness.[26] Plagues of smallpox were sometimes of similar dimensions.

Even without pestilence, deaths might bring a planter's ruin. A series of them drove M. W. Philips to exclaim in his plantation journal: "Oh! my losses almost make me crazy. God alone can help." In short, planters must guard their slaves' health and life as among the most vital of their own interests; for while crops were merely income, slaves were capital. The tendency appears to have been common, indeed, to employ free immigrant labor when available for such work as would involve strain and exposure. The documents bearing on this theme are scattering but convincing. Thus E. J. Forstall when writing in 1845 of the extension of the sugar fields, said thousands of Irishmen were seen in every direction digging plantation ditches;[27] T. B. Thorpe when describing plantation life on the Mississippi in 1853 said the Irish proved the best ditchers;[28] and a Georgia planter when describing his drainage of a swamp in 1855 said that Irish were hired

[23] MS. preserved on the plantation, owned by ex-Governor H. C. Warmoth.
[24] William Allen, *Life of John McDonogh* (Baltimore, 1886), p. 54.
[25] *Niles' Register*, XLV, 84.
[26] *Federal Union* (Milledgeville, Ga.), Sept. 14 and 17 and Oct. 22, 1834.
[27] Edward J. Forstall, *The Agricultural Productions of Louisiana* (New Orleans, 1845).
[28] *Harper's Magazine*, VII, 755.

for the work in order that the slaves might continue at their usual routine.[29] Olmsted noted on the Virginia seaboard that "Mr. W. . . . had an Irish gang draining for him by contract." Olmsted asked, "why he should employ Irishmen in preference to doing the work with his own hands. 'It's dangerous work,' the planter replied, 'and a negro's life is too valuable to be risked at it. If a negro dies, it is a considerable loss you know.' " [30] On a Louisiana plantation W. H. Russell wrote in 1860: "The labor of ditching, trenching, cleaning the waste lands and hewing down the forests is generally done by Irish laborers who travel about the country under contractors or are engaged by resident gangsmen for the task. Mr. Seal lamented the high prices of this work; but then, as he said, 'It was much better to have Irish do it, who cost nothing to the planter if they died, than to use up good field-hands in such severe employment.' " Russell added on his own score: "There is a wonderful mine of truth in this observation. Heaven knows how many poor Hibernians have been consumed and buried in these Louisianian swamps, leaving their earnings to the dramshop keeper and the contractor, and the results of their toil to the planter." On another plantation the same traveller was shown the débris left by the last Irish gang and was regaled by an account of the methods by which their contractor made them work.[31] Robert Russell made a similar observation on a plantation near New Orleans, and was told that even at high wages Irish laborers were advisable for the work because they would do twice as much ditching as would an equal number of negroes in the same time.[32] Furthermore, A. de Puy Van Buren, noted as a common sight in the Yazoo district, "especially in the ditching season, wandering 'exiles of Erin,' straggling along the road"; and remarked also that the Irish were the chief element among the straining roustabouts, on the steamboats of that day.[33] Likewise Olmsted noted on the Alabama River that in lading his boat with cotton from a towering bluff, a slave squad was appointed for the work at the top of the chute, while Irish deck hands were kept below to capture the wildly bounding bales and stow them. As to the reason for this division of labor and concentration of risk, the traveller had his own surmise confirmed when the captain answered his question by saying, "The niggers are worth too much to be risked here; if the Paddies are knocked overboard, or get their backs broke, nobody loses anything!" [34] To these chance observations it may be added that many newspaper items and canal and railroad company reports from the 'thirties to the 'fifties record that the construction gangs were largely of Irish and Germans. The pay attracted those whose labor

---

[29] *DeBow's Review*, XI, 401.   [30] Olmsted, *Seaboard Slave States*, pp. 90, 91.

[31] W. H. Russell, *My Diary North and South* (Boston, 1863), pp. 272, 273, 278.

[32] Robert Russell, *North America, Its Agriculture and Climate* (Edinburgh, 1857), p. 272.

[33] A. de Puy Van Buren, *Jottings of a Year's Sojourn in the South* (Battle Creek, Mich., 1859), pp. 84, 318.

[34] Olmsted, *Seaboard Slave States*, pp. 550, 551.

was their life; the risk repelled those whose labor was their capital. There can be no doubt that the planters cherished the lives of their slaves.

Truancy was a problem in somewhat the same class with disease, disability and death, since for industrial purposes a slave absent was no better than a slave sick, and a permanent escape was the equivalent of a death on the plantation. The character of the absconding was various. Some slaves merely took vacations without leave, some fled in postponement of threatened punishments, and most of the rest made resolute efforts to escape from bondage altogether.

Occasionally, however, a squad would strike in a body as a protest against severities. An episode of this sort was recounted in a letter of a Georgia overseer to his absent employer: "Sir: I write you a few lines in order to let you know that six of your hands has left the plantation—every man but Jack. They displeased me with their worke and I give some of them a few lashes, Tom with the rest. On Wednesday morning they were missing. I think they are lying out until they can see you or your uncle Jack, as he is expected daily. They may be gone off, or they may be lying round in this neighbourhood, but I don't know. I blame Tom for the whole. I don't think the rest would of left the plantation if Tom had not of persuaded them of for some design. I give Tom but a few licks, but if I ever get him in my power I will have satisfaction. There was a part of them had no cause for leaving, only they thought if they would all go it would injure me moore. They are as independent a set for running of as I have ever seen, and I think the cause is they have been treated too well. They want more whipping and no protecter; but if our country is so that negroes can quit their homes and run of when they please without being taken they will have the advantage of us. If they should come in I will write to you immediately and let you know." [35]

Such a case is analogous to that of wage-earning laborers on strike for better conditions of work. The slaves could not negotiate directly at such a time, but while they lay in the woods they might make overtures to the overseer through slaves on a neighboring plantation as to terms upon which they would return to work, or they might await their master's posthaste arrival and appeal to him for a redress of grievances. Humble as their demeanor might be, their power of renewing the pressure by repeating their flight could not be ignored. A happy ending for all concerned might be reached by mutual concessions and pledges. That the conclusion might be tragic is illustrated in a Louisiana instance where the plantation was in charge of a negro foreman. Eight slaves after lying out for some weeks because of his cruelty and finding their hardships in the swamp intolerable returned home together and proposed to go to work again if granted amnesty. When the

---

[35] Letter of I. E. H. Harvey, Jefferson County, Georgia, April 16, 1837, to H. C. Flournoy, Athens, Ga. MS. in private possession. Punctuation and capitals, which are conspicuously absent in the original, have here been supplied for the sake of clarity.

foreman promised a multitude of lashes instead, they killed him with their clubs. The eight then proceeded to the parish jail at Vidalia, told what they had done, and surrendered themselves. The coroner went to the plantation and found the foreman dead according to specifications.[36] The further history of the eight is unknown.

Most of the runaways went singly, but some of them went often. Such chronic offenders were likely to be given exemplary punishment when recaptured. In the earlier decades branding and shackling were fairly frequent. Some of the punishments were unquestionably barbarous, the more so when inflicted upon talented and sensitive mulattoes and quadroons who might be quite as fit for freedom as their masters. In the later period the more common resorts were to whipping, and particularly to sale. The menace of this last was shrewdly used by making a bogey man of the trader and a reputed hell on earth of any district whither he was supposed to carry his merchandise. "They are taking her to Georgia for to wear her life away" was a slave refrain welcome to the ears of masters outside that state; and the slanderous imputation gave no offence even to Georgians, for they recognized that the intention was benevolent, and they were in turn blackening the reputations of the more westerly states in the amiable purpose of keeping their own slaves content.

Virtually all the plantations whose records are available suffered more or less from truancy, and the abundance of newspaper advertisements for fugitives reinforces the impression that the need of deterrence was vital. Whippings, instead of proving a cure, might bring revenge in the form of sabotage, arson or murder. Adequacy in food, clothing and shelter might prove of no avail, for contentment must be mental as well as physical. The preventives mainly relied upon were holidays, gifts and festivities to create lightness of heart; overtime and overtask payments to promote zeal and satisfaction; kindliness and care to call forth loyalty in return; and the special device of crop patches to give every hand a stake in the plantation. This last raised a minor problem of its own, for if slaves were allowed to raise and sell the plantation staples, pilfering might be stimulated more than industry and punishments become more necessary than before. In the cotton belt a solution was found at last in nankeen cotton.[37] This variety had been widely grown for domestic use as early as the beginning of the nineteenth century, but it was left largely in neglect until when in the thirties it was hit upon for negro crops. While the prices it brought were about the same as those of the standard upland staple, its distinctive brown color prevented the admixture of the planter's own white variety without certain detection when it reached the gin. The scale which the slave crops attained on some plantations is indicated by the proceeds of $1,969.65 in 1859 from the nankeen of the negroes on the state of Allen McWalker in

---

[36] *Daily Delta* (New Orleans), April 17, 1849.
[37] John Drayton, *View of South Carolina* (Charleston, 1802), p. 128.

Taylor County, Georgia.[38] Such returns might be distributed in cash; but planters generally preferred for the sake of sobriety that money should not be freely handled by the slaves. Earnings as well as gifts were therefore likely to be issued in the form of tickets for merchandise. David Ross, for example, addressed the following to the firm of Allen and Ellis at Fredericksburg in the Christmas season of 1802: "Gentlemen: Please to let the bearer George have ten dollars value in anything he chooses"; and the merchants entered a memorandum that George chose two handkerchiefs, two hats, three and a half yards of linen, a pair of hose, and six shillings in cash.[39]

In general the most obvious way of preventing trouble was to avoid the occasion for it. If tasks were complained of as too heavy, the simplest recourse was to reduce the schedule. If jobs were slackly done, acquiescence was easier than correction. The easy-going and plausible disposition of the blacks conspired with the heat of the climate to soften the resolution of the whites and make them patient. Severe and unyielding requirements would keep everyone on edge; concession when accompanied with geniality and not indulged so far as to cause demoralization would make plantation life not only tolerable but charming.

In the actual régime severity was clearly the exception, and kindliness the rule. The Englishman Welby, for example, wrote in 1820: "After travelling through three slave states I am obliged to go back to theory to raise any abhorrence of it. Not once during the journey did I witness an instance of cruel treatment, nor could I discover anything to excite commiseration in the faces or gait of the people of colour. They walk, talk and appear at least as independent as their masters; in animal spirits they have greatly the advantage." [40] Basil Hall wrote in 1828: "I have no wish, God knows! to defend slavery in the abstract; . . . but . . . nothing during my recent journey gave me more satisfaction than the conclusion to which I was gradually brought that the planters of the Southern states of America, generally speaking, have a sincere desire to manage their estates with the least possible severity. I do not say that undue severity is nowhere exercised; but the discipline, taken upon the average, as far as I could learn, is not more strict than is necessary for the maintenance of a proper degree of authority, without which the whole framework of society in that quarter would be blown to atoms." [41] And Olmsted wrote: "The only whipping of slaves that I have seen in Virginia has been of these wild, lazy children as they are being broke in to work." [42]

---

[38] Macon, Ga., *Telegraph*, Feb. 3, 1859, quoted in *DeBow's Review*, XXIX, 362 note.

[39] MS. among the Allen and Ellis papers in the Library of Congress.

[40] Adlard Welby, *Visit to North America* (London, 1821), reprinted in Thwaites ed., *Early Western Travels*, XII, 289.

[41] Basil Hall, *Travels in the United States*, III, 227, 228.

[42] Olmsted, *Seaboard Slave States*, p. 146.

As to the rate and character of the work, Hall said that in contrast with the hustle prevailing on the Northern farms, "in Carolina all mankind appeared comparatively idle." [43] Olmsted, when citing a Virginian's remark that his negroes never worked enough to tire themselves, said on his own account: "This is just what I have thought when I have seen slaves at work —they seem to go through the motions of labor without putting strength into them. They keep their powers in reserve for their own use at night, perhaps." [44] And Solon Robinson reported tersely from a rice plantation that the negroes plied their hoes "at so slow a rate, the motion would have given a quick-working Yankee convulsions." [45]

There was clearly no general prevalence of severity and strain in the régime. There was, furthermore, little of that curse of impersonality and indifference which too commonly prevails in the factories of the present-day world where power-driven machinery sets the pace, where the employers have no relations with the employed outside of work hours, where the proprietors indeed are scattered to the four winds, where the directors confine their attention to finance, and where the one duty of the superintendent is to procure a maximum output at a minimum cost. No, the planters were commonly in residence, their slaves were their chief property to be conserved, and the slaves themselves would not permit indifference even if the masters were so disposed. The generality of the negroes insisted upon possessing and being possessed in a cordial but respectful intimacy. While by no means every plantation was an Arcadia there were many on which the industrial and racial relations deserved almost as glowing accounts as that which the Englishman William Faux wrote in 1819 of the "goodly plantation" of the venerable Mr. Mickle in the uplands of South Carolina.[46] "This gentleman," said he, "appears to me to be a rare example of pure and undefiled religion, kind and gentle in manners. . . . Seeing a swarm, or rather herd, of young negroes creeping and dancing about the door and yard of his mansion, all appearing healthy, happy and frolicsome and withal fat and decently clothed, both young and old, I felt induced to praise the economy under which they lived. 'Aye,' said he, 'I have many black people, but I have never bought nor sold any in my life. All that you see came to me with my estate by virtue of my father's will. They are all, old and young, true and faithful to my interests. They need no taskmaster, no overseer. They will do all and more than I expect them to do, and I can trust them with untold gold. All the adults are well instructed, and all are members of Christian churches in the neighborhood; and their conduct is becoming their professions. I respect them as my children, and they look on me as their friend and father. Were they to be taken from me it would be

---

[43] Basil Hall, III, 117.   [44] *Seaboard Slave States,* p. 91.
[45] *American Agriculturist,* IX, 93.
[46] William Faux, *Memorable Days in America* (London, 1823), p. 68, reprinted in Thwaites, ed., *Early Western Travels,* XI, 87.

the most unhappy event of their lives.' This conversation induced me to view more attentively the faces of the adult slaves; and I was astonished at the free, easy, sober, intelligent and thoughtful impression which such an economy as Mr. Mickle's had indelibly made on their countenances."

U. B. Phillips' Use of Sources

Ruben F. Kugler

Apparently, the debate among historians over the merits of the writings of Ulrich Bonnell Phillips (1877–1934) will continue as long as there is interest in the Civil War and subsequent racial issues. One reason for this debate is that Phillips has been considered the leading authority on slavery and the Southern plantation system.[1] Many textbook writers, for example, cite his works as the "standard" and "best" on slavery.[2] Donald Sheehan, who edited a collection of historical writings, wrote in this work:

> Probably Phillips is in no small way responsible for the now commonly held view that the slaves took kindly to their school [slavery] and that the schoolmasters [slaveholders] were as often fatherly as avaricious and more often indulgent than cruel.[3]

One reason for the authoritative position of Phillips' works is that they reflect extensive research, particularly on plantation records. As will be discussed below, however, recent criticism and findings have thrown doubt on his accuracy and objectivity. Did Phillips follow the scientific method in quoting and paraphrasing sources? This article will confine itself to this phase of his historical method, although criticism of historians on other aspects will be briefly mentioned.

From *Journal of Negro History*, XLVII (July 1962), 153–168. Reprinted by permission. Published by the Association for the Study of Negro Life and History, Inc.

[1] Frederick Jackson Turner, *The United States, 1830–1850; the Nation and Its Sections* (New York, 1935), p. 149 n. Ulrich B. Phillips, *The Course of the South to Secession* (New York, 1939), p. vii. E. Merton Coulter, the editor of this work by Phillips, wrote: "It is generally agreed that no one had a more thorough knowledge and a keener appreciation of the ante-bellum South than Ulrich Bonnell Phillips."

[2] Dumas Malone and Basil Rauch, *Empire for Liberty* (New York, 1960), I, 863. John Hicks, *A Short History of American Democracy* (Boston, 1946), p. 289 n. Leland Baldwin, *The Stream of American History* (New York, 1952), I, 170–71. Homer C. Hockett, *Political and Social Growth of the United States* (New York, 1935), p. 574. In each of seven libraries visited, this writer found additional examples.

[3] Donald Sheehan, ed., *The Making of American History* (New York, 1954), I, 324.

Throughout his career, Phillips espoused the scientific method. In one of his first works, he stated that he had attempted to exhaust the sources of his subject:

> It not difficult for one whose native environment is the Cotton Belt to orient himself into antebellum Georgia. I have made little use, however, of the historical imagination. The method is that of the investigator rather than the literary historian. The work is intended to be a thorough scientific treatment of its subject. No pains have been spared in obtaining exhaustive and accurate information.[4]

A decade later he wrote:

> The historian who would give a sound exposition of the great issues must be critically cognizant of all the doctrines influential in the period of which he treats; he must view them all as phenomena and be dominated by no one of them.[5]

Toward the end of his career he declared that his "fancy" was "restricted by records." [6]

Many reviewers could be quoted on their praise of Phillips' scholarship. For example, Theodore D. Jervey, who has written on slave history, stated that Phillips let the facts speak for themselves.[7] Ellis Merton Coulter, a prominent historian of Southern history, declared that Phillips became the greatest authority of his time in his field.[8] Others, historians such as Wood Gray, Thomas Pressly, Wendell H. Stephenson and Sam E. Salem, praised Phillips' contribution to his subject, but admitted his Southern self-consciousness.[9]

Inasmuch as few persons, except for concerned historians, are aware of the growing unfavorable criticism of Phillips' works, this article will dis-

---

[4] Ulrich B. Phillips, "Georgia and State Rights," *Annual Report of the American Historical Association for the Year 1901* (Washington, D. C., 1902), II, 5–6.

[5] Ulrich B. Phillips, "On the Economics of Slavery, 1815–1860," *Annual Report of the American Historical Association for the Year 1912* (Washington, D. C., 1914), p. 151.

[6] Ulrich B. Phillips, *Life and Labor in the Old South* (Boston, 1929), pp. vii–viii. Hereafter referred to as Phillips, *Life and Labor.* Ulrich B. Phillips, *American Negro Slavery* (New York, 1918), p. 514. Hereafter referred to as Phillips, *Slavery.*

[7] Theodore D. Jervey's review of Phillips, *Slavery,* in *American Historical Review,* XXV (October, 1919), 117–18. C. P. Patterson's review of Phillips, *Slavery,* in *Political Science Quarterly,* XXXIII (September, 1918), 454–56. William K. Boyd's review of Phillips, *Life and Labor,* in *American Historical Review,* XXXV (October, 1929), 133–35. For a listing of reviews see Everett E. Edwards, "A Bibliography of the Writings of Professor Ulrich Bonnell Phillips," *Agricultural History,* VIII (October, 1934), 196–218.

[8] E. Merton Coulter, "Ulrich Bonnell Phillips," *Dictionary of American Biography* (New York, 1944), suppl. I, 597.

[9] Wood Gray, "Ulrich Bonnell Phillips," William T. Hutchinson, ed., *Marcus W. Jernegan Essays in American Historiography* (Chicago, 1937), pp. 369–72. Thomas J. Pressly, *Americans Interpret Their Civil War* (Princeton, 1954), pp. 231–38. Sheehan, *The Making of American History,* I, 234. Wendell H. Stephenson, *The South Lives in History* (Baton Rouge, La., 1955), pp. 72–94. Sam E. Salem, "U. B. Phillips and the Scientific Tradition," *Georgia Historical Quarterly,* XLIV (June, 1960), 172–85.

cuss such disapproval in more detail than the favorable comments. In general, while some of the unfavorable critics lauded his pioneer contributions to the historiography of the plantation system, they indicated more or less disagreement with his subjective historical method.

Carter G. Woodson, former editor of the *Journal of Negro History*, was one of the few early critics of Phillips' first major writing on slavery, *American Negro Slavery* (1918). An unsigned review in this journal, which Dr. Woodson probably wrote, stated that a major defect of the book was "a failure to understand what the Negroes have thought and felt and done. . . ."[10] The *Mississippi Valley Historical Review* also printed a review by Woodson in 1919.[11]

Frederic Bancroft, specialist on Southern history, irritated by Phillips' bias and inaccuracies, produced in 1931 a scholarly study of slave-trading. Bancroft discovered that many farmers and planters had engaged in slave-trading, while *American Negro Slavery* claimed that professional slave-traders carried on almost all of this traffic.[12] As will be seen, in *Life and Labor in the Old South* (1929), Phillips admitted that many planters had engaged in slave-trading.

In 1944 Richard Hofstadter attacked Phillips' methodology. Hofstadter stated that Phillips had neglected the records of smaller slaveholders, and, instead, concentrated on the documents from large plantations. Hofstadter also declared that Phillips chose as examples of plantation rules those which were written by unusually kind planters.[13] Phillips, himself, had conceded in an early writing that such rules described a too idyllic view of the system. He wrote: "What they show in fact is rather the aspirations of the high class planters than the actuality on the average plantation." Later, when Phillips wrote *American Negro Slavery*, he quoted at length from the very plantation manuals which he had previously described as not showing typical conditions, and he failed to warn his readers against making sweeping generalizations therefrom.[14]

Kenneth M. Stampp, who had studied many kinds of original plantation

[10] Review of Phillips, *Slavery*, in *Journal of Negro History*, IV (January, 1919), 102–03. Dr. W. M. Brewer, editor of this journal, in a letter to this writer (9/12/61) wrote that he believed that Woodson wrote this review. Woodson's unsigned review shows a similarity of language used in his signed review cited below.

[11] Carter G. Woodson, review of Phillips, *Slavery*, in *Mississippi Valley Historical Review*, V (March, 1919), 480–82. W. E. B. DuBois wrote a similar review for the *American Political Science Review*, XII (November, 1918), 722–26.

[12] Frederic Bancroft, *Slave-Trading in the Old South* (Baltimore, 1931), pp. 24, 208, 213, 234–35 n, 283 n. For Bancroft's frank criticism of Phillips, see his letter to H. A. Traxler, October 23, 1929, in Jacob E. Cooke, *Frederic Bancroft, Historian* (Norman, Okla., 1957), p. 120. Cooke's book is an extended evaluation of Bancroft.

[13] Richard Hofstadter, "U. B. Phillips and the Plantation Legend," *Journal of Negro History*, XXXIX (April, 1944), 109–24.

[14] John R. Commons, Ulrich B. Phillips, *et al.*, eds., *A Documentary History of American Industrial Society* (Cleveland, Ohio, 1910), I, 98–99, 109–30. Phillips, *Slavery*, pp. 261–88, 306–07. Phillips, *Life and Labor*, pp. 214, 323.

records, pointed out that planters would demand more work from slaves than their instructions to overseers indicated. Stampp granted that some slaves, particularly domestic servants, may not have exerted themselves unduly. "From these models," he wrote, "proslavery writers drew their sentimental pictures of slave life." He charged that "their profound error was in generalizing from them." [15] This, as shown above, was the error which Hofstadter attributed to Phillips.

In 1948 John Hope Franklin challenged Phillips' interpretation of slave history and declared that he tended to apologize for that institution.[16] Michael Kraus expressed mixed feelings about Phillips in his 1953 historiographical work. In a history of the United States published six years later, Kraus made the following bibliographical note:

> U. B. Phillips, *Life and Labor in the Old South* (Boston, 1929) is the culmination of long, though not always critical, study. Frederic Bancroft, *Slave-Trading in the Old South* (Baltimore, Md.: T. H. Furst Co., 1931) is good. K. M. Stampp, *The Peculiar Institution* (New York: Knopf, 1956) is a splendid re-examination of slave society.[17]

Kenneth M. Stampp, University of California (Berkeley) historian, stated in his 1952 article in the *American Historical Review* that Phillips' writings were based on his belief in the inherent inferiority of the Negro.[18] Stampp's *The Peculiar Institution: Slavery in the Ante-Bellum South* (1956) cited much evidence—using some of Phillips' sources—to support anti-slavery interpretations.

Writing for the *Saturday Review*, Clement Eaton expressed his belief that *The Peculiar Institution* judged slavery too harshly, although Eaton praised Stampp's research into primary sources. Eaton apparently supported Phillips' belief in the masters' kind treatment of their slaves. Frank W. Klingberg's review in the *American Historical Review* (October, 1957) generally praised Stampp's book, and stated that it would inevitably be compared with Phillips' *American Negro Slavery*.[19]

---

[15] Kenneth M. Stampp, *The Peculiar Institution: Slavery in the Ante-Bellum South* (New York, 1956), pp. 77, 80. Phillips quoted from the rules of James H. Hammond, who instructed his overseer not to punish severely. (Phillips, *Slavery*, p. 274.) The writer has a photostat of a letter written by Hammond, which indicated that he used severe methods to break in his slaves. Phillips did not quote this letter: James H. Hammond, letter to Walker, Rome, Italy, Dec. 27, 1836, in James H. Hammond Papers, Library of Congress. Walker, whose first name is not given, was one of Hammond's overseers.

[16] John Hope Franklin, *From Slavery to Freedom* (New York, 1948), pp. 194–95, 602–03.

[17] Michael Kraus, *The Writing of American History* (Norman, Okla., 1953), p. 308. Michael Kraus, *The United States to 1865* (Ann Arbor, Mich., 1959), p. 526.

[18] Kenneth M. Stampp, "The Historian and Southern Negro Slavery," *American Historical Review*, LXII (April, 1952), 619–20. Stampp, *Peculiar Institution*, pp. 8–9.

[19] Clement Eaton, review of Stampp, *Peculiar Institution*, in *Saturday Review*, XXXIX (September 22, 1956), 24. Frank W. Klingberg, review of Stampp, *Peculiar Institution*, in *American Historical Review*, LXIII (October, 1957), 139–40.

In 1959 Stanley Elkins' work on slavery, although giving Phillips credit for his contributions to the subject, criticized his biased approach. Elkins pointed out that a pro-Stampp trend was supplanting Phillips as the authority on slavery.[20] A Library of Congress bibliography on the history of the United States made essentially the same statement as did Elkins in regard to the ascendancy of Stampp.[21]

In his historiographical study (1960), Harvey Wish wrote about Phillips:

> Among his shortcomings was that he ordered his evidence in such a way as to justify slavery; the initial sin of the slave trade had been committed [not by slaveholders but] by others. . . . The case of Ulrich B. Phillips illustrates how the subjective values of a historian may neutralize the most meticulous empirical research.[22]

C. Vann Woodward, a Southern historian, criticized (1960) Phillips' preoccupation with race consciousness. Woodward wrote that Phillips believed that the central theme of Southern history was the resolve that the South "shall be and remain a white man's country," to use Phillips' words. Woodward also stated that the Plantation Legend, which held that the antebellum plantation was a paternalistic institution designed to civilize the Negro, had suffered irreparable damage.[23]

The first edition of the American Historical Association, *Guide to Historical Literature* (1931), had praised Phillips' *American Negro Slavery* as the "best," "fair," and "accurate" work in its field.[24] The 1961 edition of the A. H. A.'s *Guide* apparently reflects recent criticism of Phillips by dropping these laudatory adjectives. This 1961 evaluation states the following: "This work, by one of the most learned students of the old South, is considered traditional in its interpretation of slavery, particularly in ascribing to the plantation a civilizing influence on the lives of Negroes." [25] The *Guide,* however, repeated its praise of *Life and Labor in the Old South.*

The second edition of a widely used college textbook, James G. Randall and David Donald, *The Civil War and Reconstruction* (Boston, 1961), contains the following in its bibliographical essay:

> For many years the standard history of slavery was Ulrich B. Phillips, *American Negro Slavery* (1918), a work based on vast research and

[20] Stanley Elkins, *Slavery* (Chicago, 1959), p. 20.

[21] U. S. Library of Congress, *A Guide to the Study of the United States of America* (Washington, D. C., 1960), p. 380.

[22] Harvey Wish, *The American Historian* . . . (New York, 1960), pp. 254–55.

[23] C. Vann Woodward, *The Burden of Southern History* (Baton Rouge, La., 1960), pp. 9–13. U. B. Phillips, "The Central Theme of Southern History," *American Historical Review,* XXXIV (October, 1928), 30–31.

[24] American Historical Association, *A Guide to Historical Literature,* edited by George M. Dutcher, *et al.* (New York, 1931), p. 1040.

[25] American Historical Association, *Guide to Historical Literature* (New York, 1961), pp. 725–26.

characterized by sympathy toward the slaveholders. . . . In recent years Phillips' views have come increasingly under attack, and Kenneth M. Stampp's authoritative *The Peculiar Institution* (1956) is a thorough-going refutation from a pronounced Northern point of view.[26]

David Donald, who revised this work and wrote the bibliographical essay, was born and raised in Mississippi but has taught mainly in Northern institutions.

The bulk of this article shows the results of a check made of them. This paper will analyze eight examples of his methods of quoting and paraphrasing sources: the first four touch on conditions of slavery, and the last four concern the Negroes' attitudes toward their bondage. The reader should keep in mind that, inasmuch as this is a limited methodological study, he should not expect a comprehensive analysis of Phillips' interpretation of slavery.

In the first example, Phillips cited sources which did not support the statements which he apparently obtained from them. The second chapter of *American Negro Slavery*, entitled "The Maritime Slave Trade," while admitting some of the deplorable conditions of the slave transport from Africa, painted a brighter picture of that traffic than most historians have done. Phillips wrote, in regard to the slave ships, that "the food if coarse was generally plenteous and wholesome, and the sanitation fairly adequate." He cited as evidence for this paragraph two summaries of a British Parliamentary investigation by W. O. Blake and Thomas Buxton; he did not, however, cite any pages in these two sources.[27] Phillips cited only chapters.

The writer could find nothing in Blake's and Buxton's writings which supported Phillips' generalizations on food and sanitation. As a matter of fact, both works reveal much worse conditions than Phillips described. Buxton quoted Falconbridge, a witness, who testified: "Numberless quarrels take place among them [the slaves] during their meals; more especially when they are put upon short allowance, which frequently happens." Both Buxton and Blake related the testimony of other witnesses who reported the lack of fresh air and other inadequacies resulting in sickness and filthy conditions. Slave-dealers estimated that the average ship lost nearly one-third of its cargo; some ships arrived with only half of the original number of Africans alive.[28] It would seem that Phillips' own opinion of the slave trade prevented his accurate reading of Blake and Buxton.

---

[26] James G. Randall and David Donald, *The Civil War and Reconstruction* (Boston, 1961), 2d ed., p. 743. See also David Donald's review of Stampp, *Peculiar Institution* in *Commentary*, XXII (December, 1956), 582–85, wherein Donald has both praised and found fault with Stampp's work.

[27] Phillips, *Slavery*, p. 37.

[28] Thomas F. Buxton, *The African Slave Trade and Its Remedy* (London, 1840), pp. 125, 172–74. W. O. Blake, *The History of Slavery and the Slave Trade . . .* (Columbus, Ohio, 1859), pp. 126–42.

Another example of such misreading is his use of Fredrika (sometimes spelled Frederika) Bremer's writings. She was a Swedish novelist who visited the ante-bellum South. Phillips wrote in his *Life and Labor in the Old South:* "Frederika Bremer had virtually nothing but praise for the slave quarters she visited or their savory food which she tasted." [29]

While Bremer found that some of the food given to slaves was better than she had expected, Phillips did not quote her description of a planter's provisions for the old and sick:

> Deeper down in the wood I saw a slave village, or houses resembling one, but which had an unusually irregular and tumble-down appearance. . . . I found the houses actually in the most decayed and deplorable condition, and in one house old and sickly negroes, men and women. In one room I saw a young lad very much swollen, as if with dropsy; the rain and wind could enter by the roof; everything was naked in the room; neither fire-wood nor fire was there, although the day was chilly. In another wretched house we saw an old woman lying among rags as in a dog-kennel.[30]

Elsewhere she saw better quarters, but the complete reading of her book makes it clear that Phillips misread it; rather than "praise" she had virtually nothing but condemnation for the institution of slavery.

By presenting Bremer's observations as he did—incompletely and inaccurately—Phillips gave the reader the incorrect impression that Bremer found that the lot of the Negro under slavery was satisfactory. In her travels she found much she loved about the South, but not its peculiar institution. The effect of the slave-trade upon children horrified her. An overseer told her that masters insisted that overseers whip the slaves in order to force them to work as they "ought." A Mississippi planter admitted that most slave-holders were not good or tender toward their slaves; passion and insanity commonly prevailed in the treatment of bondsmen.[31] Phillips did not quote any of these unpleasant facts observed by Bremer.

Another example of giving the reader an incorrect impression is seen in the manner in which Phillips quoted Frederick Law Olmsted. Olmsted was a Northerner who traveled extensively in the South. By quoting Olmsted out of context, Phillips was able to draw a conclusion which supported a pro-slavery interpretation. Phillips wrote:

> With physical comforts provided, the birth-rate would take care of itself. The pickaninnies were winsome, and their parents, free of expense and anxiety for their sustenance, could hardly have more of them than they wanted.[32]

---

[29] Phillips, *Life and Labor*, p. 214.

[30] Fredrika Bremer, *The Homes of the New World* (New York, 1854), I, 293–94. Phillips' citation in Bremer was to "I, 293 *et passim*."

[31] *Ibid.*, I, 366–67, 373; II, 188–90. Stampp, *Peculiar Institution, op. cit.*, p. 295, quoted Bremer as finding slave quarters "in the most decayed and deplorable condition."

[32] Phillips, *Slavery*, p. 298.

By not quoting Olmsted's complete story, Phillips left an inaccurate impression of the facts. Phillips' version, quoted in the left-hand column, should be compared with the more complete passage as Olmsted himself told it:

Phillips, *Slavery*, p. 298:

[The above quotation from Phillips about slave parents being free from anxiety introduced the following:]

A Virginian told Olmsted, "he never heard of babies coming so fast as they did on his plantation; it was perfectly surprising";[17] and in Georgia, Howell Cobb's negroes increased "like rabbits." [18] [Phillips' 17th citation referred to Olmsted, p. 57; the 18th citation was to another source.]

Olmsted, *Seaboard Slave States,* pp. 57–58:

But this proportion was somewhat smaller than usual, he [the Virginian] added, "because his women were uncommonly good breeders; he did not suppose that there was a lot of women anywhere that bred faster than his; he never heard of babies coming so fast as they did on his plantation; it was perfectly surprising; and every one of them, in his estimation was worth two hundred dollars, as negroes were selling now, the moment it drew breath."

Phillips also omitted the further remarks of the Virginian who told Olmsted that he intended to sell his slaves in Louisiana, Texas or California— depending on where he could get the highest price. In Stampp's *Peculiar Institution,* this same passage in Olmsted is cited with the inclusion of the significant words omitted by Phillips. It becomes obvious, after comparing Stampp's and Phillips' use of Olmsted, that the full text in Olmsted supports Stampp's but not Phillips' conclusion therefrom.[33]

Phillips' *Life and Labor in the Old South,* unlike his *American Negro Slavery,* admitted some of the slave-trading activities of planters. In the former work, Phillips wrote:

> The social stigma laid upon them [the slave-traders] can hardly have been so stringent as tradition tells, for many a planter and perhaps most of the general merchants turned a trade on favorable occasion, and sundry citizens of solid worth and esteem can be identified as regular participants.[34]

Life and Labor in the Old South, however, followed *American Negro Slavery* in giving an inaccurate impression of the slave-trading firm of Franklin and Armfield by not quoting a key source completely. Phillips used as his main source of information on this company the work of E. A. Andrews, a Northerner who went South to study slavery in behalf of the

---

[33] Stampp, *Peculiar Institution*, p. 246. Both Stampp and Phillips cited the same page in Frederick Law Olmsted, *A Journey in the Seaboard Slave States* (New York, 1856), p. 57.

[34] Phillips, *Life and Labor*, p. 158.

American Union for the Relief and Improvement of the Colored Race.

In *American Negro Slavery* Phillips devoted almost a page to Andrews' description of the slave pen of Franklin and Armfield. On the whole, it appeared that, according to Phillips, Andrews liked what he saw there. A similar incorrect impression is given in *Life and Labor in the Old South*:

> The clearest account of this traffic at large is by E. A. Andrews, *Slavery and the Domestic Slavetrade* (Boston, 1836), describing particularly the well-ordered assembling house of Franklin and Armfield at Alexandria, Virginia.[35]

Reading the full account in Andrews' work, however, reveals that Andrews did not like what he saw at Alexandria. While Armfield's assistant was telling Andrews about the happy condition of the inmates, one of the slaves looked earnestly at Andrews,

> and as often as the keeper turned away his face, he shook his head, and seemed desirous of having me understand, that he did not feel any such happiness as was described, and that he dissented from the representation made of his condition.[36]

Phillips did not quote the above nor Andrews' statement that the female quarters had a neat and comfortable appearance "for a prison." Andrews wrote:

> In most respects, however, the situation of the convicts at the penitentiary was far less deplorable than that of these slaves, confined for the crime of being descended from ancestors who were forcibly reduced to bondage.

Phillips also failed to quote Andrews' conclusion:

> After resting myself a few minutes, I took leave of Mr. Armfield and of his establishment, and returned to my lodging in the city, ruminating, as I went, upon the countless evils, which "man's inhumanity to man," has occasioned in this world of sin and misery.[37]

When one reads Andrews' book, it is evident that Phillips failed to inform the reader of the important passages in Andrews. Frederic Bancroft, who cited the same passage in Andrews, quoted the significant lines omitted by Phillips. The full text in Andrews' work supports Bancroft's conclusion; it does not support Phillips' interpretation which gave the incorrect impression that Andrews had a favorable opinion of Franklin and Armfield.[38]

---

[35] Phillips, *Slavery*, pp. 194–95; Phillips, *Life and Labor*, p. 155 n.
[36] E. A. Andrews, *Slavery and the Domestic Slave-Trade in the United States* (Boston, 1836), p. 138.
[37] *Ibid.*, pp. 141–43.
[38] Bancroft, *Slave-Trading*, pp. 26 n., 55, 59–62, 207.

In another case, Phillips omitted a significant phrase from an article by Judge J. B. O'Neall, although he did show the omission with ellipses. This South Carolina judge wrote a legal analysis of slavery published before the Civil War. Phillips quoted him as follows, with the exception of the italicized words:

> Experience and observation fully satisfy me that the first law of slavery is that of kindness from the master to the slave. With that *properly inculcated, enforced by law and judiciously applied,* slavery becomes a family relation, next in its attachment to that of parent and child.[39] [Italics not in original]

Without the phrase "enforced by law," the reader is given the impression that the Judge believed that slavery was generally a paternalistic relationship without legal enforcement. If, however, one reads the entire article by Judge O'Neall, it is evident that he held a different opinion.

O'Neall pointed out that South Carolina law required slaveholders to provide their bondsmen with sufficient clothing, housing and food. Then he commented: "I regret to say, *that there is, in such a state as ours,* great occasion for the enforcement of such a law, *accompanied by severe penalties.*" (Italics in the original.) The Judge told of the frequent changes of masters resulting in rending of family ties, he cited laws which did not punish severely enough those who tortured and killed slaves, and he objected to legislation which forbade the education of slaves.[40] None of this is mentioned by Phillips. If he had not omitted from his quotation of O'Neall the phrase "enforced by law" and had summarized the article, this source would then be seen as evidence against his argument that slavery was a patriarchal institution.[41]

Phillips paraphrased inaccurately in his use of another source. In *American Negro Slavery,* the chapter, "Types of Large Plantations," summarized the findings of Fanny Kemble, the English actress who married Pierce Butler, a Georgia planter. Phillips concluded, on the basis of her journal, that she found that the "swarms of negroes were stupid. . . ." [42] Phillips did not cite any pages for this reference. In turning to the source of this information, *Journal of a Residence on a Georgian Plantation in 1838–1839,* one finds instead that Fanny Kemble did not hold the opinion which Phillips ascribed to her. She wrote that, if the laws allowed slaves to read books, they "would seize them with avidity—receive them gladly, comprehend them quickly; and the masters' powers over them would be an-

---

[39] Phillips, *Slavery,* p. 513, quoting J. B. O'Neall, in J. D. B. DeBow, *The Industrial Resources* . . . (New Orleans, 1852), II, 278.

[40] DeBow, *Industrial Resources,* II, 276–79. Bancroft, *Slave-Trading,* p. 200 n, quoted a passage from O'Neall about the "rending of family ties. . . ."

[41] Phillips, *Slavery,* pp. 306–07, 327, 514. Phillips, "Georgia and State Rights," *loc. cit.,* II, 154. Phillips, *Course of the South to Secession,* p. 125.

[42] Phillips, *Slavery,* p. 251.

nihilated at once and forever." She also declared that "if they are incapable of profiting by instruction, I do not see the necessity for laws inflicting heavy penalties on those who offer it to them." [43] It would seem that Phillips allowed his own opinion of the mentality of Negroes to color his summary of Fanny Kemble's experiences.[44]

In another instance of misreading Olmsted, Phillips used a story told to Olmsted by the executor of an estate. The executor related how a lazy slave became energetic when promised that he could buy his freedom by performing extra work. Phillips told only that part of the story in which the freed Negro went North, did not like it there and returned to Virginia. By not completing the tale, Phillips' version made it appear that the ex-slave preferred slavery to freedom. A reading of the complete narrative in Olmsted reveals that the Negro did not return to his ex-master (the executor); actually, he went to a nearby place to work for wages. Compare Phillips' account in the left-hand column with Olmsted's telling:

Phillips, *Slavery*, p. 440:

And at Richmond Olmsted learned of a negro who after buying his freedom had gone to Philadelphia to join his brother, but had promptly returned. When questioned by his former owner [the executor] this man said: "Oh, I don't like dat Philadelphy, massa; ant no chance for colored folks dere; spec' if I'd been a runaway de wite folk dere take care o' me; but I couldn't git anythin' to do, so I jis borrow ten dollar of my broder an' cum back to old Virginny."

Olmsted, *Seaboard Slave States*, pp. 103–04:

[Phillips' version in the left column is part of the story, but he did not quote the following ending]:

"But you know [said the executor] the law forbids your return. I wonder that you are not afraid to be seen here; I should think Mr. —— (an officer of police) would take you up."

"Oh! I look out for dat, Massr, I juss hire myself out to Mr. —— himself, ha! ha! He tink I your boy."

By not quoting the pertinent facts in the beginning of Olmsted's story and by deleting the ending, Phillips minimized this Negro's antipathy toward slavery. Phillips, as shown by the use he made of this story, turned it into an argument against the North in respect to its treatment of Negroes. This may be an example of what psychologists call projection. In addition, he failed to point up Olmsted's sub-title of the account: "Ingenuity of the Negro." [45]

---

[43] Frances Anne Kemble, *Journal of a Residence on a Georgian Plantation in 1838–1839* (New York, 1863), pp. 8–9.

[44] The following works reveal aspects of Phillips' racial beliefs: U. B. Phillips, "The Economic Cost of Slaveholding in the Cotton Belt," *Political Science Quarterly*, XX (June, 1905), 257–59. Phillips, *Slavery*, pp. viii, 339–43. Phillips, *Life and Labor*, pp. 261–66.

[45] Olmsted, *Seaboard Slave States*, p. 103.

The eighth and last example of subjectivity illustrates one-sided selection of passages. Concerning the feelings of recently enslaved Africans, Phillips wrote in his *American Negro Slavery:* "That by no means all the negroes took their enslavement grievously is suggested by a traveler's note at Columbia, South Carolina, in 1806." The traveler, Edward Hooker, an attorney, was told upon inquiry of a sixteen year old slave that he saw no injustice in being enslaved.[46]

Phillips did not question the probability that this "bright" Negro replied to the question about his feelings toward slavery in such a manner as to avoid punishment for insubordination. The same page in Hooker contains a report of recent rumors and fears of a slave insurrection, and the killing of a slave who was perhaps falsely suspected of plotting the revolt. Would a bright slave, knowing of such events, complain to a white man about mistreatment? Also it seems that Phillips, by inferring that an appreciable number of Africans saw no injustice in being enslaved, drew an illogical conclusion. The writer found similar examples in which Phillips quoted sources in a one-sided manner.[47] This subjective method revealed a pattern of selection in which he would often cite pro-slavery passages, while ignoring anti-slavery findings related to the same incident sometimes located on the same page.

Allowing for some unavoidable subjectivity, the writings of a leading authority should demonstrate more consistency than Phillips' writings did. Of course, in order to make a definitive judgment on his works, one would need more instances of misused sources than have been presented in this article. The writer believes, however, that the criticisms of the historians cited above, as well as the eight examples of unbalanced selection, misquoting and inaccurate paraphrasing, raise a strong doubt in regard to the objectivity of Phillips' works.

It has been seen that Phillips cited three writers (Blake, Buxton and Bremer) to support an interpretation which their writings did not support. He quoted Olmsted out of context, and he left out a key phrase from a sentence in Judge O'Neall's article. A reading of that article in full re-

---

[46] Edward Hooker, "Diary of Edward Hooker," in *Annual Report of the American Historical Association for the Year 1896* (Washington, D. C., 1897), I, 882. Phillips, *Slavery*, p. 42 n, incorrectly cited the A. H. A. report for 1906.

[47] Compare Phillips, *Slavery*, p. 287, with Harriet Martineau, *Society in America* (London, 1837), II, 315–17, 320–21; cf. Phillips, *Slavery*, p. 241, with Estwick Evans, "A Pedestrious Tour . . . ," in Reuben G. Thwaites, ed., *Early Western Travels, 1748–1846* (Cleveland, 1904), VIII, 325–26, 332; cf. Phillips, *Slavery*, pp. 324–25, and Phillips, *Life and Labor*, pp. 219, 222–28, with Philip Vickers Fithian, *Journal and Letters, 1767–1774* (Princeton, 1900), pp. 68–69, 128–32, 248, 279, 287; cf. Phillips, *Slavery*, p. 129, with Max Farrand, ed., *The Records of the Federal Convention of 1787* (New Haven, 1911–12), II, 369–70; cf. Phillips, *Slavery*, p. 307, with William Faux, *"Memorable Days in America* . . . ," in Reuben G. Thwaites, ed., *Early Western Travels* (Cleveland, 1905), XI, 62, 74, 77, 80, 91 ff. Phillips often fell into methodological errors in his unrepresentative selections from Olmsted; random choices from the citations in *American Negro Slavery* will reveal this.

veals the significance of the omitted phrase. In his use of Olmsted, Kemble and Andrews, Phillips left the reader with incorrect impressions regarding their findings and opinions. On the basis of a single incident, which he found in Hooker, he made a sweeping generalization; furthermore, on the same page in Hooker there is contrary evidence which Phillips omitted. Phillips committed another type of methodological error when he used Blake, Buxton and Kemble without citing pages therein. In general, it appears that Phillips did not comply with his own standards of the scientific historical method described at the beginning of this article.

XIII

The Jacksonians and the Bank: Democrats in Principle or Democrats by Trade?

INTRODUCTION

The brilliant Age of Jackson and the provocative figure of the President himself have challenged the imagination of historians from James Parton, his first biographer, to the present-day "urban school" of historians.[1] More and more the issue of the "killing" of the Second Bank of the United States by Jackson and his party appears as the most comprehensive single issue of the period. Around it are grouped and focused the strongest political, economic, social, and even cultural ideologies and folklore of the day.

On the bank issue, there developed in the Democratic Party two divergent points of view. There was the hard-money, loco-foco, left wing of the party: "Its aim was to clip the wings of commerce and finance by restricting the credit that paper money enabled them to obtain. There would be no vast debt, no inflation, no demoralizing price changes; there would be no fluctuant or disappearing values and no grinding poverty. The precious metals would impose an automatic and uncompromising limit on the volatile tendencies of trade."[2] The members of this wing of the party were known as "Democrats in principle."

The other wing of the party represented the new laissez faire, democratized, acquisitive business interest. It was quite un-Hamiltonian in its outlook and its ambitions: "Its strength lay with free enterprise, that is with the new generation of businessmen, promoters, and speculators, who found the old Hamiltonian order of the Federalists too stodgy and confining."[3] These were "Democrats by trade."

The first selection below from Arthur M. Schlesinger, Jr., The Age of Jackson *(1945), contends that the hard-money doctrine appealed primarily not to the frontier but "to the submerged classes of the East and to the farmers of the South" and that this doctrine "was the controlling policy of the administration from the winter of 1833 on." Bray Hammond in his recent Pulitzer prize-winning* Banks and Politics in America *(1957), from which the second selection is taken, strongly rejects this interpretation and argues that the dominating group among the Jacksonians were "Democrats by trade" rather than Schlesinger's "Democrats in principle" and that the former, "though their cause was a sophisticated one of enterpriser against capitalist, of banker against regulation, and of Wall Street against Chestnut, the language was the same as if they were all back on the farm."*

---

[1] C. G. Sellers, "Andrew Jackson versus the Historians," *Mississippi Valley Historical Review,* XLIV (1958), 615–634.

[2] Bray Hammond, "Jackson, Biddle, and the Bank of the United States," *Journal of Economic History,* VII (May 1947), 6.

[3] *Ibid.,* p. 6.

Hard Money

Arthur M. Schlesinger, Jr.

The determination which enabled Jackson to resist the hysteria of panic came basically from the possession of an alternative policy of his own. Madison had surrendered to a corresponding, though less intense, pressure in 1816 because he had no constructive program to offer. But, for Jackson, the emotions and ideas which underlay the hard-money case against the Bank were crystallizing into a coherent and concrete set of measures, designed to capture the government for "the humble members of society," as Hamilton's system had captured it for "the rich and powerful."

1

The Jeffersonian tradition provided the main inspiration for this program. The Virginia condemnation of paper money, pronounced by Jefferson, formulated profoundly by Taylor, kept pure and uncompromising by Macon and Randolph, had passed on as a vital ideological legacy to Jackson, Benton, Van Buren, Polk, Cambreleng. Yet it was handed down as a series of keen but despairing criticisms delivered in the shadow of an invincible industrialism. The creative statesmen of the Jackson administration now proposed to transform it into a positive governmental policy.

The Bank War played an indispensable role in the precipitation of hard-money ideas. It dramatized currency questions in a way which captured the imagination of the people and excited their desire for further action on the financial front. It enlisted the enthusiasm of intellectuals, stimulating them to further analysis, widening the range and competence of economic theory. It tightened class lines, and the new bitterness of feeling sharpened the intellectual weapons.

Above all, the Bank War triumphantly established Jackson in the confidence of the people. Their faith in him had survived ordeals and won vindication: thereafter, when faced by a choice between Jackson and a cherished policy, most of them would choose Jackson. The effect of this mandate was particularly to sell the West on an intricate economic program, which many Westerners did not understand and which ran counter to their preconceptions.

The uncertainty about the West had postponed the avowal of the hard-money system.[1] The veto message, written by three men of known hard-money convictions, Jackson, Taney and Kendall, suppressed mention of the doctrine, as if by main force. But the election of 1832 increased Jackson's confidence. He could have lost the entire West and still have broken even with Clay, but he carried the whole West except for Kentucky.[2] He now felt certain of vigorous national support, and also of probable Western support, even for his economic ideas. Not all the West would follow, of course, and even three leaders from his own state turned against him on the currency question: his old friend Hugh Lawson White, young and able John Bell, and the picturesque if somewhat phony frontiersman, Davy Crockett. Others of his Western supporters, like Robert J. Walker of Mississippi, were careful to disclaim any hard-money leanings.[3] But, on the whole, the magic of Jackson's name was fairly certain to win Western approval for almost anything.

He thus was emboldened to come out publicly for the hard-money policy, expressing himself first in his interview with the Philadelphia delegation a few days before his second inaugural. His objective, he said, was gradually to reduce the circulation of paper, by forbidding deposit banks to issue small notes and by refusing such notes in payment for taxes, until all notes under twenty dollars would be eliminated and "thus a metallic currency be ensured for all the common purposes of life, while the use of bank notes would be confined to those engaged in commerce."[4]

---

[1] Orestes A. Brownson later declared that he had been urged in 1831 by "men high in the confidence of the party . . . to support the administration of that day, on the ground that it was opposed to all corporate banking, whether state or national." This was, of course, long before any such purpose was avowed as party policy. *Boston Reformer,* August 4, 1837.

[2] The "West" here includes Alabama, Mississippi, Louisiana, Kentucky, Tennessee, Ohio, Indiana, Illinois and Missouri. Jackson had only to carry one Western state to get a majority of the electoral votes.

[3] "God save us from the wild, visionary, ruinous, and impracticable schemes of the senator of Missouri," Walker cried in 1837. ". . . Sir, in resistance to the power of the Bank of the United States, in opposition to the re-establishment of any similar institution, the Senator from Missouri would find Mr. W. with him; but he could not enlist as a recruit in this new crusade against the banks of his own and every other State in the Union. . . . [It] was not, he believed, anticipated by any one of his constituents." Walker in the Senate, January 28, 1837, *Register of Debates,* 24 Congress 2 Session, 621–622. Note Walker's emphasis on "resistance to the power of the Bank" as his main motive in fighting it. In 1840, when Walker, now a strong hard-money man, undertook to explain the origins of the hard-money policy, he correctly declared: "The workingmen of the city of New York, next, perhaps to the patriot Jackson and the Senator from Missouri, may be justly considered the original Loco Focos and hard money men of the Union." Walker in the Senate, January 21, 1840, *Congressional Globe,* 26 Congress 1 Session, Appendix, 140.

[4] *Niles' Register,* March 1, 1834.

Soon after, he reorganized his cabinet, turning it for the first time into an effective unit. McLane and Duane, both evidently hostile to a radical economic policy, were replaced by John Forsyth in the State Department and Roger B. Taney in the Treasury. William T. Barry, whose incompetence as Postmaster General finally drove even Jackson to despair, was succeeded by Amos Kendall. Benjamin F. Butler of New York, Van Buren's former law partner, followed Taney as Attorney General, and, after Taney's eventual rejection by the Senate, Levi Woodbury was promoted to the Treasury. In this circle of staunch hard-money men Lewis Cass could only relapse into mournful silence. The administration was now streamlined for action.

2

The hard-money system owed many of its maxims and dogmas to the Jeffersonians, and much of its vitality to the Northern workingmen who backed it so warmly; but the man to whom, after Jackson, Benton and Taney, it perhaps owed most for its emergence as a constructive policy was William M. Gouge, the Philadelphia editor and economist. Gouge put the hard-money doctrines in the clearest form, furnished the most cogent indictment of the paper system, stated the general problems in a way (unlike the Jeffersonian) relevant to a society where finance capitalism was well entrenched, and proved unfailingly resourceful in working out the practical measures to realize his policy. Thirty-seven years old in 1833, he had been from 1823 to 1831 editor and part proprietor of the *Philadelphia Gazette*. For the next two years, he busied himself with a treatise on the banking system, published in Philadelphia in February, 1833, under the title *A Short History of Paper Money and Banking in the United States*.[5]

The work consisted of an analysis of the social consequences of the paper system, followed by a detailed account of the history of paper money in America. The first section set forth the broad theoretical case, while the second provided the crushing documentation. Facts were Gouge's most powerful weapons; and in a plain, circumstantial way, occasionally flavored by irony, constantly buttressed by names, dates and citations, he supplied a crisp and comprehensive statement of the hard-money position.

The book became an instant success. Probably no work in economics had ever circulated so widely in the United States. The first edition was nearly exhausted by the fall of 1834, and, in 1835, it was reprinted in cheap stereotyped form to sell for twenty-five cents. By 1837 it had gone into a third edition. It was serialized in the *New York Evening Post* in 1834, and later in the *Washington Globe* and many other papers. William Cobbett published an English edition, and an abridged version was translated into

---

[5] Gouge's own copy, with interleaved notes, is in the Harvard College Library.

French and printed at Brussels. All the radicals of the day read it voraciously—William Leggett, Theophilus Fisk, Orestes A. Brownson, William Cullen Bryant—and paid cordial tribute to the author. It delighted Frank Blair, was passed from hand to hand in the inner circle of government; and early in 1835 Gouge was called down to Washington to take a job under Levi Woodbury in the Treasury Department. There his terse and hard-hitting memoranda were to exert for many years an important influence on financial policy.[6]

The book's success was deserved. Its historical sections went unchallenged, even by the most ardent defenders of the system; and Gouge's keenness of analysis, as well as his accuracy, has won the approval of our ablest historians of banking. When it was first published Condy Raguet called it "decidedly the best work on Banking that we have ever met with." Modern students have treated it with similar respect. As William Graham Sumner, no friend of Jacksonian democracy, put it, Gouge "studied this system [of paper money] in its operation more thoroughly and with more intelligence than anybody else." A popular jingle expressed contemporary appreciation:—

> Of modern books, the best I know—
>   The author all the world is thanking—
> One written more for use than show,
>   Is quaintly titled, "*Gouge* on Banking."
>
> But still improvements might be made,
>   Whilst books on books the world is scrouging,
> Let *Biddle* try to help the trade,
>   And write one titled, "Banks on *Gouging*." [7]

3

The hard-money policy was conceived by Gouge and its other champions as a total alternative to the Hamiltonian system. Its central point was the exclusion of banks from control over the currency. It was not, as its opponents persisted in describing it, a demand for the annihilation of the banking system and the establishment of an exclusively metallic currency.

---

[6] *Journal of Banking*, July 7, 1841; *New York Evening Post*, September 15, 1834, June 29, 1837.

[7] *The Examiner, and Journal of Political Economy*, October 30, 1833; W. G. Sumner, *History of Banking in the United States*, 181; *Journal of Banking*, August 18, 1841. The leading modern historian of early banking theories remarks: "Gouge was one of the most thorough students of our early banking and also one of its keenest and most influential critics." Miller, *Banking Theories in the United States before 1860*, 86 n. For Nicholas Biddle's characteristic misjudgment of Gouge's work and its significance, see Biddle to J. S. Barbour, July 11, 1833, Biddle, *Correspondence*, 211. For the impact of Gouge on an ordinary intelligent and untutored young man, see Lucian Minor, "Diary of a Journey to the West in 1836," *Proceedings of the Massachusetts Historical Society*, XXVII, 284, 286.

It proposed merely to limit bank paper to commercial transactions, and to confine banks to the functions of deposit and discount, slowly withdrawing from them the privilege of note issue.[8]

The main purposes were three. One was essentially economic: to prevent periodic depressions; another essentially political: to prevent the rise within the state of independent powers, not responsible to the people and able to defy the government; and the third essentially social: to prevent the rule of a moneyed aristocracy systematically exploiting the "humble members of society."

The economic argument was brought to the public attention largely by Benton and Gouge, and it drew somewhat on the reports of the English bullionists. The political was, of course, central in the American tradition; it was perhaps the particular contribution of the frontier to this controversy, and had been thrust forward during the Kentucky Relief War. The social argument represented the Jeffersonian legacy and was indebted considerably in its details to John Taylor of Caroline. As political expediency dictated, one could be stressed at certain times and others concealed. The Bank veto, for example, confined itself mainly to the second argument, with some suggestions of the third. But, after the election of 1832 had demonstrated the national confidence in Jackson, the administration began to urge all three. Gouge's book stated them conveniently, and Jackson's Farewell Address provided an excellent brief summary.

The economic argument turned ultimately on varying attitudes toward the concrete economy as an environment for living, rather than on disagreement over abstract principles. Alexander Hamilton in his eagerness to make out a case for paper money had once argued that note issue constituted "an absolute increase of capital," but this obviously untenable view was pretty well abandoned by 1830.[9] Even the most fervent admirers of paper money acknowledged the value of increasing the proportion of specie in the circulating medium. Nicholas Biddle himself in some moods was a hard-money man.[10] Daniel Webster loudly and constantly proclaimed the evils of overissue, except when he had to vote on a measure intended to prevent it.

Yet men like Biddle and Webster plainly preferred in last analysis a speculative economy, with quick expansion, huge gains and huge risks. During the investigation of the Bank by the Clayton Committee, when

---

[8] See Appendix.   [9] Miller, *Banking Theories,* 30–34.

[10] In 1832 Biddle recommended the following reforms: "First, to widen the basis of the metallic circulation, by abolishing the use of small notes. . . . And second, to annex to the non-payment of specie by the banks, so heavy a penalty . . . as would deprive the banks of all temptation to incur the risk of insolvency." *House Report,* 22 Congress 1 Session, no. 460, "Bank of the United States," 367. For a typical expression of a theoretical preference for hard money hedged round by practical arguments against it, see Edward Everett, "Address to the Legislature," Massachusetts *House Document,* no. 6 (1836), 16–18.

Cambreleng asked whether the existing banking system did not encourage speculation, Biddle replied: "Until the nature of man is changed, men will become speculators and bankrupts—under any system—and I do not perceive that our own is specially calculated to create them." Cambreleng became more specific. Would not the system be more healthy if note issue were forbidden? Biddle hedged: "I fear I do not comprehend all this. . . . That banks do occasional mischief there can be no doubt; but until some valuable improvement is found which supplies unmixed good, this is no objection to them. And constituted as they now are, the banks of the United States may be considered safe instruments of commerce." [11]

Biddle and men like him were willing to take the chance of depression in exchange for the thrills and opportunities of boom. But others confronted a speculative situation with much less confidence. Men of small and fairly fixed income—farmers, laborers, mechanics, petty shopkeepers, many of the Southern planters—felt themselves the victims of baffling and malevolent economic forces which they could not profit by or control.

On the most obvious level, the working classes believed that they were regularly cheated by paper money. A good portion of the small notes they received in wages were depreciated, worthless or counterfeit. Unscrupulous employers even bought up depreciated notes and palmed them off on their workingmen at face value. And, in the larger economic picture, all the stable-income classes had to stand by helpless and impotent during the unpredictable rise and fall of prices or ebb and flow of credit. Their reaction to a gambling economy was not delight at the opening up of chances for gain, but an intense feeling of insecurity. Jackson expressed their pent-up exasperation in his exclamation to the Baltimore committee on stock-jobbers, brokers and gamblers—"would to God, they were all swept from the land!" [12]

The administration proposed to rescue the working classes from this treacherous economic order. "It is time," declared Taney, "that the just claims of this portion of society should be regarded in our legislation in relation to the currency. So far we have been providing facilities for those employed in extensive commerce, and have left the mechanic and the laborer to all the hazards of an insecure and unstable circulating medium." Jackson pronounced it "the duty of every government, so to regulate its currency as to protect this numerous class, as far as practicable, from the impositions of avarice and fraud." [13]

---

[11] *House Report,* 22 Congress 1 Session, no. 460, "Bank of the United States," 362, 364, 365, 367.

[12] See also his remark to the Philadelphia delegation that *"brokers* and *stock speculators,* and *all who were doing business upon borrowed capital* . . . all such people ought to break." *Niles' Register,* March 1, 8, 1834.

[13] Taney, "Letter to the Ways and Means Committee," April 15, 1834, *Register of Debates,* 23 Congress 1 Session, Appendix, 161; Richardson, comp., *Messages and Papers,* III, 302.

Prompted by these aims, the Jacksonians began to sketch out fairly coherent theories of self-generating business cycles. Condy Raguet was perhaps the first to adumbrate the general theory, and Gouge set forth the classic description in his *Paper Money*.

In its simplest outline the theory was this: Banks incline to overissue their notes. Prices then rise, and a speculative fever begins to spread. Excited by the appearance of prosperity that accompanies boom, people spend freely. The general expansion of credit leads to overtrading and inflation. Every new business operation on credit creates more promissory notes, and these increase the demand for discounts, till finally the currency depreciates so greatly that specie is required for export in order to pay foreign debts. With specie at a premium, contraction sets in. Banks call in their loans, timid people start runs on banks, contraction turns to panic, and panic to collapse. "One man is unable to pay his debts," wrote Gouge. "His creditor depended on him for the means of paying a third person to whom he is himself indebted. The circle extends through society. Multitudes become bankrupt, and a few successful speculators get possession of the earnings and savings of many of their frugal and industrious neighbors." [14]

The more careful analysts pointed out the complex interdependence of bank credit and general business activity, but political pamphleteers skipped the subtleties and blamed depressions on the paper-money system alone. Bank paper, they argued, stimulated the original boom psychology by beguiling businessmen into overtrading at times of rising prices. It linked the whole system so intimately that the failure of one merchant might prevent a dozen others from meeting their obligations. And most particularly, the expansion or contraction of paper in circulation bore only a perverse and futile relation to actual business needs. In the words of George Bancroft, it "expands when rising prices require a check to enterprise, and contracts when falling prices make credit most desirable." Or, as Theophilus Fisk put it with more vernom, "The moment a spirit of speculation can be excited, the banks increase the flame by pouring oil upon it; the instant a reaction takes place, they add to the distress a thousand fold." [15]

If by modern standards highly inadequate, this currency theory of depression yet represented a considerable advance over no theory at all. Very little was then said of general overproduction as a cause of depression. Some men, like Robert Rantoul, Jr., laid special stress on the glutting of markets as a factor in crisis; but many would agree with Gouge's note on such arguments, that "if the real wants of the community, and not their

---

[14] Gouge, *Paper Money*, Part I, 24–25. See also Condy Raguet in the *Free Trade Advocate*, July 4, 1829, and the admirable discussion in Miller, *Banking Theories*, 192–205.

[15] George Bancroft, *Address at Hartford, . . . Feb. 18, 1840*, 14; Theophilus Fisk, *The Banking Bubble Burst; or the Mammoth Corruptions of the Paper Money System Relieved by Bleeding*, 25.

ability to pay, be considered, it will not, perhaps, be found that any one useful trade or profession has too many members," and accept his emphasis on the problem of "ability to pay." In 1843 Orestes A. Brownson in a brilliant passage placed the blame squarely on "our vicious method of distributing the products of labor." "More can be produced, in any given year," he wrote, "with the present productive power, than can be sold in any given five years." The fault lies in distribution.

> We create a surplus—that is a surplus, not when we consider the wants of the people, but when we consider the state of the markets— and then must slacken our hand till the surplus is worked off. During this time, while we are working off the surplus, while the mills run short time, or stop altogether, the workmen must want employment. The evil is inherent in the system.

But this line of thought evidently failed to strike much response and was carried no farther.[16]

4

The political argument—opposition to the rise of independent powers within the state—had general premises deeply entrenched in the national consciousness. Everyone, from right to left, believed, with more or fewer qualifications, that sovereignty belonged to the people. It was but one step from this to declare that the people's government, therefore, should not be defied by private institutions; and it was easy to extend this proposition to economic institutions, as well as political.

In their nature as corporations, banks gave rise to one set of objections, springing from their monopoly of financial prerogative through special charter. Indeed, they provided so much the most flagrant instances of abuse of corporate privilege that they were mainly responsible for fixing national attention on the problem.

Their power over the currency was viewed as an especially grave encroachment on the domain of government. The regulation of the currency, in the words of Benton, was "one of the highest and most delicate acts of sovereign power . . . precisely equivalent to the power to create currency"; and he considered it "too great a power to be trusted to any banking company whatever, or to any authority but the highest and most responsible which was known to our form of Government." Commercial credit was another matter, "an affair of trade," as Cembreleng put it, "and not of government"; and the logic of this position pointed to the abolition of banks of

---

[16] Robert Rantoul, Jr., speech at Salem, March 31, 1834, Luther Hamilton, *Memoirs, Speeches and Writings of Robert Rantoul, Jr.*, 537; Gouge, *Paper Money*, Part I, 27–28; O. A. Brownson, "The Present State of Society," *Democratic Review*, XIII, 34 (July, 1843); see also O. A. Brownson, *Address on Social Reform*, 5–6.

note issue, on the one hand, and the establishment of free competition among banks of discount and deposit, on the other. The crucial error of the federal government, according to the hard-money advocates, lay in accepting bank notes in the payment of federal dues, by which it thus extended and virtually underwrote the credit of the banks. The remedy was to exclude bank notes from government payments.[17]

The behavior of banks in practice, moreover, violated the national faith in popular rule. The most powerful argument against Biddle's Bank was always its calm assumption of independence. "The Bank of the United States," Jackson charged, "is in itself a Government which has gradually increased in strength from the day of its establishment. The question between it and the people has become one of power." Biddle's conduct, in 1834, in refusing to allow a House committee to investigate the Bank records or examine the Bank officers, was simply the climax of his oft-expressed theory of the Bank's independence. "This powerful corporation, and those who defend it," as Taney said, without much exaggeration, "seem to regard it as an independent sovereignty, and to have forgotten that it owes any duties to the People, or is bound by any laws but its own will." [18]

But Biddle was simply exhibiting on a larger scale habits long established in banking experience. William Graham Sumner concisely summed up the pretensions of the banks:—

> The bankers had methods of doing things which were customary and conventional, but . . . contrary both to ordinary morality and to law as applied to similar matters outside of banks. . . . The banks also disregarded law so habitually that it became a commonplace that law could not bind them. . . . We search almost in vain through the law reports for any decisions on the rights or authority of the State over banks or the duties of banks to the State. It may be said that no attempts were made to test or enforce the right of the State against banks, and that, as a matter of practice, it had none. The banks were almost irresponsible. Such decisions as bear at all on the authority of the State over banks proceed from the attempts of the banks to resist the exercise of any authority whatever.

Such a situation obviously could not be long borne. As Theophilus Fisk put it, "Either the State is sovereign, or the Banks are." [19]

---

[17] Benton in the Senate, March 22, 1834, *Register of Debates*, 23 Congress 1 Session, 1092–1093; Cambreleng to Van Buren, November 2, 1835, Van Buren Papers. Cf. Gouge, *Paper Money*, Part I, 53: "The regulation of the currency is one of the most important prerogatives of sovereignty. This prerogative is now, in point of fact, surrendered to the Banks."

[18] Jackson's first draft of the "Paper Read to the Cabinet," Jackson, *Correspondence*, V, 194; *Washington Globe*, October 1, 1834.

[19] Sumner, *History of Banking in the United States*, 351–352; Fisk, *Banking Bubble Burst*, 72.

5

The social argument—the battle against domination by "the rich and powerful"—represented the culmination of the hard-money doctrine. The economic and political arguments, though capable of standing by themselves, were ultimately directed at conditions preliminary to the question: who shall rule in the state? The recurrent economic crises were evil, not only in themselves, but because they facilitated a redistribution of wealth that built up the moneyed aristocracy. The irresponsible political sovereignties were evil, not only in themselves, but because they provided the aristocracy with instruments of power and places of refuge.

The Bank War compelled people to speculate once again about the conflict of classes. "There are but two parties," exclaimed Thomas Hart Benton, giving the period its keynote; "there never has been but two parties . . . founded in the radical question, whether PEOPLE, or PROPERTY, shall govern? Democracy implies a government by the people. . . . Aristocracy implies a government of the rich. . . . and in these words are contained the sum of party distinction." [20]

The paper banking system was considered to play a leading role in this everlasting struggle. Men living by the issue and circulation of paper money produced nothing; they added nothing to the national income; yet, they flourished and grew wealthy. Their prosperity, it was argued, must be stolen from the proceeds of productive labor—in other words, from the honest but defenseless "humble members of society"; and Gouge extensively annotated the modes of plunder.

The system was further important in the strategy of the warfare. Taney described the big Bank as "the centre, and the citadel of the moneyed power." "A national bank," declared the Massachusetts Democratic convention of 1837, "is the bulwark of the aristocracy; its outpost, and its rallying point. It is the bond of union for those who hold that Government should rest on property." [21] To a lesser degree all banks acted as strongholds of conservatism. They provided the funds and often the initiative for combat. Their lawyers, lobbyists and newspapers were eternally active. Politicians would gather in their board rooms and consult their presidents and accept gifts of stock. More than any other kind of corporate enterprise, banks boldly intervened in politics when they felt their interests menaced.

The hard-money policy attacked both the techniques of plunder and the general strategy of warfare. By doing away with paper money, it proposed to restrict the steady transfer of wealth from the farmer and laborer to the business community. By limiting banks to commercial credit and denying them control over the currency, it proposed to lessen their influ-

---

[20] *Niles' Register,* August 29, 1835.
[21] *Washington Globe,* August 25, 1834, October 27, 1837.

ence and power. By reducing the proportion of paper money, it proposed to moderate the business cycle, and order the economy to the advantage of the worker rather than the speculator. It was a coherent policy, based on the best economic thought of the day, and formulated on a higher intellectual level than the alternatives of the opposition.

By origin and interest, it was a policy which appealed mainly to the submerged classes of the East and to the farmers of the South rather than to the frontier. Historians have too long been misled by the tableau of Jackson, the wild backwoodsman, erupting into the White House. In fact, the hard-money doctrine, which was not at all a frontier doctrine, was the controlling policy of the administration from the winter of 1833 on; and for some time it had been the secret goal of a small group, led by Jackson, Taney, Benton and Kendall, and passively encouraged by Van Buren. From the removal of the deposits to the end of Van Buren's presidency in 1840 this clique of radical Democrats sought to carry out the policy in its full implications. As soon as the hard-money program was divorced from the glamour of the Hero of New Orleans and had to rest on its inherent appeal, it did very badly in the West.

Andrew Jackson ably summed up its broad aims. "The planter, the farmer, the mechanic, and the laborer," he wrote, "all know that their success depends upon their own industry and economy, and that they must not expect to become suddenly rich by the fruits of their toil." These classes "form the great body of the people of the United States; they are the bone and sinew of the country." Yet "they are in constant danger of losing their fair influence in the Government." Why? "The mischief springs from the power which the moneyed interest derives from a paper currency, which they are able to control, from the multitude of corporations with exclusive privileges which they have succeeded in obtaining in the different States." His warning to his people was solemn. "Unless you become more watchful . . . you will in the end find that the most important powers of Government have been given or bartered away, and the control over your dearest interests has passed into the hands of these corporations." [22]

6

Taney and Benton worked out the details of the immediate hard-money measures. They proposed to increase the metallic basis of the currency in two directions: by the restoration of gold to circulation, and by the suppression of small notes. The first measure had been for many years close to Benton's heart. Gold had long been undervalued, at the ratio of 15 to 1, with the result that no gold eagles and only a scattering of other gold coins had been minted since 1805, and most of these rapidly left the

---

[22] Richardson, comp., *Messages and Papers*, III, 305–306.

country. Benton argued that, if the gold were not thus expelled, the amount of specie derivable from foreign commerce, added to the amount obtained from American mines, could supply all financial needs without recourse to small notes or "shinplasters." [23] In June, 1834, his bill to revise the valuation to 16 to 1 passed Congress. As an expression of the strictly economic intentions of the hard-money policy, it made a broad appeal to all men of good will, winning the support of John Quincy Adams, Webster and Calhoun. Only diehards like Clay and Horace Binney opposed it.

The change in the coinage ratio was one of Benton's greatest triumphs. He exulted in the new flow of gold to the government mints. "This is the money the Constitution provides," he would say, "and I will not have anything to do with any other kind." Or, in another mood, "What! Do you want a coroner's jury to sit and say, 'Old Bullion died of shin-plasters?' " [24] Old Bullion was the name his hard-money fixation had won him, among his friends, at least; his enemies called him sarcastically the Gold Humbug. For a time, foes of the hard-money policy sought to ridicule Benton's reform out of existence. Gilt counters were circulated, with grotesque figures and caustic inscriptions—the "whole hog" and the "better currency." But no one dared argue directly that this infusion of specie would not improve the health of the economy.

The effects of revaluation were immediate. Levi Woodbury reported in December, 1836, that more gold had been coined in the twelve months preceding than in the first sixteen years of the mint's existence, and more in the two and a half years since revaluation than in the thirty-one before. In October, 1833, there had been only thirty million dollars of specie in the country, of which twenty-six million was in banks. In December, 1836, there was seventy-three million dollars, of which only forty-five million was in banks. [25]

Yet the revival of gold would hardly be enough without measures to suppress small notes. This proposal had the sanction, not only of the theory of Adam Smith (and of Nicholas Biddle), but of the example of Great Britain, which had established a £5 minimum in 1829. Most economically literate conservatives acknowledged the theoretical advantages of suppres-

---

[23] See Benton's great speech on the gold currency, in the Senate, March 21–22, 1834, *Register of Debates,* 23 Congress 1 Session, especially 1073–1084; Benton, *Thirty Years' View,* I, 436–457.

[24] Meigs, *Benton,* 263.

[25] Levi Woodbury, "Report from the Secretary of the Treasury," December 6, 1836, *Register of Debates,* 24 Congress 2 Session, Appendix, 79. It is hard to assess the hard-money claim that specie could have altogether displaced small notes. Gouge calculated in 1841 that "barely by detaining in the country such amounts of gold and silver as come to us in the present course of trade, we should, in ten or twelve years, have a perfectly sound circulating medium." *Journal of Banking,* December 22, 1841. Whether or not one-hundred-per-cent displacement was possible, or desirable, an increase in the proportion of specie was badly needed.

sion;[26] and Congress and the Treasury, drawing on their authority to define the kind of money receivable in federal payments, could exert real, if limited, influence on the issues of state banks. A joint resolution of 1816 had made all notes from specie-paying banks acceptable in tax payments. In a Treasury circular of April, 1835, all notes under $5 were banned, and banks holding government deposits were forbidden to issue such notes. In February, 1836, a similar circular banned notes under $10, and a congressional act of April, 1836, prohibited notes under $20 after March 3, 1837, and required immediate convertibility for all notes. The conditions imposed on the deposit banks controlled their stock transactions, as well as their note issue, calling for weekly statements and ordering that they should always be open for examination. Declared Secretary Woodbury, "All mystery on the subject of banking should cease." [27]

But these regulations had little effect on the general banking situation. Only by deliberately rousing public opinion within the states could the administration hope to abolish small notes. In some states tattered shinplasters circulated with face values of 12½ or even 6¼ cents. In December, 1834, Jackson appealed to the states to follow the national example. Pennsylvania, Maryland and Virginia already had legislation against small bills. In 1835 Maine, Connecticut and New York outlawed notes below $5, while North Carolina, Georgia, Alabama, Ohio, Indiana and Missouri also passed restrictive measures.[28]

7

But the administration's campaign came too late. The wise counsels of the hard-money advocates were drowned out by the roar of the nation's greatest boom in years. The Bank of the United States alone enlarged its loans an average of two and a half million dollars a month and its paper circulation by a total of ten million dollars between December, 1834, and July, 1835.[29] Smaller banks rushed to follow, increasing the amount of paper money from eighty-two million dollars on January 1, 1835, to one hundred and eight million, a year later, and one hundred and twenty million by December 1, 1836.[30]

---

[26] Some conservatives would argue of shinplasters, however, like a Massachusetts committee in 1840, "They float as free as the snow flakes, and every hand is held out to catch as much as it can of the beneficial shower. If they were found to be unsafe or inconvenient, they would instantly be rejected." Massachusetts *House Document*, no. 66 (1840), 5.

[27] Levi Woodbury, "Report on the Present System of Keeping and Disbursing the Public Money," December 12, 1834, *Register of Debates*, 23 Congress 2 Session, Appendix, 105.

[28] D. R. Dewey, *State Banking before the Civil War*, 68–71.

[29] *Washington Globe*, June 10, 1835, May 12, 1836.

[30] Levi Woodbury, "Report from the Secretary of the Treasury," December 6, 1836, *Register of Debates*, 24 Congress 2 Session, Appendix, 80.

Wages climbed, opportunity seemed limitless and riches appeared to lie everywhere. A popular tract of 1836—*The Book of Wealth; in Which It Is Proved from the Bible, that It Is the Duty of Every Man to Become Rich*—suggests the temper of the day. Designed to allay any religious misgivings about joining at the trough, the book earnestly declared one thing to be certain: "no man can be obedient to God's will as revealed in the Bible, without, as the general result, becoming wealthy." [31]

The administration watched the speculative mania with profound alarm. In the *Globe* Frank Blair repeatedly voiced the deep anxieties of the hard-money circle. "We have again and again warned the community," he wrote in the spring of 1835, "of the infatuation which had seized them since the panic, to embark in every species of extravagant speculation." A month later: "this state of things cannot last. . . . A reaction is as certain to take place as the sun is to continue its diurnal course." After a year of similar remarks: "The only remedy is to be found in banking less and trading less." [32]

Jackson, in the early months of 1836, lifted his voice in conversation against "the mad career" in which the nation was rushing to ruin. Benton declared angrily in the Senate: "I did not join in putting down the Bank of the United States, to put up a wilderness of local banks. I did not join in putting down the paper currency of a national bank, to put up a national paper currency of a thousand local banks. I did not strike Caesar," he concluded in magnificent wrath, "to make Anthony master of Rome. . . . The present bloat in the paper system cannot continue. . . . The revulsion will come, as surely as it did in 1819–'20." When Secretary Woodbury made his report in December, 1836, he had to predict that the inflation would "produce much distress, embarrassment, and ruin, before this specie can be duly equalized, the excesses of paper sufficiently curtailed, and the exorbitant discounts gradually lessened." [33]

A basic cause of the inflation was land speculation, and the administration had already moved to plug up this great hole in the national economy. The receivability of bank notes in payment for the public lands had practically converted the national domain into a fund for the redemption of the notes, providing in effect a capital for seven or eight hundred institutions to bank on, and filling the Treasury with more or less worthless paper. Benton had pointed out in detail how land sales passed on to the government the job of underwriting the whole banking system. Speculators would borrow five, ten, twenty, fifty thousand dollars in paper from

---

[31] Thomas P. Hunt, *The Book of Wealth*, 5, 22, 24.

[32] *Washington Globe*, May 23, June 10, 1835, May 31, 1836.

[33] Jackson's conversation reported by "A Yeoman," *Washington Globe*, August 11, 1837; Benton in the Senate, January 27, 1837, *Register of Debates*, 24 Congress 2 Session, 610; Levi Woodbury, "Report from the Secretary of the Treasury," December 6, 1836, *Register of Debates*, 24 Congress 2 Session, Appendix, 80.

banks on the condition of using it on the frontier. They would then pay the notes to government land offices in exchange for land, which served as security for additional loans; meanwhile, the notes circulated freely as land-office money, some never returning to the original bank for redemption, the rest only after a long interval. This racket not only subsidized the banking interest—land sales had risen from four million dollars a year to five million a quarter—but it also, in Benton's words, irretrievably entangled "the federal Government with the ups and downs of the whole paper system, and all the fluctuations, convulsions, and disasters, to which it was subject." [34]

Benton introduced a resolution requiring that the public lands be paid for in specie. Webster, with his usual policy of supporting sound money except when concrete measures were proposed which might secure it, led the attack on this measure, and a combination of Whigs and conservative Democrats killed it in the Senate. But after adjournment Jackson had Benton draw up an executive order embodying his idea, and the famous "Specie Circular" was issued.

The business community grew furious over this latest evidence of executive despotism. When Congress reassembled in December, the Whigs demanded the repeal of the Circular and the reopening of the land offices to wildcat money, and the Democrats split wide under the pressure. One wing, led by William Cabell Rives of Virginia and N. P. Tallmadge of New York, emerged as defenders of the state banks. Benton vainly urged the imminence of a financial explosion which would leave the Treasury holding the bag; but his efforts won him little more than denunciation as "that most miserable Jacobin of the woods of Missouri, who, with an impudence and insolence unparalleled, has attempted to overthrow the commercial and financial relations and institutions of this country." [35] The final vote disclosed a tiny group of five men, led by Benton and Silas Wright, upholding the hard-money position. The bill passed the House and went to the President on the day before adjournment. Firm to the end, the old General returned it with his veto.

Jackson thus had to overrule Congress to sustain the hard-money policy. But the Specie Circular furnished the only tense financial issue in the last years of his administration. After the panic session the great scenes of battle began to shift to the states. Here, in places inaccessible to the long arm and grim energy of General Jackson, little bands of devoted Jacksonians fought to stem the rush for bank and corporate charters, unfolding the potentialities of the Jacksonian program, enriching the techniques and amplifying the intellectual resources.

Above all, these local battles called forth the common people in cities,

---

[34] Benton in the Senate, April 23, 1836, *Register of Debates*, 24 Congress 1 Session, 1255–1257. See also *Washington Globe*, July 12, 1836.
[35] *Boston Commercial Gazette*, February 27, 1837.

towns and country—the poor day laborer, the industrious mechanic, the hard-handed farmer—the "humble members of society" everywhere. They listened for hours on hot summer days to dry expositions of financial policy. They crowded in bare and unheated halls on cold winter nights to hear about the evils of banking. They read, and thumbed, and passed along tracts and speeches attacking the paper system. They saw the dizzy climb of prices, wages lagging behind, raged silently at discounted bank notes, and wondered at the behavior of Democratic politicians pledged against voting for incorporations. They talked among themselves, with shrewdness and good sense and alarm. . . . Their discontent was real and widespread. It found its leaders, and the experience of these years prepared them for one great final drive on the national scene.

The Jacksonians, 1829–1841

Bray Hammond

I

During the half century that ended with General Jackson's election, America underwent changes perhaps the most radical and sweeping it has ever undergone in so short a time. It passed the climacteric separating a modern industrial economy from an older one of handicraft; it passed from colonial weakness through bare independence to actual power and from an unjostled rural culture to the complexities of populousness, sectionalism, urban slums, mechanized industry, and monetary credit. Men who had spent their childhood in a thin line of sea-board colonies, close even in their little cities to the edge of the westward continental wilderness, spent their late years in a tamed and wealthy land spread already to the Missouri and about to extend beyond it. They lived to ride on railways and steamships, to use the products of steam-driven machinery, to dwell in metropolitan centers, and to feel within their grasp and the grasp of their sons more potential and accessible wealth than had ever before excited the enterprise of man.

An outstanding factor in the changes that came about was the flow of

---

Reprinted from *Banks and Politics in America from the Revolution to the Civil War* by Bray Hammond by permission of Princeton University Press. Copyright © 1957, by Princeton University Press. Editor's note: Part of Section III and all of Section V of Chapter XII are omitted.

immigration from Europe. Between 1790 and 1840 the population grew from 4,000,000 to 17,000,000. In the latter year an average of 230 immigrants entered the country daily. Ten years later it was over 1,000 daily. The area of settlement and exploitation expanded swiftly under the pressure of this movement. While General Jackson was President the federal union came to include twice as many states as it had begun with and held territory that recently had belonged to Spain and France. It was shortly to add regions in the South and West taken from Mexico and regions in the Northwest that Great Britain claimed. Its expansion seemed irresistible.

The changes in social outlook were profound. Steam was generating conceptions of life, liberty, and the pursuit of happiness that were quite alien to Thomas Jefferson's; and the newcomers pushing into the country from Europe had more impatient economic motives than their 18th century predecessors. People were led as they had not been before by visions of money-making. Liberty became transformed into *laisser faire*. A violent, aggressive, economic individualism became established. The democracy became greedy, intolerant, imperialistic, and lawless. It opened economic advantages to those who had not previously had them; yet it allowed wealth to be concentrated in new hands only somewhat more numerous than before, less responsible, and less disciplined. There were unenterprising and unpropertied thousands who missed entirely the economic opportunities with which America was thick. There was poverty in the eastern cities and poverty on the frontier. Those who failed to hold their own in the struggle were set down as unfit.

Wealth was won and lost, lost and won. Patient accumulation was contemned. People believed it was not what they saved but what they made that counted. Jay Cooke, one of America's future millionaires, who was scarcely born poor on a farm but primitively at least, in a frontier settlement, was already on his way to fortune in a private banking firm before the age of twenty and writing home about his work with enthusiasm. This was in the winter of 1839–1840. "My bosses are making money fast," he said. "This business is always good, and those who follow it in time become rich. . . . Among our customers are men of every age and every position in society, from the hoary miser to the dashing buck who lives upon his thousands. Through all grades I see the same all-pervading, all engrossing anxiety to grow rich." Something of the same sort, to be sure, was taking place in western Europe and especially in Great Britain. Half the people and most of the money for America's transformation came from there. But though industrial and technological revolution occurred also in the Old World, in the New, where vast resources awaited exploitation, it produced a dazzling, democratic expansion experienced nowhere else. The situation was such that the rallying cry, *"Laissez nous faire!"* expressed the views of Americans perfectly, when translated.

Socially, the Jacksonian revolution signified that a nation of democrats was tired of being governed, however well, by gentlemen from Virginia and Massachusetts. As Professor Sumner observed, what seems to have enchanted people with General Jackson when he became a candidate for President was not any principles or policies he advocated but his breaches of decorum, real or alleged.[1] Economically, the revolution signified that a nation of potential money-makers could not abide traditional, conservative limitations on business enterprise, particularly by capitalists in Philadelphia. The Jacksonian revolution was a consequence of the Industrial Revolution and of a farm-born people's realization that now anyone in America could get rich and through his own efforts, if he had a fair chance. A conception of earned wealth arose which rendered the self-made man as superior morally to the hereditary well-to-do as the agrarian had been. It was like the conception which led Theodoric the Great to boast that he held Italy solely by right of conquest and without the shadow of legal, that is, hereditary right. The humbly born and rugged individualists who were gaining fortunes by their own toil and sweat, or wits, were still simple Americans, Jeffersonian, anti-monopolistic, anti-governmental, but fraught with the spirit of enterprise and fired with a sense of what soon would be called manifest destiny. They envied the social and economic advantages of the established urban capitalists, mercantile and financial; and they fought these aristocrats with far more zeal and ingenuity than the agrarians ever had. They resented the federal Bank's interference with expansion of the monetary supply. They found it bestriding the path of enterprise, and with Apollyon's brag but Christian's better luck they were resolved to spill its soul. They democratized business under a great show of agrarian idealism and made the age of Jackson a festival of *laisser faire* prelusive to the age of Grant and the robber barons.

In their attack on the Bank of the United States, the Jacksonians still employed the vocabulary of their agrarian backgrounds. The phraseology of idealism was adapted to money-making, the creed of an earlier generation becoming the cant of its successor. Their terms of abuse were "oppression," "tyranny," "monied power," "aristocracy," "wealth," "privilege," "monopoly"; their terms of praise were "the humble," "the poor," "the simple," "the honest and industrious." Though their cause was a sophisticated one of enterpriser against capitalist, of banker against regulation, and of Wall Street against Chestnut, the language was the same as if they were all back on the farm. Neither the President, nor his advisers, nor their followers saw any discrepancy between the concept of freedom in an age of agrarianism and the concept of freedom in one of enterprise. Only the poets and philosophers were really aware that a discrepancy existed and though troubled by it their vision was far from clear. Notwithstanding their language, therefore, the Jacksonians' destruction of the Bank of the United States was in no sense a blow at capitalism or property or the "money

---

[1] Oberholtzer I, 57–58; Sumner, *Jackson*, 179.

power." It was a blow at an older set of capitalists by a newer, more numerous set. It was incident to the democratization of business, the diffusion of enterprise among the mass of people, and the transfer of economic primacy from an old and conservative merchant class to a newer, more aggressive, and more numerous body of business men and speculators of all sorts.

The Jacksonians were unconventional and skillful in politics. In their assault on the Bank they united five important elements, which, incongruities notwithstanding, comprised an effective combination. These were Wall Street's jealousy of Chestnut Street, the business man's dislike of the federal Bank's restraint upon bank credit, the politician's resentment at the Bank's interference with states' rights, popular identification of the Bank with the aristocracy of business, and the direction of agrarian antipathy away from banks in general to the federal Bank in particular. Destruction of the Bank ended federal regulation of bank credit and shifted the money center of the country from Chestnut Street to Wall Street. It left the poor agrarian as poor as he had been before and it left the money power possessed of more money and more power than ever.

II

By the term "Jacksonian" I mean not merely the President's Democratic supporters, whom he still called Republican, but in particular his closest advisers and sharers in responsibility. These included most of his "Kitchen Cabinet," some of his official Cabinet, and a number of others. Those most responsible for the destruction of the Bank, without whose urgency and help it might not have been undertaken or achieved, were all either business men or closely concerned with the business world. Named in the approximate order of their appearance, they were Duff Green, Samuel Ingham, Isaac Hill, Martin Van Buren, Amos Kendall, Francis Preston Blair, Churchill C. Cambreleng, Roger B. Taney, and David Henshaw—all but Taney being or becoming men of wealth. They did not include Major William B. Lewis, a Tennessee planter, one of the General's oldest friends and the only one of his intimates not openly hostile to the Bank. Others of importance were Thomas Hart Benton, James K. Polk, Levi Woodbury, Benjamin F. Butler, Jacob Barker, Reuben M. Whitney, William Gouge, and James A. Hamilton.

Duff Green was born in Kentucky but as a young man he went on to Missouri, where he became a land speculator and merchant, with a substantial business centering in St. Louis. By the time he left there a decade later, he says: "I had established the first line of stages west of the Mississippi. I had a profitable contract for carrying the mail. I had placed the line under the charge of trustworthy partners, who paid me a large fixed income. I had a valuable business as an attorney. I was the editor and proprietor of a leading paper, giving me considerable profit, and I was investing my income in and adjoining the city of St. Louis." He moved to Washington in 1825, where he owned the *United States Telegraph* and edited it in support of Andrew Jackson for President and in denunciation of the Bank of the United States. Newspaper publishing was apparently a simpler, less specialized, and perhaps more generally profitable form of business then than it has since become. He at first belonged to the Kitchen Cabinet, but before long he was thrust out because he was a friend of John C. Calhoun. Though Duff Green borrowed from the Bank, he approved its destruction. But his dislike of it was offset by his dislike of Amos Kendall and other Jacksonians and by his ties of family and friendship with Mr. Calhoun. He continued a long, successful career in business enterprise, being banker, railway-builder, manufacturer, and promoter in divers fields.[2]

Andrew Jackson's first Secretary of the Treasury was Samuel Ingham of Pennsylvania, farm-born but apprenticed to a paper-maker. He remained active in farming while engaged mainly in paper-manufacturing, coal-mining, railways, and eventually banking. Though primarily a business man he was always active in politics. As Secretary of the Treasury he opened the official assault on the federal Bank.

An assistant of his in the Treasury who instigated the attack was Isaac Hill of New Hampshire, also an appointee of General Jackson's. He was frail and lame, an abusive editorial-writer, an acrid partisan, a publisher, a bank director, a bank president, and a substantial man of business. He too was a member of the Kitchen Cabinet. He failed to be confirmed in his Treasury appointment by the Senate, but promptly got elected a member thereof. As an editor, in Professor Sumner's words, "His main 'principle' was that things were in the hands of an 'aristocracy' and that he ought to organize the 'honest yeomanry' in order to oust that aristocracy from power. . . . He had the rancorous malignity of those men who have been in a contest with persons who have treated them from above downwards." When a candidate for Governor of New Hampshire in 1835 he had to be defended from the "grave reproach" of being wealthy. But if wealthy, it was urged, he had not always been so; "Isaac Hill was born of poor but respectable parentage." He was a self-made man and not one of "those sons of fortune who have been from their very cradle nursed in the lap of luxury, who have never known what it is to grapple with adversity, who have found every wish anticipated and every want supplied almost before it was experienced." Such "may thank their God that they are not as this mechanic," but they "will generally be found, in their race through life, . . . outstripped by those whose experience and whose training have prepared them by their very severity for a certain victory."[3]

Martin Van Buren, President Jackson's first Secretary of State, later Vice President with him, and his successor in the Presidency, was probably the

---

[2] Green, 27, 80–81; Washington *Telegraph*, 11 July 1832.

[3] Sumner, *Jackson*, 186; Bradley, 1, 141–44.

most influential of the President's advisers and highest in his esteem. His father had been a farmer and tavern-keeper of very modest estate, and he himself was without formal education. He achieved polish, eminence, and wealth. In his early career he was an associate of Jacob Barker, a Wall Street banker of more enterprise than substance. He left the bar at the age of forty-six, when he became Governor of New York, "with a competence fairly earned, which his prudence and skill made grow into an ample fortune." Baring Brothers were informed by a New York correspondent, the banker Jonathan Goodhue, 16 March 1837, respecting the new President, that "Mr. Van Buren is a very rich man," with an understanding of business "vastly better" than General Jackson's.[4] The Albany Regency, the New York political oligarchy of which he was the creative spirit, maintained banks and politics in the most intimate union. Mr. Van Buren sponsored, as Governor, a law enacted in 1829 authorizing a system of state banks under a Safety Fund. He was always an efficient promoter of New York's economic interests. He did not openly oppose the Bank of the United States till late, or even then conspicuously, and Nichloas Biddle long refused to believe he was not the friend he had seemed to be. Mr. Van Buren's tact was extraordinary; he had superlative skill in political manipulation and the advancement of his own interest without friction or apparent effort. Though self-made, like most of the men on whom General Jackson relied, Mr. Van Buren differed from the others in performing his task with modesty and grace; he was without rancor, without assertiveness, and without the psychotic sense of insecurity and inferiority that seemed to torment many of his Jacksonian associates.

Francis Preston Blair replaced Duff Green as journalist spokesman of the Jacksonians. The new journal set up for him was the *Globe*. Amos Kendall said the *Globe* was originated by "those friends of General Jackson who regarded measures more than men and desired his re-election for another four years, not so much for his own sake, as to effect reforms in the government which no other man was capable of bringing about." Chief of these reforms, Mr. Kendall said, was an end to the Bank. Blair, the *Globe*'s proprietor, had been president of the Commonwealth Bank of Kentucky and co-editor with Amos Kendall of the *Argus of Western America*. He was "heavily indebted" to the Bank of the United States—the amount exceeded $20,000—but the difficulty was got around by a settlement at about ten cents on the dollar, and he was fetched to Washington, where he began publication of the *Globe* in December 1830.[5] The paper was very profitable and with the government printing made Blair a rich man.[*]

---

[4] Shephard, 30; Baring Papers OC, 16 March 1837.

[5] Catterall, 171; Biddle Papers 28, Folio 5730; 4 PLB, 220; Mackenzie, *Butler and Hoyt,* 87–88; Kendall, *Autobiography,* 372, 374.

[*] Blair's indebtedness was to one of the Kentucky offices of the federal Bank. As already said, branches of the Bank, though legally offensive because of their subordination

Amos Kendall was a native of New England, the son of a typically poor but independent Massachusetts farmer of a typically puritan background. He was educated at Dartmouth. In 1814 he emigrated to Kentucky, where in time he became proprietor and editor in Frankfort of the *Argus of Western America*. Although scarcely a personal acquaintance before they came to Washington, Mr. Kendall became invaluable to President Jackson directly thereafter. He was foremost in the Kitchen Cabinet. He held the office of Fourth Auditor of the Treasury but was far beyond his official superiors in influence. It was said that "whatever Kendall went for he fetched." He was known to the generality in Washington as an invincible, sallow, white-haired, unhealthy creature, but seldom seen. Harriet Martineau was fortunate enough to catch a glimpse of him once, and a Congressman who saw him at the same time told her that "he had watched through four sessions for a sight of Kendall and had never obtained it till now." The "invisible Amos Kendall," she reported, was "one of the most remarkable men in America, . . . supposed to be the moving spring of the whole administration; the thinker, planner, and doer; but it is all in the dark." His were the terse and commanding words repeated daily in the Jacksonian press: "The world is governed too much." Being made Postmaster General in 1835, he showed signal administrative ability in reforming the postal service. In 1845 he became associated with Samuel F. B. Morse in the commercial development of the telegraph. He had found Mr. Morse "endeavoring, with little prospect of success, to get an appropriation from Congress to extend a line of his telegraph from Baltimore to New York; it being already in operation between Washington and Baltimore." He asked Mr. Morse "whether he had no project to render his telegraph profitable as a private enterprise." Out of his enquiry an agreement arose which "vested Mr. Kendall with full power to manage and dispose of Morse's interest in his patent-right, according to his discretion." And from this in turn came the erection of telegraph lines everywhere in the country, determined suits in defense of patents, the formation of numerous separate companies, and their eventual consolidation into a nation-wide system. One could not imagine a more explicit example of entrepreneurial behavior. Mr. Kendall fought his way to such wealth and success that in time he had to defend himself from the charge, echoing one he had so often made against the Bank of the United States, that he and his business associates were "autocrats of the telegraph" and that "a more infamous monopoly than the American Telegraph Company" never existed. With Mr. Van Buren, whose

---

to Philadelphia, seem generally to have been well regarded as local or regional institutions in spirit. In 1836 Mr. Blair occupied the handsome Washington residence since known as the Blair House, which remained in his family a century or more till acquired by the government to be maintained as an adjunct to the White House for the lodging of visitors of state.

talents were of a different order, he was the ablest of the Jacksonians and an outstanding figure in American business enterprise.[6]

Mr. Kendall's progress was a consistent one. As early as 1820 he was denying that labor was a source of value. He had always taken a harsh, puritanical view of things and scorned governmental relief in the days of western distress. He had favored "some degree of relief" but condemned Kentucky's interference with foreclosures. "Things will take their course in the moral as well as in the natural world," he had written. Legislatures could not relieve man of his responsibilities. "The people must pay their own debts at last." He had considered the Bank of the United States an artificial monopoly poisonous to individualism and its annihilation the paramount aim of "the Democracy." Speaking years later of "reforms in the government" in which he had participated, he said that "chief of these was its severance from the banking power organized and exercised under the charter of the Bank of the United States." It was his belief that Congress should "be content to let currency and private business alone." He never abandoned this view. He was an apostle and exemplar of *laisser faire*. Government, he said, "cannot make the people rich but may make them poor." Americans, in his opinion, were demanding "that their governments shall content themselves with protecting their persons and property, leaving them to direct their labor and capital as they please, within the moral law; getting rich or remaining poor as may result from their own management or fortune." [7] Mr. Kendall turned to religion and philanthropy in his later years; he was a founder and benefactor of what is now Gallaudet College, for the deaf, Kendall Green, Washington, D. C. It was the only such college in the world, and he was its first president.*

Churchill C. Cambreleng, member of Congress from New York City, was a close associate of Martin Van Buren and an administration leader in the lower house, where he was known as New York's "commercial representative." He was a self-made man of modest North Carolina origins who had become a confidential agent and friend of John Jacob Astor. He had been friendly to the Bank of the United States before Jackson's election. About 1825 he had visited western New York at the request of the Bank, and for a fee, to study the relative advantages of Rochester, Utica, and Buffalo for a

---

[6] Martineau I, 257–59; Kendall, *Autobiography*, 372, 527; Kendall, *Circular*.

[7] Kendall, *Autobiography*, 228, 229, 246, 374, 504–05, 510–13, 559.

* In 1813, while still at Dartmouth, Amos Kendall had submitted some poetry he had written to the *Port Folio* in Philadelphia, whose editors had offered a prize. He failed even of mention. He was naturally peevish about it; he thought the winning pieces were miserable. So do I, but they were not worse than his. If he later recognized in the president of the Bank of the United States the editor who had rejected his work, I can imagine it spurred the politician to avenge the poet; and in the end the smiling, insufferable aristocrat in Philadelphia who lorded it over borrowers and lenders got punished also for lording it over poor versifiers. Kendall, *Autobiography*, 82.

new branch office to be established in that region. He understood the operations of the Bank fully; Nicholas Biddle said it would be "difficult to describe more accurately the plan of circulation of the Bank" than he had
done. Like Martin Van Buren, Mr. Cambreleng was an efficient promoter
of New York's interests, both political and economic. He was tireless and
highly capable in his congressional leadership against the Bank.[8]

Roger B. Taney (pronounced Tawney) was President Jackson's second
Attorney General and his fourth Treasury Secretary. He shared first place
with Kendall and Cambreleng among the President's advisers in relentless,
aggressive, resourceful enmity for the Bank of the United States. He was a
Baltimore attorney and member of a family belonging to the landed aristocracy of southern Maryland, where he was reared. He was a shareholder in
the Union Bank of Baltimore, its counsel, and an intimate friend of its
president, Thomas Ellicott. This bank was one to which federal funds were
transferred when he and President Jackson removed them from the federal
Bank. Mr. Taney had been interested previously in three other banks and a
director of two. In an influential letter to President Jackson, 27 June 1832,
he denied the constitutionality and expediency of the Bank on the ground
that it bestowed privileges on some and refused them to others. He ignored
the regulatory duties of the government and of the Bank, except as an "absolute dominance over the circulating medium of the country," and confined the Bank's usefulness to its safekeeping and transport of federal funds.
As he disingenuously put it, "the simple question of selecting the most
appropriate agent for conveying the public revenues from place to place
has excited as much heat and passion as even the great question of the
tariff." The question was not the simple one he said it was, and the regulation of banking and money is no less important than the tariff. He dwelt
on the unfairness to the state banks of chartering a federal Bank, exempt
from state taxation, on "the burthens now borne by the state banks," and
on the "heavy impositions" invidiously put on "the property of individuals
in the state banks." For, he said, "the stockholders in the state banks, who
are generally men in moderate circumstances, are subject to the weight of
unlimited war taxation whenever the public exigency may require it—
why should the stock in the Bank of the United States, which is generally
held by the most opulent monied men, many of them wealthy foreigners,
be entirely free from the additional taxation which war or any other calam-
ity may bring upon the rest of the community? . . . The money of the
citizens employed in the state banks is to be diminished in value by new
burthens whenever the wants of the country require it, while the money
of the opulent citizen and of the wealthy foreigner . . . is not to be allowed
to feel the pressure. . . ." This was false. No such line could be drawn be-

---

[8] 22nd Congress, 1st Session, HR 460, p. 357–58; Mackenzie, *Van Buren*, 101 n; *Butler
and Hoyt*, 104–06.

tween the wealth of the federal Bank's stockholders and that of state bank stockholders, nor had the federal Bank any immunity from taxation, save by the states.[9]

Mr. Taney was eventually appointed Chief Justice of the Supreme Court by President Jackson, where his decisions regularly favored free enterprise and competition—and typically so in the Charles River Bridge case, 1837. In this major decision he denied that rights had been vested in one toll-bridge corporation which must be allowed to obstruct the erection of other bridges needed by the community. The rights of the first, the Charles River Bridge, ran back by succession almost two centuries to a legislative grant to Harvard College for a ferry between Cambridge and Boston. The income from tolls on the bridge that replaced the ferry made it a very profitable investment. But one bridge in time proved not to be enough; and the new bridge that was built being eventually passable without toll, to the loss of income and investment by the Charles River Bridge's proprietors, the latter sued in the Supreme Court for redress. Their suit was rejected. The State, according to Taney's opinion, could not be supposed to have surrendered "its power of improvement and public accommodation in a great and important line of travel along which a vast number of its citizens must daily pass." For though the rights of property are to be "sacredly guarded, we must not forget that the community also have rights and that the happiness and well being of every citizen depends on their faithful preservation." Especially "in a country like ours," declared Chief Justice Taney, "free, active, and enterprising, continually advancing in numbers and wealth, new channels of communication are daily found necessary, both for travel and trade, and are essential to the comfort, convenience, and prosperity of the people." [10]

It does not derogate from the propriety of this opinion to point out that though it is compatible with agrarian doctrine its real affinity is with *laisser faire*. It favored free enterprise, and at the same time it contributed to a new concept of the corporation. Though it seemed at the moment a blow at corporate rights in the sense that it refused to preserve a monopoly of bridge traffic anciently conferred, its beneficiary was not an individual or several individuals but a new and rival corporation competing with the old. It therefore further familiarized people with corporate competition as well as corporate monopoly and definitely helped the corporation replace the individual as an agent of free enterprise in the economy. Mr. Taney, I am sure, intended no such eventuality. Nor, I am sure, did Justice Story and Daniel Webster, by insisting on the preservation of the rights long vested in the original bridge company, intend that future material progress be shackled to 17th century grants appropriate to 17th century life. But

---

[9] Swisher, 190–93; Jackson Papers 81, Folio 15985, 16008, 16011.
[10] *Charles River Bridge* v. *Warren Bridge*, 11 Peters 419, 546.

Taney just as surely was on the side of *laisser faire* and rampant business individualism as Story and Webster were on the side of economic and technical conservatism. He was not attacking vested rights *per se,* or corporate rights, or property rights, or wealth, or capitalism, but propounding a new democratic concept that within his own lifetime was to be more typical of capitalism than was the clumsy, antediluvian monopoly that he refused to sanction.

And so of his interposition in banking—to say that it was agrarian and anticapitalistic is absurd. By siding with the state banks against the federal Bank, he simply contributed to a new and democratic concept then current, which in New York in 1838 achieved what at the time seemed one of the notable glories of the age of Jackson—the authorization of "free banking." Yet even if *laisser faire* be deemed beneficent on the whole, it does not follow that it was properly applicable to the monetary function or warranted Taney's advocacy, in Horace Binney's words, of "an unregulated, uncontrolled, state bank paper currency." The monetary function is within the province of governmental responsibility, and though Mr. Taney and the other Jacksonians did not deny it, they did deny, to their own stultification, that banking was a monetary function. Instead they were interested in banking for the good, earthy reason that it was a fine way to make money. As Secretary of the Treasury in the Cabinet of a President who believed banks to be unconstitutional as well as morally evil, Mr. Taney said publicly and officially that "there is perhaps no business which yields a profit so certain and liberal as the business of banking and exchange; and it is proper that it should be open as far as practicable to the most free competition and its advantages shared by all classes of society." Mr. Taney made little money himself but both in administrative office and on the bench he propounded the philosophy of competitive enterprise with remarkable success. And such was his command of the arts of sycophancy and misrepresentation—always, however, in furtherance of democratic rights—that he readily got the old hero he served to face the opposite way from his real convictions and knife his own agrarian cause.[11]

David Henshaw, one of the most important business men who helped in the assault on the federal Bank, was a poor farmer boy who became a banker, a railway-builder, newspaper-publisher, business-promoter generally, Collector of the Port of Boston, and Jacksonian political boss of Massachusetts. "Though a wealthy man," Professor Arthur M. Schlesinger, Jr., observes, "Henshaw had many of the prejudices of his humble origin. His personal rancor toward the aristocracy which had snubbed him was not unlike that of his good friend, Isaac Hill." Professor Arthur B. Darling says of Henshaw and his associates that "in order to develop political influence over the poorer classes, they themselves made capital of their hostility to-

[11] Congress, *Register of Debates* x, Part 2, 2322; Treasury Department, Secretary, *Reports on Finances, 1789–1849* III, 457.

ward the wealthy." Henshaw's *Remarks upon the Bank of the United States,* 1831, and his proposal in 1832 for a new bank with $50,000,000 of Jacksonian capital which should replace the aristocratic monster in Philadelphia that had a capital of only $35,000,000, were echoed in the message President Jackson sent to Congress when he vetoed the federal Bank's charter in 1832. His arguments were echoed again in the reasons given to Congress by Secretary Taney in 1833 for having ceased to deposit the public funds in the public Bank. "Even if it be expedient to grant a Bank upon the same plan," Henshaw said, "it ought not to be exclusively to the present stockholders. . . . The whole community should be offered the opportunity to have an interest in the institution on equal terms." This argument, though false in its implication, impressed the President. Henshaw in 1830 had deposited in his own bank the public funds he took in as Collector of the Port of Boston, thus pioneering in the action that Jackson and Taney took three years later in removing the federal funds from the federal depository and putting them in pet state banks.[12]

David Henshaw's views on vested rights received still more formidable confirmation. Having had land to sell in South Boston to which free access must be provided, he and his associates had built a bridge, given it to the state, and sold the land profitably. Later Henshaw championed the new Warren Bridge against the old Charles River Bridge in the controversy to which I have just referred in speaking of Roger B. Taney. He was scorned by the more intellectual and idealistic Jacksonians, but the irrefragable arguments he offered in the Boston press against the sanctity of charter grants and in favor of free bridges and free enterprise can be found again in the learned opinion which Chief Justice Taney rendered in the Charles River Bridge case.*

From among the foregoing Jacksonians, Major William B. Lewis is missing. He was one of Andrew Jackson's oldest and closest friends, a neighbor in Tennessee, Second Auditor of the Treasury, and a resident with the General at the White House. He was an expert politician, adept in the manipulation and creation of "public opinion," but seems to have had no economic interest other than that of southern planter. He was the only cultivator of the soil, the only real agrarian, the President kept close to him in Washington, and he was of the well-to-do sort, not the horny-handed. He was also the only one of the President's closest associates to befriend the Bank of the United States. He seems to have thought it more sensible to

---

[12] Schlesinger, 147; Darling, 7; Henshaw, 36; New England Historical and Genealogical Society, *Memorial Biographies* I, 491.

* Since writing this, I find that Professor Darling has also compared Jackson's veto with Henshaw's compositions and noticed "that Jackson was familiar with Henshaw's arguments." More than familiar, I should say; and so was Taney. It was sensible of Jackson and Taney to heed Henshaw's advice, which for their purposes was invaluable, and Henshaw deserves credit that he has never got for his help in achieving Jacksonian aims. Darling, 136, note 13.

make the Bank Jacksonian than to destroy it. His was the sole agrarian element in the administration's relations with the Bank, and it was not hostile.

III

. . . With the business interests and objectives of the Jacksonians I have no quarrel save for the cant which made the conflict over the Bank of the United States appear to be one of idealism against lucre and of human rights against property rights. The Jacksonians were no less drawn by lucre than the so-called conservatives, but rather more. They had no greater concern for human rights than the people who had what they were trying to get. The millionaires created by the so-called Jacksonian revolution of "agrarians" against "capitalists"—of the democracy against the money-power—were richer than those they dispossessed, they were more numerous, they were quite as ruthless; and *laisser faire,* after destroying the monopolies and vested rights the Jacksonians decried, produced far greater ones. There was nothing sacred about the federal Bank. The defense of it is simply that it was very useful and if not perfect it could have been improved, had its enemies felt any interest in improving it. The Jacksonians paid no heed to its merits but canted virtuously about the rich and the poor, hydras, and other irrelevancies. This was good politics. But it cannot conceal the envy and acquisitiveness that were their real motives. What the Jacksonians decided on, they directed their propaganda toward, and got. What they went for, they fetched, like Amos Kendall. An unusual number of them were not only business men but journalists, and gained both profit and influence through the press—notably Duff Green, Amos Kendall, Francis Preston Blair, Isaac Hill, and David Henshaw. They told the world it was governed too much. They vied with their great contemporary James Gordon Bennett in a glib and vigorous style. The Washington *Globe,* the organ of the administration, was attractively printed on good paper, every active Jacksonian had to take it, and, its contents aside, even the best people could feel satisfied to have it lying on the parlor table. It relied otherwise on unashamed, repetitious adulation of Andrew Jackson and defamation of his enemies. It presented matters in black and white, Bank and President, hydra and hero. "Many a time," Amos Kendall is made to say in John Pendleton Kennedy's satire, *Quodlibet,* "have I riveted by diligent hammering, a politic and necessary fabrication upon the credulity of the people—so fast that no art of my adversary could tear it away to make room for the truth. Therefore, I say to you and our democratic friends—hammer without ceasing." [13]

---

[13] Kennedy, 178.

IV

Andrew Jackson himself had been lawyer, legislator, jurist, merchant, and land speculator, but principally planter and soldier. His origin was humble and agrarian. He was a self-made man. He belonged to an aristocracy of a frontier sort peculiar to the Southwest of his day—landed, proud, individualistic, slave-owning, and more bound by the cruder conventions than the politer ones. Cock-fighting, betting, horse-racing, and the punctilio of the duel seem to have satisfied its cultural needs. It was without the education and discipline of the older aristocracies of the sea-board. It possessed more of the aristocrat's assertive and obnoxious vices than his gentler, liberal virtues and stood on property and pretension rather than birth and breeding. In a quarrel General Jackson would resort to the field of honor if his enemy were a "gentleman" but merely beat him with a stick on sight if he were not. Such distinctions seem to have been lost on Albert Gallatin, an aristocrat of a different water, in whose fastidious judgment President Jackson was "a pugnacious animal." [14]

Yet the distinction and courtesy of the General's manners took by surprise those who knew him first as President; he was by then unwell, grieving over the death of his wife, and softened besides by what age will sometimes do to men. He was not now the brawler in taverns and at racetracks. "I was agreeably disappointed and pleased," wrote William Lyon Mackenzie of Upper Canada in 1829—a man of considerable violence himself in word and deed—"to find in General Jackson great gentleness and benevolence of manner, accompanied by that good natured affability of address which will enable persons who wait upon him to feel at ease in his presence. . . ." When he chose, however, the General still could storm outrageously enough. He could simulate bursts of passion that terrified strangers, who shrank from having the President of the United States burst a blood vessel on their account, even though they were not fond of him. But his tongue seldom slipped. No one profited from blunders of his. What mistakes he made arose from a child-like trust in his friends and not from carelessness with his adversaries.[15]

He was exceptionally susceptible to the flattery and suggestion of his friends. This did not impair his maintaining a forceful, determined leadership. He listened to his advisers individually and chose his plan of action himself. His native views were agrarian and Jeffersonian, though of Jefferson himself he could entertain very low opinions, and no one—not Alexander Hamilton himself—ever went further from the constitutional principles of Jefferson than Jackson did in his nullification proclamation of December 1832. With him, moreover, as with other self-made men of his

---

[14] Marquis James, 109; Henry Adams, *Gallatin,* 651.
[15] Mackenzie, *Sketches,* 46–47.

time, agrarian and Jeffersonian views faded into *laisser faire*. He was a rugged individualist in all directions. He was no friend to the shiftless and indigent who got into debt and then could not get out. He paid his own debts, no matter how hard he found it to do so, and he expected others to pay theirs.

"Andrew Jackson was on the side of the capitalists," writes Mr. Marquis James of his earlier career. "His first case in Nashville in 1788 had landed him as champion of the creditors against the debtors. Jackson desired wealth." He had been opposed to western relief measures taken on behalf of debtors in the ten years preceding his election to the Presidency. They were wicked, pernicious, profligate, and unconstitutional. Opinions like this put him logically on the side of the Bank of the United States, which was the pivotal creditor, and opposed him to the banks made of paper, such as the Bank of the Commonwealth of Kentucky, over which his kitchen adviser, Francis Preston Blair, had presided. But solecisms embarrassed the General very little. On the frontier more than elsewhere, the modification of an agrarian economy into an industrial and financial one was such, in William Lyon Mackenzie's words, as to "make speculation as extensive as life, and transform a Jeffersonian democracy into a nation of gamesters and our land into one great gaming house where all are forced to play, while but few can understand the game." General Jackson's prejudices were stronger than his convictions, and he was himself among the least consistent and stable of the Jacksonians. "Not only was Jackson not a consistent politician," says Professor Thomas P. Abernethy, "he was not even a real leader of democracy. He had no part whatever in the promotion of the liberal movement which was progressing in his own state. . . . He was a self-made man . . . he always believed in making the public serve the ends of the politician. Democracy was good talk with which to win the favor of the people and thereby accomplish ulterior objectives. Jackson never really championed the cause of the people; he only invited them to champion his. He was not consciously hypocritical in this. It was merely the usual way of doing business in these primitive and ingenuous times." Of his election to the Presidency Professor Richard Hofstadter writes that it was not "a mandate for economic reform; no financial changes, no crusades against the national Bank, were promised. . . . Up to the time of his inauguration Jackson had contributed neither a thought nor a deed to the democratic movement, and he was elected without a platform." [16]

What counts is that Jackson was popular. He was a picturesque folk character, and it does his memory an injustice to make him out a statesman. "All the remodelling and recoloring of Andrew Jackson," says Professor Abernethy, "has not created a character half so fascinating as he was in reality." To the dissatisfied, whether through distress or ambition, Andrew Jackson

---

[16] Marquis James, 89; Mackenzie, *Butler and Hoyt,* 105 n; Abernethy, 248–49; Hofstadter, 54.

offered a distinct and attractive change from the old school of leaders the country had had—and not the least by his want of real ideas. He became the champion of the common man, even though the latter might be no longer either frontiersman or farmer but speculator, capitalist, or entrepreneur of a new, democratic sort, who in every village and township was beginning to profit by the Industrial Revolution, the growth of population, and the expanding supply of bank credit. This new common man was manufacturer, banker, builder, carrier, and promoter. He belonged to the "active and enterprising," in the luminous contrast put by Churchill C. Cambreleng, as against the "wealthier classes." And his conflict was not the traditionary one between the static rich and the static poor but a dynamic, revolutionary one between those who were already rich and those who sought to become rich.[17]

General Jackson was an excellent leader in the revolt of enterprise against the regulation of credit by the federal Bank. Though the inferior of his associates in knowledge, he was extraordinarily effective in combat. And as a popular leader he combined the simple agrarian principles of political economy absorbed at his mother's knee with the most up-to-date doctrine of *laisser faire*. Along with several of the best constitutional authorities of his day—but not Mr. Taney—General Jackson believed that the notes issued by state banks were unconstitutional. In 1820 he wrote to his friend Major Lewis: "You know my opinion as to the banks, that is, that the constitution of our state as well as the Constitution of the United States prohibited the establishment of banks in any state. Sir, the tenth section of the first article of the federal Constitution is positive and explicit, and when you read the debates in the convention you will find it was introduced to prevent a state legislature from passing such bills." Seventeen years later, in 1837, he wrote to Senator Benton: "My position now is and has ever been since I have been able to form an opinion on this subject that Congress has no power to charter a Bank and that the states are prohibited from issuing bills of credit or granting a charter by which such bills can be issued by any corporation or order." Yet in effect he did as much as could be done to augment the issue of state bank notes and was proud of what he did. Most statesmen would feel some embarrassment in such a performance.[18]

The Jacksonians were anything but rash. Once decided that they should fight the Bank rather than wed with it, they developed their attack patiently, experimentally, shrewdly, probing the aristocratic victim and teasing public interest into action. The President himself took no unnecessary chances, but those he had to take he took without fear. He was a man of "sagacious temerity," in the words of one of his contemporaries. His attack

[17] Abernethy, 124; 22nd Congress, 1st Session, HR 460, p. 333.
[18] New York Public Library, *Bulletin* IV (1900), 190; Jackson, *Correspondence* IV, 446; Bassett II, 590.

on the Bank was like his careful slaying of Charles Dickinson in a duel thirty years before. His opponent had been formidable—much younger than he and an expert marksman, which he himself was not. Each was to have one shot. Jackson and his second had gone over the prospects carefully and decided it would be best to wait for Dickinson to fire first. For though Jackson would probably be hit, "he counted on the resource of his will to sustain him until he could aim deliberately and shoot to kill, if it were the last act of his life." So he awaited his adversary's fire and, as he had expected, he was hit. But his coat, buttoned loosely over his breast, as was his wont, had presented a deceptive silhouette, and the ball had missed his heart. He concealed his hurt and concentrated on his helpless enemy, whose life he now could take. "He stood glowering at him for an instant, and then his long pistol arm came slowly to a horizontal position." He aimed carefully and pulled the trigger. But the hammer stopped at half-cock. The seconds consulted while the principals stood, and Jackson was allowed to try again. Once more he took deliberate aim, his victim waiting in evident horror, and fired. Dickinson fell, mortally hurt. "I should have hit him," Jackson asserted later, "if he had shot me through the brain." The same mystical will power, the same canny and studious appraisal of probabilities and of relative advantages and disadvantages, weighed in the conflict with the Bank. The President tantalized the frank and impatient Mr. Biddle, he waited for him to make the appropriate mistakes, and then with care and effectiveness he struck. His adversaries' weaknesses were no less at his command than his own skill.[19]

*　　*　　*

VI

Despite the fact of a strong and determined rebellion within the business world against the Bank of the United States, the fiction that the attack on the Bank was on behalf of agrarians against capitalists, of humanity against property, of the poor against the rich, and of "the people" against "the money power," has persisted. There was, to be sure, an extremely respectable minority comprising the more conservative and thoughtful men of business, Mr. Gallatin, for example, and Nathan Appleton, who defended the Bank till near the end, but it will scarcely do to say that they represented the business world while C. C. Cambreleng, David Henshaw, and Reuben Whitney did not.

It is obvious that New York, besides gaining most from a successful attack on the Bank, risked the least; for it did not need, as the South and West did, the capital brought in by the Bank's branches. The West's aversion for the federal Bank was like the nationalistic resentment in a 20th century

---

[19] Ingersoll, 264; Marquis James, 116–18; Bassett, 63–64.

underdeveloped economy which wants and needs imported capital but growls at the "imperialism" of the country that is expected to provide it. The western enemies of the Bank were moved by complex psychological and political considerations—including past distress and present dependence—while its New York enemies were moved, much more simply, by covetousness and rivalry. This was the decisive new ingredient provided in the Jacksonian attack. The agrarian prejudice had been alive since 1791 and most dangerous to the Bank a few years past during its critical days and the distress in the Ohio valley. The state bank opposition was almost as old as the agrarian. And the relative importance of the two varied with the decline of agrarianism and the growth of enterprise. New York, now the center of enterprise, added to the long-lived antagonism a hearty and acute self-interest. That Andrew Jackson proved to be the instrument of her interest was the happy result of Mr. Van Buren's skill and devotion.

It goes without saying that Andrew Jackson himself did not understand what was happening. He had started with a vague, agrarian prejudice against banking which on occasion cropped up throughout his life but never led him to deny himself the service of banks or the friendship and support of bankers.* It was no great task for his advisers to arouse this dormant distrust, nourished on what he had read about the South Sea Bubble, and focus it upon the Bank in Philadelphia, a city whence he had suffered years before, at the hands of a bankrupt merchant and speculator, a harsh financial misfortune. Nor was an elaborate plot required to be agreed upon among conspirators. The first harassment of the Bank from the administration group was evidently spontaneous and simply aimed at making the Bank Jacksonian. Some time elapsed before it got under directed control. Even then there is no reason to suppose that the program was not mainly opportunistic. In the early stages the object need have been only to make sure that the charter be not renewed. To this end the General's mind must be fixed against the Bank, and the proper improvement of opportunities could be left to the discretion of those in whose path the opportunities appeared. The adviser who influenced the General most directly or who perhaps left the best record of what he did was Roger B. Taney, though he joined the Jacksonian circle late. He succeeded in filling the General's mind with a vindictiveness that Martin Van Buren or Amos Kendall would probably not have produced. They too would have killed the Bank but with less emotion and less cant. "When a great monied institution," Mr. Taney told the General, "attempts to overawe the President in the discharge of his high constitutional duties, it is conclusive evidence

---

* He did not cease transacting personal and family business with the Nashville office of the Bank of the United States, which he presumably dissociated from the main office in Philadelphia. The view was reasonable. Gravitation of the branches toward independence was a perennial source of weakness to the Bank; and eventually they became local banks in fact.

that it is conscious of possessing vast political power which it supposes the President can be made to feel." The Taney reasoning is sound, but the premises are misrepresented, and the effect was to fill the President with bitter suspicion of the Bank; though the alleged "attempts to overawe the President"—this was written in June 1832—were the reasonable attempts of Mr. Biddle to gain support for the Bank, find out what the scowls and rumblings from Washington signified, and remove the doubts that he thought were troubling the President.[20]

But thanks to the sort of thing Mr. Taney kept telling him, the President by now had few doubts such as Mr. Biddle imagined. He was merely considering how best to proceed against the Bank. Replacement, he realized, was necessary, and for a long time he was fumbling over unintelligible projects to that end. One of these projects, which may be intelligible to those whose understanding has not been corrupted by some knowledge and experience of the subject, was described to James A. Hamilton, 3 June 1830. The President had in mind "a national bank chartered upon the principles of the checks and balances of our federal government, with a branch in each state, the capital apportioned agreeably to representation and to be attached to and be made subject to supervision of the Secretary of the Treasury." He recalls having shown Mr. Hamilton "my ideas on a bank project, both of deposit (which I think the only national bank that the government ought to be connected with) and one of discount and deposit, which from the success of the State Bank of South Carolina I have no doubt could be wielded profitably to our government with less demoralizing effects upon our citizens than the Bank that now exists. But a *national* Bank, entirely *national* Bank of deposit is all we ought to have: but I repeat a national Bank of discount and deposit may be established upon our revenue and national faith pledged and carried on by salaried officers, as our revenue is now collected, with less injury to the morals of our citizens and to the destruction of our liberty than the present hydra of corruption and all the emoluments accrue to the nation as part of the revenue." But these ruminations belonged merely to a period of waiting. As soon as a promising arrangement offered, the President acted. He ordered the federal funds removed from the Bank and put in the banks of his friends.[21]

Besides contributing mainly, by this course, to a shift of the money market from Chestnut Street to Wall Street, the General contributed to the inflation, the speculation, and the various monetary evils which, with a persistent agrarian bias, he blamed on banks and paper money. There were plenty of men in his own party, among them better agrarians than himself, who would have cleared his vision and tried to, but the old gentleman preferred the sycophantic advisers who stimulated his suspicions and prejudices, blinded him to facts, confused him about the nature of the federal

---

[20] Jackson Papers 81, Folio 16006.
[21] J. A. Hamilton, *Reminiscences*, 167–68.

Bank's usefulness, diverted his attention from the possibility that it be amended and corrected instead of being destroyed, and allowed him to declaim the most ignorant but popular clap-trap.[22]

VII

Although the Bank was by no means the only thing that occupied the Jacksonians, its destruction was apparently esteemed by many of them their finest accomplishment. It rumpled and demoralized the aristocrats they envied. It redistributed vested rights. It established *laisser faire*. It freed banks from federal credit regulation. It reduced the government's monetary powers by more than half. It stimulated business. It furthered the interests of New York City, Boston, and Baltimore at the expense of Philadelphia. In all this there was abundant satisfaction for Van Buren, Kendall, Henshaw, Cambreleng, Taney, and others who were like-minded.

There were many dissidents among the Jacksonians, however, who deplored the materialism of the Democracy. To the intellectuals prominent in the party, and especially to George Bancroft, David Henshaw was an abomination. The *Pennsylvanian* of Philadelphia, itself Jacksonian, felt the presence in the party of too many "Wall Street gamblers." Erastus Root, the up-state New York agrarian in Congress, defended the federal Bank from Martin Van Buren's Albany Regency and the New York banks and got purged for it. When the New York *Evening Post* protested in 1835 at Amos Kendall's order forbidding the use of the mails for abolitionist literature, it was excommunicated by the administration's mouthpiece in Washington: "The *Evening Post* has on various occasions shown a disposition to fly off from the Democratick Party by running into extremes. . . . The spirit of agrarianism was perceivable in all the political views of the editor, and it seemed as if he was inclined to legislate altogether upon abstraction and allow the business of the world and the state of society to have nothing to do with it." A writer in the *Democratic Review* in December 1838 distinguished Democrats by trade from Democrats in principle, ironically disparaging the latter in favor of the more sensible Democrat by trade, who "got a snug slice of the public deposits" for his bank.[23]

From a very different viewpoint, the Canadian patriot, William Lyon Mackenzie, whose great-grandson a century later was Canada's premier, had much to say of the Jacksonians. He had contrasted the economic and political backwardness of the Provinces under British rule with the progress and prosperity of the States and had tried to make both the British government and his fellow subjects learn something from American experience. But in his own province of Upper Canada, and in the others, authority had re-

---

[22] [J. R. McCulloch], *Edinburgh Review* LXV (1837), 227–28.
[23] Niles XLV (1833), 39; Congress, *Register of Debates* VIII, Part 2, 2036 ff, 2069 ff; New York *Evening Post*, 24 September 1835; *Democratic Review* III (1838), 368.

mained unyielding, with Family Compact, Church, and Seigneury. So, like George Washington and his compatriots sixty years before, Mr. Mackenzie had been driven to conclude that armed rebellion was necessary. With the sentiments of the American Declaration of Independence in mind, he had "engaged at last," he said, "in a desperate though for the time an unsuccessful attempt to transplant the same institutions" into Canada. He had failed and fled to the States, where, expecting to remain, for there was a price on his head in the Provinces and some of his associates had been hanged, he supported the Jacksonians. He was a journalist. In singular circumstances he came in possession of the private correspondence of prominent New York Jacksonians—Van Buren, Cambreleng, and others.[24] Reading it, he asked himself, "Is this, can it be, free, enlightened, democratic America? The America of my early dreams it surely is not." No idea, he thought, "can be more erroneous than that men of humble origin are more friendly to the class among whom they were reared than the dwellers in palaces and among the opulent of the land." *

Popular propaganda has acquired more general and familiar use since the age of Jackson, but none more skillful. With the exception of a few persons who, with John Pendleton Kennedy, could appreciate the art of Amos Kendall and his associates, Americans were hypnotized by the Jacksonian propaganda, and Andrew Jackson himself—its main object—got guidance and inspiration from it. That many historians still follow the Jacksonian formula points to its effectiveness. In the words of one, for example, "The poor men of the East and of the West were asserting the power of their mass strength and, putting Andrew Jackson in the presidency, were smashing that symbol of financial autocracy, the great Bank of the United States." I take this quotation not as the isolated judgment of one historian but as typical of the view that seems in recent years to have gained in conventional favor, despite the record of the conspicuous business interests of the leading Jacksonians, of the accomplishments of the federal Bank, and of the disposition of the state banking interests toward it, especially in New York and Boston.[25]

The words of another historian are equally typical. "By doing away with paper money," he says, Jacksonian policy "proposed to restrict the steady transfer of wealth from the farmer and laborer to the business community.

---

[24] Mackenzie, *Van Buren,* 16, 90 n; *Butler and Hoyt,* 140 n.

* He published the correspondence he had found, and it was never repudiated. To Mr. Van Buren, however, he was "that somewhat notorious person" who found an old trunk, rifled it of its contents, and published them—a "pitiful enterprise." Upon the grant of amnesty in 1849, Mr. Mackenzie, his mind completely changed about America, returned to Canada, where the efforts in which he had risked hanging had already borne fruit in Lord Durham's brilliant report and in the achievement of responsible government for the Provinces through the further efforts of Robet Baldwin and Louis H. La Fontaine. Van Buren, *Autobiography,* 536–69; Lindsey, 458, 470 ff.

[25] Gabriel, *American Democratic Thought,* 44.

By limiting banks to commercial credit and denying them control over the currency, it proposed to lessen their influence and power. By reducing the proportion of paper money, it proposed to moderate the business cycle, and order the economy to the advantage of the worker rather than the speculator." [26]

These statements seem to me fallacious, individually and collectively. For one thing I do not believe that Van Buren, Kendall, Cambreleng, Henshaw, and Taney ever proposed restricting the transfer of wealth from the farmer and laborer to the business community, or lessening the influence and power of banks, or moderating the business cycle, or ordering the economy to the advantage of the worker. The passage reflects the Jacksonians' views neither of men nor of money. The two latter aims they never thought of, in modern terms, and the two former were nearer the opposite of what they sought. And if Van Buren, Kendall, Cambreleng, Henshaw, and Taney ever supposed that any of these aims could be achieved by getting rid of paper money and limiting banks to commercial credit, then I shall have to acknowledge that they were less bright than I supposed. They probably understood the equivalence of note and deposit liabilities as well as Albert Gallatin did, and they certainly knew that a greater volume of business payments could be made by check more conveniently than by bank notes, if not already so made. Their attack on banking powers, except as exercised by the federal Bank, was pretense. But it was pretense conveniently obscured by the current confusion as to what comprised banking powers. So long as most people identified banking with note issue, an attack on note issue seemed deadly to bankers and the money power. Instead, it would be bad for bankers in the backwoods, for whom note issue was still important, but the bankers in Wall Street it would never touch.

But, of course, the notion that even the note issue function of banks was seriously threatened was not entertained by any sophisticated Jacksonian. Senator Thomas Hart Benton, it is true, seems to have entertained it, for when in 1837 he saw banks and bank issues increasing, he showed signs of real surprise. "I did not join in putting down the Bank of the United States," he said, "to put up a wilderness of local banks. I did not join in putting down the paper currency of a national bank to put up a national paper currency of a thousand local banks." It is doubtful if many Jacksonian leaders shared his naïveté. They may rather have been amused at Old Bullion's primitive ideas. [27]

That the party should have been so largely a party of business enterprise and that its leaders should have been men so devoted to the principle of *laisser faire* is not in itself to be reprehended, of course. Even the critics of that principle can excuse the Jacksonians for being impressed by it. In a sense *laisser faire* was idealistic in that it assumed human nature to be good

---

[26] Schlesinger, 125.   [27] Congress, *Register of Debates* XIII (1837), Part 1, 610.

and governments, save at their simplest, evil. But the preoccupations of *laisser faire* were in fact materialistic. It was the device of men who wished to make money. They clothed their new aspirations in the familiar, idealistic language of the religious and agrarian traditions in which they had been reared. There was no other period in American history, one would hope, when language was more idealistic, endeavor more materialistic, and the tone of public life more hypocritical than during the Jacksonian revolution.

On the Bank itself, of course, the party was divided, though the close associates of the President who befriended it, William B. Lewis, Louis McLane, and Edward Livingston, were exceptional. On the tariff, which rivaled the Bank in importance, the division was far more confusing; though the party was professedly for low tariffs, it was responsible for schedules that provoked the doctrine of nullification. Logically, free trade should have been deduced as directly from Amos Kendall's dictum, "the world is governed too much," as was the quashing of currency and credit regulation, and a substantial number of Jacksonians contended consistently for both, as Cambreleng did. But others, including Jackson himself, and the country as a whole, chose governmental interposition in the form of protective tariffs and rejected it in the form of credit restriction. These were choices that followed the higher logic of what was most profitable: government should boost business but should not bother it—becoming at its best Hamiltonian in one direction and Jeffersonian in the other. Party-wise, and reduced to the simplest terms, the Jacksonian aims—that is, Mr. Van Buren's —were to end Philadelphia's rivalry of New York as financial center and Mr. Calhoun's rivalry of Mr. Van Buren himself as successor to Andrew Jackson in the presidency. Both aims were achieved, at the sacrifice of monetary regulation on the one hand and of low tariffs on the other.*

VIII

Nicholas Biddle, who seems to have been a Jacksonian himself to the extent of having voted for the General in place of his old friend John Quincy Adams, had no such band of helpers to defend the Bank of the United States as General Jackson had to attack it. The older, more conservative, non-political part of the business world supported the Bank with enough decorum but too little energy. Those who defended it the loudest did so because they disliked Andrew Jackson. Henry Clay and Daniel Webster, though they were committed to the Bank on principle, were far more committed to anything that would thwart the General.[28]

---

* My analysis is the same in substance as Mr. Wiltse's in his biography of Calhoun: "Opposition to internal improvements and opposition to the Bank were the basic economic interests of New York and were therefore the corner stones of Van Buren's policy." Charles M. Wiltse, *John C. Calhoun, Nullifier,* 40; also chap. 10.

[28] Biddle, *Correspondence,* 55–56.

Henry Clay was himself a very popular westerner, skillful in politics, ambitious, and able. He too had been a poor boy but singularly fortunate in winning important friends to ease his rise. Except for farming and cattle-breeding, statecraft absorbed him. His policy of fostering American industry with protective tariffs was much approved in the North, though it conflicted in principle and even in practice with *laisser faire*. Clay's policy ultimately prevailed and was of immense consequence to business enterprise, but he was not himself a successful money-maker.

Neither was Daniel Webster. The impracticality and improvidence in business matters of these two brilliant men contrasts interestingly with the shrewd acquisitiveness of their Jacksonian opponents, who knew how to make money and hold on to it. For Henry Clay and Daniel Webster, champions of the "money power," of "monopoly," and of "privilege," were always going beyond their means, floundering in debt, and dependent on their friends to keep them on their feet. Thomas Wren Ward, of Boston, a business man of the foremost ability and character, reported to his principals, the Barings, that he considered Mr. Webster "by far the greatest man we have," and "in bringing power on a given point . . . probably greater than any man now living." Yet, he also said, "great as Mr. Webster unquestionably is, and sound as are his views generally, and able as he is on great occasions in defending the true principles of the Constitution and upholding the rights of property, still I do not give him my esteem and confidence." This was because, in Mr. Ward's opinion, he showed "a disregard to his moral obligations and a recklessness in pecuniary matters." Mr. Ward depicts Mr. Webster as living largely by passing the hat among wealthy men, who lent him money because of his public importance and scarcely expected him to repay it; in England he would try to do the same. "It will be easy to have him in your books if you desire it, but whatever he may owe you, I think you will be very safe in writing off to profit and loss." [29]

The two best aides Mr. Biddle had were Horace Binney and John Sergeant, Philadelphia lawyers of great competence. The latter was a personal friend of Nicholas Biddle from the literary days of the *Port Folio*. Neither Binney nor Sergeant had had so golden a social and economic background as Nicholas Biddle, but neither could they be called poor farm boys and self-made men. They were the best of Mr. Biddle's aides in the inadequate sense that they were highly intelligent, judicious, and reputable gentlemen; which, of course, made them no match whatever for President Jackson's array of experts. Unlike Henry Clay and Daniel Webster, they had something of the sincere, understanding loyalty to the Bank that Nicholas Biddle had. They knew its purpose and value as he did. Mr. Webster knew its purpose and value long enough to make a speech; I doubt if Mr. Clay ever bothered to go beyond the simple generalization that the Bank was an important institution which Andrew Jackson did not like.

---

[29] Baring Papers, T. W. Ward to Baring Brothers, 29 April 1839.

Politics also kept John C. Calhoun from helping the Bank as he might have done. More than anyone else, he could claim the chartering of the Bank in 1816 as his work, and he understood the Bank's operation better than anyone else in Washington. But just at the time when the assault on the Bank was most critical—in 1832 and 1833—Mr. Calhoun was wholly absorbed in resistance to the tariff. In January 1834, however, he passed a scathing and accurate judgment on removal of the public deposits from the government Bank and on the reasons offered to Congress by Secretary Taney for this removal. In this address and in another in March, no less brilliant, he discussed the functions of the Bank clearly and objectively. His thorough understanding of its functions in the economy was based, as Nicholas Biddle's had originally been, on intelligent study and not at all on experience. Yet even more forcefully than the Bank had ever done he rested his argument where it belonged—on the constitutional responsibility of the government for the currency. He was distinguished among American statesmen in his realization that banking is a monetary function, that regulation of all the circulating medium is the duty of the federal government, and that the duty is to be exercised through a central bank; not for more than a century was such understanding of the subject to be expressed again in Congress. Daniel Webster in particular had never asserted the positive and proper defense of the Bank of the United States as Mr. Calhoun had. His arguments were merely legal, not economic. According to Webster, the Bank was authorized by the Constitution if necessary to the government's operations. This fell far short of seeing in the Bank the one effective means of meeting the federal government's responsibility, under the Constitution, for the circulating medium. Further, Daniel Webster leaned on the jejune defense of vested rights, an obsolescent contention which weakened the Bank's case by the antagonisms it raised and failed entirely to take it off the ground prepared for it by its selfish enemies. Mr. Calhoun's argument, practically alone, put the case on the high, affirmative, responsible ground of monetary powers, where it belonged. But politically it had no effect. The idea that the federal Bank regulated the monetary supply in accordance with the Constitution's assignment of powers made no appeal to people who did not see that bank credit was part of the monetary supply, or, if they did see, were unwilling to have it regulated.

XIV

John C. Calhoun:
Philosopher of Liberty or
Marx of the Master Class?

INTRODUCTION

Calhoun has been called the "darling of students of American political thought, the thinker who is almost invariably advanced when someone of European stature is asked for in the American tradition." [1] *The contemporary of Clay and Webster, he was undoubtedly their intellectual superior, and he was as Richard Hofstadter says, "probably the last American statesman to do any primary political thinking."*

It has been generally conceived that the fundamental contribution of Calhoun to the art and science of politics lay in his exposition and resolution of the problem of the minority under the democratic form of government. De Tocqueville, a friendly French critic of American democracy in Calhoun's own generation, and Lord Acton, an English-Catholic historian in the succeeding generation, were to emphasize the dangers to human liberty inherent in majoritarian democracy. Neither of these, however, created a political device by which the minority might be protected. Calhoun's fertile and inventive mind created two such devices: the doctrines of nullification and concurrent majorities.

R. H. Gabriel, represented in our first selection below, says of Calhoun, "Political scientists have charted his theories, have pronounced them brilliant, and then have tossed them into the scrap-heap of discarded ideas. Perhaps the scholars have been too pre-occupied with his political devices to consider fully the ideas lying behind them. When his philosophy is analysed in terms of the American democratic faith, some new insights are achieved both concerning that faith and in the understanding of his thought." Gabriel, however, points out clearly that all Calhoun's statements regarding the fundamental law and human liberty must be premised and modified by Calhoun's acceptance and approval of the institution of chattel slavery. To Calhoun, slavery rather than being an evil was a good—a positive good.

Richard Hofstadter, in our second selection below, like Gabriel regards the doctrines of nullification and concurrent majorities as possessing "only antiquarian interest for the twentieth-century mind." He admits that Calhoun's theoretical formulation of the problems of a minority under the democratic form of government may have some "permanent significance," but his practical solutions were designed to protect only a very special kind of minority right, that is, a propertied minority right. "Not in the slightest," Hofstadter writes, "was he concerned with minority rights as they are chiefly of interest to the modern liberal mind—the rights of dissenters to

---

[1] Louis Hartz, "The Reactionary Enlightenment: Southern Political Thought before the Civil War," *Western Political Quarterly*, V (March 1952), 39.

express unorthodox opinions, of the individual against the State, least of all of ethnic minorities." Hofstadter sees the chief interest of Calhoun's thought for the mid-twentieth century to lie in his consciousness of social structure and class forces. Before Marx published the Communist Manifesto, *"he placed the central ideas of 'scientific' socialism in an inverted framework of moral values and produced an arresting defense of reaction, a sort of intellectual Black Mass."*

A Footnote on John C. Calhoun

Ralph Henry Gabriel

Calhoun died in 1850 as Melville was rising to his greatest heights. As a brilliant youngster in the arena of Washington politics, Calhoun, like Clay, was a nationalist, ardent in the defense of American honor against British insults. After the War of 1812, his wide-ranging imagination visioned a union of far-separated sovereign states through a system of military roads constructed by the central government. Long before his death, however, he became to both North and South the principal leader of a section. As an old man he seemed to his enemies to personify sectional intransigence. He forged in the busy smithy of his mind the intellectual weapons with which the champions of the Cotton Kingdom sought to defeat the democratic principle of majority rule. Before Robert E. Lee rose to fame, Calhoun was the greatest of the sectionalists, the most brilliant among the champions of a cause which was ultimately lost. In Washington a few weeks after Appomattox, Walt Whitman overheard a conversation of two Union soldiers discussing a monument to Calhoun in the South. One man remarked that the true monuments to the South Carolinian were to be found scattered over the Confederacy in wasted farms, in broken railroads, in destroyed shops, and in the gaunt chimneys which marked the places where families once had made their homes. This soldier expressed a harsh judgment. But his generation in the victorious North was in a mood to agree with him.

Since 1865 Calhoun's thought almost always has been studied by Americans only against the background of sectional conflict. Among the conventions in the teaching of American history in the schools is one which assigns Calhoun and his theory of nullification irrevocably to the past. Wash-

From Ralph Henry Gabriel, *The Course of American Democratic Thought*, Second Edition. Copyright © 1956. The Ronald Press Company. Reprinted by permission.

ington, Hamilton, and Jefferson, through their beliefs and admonitions, still speak to the present. The issues which they debated still live. The same is not true of Calhoun. Unlike his contemporaries Webster and Marshall, his words are seldom used by moderns to point an argument. Political scientists have charted his theories, have pronounced them brilliant, and then have tossed them into the scrap-heap of discarded ideas. Perhaps the scholars have been too preoccupied with his political devices to consider fully the ideas lying behind them. When his philosophy is analyzed in terms of the American democratic faith, some new insights are achieved both concerning that faith and in the understanding of his thought. The simplest approach is to interrogate the dead Calhoun with respect to the ruling ideas of those decades when he was the champion of the South.

What was his stand on the tenet of the fundamental law? This concept included both the natural law of the Enlightenment and the moral law of the Christians. Emerson in his transcendentalism had united the two in his theory that the moral sense pervaded nature from the center of the cosmos to its circumference. Calhoun, unlike Melville, did not reject such absolutism. The opening sentences of his *Disquisition on Government,* published in the year after his death, state his position: "In order to have a clear and just conception of the nature and object of government, it is indispensable to understand correctly what the constitution or law of our nature is, in which government originates; or, to express it more fully and accurately,— that law, without which government would not, and with which, it must necessarily exist. Without this, it is as impossible to lay any solid foundation for the science of government as it would be to lay one for that of astronomy, without a like understanding of that constitution or law of the material world, according to which several bodies composing the solar system mutually act on each other, and by which they are kept in their respective spheres."

In these somewhat ponderous phrases Calhoun repeated the doctrine of the fundamental law. Whence comes this unwritten constitution or law ultimately governing human life? Calhoun answered simply that the fundamental law of human nature compels men to live in society, and that existence in society requires a government. But of the two, thought Calhoun, society is the more important. "Both are, however," he added, "necessary to the existence and well-being of our race, and equally of Divine ordination." [1] The fundamental law comes of God. Calhoun accepted also the concept of the moral law. In the Senate on February 13, 1840, in discussing the right of petition, he elaborated an argument that if they are to be protected at all, rights must be defended at the first challenge. The individual or group that gives way when a moral issue is raised is, therefore, irreparably weakened in its efforts to maintain the justice of its cause. "The moral is

---

[1] John C. Calhoun, *A Disquisition on Government, and a Discourse on the Constitution of the United States,* 1852 ed., 5.

like the physical world," he said, employing an unusual metaphor, "Nature has incrusted the exterior of all organic life, for its safety. Let that be broken through, and it is all weakness within. So in the moral and political world. It is at the extreme limits of right that all wrong and encroachments are the most sensibly felt and easily resisted." [2]

One must understand the application of these generalizations in the affairs of everyday life to comprehend their meaning for the man who during Jackson's administration became the acknowledged and militant leader of a section. Calhoun concurred in the general assumption of Southerners concerning the relation between chattel slavery and the fundamental law. "Negroes are not free," said Calhoun's contemporary George Fitzhugh, "because God and nature, and the general good, and their own good, intended them for slaves." [3] Nature, thought Fitzhugh, had created the races unequal and slavery was the institution through which civilized man gave to the African that share in civilization of which he was capable of making use. Slave owners, moreover, found in Holy Writ divine sanction for the institution. This premise must be read into all Calhoun's statements concerning the fundamental law and concerning liberty.

What was his stand on the doctrine of the free individual? Calhoun felt himself to be more sensitive than his age to the problems of liberty. "We have had so many years of prosperity," he said in 1848 as the Mexican War was closing, "we have passed through so many difficulties and dangers without loss of liberty—that we begin to think that we hold it by divine right from heaven itself." "It is harder to preserve than to obtain liberty," he added. "After years of prosperity, the tenure by which it is held is but too often forgotten; and, I fear, Senators, that such is the case with us. There is no solicitude now about liberty. It was not so in the early days of the Republic." [4]

The threat of tyranny which Calhoun saw close at hand was that of a numerical majority within the nation seeking to use the power of the central government to build up an agricultural, commercial, and industrial economy based on free labor to the disadvantage of an agrarian economy resting on the institution of slavery. After 1831, the year of the Nat Turner uprising in Virginia and the first issue of William Lloyd Garrison's *Emancipator* in Massachusetts, Southerners became a "conscious minority" within the nation. Until his death in 1850 Calhoun remained the chief spokesman in Washington for that minority. For him liberty meant freedom for the Southern people to carry on their lives and to develop their institutions in ways that seemed best to them. He saw in the rising anti-slavery movement in the North a threat that must be faced and countered. He embodied his proposals in the theories of nullification and of the concurrent majority.

Calhoun proclaimed and insisted upon the rights of the states, thirteen of

---

[2] R. K. Cralle, ed., *The Works of Calhoun*, 1867, III, 445.

[3] George Fitzhugh, *Cannibals All*, 1857, 116.   [4] Cralle, *Works*, IV, 417–418.

which were older as independent sovereignties than the Constitution. He described this instrument as a compact among sovereign states to set up a central government to perform certain general functions as an agent of the states. In the midst of Jackson's administration, when the protective tariff became an issue, Calhoun developed the theory of nullification. This theory stated, in brief, that when one of the principals (one of the states) believed that the agent had exceeded the authority given it by the compact, the state might nullify the act. South Carolina took such action in 1832 in the matter of a protective tariff. Only South Carolina, however, actively supported so drastic a measure as nullification. This device in Calhoun's mind was merely an aspect of a larger theory, namely, that of the "concurrent majority." Phrased simply, the idea of the concurrent majority meant that each of the major interests—agriculture, commerce, manufacturing—and each of the great sections—North, South, West—should have the power to prevent or halt national actions deemed adverse to its vital interests. On the questions of high policy unanimous consent among major interests must replace decisions by mere majorities. Calhoun devoted the two final decades of his life to the building up of a set of principles which, if accepted throughout the nation, would protect the Southern minority and permit it to carry on without external coercion its chosen way of life. Calhoun supported his theory with an analysis of the doctrine of the free individual and of the sentiment of nationalism unrivaled in his generation.

Calhoun, in his assumptions concerning human nature, was under an unconscious, but nonetheless heavy, debt to Calvin. Man, thought the South Carolinian, was created to live in society but, paradoxically, his egoistic tendencies outweigh the altruism in his nature. Because of this fact government is necessary to prevent self-seeking individuals from overreaching and exploiting their fellows. The purpose of the State is to enable society to function. Government is the policeman of society. "But government," Calhoun went on, "although intended to protect and preserve society, has a strong tendency to disorder and abuse of its powers, as all experience and almost every page of history testify. The cause is to be found in the same constitution of our nature which makes government indispensable. The powers which it is necessary for government to possess, in order to repress violence and preserve order, cannot execute themselves. They must be administered by men in whom, like others, the individual are stronger than the social feelings. And hence, the powers vested in them to prevent injustice and oppression on the part of others, will, if left unguarded, be by them converted into instruments to oppress the rest of the community. That, by which this is prevented, is what is meant by CONSTITUTION, in its most comprehensive sense, when applied to GOVERNMENT." [5]

Calhoun had Calvin's low opinion of human nature. The lawyers ex-

---

[5] *Disquisition*, 7.

pressed the same attitude in the maxim *caveat emptor*. Upon such assumptions of human fallibility American politics had been founded. It was this skepticism which held in check, in the politics of the United States, the tendencies toward doctrinaire extremism found in the constitutions written during the French Revolution. Calhoun's words were those of the scholar and the theorist, but his thought was that of the run-of-the-mill American democrat. A realism harvested from a life spent in the practice of the political art prevented Calhoun from putting faith in the power of words, even if written on parchment, to restrain the activities of government officials. For him, in spite of the Constitution, the federal Republic was governed by men. The Constitution could not enforce itself. What power it had to restrain public officials must come from its use as an instrument of protection by free citizens. "Power can only be resisted by power,—and tendency by tendency," said Calhoun. "Those who exercise power and those subject to its exercise,—the rulers and the ruled,—stand in antagonistic relations to each other. The same constitution of our nature which leads rulers to oppress the ruled,—regardless of the object for which government is ordained, —will, with equal strength, lead the ruled to resist, when possessed of the means of making peaceable and effective resistance." [6]

Calhoun's was not exactly the doctrine of the malevolent State. It was rather the doctrine that no public official can be trusted unless he knows that he is being watched by citizens who have the power to check usurpations. But, for all his realism, the South Carolinian was an idealist. He believed that he had discovered a political device which, by making constitutional democracy work, would guarantee liberty. Human liberty, the dream of the free individual, was the vision that beckoned him and urged him on. "With me," he said in 1848, two years before his death, "the liberty of the country is all in all. If this be preserved, every thing will be preserved; but if lost, all will be lost." [7]

It is difficult to picture Calhoun outside that small semicircular Senate chamber in the old Capitol which the Supreme Court later occupied for more than half a century. In this almost intimate room he presided in the prime of life as Vice-President. Here, as Senator, he grew old. In this chamber one day, when his failing strength was proclaimed by his pinched features and his sunken cheeks, he spoke of the destiny of America. He had never been more impressive. "It has been lately urged in a very respectable quarter," he said, "that it is the mission of this country to spread civil and religious liberty over all the globe, and especially over this continent— even by force, if necessary. It is a sad delusion. . . . To preserve . . . liberty it is indispensable to adopt a course of moderation and justice toward all nations; to avoid war whenever it can be avoided; to let those great causes which are now at work, and by which the mere operation of time

---

[6] *Ibid.*, 12.   [7] Cralle, *Works*, IV, 420.

will raise our country to an elevation and influence which no country has ever heretofore attained, continue to work. By pursuing such a course, we may succeed in combining greatness and liberty—the highest possible greatness with the largest measure of liberty—and do more to extend liberty by our example over this continent and the world generally, than would be done by a thousand victories." [8] In such a mood the author of the theory of nullification approached that last doctrine of the democratic faith, that doctrine of destiny which was the essence of the spirit of American nationalism.

Nationalism is a sentiment. It is a thing which is less of the mind than of the emotions. It is a consciousness of the group, a feeling in the heart of the individual that his fate is inextricably bound up with those of his people. It is enhanced by external danger. It deteriorates when the population spreads over an area so wide that communication across the nation becomes difficult. During the decades in which Calhoun urged the adoption of his device of nullification, the American people, with the exception of a brief threat of war with England in 1837, felt secure from attack by foreigners. They did not fear the Mexicans. The civil liberty enjoyed by American citizens was founded upon this sense of security. This liberty, greater than that possessed by any other people in the mid-nineteenth-century world, became the boast of American nationalism. It was the trait which was pointed out to distinguish the civilization of the United States from that of other nations.

Calhoun looked deeper than the superficialities of Independence Day orations. As he felt that liberty was a boon easily lost, so also he was convinced that the sentiment of nationalism might under certain circumstances disappear and leave the citizens of the Republic confounded. Almost alone among his contemporaries, Calhoun saw that nationalism in the United States also depends upon security. The loyalty of the individual or of the local community to the national group is primarily the product of the conviction, often unrecognized, that safety lies in merging the life of the locality with that of the nation. As the middle of the century approached, the growing anti-slavery movement in the North threatened the civilization of the South with disruption. The people of the Cotton Kingdom believed that they had accomplished a practicable solution of that most difficult of all social puzzles, the problem of getting two unlike races to live and work together with a minimum of disorder and a reasonable amount of mutual profit. The solution was the ancient institution of slavery. In communities where Negroes outnumbered the white population by two or three to one, it was impossible in the middle decades of the century for the dominant race to see how civilization could be preserved, if the discipline of slavery were relaxed. The appearance in the North of

---

[8] *Ibid.*, 416, 420.

a vociferous and determined movement to bring African servitude to an end filled the South with apprehension. Calhoun foresaw, what ultimately turned out to be the fact, that this sense of insecurity would erode the sentiment of nationalism until, if measures were not taken to protect the South, the old group loyalty would disappear and the nation would fall apart.

Calhoun saw that the numerical majority offered no security to endangered Southern civilization. A majority is made up of men; and, according to the Calhoun theory of human nature, men in the mass can be as selfish and as tyrannical as they are as individuals. He proposed, therefore, the political doctrine of the concurrent majority. Calhoun thought that the sentiment of nationalism can live only so long as the vital interests of all groups within the nation are equally protected. Guarantee such security to all men, to all interests, and to all sections, argued the South Carolinian, and the sentiment of nationalism will flourish as a garden in the warmth of the summer sun. "The concurrent majority . . . ," he said, "tends to unite the most opposite and conflicting interests, and to blend the whole into one common attachment to the country. By giving to each interest, or portion, the power of self-protection, all strife and struggle between them for ascendency is prevented. . . . Under the combined influence of these causes, the interests of each would be merged in the common interests of the whole; and thus, the community would become a unit, by becoming a common centre of attachment of all its parts. And hence, instead of faction, strife, and struggle for party ascendency, there would be patriotism, nationality, harmony, and a struggle only for supremacy in promoting the common good of the whole." [9] Calhoun defined nationalism in terms of a satisfied and happy minority. He was a nationalist in the sense that he preferred that the Union be preserved. But he made the principle of the concurrent majority the condition of union. Give the South autonomy in matters it deemed vital and "patriotism, nationality, and harmony" would follow.

---

[9] *Disquisition*, 48–49.

John C. Calhoun: The Marx

of the Master Class

Richard Hofstadter

It would be well for those interested to reflect whether there now
exists, or ever has existed, a wealthy and civilized community in which
one portion did not live on the labor of another; and whether the
form in which slavery exists in the South is not but one modification
of this universal condition. . ... . Let those who are interested remember that labor is the only source of wealth, and how small a portion
of it, in all old and civilized countries, even the best governed, is left
to those by whose labor wealth is created.   *John C. Calhoun*

I

Jackson led through force of personality, not intellect; his successors in the
White House were remarkable for neither, and yielded pre-eminence to
Congressional politicians. Of the three greatest, Clay, Webster, and Calhoun,
the last showed the most striking mind. His problem, that of defending a
minority interest in a democracy, offered the toughest challenge to fresh
thinking.

As nationalists closely allied with capitalistic interests, Clay and Webster
could both use the ideas of the Founding Fathers as they were transmitted
through the Federalist tradition. Clay, content to leave theoretical elaboration of his "American system" to economists like Mathew Carey and
Hezekiah Niles, never presumed to be a thinker, and his greatest contribution to the political art was to demonstrate how a Hamiltonian program
could gain strength by an admixture of the Jeffersonian spirit. Webster,
who was satisfied, on the whole, to follow the conservative republicanism
of the Fathers, is rightly remembered best as the quasi-official rhapsodist of
American nationalism. He felt no need to attempt a new synthesis for his
own time.

Calhoun, representing a conscious minority with special problems,

Reprinted from *The American Political Tradition*, Vintage Edition, by Richard Hofstadter, by permission of Alfred A. Knopf, Inc. Copyright, 1948 by Alfred A. Knopf, Inc.
Pp. 68–92.

brought new variations into American political thinking. Although his concepts of nullification and the concurrent voice have little more than antiquarian interest for the twentieth-century mind, he also set forth a system of social analysis that is worthy of considerable respect. Calhoun was one of a few Americans of his age—Richard Hildreth and Orestes Brownson were others—who had a keen sense for social structure and class forces. Before Karl Marx published the *Communist Manifesto,* Calhoun laid down an analysis of American politics and the sectional struggle which foreshadowed some of the seminal ideas of Marx's system. A brilliant if narrow dialectician, probably the last American statesman to do any primary political thinking, he placed the central ideas of "scientific" socialism in an inverted framework of moral values and produced an arresting defense of reaction, a sort of intellectual Black Mass.

Calhoun was born in 1782 into a Scotch-Irish family that had entered the colonies in Pennsylvania and migrated to the Southern back country in the middle of the century. His paternal grandmother had been killed by Indians on the frontier in 1760 and his mother's brother, John Caldwell, after whom he was named, had been murdered by Tories during the Revolution. Patrick Calhoun, his father, acquired over thirty slaves in an area where slaves were rare, became a prominent citizen of the South Carolina hinterland and a member of the state legislature, and opposed the federal Constitution. When John was fourteen, Patrick died. The boy was tutored for a time by his brother-in-law, Moses Waddel, soon to become one of the South's outstanding educators; he graduated from Yale in 1804, studied law at Tapping Reeve's famous school in Litchfield, and joined the Carolina bar.

Calhoun's warmest attachment during these years, and perhaps all his life, was to an older woman, Floride Bonneau Calhoun, his father's cousin by marriage. After years of close friendship and constant correspondence, he married her eighteen-year-old daughter, whose name was also Floride. It was customary for a bride to keep control of her own fortune, but the young planter indelicately insisted that she place her property in his hands. It was so arranged. Besides these extensive landholdings, the connection brought Calhoun an assured position among gentlefolk of the seaboard.

In 1808, three years before his marriage and shortly after his admission to the bar, Calhoun was elected to the South Carolina legislature. In 1810 he was elected to Congress, where he promptly became a leader among the young "war hawks." When the war with Britain began, he became the foremost advocate of war appropriations, and for fifteen years he remained the most ardent worker for national unity and national power. He was for more troops, more funds, for manufactures, federal roads, a higher tariff, and a new national bank. Impatient with "refined arguments on the Constitution," he waved all constitutional objections aside. In 1817 he became

Secretary of War in James Monroe's Cabinet and put through an ambitious program of fortifications and administrative improvement. John Quincy Adams, his colleague in the Cabinet, wrote in his diary that Calhoun was

> a man of fair and candid mind, of honorable principles, of clear and quick understanding, of cool self-possession, of enlarged philosophic views, and of ardent patriotism. He is above all sectional and factional prejudices more than any other statesman of this Union with whom I have ever acted.

Calhoun took a conciliatory view of sectional issues. When the question of slavery first appeared in the controversy over Missouri, he stood for moderation. "We to the South ought not to assent easily to the belief that there is a conspiracy either against our property or just weight in the Union," he wrote to a friend, adding that he favored supporting such measures and men "without a regard to sections, as are best calculated to advance the general interest." One must agree with William E. Dodd: Calhoun's whole early life as a public man had been built upon nationalism, and at heart he remained a Unionist as well as a Southerner. What he wanted was not for the South to leave the Union, but to dominate it. Even as late as 1838 he cautioned his daughter against the disunionist school of thought. "Those who make it up, do not think of the difficulty involved in the word; how many bleeding [pores] must be taken up on passing the knife of separation through a body politic. . . . *We must remember, it is the most difficult process in the world to make two people of one.*"

Changes at home converted the reluctant Calhoun from a nationalist to a sectionalist. As the cotton economy spread, South Carolina became entirely a staple-growing state. Her planters, working exhausted land, and hard pressed to compete with the fresh soil of the interior, found it impossible to submit quietly any longer to the exactions of the protective tariff. Before long a fiery local group of statesmen made it impossible for any politician to stay in business who did not take a strong stand for sectional interests.

Calhoun, who aspired to be much more than a regional leader, managed for some years to soft-pedal his swing to a sectional position. His initial strategy was to make an alliance with the Jackson supporters in the hope that Jackson, himself a Southern planter and an old Republican, would pursue policies favorable to the South and eventually pass the presidency on to Calhoun. Then Calhoun would cement an alliance between the agrarian South and West against the capitalistic East. Both in 1824, when Jackson was defeated by the Clay-Adams bargain, and in 1828, when he was elected, Calhoun was his vice-presidential running mate.[1]

During the campaign of 1828 the exorbitant Tariff of Abominations be-

---

[1] Because of the unusual circumstances of the election of 1824, Calhoun became Vice President although Jackson was defeated.

came law, and Calhoun wrote his first great document on the sectional question, the *Exposition and Protest,* the authorship of which remained secret for some time for political reasons.[2] Denouncing the tariff bitterly, Calhoun declared: "We are the serfs of the system." After giving an impressive analysis of the costs of the tariff to the plantation economy, he came to political remedies. "No government based on the naked principle that the majority ought to govern, however true the maxim in its proper sense, and under proper restrictions, can preserve its liberty even for a single generation." Only those governments which provide checks on power, "which limit and restrain within proper bounds the power of the majority," have had a prolonged and happy existence. Seeking for some constitutional means, short of secession, of resisting the majority, Calhoun seized upon the idea of state nullification. The powers of sovereignty, he contended, belonged of right entirely to the several states and were only delegated, in part, to the federal government. Therefore the right of judging whether measures of policy were infractions of their rights under the Constitution belonged to the states. When a state convention, called for the purpose, decided that constitutional rights were violated by any statute, the state had a right to declare the law null and void within its boundaries and refuse to permit its enforcement there. Nullification would be binding on both the citizens of the state and the federal government. The *exposition* closed with the hope that Jackson would be elected and would make a practical test of nullification unnecessary.

Calhoun and the South were soon disappointed with Old Hickory. Personal grievances—among them Jackson's discovery that Calhoun as Secretary of War had wanted to repudiate his free and easy conduct in the Seminole campaign—caused the general to break with the Carolinian. The final breach came during the nullification crisis of 1832, when Jackson turned all his wrath upon South Carolina and incontinently threatened to hang Calhoun. At its close Calhoun, having resigned from the vice-presidency, sat in the Senate for his state, planning to join the anti-Jackson coalition, and militant Southerners were thinking about new ways of stemming Northern capital. Calhoun's trajectory toward the presidency had been forcibly deflected. Henceforth his life became a long polemical exercise, his career a series of maneuvers to defend the South and propel himself into the White House. Nourished on ambition and antagonism, he grew harder, more resolute, and more ingenious.

II

Charleston was the great cultural center of the Old South, a city with a flavor of its own and an air of cosmopolitan taste and breeding, and

---

[2] Calhoun's report was not officially adopted, but because the lower house of the Carolina legislature ordered a printing of five thousand copies, it was generally taken as an official statement.

Charleston was the one part of South Carolina for which Calhoun had no use. He hated the life of ease and relaxation enjoyed by the absentee planters who were the mainstay of its social and cultural distinction. In 1807, when malaria was ravaging the city, he wrote to Floride Bonneau Calhoun with ill-disguised relish that every newspaper brought a long list of deaths. This, he thought, was due far less to the climate of the place than to "the misconduct of the inhabitants; and may be considered as a curse for their intemperance and debaucheries."

Debaucheries of any kind Calhoun was never accused of. There is no record that he ever read or tried to write poetry, although there is a traditional gibe to the effect that he once began a poem with "Whereas," and stopped. Once in his life he read a novel—this at the request of a lady who asked for his judgment on it. A friend, Mary Bates, observed that she "never heard him utter a jest," and Daniel Webster in his eulogy said he had never known a man "who wasted less of life in what is called recreation, or employed less of it in any pursuits not immediately connected with the discharge of his duty." Duty is the word, for duty was the demonic force in Calhoun. "I hold the duties of life to be greater than life itself," he once wrote. ". . . I regard this life very much as a struggle against evil, and that to him who acts on proper principle, the reward is in the struggle more than in victory itself, although that greatly enhances it." In adult life to relax and play are in a certain sense to return to the unrestrained spirits of childhood. There is reason to believe that Calhoun was one of those people who have had no childhood to return to. This, perhaps, was what Harriet Martineau sensed when she said that he seemed never to have been born. His political lieutenant, James H. Hammond, remarked after his death: "Mr. Calhoun had no youth, to our knowledge. He sprang into the arena like Minerva from the head of Jove, fully grown and clothed in armor: a man every inch himself, and able to contend with any other man."

For men whom he took seriously, this white-hot intensity was difficult to bear. Senator Dixon Lewis of Alabama, who weighed four hundred and thirty pounds and found relaxation a natural necessity, once wrote to Calhoun's friend Richard K. Crallé during an election year:

> Calhoun is now my principal associate, and he is too intelligent, too industrious, too intent on the struggle of politics to suit me except as an occasional companion. There is no *relaxation* with him. On the contrary, when I seek relaxation with him, he screws me only the higher in some sort of excitement.

Judge Prioleau, when he first met Calhoun, told an inquirer he hoped never to see him again. For three hours he had been trying to follow Calhoun's dialectic "through heaven and earth," and he was exhausted with the effort. "I hate a man who makes me think so much . . . and I hate a man who makes me feel my own inferiority." Calhoun seldom made himself congenial. He once admitted that he was almost a stranger five miles from his home, and we can be sure that his political popularity was not personal, but abstract. Nor is there any reason to believe that he often felt lonesome, except for his family. He loved an audience, but did not especially care for company. He enjoyed spending long hours in solitary thought.

Colleagues in the Senate who were used to harangues of this tall, gaunt, sickly man with his traplike mouth and harsh voice, suited, as someone said, to a professor of mathematics, respected him deeply for his extraordinary mind and his unquestionable integrity, but found him on occasion just a bit ludicrous. Clay has left a memorable caricature of him—"tall, careworn, with furrowed brow, haggard and intensely gazing, looking as if he were dissecting the last abstraction which sprung from metaphysician's brain, and muttering to himself, in half-uttered tones, 'This is indeed a real crisis.'"

There is testimony to Calhoun's gentleness and charm, to the winning quality of his very seriousness at times. "He talked," reports one admirer, "on the most abstruse subjects with the guileless simplicity of a prattling child." Benjamin F. Perry, a bitter political opponent, testified to his kindness, but observed: "He liked very much to talk of himself." He saved his charm and indulgence particularly for women and children, whose world, one imagines, he considered to be a world entirely apart from the serious things of life. There is a brief and touching picture of him at his daughter's wedding removing the ornaments of a cake to save them for a little child. It is easy enough to believe that he never spoke impatiently to any member of his family, for he could always discharge his aggressions upon a senator. And two of the most effective characterizations have been left by women: it was Harriet Martineau who called him "the cast iron man who looks as if he had never been born, and could never be extinguished," and Varina Howell Davis who described him as "a mental and moral abstraction."

It would be interesting to know what Mrs. John C. Calhoun thought of him. That he was devoted to her one can readily imagine, but devotion in a man like Calhoun is not an ordinary man's devotion. When he was thinking of marrying her, he wrote to her mother: "After a careful examination, I find none but those qualities in her character which are suited to me." In the course of their exemplary married life she bore him nine children, whom he treated with paternal tenderness. But there survives a curious letter written to his cherished mother-in-law on the death of his first-born daughter in her second year of life, which reads in part:

> So fixed in sorrow is her distressed mother that every topick of consolation which I attempt to offer but seems to grieve her the more. It is in vain I tell her it is the lot of humanity; that almost all parents have suffered equal calamity; that Providence may have intended it in kindness to her and ourselves, as no one can say what, had she lived,

would have been her condition, whether it would have been happy or miserable; and above all we have the consolation to know that she is far more happy than she could be here with us. She thinks only of her dear child; and recalls to her mind every thing that made her interesting, thus furnishing additional food for her grief.

Here surely is a man who lived by abstractions; it is amazing, and a little pathetic, that he sought to make his business the management of human affairs.

Calhoun had a touching faith in his ability to catch life in logic. His political reasoning, like so many phases of his personal life, was a series of syllogisms. Given a premise, he could do wonders, but at times he showed a fantastic lack of judgment in choosing his premises, and he was often guilty of terrible logic-chopping.[3] His trust in logic led to an almost insane self-confidence. "Whether it be too great confidence in my own opinion I cannot say," he once wrote, "but what I think I see, I see with so much apparent clearness as not to leave me a choice to pursue any other course, which has always given me the impression that I acted with the force of destiny." "In looking back," he wrote to Duff Green six years before his death, "I see nothing to regret and little to correct."

That all Calhoun's ability and intensity were focused on making himself president was the accepted view of his contemporaries, friend and foe, and has not been denied by his friendliest biographers. But he himself never acknowledged or understood it. "I am no aspirant—never have been," he declared fervently to the Senate in 1847. "I would not turn on my heel for the Presidency." On this score he thought himself "the most misunderstood man in the world." A certain relative purity of motive, however, must be credited to him. He was not primarily an opportunist. He generally sought to advance himself on the basis of some coherent and well-stated body of principles in which he actually believed. It was quite in keeping that he could on occasion be devious with individual men—as he was with Jackson for years—but not with ideas. His scruples about money were matched only by those of Adams, and might have been held up as an example to Webster. He supported a large family—seven of the nine children survived to adulthood—on his declining plantation enterprises, and sincerely professed his indifference to money-making. In 1845 he applied to Webster's rich Boston patron, Abbott Lawrence, for a loan of thirty thousand dollars, and when Lawrence replied in language suggesting that for

---

[3] Typical of Calhoun at his worst was his assault on the philosophy of the Declaration of Independence, which he read as "all men are born free and equal": "Taking the proposition literally . . . there is not a word of truth in it. It begins with 'all men are born,' which is utterly untrue. Men are not born. Infants are born. They grow to be men. . . . They are not born free. While infants they are incapable of freedom. . . ." Anyone whose introduction to Calhoun came through such portions of his work would find it hard to believe that he had sound and trenchant criticisms of the natural-rights philosophy, and yet he did.

a man of Calhoun's personal eminence he might be generous beyond the call of commercial duty, Calhoun withdrew his request in a letter of supreme dignity.

Calhoun's failure to understand that politics works through people and requires sustained personal loyalty as well as fidelity to ideas was resented by his followers and partisans. James H. Hammond once complained that the leader was "always buying over enemies and never looks after friends." Again: "He marches and countermarches all who follow him until after having broken from the bulk of his followers he breaks from his friends one by one and expends them in breaking down his late associates—so all ends in ruin." Rhett and Hammond both agreed that he was too unyielding and impersonal to be a great party leader. As Rhett put it, "he understood principles . . . but he did not understand how best to control and use . . . man."

Calhoun, of course, was a slavemaster, and his view of himself in this capacity was what might be expected: "My character as a master is, I trust, unimpeachable, as I hope it is in all the other relations of life." He looked upon his relation to his slaves, he asserted, "in the double capacity of master and guardian." His neighbors testified that he was kind to them, and by the lights of his section and class there is little reason to doubt it. But the only record of his relation to a slave suggests that kindness to slaves was a mixed quality in the South. In 1831 a house servant, Aleck, committed some offense to Mrs. Calhoun for which she promised a severe whipping, and he ran away. When he was caught in Abbeville a few days later, Calhoun left instructions with a friend:

> I wish you would have him lodged in jail for one week, to be fed on bread and water, and to employ some one for me to give him 30 lashes well laid on at the end of the time. . . . I deem it necessary to our proper security to prevent the formation of the habit of running away, and I think it better to punish him before his return home than afterwards.

The case of Aleck and the "thirty lashes well laid on" does more for our understanding of the problem of majorities and minorities than all Calhoun's dialectics on nullification and the concurrent majority.

III

In 1788 Patrick Henry, arguing against the federal Constitution, asked: "How can the Southern members prevent the adoption of the most oppressive mode of taxation in the Southern States, as there is a majority of the Northern States?" This anxiety about the North's majority ripened like the flora of the Southern swamplands. As the years went by, the South grew, but the North grew faster. In 1790, when Calhoun was eight years old, populations North and South were practically equal. By 1850, the year of his death, the North's was 13,527,000, the South's only 9,612,000. This preponderance was reflected in Congress. Although Southern politicians held a disproportionate number of executive offices, federal policy continued to favor Northern capital, and Southern wealth funneled into the pockets of Northern shippers, bankers, and manufacturers. Of course, the greater part of the drain of Southern resources was the inevitable result of a relationship between a capitalistic community and an agrarian one that did little of its own shipping, banking, or manufacturing. But a considerable portion too came from what Southerns considered an "artificial" governmental intrusion—the protective tariff. It was tariffs, not slavery, that first made the South militant. Planters were understandably resentful as the wealth of the Southern fields, created by the hard labor of the men, women, and children they owned, seemed to be slipping away from them. "All we want to be rich is to let us have what we make," said Calhoun.

Southern leaders began to wonder where all this was going to stop. Given its initial advantage, what was to prevent the North from using the federal government to increase the span between the political power of the sections still further, and then, presuming upon the South's growing weakness, from pushing exploitation to outrageous and unbearable extremes? Humiliated by their comparative economic backwardness, frightened at its political implications, made uneasy by the world's condemnation of their "peculiar institution," Southern leaders reacted with the most intense and exaggerated anxiety to every fluctuation in the balance of sectional power. How to maintain this balance was Calhoun's central problem, and for twenty-two years his terrible and unrelenting intensity hung upon it. "The South," he lamented as early as 1831, ". . . is a fixed and hopeless minority," and five years later he declared in significant hyperbole on the floor of the Senate: "We are here but a handful in the midst of an overwhelming majority." In 1833, speaking on the Force Bill, he saw the South confronted with "a system of hostile legislation . . . an oppressive and unequal imposition of taxes . . . unequal and profuse appropriations . . . rendering the entire labor and capital of the weaker interest subordinate to the stronger."

After 1830, when abolitionism began to be heard, the South's revolt was directed increasingly against this alleged menace. There is little point in debating whether fear of abolition or fear of further economic exploitation was more important in stimulating Southern militancy and turning the Southern mind toward secession. The North, if the balance of power turned completely in its favor, could both reduce the planter class to economic bondage and emancipate its slaves. Southern leaders therefore concentrated on fighting for the sectional equilibrium without making any artificial distinctions about their reasons. As Calhoun put it in 1844, "plunder and agitation" were "kindred and hostile measures." "While the tariff takes from us the proceeds of our labor, abolition strikes at the labor itself."

Of course, voluntary emancipation was out of the question. To understand the mind of the Old South it is necessary to realize that emancipation meant not merely the replacement of slave labor by hired labor, but the loss of white supremacy, the overthrow of the caste system—in brief, the end of a civilization. Although Calhoun once condemned the slave trade as an "odious traffic," there is no evidence that he ever shared the Jeffersonian view of slavery, widespread in the South during his youth, that slavery was a necessary but temporary evil. During a conversation with John Quincy Adams in 1820 he revealed how implicitly he accepted the caste premises of slavery. Adams spoke of equality, of the dignity and worth of human life. Calhoun granted that Adams's beliefs were "just and noble," but added in a matter-of-fact way that in the South they were applied only to white men. Slavery, he said, was "the best guarantee to equality among the whites. It produced an unvarying level among them . . . did not even admit of inequalities, by which one white man could domineer over another."

Calhoun was the first Southern statesman of primary eminence to say openly in Congress what almost all the white South had come to feel. Slavery, he affirmed in the Senate in 1837, "is, instead of an evil, a good— a positive good." By this he did not mean to imply that slavery was always better than free labor relations, but simply that it was the best relation between blacks and whites. Slavery had done much for the Negro, he argued. "In few countries so much is left to the share of the laborer, and so little exacted from him, or . . . more kind attention paid to him in sickness or infirmities of age." His condition is greatly superior to that of the poorhouse inmates in the more civilized portions of Europe. As for the political aspect of slavery, "I fearlessly assert that the existing relation between the two races in the South . . . forms the most solid and durable foundation on which to rear free and stable political institutions."

The South thought of emancipation as an apocalyptic catastrophe. In a manifesto prepared in 1849 Calhoun portrayed a series of devices by which he thought abolitionists would gradually undermine slavery until at last the North could "monopolize all the territories," add a sufficient number of states to give her three fourths of the whole, and then pass an emancipation amendment. The disaster would not stop with this. Since the two races "cannot live together in peace, or harmony, or to their mutual advantage, except in their present relation," one or the other must dominate. After emancipation the ex-slaves would be raised "to a political and social equality with ther former owners, by giving them the right of voting and holding public offices under the Federal Government." They would become political associates of their Northern friends, acting with them uniformly, "holding the white race at the South in complete subjection." The blacks and the profligate whites that might unite with them would become the principal recipients of federal offices and patronage and would be "raised above the whites of the South in the political and social scale." The only resort of the former master race would be to abandon the homes of its ancestors and leave the country to the Negroes.[4]

Faced with such peril, the South should be content with nothing less than the most extreme militancy, stand firm, meet the enemy on the frontier, rather than wait till she grew weaker. Anything less than decisive victory was unthinkable. "What! acknowledged inferiority! The surrender of life is nothing to sinking down into acknowledged inferiority!"

It was one of Calhoun's merits that in spite of his saturation in the lore of constitutional argument he was not satisfied with a purely formal or constitutional interpretation of the sectional controversy, but went beyond it to translate the balance of sections into a balance of classes. Although he did not have a complete theory of history, he saw class struggle and exploitation in every epoch of human development. He was sure that "there never has yet existed a wealthy and civilized society in which one portion of the community did not, in point of fact, live on the labor of the other." It would not be too difficult "to trace out the various devices by which the wealth of all civilized communities has been so unequally divided, and to show by what means so small a share has been allotted to those by whose labor it was produced, and so large a share to the non-producing classes." Concerning one such device he had no doubts; the tariff was a certain means of making "the poor poorer and the rich richer." As early as 1828 he wrote of the tariff system in his *Exposition and Protest:*

> After we [the planters] are exhausted, the contest will be between the capitalists and operatives [workers]; for into these two classes it must, ultimately, divide society. The issue of the struggle here must be the same as it has been in Europe. Under the operation of the system, wages must sink more rapidly than the prices of the necessaries of life, till the operatives will be reduced to the lowest point,—when the portion of the products of their labor left to them, will be barely sufficient to preserve existence.

In his *Disquisition on Government* Calhoun predicted that as the community develops in wealth and population, "the difference between the rich and poor will become more strongly marked," and the proportion of "ignorant and dependent" people will increase. Then "the tendency to conflict between them will become stronger; and, as the poor and dependent become more numerous in proportion there will be, in governments of

---

[4] Setting aside its valuations and demagogic language, Calhoun's forecast bears a strong resemblance to the plans actually adopted by the Radical Republicans during Reconstruction.

the numerical majority, no want of leaders among the wealthy and ambitious, to excite and direct them in their efforts to obtain the control."

Such arguments were not merely for public consumption. In 1831 a friend recorded a conversation in which Calhoun "spoke of the tendency of Capital to destroy and absorb the property of society and produce a collision between itself and operatives." "The capitalist owns the instruments of labor," Calhoun once told Albert Brisbane, "and he seeks to draw out of labor all the profits, leaving the laborer to shift for himself in age and disease." In 1837 he wrote to Hammond that he had had "no conception that the lower class had made such great progress to equality and independence" as Hammond had reported. "Modern society seems to me to be rushing to some new and untried condition." "What I dread," he confessed to his daughter Anna in 1846, "is that progress in political science falls far short of progress in that which relates to matter, and which may lead to convulsions and revolutions, that may retard, or even arrest the former." During the peak of the Jacksonian bank war he wrote to his son James that the views of many people in the North were inclining toward Southern conceptions. They feared not only Jackson's power, but "the needy and corrupt in their own section. They begin to feel what I have long foreseen, that they have more to fear from their own people than we from our slaves."

In such characteristic utterances there is discernible a rough parallel to several ideas that were later elaborated and refined by Marx: the idea of pervasive exploitation and class struggle in history; a labor theory of value and of a surplus appropriated by the capitalists; the concentration of capital under capitalistic production; the fall of working-class conditions to the level of subsistence; the growing revolt of the laboring class against the capitalists; the prediction of social revolution. The difference was that Calhoun proposed that no revolution should be allowed to take place. To forestall it he suggested consistently—over a period of years—what Richard Current has called "planter-capitalist collaboration against the class enemy." In such a collaboration the South, with its superior social stability, had much to offer as a conservative force. In return, the conservative elements in the North should be willing to hold down abolitionist agitation; and they would do well to realize that an overthrow of slavery in the South would prepare the ground for social revolution in the North.

> There is and always has been [he said in the Senate] in an advanced stage of wealth and civilization, a conflict between labor and capital. The condition of society in the South exempts us from the disorders and dangers resulting from this conflict; and which explains why it is that the political condition of the slave-holding states has been so much more stable and quiet than that of the North. . . . The experience of the next generation will fully test how vastly more favorable our con-

dition of society is to that of other sections for free and stable institutions, provided we are not disturbed by the interference of others, or
shall . . . resist promptly and successfully such interference.

On January 9, 1838 Calhoun explained further why it was impossible
in the South for the conflict "between labor and capital" to take place,
"which makes it so difficult to establish and maintain free institutions in
all wealthy and highly civilized nations where such institutions as ours do
not exist." It was because the Southern states were an aggregate of communities, not of individuals. "Every plantation is a little community, with
the master at its head, who concentrates in himself the united interests
of capital and labor, of which he is the common representative." In the
Southern states labor and capital are "equally represented and perfectly
harmonized." In the Union as a whole, the South, accordingly, becomes

> the balance of the system; the great conservative power, which prevents
> other portions, less fortunately constituted, from rushing into conflict.
> In this tendency to conflict in the North, between labor and capital,
> which is constantly on the increase, the weight of the South has been
> and ever will be found on the conservative side; against the aggression
> of one or the other side, whichever may tend to disturb the equilibrium
> of our political system.

In 1836 Calhoun had pointed out to "the sober and considerate" Northerners

> who have a deep stake in the existing institutions of the country that
> the assaults which are now directed against the institutions of the
> Southern States may be very easily directed against those which uphold
> their own property and security. A very slight modification of the
> arguments used against the institutions [of the South] would make them
> equally effectual against the institutions of the North, including bank-
> ing, in which so vast an amount of its property and capital is invested.

In 1847 he again reminded Northern conservatives how much interest
they had "in upholding and preserving the equilibrium of the slaveholding states." "Let gentlemen then be warned that while warring on us, they
are warring on themselves." Two years later he added that the North, without the South, would have no central point of union, to bind its various
and conflicting interests together; and would . . . be subject to all the
agitations and conflicts growing out of the divisions of wealth and poverty."
All these warnings were merely the consequence of a long-standing conviction which Calhoun had expressed to Josiah Quincy that "the interests
of the *gentlemen* of the North and of the South are identical." The Carolinian had no serious expectation that his appeals and predictions would
change Northern public opinion, but he hoped that events might. Growing
discontent among the masses might drive Northern conservatives into the
arms of the planters, but as he confessed to Duff Green in 1835, whether

the intelligence of the North would see the situation "in time to save themselves and the institutions of the Country God only knows."

Calhoun had an ingenious solution for the sectional problem: in return for the South's services as a balance wheel against labor agitation, the solid elements in the North should join her in a common front against all agitation of the slavery issue. His program for the tariff problem was best expressed in a letter to Abbott Lawrence in 1845: Northern manufacturers should join the planters in producing for the export market. At best it would be impossible for manufacturers to attain prosperity in the home market alone; "the great point is to get possession of the foreign market," and for that the high-duty tariff is nothing but an obstruction. The North should emulate English manufacturers by lowering duties, importing cheap raw materials, and competing aggressively for foreign trade. "When that is accomplished all conflict between the planter and the manufacturer would cease."

IV

During the last seven years of Calhoun's life the sectional conflict centered more and more on the acquisition of new territory and its division between slave and free society. Nullification had failed for lack of unity within the South. The alliance with the West was unstable and uncertain. The proposed alliance with Northern capital Calhoun could not bring about. Hence the problem of defense turned increasingly upon the attempt to acquire new slave territory in Texas, Mexico, and the vast area wrested from Mexico by war, and keeping the North from taking the West for free labor.

Calhoun's interest in Texas was defensive in intent, but exorbitantly aggressive in form. Great Britain, eager for a new market and an independent source of cotton, was encouraging Texas to remain independent by offering financial aid and protection. During 1843, when Lord Brougham and Lord Aberdeen both openly confessed Britain's intent to foster abolition along with national independence in Texas, Calhoun, then Secretary of State, stepped forward in alarm to link the annexation issue with a thoroughgoing defense of slavery. Southerners feared that another refuge for fugitive slaves and the example of an independent, free-labor cotton-producing country on their border would be a grave menace to their social structure. Britain, Calhoun frankly told the British Minister, was trying to destroy in Texas an institution "essential to the peace, safety, and prosperity of the United States"! In 1844 he published an interpretation of Britain's motives. Having freed the slaves in her own colonial empire, he charged, she had lost ground in world production of tropical products, including cotton, had endangered the investment in her empire, and had reduced it to far poorer condition than such areas as the Southern United

States and Brazil, where slavery survived. Britain, in her effort "to regain and keep a superiority in tropical cultivation, commerce, and influence," was desperately trying to "cripple or destroy the productions of her successful rivals" by undermining their superior labor system.

Ardent as he had been for annexation of Texas, Calhoun was frightened during the war with Mexico by sentiment in the South for conquest and annexation of all Mexico. If Mexico were taken, he feared that the necessity of controlling her would give the executive tremendous powers and vast patronage, bring about precisely the centralization of federal power that he so feared, and finally destroy the constitutional system. He predicted that conflict between North and South over disposition of the acquired territory might easily disrupt the Union. "Mexico is for us the forbidden fruit; the penalty of eating it would be to subject our institutions to political death."

In 1846 the introduction of the Wilmot Proviso, which banned slavery from all territory to be taken from Mexico, excited the South as nothing had before. Calhoun felt that it involved a matter of abstract right upon which no compromise should be considered, even though it was unlikely that slavery would go into the territories in question. In December he told President Polk that he "did not desire to extend slavery," that it would "probably never exist" in California and New Mexico. Still he would vote against any treaty that included the Wilmot Proviso, because "it would involve a principle." [5]

Calhoun became obsessed with the North's tendency to "monopolize" the territories for free labor. In 1847, when Iowa had entered the Union and Wisconsin was ready for statehood, he expressed his fear that the territories would yield twelve or fifteen more free states. The South was fast losing that parity in the Senate which was its final stronghold of equality in the federal government. In March of that year he called for a united Southern party to force a showdown on Southern rights. In his last great speech, which was read to the Senate for him because he was dying, he declared with finality that the balance of power had already been lost. The South no longer had "any adequate means of protecting itself against . . . encroachment and oppression." Reviewing the growth of Northern preponderance, the exploitation of the South, and the progressive disintegration of the moral bonds of Union, Calhoun warned that the nation could be saved only by conceding to the South an equal right in the newly acquired Western territory[6] and amending the Constitution to restore

---

[5] This was not his view alone. "It cannot be a slave country," wrote Robert Toombs to J. J. Crittenden, January 22, 1849. "We have only the point of honor to save . . . and [to] rescue the country from all danger of agitation."

[6] It is not certain whether Calhoun had changed his mind about not expecting slavery to go into the territory, as he had admitted to Polk, or whether he still considered that the mere victory on principle was of that much importance.

to her the power of self-protection that she had had before the sectional balance was destroyed.

An amendment to the Constitution would be a guarantee of equality to the South. Calhoun demanded that this guarantee should take the form of the concurrent majority, which was the king pin in his political system. All through his sectional phase Calhoun had been preaching for the concurrent majority. He expressed it as early as 1833 in his speech on the Force Bill and last formulated it in the *Disquisition on Government,* published after his death. Government by numerical majorities, he always insisted, was inherently unstable; he proposed to replace it with what he called government by the whole community—that is, a government that would organically represent both majority and minority. Society should not be governed by counting heads but by considering the great economic interests, the geographical and functional units, of the nation. In order to prevent the plunder of a minority interest by a majority interest, each must be given an appropriate organ in the constitutional structure which would provide it with "either a concurrent voice in making and executing the laws or a veto on their execution." Only by such a device can the "different interests, orders, classes, or portions" of the community be protected, "and all conflict and struggle between them prevented." [7]

Time had persuaded Calhoun that a dual executive would be the best means of employing the concurrent majority in the United States. The nation should have two presidents, each representing one of the two great sections, each having a veto power over acts of Congress. No measure could pass that did not win the approval of the political agents of both sections. The equality between sections that had existed at the beginning of the government would thus be restored.

Calhoun's analysis of American political tensions certainly ranks among the most impressive intellectual achievements of American statesmen. Far in advance of the event, he forecast an alliance between Northern conservatives and Southern reactionaries, which has become one of the most formidable aspects of American politics. The South, its caste system essentially intact, has proved to be for an entire century more resistant to

---

[7] The concurrent majority was actually operative in South Carolina from the time of Calhoun's entrance into politics, when apportionment of the state legislature was so arranged as to give one house to the seaboard plantation area and the other to the upcountry farmers. William A. Schaper has pointed out, however, that the concurrent-majority principle could work there because the minority, the planters, kept possession of power "until it had won over the majority to its interests and its institutions." Some Southerners hoped that since the South had a faction in both major parties, she could exercise an informal equivalent of the concurrent majority within the bisectional party system rather than the Constitution itself. This plan worked for some time, but Calhoun had no faith in it for the long run. He argued that parties must ultimately partake "more or less of a sectional character," a tendency that would grow stronger with the passage of time. And if parties became sectional, the concurrent voice could be found only in a formal constitutional amendment.

change than the North, its influence steadily exerted to retard serious reform and to curb the power of Northern labor. Caste prejudice and political conservatism have made the South a major stronghold of American capitalism.

But prescient and ingenious as Calhoun was, he made critical miscalculations for the sectional struggle of his own time. He had a remarkable sense for the direction of social evolution, but failed to measure its velocity. His fatal mistake was to conclude that the conflict between labor and capital would come to a head before the conflict between capital and the Southern planter. Marx out of optimism and Calhoun out of pessimism both overestimated the revolutionary capacities of the working class. It was far easier to reconcile the Northern masses to the profit system than Calhoun would ever admit. He failed to see that the expanding Northern free society, by offering broad opportunities to the lower and middle classes, provided itself with a precious safety valve for popular discontents. He also failed to see that the very restlessness which he considered the North's weakness was also a secret of its strength. "The main spring to progress," he realized, "is the desire of individuals to better their condition," but he could not admit how much more intensely free society stimulated that essential desire in its working population than his cherished slave system with its "thirty lashes well laid on."

Calhoun, in brief, failed to appreciate the staying power of capitalism. At the very time when it was swinging into its period of most hectic growth he spoke as though it had already gone into decline. The stirrings of the Jackson era particularly misled him; mass discontent, which gained further opportunities for the common man in business and politics, and thus did so much in the long run to strengthen capitalism, he misread as the beginning of a revolutionary upsurge. Calhoun was, after all, an intense reactionary, and to the reactionary ear every whispered criticism of the elite classes has always sounded like the opening shot of an uprising.

Calhoun's social analysis lacked the rough pragmatic resemblance to immediate reality that any analysis must have if it is to be translated into successful political strategy. He never did find a large capitalist group in the North that would see the situation as he did. Although he joined the Whig Party for a few years after his disappointment with Jackson, a long-term alliance with such firm spokesmen of capitalist tariff economics as Clay and Webster was unthinkable. Under the Van Buren administration he returned to the Democratic fold on the subtreasury issue, and there he remained. During the late thirties, while he was still appealing to Northern conservatives to join hands with the planters, he admitted that the Whig Party, the party most attractive to Northern capital, was more difficult than the Democrats on both the tariff and abolition.

Ironically, for a long time Northern labor was ideologically closer than Northern capital to the planters. The workers had little sympathy for abolitionism, but responded with interest when Southern politicians unleashed periodic assaults on Northern wage slavery. When Francis W. Pickens, one of Calhoun's own lieutenants, rose in the House in the fall of 1837 to point out that the planters stood in relation to Northern capital "precisely in the same situation as the laborer of the North" and that they were "the only class of capitalists . . . which, as a class, are identified with the laborers of the country," Ely Moore, a labor spokesman, endorsed his position. And eight years after Calhoun's death, when James H. Hammond lashed out in a famous speech against "wage slavery," he received many letters of thanks from Northern workers for exposing their condition. Calhoun himself, organizing his presidential drive between 1842 and 1844, found strong support among many members of the former left wing of Northern democracy. Fitzwilliam Byrdsall, ardent democrat and historian of the Locofocos, wrote to him from New York City that "the radical portion of the Democratic party here, to whom free suffrage is dear and sacred, is the very portion most favorable to you." Calhoun had not long before expected this sort of man to frighten the capitalists into the arms of the planters!

The essence of Calhoun's mistake as a practical statesman was that he tried to achieve a static solution for a dynamic situation. The North, stimulated by invention and industry and strengthened by a tide of immigration, was growing in population and wealth, filling the West, and building railroads that bound East and West together. No concurrent majority, nor any other principle embodied in a parchment, could stem the tide that was measured every ten years in the census returns. William H. Seward touched upon the South's central weakness in his speech of March 11, 1850, when he observed that what the Southerners wanted was "a *political* equilibrium. Every political equilibrium requires a physical equilibrium to rest upon, and is valueless without it." In the face of all realities, the Southerners kept demanding that equality of territory and approximate equality of populations be maintained. "And this," taunted Seward, "must be perpetual!"

Moreover, the Calhoun dialectic was so starkly reactionary in its implications that it became self-defeating. There was disaster even for the South in the premise that every civilized society must be built upon a submerged and exploited labor force—what Hammond called a "mud-sill" class. *If* there must always be a submerged and exploited class at the base of society, and *if* the Southern slaves, as such a class, were better off than Northern free workers, and *if* slavery was the safest and most durable base on which to found political institutions, then there seemed to be no reason why *all* workers, white or black, industrial or agrarian, should not be slave rather than free. Calhoun shrank from this conclusion, but some Southerners did not. George Fitzhugh won himself quite a reputation in the fifties arguing along these lines. The fact that some Southerners, however few, followed

Fitzhugh was an excellent one for Northern politicians to use to rouse free-men, especially those who were indifferent to the moral aspects of slavery, to take a stand against the spread of the institution.

Calhoun could see and expound very plausibly every weakness of Northern society, but his position forced him to close his eyes to the vulnerability of the South. Strong as he was on logical coherence, he had not the most elementary moral consistency. Here it is hard to follow those who, like Professor Wiltse, find in him "the supreme champion of minority rights and interests everywhere." It is true that Calhoun superbly formulated the problem of the relation between majorities and minorities, and his work at this point may have the permanent significance for political theory that is often ascribed to it. But how can the same value be assigned to his practical solutions? Not in the slightest was he concerned with minority rights as they are chiefly of interest to the modern liberal mind—the rights of dissenters to express unorthodox opinions, of the individual conscience against the State, least of all of ethnic minorities. At bottom he was not interested in any minority that was not a propertied minority. The concurrent majority itself was a device without relevance to the protection of dissent, but designed specifically to protect a vested interest of considerable power. Even within the South Calhoun had not the slightest desire to protect intellectual minorities, critics, and dissenters. Professor Clement Eaton, in his *Freedom of Thought in the Old South,* places him first among those politicians who "created stereotypes in the minds of the Southern people that produced intolerance." Finally, it was minority privileges rather than rights that he really proposed to protect. He wanted to give to the minority not merely a proportionate but an *equal* voice with the majority in determining public policy. He would have found incomprehensible the statement of William H. Roane, of Virginia, that he had "never thought that [minorities] had any other *Right* than that of freely, peaceably, & *legally* converting themselves into a *majority* whenever they can." This elementary right Calhoun was prompt to deny to any minority, North or South, that disagreed with him on any vital question. In fact, his first great speeches on the slavery question were prompted by his attempt to deny the right of petition to a minority.

Calhoun was a minority spokesman in a democracy, a particularist in an age of nationalism, a slaveholder in an age of advancing liberties, and an agrarian in a furiously capitalistic country. Quite understandably he developed a certain perversity of mind. It became his peculiar faculty, the faculty of a brilliant but highly abstract and isolated intellect, to see things that other men never dreamt of and to deny what was under his nose, to forecast with uncanny insight several major trends of the future and remain all but oblivious of the actualities of the present. His weakness was to be inhumanly schematic and logical, which is only to say that he thought as he lived. His mind, in a sense, was *too* masterful—it imposed itself upon

John C. Calhoun: The Marx of the Master Class

realities. The great human, emotional, moral complexities of the world escaped him because he had no private training for them, had not even the talent for friendship, in which he might have been schooled. It was easier for him to imagine, for example, that the South had produced upon its slave base a better culture than the North because he had no culture himself, only a quick and muscular mode of thought. It may stand as a token of Calhoun's place in the South's history that when he did find culture there, at Charleston, he wished a plague on it.

XV

Manifest Destiny: A Mystique or an Extension of the Area of Freedom?

INTRODUCTION

"Let me live where I will, on this side is the city, on that the wilderness, and ever I am leaving the city more and more and withdrawing into the wilderness. I should not lay so much stress on this fact if I did not believe that something like this is the prevailing tendency of my countrymen. I must walk toward Oregon and not toward Europe." So Henry David Thoreau (1817–1862) wrote of himself and his generation.

The decade of the 1840's (the Roaring, the Fabulous Forties) is preeminently the decade of the achievement in a continental territorial sense of the "Manifest Destiny" of the United States of America. The "re-annexation" of Texas, the "re-occupation" of Oregon, the acquisition by war with Mexico of the provinces of New Mexico and California (comprehending the present states of California, Nevada, Utah, Arizona, New Mexico, and parts of Wyoming and Colorado)—these supply the gross material image of the accomplishment of American Manifest Destiny. But Manifest Destiny in this decade meant something else as well—something that lay deep in the ethos of the American people. Viewed as an essential part of the history of ideas in America, the motivation and ideology of Manifest Destiny, when subjected to acute analysis, throw strong light upon the spiritual, emotional, ethical, and romantic life of that day, as well as setting in a new perspective the more conventional political and economic life of the times.

As acute analysis, as perceptive interpretation, and as poetic appreciation, the works of Bernard DeVoto and of Albert K. Weinberg on this theme have surely never been equaled, if, indeed, they have been approached. De Voto and Weinberg are not oppositional in their views of the inner meaning of "Manifest Destiny." Rather they complement each other. Yet read together, they are quite different, quite separate, quite distinct. Through De Voto's work—he wrote three large volumes on the westward movement during the first half of the nineteenth century—there runs a quality of warmth, of romance, of poetical conception that seem to catch the very mystique of Manifest Destiny. Weinberg's work is distinguished by the qualities of the intellect and of the mind. His analysis, clear and sensitive, applies "the methods of ideological analysis to political attitudes" and leads on to generalizations that illuminate and give new meaning to this whole period.

Build Thee More Stately Mansions

Bernard De Voto

The First Missouri Mounted Volunteers played an honorable part in the year of decision, and looking back, a private of Company C determined to write his regiment's history. He was John T. Hughes, an A.B. and a schoolmaster. Familiarity with the classics had taught him that great events are heralded by portents. So when he sat down to write his history he recalled a story which, he cautions us, was "doubtless more beautiful than true." Early in that spring of 1846, the story ran, a prairie thunderstorm overtook a party of traders who were returning to Independence, Missouri, from Santa Fe. When it passed over, the red sun had sunk to the prairie's edge, and the traders cried out with one voice. For the image of an eagle was spread across the sun. They knew then that "in less than twelve months the eagle of liberty would spread his broad pinions over the plains of the west, and that the flag of our country would wave over the cities of New Mexico and Chihuahua."

Thus neatly John T. Hughes joined Manifest Destiny and the fires that flamed in the midnight sky when Caesar was assassinated. But he missed a sterner omen.

The period of Biela's comet was seven years. When it came back in 1832 many people were terrified for it was calculated to pass within twenty thousand miles of the earth's orbit. The earth rolled by that rendezvous a month before the comet reached it, however, and the dread passed. In 1839 when the visitor returned again it was too near the sun to be seen, but its next perihelion passage was calculated for February 11, 1846. True to the assignment, it traveled earthward toward the end of 1845. Rome identified it on November 28 and Berlin saw it two days later. By mid-December all watchers of the skies had reported it. The new year began, the year of decision, and on January 13 at Washington, our foremost scientist, Matthew Maury, found matter for a new report.

Maury was a universal genius but his deepest passion was the movement of tides. In that January of '46 he was continuing his labor to perfect the basis for the scientific study of winds and current. Out of that labor came the science of oceanography, and methods of reporting the tides not only of

From Bernard DeVoto, *The Year of Decision: 1846* (Boston: Houghton Mifflin Company, 1950), pp. 3–10; 30–50. Reprinted by permission.

the sea but of the air also that have been permanent, and a revolution in the art of navigation. But he had further duties as Superintendent of the Naval Observatory, and so by night he turned his telescope on Biela's comet. That night of January 13, 1846, he beheld the ominous and inconceivable. On its way toward perihelion, Biela's comet had split in two.

This book tells the story of some people who went west in 1846. Its purpose is to tell that story in such a way that the reader may realize the far western frontier experience, which is part of our cultural inheritance, as personal experience. But 1846 is chosen rather than other years because 1846 best dramatizes personal experience as national experience. Most of our characters are ordinary people, the unremarkable commoners of the young democracy. Their story, however, is a decisive part of a decisive turn in the history of the United States.

Sometimes there are exceedingly brief periods which determine a long future. A moment of time holds in solution ingredients which might combine in any of several or many ways, and then another moment precipitates out of the possible the at last determined thing. The limb of a tree grows to a foreordained shape in response to forces determined by nature's equilibriums, but the affairs of nations are shaped by the actions of men, and sometimes, looking back, we can understand which actions were decisive. The narrative of this book covers a period when the manifold possibilities of chance were shaped to converge into the inevitable, when the future of the American nation was precipitated out of the possible by the actions of the people we deal with. All the actions it narrates were initiated, and most of them were completed, within the compass of a single calendar year. The origins of some of them, it is true, can be traced back as far as one may care to go, and a point of the book is that the effects of some are with us still, operating in the arc determined by 1846. Nevertheless, the book may properly be regarded as the chronicle of a turning point in American destiny within the limits of one year.

This is the story of some people who went west in 1846: our focus is the lives of certain men, women, and children moving west. They will be on the scene in different groupings: some emigrants, some soldiers, some refugees, some adventurers, and various heroes, villains, bystanders, and supernumeraries. It is required of you only to bear in mind that while one group is spotlighted the others are not isolated from it in significance.

Our narrative will get them into motion in the month of January, 1846. But the lines of force they traveled along were not laid down on New Year's Day, and though our stories are clear and simple, they are affected by the most complex energies of their society. They had background, they had relationships, and in order to understand how an inevitability was precipitated out of the possible, we must first understand some of the possibilities.

We must look not only at our characters but at their nation, in January, 1846.

The nation began the year in crisis. It was a crisis in foreign relations. The United States was facing the possibility of two wars—with Great Britain and with Mexico. But those foreign dangers had arisen out of purely domestic energies. They involved our history, our geography, our social institutions, and something that must be called both a tradition and a dream.

Think of the map of the United States as any newspaper might have printed it on January 1, 1846. The area which we now know as the state of Texas had been formally a part of that map for just three days, though the joint resolution for its annexation, or in a delicate euphemism its "re-annexation," had passed Congress in February, 1845. Texas was an immediate leverage on the possible war with Mexico. Texas had declared itself a republic in 1836 and ever since then had successfully defended its independence. But Mexico had never recognized that sovereignty, regarded Texas as a Mexican province, had frequently warned the United States that annexation would mean war, and had withdrawn her minister immediately on the passage of the joint resolution which assured it.

In the far northwestern corner our map would tint or crosshatch a large area to signify that it was jointly occupied by the United States and Great Britain. This area would include the present states of Oregon, Washington, and Idaho, and small parts of Montana and Wyoming lying west of the continental divide. It would also include a portion of Canada, extending northward to agree with the political sentiments of the map maker, perhaps as far north as a line drawn east from the southern tip of Alaska. The whole area was known simply as "Oregon" and it was an immediate leverage on the possible war with Great Britain. For the President of the United States had been elected on a platform which required him to assert and maintain the American claim to sole possession of all "Oregon," clear up to 54° 40', that line drawn eastward from southern Alaska,* and on January 1 the British press was belligerently resenting his preparations to do so.

West of Texas and south of Oregon, from the Pacific Ocean to the continental divide and the Arkansas River, was a still larger area which our map would show as Mexican territory. This area included the present states of California, Nevada, Utah, Arizona, New Mexico, and parts of Wyoming and Colorado. It was composed of two provinces, "California," and "New Mexico," but no American map maker could have approximated the theoretical boundary between them. It too was a powerful leverage, though not often a publicly acknowledged one, on the possible war with Mexico.

It is of absolute importance that no map maker of any nationality, even

---

* Really from the southern tip of Prince of Wales Island.

if he had been able to bound these vast areas correctly, could have filled them in. Certain trails, certain rivers, long stretches of certain mountain ranges, the compass bearings of certain peaks and watersheds, the areas inhabited by certain Indian tribes—these could have been correctly indicated by the most knowledgeful, say Thomas Hart Benton and the aged Albert Gallatin. But there were exceedingly few of these and the pure white paper which the best of them would have had to leave between the known marks of orientation would have extended, in the maps drawn by anyone else, from the Missouri River and central Texas, with only the slightest breaks, all the way to the Pacific. That blank paper would almost certainly have been lettered: "Great American Desert."

The Great American Desert is our objective—"Oregon," "New Mexico," and "California"—the lands lying west of the Louisiana Purchase. Like the Americans who occupied them, however, we must also deal with Texas, the newly annexed republic. The sum of these four geographical expressions composed, on January 1, 1846, the most acute crisis in foreign relations since the Treaty of Ghent had ended the second war with Great Britain in December, 1814, and they were bound together in what can now be understood as a system of social energies. Just how they were bound together will (the hope is) be clear by the end of this book, and we must begin by examining some of the far from simple reasons why they had produced the crisis. It will be best to lead into them by way of the man who in part expressed and in part precipitated the crisis, the President, hopefully called by some of his supporters "Young Hickory," James K. Polk.

Two years before, in the summer of 1844, the first telegraph line brought word to Washington that the Democratic convention, meeting in Baltimore, had determined to require a two-thirds vote for nomination. The rule was adopted to stop the comeback of ex-President Martin Van Buren, who had a majority. That it was adopted was extremely significant—it revealed that Van Buren had defeated himself when he refused to support the annexation of Texas. The convention was betting that the spirit of expansionism was now fully reawakened, that the annexation of Texas was an unbeatable issue, that the Democrats would sweep the country if factionalism could be quelled. Smoke-filled rooms in boarding houses scorned President Tyler (whose renomination would have split the party in two), and would not take General Cass, John C. Calhoun, or Silas Wright, all of whom were identified with factions that were badly straining the party. Factionalism, it became clear, was going to be quelled by the elimination of every prominent Democrat who had ever taken a firm stand about anything. So presently the telegraph announced that George Bancroft, with the assistance of Gideon Pillow and Cave Johnson and the indorsement of Old Hickory in the Hermitage, had brought the delegates to agree on the first dark horse ever nominated for the Presidency, Mr. Pillow's former law partner, James K. Polk.

"Who is James K. Polk?" The Whigs promptly began campaigning on that derision, and there were Democrats who repeated it with a sick concern. The question eventually got an unequivocal answer. Polk had come up the ladder, he was an orthodox party Democrat. He had been Jackson's mouthpiece and floor leader in the House of Representatives, had managed the anti-Bank legislation, had risen to the Speakership, had been governor of Tennessee. But sometimes the belt line shapes an instrument of use and precision. Polk's mind was rigid, narrow, obstinate, far from first-rate. He sincerely believed that only Democrats were truly American, Whigs being either the dupes or the pensioners of England—more, that not only wisdom and patriotism were Democratic monopolies but honor and breeding as well. "Although a Whig he seems a gentleman" is a not uncommon characterization in his diary. He was pompous, suspicious, and secretive; he had no humor; he could be vindictive; and he saw spooks and villains. He was a representative Southern politician of the second or intermediate period (which expired with his Presidency), when the decline but not the disintegration had begun.

But if his mind was narrow it was also powerful and he had guts. If he was orthodox, his integrity was absolute and he could not be scared, manipulated, or brought to heel. No one bluffed him, no one moved him with direct or oblique pressure. Furthermore, he knew how to get things done, which is the first necessity of government, and he knew what he wanted done, which is the second. He came into office with clear ideas and a fixed determination and he was to stand by them through as strenuous an administration as any before Lincoln's. Congress had governed the United States for eight years before him and, after a fashion, was to govern it for the next twelve years after him. But Polk was to govern the United States from 1845 to 1849. He was to be the only "strong" President between Jackson and Lincoln. He was to fix the mold of the future in America down to 1860, and therefore for a long time afterward. That is who James K. Polk was.

The Whigs nominated their great man, Henry Clay. When Van Buren opposed the annexation of Texas, he did so from conviction. It was only at the end of his life, some years later, that Clay developed a conviction not subject to readjustment by an opportunity. This time he guessed wrong— he faced obliquely away from annexation. He soon saw that he had made a mistake and found too clever a way out of the ropes which he had voluntarily knotted round his wrists. Smart politics have always been admired in America but they must not be too smart. The Democrats swept the nation, as the prophets had foretold. It was clear that the Americans wanted Texas and Oregon, which the platform had promised them. Polk, who read the popular mind better than his advisers did, believed that the Americans also wanted the vast and almost unknown area called New Mexico and California.

They did. Polk's election was proof that the energy and desire known as expansionism were indeed at white heat again, after a period of quiescence. This reawakening, which was to give historians a pleasant phrase, "the Roaring Forties," contained some exceedingly material ingredients. Historians now elderly made a career by analyzing it to three components: the need of certain Southern interests and Southern statesmen to seize the empty lands and so regain the power which the increasing population of the North was taking from them, the need of both Northern and Southern interests to dominate the Middle West or at least maintain a working alliance with it, and the blind drive of industrialism to free itself to a better functioning.

Now all those elements were certainly a part of the sudden acceleration of social energies signified by the election of 1844. But society is never simple or neat, and our elder historians who thus analyzed it forgot what their elders had known, that expansionism contained such other and unanalyzable elements as romance, Utopianism, and the dream that men might yet be free. It also contained another category of ingredients—such as the logic of geography, which the map of January 1, 1846, made quite as clear to the Americans then as it is to anyone today. You yourself, looking at a map in which Oregon was jointly occupied by a foreign power and all the rest of the continent west of Texas and the continental divide was foreign territory, would experience a feeling made up of incompletion and insecurity. Both incompletion and insecurity were a good deal more alive to the 1840's than anything short of invasion could make them now. And finally, expansionism had acquired an emotion that was new—or at least signified a new combination. The Americans had always devoutly believed that the superiority of their institutions, government, and mode of life would eventually spread, by inspiration and imitation, to less fortunate, less happy peoples. That devout belief now took a new phase: it was perhaps the American destiny to spread our free and admirable institutions by action as well as by example, by occupying territory as well as by practising virtue. . . . For the sum of these feelings, a Democratic editor found, in the summer of '45, one of the most dynamic phrases ever minted, Manifest Destiny.

In that phrase Americans found both recognition and revelation. Quite certainly, it made soldiers and emigrants of many men (some of them among our characters) who, without it, would have been neither, but its importance was that it expressed the very core of American faith. Also, it expressed and embodied the peculiar will, optimism, disregard, and even blindness that characterized the 1840's in America. As we shall see, the nation which believed in Manifest Destiny came only by means of severe shock and after instinctive denial to realize that Manifest Destiny involved facing and eventually solving the political paradox, the central evasion, of the Constitution—slavery. But it is even more indicative of the 1840's that those who rejected the innumerable statements of Manifest Destiny, repudiated its agencies, and denied its ends, believed in Manifest Destiny. Let Brook Farm speak for them—Brook Farm, the association of literary communists who had withdrawn from the world to establish Utopia a few miles from Boston.

For the Brook Farmers, certainly, did not speculate in Western lands and so cannot come under the economic interpretation of expansionism. Neither were they the spirit of industrialism: they had organized with the declared purpose of nullifying industrialism. Nor were they political adventurers, conspirators, or opportunists: they had formally announced their refusal to adhere to the American political system. But Manifest Destiny had no clearer or more devout statement, and the 1840's had no more characteristic expression, than the editorial which the Brook Farmers published in optimism's house organ, *The Harbinger,* when the curve of the year 1846 began to be clear:—

There can be no doubt of the design being entertained by the leaders and instigators of this infamous business, to extend the "area of freedom" to the shores of California, by robbing Mexico of another large mass of her territory; and the people are prepared to execute it to the letter. In many and most aspects in which this plundering aggression is to be viewed it is monstrously iniquitous, but after all it seems to be completing a more universal design of Providence, of extending the power and intelligence of advanced civilized nations over the whole face of the earth, by penetrating into those regions which seem fated to immobility and breaking down the barriers to the future progress of knowledge, of the sciences and arts: and arms seem to be the only means by which this great subversive movement towards unity among nations can be accomplished. . . . In this way Providence is operating on a grand scale to accomplish its designs, making use of instrumentalities ignorant of its purposes, and incited to act by motives the very antipodes of those which the real end in view might be supposed to be connected with or grow out of.

Thus the literary amateurs: it violates our principles but is part of a providential plan. As Providence's instrumentality Polk was much less woozy. Shortly after he was inaugurated, he explained his objectives to George Bancroft, the scholar, historian, and man of letters who had been a Democratic Brain-Truster since Jackson's time, and whom Polk would make acting Secretary of War, Secretary of the Navy, and finally Minister to Great Britain. His objectives were: the revision of the protective tariff of 1842, the re-establishment of the independent treasury, the settlement of the Oregon question, and the acquisition of California. He was to achieve them all.

. . . There were sixteen inches of ice on Walden Pond, and it undulated under a slight wind like water. Mornings, Henry Thoreau woke with a

461

feeling that he had not answered some question asked him during sleep, but there was no question on Nature's lips. He took an axe and chopped through snow and ice but, before drinking, gazed at the sandy bottom where "waveless serenity reigns as in the amber twilight sky." Heaven, he decided, is under our feet as well as over our heads. He watched men fish through the ice for pickerel and went about a job he had set himself, to plumb the bottom of Walden, which was locally believed to have no bottom. He found it at one hundred and two feet, then, after plotting a chart, discovered that the line of greatest length intersected the line of greatest width exactly at the point of greatest depth. Might this not correspond to the law of average? Might not the two diameters of a man's thought similarly be used to determine exactly how and where his depth went down? Henry thought so, and he went on to see whether White's Pond would show the same regularity. It did.

He had cleared his plot above the lake front the preceding spring, while Polk pushed his foreign policy in the direction of war. He had planted his beans and raised the walls of his shack while Frémont and Kearny headed west, had mortared his chimney while Buchanan prepared Gillespie's instructions, and had plastered the walls while Pakenham fished through the President's ice to determine how much he must concede. These things had no present notice in Henry Thoreau's mind. He was conducting an experiment in economy. He had looked at the twin wonders of the age, the developing industrial system and the certainty of universal moral reform, and had seen no need to pay tribute to either. The first chapter of *Walden* accurately analyzes the bank failures, bond repudiations, mortgages, farmsteads, and factories of the thirties and forties, but Thoreau's experiment dealt with a preliminary, or antecedent, problem, the survival of the mind's integrity in such a system. In Arcadia he had seen no one pounding stone, and he wanted to free himself from subjection to horses, plowing, and the day's waste—as the system would have to do if it were to inclose his loyalty. His house cost him twenty-eight dollars and a shilling; at the end of a year he had needed $25.21¾ to live on. (He appears not to have discussed capitalization with the Provident Institution.) Meanwhile he had written *A Week on the Concord and Merrimac Rivers*, beginning it, very likely, during the January of Mr. Buchanan's insubordination, and had begun the notes that were to acquire form in *Walden*. He had also acted as inspector of snowstorms and rainstorms, and had proved conclusively that "it is not necessary that a man should earn his living by the sweat of his brow, unless he sweats easier than I do." . . . What else he had proved we shall see.

There was a further element in Thoreau's expatriation from Concord. The village had reached a tension of conversational reform. Emerson had observed that "Mr. Alcott and Mr. Wright cannot chat or so much as open the mouth on aught less than a new solar system and the prospective education in the nebulae." Thoreau, though he inexplicably thought Alcott so great a man that nature could not let him die, began to repudiate his conversation as soon as the Walden pines shut off the rhythms of that noble drool. Henry had stayed too long among the pure and garrulous; he felt that his manners had "been corrupted by communication with the saints." Concord had suggested to him that the reforms and liberations it exhaled in sitting rooms might not be a cure of the world's ills but only for dyspepsia. "What so saddens the reformer," he had come to think, "is not his sympathy with his fellows in distress but though he be the holiest son of God, is his private ail." Truly, wailing did come up from Southern plains, but was it the wailing alone of blacks, and just how shall we begin to act on it? Just what intemperance and brutality would best serve for the beginning of redemption? "If anything ail a man, so that he does not perform his functions, if he have a pain in the bowels even, for that is the seat of sympathy, he forthwith sets about reforming—the world."

Here Henry was glancing at Harvard Village, ten miles northwest of Walden, where at Fruitlands the pain in Mr. Alcott's bowels had not succeeded in bringing in the rule of right reason, though it had reformed the world for some months. More particularly, toward West Roxbury, where the far happier Brook Farmers, in smocks, ignorant of the catastrophe preparing for them, hated Polk but praised Providence for using him as an instrument, and spent the January evenings chatting and munching apples before log fires, reading *Consuelo* for beautiful sentiments and, as preparation for the more stately mansion they were building, Fourier's *Theory of the Human Passions*.

The smock wearers also were making an experiment in economy, and they were very happy. The newest Newness made amazing progress, they loved one another and humanity, the children did so marvelously well in the progressive school. Everything was so clear, so easily hand-tinted with pretty words, though it was among the benefits of Association that they came less and less to need words, the twitch of an eyebrow conveying a philosophy and the intuitions so sharpening that they could read letters by simply pressing the envelope against the forehead. This showed how their "right development" refined the passions. Wrong development, which the world's people suffered, produced selfishness, injustice, duplicity; but right development produced harmony, justice, unity. Charles Fourier told them so, who was part Alcott and part Marx. Under Association, which was Fourier's principle of economy, right development would go farther still. It would soften and regulate the temperature (a desirable achievement in January at West Roxbury) and increase the warmth at the poles, correct the heat of the equator, bring on eternal springtime, fertilize the desert, and prevent the drying up of streams. Moreover, it would domesticate the beaver and zebra to man's uses and increase the fish in lakes and rivers some twenty-fold. (Thus Mr. Albert Brisbane, translating Fourier. He omitted Fourier's further promise that lions would turn into anti-lions, a soothed, humanitarian species, other savage carnivores into playful anti-beasts, and the great sea itself into soda pop.) Association would also put an end to larceny, there would be no theft, no sharp business practices; nine tenths or more of the diseases that afflict man under incoherence or Civilization would disappear, and men would live three times as long. Moreover, Zachary Taylor's profession would be obsolete and fleets and armies would wither away. So much for Polk.

(Right development had not yet, however, produced the anti-cow. Na-thaniel Hawthorne, who had bought two $500 shares in Brook Farm and would later sue to get his money back, had had to flee Association because he could no longer bring himself to fork the bright, symbolic gold out of the stalls.)

Two months short of final extinction, there burned here more appeal-ingly than anywhere else a hope that had built more than two score com-munities in the last two decades, most of them already dead. It was the de-sign of Brook Farm: "1. To indoctrinate the whole people of the United States with the principles of associative unity. 2. To prepare for the time when the nation, like one man, shall reorganize its townships on the basis of perfect justice." Thus American millennialism had changed its phase: it had given up Christ in favor of Refined Passions and Virtuous Labor. In the earlier phase, the expectation of perfect sainthood in the immediate (or the oncoming) Kingdom of God had begotten such associations as the Shakers, the Latter-day Saints, the Rappites, and the Disciples of Christ. In the new phase a different perfection was expected, perfect justice as an outgrowth of perfect co-operation—the co-operation, that is, of literary people.

Industrialism had spread its first great wave across the countryside, and a misunderstood abhorrence of its bleak factories oppressed sensitive spirits. The sensitive found only two courses: they could flee from industrialism or they could master it with virtue. The first era of Brook Farm, now over, had attempted flight: the literary raking hay in yellow pantaloons, a small but elevated company baking their bread from their own handmade flour to Plato's dream, presumably as an inspiration to greasy mechanics and stunted factory girls. There were many similar companies of the sensitive, and they had reached perihelion at Fruitlands, where the Great Inane voiced thoughts while Mrs. Alcott and the children gathered in the barley, a poor wench was excommunicated for eating a shred of vile flesh, and in the end Alcott turned his face to the wall and hoped to die because virtue had failed. Of forty such congregations, John Humphrey Noyes, who may be granted authority, said that they failed because right reason was not a working substitute for the grace of God, and because you could not defeat industrialism with plow and scythe.

For the others, those who would master industrialism with virtue, Charles Fourier was the way and the light, and the second era of Brook Farm was dedicated to him. Fourier promised the sensitive that the hideous factories could be transformed into beauty. You refined the passions. You dignified and ennobled labor. You made industry the more attractive as its operations were the more laborious and unpleasant. You put Corinthian columns round the prison house of labor and built it in "fields beautifully laid out and diversified by clusters of fruit and forest trees, flower beds, and fountains." You supplied band concerts and bright uniforms and a series of Eagle Scout badges for the ennobled mechanics. You beguiled the children by inducing them to play in little workshops with little tools. And again and always you refined the passions, inviting mankind to change its heart, to enter into the womb and be born again a second time, to sink the brute and bring the angel in.

Yet mortgages had to be paid, the brute lingered and the angel delayed, and the literary ended in despair. Between Charles A. Dana of Brook Farm, going out to sound Association's trumpet call by lecturing on "Reform Movements Originating among the Producing Classes," and Charles A. Dana of the *Sun,* the century's ablest public disbeliever in mankind, is just the paradox that in all ages overcomes the literary dream. The literary will accept no hybrid of brute and angel; they desire Utopia and will not settle for the human race. They love the people but they hate the mob. On George Ripley's word, and he was the founder of Brook Farm, mankind is dwarfed and brutish. In that common despair ended all that Association had to say.

We are to see several answers to George Ripley worked out to the westward. And at Walden another answer was worked out, to Ripley and to all the decade's reforms as Henry Thoreau saw them. Might not the pain in a reformer's bowels, Thoreau wondered, be just an egoism that debauched his cause? It was necessary to rescue the drowning but also you must tie your shoestrings. Most men lived lives of quiet desperation, and Thoreau could not see that they grew more desperate in factories than on farms, in colleges, or at reason's feast in Mr. Alcott's house. He went down to talk to the Irishmen who were building the Fitchburg railroad, whose whistle he welcomed without a shudder. The railroad was industrialism but also it was making toward Oregon. He anticipated Mr. MacLeish in perceiving that "the rails are laid on them and they are covered with sand, and the cars run smoothly over them." But he would waste no sorrow on them so long as farmers must be subject to their cattle or any man whatsoever was involved in "bankruptcy and repudiation, the springboards from which much of our civilization vaults and turns its somersets."

In short, Thoreau believed that the factory could not be fled from and that it could not be beautified by refining the passions. Labor was dignified only as the laborer was not thought dwarfed and brutish but granted membership in the human race. And with the race, he told his listeners, you must go much farther back than you have ever dreamed. He who wants help wants everything. Nothing can be effected but by one man. You may begin by sawing the little sticks, or you may saw the great sticks first, but sooner or later you must saw them all. So on the banks of Walden he sat him down, "in the Presidency of Polk, five years before the passage of Webster's Fugitive Slave Bill," to grow his beans and write his book. It was not by chance that when Henry Thoreau went out to walk his needle settled west.

American literature gained a flowerier Brook Farm, this spring of '46. The minister in London who was interpreting the Peel government and the jingo press to Buchanan was Louis McLane. A Tammany technician who had assisted the campaign was sent with him as secretary of legation. In May Buchanan was to receive a letter from McLane earnestly desiring the removal of his secretary of legation, "for the sake of the honor as well as the interest of the country." Mr. Gansevoort Melville, the secretary in question, had taken to London with him the manuscript of a younger brother's book about the Marquesas Islands. Gansevoort had sold it and now *Typee* was being printed in both England and America. Sweet, artless, prismatic with an aspiration that was not Concord Village nor the United States Senate nor the Oregon emigration but partook of all three, it described a poet's stay among some gentle cannibals. Chatting with his Mehevis and Kory-Kory's, Melville feels a splendid scorn for Alcott's orphic platitudes and the colonists sweating with hayforks at West Roxbury. Better in coral bays to swim with islanders uncorrupted by reason, to sleep beside them under thatched palm leaves unregardful of factories, to dine on pork in the pi-pi where the gorged chiefs smoke their coconut-shell pipes. The city of Lowell is obliterated altogether and nothing need be considered but sunrise and violet lagoons and the surf coming in. Moreover Fayaway's shoulders wear epaulettes of tattoo, her tappa skirt ends at the knees, and her tunic makes no effort to conceal her young breasts. . . . This mansion opening to the westward, though built of dream, is also part of expansionism, and though Melville might despise Alanno of Hio-Hio, he breathed the same air.

(But Fayaway's breasts were too sweetly displayed, her olive-tinted thighs were bare when Melville swam with her, and many readers exercised their privilege of conjecture. Moreover, Melville had denounced the missionaries, who were too much debauching paradise with a sense of shame and the city of Lowell's cotton cloth. The nation would hear no criticism of righteousness, and his publishers hurriedly altered such sheets as were not yet bound and rushed another printing which omitted comment on the godly. Meanwhile, in early '46, he sat down to write *Typee's* successor, in Lansingburg, New York, and began to court the daughter of Lemuel Shaw. In the end he married her and found no tattooing on her shoulders; if she had breasts, no one crushed flowers between them. She is implacable in our literature. Her husband's work turned aside, after *Omoo,* into phantasies of incest and at last an orphic impotence that has too much in common with Bronson Alcott's noblest thoughts.)

Mr. Hawthorne was back in Salem, where a happy marriage had freed him of the old phobia that had kept him from coming outdoors by day. He was writing to his friend George Bancroft, Secretary of the Navy, in hope of the Salem post office, and was due, by summer, to get the custom-house where he was to meet certain ghosts and in old papers was to find a scarlet initial embroidered with threads of gold. Mr. Emerson was finishing his lectures on Representative Men in Boston and making notes quite as acute as Thoreau's about Fourier, reform, politicians, and slavery. Though he was whiggish, he was no Whig. "These rabble at Washington are really better than the snivelling opposition. They have a sort of genius of a bold and manly cast, though Satanic. They see, against the unanimous expression of the people [the seer was wrong, here, and would amend that judgment before the spring was out], how much a little well-directed effrontery can achieve, how much crime the people will bear, and they proceed from step to step. . . ."

Longfellow heard Emerson lecture and worked on *Evangeline,* the second canto, where the lovers' marriage contract is signed in Acadia just when the English ships "ride in the Gaspereau's mouth with their cannon pointed against us." The menace of those guns or something graver oppressed him through January and he could not shake off a heaviness of spirit. Perhaps his gloom was just the Cambridge winter: "This dull dismal cold crushes me down, as if the sky were falling; or as if I were one of the four dwarfs of the northern mythology, who uphold the dome of heaven upon their shoulders." Or maybe it was a poet's premonition as, foreboding but helpless, he saw his country moving inexorably toward war. And, seeing, could remember what he had written four years before:—

> There is a poor, blind Samson in this land,
>> Shorn of his strength and bound in bonds of steel,
> Who may, in some grim revel, raise his hand,
>> And shake the pillars of this Commonweal,
> Till the vast Temple of our liberties
> A shapeless mass of wreck and rubbish lies.

Walking to Boston with Longfellow, hoping to lighten his dull mood, James Russell Lowell felt the pillars of the commonweal begin to shake. It was a literary achievement of Polk's election that it had stiffened a dilettante into a serious writer. Lowell had written when the Democrats triumphed:—

> Careless seems the great Avenger; history's pages but record
>> One death-grapple in the darkness 'twixt old systems and the Word;
> Truth forever on the scaffold, Wrong forever on the throne,
>> Yet that scaffold sways the future and, behind the dim Unknown,
> Standeth God within the shadow, keeping watch above his own.

Thereafter he could not be satisfied with the sweet-lavender asininity of Brook Farm; he had found steel and an edge. Since writing it he had married his beloved bluestocking, Maria White, had honeymooned in Philadelphia, had done some prentice work writing tracts for the Abolitionists, and now had come home to Elmwood. On the last day of '45 his daughter Blanche was born and James is seen briefly in January dreaming of a time when she will be "a great, strong, vulgar, mud-pudding-baking, tree-climbing little wench" . . . and beginning some articles for a London paper that will be Lowell taking up arms and going forth to war.

But do not suppose that Mr. Polk lacked literary support. The Democratic Party had an organ in Brooklyn and now there began to resound from it the barbaric if adolescent yawp of Mr. Walter, as he still signed it, Whitman.

Whitman could discern no danger to the eastward: "As for the vaunted ocean-sway of Great Britain, we laugh it to scorn! It can never compete with us, either in time of peace or war. Our Yankee ingenuity has built better ships and manned them with hardier crews than any other nation on earth." A flag goes up on the *Eagle* building, and "Ah! its broad folds are destined to float yet—and we, haply, shall see them—over many a good square mile which now owns a far different emblem." Where? "The more we reflect on the matter of annexation as involving a part of Mexico, or even the main bulk of that Republic, the more do doubts and obstacles resolve themselves away, the more plausible appears that at first glance most difficult consummation. . . . Then there is California, in the way to which lovely tract lies Santa Fe; how long a time will elapse before *they* shine as two new stars in our mighty firmament?" Expansion finds its incident: "Mexico, though contemptible in many respects, is an enemy deserving a vigorous 'lesson.' We have coaxed, excused, listened with deaf ears to the insolent gasconade of her government, submitted thus far to a most offensive rejection of an ambassador personifying the American nation, and waited for years without payment of the claims of our injured merchants." And Manifest Destiny its broadest sentiment: "It is from such materials—from the Democracy, with its manly heart and its lion strength spurning the ligatures wherewith drivellers would bind it—that we are to expect the great FUTURE of this Western World! a scope involving such unparalleled human happiness and rational freedom, to such unnumbered myriads, that the heart of a true *man* leaps with a mighty joy only to think of it!"

Adolescent but perfectly expressive of Walter Whitman's countrymen, in January, 1846.

California, January 24, 1846.

"Many weeks of hardships, close trials, and anxieties have tried me severely, and my hair is turning gray before its time. But all this passes, *et le bon temps viendra*." Thus Childe Harold's American heir, writing to his wife from Yerba Buena, on the Bay of San Francisco. And, receiving that letter of January 24 in Washington and learning that a Mr. James Magoffin (who will be an actor in our drama) can take an answer to Bent's Fort on the Arkansas, whence it will be forwarded to California, Jessie Benton Frémont grieves: "Poor papa, it made tears come to find that you had begun to turn gray. [He was thirty-three.] You must have suffered much and been very anxious 'but all that must pass. . . . . I have not had so much pleasure in a very great while as today. The thought that you may hear from me and know that all are well and that I can tell you again how dearly I love you makes me as happy as I can be while you are away."

Young Francis Parkman found it natural to prefix quotations from *Childe Harold* to the chapters of *The Oregon Trail*. But it was in the person of John Charles Frémont that the nation's enthusiasm for the poetry of Lord Byron found a career. We are to follow him through knotty and hardly soluble controversies. They will be less obscure if it is kept in mind that Frémont was primarily a literary man . . . who had a literary wife.

Greatness was a burden on Childe Harold's soul but nature kept the lines a little out of drawing. Born in high romance outside the law, he had grown up a young Rousseau. He had found a profession plotting the wilderness for the Topographical Corps. His native poetry responded to the solitudes and he had mastered the skilled crafts of living there. If his father's romance was out of Alexandre Dumas, his own was out of Italian opera. It rose in a fine cadenza when, secretly married to Jessie, the beautiful, bluestocking daughter of Thomas Hart Benton, he stood before the Senator to announce defiance of his will. Benton's rage had been known continentally ever since he had shot it out with Andrew Jackson in a community brawl. It now turned on Frémont but to violins Jessie stepped forward and sang her aria, "Whither thou goest I will go, and where thou lodgest I will lodge." Benton, who was one of the best-educated men in Congress, surrendered to a literary allusion.

An obscure lieutenant of topographical engineers had become the son-in-law of the most powerful Senator, of the Senator, furthermore, who was the greatest expansionist, whose lifelong vision it had been to make all the West American. Also, greatness had secured the assistance of a national spotlight. Benton and his colleague Linn had Frémont put in command of two explorations of the West whose sole purpose was to advertise the Oregon country. The first took him to South Pass and a little beyond; the second to Oregon and, looping back, to California by a spectacular if injudicious winter crossing of the Sierra. He proved himself a first-rate wilderness commander, learning his new trade from two of its masters, Kit Carson and Tom Fitzpatrick. He traveled little country that his instructors had not had by heart for twenty years, blazed no trails, though the Republicans were to run him for the Presidency as the Pathfinder, and did little of importance beyond determining the latitude and longitude of many sites which the mountain men knew only by experience and habit. But he learned mountain and desert skills well, was tireless in survey and analysis, and enormously enjoyed himself.

Also he was a literary man and the Thunderer was his father-in-law. Benton roared in the Senate, the other expansionists chimed in, and Frémont had given the West to the American people. With Jessie's eager help he wrote his two reports, which were far more important than his travels. The government printed them, first separately, then together, and sowed them broadcast. The westering nation read them hungrily. Frémont chasing buffalo, Galahad Carson reclaiming the orphaned boy's horses from the Indians, Odysseus Godey riding charge against hordes of the red butchers —there was here a spectacle that fed the nation's deepest need. They were adventure books, they were charters of Manifest Destiny, they were texts of navigation for the uncharted sea so many dreamed of crossing, they were a pageant of daring, endurance, and high endeavor in the country of peaks and unknown rivers. With Benton's advertising, they made Frémont a popular image of our Western wayfaring. Now he could come downstage center with the light on him and begin his role as a hero of romantic drama.

We have noted the start of his third expedition, from St. Louis, in June, 1845. Carson was his adjutant again. Fitzpatrick was with him for a while but was detached to accompany Lieutenant Abert on that other subtly motivated "exploration" to the Southwest. He had such other mountain men as Dick Owens, Lucien Maxwell, Basil Lajeunesse, Alexis Godey, and Joe Walker. The usefulness to Polk of this third expedition, its part in the great game, is clear. While the crises with Mexico and Great Britain were intensifying, on the frontier of Oregon and California there would be an army officer and sixty armed men, most of them thirty-third-degree mountain men. . . . Now there was making toward him a lieutenant of marines vastly impressed by anti-American demonstrations in Mexico City. The lieutenant had been ordered to show him instructions directing the consul at Monterey to procure a peaceful revolution in California, and also carried private letters from Benton and Benton's daughter. In January, Lieutenant Gillespie was crossing Mexico with exceeding slowness, to sail for Honolulu on February 22.

In January greatness burgeoned in Frémont's soul. He had reached his stage and time was on the march. It might be that some great deed could be done. And from then on to the end of his life he was to go, always subtly, astray. Nothing came out quite the way it should have done. Lord Byron, who had imagined him, could not make him rhyme.

He had reached Sutter's Fort (the site of Sacramento) on December 9 of '45, after the outstanding exploration of his career which broke a trail across the Salt Desert west of Great Salt Lake to Ogden's or Mary's River, which Frémont renamed the Humboldt. . . . Well, not quite the first passage of that white waste, though Frémont sincerely believed that it was.

Jedediah Smith, the great mountain man, had crossed it from the west, east, south of Frémont's trail, in 1827. Carson seems not to have known of Smith's crossing, though both he and Joe Walker should have known, and it was indicated on at least two well-known maps with which it was Frémont's business to be wholly familiar. No matter, that crossing (under Walker's guidance) was notable enough, and so was the earlier stretch (under Carson's guidance) which had brought the party from the Grand River to the White River and on to the Green.

At the Humboldt Frémont sent the larger part of his force into California under Joe Walker. Then, after another valuable survey, he divided his force again and led a picked party in a forced winter crossing of the high Sierra. The venture was foolhardy, was disapproved by Carson, served only Frémont's consciousness of brave deeds—and beat the snows by just a little while. He and his gaunt companions came down into the great green valley. Sutter fed them and they waited for Walker's party to join them.

Walker delayed, having mistaken the rendezvous appointed. Frémont had now reached his theater and he was restless. He marched his little group vaguely toward Oregon, whither he had been ordered, turned back to Sutter's again (past a site on the American River where Sutter had considered building a sawmill), and on January 14 started south to find his larger party. He met some of the California Indians who lived on horses stolen from their decayed relatives, the mission peons. So he redressed an injury they had done him on his last visit, two years before. Owens, Carson and the Delaware scouts got fresh scalps for their leggins in three sharp, unnecessary skirmishes. It was at least a theatrical deed but it was not judicious. There had arrived in California, from a Mexican government that feared war, orders to warn out of the province all foreigners who were not licensed to hold land. The warning had not been issued but the orders directing it had begot suspicion and unrest. And now a foreigner, accompanied by the mountain men whom the Californians knew from years of forays against their horse herds, was marching through their province killing Indians. To what end? If he meant nothing worse, did he mean to stir up an Indian war?

Frémont went back to Sutter's Fort. He got a passport from Sutter and went to Yerba Buena, where he wrote the letter quoted above. Then he moved down the coast to Monterey, the seagirt town where Richard Henry Dana had first sent down a royal yard and heard the mate's "Well done" with as much satisfaction as ever he had felt in Cambridge on seeing a *"bene"* at the foot of a Latin exercise. Here he called formally on the consul, Larkin, to whom Gillespie was bringing secret instructions.

Sea and sky are pleasant at Monterey, and Frémont stayed on drinking the excellent native wines and talking with the shrewd, hard-bitten consul. On January 29 the prefect, Don Manuel Castro, inquired through

Larkin what errand had brought an American army officer to the golden shore. Frémont answered that though he was an army officer his errand was not military but peaceful, to determine the best trade route to the Pacific, and that his company were not soldiers but civilians. That was true. He was a touch diplomatic, however, when he added that he had left his party on the frontier—he did not know where they were but did know that they were moving through the interior—and that he had come to Monterey for supplies. Then another Castro, Don José, the military commander of California (who was bickering with the governor, Don Pío Pico, and whom Larkin had cozened a good way toward revolution), gave Frémont permission to winter in the valley of the San Joaquin. Frémont told Don José that, eventually, he would want to go home along the southern route, up the Gila River.

But he did not go to the San Joaquin Valley, which was east of the coastal mountains and distant from the settlements. He stayed on where he was. Later he was to explain that he had lingered here like any tourist, in the hope of finding a place to build a house for his mother. Maybe. But he was hearing stories from resident Americans. And destiny was stirring in his soul.

On January 14 James Clyman, encamped in the mountain chaos of northern California, wrote in his journal:—

> Heard that Mr. Fremont had arived at suitors Fort and still more recently that Mr. Hastings and Party had likewise arived Both from the U. States. But no information has yet arived of the Politicks in the states in fact information of all Kinds Travels slow and is very uncertain when it has arived you know nothing certain unless you see it yourself.

Jim Clyman, a master mountain man, thus notes the coming of two California authors. Clyman's own role in our story will unfold presently; his immediate convenience here is that he also had literary moments. He had written into his journal a treatise on the hunting of grizzly bears and, just before it, a more extended one on California and the Californians. He found the latter "a proud Lazy indolent people doing nothing but ride after herds from place to place without any appearent object," whose labor and drudgery were done by Indians "kept in a state of Slavery haveing or Receiving no compensation for their labour except a scanty allowance of subsistence . . . and perhaps a cotton Shirt and wool sufficient to make a coarse Blanket." Their government was a series of revolutions, "every change for the worse," and the change meaning merely that "the revenue has fallen into other hands." And "in fact the Military and all parts of the Government are weak imbecile and poorly organized and still less respected."

Jim Clyman, however, liked the California scenery. And he was quite clear about such countrymen of his as he met there. "The Foreigners which have found their way to this country are mostly a poor discontented set of inhabitants and but little education hunting for a place as they [want] to live easy only a few of them have obtained land and commenced farming and I do not hear of but one man that has gone to the trouble and Expence to get his title confirmed and fixed beyond altiration and dispute."

Clyman lingered along the Putah and other mountain creeks during January, chronicling the rains and watching the lush spring come on. And, doubtless, remembering his past. It was his private past, but to saturation it was the American past also.

January in California was already spring. The rains had wrought their resurrection and Jim Clyman "noticed the manseneto trees in full Bloom . . . an evergreen shrub growing in a thick gnarled clump . . . and would make a beautiful shade for a door yard." The season was "fine growing weather verry much resembling a Missouri April or an Eastern May."

But in Missouri and the East January was still winter, an uncommon hard winter. The prairies were deep under snow, frost sank deep in the ground, the wind whistled by from the north and the boughs of trees fired pistol shots when they moved in it. It was a season suspended, a time to finish jobs while the stock stamped in the barn all day long, a time for talking.

They talked in country stores, at the post offices, in the kitchens of farmhouses—along the Sangamon, in the Western Reserve, in the bluegrass country, under the shadow of Mount Equinox. The little weeklies—*Journal, Sentinel, Freedom's Herald*—reprinted what the Washington *Union* said about Texas, the *National Intelligencer's* appraisal of the British fleet, a summary of the impending crisis based on *Niles' Register*. Gittin' on to war, I guess. Polk's bound to take no sass from Johnny Bull, no, nor the Greasers, neither. Or Polk's set to make us fight a war if he can't get slave territory noways else. ("They just want this Californy So's to lug new slave states in, to abuse ye an' to scorn ye', An' to plunder ye like sin.") They talked very much like Benton, Buchanan, Webster, Lincoln, Whitman, Emerson, Dana, Thoreau. Fist on the table, Pa brought the verdict in. Dave listened and had his say but would not mention a young dream of Her Majesty's frigate striking her colors in humiliation or dark-skinned lancers dying in the Halls of Montezuma while a Hoosier farm boy waved an unfamiliar sword. And Ma looked at Dave, a firstborn son whom President Polk might send to war.

But to a long-peaceful nation war was an unreal haze on the far horizon. Whereas here at hand, in the Sangamon country or in the Green Mountains, next to Perkins' store or half a mile up the crick, someone who might be named, say, Bill Bowen had sold his place. Bill and Mother, the girls, and three of the boys were going west.

Strange paraphernalia gathered in the Bowen barn and the Bowens were preparing a granary that would have seen the family through a famine year. At least two hundred pounds of flour or meal per person, the *Guide* said, *The Emigrants' Guide to Oregon and California* by Lansford W. Hastings, whose arrival in California Jim Clyman had recorded. All the Bowens thumbed that small volume, arguing, checking, refuting. Twenty pounds of sugar, ten pounds of salt . . . everyone will require at least twice as much as he would need at home, since there will be no vegetables . . . some buffalo can be counted on—and along the icebound Sangamon Bill Bowen sees himself riding down a shaggy beast straight out of fable . . . such goods for the Indian trade as beads, tobacco, handkerchiefs, cheap pantaloons, butcher knives, fish hooks—so young Bill and Nancy and Henry Clay and Joe will truly trade fish hooks for moccasins with a feathered topknot beside streams that are also straight out of fable. That topknot looks just like Tecumseh or Pontiac, and the streams of fable, the Platte, the Snake, the Green, are just such known rivers as the Sangamon, the Connecticut, the Maumee. While the north wind howls over the rooftree, it seems impossible that, come summer, Bill and Nancy Bowen will be unyoking the oxen while the "caral" forms on the banks of the Sweetwater, but they will be, for on page 147 Mr. Hastings says so.

This Hastings was a Frémont in miniature. He is an elusive soul, not much can be said about him with certainty. A young man on the make, he was at this moment engaged in a grandiose and still wholly theoretical real-estate enterprise on the golden shore, and he was the local agent of a bigger one managed from Washington which was a kind of gaudy bet on an insider's guess that there would be war. But he also had speculations —or visions—more gaudily ambitious. He may have meditated another overlordship on the frontier of empire, like the one which Sutter had actually established at New Helvetia. He may have seen himself—he would only have been one of a good many—as a kind of Sam Houston, president of another Lone Star Republic. He may have intended to utilize the opportunities provided for a smart man with nerve—precisely as Frémont did. Rumors connected him—loosely—with the Mormons and, on grounds that are apparently more substantial, with one of the current revolutionary intrigues. Whatever was in his mind, he did not have quite enough stuff. Put him down as a smart young man who wrote a book—it is not a unique phenomenon in literature—without knowing what he was talking about. As the first head of the California Chamber of Commerce, the first Booster on the golden shore. He went from his home town, Mount Vernon, Ohio, to Oregon in 1842 with Elijah White's famous caravan. He found no opening for his talents in that sober commonwealth and moved on to California. He liked what he saw, he perceived there were opportunities for smart men, so he wrote a prospectus and took it east in 1844. It was published at Cincinnati in 1845 and Hastings went back to California. Jim Clyman heard of him just when the Bowens and the Smiths and the Does were reading it. And while they were reading it Mr. Hastings formed a new design, one which shifted him from merely mischievous advertising to really dangerous activity. As, farther along, we shall see.

"Here perpetual summer is in the midst of unceasing winter; perennial spring and never failing autumn stand side by side, and towering snow clad mountains forever look down upon eternal verdure." That strain was not as familiar in '46 as the years have made it now. Bill Bowen, who has to plunge between frozen walls of snow to lug in endless armfuls of hickory lengths, reads with an understandable fascination that no fires are needed in California except to cook by, and those usually outdoors. Mother's knuckles are gnarled and stiff with rheumatism begotten by prairie winters —but by that violet sea it is warmer in winter than in summer, and even in December vegetation is in full bloom. (My sakes! hollyhocks, sweet william, carnation pinks at Christmas time in your own dooryard!) Aunt Esther is racked by chills and fever every autumn, her thin shoulders wrapped with a shawl even in August. But "there being no low, marshy regions, the noxious miasmatic effluvia . . . is here nowhere found" and "while all this region . . . is entirely exempt from all febrific causes, it is also entirely free from all sudden changes and extreme variableness of climate or other causes of catarrhal or consumptive affections." So Aunt Esther can ease her tired old bones in California, and Nancy will not sniffle all winter long, and pink will come back to little Bob's cheeks, they will not have to watch him die of lung fever, after all.

And such farms! Young Bill, chipping at the frozen droppings of the cows, may meditate on the information that California stock require neither feeding nor housing, nor other care, nor any expense. Moreover, Mr. Hastings has seen oats half an inch thick through the stalk and eight feet high, thousands of acres at a stretch. Clover grows to five feet, covering the hills with natural hay. A single stalk of wheat forms seven heads and the grain runs four pounds to the bushel heavier than any the Bowens know. Seventy bushels to the acre, often up to a hundred and twenty bushels—and next year sixty-one bushels spontaneously, with no sowing at all. Also two crops in one twelvemonth, and up to sixty bushels of corn per acre, and wild flax waves as far as the eye can see, and the soil grows everything, tobacco, rice, cotton, crabapples, plums, strawberries the largest and most delicious in the world, peaches blossoming in January, such grapes as you cannot believe in.

Bill Bowen had no reason to know that there were optimisms in Hastings' book. The advertiser told him too candidly that there was no scarcity of fuel east of the Platte River, that all the streams he would cross were easily fordable, that buffalo would be plentiful for hundreds of miles beyond the Rockies, that they could be herded like cattle, that the California Indians were inoffensive, and so on. Publicity is an art of omission—and Hastings' need was to trump Oregon, which drew most of the emigration.

There were few difficulties, he said, till you reached the place where the road forked. On the fork that led to Oregon the travel became dreadful and hazardous at once—and even if you survived it you would have only unfruitful Oregon for all your labors. Some remarks here about five months of rain and sleet, whereas rain in California was California rain. They read this in the Sangamon country. They also read the barker's light suggestion that a fine way to shorten the trip would be to try a route which Mr. Hastings had so far not bothered to try (and no one had yet broken), a possible cutoff from Fort Bridger (which Hastings had barely seen) to the southern end of Great Salt Lake and thence due west to Ogden's river (country about which Hastings knew nothing whatever). The saving of several hundred miles seemed promising on a winter evening in the kitchen.

Much more widely read, Frémont's was a much better book. It knew what it was talking about, and when Bill Bowen read that there was wood or water in a given place, or good soil, or difficult travel, he could count on it. The myth of the Great American Desert went down before this literary man's examination—and before his vision (like his father-in-law's) of cities rising in wasteland and the emptiness filling with fat farms. It was filled with solid facts that solid minds could use: it told about the winds, the water, the timber, the soil, the weather. It was extraordinarily seeing and intuitive, remarkably accurate. In the book he wrote, Frémont deserves well of the Republic.

But the book had a much greater importance than this: it fed desire. The wilderness which was so close to Frémont's heart that he has dignity only when he is traveling it was the core of the nation's oldest dream. Kit Carson, Tom Fitzpatrick, Alexis Godey, Basil Lajeunesse, his mountain men, were this generation's embodiment of a wish that ran back beyond Daniel Boone, beyond Jonathan Carver, beyond Christopher Gist, innumerable men in buckskins, forest runners, long hunters, rivermen, *gens du nord,* the company of gentlemen and adventurers of the far side of the hill. Something older than Myles Standish or Captain John Smith fluttered a reader's pulse when the mountain men worked their prodigies before Frémont's admiring eyes. It responded to his exaltation when, pounding his rifle on the saddle to seat a fresh load, he charged through dust clouds at the snorting buffalo. It quickened when he reached the highest peak of the Wind River divide and there pressed between leaves of his notebook a honey bee that was making westward. He went on—across deserts, through untrodden gulches, up slopes of aspen, over the saddle, along the ridge, down the far side. He smelled sagebrush at dawn, he smelled rivers in the evening—alkali in sun-hardened earth when a shower had passed, pines when the pollen fell, roses and sweet peas and larkspur, carrion, sulphur, the coming storm, greasewood, buffalo dung in the smoke of campfires. He saw the Western country with eager eyes—saw it under sun, bent and swollen by mirage, stark, terrible, beautiful to the heart's longing, snow on the peaks, infinite green and the night stars.

That was what the pulse answered in Frémont's book. And, looking at Bill Bowen, asking why this settled citizen of Sangamon County or Brattleboro or the Mohawk Valley was selling out and heading west, one finds no dependable answer except in that answering pulse. Now it is true that Bill Bowen, reading Frémont by candlelight beside the Cumberland or the Delaware, could jot down a well-considered memorandum that there was first-rate farm land along the Willamette. It is true that the dispossessed Mormons, scrutinizing in their beleaguered city every page he wrote and every similar page they could find, could plot an itinerary toward a destination unknown but known to offer their only chance of surviving. But that is of the slightest importance, and it is not what a young man named Francis Parkman read painfully, with eyes beginning to be diseased, that winter in Boston. Or a boy named Lewis Garrard, reading him in Cincinnati and tossing away his schoolbooks because "the glowing pages of Frémont's tour to the Rocky Mountains . . . were so alluring to my fancy that my parents were persuaded to let me go westward." Or a thousand men named Bill Bowen, from Missouri eastward to the state of Maine.

It was certainly an important, an irrevocable climax when Bill Bowen sold his place, and certainly there went into it the hardest, most reasoned motives. Bodies bent by the labor of New England farms would find a longing crystallized in the tidings that the Oregon soil was deep and without stones, in gentle weather, beside broad waters, below the brows of timbered hills. Bodies sapped by malarial autumns and prairie winters would feel the tug of a California where there was neither cold nor hard work nor any distempers of the flesh. Furthermore, the prairie crops had slackened for the past several seasons and over a wide area had failed—and, on Mr. Hastings' promise, crops never slackened or failed where rolled the Sacramento. Also, neither the tariff of '42 nor all the rhetoric of Congress had succeeded in fully restoring the farmers' market which had been shattered in '37—and there was a belief that in Oregon the trade with China and the Sandwich Islands would absorb all crops that could be grown, a knowledge that there was a great grazing industry in California, a promise that the same herds could be developed in Oregon. We may also make the conventional genuflection to the texts which tell us that the victims of industrialism's earliest American failures were going westward in new hope— though, after due search, exceedingly few of them have been found in any of the events we deal with and none at all along the Western trails. Finally, those Congressmen who talked so gloriously about stretching the eagle's wing across the setting sun were talking about a fundamental reality, a belief that plumbed deep in Bill Bowen's heart. Bill Bowen had long believed and now believed more passionately than ever before that the

Americans must occupy their continent, and if others won't do it while there is yet time, maybe I'd better start right now.

Nevertheless, when all these reasons are totaled up they make a sum far from large enough to explain why, suddenly, the Americans were marching on their last frontier—to explain the evening talk in farm kitchens in January, 1846. One comes much closer to the truth with Boone and Carver and Gist, with the venturers crossing the fixed frontier of Sudbury toward the new land in the Connecticut bottoms—with all those who in two and a quarter centuries had moved up to the Fall Line and beyond it, across to the Mississippi, and, a few years since, beyond that. . . . When Bill Bowen sold his house a national emotion welled in the secret places of his heart and he joined himself to a national myth. He believed with Henry Thoreau in the forest and in the meadow and in the night in which the corn grows. Eastward Thoreau went only by force, but westward, ever since Columbus dared the Ocean Sea, westward he had gone free. The lodestone of the West tugged deep in the blood, as deep as desire. When the body dies, the Book of the Dead relates, the soul is borne along the pathway of the setting sun. Toward that Western horizon all heroes of all peoples known to history have always traveled. Beyond it have lain all the Fortunate Isles that literature knows. Beyond the Gates of Hercules, beyond the Western Ocean, beyond the peaks where the sun sinks, the Lapps and the Irish and the Winnebago and all others have known that they would find the happy Hyperboreans—the open country, freedom, the unknown. Westward lies the goal of effort. And, if either Freud or the Navajo speak true, westward we shall find the hole in the earth through which the soul may plunge to peace.

These people waiting for spring to come are inclosed by our myth. But think of them as hard-handed, hard-minded Americans seeking a new home in the West. Think of them also as so certain in their desire that James K. Polk's war seems trivial and wasted. . . . If the dream filled the desert with a thousand brooks like the one that tinkled in the north pasture, built in the Rocky Mountains a thousand white cottages like those that line a New Hampshire common, sowed alkali plains with such crops as the oak openings knew in Michigan, and sketched on the unknown a familiar countryside of rich green slopes, farm cattle lying in noon shade beside familiar pools, and the jeweled miniature of neighbors striking whetstone to scythe within a shout's reach of one another—why, they would learn about the West soon enough.

Extension of the Area of Freedom

Albert K. Weinberg

In the "roaring 'forties," a decade thus designated because the spirit of American life rose into high and turbulent flame, there was welded an association of two ideals which gave a new integration to the American's consciousness of national destiny. One of the two ideals was territorial expansion. After several decades of relative quiescence, expansionism was rekindled by the issues of Texas and Oregon and was fanned to white heat by the oratory of Democrats in the presidential election of 1844. For the first time the wish of numerous Americans fathered the thought that their eventual possession of no less a domain than the entire North American continent was "manifest destiny"—a phrase which now passed into the national vocabulary.

The central implication of "manifest destiny" in the 'forties, however, was less a matter of the scope of expansion than of its purpose. The conception of expansion as a destiny meant primarily that it was a means to the fulfilment of a certain social ideal the preservation and perfection of which was America's providential mission or destiny. This ideal, conceived as "the last best revelation of human thought," was democracy—a theory of mass sovereignty but in a more important aspect a complex of individualistic values which, despite Fisher Ames's observation that America was too democratic for liberty,[1] Americans most frequently summarized by the inspiring word "freedom." It was because of the association of expansion and freedom in a means-end relationship that expansion now came to seem most manifestly a destiny.

While the championship of the rights of man appeared from the beginning of national life to be America's special destiny, expansion had not seemed in general to be a necessary element in this preeminent national purpose. It is true that expansionists of the Revolution and the War of 1812 tendered "liberty"[2] to the "oppressed" Canadians, and that Jefferson once included not only Canada but Cuba and Florida as well in America's

From *Manifest Destiny: A Study of Nationalist Expansionism in American History* (Baltimore: The Johns Hopkins Press, 1935), pp. 100–129. Reprinted by permission.

[1] *Works of Fisher Ames*, I, 328.

[2] Representative Johnson, *Annals of Cong.*, 12th Cong., 1st sess., col. 458.

"empire for liberty." [3] Yet in all these instances, as foregoing evidence has suggested, the extension of democracy was probably neither a primary motive of any expansionists nor even a secondary motive of many of them. It was not until the 'forties that the popular ideology of expansionism centered in democracy. The new importance of this ideal to the expansionist was shown by the words which rang through the land as his slogan, "extension of the area of freedom."

It was because of its infusion with this ideal that American expansionism of the middle 'forties became possessed, as Professor Adams says in his valuable essay on "Manifest Destiny," of a "spiritual exaltation" in contemplation of the assumed superiority of American institutions. A recognition of the rôle played by idealistic American nationalism in this expansion movement has led to an explanation which is very different from that of most early American historians. Writers close to the passions of the Civil War attributed expansionism to "the glut of our slaveholders," [4] the desire of the Southern States to extend the system of slavery. More objective contemporary historians believe that the intensity and extensity of expansionism, while due partly to sectional interests, were caused primarily by nationalistic attitudes resting not merely upon practical interests but also upon the "emotion" of "manifest destiny" [5] and its correlate, the "idealism" [6] of the spirit of democracy.

However, it is as yet more common to refer to democracy as an explanation of American expansionism than to attempt an explanation of expansionist democratic idealism itself. The zeal for extending the area of freedom raises several interesting and important problems. Why is it that, despite the fact that neither expansionism nor the attachment to democracy was new, the two did not come into fusion before? What were the historical circumstances which overcame the previous estrangement of these pieties? Most important of all, what was the true meaning of the ideal described vaguely as extension of the area of freedom?

The point of the last question is made sharper by the fact that the most usual connotation of such words as "extension of the area of freedom" does not make sense in the light of the historical context. The phrase was used primarily by those who urged the annexation of Texas. But Texas already had a republican government, as was pointed out by anti-expansionists attacking the slogan. Thus Representative McIlvain asked "how, if freedom mean republican liberty, can its area be extended by the union of the two governments?" [7] Perplexed by the same question, Repre-

---

[3] *The Writings of Thomas Jefferson,* ed. H. A. Washington (Philadelphia, 1854), V, 444.

[4] James Schouler, *History of the United States of America* (Washington, 1889), IV, 519.

[5] Ephraim Douglass Adams, *The Power of Ideals in American History* (New Haven, 1926), p. 93.

[6] William Archibald Dunning, *The British Empire and the United States* (New York, 1914), p. 138.

[7] *Cong. Globe,* 28th Cong., 2d sess., App., p. 373.

sentative Marsh characterized "extension of the area of freedom" as "an argument addressed to the ear and not the understanding—a mere jingle of words without meaning, or, if significant, false in the only sense which the words will fairly bear." [8]

Unfortunately the matter cannot be so quickly dismissed. The popular slogan is often vapid, but in this case it did have a meaningful content. Only, it was very different from the significance which contemporary anti-expansionists and even later historians attached to the shibboleth. To understand its rather surprising implication, it will be necessary to turn first to the historical background of the expansionist ideal in order to survey briefly the previous development of the relationship between the ideas of democracy and expansion.

When Representative Severance urged in the 'forties that Americans "rather extend the 'area of freedom' by . . . our bright and shining example as a pattern republic," [9] he was reverting to the conception which had been held by the founders of the nation. Originally "the extension of the area of freedom" signified extension of freedom regardless of political connection. Moreover the chief method chosen for extending freedom was the purely passive one of radiating democratic influence through impressive example. Thus Joel Barlow said in 1787 that "the example of political wisdom and felicity, here to be displayed, will excite emulation throughout the kingdoms of the earth, and meliorate the condition of the human race." [10] Thomas Jefferson spoke of America as "a standing monument and example" which would "ameliorate the condition of man over a great portion of the globe." [11] Jefferson also suggested another non-expansionist method of extending freedom. It was the pioneer migration covering even the Western Coast "with free and independent Americans, unconnected with us but by the ties of blood and interest, and employing like us the rights of self-government." [12] It is clear from many such utterances that Americans at first perceived no necessary logical relationship between the extension of democracy and the extension of America's boundaries.

Why did early Americans see no logical nexus between the two ideals which were firmly associated by their descendants? One reason for the original disassociation of democracy and expansion was the internationalist orientation of many of the founders of the Republic. Early idealists, as the nationalistic Gouverneur Morris complained, had a *penchant* for referring to themselves as "citizens of the world." [13] Associated with this internationalism was a devotion to democracy for its own sake. If only the offshoots of the American Republic blossomed into freedom, the retention of politi-

---

[8] *Ibid.*, p. 316.   [9] *Ibid.*, p. 371.

[10] Joel Barlow, *An Oration, Delivered . . . July 4, 1787* (Hartford, 1787), p. 20.

[11] *Writings of Thomas Jefferson*, Memorial ed., X, 217.

[12] *Writings of Thomas Jefferson*, IX, 351.

[13] S. E. Morison, ed., *Sources and Documents Illustrating the American Revolution, 1764–1788, and the Formation of the Federal Constitution* (Oxford, 1923), pp. 281–82.

cal connection seemed to Jefferson "not very important to the happiness of either part." [14]

Yet it is doubtful whether these magnanimous attitudes account fundamentally for the non-expansionist character of early democratic philosophy. Indifference to the national label of expansive democracy may be explicable basically by the aspect in which expansion of territory presented itself from the viewpoint of self-interest. It did not seem originally that wide extent of territory was needful to the American democracy. Its original domain appeared, Thomas Paine said, as a world; as late as 1801 Jefferson thought that it would suffice unto the thousandth generation. But in addition to those who thought territorial expansion unnecessary there were many who believed it dangerous to democracy. Thus a large group attached to State sovereignty opposed the Constitution on the ground, largely derived from the theory of Montesquieu, that the existing domain even of the thirteen States was too large for one national government. The authors of the *Federalist* countered by distinguishing between a pure democracy and a representative republic and by assuming the greater immunity of the large republic to faction. Even they, however, had reference not to expansion but only to the amalgamation of the thirteen States.

After adjusting themselves to the new Federal Union the small-territory party took renewed alarm from the proposal to purchase the "vast new world" of Louisiana. A republican government, declared Fisher Ames on this occasion, could not be practicable, honest, or free, if applied to the government of a third of God's earth.[15] The anti-expansionist arguments in this and the later issue of Orleans Territory reveal clearly the ideas which made democracy and expansion seem incompatible. The chief objection to expansion was that it would cause, sooner or later, the very destruction of a republican government. The reasons for this view were set forth by Representative Griswold:

> The vast and unmanageable extent which the accession of Louisiana will give to the United States; the consequent dispersion of our population; and the destruction of that balance which it is so important to maintain between the Eastern and Western States, threatens, at no very distant day, the subversion of our Union.[16]

Eight years later Josiah Quincy, opposing the incorporation of Orleans Territory, asserted similarly that the bill contained "a principle incompatible with the liberties and safety of my country," and if passed would be "a death-blow to the Constitution." [17]

A second objection, felt by some more keenly than the first, was that expansion endangered the rights and liberties of the individual States.

---

[14] *Writings of Thomas Jefferson*, VIII, 295.   [15] *Works of Fisher Ames*, I, 329.
[16] *Annals of Cong.*, 8th Cong., 1st sess., col. 465.   [17] *Ibid.*, 11th Cong., 3d sess., col. 542.

This objection was offered in the Louisiana discussion, and again in Josiah Quincy's speech opposing the creation of Orleans Territory. Quincy avowed frankly that his first public love was the Commonwealth of Massachusetts, whereas his love of the Union was merely devotion to a safeguard of the prosperity and security of his State. He opposed expansion because it introduced a new power to overbalance the political weight of any one State. He decried as an "effective despotism" that condition of things in which the original States must lose their political control to the new States, which, taking advantage of a conflict of interests, would throw themselves into the scale most conformable to their purposes.[18]

A third type of criticism alleged the danger of expansion to the liberties of individual citizens. Representative Griswold opposed the Louisiana Purchase because of fear that "additional territory might overbalance the existing territory, and thereby the rights of the present citizens of the United States be swallowed up and lost." [19] Certain Americans, like Josiah Quincy, not merely feared to throw their "rights and liberties" into "hotch-pot" with those of an alien race.[20] They even feared, as Senator White declared in the Louisiana debate, that their own citizens who roved so far from the capital would lose their affection for the center and develop antagonistic interests.[21] Both fears motivated John Randolph's words of 1813:

> We are the first people that ever acquired provinces . . . not for us to govern, but that they might *govern us*—that we might be ruled to our ruin by people bound to us by no common tie of interest or sentiment.[22]

Thus the original failure to relate democracy and expansion was due not merely to altruism, but also, and perhaps primarily, to egoistic fear for the liberties of the American nation, States, and individual citizens. A general tendency to associate democracy and expansion could not possibly develop before these fears had disappeared.

The years following America's first territorial acquisition did in fact witness the gradual dissipation of one after another of the anti-expansionist's apprehensions. The first to pass was the morbid notion that the Union itself could be destroyed through plethora of territory. Louisiana was scarcely incorporated before it seemed an increment of natural growth rather than of elephantiasis. In his oration of 1804 on the acquisition, Dr. David Ramsay taunted those who had prophesied that the Constitution would never answer for a large territory.[23] Jefferson's inaugural address of 1805 re-

---

[18] *Ibid.*, col. 536.   [19] *Ibid.*, 8th Cong., 1st sess., col. 433.

[20] *Ibid.*, 11th Cong., 3d sess., col. 538.   [21] *Ibid.*, 8th Cong., 1st sess., col. 34.

[22] Quoted by William Cabell Bruce, *John Randolph of Roanoke 1773–1833* (New York, 1922), I, 402.

[23] David Ramsay, *An Oration on the Cession of Louisiana to the United States, Delivered on the 12th May, 1804* . . . (Charleston, 1804), pp. 20–21.

minded those once fearful of Louisiana that "the larger our association the less will it be shaken by local passions." [24]

The fear that extended territory would prove injurious to the liberties of the individual States also quickly evaporated. By 1822 President Monroe could say with an expectation of general approbation:

> The expansion of our Union over a vast territory can not operate unfavorably to the States individually. . . . With governments separate, vigorous, and efficient for all local purposes, their distance from each other can have no injurious effect upon their respective interests.[25]

State anti-expansionism was lessened not only by the defeat of the particularists in the War of 1812 but also by the rise of the political theory which Monroe's words intimated. The years following the War of 1812 witnessed the increasing popularity of the view that the United States Government was based upon a distinctive principle of federation dividing power between State and Federal Government in a manner safe and efficacious for both. The encouraging implication of this theory for expansion was stated by Edward Everett in an address of 1824:

> . . . by the wise and happy partition of powers between the national and state governments, in virtue of which the national government is relieved from all the odium of internal administration, and the state governments are spared the conflicts of foreign politics, all bounds seem removed from the possible extension of our country, but the geographical limits of the continent. Instead of growing cumbrous, as it increases in size, there never was a moment, since the first settlement in Virginia, when the political system of America moved with so firm and bold a step, as at the present day.[26]

The fear that the inhabitants of the distant sections would subvert the liberties of their eastern fellow citizens also proved unfounded. The Eastern States learned that their western kinsmen were not only the strongest of Unionists but also the most democratic of the democrats. One may again turn to an address by Everett, who, though of the same State as the particularist Josiah Quincy, spoke in 1829 to citizens of Tennessee with utmost friendliness. After prophesying that the sceptre of political power would depart from Judah, the East, to the multiplying States of the West, he said:

> We look forward to that event without alarm, as in the order of the natural growth of this great Republic. We have a firm faith that our interests are mutually consistent; that if you prosper, we shall prosper; if you suffer, we shall suffer; . . . and that our children's welfare,

---

[24] Richardson, *Messages*, I, 379.   [25] *Ibid.*, II, 177.
[26] Edward Everett, *Orations and Speeches on Various Occasions* (2d ed.: Boston, 1850–1868), I, 33.

honor, and prosperity will not suffer in the preponderance, which, in the next generation, the west must possess in the balance of the country.[27]

Not only did Everett trust the West but he regarded westward migration as the *"principle* of our institutions" going forth to take possession of the land.[28]

By the decade of the 'thirties there had disappeared every apprehension of incompatibility between the principle of democracy and America's existing domain; the course of this decade was to witness the beginnings of the belief in the compatibility of democracy and future increased domain. One factor in this development was a growing confidence in the flexibility of the federative principle. Thus a writer in the *Democratic Review* of 1838 affirmed that "the peculiar characteristic of our system . . . is, that it may, if its theory is maintained pure in practice, be extended, with equal safety and efficiency, over any indefinite number of millions of population and territory." [29] Favorable contemplation of indefinite future expansion was also induced by the fact that the self-consciousness and spiritual inflammability of Jacksonian equalitarianism brought to most intense fervor, not only the appreciation of democracy, but also the belief that, as Jackson's Farewell Message asserted, Providence had chosen Americans as "the guardians of freedom to preserve it for the benefit of the human race." [30] So grandiose a status seemed to some to demand as its symbol a grandiosity of territorial extent. Thus an essay in the *Democratic Review* of 1838, depicting America as "The Great Nation of Futurity," not only foreshadowed its editor's later coinage of the phrase "manifest destiny" but also exemplified the incipient transition of the idea of manifest destiny from its non-expansionist to its expansionist form:

> The far-reaching, the boundless future will be the era of American greatness. In its magnificent domain of space and time, the nation of many nations is *destined to manifest* [italics mine] to mankind the excellence of divine principles; to establish on earth the noblest temple ever dedicated to the worship of the Most High—the Sacred and the True. Its floor shall be a hemisphere—its roof the firmament of the star-studded heavens, and its congregation an Union of many Republics, comprising hundreds of happy millions, calling, owning no man master, but governed by God's natural and moral law of equality, the law of brotherhood—of 'peace and good will amongst men'.[31]

While the conception of the United States as embracing an entire hemisphere outdid even the ambition of the 'forties, the very ambitiousness of

---

[27] *Ibid.,* p. 196.
[28] *Ibid.,* p. 210.
[29] *Democratic Review,* "The Canada Question," I (1838), 217.
[30] Richardson, *Messages,* III, 308.
[31] *Democratic Review,* "The Great Nation of Futurity," VI (1839), 427.

the vision indicates the relegation of its fulfilment to the distant future. With respect to the present, the 'thirties were not a decade of active expansionism. Like others the *Democratic Review* was cool toward the vague possibility of annexation raised by the Canadian revolts.[32] The definite proffers of annexation by Texas after its successful rebellion were successively rebuffed, despite the recognition by Senator Niles and other Americans that "destiny had established intimate political connexion between the United States and Texas." [33] In some measure the apathy regarding immediate expansion was due to the persistence of the sedentary ideal of radiating freedom by example—an ideal expressed by a writer in the *North American Review* of 1832 when he affirmed that "we can wait the peaceful progress of our own principles." [34] But this attitude is an inadequate explanation of the fact that Americans rejected an opportunity to render greatly needed assistance in the progress of their democratic principles. Such assistance was refused the Texans when they appealed for annexation after falling into deplorable difficulties. The reserve of Americans toward their former compatriots was caused not only by the fear of difficulty over annexation with both Mexico and American abolitionists, but also by the absence of any belief in the urgent need for expansion. The speeches of Jackson as president exude the complacency and sense of self-sufficiency of this decade. Especially noteworthy is his confident observation concerning an issue always highly determinative of the attitude toward expansion: "You have no longer any cause to fear danger from abroad . . ." [35]

One finally comes to the task of explaining the sudden rise in the 'forties of the ideal of extending the area of freedom by expansion. Is it conceivable that, after having been cold to the sufferings of the Texans for seven years, Americans quite spontaneously developed an overwhelming desire to enfold them with their protective democracy? Such a conception is the more difficult because the expansionists themselves made no pretension to undiluted altruism. On the other hand, only a priori cynicism would suppose that the democratic ideology was merely a hypocritial grace whereby the American appeased conscience before indulging the land-hunger of this decade. An examination of the circumstances and ideas attending the inception of the expansionist movement reveals that a definite international development, suddenly placing new problems in the center of the American's political horizon, was the factor which brought into play the spirit of democracy as well as other motives of expansionism.

The development was the emergence of that "danger from abroad" which Jackson had declared to be absent in the 'thirties. "In Texas, in California,

---

[32] *Ibid.,* I (1838), 216–17.
[33] *Reg. of Debates,* 24th Cong., 1st sess., col. 1918.
[34] *North American Review,* "North-Eastern Boundary," XXXIV (1832), 563.
[35] Richardson, *Messages,* III, 307.

and in Oregon," as Professor Perkins writes with reference to the years following 1841, "the ambition or the intrigue of European nations seemed to the dominant political generation of Americans to threaten fundamental American interests." [36] British and French attempts to establish sovereignty or political influence in adjacent countries appeared to threaten not merely economic and strategic interests but also the security of democracy. The expansionism of the 'forties arose as a defensive effort to forestall the encroachment of Europe in North America. So too, as one can see in the most numerous utterances, the conception of an "extension of the area of freedom" became general as an ideal of preventing absolutistic Europe from lessening the area open to American democracy; extension of the area of "freedom" was the defiant answer to extension of the area of "absolutism."

The European scare started with Texas and at least as early as 1843. In the early months of that year President Tyler was brought by information about British influence in Texas to the fear which was reflected in the reference of his annual message to "interference on the part of stronger and more powerful nations." [37] In 1843, also, Andrew Jackson wrote his famous letter on Texas to Aaron V. Brown, in which, amid warnings of British intrigue, he coined a famous phrase by advocacy of "extending the area of freedom." [38] The year 1844, which witnessed the negotiation of Tyler's unratified treaty of annexation, saw also the publication of Jackson's letter, and the popularization of his felicitous phrase. Although many Southerners wished for annexation primarily to forestall British abolitionist efforts, they also used, without sense of inconsistency, the democratic argument of Andrew Jackson. Texas, Senator Lewis of Alabama wrote to his constituents, was the "great Heritage of Freedom," to be held "in defiance of that power which has well-nigh enslaved the world." [39] The New Orleans *Jeffersonian Republican* represented press economico-ethical sentiment in arguing that unless American supremacy were extended to the Rio Del Norte a few years would suffice for the establishment of an influence near us "highly dangerous to our prosperity, and inimical to the spread of Republican institutions." [40] The discussions of annexation in the congressional debates gave rise to numerous similar observations, and the passage by the Senate of the resolution for annexation of Texas was acclaimed by the New Orleans *Picayune* as "the triumph of republican energy over royal finesse; as the triumph of free minds over the diplomacy of

---

[36] Dexter Perkins, *The Monroe Doctrine 1826–1867* (Baltimore, 1933), p. 64.

[37] Richardson, *Messages*, IV, 261.

[38] James Parton, *Life of Andrew Jackson* (New York, 1860), III, 658.

[39] *A Letter of the Hon. Dixon H. Lewis, to His Constituents of the Third Congressional District of Alabama* (n.p., 1844), p. 8.

[40] New Orleans *Jeffersonian Republican*, reprinted in *Richmond Enquirer*, January 7, 1845.

foreign task-master." [41] President Polk's message announcing the acceptance of annexation by Texas gave prominent place to an attack upon the attempted application of the European doctrine of the balance of power to America—an application which he attributed to hostility to "the expansion of free principles." [42]

No less frequently did the ideal of defending democracy figure in the Oregon issue, in which the claims of the United States were again pitted against those of Great Britain. This question seemed to Senator Dickinson to be "a question between two great systems; between monarchy and republicanism." [43] The annexation of Oregon, Representative Sawyer declared, would rid the continent of British power and thereby "hand down to posterity, pure and unadulterated, that freedom we received from the fathers of the Revolution." [44] For it seemed, as Representative Levin said, that the spirit of republicanism "permits not the contaminating proximity of monarchies upon the soil that we have consecrated to the rights of man." [45] Such an attitude toward the Oregon issue also occasioned Senator Allen's resolution affirming that European political interference or colonization upon this hemisphere would be "dangerous to the liberties of the people of America." [46]

With justification Americans also feared the British lion in the wilderness of California. The Whig *American Review* spoke typically in accusing Great Britain of seeking sovereignty over California in order to interpose a barrier to the general growth of the American Union and thereby to "the progress of republican liberty, by which she believes her own institutions and the position of the family of European sovereigns, to be seriously menaced." [47] Such interposition, it declared, was dangerous to the self-preservation of the United States and therefore unallowable. Secretary of State Buchanan's despatch of 1845 to Consul Larkin, indicating the favorable view which a petition of the colonists for annexation would receive, spoke of Great Britain's designs as conflicting with the desire of the colonists for republican institutions.[48] The *New York Herald,* calling likewise for protection of free institutions, wished to annex the whole of Mexico instead of merely California.[49] Stephen Douglas hoped to check absolutism by annexing Canada. Representative Cary stated his constituents' broader doctrine:

> Their doctrine was, that this continent was intended by Providence as a vast theatre on which to work out the grand experiment of Republican government, under the auspices of the Anglo-Saxon race. If

[41] New Orleans *Daily Picayune,* reprinted in *Nashville Union,* March 25, 1845.
[42] Richardson, *Messages,* IV, 398.   [43] *Cong. Globe,* 29th Cong., 1st sess., p. 424.
[44] *Ibid.,* App., p. 229.   [45] *Ibid.,* 95.   [46] *Ibid.,* 29th Cong., 1st sess., p. 197.
[47] *American Review,* "California," III (1846), 98.
[48] *The Works of James Buchanan,* ed. J. B. Moore (Philadelphia, 1908–1911), VI, 276.
[49] *New York Herald,* January 6, 1846.

the worn-out and corrupt monarchies of the Old World had colonies here; let them be kept within the narrowest limits, consistent with justice and the faith of treaties. Let all which remains be preserved for the growth and spread of the free principles of American democracy.[50]

However, the toleration of existent European colonies seemed to still bolder spirits to be contrary to the true purpose of Providence. In the July number of the *Democratic Review* of 1845 an article on the Texas question affirmed nothing less than continental dominion to be America's "manifest destiny." The historic phrase, as the researches of Professor Pratt indicate, seems to have been used for the first time in this article. The article is attributed by Professor Pratt[51] on the ground of internal evidence to John L. O'Sullivan, editor of the *Democratic Review* and the *New York Morning News,* later Minister to Portugal, who was called by John St. Tammany rather fulsomely "one of the ablest writers and most accomplished scholars and gentlemen of the times." [52] The passage using the later famous phrase is as follows:

> Why, were other reasons wanting, in favor of now elevating this question of the reception of Texas into the Union, out of the lower region of our past party dissensions, up to its proper level of a high and broad nationality, it surely is to be found, found abundantly, in the manner in which other nations have undertaken to intrude themselves into it, between us and the proper parties to the case, in a spirit of hostile interference against us, for the avowed object of thwarting our policy and hampering our power, limiting our greatness and checking the fulfilment of our manifest destiny to overspread the continent allotted by Providence for the free development of our yearly multiplying millions.[53]

European encroachment must thus be thanked for making manifest the destiny of continental dominion. With truth Professor Rippy remarks that "manifest destiny never pointed to the acquisition of a region so unmistakably as when undemocratic, conservative Europe revealed an inclination to interfere or to absorb." [54] What was not manifest to Americans was the vicious circle which their defensive expansion created; for Europe's inclination to interfere in North America was caused chiefly by fear of the growing economic and political ambition of the United States.

The view that European interference in America menaced American democracy apparently rested on three principal grounds. The first was the belief that whatever threatened American security was a danger to the

---

[50] *Cong. Globe,* 28th Cong., 2d sess., App., pp. 161–62.

[51] Julius W. Pratt, "The Origin of 'Manifest Destiny,' " *American Historical Review,* XXXII (1927), 795–98.

[52] *Tri-Weekly Nashville Union,* January 28, 1845.

[53] *Democratic Review,* "Annexation," XVII (1845), 5.

[54] Rippy, *The United States and Mexico,* p. 29.

political principle which the nation embodied. The second was the supposition that, irrespective of strategic menace, European absolutism would "pollute" American democracy by its very contiguity. The third and perhaps most influential of all was the recognition that adjacent European power threatened the extension of American democracy—an ideal which was made more precious by this very menace.

European adjacency doubtless entailed commercial and political disadvantages, but the foregoing assumptions may seem great exaggerations in respect to danger to the life of the Republic or its democratic institutions. Though the fear expressed was doubtless sincere—for the fears of nations seldom develop in strict accord with logic—there was much more to the question than the fear of the European menace. Considerations which were logically independent—however much the European menace acted as a catalytic agent in their generation—also caused Americans of the 'forties to believe that expansion was essential to the life or healthful development of American democracy.

Whereas it had once been feared that the existence of the Union was jeopardized by expansion, it was now apprehended that the Union might be imperilled by failure to expand through annexing Texas. The Southern States held Texas to be necessary to their economic prosperity, the security of their "peculiar institution," and their maintenance of a balance of political power with the North. It therefore seemed to many that, as Robert J. Walker wrote in his widely read letter on Texas, the defeat of annexation by the North might lead to a union of the South and Southwest with Texas.[55] Ground for this fear was given by certain statements of some Southerners, such as the observation by Senator Lewis of Alabama that if the treaty were rejected he would consider the Union at an end.[56] The fact that the Union seemed synonymous with republicanism created a logical link between solicitude for the Union and zeal for the extension of freedom. Thus Senator Merrick, who warned his colleagues that the failure of annexation would endanger sectional tranquillity, affirmed that the success of annexation would mean the formation of a more perfect union and the securing of the blessings of liberty to ourselves and our posterity.[57] It seemed similarly to Thomas W. Gilmer that "our union has no danger to apprehend from those who believe that its genius is expansive and progressive, but from those who think that the limits of the United States are already too large and the principles of 1776 too old-fashioned for this fastidious age." [58] In fact it is difficult to know which side endangered the Union more. For the threats of Northern abolitionists to dissolve the

---

[55] Walker, *Letter . . . Relative to the Reannexation of Texas*, p. 15.

[56] Dixon H. Lewis to John Calhoun, March 6, 1844, *Correspondence of John C. Calhoun,* ed. J. F. Jameson, *Fourth Annual Report of the Historical Manuscripts Commission, American Historical Association* (Washington, 1900), p. 936.

[57] *Cong. Globe*, 28th Cong., 2d sess., App., p. 233.   [58] *Niles' Register*, LXIV (1843), 285.

Union in the event of annexation were just as numerous as those of the Southern expansionists with reference to its failure.

A second line of argument gives the impression that to many the chief consideration was not the Union but.the individual State. For, just as the traditional argument regarding the effect of expansion on the Union was inverted, so was also the traditional argument regarding the State. It was the original fear of New England particularists that expansion would be prejudicial to States' rights. After the War of 1812, as already stated, this fear was destroyed by a theory of the distribution of powers according to which the needful powers of the State need not be prejudiced by expansion. In the 'forties this theory was developed by circumstances into the view that expansion was not only not injurious to the individual States but was in fact essential to the preservation of their liberties.

The general logic of this view was stated briefly by Representative Belser of Alabama, during the Texas debate, in the words: "Extension . . . was the antagonistical principle of centralization." [59] In amplification of this view one may quote from Representative Duncan's speech on the Oregon bill:

> There is a strong and constant tendency towards consolidation of power toward the centre of federal government; and that tendency has been favored by a party in this country, who desired at first that our federal government should possess unlimited powers. . . .
>
> To oppose that constant tendency to federal consolidation, I know no better plan than to multiply States; and the farther from the centre of federal influence and attraction, the greater is our security.[60]

From this point of view, extension of the area of freedom meant increase of the security of American States against a curious enemy, their own federal government.

Whereas Representative Duncan was an Ohioan, the theory which he expressed was espoused more frequently by Americans of the Southern slaveholding States. The theory came to the fore at this time principally because of the bearing of the annexation of Texas upon the economic and political interests of the South. Opposition to the annexation desired by these interests was attributed by Southerners both to inimical abolitionists and to advocates of a federal authority overriding States' rights. Thus an advocate of the annexation of Texas in the *Southern Quarterly Review* of 1844 attributed such wicked opposition to those using the epithets "general," "national," and "American" to derogate from rights guaranteed to the States by the Constitution.[61] Representative Rhett of South Carolina called for annexation as a means of defeating those antagonistic to the rights of

---

[59] *Cong. Globe*, 28th Cong., 2d sess., App., p. 43. [60] *Ibid.*, p. 178.
[61] *Southern Quarterly Review*, "The Annexation of Texas," VI (1844), 498.

Southern States. Having declared that the South must be permitted to participate in the nation's expansion, he added:

> Every census has added to the power of the non-slaveholding States, and diminished that of the South.* We are growing weaker, and they stronger, every day. I ask you, is it the spirit of the constitution to strengthen the strong against the weak? What are all its checks and balances of power, but to protect the weak and restrain the strong? The very object of a constitution, in all free governments, is to restrain power. . . . If this measure, therefore, will tend to strengthen the weaker interest in the Union it will be moving in strict accordance with the whole spirit of the constitution.[62]

It was thus true that, as anti-expansionists charged, "we were to extend the area of freedom by enlarging the boundary of slavery." [63] But it was not true that, as anti-expansionists also charged, the phrase about extending freedom was used merely to cover up the design of extending slavery. The strange truth of the matter is that the extension of slavery, which virtually no Southern expansionist denied to be one of his motives, did not seem to the slaveholder incompatible with the ideal of diffusing democracy. The harmonization of the two purposes is explained in part by the Southerner's belief that religious and natural law made the negro a necessary exception to the principle of political equality. But it is also explained by the fact that the extension of slavery appeared essential to States' liberties. In this view the Southerner overlooked the consideration that slavery seemed to abolitionist sections an equal infringement of their right to a union based on universal individual liberty.

North and South saw with one eye, however, on one topic—the liberty of the American (white) individual. Here again, as though some Hegelian metaphysical dialectic of antitheses were at work, one meets the inversion of a traditional argument. Anti-expansionists had maintained originally that the political untrustworthiness of a remote pioneer population made extended territory dangerous to individual liberties. Now, with particular view to the very pioneers who were once feared, expansionists declared that territorial extension was essential to the fullest liberty of the individual.

The idea of individualism perhaps did more than anything else to cement the association between democracy and expansion. For the sturdiest element in democracy was its valuation of individualism—the thesis of the individual's right not only to exemption from undue interference by government but also to the most abundant opportunity for self-development. Those entirely misread its spirit who believe that the enthusiasm for democracy was merely enthusiasm over a form of government as such. Fundamentally, indeed, the Jeffersonian American rather disliked government;

---

[62] *Cong. Globe*, 28th Cong., 2d sess., App., p. 146.
[63] Representative Sample, *ibid.*, p. 73.

though recognizing the necessity of giving some power to the State, he at least verged on anarchism in his belief that "the best government is that which governs least." Whereas individualism in its negative phase meant restraint from undue interference with individual rights, in its positive phase it signified that "care of human life and happiness" which Jefferson called the only legitimate object of government.[64]

Although both individualism and the pioneer spirit had prevailed from the beginning, it was not until the 'forties that the enterprise of the pioneer seemed the most perfect expression of American individualism. The coming of the pioneer movement to self-consciousness in this decade was due to various factors: the popular interest aroused by the accelerating trek to Oregon and the Southwest; the fact that the pioneer movement now became involved with territorial issues of national concern; and above all, perhaps, the general land-hunger which caused the pioneer to seem now not a deviation from but the very expression of Americanism. It was in the fervent appreciation of the pioneer movement that there were forged all the links uniting individualism and expansionism.

Among such links was the conception of the economic value of expansion to the individual. Expansion, later to be depicted by anti-imperialists as a means to economic exploitation and slavery, was seen in this period as a means to economic liberty. Economic freedom had become as important as political freedom to the philosophy of democracy, which, giving full recognition to the Platonic truth that before one can live well one must live, was unhesitant about attaching an almost moral valuation to even the material values of land-ownership. Land, as Professor Fish has pointed out, seemed to the American of the 'forties the very key to happiness.[65] The demand for abundant territory in the name of economic liberty is exemplified by the words of Representative Duncan in support of the Oregon Bill:

> First, to extend our population we require the possession of Oregon. I have before remarked that personal liberty is incompatible with a crowded population. . . .
>
> By whatever means the lands and wealth of a country fall into the hands of a few individuals, it establishes a feudal system as oppressive and destructive of the liberties of the people as if it were established by conquest, and equally enslaves the people. . . . The inability of the weak, the humble, and the non-assuming, to contend with the overbearing, the cunning, and the grasping monopolist makes it necessary, to the equality of circumstances and personal liberty, that the advantages of territory should constantly be kept open to all who wish to embrace it.[66]

---

[64] *Writings of Thomas Jefferson*, ed. Washington, VIII, 165.
[65] Carl Russell Fish, *The Rise of the Common Man 1830–1850* (New York, 1929), p. 125.
[66] *Cong. Globe*, 28th Cong., 2d sess., App., p. 178.

The foregoing is unimpeachable in logic so far as concerns the privileges of homestead. It is not clear, however, that the enlargement of individual agrarian opportunities required further national expansion. The anti-expansionist maintained correctly that the Republic already "had an ample area for hundred millions of human beings," [67] with vast regions as yet scarcely explored. Indeed the boast of the average American was like that of Mr. Bovan in *Martin Chuzzlewit:* "We have a vast territory, and not—as yet—too many people on it."

The rub lay precisely in the "as yet." Just as in the issue of Indian lands, the expansionist took his main position on the ground of need of territory for posterity. In calculating the territorial needs of posterity Americans used the rate of population growth which had been maintained as late as the census of 1840—approximately a doubling of population every twenty-five years. According to the typical estimate of John L. O'Sullivan, a century from 1845 would see an American population of approximately three hundred millions.[68] These calculations were a favorite occupation of American nationalists, who agreed with the biblical writer that in the multitude of the people is the king's honor—or more correctly the honor of democracy, to which they actually attributed American fecundity. It seemed, then, a duty to the hasty American to provide territory for a future population even before the need arose. Referring to reproductive capacity as the American multiplication table, Representative Kennedy asked how room would be found for posterity without the acquisition of Oregon.[69] Representative Belser, prophesying the three hundred millions of a century thence, declared confinement of the area of freedom an impossibility.[70] Presentiment of this "stupendous" growth of population seemed to John L. O'Sullivan the fundamental cause of the popular movement toward territorial extension.[71]

But today, nine decades after O'Sullivan's prophecy of three hundred million in a century, America's population is still not much more than a third of that estimate. The gross miscalculation arose from an erroneous statistical method. As an anti-expansionist writer pointed out in 1849, expansionists overlooked the consideration that as a people become denser they multiply more slowly.[72] The unusual growth-rate of American population was ascribed in Alison's work of 1840 on *Principles of Population* to the continual influx of immigrants to better their fortunes on the unappropriated lands of the West.[73] With the settlement of surplus land immigration and likewise the rapid growth of population would subside. The true cure for the overgrowth of population was thus to cease expanding. But instead

---

[67] Senator Rives, *ibid.*, p. 382.   [68] *New York Morning News,* January 5, 1846.

[69] *Cong. Globe*, 29th Cong., 1st sess., p. 180.   [70] *Ibid.*, 28th Cong., 2d sess., App., p. 43.

[71] *New York Morning News,* January 5, 1846.

[72] Charles T. Porter, *Review of the Mexican War* (Auburn, 1849), pp. 165–66.

[73] Archibald Alison, *The Principles of Population* (Edinburgh, 1840), I, 548.

of adopting this disagreeable cure, the American nationalist proposed to continue expanding. Thus he was laying the basis for the very superfluity of population which he cited as the justification of expansion.

But reasoning in regard to needs of population was not responsible fundamentally for the association of expansion and individual liberty. The pioneer was not rational as he rushed from the abundant fertile land at hand to stake his claim on land more distant. He was impelled onward, if the contemporary interpretation does not over-romanticize him, by some fever in the blood, some spirit of adventure. So, too, the philosopher of the pioneer movement was thinking of liberty in a sense broader than the freedom to satisfy economic needs. He was envisaging a liberty for the pioneer impulse as such, an impulse of adventure and self-expression. This impulse seemed good in and of itself as an essential element in the energetic spirit produced by free institutions. It was the fact that it gave scope for the satisfaction of such an impulse which primarily caused expansion to be related to individual liberty.

Observations illustrative of this association received at times a naïvely naturalistic expression, as in the words of Major Daveznac at the New Jersey Democratic State Convention of 1844:

> Land enough—land enough! Make way, I say, for the young American Buffalo—he has not yet got land enough; he wants more land as his cool shelter in summer—he wants more land for his beautiful pasture grounds. I tell you, we will give him Oregon for his summer shade, and the region of Texas as his winter pasture. (Applause.) Like all of his race, he wants salt, too. Well, he shall have the use of two oceans—the mighty Pacific and turbulent Atlantic shall be his . . . He shall not stop his career until he slakes his thirst in the frozen ocean. (Cheers.)[74]

So far was Representative McClernand from shame of such cravings that he called the American impulse of expansion "glorious" and "divine." He thought it "a new impulse called into action by free institutions operating upon the restless and daring spirit of the Anglo-Saxon blood." [75] Similarly, Representative Ficklin apotheosized the unmercenary, exploratory spirit which sent Americans to distant Oregon:

> This wild spirit of adventure gives nerve and energy to the mental and physical man, and prompts its possessor to deeds of peril and of danger, from which the tame and timorous would shrink with horror; it expands the heart, and unfetters its joys, its hopes, its aspirations; it lends a new charm to life, a new spring to human energies and desires, and wakens in the breast a kindred feeling with that which animated our first parents in the garden of Eden.[76]

---

[74] *Young Hickory Banner,* October 15, 1845.
[75] *Cong. Globe,* 29th Cong., 1st sess., App., p. 277.   [76] *Ibid.,* p. 175.

"Wide shall our own free race increase," [77] wrote an American poet who was quoted by a congressional expansionist. But what limits would this free race, irresistible to others, set for itself? Even the least grandiose conceptions assumed that under "the influence of free institutions" the pioneer movement would cover "everything in the shape of land not already occupied by comparatively large numbers from some foreign nation." [78] This embraced at least Texas, California, and Oregon. But there was a much broader vision which was confessed by many expansionists and was in the subliminal expectation of nearly all. It was identical with that which De Tocqueville, his dazzled imagination following the course of the deluge of pioneers, expressed in the 'thirties:

> At a period which may be said to be near,—for we are speaking of the life of a nation,—the Anglo-Americans alone will cover the immense space contained between the polar regions and the tropics, extending from the coasts of the Atlantic to those of the Pacific Ocean.[79]

If the detached foreigner could believe that "the continent which they inhabit is their dominion," [80] would not the same belief suggest itself the more readily to self-confident Americans? The literature of the time is replete with the expression of that belief. The toast at a political banquet urged the march of the "Spirit of Democratic progression" until *the whole unbounded continent is ours.*" [81] In an article of 1844 on "The Texas Question" a writer in the *Democratic Review* declared that the increase and diffusiveness of America's population, occupying all territory until checked by great natural barriers, would at no distant day cover "every habitable square inch of the continent." [82] Continental dominion was predicted by John L. O'Sullivan in the light of both natural law and providential design:

> Texas has been absorbed into the Union in the inevitable fulfilment of the general law which is rolling our population westward; the connexion of which with that ratio of growth in population which is destined within a hundred years to swell our numbers to the enormous population of *two hundred and fifty millions* (if not more), is too evident to leave us in doubt of the manifest design of Providence in regard to the occupation of this continent.[83]

Jefferson and other imaginative early Americans also foresaw a time when "our rapid multiplication will . . . cover the whole northern, if not the

[77] Representative Hamlin, *ibid.*, 29th Cong., 1st sess., p. 187.
[78] John M. Galt, *The Annexation of Texas,* reprinted in *Political Essays* (n.p., 1852?), p. 5.
[79] Alexis de Tocqueville, *Democracy in America,* tr. Henry Reeve (New York, 1898), I, 557.
[80] *Ibid.,* p. 519.   [81] *New York Morning News,* January 9, 1846.
[82] *Democratic Review,* "The Texas Question," XIV (1844), 429.
[83] *Ibid.,* XVII (1845), 17.

southern continent." [84] But whereas Jefferson did not care about the political tie, expansionists of the 'forties insisted upon it as essential to the realization of freedom. They held that seekers for economic and social liberty must be followed by a government solicitous for their political liberty. Thus Representative Bowlin, describing the progress of the pioneer race, declared that the Government should follow them with the laws and instructions which they love and cherish, and thereby also add strength and permanent glory to the Republic.[85] So too, Senator Linn, champion of the Oregon settlers, proclaimed that the irresistible advance of American population should march "with every public right in the lead." [86] The association between the ideal of the free pioneer and that of the extension of the political area of freedom appears in the lines of a contemporary poet who said that the increase of our "free race" would extend widely the elastic chain

> That binds in everlasting peace
> State after State—a mighty train.[87]

"We are the pioneers of the continent," proclaimed an expansionist editorial in the organ of the author of the phrase "manifest destiny." [88] It is in the light of this pioneer ideal that one must interpret not only the immediate territorial ambitions but even the dream of eventual continental dominion. This future empire, like the immediate annexation of Texas, was not to be achieved through the military conquest which imperialists of 1898 were to conduct in the name of liberty. The continental republic was rather to be the natural consummation of what O'Sullivan called the "destiny to overspread the whole North American continent with an immense democratic population." [89] To paraphrase Walt Whitman, the expansionist proposed to "make the continent indissoluble" [90] by filling it with the spreading but politically cohesive American race.

Freedom for the American nation; freedom for the American State; freedom for the American individual: such, then, were the principal elements in the fundamentally egoistic program of extending the area of freedom. One sees finally why the anti-expansionists talked beside the mark when they pointed out that Texas was already republican. The freedom sought by expansionists was a distinctively American freedom which went far beyond nominal republicanism. The area in question was the domain in which American pioneers might freely spread themselves and all their institutions. The extension of the area of freedom could thus be only the expansion of the United States. Freedom, in sum, had become nationalized.

It is an exaggeration, indeed, to suppose that international philanthropy

---

[84] *Writings of Thomas Jefferson,* VIII, 105
[85] *Cong. Globe,* 28th Cong., 2d sess., App., p. 93.
[86] *Ibid.,* 27th Cong., 3d sess., App., p. 79.   [87] *Ibid.,* 29th Cong., 1st sess., p. 187.
[88] *New York Morning News,* November 15, 1845.   [89] *Ibid.,* January 5, 1846.
[90] Walt Whitman, *Leaves of Grass,* ed. Emory Holloway (New York, 1928), p. 98.

was entirely absent from the expansionist ideal. However, even its elements of altruism, as analysis will show, were restricted in a manner which can be explained only by the nationalistic orientation of the ideal.

Thus the altruistic phase of democratic expansionism had as one presupposition an egoistic disparagement of the capacity of other peoples to help themselves. This disparagement reflected in some measure, to be sure, the disillusionment which experience had brought to the original hope of extending freedom by mere example. Most of the New World peoples who had followed the example of the American Revolution fell shortly into ways of political disorder which seemed to an American of 1838 to "depress the hopes of those who desire to see civil liberty established throughout the world." [91] Most depression came from those of whom most had been hoped, the Texans. As though they had lost the talent for democracy in losing contact with their native soil, these former Americans exhibited a political and social confusion prompting one American editor's description of Texas as a "Quasi Republic." [92] Despite previous belief in the triumph of democracy through man's "eternal principle of progress," [93] Americans now saw reason to believe that not every Tom, Dick and Harry among nations had the genius for democracy. The disappointment to undue impatience caused the pendulum to swing to a pessimism as extreme as the former optimism.

Abandonment of the hope of teaching democracy by remote example led to acceptance of the alternative pedagogical method, that of taking other peoples into "the district school of democracy." Of course, the Texans strongly resented any patronizing attitude; a prominent Texan diplomat believed that the annexation of Texas was "coupled with the paramount security of Republican institutions in the United States." [94] But Representative Dean and other expansionists regarded it as "philanthropy" to extend to Texans America's blessing of civil, political, and religious liberty.[95] America's expansion seemed even more essential to the liberation of peoples non-American in blood; and Dean saw annexation as a means of releasing from their "shackles" every nation on the continent.[96] While only Canada was subjected to a monarchy, all these republican nations were in shackles in so far as they had not attained American or true freedom.

Above all, the oppressed of Europe, a section of the world in which the American had almost lost hope, were supposed to see in the United States

---

[91] *Democratic Review,* "Retrospective View of the South-American States," II (1838), 99.

[92] *Newark Daily Advertiser,* November 14, 1836, quoted by Justin H. Smith, *The Annexation of Texas* (New York, 1911), p. 66.

[93] *Democratic Review* "Democracy," VII (1840), 228.

[94] Memucan Hunt to John C. Calhoun, October 2, 1844, *Correspondence of John C. Calhoun,* p. 975.

[95] *Cong. Globe,* 28th Cong., 2d sess., App., p. 105.   [96] *Ibid.*

their only refuge. Still far removed from the "one-hundred-per-cent Americanism" of the twentieth-century immigration policy, Americans of the 'forties felt toward their gracious country as did Bryant:

> There's freedom at thy gates and rest
> For Earth's down-trodden and opprest,
> A shelter for the hunted head,
> For the starved laborer toil and bread.[97]

Benjamin Franklin's still vital conception of America as "an asylum for those who love liberty" [98] easily became an argument for expansion. Thus Representative Duncan proclaimed: "If ours is to be the home of the oppressed, we must extend our territory in latitude and longitude to the demand of the millions who are to follow us, as well of our own posterity as those who are invited to our peaceful shores to partake in our republican institutions." [99] There were those who, disregarding De Tocqueville's observation that the movement toward equality was world-wide, believed as did Governor Brown that "in the order of Providence, America might become the last asylum of liberty to the human family," [100] and must therefore lay its foundations deep and wide for the innumerable refugees of later ages. Similarly Representative Stone, advocating the annexation of Texas and an ocean-bound republic, affirmed that "Providence intended this western hemisphere to be an asylum for the oppressed." [101] Representative Belser related the salvation in freedom to biblical conceptions:

> Long may our country prove itself the asylum of the oppressed. Let
> its institutions and its people be extended far and wide, and when
> the waters of despotism shall have inundated other portions of the
> globe, and the votary of liberty be compelled to betake himself to his
> ark, let this government be the Ararat on which it shall rest.[102]

Thus the American expansionist's nationalism was so little exclusive that it offered refuge to all the devotees of freedom in a world elsewhere threatened with a rising deluge of despotism.

None the less the typical expansionist's altruism was not only conditioned by but distinctly secondary to his interest in his own people. That expansionist altruism was influenced by nationalism is clear from the fact that the expansionist became concerned about other peoples only as he conceived of them as in some sense American. There was never a period (reference is made to the years of the 'forties preceding the European

---

[97] *The Poetical Works of William Cullen Bryant,* Roslyn ed. (New York, 1908), p. 215.
[98] Van Tyne, *The American Revolution,* p. 333.
[99] *Cong. Globe,* 28th Cong., 2d sess., App., p. 178.
[100] "Inaugural Address as Governor of Tennessee, October 15, 1845," *Speeches Congressional and Political, and Other Writings of ex-Governor Aaron V. Brown, of Tennessee* (Nashville, 1854), p. 373.
[101] *Cong. Globe,* 28th Cong., 2d sess., App., p. 227.   [102] *Ibid.,* p. 43.

revolutionary movements of 1848) when the average American was less interested in world developments not bearing directly upon his own hemisphere. But even in viewing his own hemisphere the American was interested primarily in those sections inhabited altogether or largely by pioneers from the United States. The Texan was a kind of *alter ego,* described affectionately as "bone of our bone, and flesh of our flesh." [103] All three of the immediate territorial interests of the United States—Texas, Oregon, and California—were, or promised to be, settled by Americans. The adjacent Latin peoples were recipients of consideration not so much for their own sake as because they inhabited the American continent, which "the God of nature" had designed for "liberty." [104] The fundamental consideration was that no despotism should "pollute" the soil adjacent to that of the pure American democracy.

The secondary character of the expansionist's altruism is evidenced partly by the fact that most of his encomia of freedom stressed liberty for the American himself. It is also indicated by the concentration of the expansionist's interest not upon territories whose inhabitants stood in greatest need of freedom, but upon territories whose inhabitants, being entirely or largely former Americans, could most advantageously be assimilated to the Union. Aside from Texas, Oregon, and California—territories where Americans had already set their stakes—the American expansionist was willing to postpone annexation until the pioneer's Americanization of the continent had succeeded, as one expansionist said, in "irrigating it for the growth and predominance of liberty." [105] Further instances of the American's long-dominant revulsion from amalgamation with supposedly inferior peoples will be given in a subsequent chapter concerned with the ideal of regenerative expansionism.

Thus, those entirely miss the spirit of the ideal of extending the area of freedom who see it as altogether or primarily an attachment to international philanthropy. Very shortly, indeed, the altruistic form of the democratic ideal was to be developed by the issue of amalgamation raised in the Mexican War. But before the Mexican War democratic expansionism was primarily a concern for the freedom of Americans themselves; the concern for others was such as overflows even from a Nietzschean's euphoria. Precisely because the idealism of the expansionist of this period was rooted in egoism, it had a sincerity and an intensity which later expansionists probably never fully attained in their somewhat forced altruism.

An interesting problem is raised by the contrast between the American's version of extending freedom and the altruistic form which prevailed among French Revolutionists, absolutistic Pan-Slavs, and most other peoples in the history of nationalism. Why did extension of freedom mean to the

---

[103] Representative Stephens, *ibid.,* p. 313.   [104] Representative Haralson, *ibid.,* p. 194.
[105] Representative McClernand, *ibid.,* 29th Cong., 1st sess., p. 984.

American of the middle 'forties less the liberation of other peoples than the aggrandizement of his own freedom—and territory?

The reasons are interesting even if not in all cases edifying. Undoubtedly one explanation was the American's healthy-minded egoism, a matter of instinct rather than of logic. Another was the fact that the American philosophy of individualism blessed egoism in its affirmation of a natural right to the pursuit of happiness. Still another factor lay in the circumstance that the annexation of the willing Texans involved no obvious transgression (Mexico to the contrary notwithstanding) upon alien rights, and thus did not cause the uneasy conscience for which professions of international altruism are so often a compensation. But none of these reasons touches on what is probably the basic ideological explanation—the influence exerted upon the American's democratic thought by his philosophy of manifest destiny.

To understand this influence one must begin by recognizing that the egoism of the American's philosophy of the destiny of democracy did not exclude a love of democracy for its own sake. When the American spoke of extending the area of freedom he had in mind not only greater freedom for Americans but also greater freedom by means of Americans. This impersonal element in the American's attachment to the cause of freedom is abundantly illustrated in the expansionist literature. The *New York Morning News,* affirming that the great experiment of democracy required nothing less than the continent, saw the end of this experiment as "the free development of humanity to the best and highest results it may be capable of working out for itself." [106] The vision which caused the American expansionist's heart to leap was described by Representative Cathcart as that of "State after State coming into this great temple of freedom, and burning their incense upon an altar consecrated to the enjoyment of civil and religious liberty." [107] The migrations which would extend American territory would also, Representative Tibbatts declared, "extend the principles of civil liberty, for they march *pari passu* with the migrations of the Anglo-Saxon race." [108]

This very attachment to freedom was one element underlying the American expansionist's self-engrossment. For in his devotion to the ideal he cast about for the best instrument to realize it and found—himself. The philosophy of American nationalism developed a belief incongruous with the equalitarianism of democracy—the belief that, however equal men might be at birth, Americans had become subsequently a super-people.

The American had never been a sufferer from self-depreciation. But the 'forties witnessed the full flowering of national self-esteem in consequence of the undeniable promise in American life, of intensified democratic self-

---

[106] *New York Morning News,* February 7, 1845.
[107] *Cong. Globe,* 29th Cong., 1st sess., p. 324.
[108] *Ibid.,* 28th Cong., 1st sess., App., p. 450.

consciousness, of heightened nationalism, and of the partial stupidity of national adolescence. It was in this period that an Iowa newspaper urged ironically that America repudiate its debts to Europe on the ground that Europe was sufficiently recompensed by having assisted the spread of American civilization! [109] National boasting was reconciled with civilization by one American orator's explanation: "It is not good taste in individuals to indulge in boasting; but a nation is allowed to assume an elevated tone." In an editorial of the *United States Journal* of 1845 one finds an observation in a very elevated tone:

> It is a truth, which every man may see, if he will but look,—that all the channels of communication,—public and private, through the school-room, the pulpit, and the press,—are engrossed and occupied with *this one idea,* which all these forces are combined to disseminate: —that we the American people, are the most independent, intelligent, moral and happy people on the face of the earth.[110]

The foregoing words are not those of a satirist but of one who admitted the truth of the proposition. It was no matter that the very same page of his editorial reported the failure of Pittsburg female operatives in their strike for a ten-hour working day!

But in the national self-complacency of the "fabulous 'forties" there was the redeeming quality of moral ambition. The *United States Journal* entitled its editorial "Forward Forward" and called from drowsy satisfaction to meliorative effort. Walt Whitman, who wrote that "we are the most beautiful to ourselves and in ourselves," also exclaimed: "I will make the most splendid race the sun ever shone upon." [111] While these words are from a later decade, in the 'forties he gave prose expression to the same ideal:

> And it is from such materials—from the democracy with its manly heart and its lion strength, spurning the ligatures wherewith drivellers would bind it—that we are to expect the great FUTURE of this western world! a scope involving such unparalleled human happiness and rational freedom, to such unnumbered myriads, that the heart of a true *man* leaps with a mighty joy only to think of it! God works out his greatest results by such means; and while each popinjay priest of the mummery of the past is babbling his alarm, the youthful Genius of the people passes swiftly over era after era of change and improvement, and races of human beings erewhile down in gloom or bondage rise gradually toward that majestic development which the good God doubtless loves to witness.[112]

---

[109] Adams, *op. cit.,* p. 90. [110] *United States Journal,* October 18, 1845.
[111] Whitman, *op. cit.,* pp. 286, 98.
[112] *The Uncollected Prose and Poetry of Walt Whitman,* ed. Emory Holloway (New York, 1931), I, 159.

These swelling periods exemplify the modern version of the chosen people, which Whitman's compatriots, on six days of the week even if not the seventh, made the chief tenet of their religious philosophy as well as of their nationalism. This thesis differed from the Hebraic in that "a kingdom of priests and a holy nation" was ordained to preserve, not the law of man's duty to God, but the law of man's duty to man—democracy. In his anthropocentric theology, in which God himself served chiefly as a Providence watchful for mankind and human values, the American approached perilously close to changing the traditional dogma, that man exists *ad majorem gloriam Dei,* into the heresy that God exists *ad majorem gloriam hominis.* And Providence had entrusted the fullest achievement of the moral glory of man to the best of human material, the mighty American democracy. It is small wonder that the American like the ancient Hebrew was self-engrossed. The "chosen people" is indifferent to the heathen because it believes that the best material for the creation of its ideal is itself.

Enshrined in expansionism, then, was this dogma of the special mission. Moral idealism divested of all intent of sacrilege the half-belief that God, who walked with Noah, rode with the American pioneer in his journeys over the continent. Even theological literature was scarcely more abundant in references to Providence than was the literature of expansionism. For it seemed that especially in expanding our territory, as a poet wrote upon the prospect of annexing Texas, "we do but follow out our destiny, as did the ancient Israelite." [113] The expansionist conception of destiny was essentially ethical in its assumption that "Providence had given to the American people a great and important mission . . . to spread the blessings of Christian liberty." [114] It was ambitiously ethical in its further assumption that "Providence" had a "design in extending our free institutions as far and as wide as the American continent." [115] But the primary providential end was no more the elevation of the Latin-American heathen than was the elevation of the adjacent Philistines the end of the Israelite's journey to the Promised Land. The end in view was, as stated by John L. O'Sullivan in his first passage on manifest destiny, "the free development of our yearly multiplying millions." But in a second reference to manifest destiny he implied the moral significance of this free development of Americans. Americans were destined to develop themselves as subjects in "the great experiment of liberty and federated self-government entrusted to us." [116]

Such was the credo which encouraged American expansionists to conceive that the free rather than the meek would inherit the earth. Its logic harmonized Calvinistic pride and equalitarianism. Still greater was its service in permitting the harmonization of the American's two deepest im-

---

[113] *Democratic Review,* "Progress in America," XVIII (1846), 92.
[114] Senator Buchanan, *Cong. Globe,* 28th Cong., 1st sess., p. 380.
[115] Representative Duncan, *ibid.,* 2d sess., App., p. 178.
[116] *New York Morning News,* December 27, 1845.

pulses—the expansionism oriented toward the good earth, and the democratic idealism oriented toward "Fair freedom's star." Believing like the Crusader that "God wills it," the expansionist had the joyful illusion of hitching his pioneer wagon to a star.

There is, of course, the quite different question whether territorial expansion was objectively essential to freedom—the American's or any one else's. The expansionist's cosmology, refreshing as it was, perhaps seemed to offer little convincing evidence that the star of democracy would not have shone as brightly in the world's firmament even with less nationalist heat in man for the addition of stars to the flag.

XVI

The Proslavery Argument:
Internal Defense or
External Aggression?

INTRODUCTION

The proslavery doctrine and argument, which characterized so much of the thought of the ante-bellum South, may be considered from two different points of view. One approach to the matter is to conceive of this doctrine and argument as an apparatus of internal defense; the other approach is to conceive of it as a weapon of external aggression. The first attitude is defensive; the second is offensive, but slavery, as an institution or as a moral and religious question, lay at the center of the disequilibrium between the sections and within the sections. Slavery was the focus of the great national and sectional dialogue, and for the South, it must be both defended at home and protected abroad.

It has been commonly supposed that the proslavery argument of southern writers—the "positive good" doctrine—arose primarily in response to the abolitionist crusade, and that it was aimed at northern critics or at the nonslaveholding yeomen of the south, to rally them, under planter leadership, for the protection of the "southern way of life." Robert Morrow, in the first essay presented below, interprets the impulse behind the proslavery argument in quite different terms. In his view the argument is directed primarily, not to the outside world, not to the North, not even to the nonslaveholding yeomen of the south, but rather to the planter leadership of the south itself. He argues that this leadership was still sensitive to the Jeffersonian tradition that slavery was an open question to be debated and, it may very well be, to be ended, and to the earlier evangelical Christian tradition, which was unequivocal and demanding and which saw slavery as sin. The proslavery argument ". . . aimed to resolve 'the interminable strife between antagonistic principles'" and ". . . to strengthen and confirm the conviction of the slaveholder." It was to assuage a sense of guilt, to build up a strong orthodoxy in the leadership of the south, and to provide for that leadership a real belief in slavery. Thus the South would be "solid," the internal defense secure, and, as it were, a place d'armes established, from which external aggression could be organized.

It is to this latter aspect of proslavery constitutional doctrine that Arthur Bestor directs our attention in the second essay below. Bestor points out that the conventional view of "states rights" or "states sovereignty" has held that the content of the doctrine has not changed through the generations and that the main thrust of the doctrine has been in the direction of local autonomy, decentralization, and interposition. It minimized national power. "Consequently the doctrine must always be looked upon as a purely defensive one, capable of weakening central authority but by its very nature incapable of being used aggressively or imperialistically."

The real fascination of Bestor's study is in its demonstration that be-

tween the Wilmot Proviso (1846) and the Secession Movement (1860–1861), "State sovereignty," as refined and projected by the sharpest minds of the South, became quite a different doctrine from the one conventionally depicted. It became a doctrine of power, of command, imperious in its statement and aggressive in its intent. It demanded for slavery, in the territories of the United States, an extraterritorial and extrajurisdictional protection provided for the institution by its definition in the slave states. The doctrine became an imperial doctrine that demanded that the national government become, not a maker of policy, but simply the executor of southern policy as defined in state sovereignty. Slavery should become a national institution save where it was prohibited in the free states.

Orthodoxy and conviction at home, combined with aggression abroad, became, in this view, the proslavery argument. (See also Arthur Bestor, "The American Civil War as a Constitutional Crisis," American Historical Review, LXIX [January 1964], 327–352.)

The Proslavery Argument Revisited

Ralph E. Morrow

The ideological conflicts of the twentieth century have provided convincing evidence that "the enemy" is not always the target of propaganda. The efforts of totalitarian regimes to insure "right thinking" on the part of their people or, closer to home, of citizens' councils to influence the thinking of local constituents, demonstrate that propaganda is likely to be beamed at the people of a nation or region from which it originates. Commonplace as this observation may be, it nevertheless suggests the advisability of another look at the arguments evolved in defense of slavery in the last three decades before the Civil War. Historians usually have discussed these arguments in juxtaposition to the abolitionist attack and construed the former as counter-propaganda addressed primarily to an audience north of the Mason and Dixon line. The standard account of southern thought on slavery asserts, for example, that "The South . . . without apology, presented her case to the world tribunal," [1] and the context prompts the inference that the people of the North constituted a large

---

From *Mississippi Valley Historical Review*, XLVIII (June 1961), 79–94. Reprinted by permission.

[1] William S. Jenkins, *Pro-Slavery Thought in the Old South* (Chapel Hill, 1935), 89.

part of the "world tribunal." On another level, the explanation that the proslavery argument was a species of counterfire aimed at northerners has been presented to several generations of students through the medium of college textbooks in American history. "The more strongly the winds of abolitionism swept down from the North," says a sprightly recent text, "the more . . . savagely [the South] struck back at its tormentors." [2]

The view that proslavery propaganda was directed toward proselytizing the people of the North or, at least, combating abolitionists apparently has grown in vitality in the years since the end of the Civil War. The antebellum southern writers themselves did not consistently entertain such sanguine expectations. In the pioneering days of the "positive good" theory, William Harper remarked on "the indisposition of the rest of the world to hear anything more on this subject." The North, he complained, "seems unaware that there is a reason to be encountered or an argument to be answered." [3] Better than some who came after them Harper and a number of his contemporaries appreciated the formidable obstacles to the effective persuasion of outsiders. Southern propagandists largely were denied access to media that would give their opinions national dissemination. The South had no newspapers whose geographical coverage compared to that of the northern metropolitan journals, its few periodicals were of restricted circulation, and southern booksellers complained of insufficient outlets even in their own section. If the complaints of some of the apologists were well founded, difficulties were compounded by the unco-operative policies of northern publishing houses. Although the North, unlike the South, did not attempt formal censorship of unwanted ideas, results were not wholly different. Thornton Stringfellow, James H. Hammond, Josiah C. Nott, and Iverson L. Brookes, apologists for slavery, all admitted to learning that a New York, Philadelphia, or Boston publisher, although reluctant to offend the South, was not eager to advertise its cause.[4]

If the North was a hard audience to reach it was an even harder one to convince. Because of its remoteness it might be won to forbearance toward slavery but hardly to sympathetic acceptance of the institution. Chancellor Harper, again anticipating many who followed him, asserted that "there seems to be something in this subject [of slavery] which blunts the perceptions, and darkens and confuses the understandings of men." Present

[2] Thomas A. Bailey, *American Pageant* (Boston, 1957), 370.

[3] William Harper, "Slavery in the Light of Social Ethics," E. N. Elliott (ed.), *Cotton Is King, and Pro-Slavery Arguments: Comprising the Writings of Hammond, Harper, Christy, Stringfellow, Hodge, Bledsoe, and Cartwright on This Important Subject* (Augusta, Ga., 1860), 550–51.

[4] Thornton Stringfellow, "The Bible Argument: or, Slavery in the Light of Divine Revelation," Elliott (ed.), *Cotton Is King*, 519; Joseph Ficklin to James H. Hammond, July 24, 1845, James H. Hammond Papers (Manuscript Division, Library of Congress); Josiah C. Nott to Ephraim G. Squier, February 14, 1849, Ephraim G. Squier Papers (Manuscript Division, Library of Congress); Iverson L. Brookes, *A Defense of the South against the Reproaches and Encroachments of the North* . . . (Hamburg, S. C., 1850).

the ablest arguments in defense of slave society to one who was not part of it, he said, and "you have done nothing." [5] Harper's judgment was confirmed by the adventures of two redoubtable champions of slavery, James H. Hammond and George Fitzhugh. In 1845, Hammond attempted to draw the patron of reform, Lewis Tappan, into an argument about the merits of slavery by sending him a copy of *Letters on Slavery*. Tappan refused the engagement with the excuse that no "rational person" could sincerely uphold the views expounded by Hammond in his pamphlet.[6] A decade later, Fitzhugh celebrated the publication of *Sociology for the South* by lecturing at New Haven, Connecticut. A reporter of the event noticed "much fog and much nonsense" in Fitzhugh's remarks, and estimated, probably correctly, that "no one was convinced by his attempted arguments." Fitzhugh subsequently confessed to his failure to dent opinion in the North by reproaching its press for treating his *Sociology* with "the affectation of silent contempt." "Why the devil," he asked pretentiously, "don't someone abuse me?" [7]

These failures, however, did not diminish the impulse to defend slavery. On the contrary, the difficulties of convincing the North aggravated the awareness that the security of slave property depended upon those closest to it. Nearly every major apology for slavery, from Thomas R. Dew's essays on the debates in the Virginia legislature in 1831–1832 to the diffuse polemics of Fitzhugh, explicitly showed concern for the state of southern opinion. Authors sometimes sought only the coercion, intimidation, or strengthening of the thought of their fellow southerners and regarded the conversion of northerners as merely extra dividends. Josiah Nott, readying one of his broadsides for publication, wrote: "All the articles I have written on *niggerology* have been eagerly sought for at the South, and in the present excited state of the political world, I think the thing will go well." [8] Southern intellectuals were assuredly in the forefront of the propaganda campaign, but with a certain constancy their foes seemed to be "the mawkish sensibilities and the imbecile ignorance of many within [their] own borders." [9]

The scattering of historians who have interpreted the patterns in proslavery literature as a reflex of the tensions within the South have emphasized the conflict between the planter and non-slaveholder. With the rise of radical sentiment in the North the spectral results of abolitionism were conjured up to paralyze effective action by southern antislavery elements

---

[5] Harper, "Slavery in the Light of Social Ethics," Elliott (ed.), *Cotton Is King*, 553.

[6] Lewis Tappan to Hammond, June 6, 1845, Hammond Papers.

[7] New Haven *Daily Palladium,* March 22, 1855, quoted in Harvey Wish, *George Fitzhugh: Propagandist of the Old South* (Baton Rouge, 1943), 133; Richmond *Examiner,* October 26, 1855; Fitzhugh to George F. Holmes, April 11, 1855, George F. Holmes Papers (Southern Historical Collection, University of North Carolina Library).

[8] Nott to Squier, May 4, 1850, Squier Papers.

[9] *Southern Literary Messenger* (Richmond), XVIII (December, 1852), 724.

and to frighten non-slaveholders into submitting to the continued rule of the gentry.[10] This hypothesis helps to explain some peculiar features of the proslavery crusade. Virginia, for instance, contributed more lustrous names to the roster of defenders than did any other state. It was also the last of the southern states to engage in official debate on emancipation, and even thereafter it was remarked for the persistent anti-slavery sentiment concentrated in the western counties where the slave population was sparse. Thomas R. Dew, who is credited with switching the South onto the "positive good" track, won his reputation by his exertions against southern displays of abolitionism. His *Review of the Debates in the Virginia Legislature* was pitched specifically toward western Virginia and generally toward the non-slaveholder. Nor did Dew bury the concern about the attitudes of many Virginians toward slavery. The Fredericksburg *News*, a newspaper to which Fitzhugh contributed, warned its readers periodically that "In Virginia are to be found some of the most detestable abolitionists in the Union." [11] In the general body of proslavery writing it seems apparent that the repetition of certain themes can be fitted into the courtship of the yeoman. The reiterations of the pervasive economic advantages of slavery, the slaveholder as the living illustration of the gospel of success, race as a guarantor of status, and miscegenation as the consequence of emancipation were suited to the hardheaded interest or ego needs of the non-slaveholder.[12]

Class antagonism, however, was only one of the southern impulses that produced the proslavery argument. Furthermore, it was one to which apologists for slavery attached decreasing significance. Worry among southern intellectuals over the yeoman and non-slaveholding population was much more evident in the 1830's than it was twenty years later. For all that the hypothesis of yeoman alienation tells us about proslavery polemics it has, in its literalness, a resemblance to the older view which sees only the North as the target of southern propaganda. Both regard proslavery writing as a simple response to antislavery elements and seem to agree that the object of the writing was to counter the activity of those elements. Differences arise only over the location of the danger. One finds it in the North; the other among the non-slaveholders of the South. Neither fully appreciates the disquietude of proslavery writers over the state of mind among southerners who entertained no hostility to the institution, or who even were committed to its preservation, and the extent to which the theoretical defenses of slavery were attuned to the needs of these people. But therein lies another dimension of the proslavery argument.

---

[10] See especially William B. Hesseltine, "Some New Aspects of the Pro-Slavery Argument," *Journal of Negro History* (Washington), XXI (January, 1936), 1–15.

[11] Quoted in Wish, *George Fitzhugh,* 112.

[12] The standard summary of these arguments is James D. B. De Bow *et al., Interest in Slavery of the Southern Non-Slaveholder* (Charleston, 1860).

The milieu in which the proslavery writers worked is more fully understood by disregarding the venerable convention of dividing the socio-intellectual history of the ante-bellum South into sharply distinguishable periods. What was increasingly called "the southern way of life" consisted not merely of institutions and affirmative beliefs concerning those institutions but of traditions and memories of enduring vitality. Much in this tradition was summed up in the historical figure of Jefferson. The Jeffersonian legacy included not only a set of positive views on man and society but also a habit of candid inquiry into the forms of social organization. It flourished on "a happy variety of minds." Whether the tradition unequivocally condemned slavery is less important than its refusal to foreclose discussion of the matter.[13] Although the thinking symbolized by Jefferson may have left most southerners untouched, the mood implicit in it reached beyond a narrow clique of disciples. A Georgia contributor to De Bow's Review in 1854, although harshly critical of this Jeffersonian tradition, testified to the radius of its influence. She recalled the textbooks that boldly presented the pros and cons of slavery, the schoolboys who declaimed against it at commencement exercises, and the monotony with which local debating societies mulled over the merits of the institution. It was a tradition of open inquiry, she rightly noted, that regularly involved members of affluent families.[14]

While this tradition held slavery to be a subject open for discussion, another put it under the condemnation of the Christian conscience. Evangelical religion in the South of the earlier nineteenth century had a strain of antislavery sentiment as strong as that of Jeffersonianism. Before 1830 local or national assemblies of Methodists, Baptists, and Presbyterians, the denominations which included the bulk of churchgoing southerners, had placed slaveholding or the practices associated with it outside the pale of holy living.[15] The stand taken by the churches was made more effectual by clerical participation in the struggling antislavery movement in the South and by a current of emancipationist sympathy rising from the rank and file of evangelical communicants. Among the later censors of southern ecclesiastical thought on slavery were children of evangelical pioneers who had entertained strong reservations about the godliness of the institution.[16] Inherent in the evangelical heritage were compulsions of a particularly

---

[13] Daniel J. Boorstin, The Lost World of Thomas Jefferson (New York, 1948), 92–98, 119–27.

[14] De Bow's Review (New Orelans), XVI (January, 1854), 22–23.

[15] William W. Sweet (ed.), Religion on the American Frontier (4 vols., New York and Chicago, 1931–1946), I, The Baptists, 78–88; II, The Presbyterians, 110–15; Wade C. Barclay, Early American Methodism (2 vols., New York, 1950), II, 1–12.

[16] John B. McFerrin, History of Methodism in Tennessee (3 vols., Nashville, 1883), II, 463–95; Henry Little to Absalom Peters, July 21, 1825, and Harvey Woods to Peters, June 29, 1836, American Home Missionary Society Papers (Hammond Theological Seminary, Chicago).

powerful character; the apocalyptic framework of sin, evil, and redemption within which the issues were discussed admitted of little evasion or compromise.

The affirmations which constituted the proslavery argument contradicted but did not obliterate the antislavery traditions which Jeffersonian and evangelical thought had fostered. The common use of Jefferson as a foil in the vindication of slavery and the indignant repudiation of evangelical excesses by a later generation of southern clergymen are as suggestive of the persistence of the older tradition as of its liquidation. Figuratively, these ancient attitudes constituted the South's conscience, and this conscience helped to condition southern reactions to the sweep of nineteenth-century history. Antislavery developments in Europe and the United States had a special meaning, not only because they menaced vested economic or social interests, but because they seemed expressive of norms once espoused or tolerated by the South but later rejected or denied. The abolition of slavery in the dependencies and nations of the New World was a forceful reminder of the correctness of Jefferson's view that the status of slavery was not beyond the purview of change. The pre-eminently moral arguments of the abolitionists stung another vein of sensitivity embedded in the experience of southerners. Charges of the sinfulness of slaveholding harked back to the earlier days of southern evangelicalism, and the South's reaction was not unlike that of a righteous person accused of philandering. An effect of the outside pressures was to intensify the conflict between the two personalities of the South. One embodied a set of beliefs that had been fashioned by past conditions; the other grew from the estimated needs of the succeeding age.

The foregoing diagnosis finds support in the works of several eminent proslavery writers. In 1856 William A. Smith, president of Randolph-Macon College, authored a publication intended to supplement existing college texts in moral philosophy inasmuch as their treatment of slavery implanted in "the minds of young men . . . a fatal direction both as regards the principles of the institution and the institution itself." The opening pages of Smith's book included a lucid exposition of the South's dilemma. "There are . . . not a few," he wrote, "spread through our Southern states . . . whose minds are in a state of great embarrassment on this subject [of slavery]." And, even more significantly, he believed that this "secret doubt of the morality of African slavery" had affected "many of [the South's] best citizens." The "painful . . . suspicion that there must be something wrong in the principle of domestic slavery" Smith blamed on the persistence of "prior views of religion" and "the great abstract doctrine of Mr. Jefferson, that the principle of African slavery is *per se* sinful." [17] Contradicting this doctrine, however, was the observable reality that "slav-

[17] William A. Smith, *Lectures on the Philosophy and Practice of Slavery* (Nashville, 1856), 15, 17, 28.

ery has become more and more practical—a fixed fact in this country." The incompatibility of the persisting ideal and the "fixed fact," Smith said, had set "men against themselves." [18] "Pressed on the one hand by what is assumed to be correct principle, and on the other by . . . the necessity of governing and providing for their slaves . . . they really find themselves in a most embarrassing situation, from which they sigh to be released." [19]

By thus identifying the problem, Smith clarified the function of the proslavery argument. It aimed to resolve the "interminable strife between antagonistic principles" and had as its end the psychological adjustment of southerners—slaveholders perhaps more than non-slaveholders—to the external conditions of their existence. Thornton Stringfellow also owned that his attempts "to prove slavery a lawful relation among men" were intended "to satisfy the conscientiousness of Christians." [20] Others with associations less intimately clerical avowed the same purpose of putting the South at peace with herself by bringing moral values into line with social practice. The debates in the state legislature during 1831–1832 prompted another Virginian, Benjamin Watkins Leigh, "to address a few remarks to those who have conscientious scruples about the holding of slaves, and therefore, consider themselves under an obligation to flee to a land where this evil does not exist." [21] Later, in the tumultuous decade of the 1850's when the South was supposed to have achieved a new moral equilibrium, George F. Holmes, professor at the University of Virginia and literary czar of major southern periodicals, asserted that "this affair of conscience must be decided promptly." He asked southern intellectuals to overcome the "speculative doubts by which slaveholders [were] troubled" by assisting them to "a clear comprehension of the reasons by which slavery is justified and proved to be right." Even Holmes's admiring correspondent, George Fitzhugh, interrupted the dismal descriptions of free society and proposals for the universalization of slavery in his *Cannibals All* to point out the vulnerability of the South's moral position. The belief entertained by many in the South that "slavery, in the general . . . is morally wrong and against common right" had compromised the defense of southern society, and as a remedy Fitzhugh urged that "we must vindicate [the] institution in the abstract." [22]

The exhortations of Smith, Leigh, and Holmes about the moral needs of the slaveowner disclose the orientation in proslavery literature often overlooked. Although propaganda was not unanimously trimmed to the needs of a single socio-economic group, members of the corps of defenders

---

[18] *Ibid.*, 26.   [19] *Ibid.*, 57–58.

[20] Stringfellow, "The Bible Argument," Elliott (ed.), *Cotton Is King,* 522.

[21] Richmond *Enquirer,* February 4, 1832.

[22] *Southern Literary Messenger,* XIX (June, 1853), 324; *De Bow's Review,* XXI (August, 1856), 132; George Fitzhugh, *Cannibals All! or, Slaves without Masters* (Richmond, 1857), 294–95.

had convincing reasons for their solicitous interest in the slaveholding population. The defenders' own associations often were of a type to encourage familiarity with the minds and feelings of the more propertied classes. Many writers were connected to slavery either through ownership or family ties. Those academicians, clergymen, literateurs, and publicists without primary ties to slavery nonetheless had regular contact with the home-grown aristocracy in the latter's various capacities as patrons, governors of educational and religious institutions, students, and parishioners. The intercourse with slaveholders which made writers party to the thinking in top social echelons also promoted concern about the quality of that thought, because the perpetuation of slavery rested first of all upon the unflinching fidelity of those who were involved in the peculiar property and who possessed much of the power to make decisions for the South. The consequences of irresolution, many propagandists were disposed to argue, grew more dangerous as one ascended the social pyramid.

These factors left a mark on proslavery writing. In the principal works produced after 1850, concern for the mind of the slaveholder is as great if not greater than concern for any other element of the southern population. Holmes believed that the dangerous dispersion of flabby opinions on slavery was attributable to those whose stake in its maintenance was largest. In an article prepared for the *Southern Literary Messenger* in 1853, he condemned "the weak minds and vacillating fancies of many . . . slaveholders." Their "lukewarm, shilly-shally convictions," he said, had "armed . . . Abolition adversaries with firebrands" which "they were hurling into the South's combustible materials." To Holmes the conduct of many aristocrats bordered "on treason . . . to the South." [23] Concern about attitudes common among employers of slave labor often brought prescriptions for correct reading. One review of Fitzhugh's *Sociology* enumerated the occupational groups likely to benefit from the book and placed planters at the head of the list. Another commentator recommended the volume as a cure for "the painful sense of inferiority" contracted by planters "on visits to Northern cities with their splendor, animation, and crowded population." [24] In a summary of twenty-five years of proslavery literature the editor of the *Southern Literary Messenger,* John R. Thompson, concluded that most of the barrage had been served up "to strengthen and confirm the convictions of the slaveholder." [25]

The therapy suggested by proslavery writers unfolded in two directions. One form, instead of coming to grips with the roots of the conflict, tended to facilitate escape into a world of unreality. A clerical apologist declared that "if masters could be prevailed upon to . . . perform their whole duty to their servants . . . all the objections to slavery . . . in reasonable minds,

---

[23] *Southern Literary Messenger,* XIX (June, 1853), 325.
[24] Charleston *Mercury,* April 21, 1855; *De Bow's Review,* XIX (October, 1855), 463.
[25] *Southern Literary Messenger,* XXIII (October, 1856), 245.

would be silenced thereby." [26] This belief, like other arguments for better treatment of the slaves, was easily made part of a larger image of the unalloyed benignity of the southern system of bondage. The wish gave way to an allusion. The vein of sentimentalism in proslavery literature offered an avenue of flight from doubts arising from the theory or workings of the peculiar institution. Warm public responses to romanticized treatments of slave society indicate both the depth of the South's disturbances and the success with which they were exploited. William J. Grayson's *Hireling and the Slave,* which appeared in 1856, chiefly impresses as a transmutation of the mottled relationships of slavery into a vision of a paradisical order. Yet a reviewer for a leading southern periodical proclaimed: "There is nothing unreal . . . in the scenes and incidents depicted. . . . It is a living representation of things as they are." [27]

Despite the popularity of the literature of escape, many polemicists saw in it a dead end. Holmes condemned "the writers of replicant romances" as "quacks" who had "injured the South" because they anesthetized the conscience without relieving it of painful antagonisms.[28] Only by planting the institution "on the firm basis of philosophical reasoning, historical testimony, and social experience" could the South be "rid . . . of the superstition that slavery is a cleaving mischief." [29] The satisfaction of this need to believe sent southern authors on heroic searches for the certitude that would dissolve guilt and doubt. John Thompson exclaimed: "Let this subject be understood . . . and we need not fear to stand alone." [30] The need to believe in slavery was inseparably wedded to the intellectual content of the proslavery argument. The finely reasoned cases by which God, nature, and history vindicated slavery were offered as assurances. One reader congratulated James Hammond on his pamphlet because the author had not left "a thread of doubt" to "unhinge minds upon the moral merits of slavery." [31]

The increasing barrage of propaganda obviously did much to scatter and demoralize southern antislavery elements. But the suppression of dissent was looked upon as an essentially negative achievement, depreciated by many of slavery's most vocal advocates. When Fitzhugh said that "agitation for the South and her institutions [was] . . . the obvious duty of every patriot" he was calling for more then the mere dispersion of heretics.[32] Those who agreed with Fitzhugh hoped to people the South with true believers—defenders of slavery who would make competition in affirming their faith the test of orthodoxy. Although the term "positive good" was

---

[26] C. F. Sturgis, "Melville Letters," *Duties of Masters to Servants* (Charleston, 1851), 54.

[27] *De Bow's Review,* XVIII (April, 1855), 460.

[28] *Southern Literary Messenger,* XIX (June, 1853), 324.

[29] *Ibid.,* XXI (March, 1855), 129; XXIII (October, 1856), 244.

[30] *Ibid.,* XXIII (October, 1856), 242.

[31] Thomas J. Butler to Hammond, July 1, 1845, Hammond Papers.

[32] Richmond *Enquirer,* March 27, 1856.

coined to describe the intellectual content of the proslavery argument, it also has a profound psychological meaning. It afforded ground for overcoming anxiety and doubt by the activity of belief. James P. Holcombe, Holmes's colleague at the University of Virginia, urged alumni of the institution to bold measures in behalf of the South, assuring them that the "final sentence of impartial history" would pronounce slavery "consistent with the purest justice, commended by the highest expediency and sanctioned by a[n] . . . enlightened humanity." [33]

The effort to rest the southern defense upon a firm ideological base turned the attention of many authors to the developing sciences of nature and society. The increasing resort to the empirical sciences was accompanied by some faint suspicions, though largely unspoken, about the validity of Scriptural evidence in controversies over social policy. It is possible to attribute fondness for the newer hypotheses concerning man and society merely to the intellectual satisfaction which they afforded southern thinkers who, like those elsewhere in the Western World, were attracted to them as offering a more rational understanding of man's behavior. Nonetheless, the choice of argumentative weapons was sometimes legitimated by referring to their anticipated effect upon public opinion in the South. The persuasiveness of the empirical sciences, it was contended, surpassed that offered by divine revelation. The Biblical defense, although it sometimes went so far as to proclaim that "God himself instituted human slavery," [34] was not always convincing. The Bible, one critic declared, did not contain "anything which would show . . . that the master commits any offense in holding slaves" but, he added, neither did it furnish the means of effectively buttressing the institution. Chancellor Harper still more emphatically discounted the use of Scripture in defenses of slavery. Slavery, he wrote, "is a civil institution with which religion has no concern." [35]

The justifications manufactured from Biblical material comprised a large part of the proslavery output, but in the fifteen years before the Civil War most authors of more than local reputation subordinated or disregarded Biblical sources to draw upon the natural and social sciences. Few notable propagandists were other than impeccably proper in their public religious observances, but their religious beliefs were generally separated from their discussions of public affairs. An exception in his outspoken enmity to religious orthodoxy was the erratic Mobile physician, Josiah Nott. Nott often justified his attitude toward revealed religion in the language of intellectual progress. He refused, he said, "to allow those worn out legends

---

[33] *Southern Literary Messenger*, XXVII (November, 1858), 419.

[34] Brookes, *A Defense of the South*, 8.

[35] *De Bow's Review*, XIX (January, 1855), 552; Harper, "Slavery in the Light of Social Ethics," Elliott (ed.), *Cotton Is King*, 552.

to obstruct the path of science." [36] Nott, nonetheless, was a propagandist as well as a scientist, and he admitted that the homage he paid to the "invincible voice of nature" bore a relationship to his concern for southern morale. Believing, as he once asserted, that slavery was "one of those importunate questions which . . . religion can never decide," he placed large hopes in biology and anthropology and predicted that the exploitation of these fields would bring "public opinion [on slavery] over to me in the South." [37]

Despite their eagerness to toughen the psychological fiber of the South, Nott and many of his collaborators usually wore a mask of complete indifference to the outcome of their inquiries into the constitution of society. Their assumed attitude was that of the objective analyst; but their professions of intellectual aloofness had a necessary connection with the problem of effective persuasion. As positivism preached, truth was the product of objectivity and objective procedures were defined as those in which human reason, undisturbed by any values or bias of the investigator, sorted and arranged the measurable evidence to arrive at conclusions of the highest degree of probability. Holmes proclaimed repeatedly that "if slavery is right let it be maintained at all costs; if it is wrong let it be abolished at all costs." And Albert T. Bledsoe, in his *Liberty and Slavery*, protested that he had eschewed appeals to "passion and sordid interest" and consulted "neither the pecuniary interests of the South nor the prejudices of the North." [38] These claims of utter detachment may have been bows to intellectual convention, but they also served to call the reader's attention to the reliability of the author's work. From an "impartial investigation of the various aspects of slavery," such as that which Holmes professed to undertake, would come the certainty "that the policy finally adopted will prove . . . unquestionably right." And what one "impartial" investigator discovered, the others stood ready to confirm. The monopoly which professional advocates of slavery held over the review columns of southern journals provided a continuing forum for mutual endorsement. The credentials given to Bledsoe were not exceptional. The Virginia mathematician was advertised as "a genius of polemics," the conqueror of "princes of philosophical theology," and "unmatched by any person in [the] country in logical encounter." These talents, enlisted in the cause of the South, said a critic, had resulted in a book that "left standing no . . . semblance of an argument against slavery." [39]

Internal strains, whether they are traced to class antagonisms or to the

[36] Nott to Squier, August 19, 1848, Squier Papers.

[37] Nott to Hammond, July 25, 1845, Hammond Papers.

[38] *De Bow's Review*, XXI (August, 1846), 133; Albert T. Bledsoe, *An Essay on Liberty and Slavery* (Philadelphia, 1856), 12.

[39] *De Bow's Review*, XXI (August, 1856), 135, 142.

conflict between tradition and practical need, were not the only influences arising within the South to give stimulus and direction to the apologists for slavery. In the fulfillment of their community function southern authors found private satisfactions that were, in different degrees, distinguishable from any larger interest. No biography of a major southern controversialist offers a basis for the assertion that he rode the flood of agitation merely for self-advantage, but writers attested to the personal compensations which lent encouragement to their work. Admirers often told James Hammond, who constantly discovered unsuspected delights in authorship, that his literary industry was certain to bring political rewards. "If you continue to strike," one of them told him, "your day must come." [40] Hammond was becomingly modest in his replies, but he confessed to William Gilmore Simms that "I am ambitious of power." The most gratifying way of attaining this power, he said, was "to send from your chest words that reach the hearts and reason of men." [41]

Josiah Nott, a curious compound of ingeniousness, opportunism, and large ambition, was likewise clearly aware of the opportunities for advancement furnished by the crisis. In commenting on the forward position he had taken in the slavery controversy he declared: "My experience has taught me that if a man wants to get on fast, he must kick up a damned fuss generally. . . . A man must get notoriety in some way or the tide will run by him." At different times, Nott identified his accrued benefits as "popularity," "money," and "professional reputation." [42] Although Nott's capabilities were not of first rank, his inclinations were intellectual and his considerable reputation, derived from works on race and slavery, suggests that the warfare of ideas opened doors to those who aspired to the life of the mind.

In later years critics have said that the South's preoccupation with the defense of slavery stifled the creativity of her intelligentsia and constricted their efforts. Ante-bellum southerners, however, reckoned the results differently. Holmes noticed that the "necessities of society in a great measure . . . give birth to . . . its literature." From this premise he reached the conclusion that southern writers were "indebted to the continuance and asperity of this slavery controversy for the creation of a genuine Southern literature." From the "avidity for information on slavery" had "sprung literary activity and the literary movement." [43] Holmes's definition was broad enough to take in most endeavor catalogued under the humanities and the social sciences. John Thompson agreed with the analysis. The peril of the South, said Thompson, had brought genuine respect for talents that once were taken lightly. Men had been raised from obscurity

---

[40] James M. Walker to Hammond, June 11, 1845, Hammond Papers.

[41] Hammond to William Gilmore Simms, July 14, 1845, *ibid.*

[42] Nott to Squier, February 14, 1849, March 26, 1851, Squier Papers; Nott to Hammond, June 3, August 12, September 4, 1845, Hammond Papers.

[43] *De Bow's Review*, XXI (August, 1846), 133.

to the centers of southern life because they possessed gifts which might previously have gone unheralded, but which now had relevance in an age of controversy. On the supposition that the South would furnish bread for its defenders, Thompson advised southern authors that "the field for their labors [was] wide." [44]

While some of the writers could total up personal rewards of self-advancement, adulation, and public influence, others who tested their mettle in controversy found satisfactions that were wholly independent of any public appreciation of their work. Nagged, like other southerners, by the moral dilemmas which slavery posed, some found in authorship a vehicle of relief from their nettlesome uncertainties. James Hammond, although alert to the tangible rewards of proslavery agitation, nevertheless averred that as he wrote his first polemic his "opinions constantly gained strength." By the time he had finished he had become certain "that slaveholding is not a sin." [45] William Gilmore Simms guessed that Hammond's experience was not unique. Simms's assertion that the re-examination of slavery had "resulted in moral reassurance . . . and in relieving . . . all that doubt, that morbid feeling of weakness" applied to authors and readers alike. And significantly, the adversaries identified by Simms—"doubt" and "that morbid feeling of weakness"—were located within the South and even within southerners themselves. [46]

If southern propagandists accurately gauged feeling in their section when they accented the conquest of guilt and doubt, an important aspect of the proslavery writing evidently has not received the attention it merits. The great body of the historical writing on the subject is primarily an analysis of the various proslavery lines of argument, with little attention to the psychological needs of the reading public. The more one studies the latter, however, the greater the temptation grows to conclude that the impact of proslavery dialectics inhered less in the quality of the presentation than in the processes of its assimilation. In other words, the satisfaction of believing in the morality of slavery was more decisive than the substance of anything believed.

The common incidence of the themes of guilt and doubt raises questions, too, as to conventional conclusions about the impulse to proslavery writing. Usually emphasized are the South's "conviction" of the justice of a condition of slavery, the "challenging temper" in which her case was delivered, and the confidence "that the verdict would be an entire vindication of her course in perpetuating her peculiar institution." [47] This view,

---

[44] *Southern Literary Messenger*, XXIII (October, 1856), 242.

[45] Hammond to Lewis Tappan, April 8, 1845, Hammond Papers.

[46] William G. Simms, "The Morals of Slavery," *The Pro-Slavery Argument: As Maintained by the Most Distinguished Writers of the Southern States . . .* (Charleston, 1852), 179.

[47] Jenkins, *Pro-Slavery Thought in the Old South*, 89; Robert E. Riegel, *Young America, 1830–1840* (Norman, 1953), 292–93.

which rules out a large body of contrary testimony, evidently supposes that the North alone was responsible for provoking the activity of slavery's apologists. Without the abolitionist crusade the intellectual talents of many southerners admittedly would have been without employment. But once the gauntlet was thrown down proslavery writers believed that the South must look first to herself and they were never quite content with the state of psychological preparedness which they found. Their immediate worry was not over those with an announced enmity to slavery but over the many southerners who asserted no hatred of the institution and often were slaveowners. Propagandists frequently denied discovering among the latter the relentless certainty commonly ascribed to them. The protestations of the "positive good" of slavery measured not only the vigor of northern abolitionism's attacks but the anxiety over the vulnerability of the South's psychological armor. Yet, it is one of the ironies of American history that southern intellectuals helped to aggravate the condition they wanted to alleviate. The propaganda fusillade caught the South in a vicious circle. Agitation heightened fear and uncertainty which seemingly called for still more agitation. A trial by arms was not an illogical exit from this cycle, for the strength that supposedly came from righteousness could then be definitively asserted.

State Sovereignty and Slavery:

A Reinterpretation of Proslavery

Constitutional Doctrine, 1846–1860

Arthur Bestor

In 1860–1861 eleven slaveholding states proclaimed their secession from the American Union. They were pushing to its logical extreme a constitutional doctrine variously known as "state rights" or "state sovereignty." The doctrine had figured in American constitutional discussion for upwards of sixty years. Moreover, during the controversy over slavery in the territories, which raged for fifteen years, from the time of the Wilmot Proviso of 1846 until the election of 1860, the arguments and slogans of state sovereignty had been reiterated so often that they became almost as familiar (and often seemed almost as ageless) as the Ten Commandments.

Historians take an impish delight in pointing out that the doctrine of state rights has been espoused on one occasion or another by virtually every section or party or interest that has ever found its opponents ensconced in power in the national capital. As Alexander Johnston put it seventy-odd years ago, "Almost every state in the Union [has] in turn declared its own 'sovereignty,' and denounced as almost treasonable similar declarations in other cases by other states."[1] Most historians stop with this

---

From *Journal of the Illinois State Historical Society*, LIV (Spring 1961), 117–180. Reprinted by permission. *Arthur Bestor, professor of history at the University of Illinois and a past president of the Illinois State Historical Society, began working on this subject in 1957 while Harmsworth Professor of American History at Oxford. The book which has resulted from his studies is tentatively titled* Slavery and the American Constitution, 1846–1860: A Historical Analysis of the Crisis That Led to Civil War *and will be published by the Clarendon Press of Oxford University. The author presented this paper to the Mississippi Valley Historical Association at its Detroit meeting on April 21, 1961. Earlier versions had been delivered as lectures at Wayne State University, the University of Illinois and the State University of Iowa. A paper on a closely related theme—"The Constitutional Issues of 1860"—was read before the Illinois State Historical Society meeting at Rockford on October 9, 1960.*

[1] "State Sovereignty," in John J. Lalor, ed., *Cyclopaedia of Political Science* (Chicago, 1884), III: 794. See also Arthur M. Schlesinger, *New Viewpoints in American History* (New York, 1922), 220–44, "The State Rights Fetish."

paradox, satisfied that they have reached the end of it. They observe that state sovereignty has made strange bedfellows, but they assume that the doctrine itself, considered simply as a doctrine, has remained essentially unaltered throughout all its changing cohabitations.

In this view of the matter, the theory of state rights, whenever invoked, has had a constant and unvarying tendency. State sovereignty, it is supposed, can always be equated with local self-determination and local autonomy. The doctrine seeks consistently to minimize the exercise of national powers. It is perennially sympathetic to the idea that a state may rightfully "interpose" its authority to prevent the central government's jeopardizing, or even interfering with, the rights or interests or customs of the state's own citizens. According to the conventional view, these three political principles are invariably associated with the idea of state sovereignty. Consequently the doctrine itself must always be looked upon as a purely defensive one, capable of weakening the central authority but by its very nature incapable of being used aggressively or imperialistically.

These assumptions are plausible enough. And the secession crisis of 1860–1861 appears to validate them completely. In defending their course, the seceding states appealed to a political philosophy that exalted local autonomy. "The slaveholding States will no longer have the power of self-government, or self-protection," complained South Carolina in a formal declaration of her reasons for seceding.[2] In an accompanying address she went on to say that "the Government of the United States has beome consolidated, with a claim of limitless powers in its operations."[3] By seceding from the Union, moreover, South Carolina was obviously interposing the sovereignty of the state in the most conclusive fashion possible. The language throughout was purely defensive. The onus for aggression was placed upon those who would uphold the Union by "coercing" the states.

Secession was obviously the culminating expression of the idea of state sovereignty, and secession can be interpreted as a defensive measure designed to vindicate the philosophy of local self-government. If, then, the doctrine of state sovereignty signified the defensive principles of local autonomy, decentralization, and interposition when invoked to justify secession, must it not have signified substantially the same three principles when earlier invoked, by the very same group, to support their policy regarding slavery in the territories? The answer, contrary to expectation, is *no*. During the crisis of 1846–1860, the doctrine of state sovereignty possessed implications for political philosophy that were almost precisely the opposite of those that had belonged to it in earlier days and that were later hastily reasserted at the time of secession.

---

[2] "Declaration of the Immediate Causes . . . [of] Secession," Dec. 24, 1860. *Journal of the Convention of the People of South Carolina, Held in 1860, 1861 and 1862* (Columbia, S. C., 1862), 465–66. The ordinance of secession was adopted on Dec. 20, 1860. *Ibid.*, 43.

[3] "Address . . . to the People of the Slaveholding States," Dec. 24, 1860. *Ibid.*, 470.

One simple fact is often forgotten. Secession was the *alternative* to, not the purposed *outcome* of, the constitutional program that proslavery forces advocated, in the name of state sovereignty, during the controversy over slavery in the territories. This alternative—dissolution of the Union—doubtless lay in the back of the minds of increasing numbers of proslavery leaders as the year 1860 approached. Nevertheless, the actual proposals they were offering from 1846 to 1860 presupposed the continued existence of the federal system. The defenders of slavery wished the constitutional machinery to function in such a way as to give maximum protection to slavery. This meant, of necessity, that they were still committed to the view that the Constitution was a machine that could and should be made to work. Only after they opted for secession did they look upon the old Constitution as a wreck to be dismantled.

In the nature of the case, the reasoning employed to support a positive program for protecting slavery in the territories and for enforcing the fugitive-slave act could not be identical with the reasoning employed to dissolve the Union. Though state sovereignty might be the premise in both instances, the two arguments were different in purpose and in logic. They were not only different, they were almost antithetical. To attempt to understand the proslavery constitutional argument of 1846–1860 by assuming it to be identical with the secessionist argument of 1860–1861 is to read history backwards and hence to misread it.

On every major point—on local autonomy, on diminution of federal power, and on interposition—the state-sovereignty position regarding slavery was almost exactly the reverse of the state-sovereignty position regarding secession.

Secession represented the principle of local autonomy pushed to its logical extreme. In discussing the question of slavery in the territories, by contrast, proponents of state sovereignty repudiated in theory and practice the idea of local autonomy. It was Stephen A. Douglas who stood consistently for self-determination in the matter of slavery. And the proslavery faction (after an initial period of hesitation) turned against Douglas's principle of territorial sovereignty so decisively that in 1860 they split the Democratic Party rather than accept it.

In the second place, secessionist documents of 1860–1861 denounced the "consolidation" of power in federal hands. By contrast, the proslavery program of 1846–1860 called for rigorous enforcement of the fugitive-slave law by federal commissioners dispersed throughout the Union. By 1860, moreover, proslavery leaders were contemplating the idea of a federally enacted slave code to be imposed in all the territories.[4]

Finally, secession represented an extreme application of the idea that a state might interpose its sovereign authority to render null and void within

---

[4] See the resolutions of Jefferson Davis, nn. 116 and 127 below.

its borders any controverted exercise of federal power. During the dispute over slavery, however, those who preached state sovereignty had no use whatever for the traditional doctrines of interposition and nullification. Instead, proslavery leaders denounced in the bitterest terms both the nullification of the fugitive-slave act by the personal-liberty laws of various northern states, and also the kind of interposition that Wisconsin attempted in the case of Sherman M. Booth.[5] Though South Carolina had, in 1832–1833, adopted the only formal ordinances of nullification in American history, she did not hesitate to proclaim in 1860 that she considered herself released from all obligations under the Constitution because thirteen northern states had "enacted laws which either nullify the Acts of Congress or render useless any attempt to execute them." [6]

These are not randon and accidental inconsistencies. They are evidence that the doctrine of state sovereignty, as applied to the issue of slavery during the fifteen years before 1860, was by no means the kind of political philosophy it is popularly supposed to have been.

What we are up against is the profound yet subtle difference between a legal concept and a political philosophy. State sovereignty is, at bottom, a *legal* postulate. The idea that government should be decentralized and local autonomy cherished is an expression of political *philosophy*. One naturally assumes a close affinity between the legal concept of state sovereignty and the political philosophy that emphasizes local self-government, just as one naturally assumes a corresponding affinity between the legal concept of national supremacy and the policy of centralization or (in the language of the early republic) "consolidation." In most periods of American history this one-to-one relationship does, in fact, hold. But it does not hold for the constitutional controversy of 1846–1860 over slavery. During that period, conclusions of a markedly consolidationist tendency were regularly being deduced from state-sovereignty premises. How this logical feat was accomplished is the subject of the present paper.

Our concern, let me make clear at the outset, will be with doctrines of constitutional law, not with the purely rhetorical use of the phrases "state sovereignty" and "state rights." Few terms in the political vocabulary are endowed with such deep emotional connotations as these, and few are so variable in meaning. Few, therefore, serve so well the purposes of political rhetoric. A cherished principle can easily be labeled a "right," without imputing to it the status of a claim enforceable at law. Similarly, "sovereignty" can bestow a majestic tone to a political argument, without implying any precisely definable constitutional theory. Arguments about state sovereignty in the full-dress debates preceding the Civil War cannot be dismissed, however, as simply rhetorical. Politicians who used the term in-

---

[5] See nn. 46, 48, and 50 below.
[6] South Carolina, "Declaration," Dec. 24, 1860. *Journal of the Convention,* 464.

sisted that it denoted a clear and definite legal conception, that it had precise constitutional consequences, and that the principles deduced from it were legally and constitutionally binding on everyone concerned with the making and enforcing of public policy. Without forgetting the emotional elements in the situation, we must here concentrate our attention upon the legal reasoning that made the controversy a constitutional one.

To understand the constitutional arguments of 1846–1860, it is obviously necessary to know precisely what the constitutional issues were. Moreover, as an essential preliminary, it is necessary to know what they were not.

ABOLITION OF SLAVERY NOT THE ISSUE

The constitutional controversy over slavery that held the nation in its grip from 1846 to 1860 did not result from any proposal before Congress that would have interfered in any way with the complete and final authority of each slaveholding state to deal in any way it chose with any and every question relating to slavery within its own boundaries. No federal measure regulating slavery within the slaveholding states was proposed in Congress or in the platform of any organized political party.[7] No responsible figure in public office questioned the plenary constitutional authority of the slaveholding states to regulate the institution within their borders, and none denied that federal interference would be palpably unconstitutional.

The simple fact that the constitutional powers of the slaveholding states within their own boundaries were never seriously contested is so often blurred in historical discussions, and the opposite has been so often insinuated, that it will be well to place the historical record clearly, though briefly, on view.

Early in the second session of the First Congress, in February and March, 1790, the issue of slavery was brought before the House of Representatives by a number of petitions urging Congress to "step to the very verge of the power vested in [it]," for the purpose of bringing slavery to an end.[8] In response the House carefully considered the extent of the powers that it believed the newly established government to possess in the matter. After a rancorous debate, two reports, somewhat different in tone though hardly

---

[7] Even the Liberty Party of 1844, which presented the most extreme platform of the entire period, stopped short of advocating a federal law abolishing slavery, even though it openly repudiated any obligation to obey the fugitive-slave clause of the Constitution. The party summed up its demands as "the absolute and unqualified divorce of the General Government from Slavery." Kirk H. Porter and Donald B. Johnson, eds., *National Party Platforms, 1840–1956* (Urbana, Ill., 1956), 4–8.

[8] Memorial of the Pennsylvania Society for Promoting the Abolition of Slavery, signed by Benjamin Franklin as president, presented Feb. 12, 1790. *Annals of Congress*, 1 Cong., 2 Sess., 1197–98. The previous day two Quaker petitions had inaugurated the discussion. *Ibid.*, 1182–84. (Hereafter, H.R. will stand, in footnotes for the House of Representatives.)

in substance, were ordered spread upon the journal. On the point in question, the decision was clear:

> That Congress have no authority to interfere in the emancipation of slaves, or in the treatment of them within any of the States; it remaining with the several States alone to provide any regulations therein, which humanity and true policy may require.[9]

The principle thus formulated in 1790 remained the unchallenged constitutional understanding until past the year 1861.

Only by amending the Constitution, therefore, could federal power be used to abolish slavery. Amendments to accomplish this end were offered in 1818 and 1839,[10] but the House immediately blocked their consideration. Between 1839 and 1863—that is to say, throughout the entire period of bitterest constitutional conflict over slavery—no proposal to amend the Constitution in this direction was so much as offered, let alone debated. On the other hand, certain amendments to *prevent* the possible abolition of slavery were proposed.[11] Indeed, the only amendment passed by Congress at the culminating moment of the crisis was of the latter character. On March 3, 1861, despite the fact that seven slaveholding states had already seceded, Congress voted to submit to the states an irrepealable amendment to the Constitution, couched in the following unambiguous (if somewhat ungrammatical) language:

> No amendment shall be made to the Constitution which will authorize or give to Congress the power to abolish or interfere, within any State, with the domestic institutions thereof, including that of persons held to labor or service by the laws of said State.[12]

---

[9] H.R., 1 Cong., 2 Sess., *Journal* (1826 ed.), 181 (March 23, 1790), Report of the Committee of the Whole House. A parallel report by a special committee had ended its discussion of this particular point with an expression of "the fullest confidence in the wisdom and humanity of the Legislatures of the several States, that they will . . . promote . . . every . . . measure that may tend to the happiness of slaves." *Ibid.*, 180. The special committee was appointed on Feb. 12 and reported on March 5; the report was debated for five days (March 16–19 and 22) in a committee of the whole house, which reported on March 22. In the end the House itself adopted neither report but instead voted, 29 to 25, that both reports "be inserted in the Journal" and then allowed to lie on the table. *Ibid.*, 157, 168, 176–81. The various debates on slavery during this session are in *Annals*, 1 Cong., 2 Sess., 1182–91, 1197–1205, 1414–17, 1450–74. See also William Maclay, *Journal . . . 1789–1791* (New York, 1890), 196, 221–22.

[10] By Arthur Livermore (N. H.), H.R., April 4, 1818, and by John Quincy Adams (Mass.), H.R., Feb. 25, 1839. Herman V. Ames, *The Proposed Amendments to the Constitution . . . during the First Century of Its History* (American Historical Association, *Annual Report for 1896*, II, Washington, 1897), 334, 349 (items 474, 697–99).

[11] For example, by John R. J. Daniel (N. C.), H.R., July 6, 1850. *Ibid.*, 354 (item 764). Others are noted, *ibid.*, 193, 195–97.

[12] Joint resolution to amend the Constitution, March 2, 1861. *U. S. Statutes at Large*, XII: 251. The inept syntax almost prevented passage. *Congressional Globe*, 36 Cong., 2 Sess., 1364–67 (hereafter cited as *Globe*).

This measure, be it noted, was not designed to inflame antislavery opinion and stir up controversy. On the contrary, it was an attempt at conciliation. As such, it was supported by Republicans who, at the very same time, were adamant against any compromise that might permit slavery to enter the territories. In its final form, the amendment was actually introduced by a Republican.[13] Republican votes contributed substantially to the two-thirds majority required for passage by the two houses.[14] The incoming Republican President, Abraham Lincoln, gave the amendment guarded approval in his Inaugural Address, delivered the day after Congress submitted the measure to the states. Pointing out that he considered "such a provision to now be implied constitutional law," Lincoln announced that he had "no objection to its being made express, and irrevocable." [15] The amendment was actually ratified by three of the states—two of them free—before events crowded it into oblivion.[16]

In supporting this iron-clad guarantee of slavery within the slaveholding states, the Republicans were not abandoning, but were reaffirming, their previously announced position. The fourth plank of their 1860 platform had said:

> That the maintenance inviolate of the rights of the states, and especially the right of each state to order and control its own domestic institutions according to its own judgment exclusively, is essential to that balance of powers on which the perfection and endurance of our political fabric depends. . . .[17]

Lincoln quoted this paragraph in his Inaugural Address, and quoted also a passage from an earlier speech of his own: "I have no purpose, directly or indirectly, to interfere with the institution of slavery in the States where it exists. I believe I have no lawful right to do so, and I have no inclination to do so." [18]

In view of this record of consistent acceptance by antislavery groups of

---

[13] Thomas Corwin (Ohio), H.R., Feb. 27, 1861. *Globe*, 36 Cong., 2 Sess., 1263. In debate, authorship was attributed to no less a figure than William H. Seward, about to become Lincoln's Secretary of State. *Ibid.*, 1284.

[14] The proposed amendment passed the House, 133 to 65, on Feb. 28, 1861. *Ibid.*, 1285. In the Senate the resolution was debated through most of the night of Sunday, March 3, 1861, the eve of Lincoln's inauguration. It finally passed 24 to 12—eight Republicans, eight Democrats from free states, and eight members from slave states joining in the affirmative vote. *Ibid.*, 1403 (legislative day, March 2). Party affiliations are in *Tribune Almanac and Political Register for 1861*, p. 17.

[15] Roy P. Basler, ed., Marion Dolores Pratt and Lloyd A. Dunlap, asst. eds., *The Collected Works of Abraham Lincoln* (New Brunswick, N. J., 1953), IV: 270.

[16] By Ohio (free state), May 13, 1861; Maryland (slaveholding), Jan. 10, 1862; Illinois (free), Feb. 14, 1862. Ames, *Proposed Amendments*, 363 (item 931).

[17] Porter and Johnson, *National Party Platforms*, 32.

[18] *Collected Works*, IV: 263; quoting from his first debate with Douglas, Ottawa, Ill., Aug. 21, 1858, *ibid.*, III: 16.

the constitutional principle that the slaveholding states possessed plenary authority over slavery within their borders, what is one to make of the charge, endlessly repeated, that the opponents of slavery, and the Republicans in particular, believed "that a war must be waged against slavery until it shall cease throughout the United States"? [19]

Part of the answer, obviously, is that such assertions represented sheer distrust and hatred of abolitionists and "Black Republicans," the kind of hatred summed up in De Bow's definition of "Yankees" as "that species of the human race who foster in their hearts lying, hypocrisy, deceit, and treason." [20] Undoubtedly multitudes of men and women in the seceding states believed that the Republicans, once installed in power, would simply repudiate their constitutional professions and proceed to launch a direct federal attack upon the system of slavery inside the boundaries of the slaveholding states.[21]

---

[19] South Carolina, "Declaration," Dec. 24, 1860. *Journal of the Convention*, 465.

[20] *De Bow's Review*, XXIII (1857): 209, quoted in J. G. de Roulhac Hamilton, "Lincoln's Election an Immediate Menace to Slavery in the States?" *American Historical Review*, XXXVII (July, 1932): 710.

[21] The fact that slavery was, in fact, abolished before the end of the Civil War is sometimes taken as proof of Republican duplicity in 1860–1861. Such a view overlooks the enormous changes wrought in the situation by the coming of war and also disregards the constitutional grounds on which successive actions, from 1862 to 1865, were based. For present purposes, it is the latter point only that calls for discussion. In 1862, the second year of the war, Congress abolished slavery in the District of Columbia and in the territories. Acts of April 16, 1862, chap. 54, and June 19, 1862, chap. 111, *U. S. Stat. at L.*, XII: 376, 432. Both measures were in accord with the avowed constitutional theory of the Republicans.

The most significant step was, of course, the Emancipation Proclamation (preliminary, Sept. 22, 1862; final, Jan. 1, 1863). This did not apply to slavery within the states that were loyal to the Union, but only to specified areas actually in arms against the United States. It did not represent the assertion of a federal power over slavery as such, but was justified solely by military necessity and was made to rest upon the so-called "war powers" of the executive. Lincoln's words were carefully chosen: "by virtue of the power in me vested as Commander-in-Chief, of the Army and Navy of the United States in time of actual armed rebellion against [the] authority and government of the United States, and as a fit and necessary war measure for suppressing said rebellion." *Collected Works*, VI: 29 (for preliminary proclamation, see *ibid.*, V: 433–36). Likewise based upon military necessity was the second confiscation act of July 17, 1862, chap. 195, the ninth section of which gave freedom to slaves belonging to Confederate owners if the slaves escaped to the Union lines or were captured. *Stat. at L.*, XII: 589, at 591.

Throughout the whole period, Union leaders recognized that only a constitutional amendment could permit interference with slavery within the *loyal* slaveholding states. Lincoln proposed such a constitutional amendment, providing for gradual emancipation with federal financial aid, in his annual message to Congress on Dec. 1, 1862. *Collected Works*, V: 529–30. He had outlined the plan in a special message of March 6, 1862. *Ibid.*, 144–46. In the end, of course, slavery was definitively abolished by constitutional amendment—the Thirteenth—introduced on Jan. 11, 1864, reported in amended form by the judiciary committee of the Senate on Feb. 10, 1864, passed by the Senate on April 8, 1864 and by the House on Jan. 31, 1865, and proclaimed a part of the Constitution (after ratification by three fourths of the states) on Dec. 18, 1865. Ames, *Proposed Amendments*, 366–67 (items 983, 985). The earliest amendments to this effect were proposed on Dec. 14, 1863—the first of the sort since 1839. *Ibid.*, 366 (items 981–82).

Distrust, however, was not the whole of the matter. When we look carefully at the phrases used by the opposing sides, we discover that their statements were not, as they first appear to be, mutually contradictory. Lincoln's pledge not to "interfere with the institution of slavery in the States where it exists" was simply a pledge not to take federal action against slavery within the confines of the slaveholding states. It did not deny the intention of the Republicans to employ against slavery every power falling within the normal domain of federal action, and did not deny the aim of constricting and hampering the institution "until it shall cease throughout the United States." On the other hand, the charge directed by South Carolina against the Republicans was not necessarily a charge that they intended to abolish slavery by direct federal action within the states. From the proslavery point of view, there was no difference between direct and indirect action. The very fact that a measure was deliberately designed to undermine slavery made it automatically unconstitutional, no matter how indirect the means employed.[22] This difference of viewpoint was the crux of the constitutional controversy of 1846–1860.

EXTRATERRITORIAL IMPLICATIONS OF SLAVERY

The question at issue—and this is a point of fundamental importance—was not the institution of slavery itself as it existed within the boundaries of a slaveholding state. These formed an impregnable barrier against federal interference, as even the most ardent opponents of slavery were bound to concede. That they did concede the point is proved by the very form the dispute over slavery assumed. The fact that the controversy of 1846–1860 turned on the extension of slavery to the territories (and, to a lesser extent, on the fugitive-slave law) showed that antislavery leaders, far from flouting the Constitution, were showing it a punctilious respect. Had they been disposed, as their opponents alleged, to ride roughshod over constitutional limitations, they would hardly have bothered with the question of the territories or the question of fugitive slaves. If direct federal action against slavery in the states had been constitutionally thinkable, there would have been no reason to fritter effort away on tangential matters involving, not the great mass of bondsmen, but only a scattered few.

There was an opposite face to this coin. Had the defenders of slavery, for their part, been confident that the institution was safe behind its state-erected bastions, they too would have had little reason to stake so much on peripheral issues like the territories and the handful of escaping slaves. Their conduct revealed their fears. Slavery, they believed, could easily be imperiled by forces that existed and events that occurred in areas beyond the limits within which the institution was established and pro-

---

[22] See n. 99 below.

tected. On one proposition both sides agreed: that slavery could be dealt a fatal blow by federal policies that were operative only outside the boundaries of the slaveholding states.

The struggle that took place between 1846 and 1860 was a struggle for control over these external policies. It was, in short, a controversy over the *extraterritorial* protection that the institution of slavery was entitled to enjoy. The extraterritorial implications of slavery—seldom described in these terms and seldom analyzed to determine their true nature—provide the indispensable key to an understanding of the constitutional controversy of 1846–1860. To explore the ramifications of this concept is the task before us.

Extraterritoriality is, first of all, a concept of international law. Significant, therefore, is the fact that the extraterritorial claims of the slaveholding states—that is to say, their assertion of a power to take action beyond their own boundaries to repress influences deemed inimical to slavery— were baldly asserted, at the very beginning of the period of controversy, in several diplomatic communications. In 1843 Great Britain was supposedly encouraging the independent Republic of Texas to undertake compensated emancipation. Alarmed by this, the American Secretary of State, Abel P. Upshur of Virginia, sent confidential instructions to the minister of the United States at the Court of St. James's, Edward Everett. Upshur wrote as follows:

> It is quite obvious that slavery could not easily be maintained in a country surrounded by other countries whose Governments did not recognise that institution. The difficulty in the present case would be increased by the fact that those countries would be inhabited by people of the same race with the slave owners, speaking the same language, having the same manners, and in many respects the same institutions. Our slaveholding States are separated from the Canadas by many intervening non-slaveholding States of our Union. Although those non-slaveholding States are as much opposed to the institution as England herself, yet the Constitution of the United States lays them under obligations in regard to it, which, if duly respected, would secure the rights of the slaveholder. . . .
>
> Texas, however, lies immediately on the border of Louisiana and Arkansas. The slave would have nothing more to do than simply to cross the Sabine or the Red river, and he would find himself a freeman. He would be very sure to profit by the opportunity. All the vigilance which the master could use, enforced even by a harsher discipline than he would be willing to exert, would avail nothing. Within a few years a large proportion of the slaves within reach of the border would seek refuge in Texas; and the remainder would be rendered valueless, by discontent and dangerous insubordination. The slaveholder ought not to submit, and would not submit, to this.[23]

[23] A. P. Upshur to Edward Everett, Sept. 28, 1843 (confidential), in Senate Document 341, 28 Cong., I Sess., 34–35.

Several weeks earlier Upshur had spelled out what he meant by saying that slaveholders "ought not to submit, and would not submit." In a communication to General W. S. Murphy, American chargé d'affaires in Texas, Upshur described the probable consequences of emancipation in that republic:

> Even if this Government should interpose for the protection of the slaveholder, it would be very difficult so to arrange the subject as to avoid disputes and collisions. The States immediately interested would be most likely to take the subject into their own hands. . . . They would assume the right to reclaim their slaves by force, and for that purpose would invade the territory of Texas.[24]

This was an extreme statement of the view that the slaveholding states were justified in attempting to control the internal policies of other states whenever those policies threatened, even indirectly, to affect the institution of slavery adversely. Upshur wished to incorporate this extraterritorial principle into our relations with foreign states, and he appeared even to condone irregular armed incursions to enforce the demand. As applied to states within the American Union, the extraterritorial claim was translated into constitutional language and the hint of violent self-help disappeared. Nevertheless the doctrine still involved the extraterritorial protection of slavery.

THE QUESTION OF FUGITIVE SLAVES

One extraterritorial right connected with slavery was clearly and explicitly recognized by the written Constitution of the United States. Upshur alluded to it. This was the right of a slaveowner to reclaim a slave who might escape into a free state. The constitutional provision on the subject had so important a bearing on all the extraterritorial claims advanced in behalf of slavery that it should be quoted in full:

> No Person held to Service or Labour in one State, under the Laws thereof, escaping into another, shall, in Consequence of any Law or Regulation therein, be discharged from such Service or Labour, but shall be delivered up on Claim of the Party to whom such Service or Labour may be due.[25]

The most significant fact about the fugitive-slave cause was that it provided for the extraterritorial operation of the laws of the slaveholding

---

[24] Upshur to Murphy, Aug. 8, 1843. *Ibid.*, 21. Further discussion of the international implications of slavery is beyond the scope of the present paper. On the abolition of the foreign slave trade and on such cases as those of the *Amistad* and the *Creole,* see any of the standard histories.

[25] Constitution of the United States, Art. IV, sec. 2, clause 3. Curiously enough, escape into a free *territory* was covered only by implication. Even the bitterest opponents of slavery, however, declined to split this particular hair.

states. If a slave escaped from his master, the laws of the state where he had been held in bondage clung to him, no matter to what part of the Union he might flee. With respect to him, the federal Constitution itself automatically annulled any law of a free state that might tend to emancipate him. The fugitive-slave clause was of unique importance to the proslavery argument. Not only was it the only provision of the Constitution that explicitly recognized the slaveowner's right of property in his slave, it was also—and more importantly—the only one that gave any extraterritorial effect to state laws establishing slavery. As such, it provided the indispensable foundation for every other type of extraterritorial claim in behalf of slavery. Whether the number of escaping slaves was large or small made little difference.[26] The fugitive-slave clause must be sustained because its collapse would mean the collapse of the entire contention that the federal government was bound to safeguard slavery outside the institution's established borders.

The principle at stake was so vital to the proslavery argument that extravagant assertions were constantly made to the effect that the fugitive-slave clause represented a fundamental bargain struck at the time the Constitution was drafted. Thus Lawrence M. Keitt of South Carolina told the House of Representatives that "the fugitive slave clause was put into the Constitution as the price of the splendid cession of the Northwest by Virginia, and as the price of the Government, too." [27] John J. Jones of Georgia insisted that "without such a constitutional guarantee it is evident that the slaveholding States never would have ratified the Constitution." [28] Robert Toombs of Georgia asserted that the obligation to return fugitive slaves, far from originating in the Constitution, "has been a fundamental principle of society for thirty centuries." [29] The facts were rather different.

---

[26] On the controversial question of the numbers involved, see Allan Nevins, *The Emergence of Lincoln* (New York, 1950), II: 489.

[27] Jan. 25, 1860. *Globe,* 36 Cong., 1 Sess., App., 96. Certain principles of the law of contracts explain this insistence that the fugitive-slave clause was an absolutely fundamental constitutional bargain. "Before partial failure of performance of one party will give the other the right of rescission, the act failed to be performed must go to the root of the contract, or the failure to perform the contract must be in respect to matters which would render the performance of the rest a thing different in substance from that which was contracted for." On the other hand, if "a breach . . . deprives the injured party of a benefit of but one of [the] subsidiary provisions or promises," then "he is left to redress his injury by an action for compensation in damages." William M. McKinney and Burdett A. Rich, eds., *Ruling Case Law,* VI (Northport, N. Y., 1915): 926. With the possibility of secession in their minds, proslavery leaders were insisting that failure to enforce the fugitive-slave clause abrogated the whole Constitution. They were outraged by a proposal that compensation for escaped slaves be substituted for enforcement of the fugitive-slave law. See Alexander H. Stephens, *A Constitutional View of the Late War between the States* (Philadelphia, 1868–1870), II: 48–49, 58, 77–79.

[28] H.R., April 23, 1860. *Globe,* 36 Cong., 1 Sess., App., 246. The seventh of Jefferson Davis's resolutions in the Senate in 1860 (see n. 116 below) dealt with the fugitive-slave clause "without the adoption of which the Union could not have been formed." *Globe,* 36 Cong., 1 Sess., 2350 (resolution adopted May 25, 1860).

[29] Senate, Jan. 24, 1860. *Globe,* 36 Cong., 1 Sess., App., 89.

A fugitive-slave clause had been inserted in the Northwest Ordinance of July 13, 1787, *coupled* with a provision prohibiting slavery throughout the entire region.[30] Near the end of the Constitutional Convention, on August 28, 1787, a similar provision for the return of fugitive slaves was proposed and briefly discussed. The next day the clause, slightly altered in form, was adopted *nemine contradicente*.[31] The following year, in the Virginia ratifying convention, James Madison put the clause in a perspective totally different from Toombs's. "At present," he said, "if any slave elopes to any of those states where slaves are free, he becomes emancipated by their laws. For the laws of the states are uncharitable to one another in this respect." The fugitive-slave clause of the proposed Constitution, Madison continued, "was expressly inserted to enable owners of slaves to reclaim them. This is a better security than any that now exists." [32]

The fugitive-slave clause was hardly a fundamental compact, but it *was* a provision of the Constitution, and a failure to enforce it was a quite legitimate grievance. The more conservative leaders of the Republican Party recognized the obligation. "It is scarcely questioned," said Lincoln in his first Inaugural Address, "that this provision was intended by those who made it, for the reclaiming of what we call fugitive slaves; and the intention of the law-giver is the law. All members of Congress swear their support to the whole Constitution—to this provision as much as to any other." Ought anyone, he asked, to "be content that his oath shall go unkept, on a merely unsubstantial controversy as to *how* it shall be kept?" [33]

Lincoln was undoubtedly sincere, but he did not speak in this matter for important segments of his own party. Ardent abolitionists had long gloried in defying and violating the fugitive-slave act. Even before the law was made harsher in 1850, the Liberty Party had declared in its platform of 1844 that the fugitive-slave clause of the Constitution was contrary both to the laws of God and to natural right, hence "utterly null and void," and that it was to be regarded "as forming no part of the Constitution of the United States." [34] After the new fugitive-slave law of 1850 was enacted, open and organized violation of its provisions—through the so-called "Underground Railway" and through deliberately publicized slave rescues— became commonplace.

OBJECTIONS TO THE FUGITIVE-SLAVE ACT

It was not defiance of the law, however, but attempted nullification of it, that made the question of fugitive slaves a constitutional issue. And nullifi-

---

[30] Clarence E. Carter, ed., *Territorial Papers of the United States,* II (Washington, 1934): 49.

[31] Max Farrand, ed., *Records of the Federal Convention of 1787* (New Haven, 1911–1937), II: 443, 453–54. A slight verbal revision was made on Sept. 15, 1787. *Ibid.,* 628.

[32] *Ibid.,* III: 325 (June 17, 1788).   [33] *Collected Works,* IV: 263–64.

[34] Porter and Johnson, *National Party Platforms,* 8.

cation did not mean a total repudiation of the constitutional obligation. It represented, instead, a denial of the constitutionality of the *statute* of 1850 by which the obligation was enforced. There were substantial grounds for such constitutional obection. The fugitive-slave law of 1850 authorized summary procedures lacking virtually all the normal legal safeguards that are summed up in the phrase of the Bill of Rights, "due process of law." Decisions were not to be made by regularly constituted courts but by court-appointed commissioners who exercised simply the powers of a justice of the peace. No jury trial was provided. The only evidence required was the deposition or affidavit of the claimant. The statute ordered that "in no trial or hearing under this act shall the testimony of such alleged fugitive be admitted in evidence." The commissioner who decided the claim would receive, for sending a Negro back into bondage, twice the fee he could col-lect were he to find the man free. And the commissioner's decision, once made, constituted a complete answer to a writ of *habeas corpus* issued by any court, state or federal.[35] Provisions like these appeared to antislavery men to subvert constitutional rights of a far more fundamental character than any the fugitive-slave clause was designed to protect. Representative James Wilson of Indiana stated the issue clearly:

> But why is this act offensive? It is not in the unwillingness on the part of the people of the free States to permit the rendition of a fugitive slave. . . . Sir, it lies deeper, and far beyond. It is in the conviction that this fugitive slave law comes in conflict with and up-roots great fundamental principles, and assumes unwarrantable and dangerous powers. Is this so? Is this true? Examine the law. Does it not recognize an officer unknown to the Constitution? Does it not deny the trial by jury in the issue of liberty? Does it not set at defiance the sovereignty of the State? . . . Does it not withhold the great writ of *habeas corpus*? I repeat again, examine the law. For this cause it is that the law has been arraigned and condemned by the people of the free States.[36]

Defenders of the fugitive-slave act of 1850 argued "that the law was not intended to try the right of property, whether the fugitive was the property of the claimant, or whether he was free; that the Constitution did not de-sign that, but that, if there was to be any question about the right of property, it was to be determined in the State whence the fugitive es-caped." [37] This answer might be technically correct, but from the anti-slavery point of view it was quite unsatisfactory. Slave property, James Wilson insisted, should "be reclaimed and surrendered under the same

---

[35] Fugitive-slave act, Sept. 18, 1850, chap. 60. *U. S. Stat. at L.*, IX: 462. The quoted sentence is from the sixth section, which included most of the other provisions mentioned; fees were prescribed in the eighth section.

[36] H.R., May 1, 1860. *Globe*, 36 Cong., 1 Sess., App., 323.

[37] James M. Mason (Va.), Senate, May 25, 1860. *Globe*, 36 Cong., 1 Sess., 2351.

rules of evidence, and with the same restrictions, as other property." [38]
Moreover, the right to property was only part of the question; the right to
liberty was involved as well. There always existed a possible doubt whether
a particular Negro who might be pointed out as a fugitive slave was so in
fact. This particular fact, insisted the opponents of the fugitive-slave law,
should be judicially determined before the individual was removed from
the jurisdiction of a free state and placed on the soil of a slaveholding one,
the laws of which made different presumptions. Because the liberty of a
man who might be a freeman was at stake, the issue should be tried by
jury; and the state of which he might in fact be a bona fide resident ought
to be able to protect him against kidnapping by issuing the writ of *habeas
corpus*. John P. Hale of New Hampshire summed up the antislavery objection in a speech to the Senate in 1860:

> The great mistake of the gentlemen who passed this law . . . is this:
> they assume at the outset that the man whom they claim is a slave, and
> they give him no sort of rights as a freeman, but only the rights of
> a slave after that. That is what I complain of; that you may go into
> one of the free States under this law, and lay your hand on a man
> who was born there, has lived there all his life, and if he comes within
> the description of your *ex parte* affidavits taken a thousand miles off,
> and [if] you can get a ten dollar commissioner to give a certificate, the
> *habeas corpus* of the State judiciary lies paralyzed at his feet, and the
> man who is claimed has to go.[39]

Though the dispute over fugitive slaves was in form a dispute over
statutory enactments and their effective enforcement, it was in reality a
dispute over the spirit in which the Constitution should be interpreted
when rights of different sorts came into conflict. Partisans of slavery could
find in the Constitution no provisions that applied in any way to Negroes,
save the one provision upholding the right of a slaveholder to his slave.
No other constitutional guarantees had any relevance, and to invoke them
was deliberate obstructionism. Representative Eli S. Shorter of Alabama put
the matter bluntly:

> If fugitive slaves are to have the benefit of the writ of habeas corpus
> and jury trial in the North, the South might as well consent at once
> to strike out from our Constitution the right of recapture. We want
> the *substance*, not the mere *shadow* of our rights.[40]

---

[38] *Globe,* 36 Cong., 1 Sess., App., 323.   [39] May 25, 1860. *Globe,* 36 Cong., 1 Sess., 2351.

[40] H.R., April 9, 1856. *Globe,* 34 Cong., 1 Sess., App., 396. Shorter destroyed whatever
foundation his argument might have had, by going on to assert that the federal "fugitive
slave law of 1850 *denies* to the slave the right of trial by jury and habeas corpus," and
by arguing from this that a state personal-liberty law is invalid because it "*confers* that
right upon him, and thereby conflicts with the act of Congress" (italics added). *Ibid.*
These contentions cannot be reconciled with any possible theory of the American Constitution, which never treats rights as having been *conferred* by government of any sort.
To say that an act of Congress *denied* the writ of *habeas corpus* in peacetime to any per-

From the antislavery point of view, on the other hand, the rights of persons, especially the right to impartial legal procedures, were guaranteed by the Constitution just as explicitly, and even more comprehensively and absolutely, than the property rights arising from slaveownership. This was, at bottom, what was meant by a "higher law." The idea foreshadowed the more generalized mid-twentieth-century doctrine that certain guarantees of the Bill of Rights occupy a "preferred position" in the hierarchy of constitutional values.[41]

This deep-lying constitutional conflict—between the right to property and the right to liberty—was never seriously considered by the Supreme Court while slavery existed. The fugitive-slave act of 1850 was, it is true, upheld by a unanimous court, but in an exceedingly offhand way:

> But although we think it unnecessary to discuss these questions, yet, as they have been decided by the state court, and are before us on the record, and we are not willing to be misunderstood, it is proper to say that, in the judgment of this court, the act of Congress commonly called the fugitive slave act is, in all of its provisions, fully authorized by the Constitution of the United States.[42]

It was not the question of personal liberty but a much more technical question—albeit one of great constitutional importance—that brought the

---

sons who might conceivably be entitled to it was to admit the unconstitutionality of the act, in view of the provision of the federal Constitution that the writ "shall not be suspended, unless when in Cases of Rebellion or Invasion the public Safety may require it." Art. I, sec. 9, clause 2. The only argument that could possibly be made to hold water was Taney's, namely that the Constitution regarded "the negro race as a separate class of persons," not "a portion of the people or citizens of the Government," and that it did not intend "to confer on them or their posterity the blessings of liberty, or any of the personal rights so carefully provided for the citizen." Dred Scott v. Sandford, 19 Howard 393, at 411 (March 6, 1857).

[41] For a concise discussion of Supreme Court opinions, pro and con, on the idea of "preferred position," see Edward S. Corwin, ed., *The Constitution of the United States of America: Analysis and Interpretation* (Washington, 1953), 789–91.

[42] Ableman v. Booth, and U. S. v. Booth, 21 Howard 506, at 526 (March 7, 1859). The Supreme Judicial Court of Massachusetts had upheld the constitutionality of the fugitive-slave law of 1850 shortly after its enactment. Thomas Sims's case, 7 Cushing 285 (April 7, 1851). Two months after the decision in Ableman v. Booth, the Supreme Court of Ohio likewise upheld the act, citing the opinion of the United States Supreme Court, of course, but also independently examining the precedents and arguments. The Ohio court divided three to two, and in the four opinions filed the various constitutional issues involved were given the most thorough consideration they were ever to receive at the hands of any judicial body. Ex parte Bushnell, and Ex parte Langston, 9 Ohio State Reports 77 (May, 1859). With the outbreak of the Civil War, the fugitive-slave act became almost a dead letter, though it was not finally repealed until June 28, 1864, chap. 166. *U. S. Stat. at L.*, XIII: 200. In the meantime, on March 13, 1862, chap. 40, Congress had expressly forbidden the use of military personnel "for the purpose of returning fugitives from service or labor, who may have escaped from any persons"—including persons in the loyal slaveholding states. *Stat. at L.*, XII: 354. Nominally the latter might still employ civil procedures under the act. Reviewing the issues from the perspective of 1921 (which is not necessarily the perspective of 1961), Allen Johnson reached the conclusion that the fugitive-slave acts were "constitutional in every particular." Johnson, "The Constitutionality of the Fugitive-Slave Acts," *Yale Law Journal*, XXXI (Nov., 1921): 161–82.

fugitive-slave act before the Supreme Court and occasioned the decision containing the perfunctory sentence just quoted.

PERSONAL LIBERTY LAWS AND THE BOOTH CASE

The written Constitution was quite clear in upholding the right of a slaveowner to recapture his escaped slave, but it was highly ambiguous in assigning responsibility for making this right effective. The fugitive-slave clause was closely associated with a clause for the extradition of criminals, and this association suggested that individual states might be expected to deal with fugitive slaves as a matter of interstate comity. On the other hand, the right to reclaim slaves was a right guaranteed by the federal Constitution, and from this could be inferred both a federal power and a federal duty. In 1842 a majority of the Supreme Court took the latter view, not only upholding the federal fugitive-slave act of 1793 (and paving the way for the subsequent act of 1850) but also asserting that the individual states had no concurrent power (and hence no concurrent responsibility) in the matter.[43] This ruling (by a divided court) was an open invitation to states with antislavery leanings not only to refuse co-operation but also to experiment with statutes—the so-called "personal libery laws" —that placed every legal obstacle that ingenuity could devise athwart the path of the would-be recoverer of an escaped slave.

These actions by the free states constituted "interposition" and "nullification," in a pure and classic sense. Indeed, the personal-liberty laws stood in a much more direct line of descent from the Kentucky and Virginia Resolutions of 1798 than did any of the ingenious theories elaborated by John C. Calhoun in the late 1820's and 1830's.[44] The personal-liberty laws applied the doctrine of interposition to exactly the kind of situation that, in 1798, prompted Jefferson and Madison to promulgate the original theory.[45] In 1798 and in the 1850's the federal law being challenged was

---

[43] Prigg v. Pennsylvania, 16 Peters 539 (1842).

[44] Calhoun's argument in 1828–1832 for nullifying the tariff diverged, in highly significant ways, from the argument used to justify interposition both in the late 1790's against the sedition act and in the 1850's against the fugitive-slave act. Calhoun was seeking to defend the economic interests of a state, not the freedom of any of its citizens. He and his followers were not arguing that the tariff infringed upon rights guaranteed to individuals by the Constitution; they merely argued that the tariff represented the *misuse* of a power—the "Power to lay and collect Taxes, Duties, Imposts and Excises"— delegated in set terms to the federal government. And South Carolina, following his lead, asserted, on the part of the state, not a mere power to protect its own citizens against the penalties they might incur for violation of an allegedly unconstitutional statute, but a power to suspend the law in its entirety and to use the full power of the state "to prevent the enforcement and arrest the operation" of the federal statute. Massachusetts, General Court, *State Papers on Nullification* (Boston, 1834); see p. 29 for the quoted phrase from the nullification ordinance of South Carolina, Nov. 24, 1832.

[45] See Adrienne Koch and Harry Ammon, "The Virginia and Kentucky Resolutions: An Episode in Jefferson's and Madison's Defense of Civil Liberties," *William and Mary Quarterly*. Third Series, V (April, 1948): 145–76.

one that, in the opinion of its opponents, not only deprived individuals of personal freedom but also, by its very manner of doing so, violated both the letter and the spirit of specific constitutional guarantees of individual rights. On both occasions the opponents of the measure were thoroughly convinced that the federal courts, in view of their existing attitude, would never rule against the validity of the statute in question. On both occasions, accordingly, opponents of the law argued that it was within the competence of a state to interpose its authority as a shield to protect persons within its own jurisdiction from deprivation of their constitutionally guaranteed personal rights.

The conflict between the constitutional philosophy embodied in the personal-liberty laws of the various northern states and the constitutional philosophy embodied in the fugitive-slave act of 1850 came to a head in the welter of cases that arose, in state and federal courts, out of the rescue of a fugitive slave who had been apprehended by his master in Wisconsin in 1854. The principal figure in the mob that snatched the slave from jail and spirited him off to Canada and freedom was an abolitionist editor named Sherman M. Booth. Prosecuted by federal authorities as a violator of the fugitive-slave act, Booth was twice freed, in 1854 and 1855, from federal custody by writs of *habeas corpus* issued by the Wisconsin Supreme Court, one writ preceding and one following his conviction in a district court of the United States. The Wisconsin judiciary declared the federal fugitive-slave act unconstitutional and argued that unless the state could liberate its own citizens from imprisonment under an invalid statute, then it "would present the spectacle of a state claiming the allegiance of its citizens, without the power to protect them in the enjoyment of their personal liberty upon its own soil." [46] Here, succinctly stated, is the original state-rights doctrine of the Kentucky and Virginia Resolutions of 1798.

The various cases, considered together on appeal, were finally decided by the United States Supreme Court on March 7, 1859, with Chief Justice Roger B. Taney speaking for a unanimous court. Taney overruled the Wisconsin Judiciary on all points and upheld the supremacy of the federal Constitution and the federal courts so forcefully as "to enhance the federal judicial power to a degree beyond that envisaged even by Marshall and Story." [47] The question of sovereignty was discussed, and the court re-

---

[46] In re Booth and Rycraft, 3 Wisconsin 157, at 176, opinion of Chief Justice Edward V. Whiton (Feb. 3, 1855). See also (for the first writ issued) In re Sherman Booth, 3 Wisconsin.

[47] Corwin, ed., *Constitution . . . Analysis*, 555. The allusions are to Justice Joseph Story's decision in Martin v. Hunter's Lessee, 1 Wheaton 304 (March 20, 1816), and Chief Justice John Marshall's decision in Cohens v. Virginia, 6 Wheaton 264 (March 3, 1821). One might add that Taney's statement of national supremacy was as sweeping as President Andrew Jackson's in his proclamation to the people of South Carolina, Dec. 10, 1832. *State Papers on Nullification*, 75–97. The precedent is apposite because Taney was Jackson's Attorney General at the time, though he did not, it is true, participate actively in the drafting of the proclamation, which was largely the work of Edward Livingston. Carl B. Swisher, *Roger B. Taney* (New York, 1935), 207.

jected completely the contention that sovereignty could not be divided, that it inhered in the states alone, and that the federal government lacked its attributes.

On the contrary, Taney argued as follows:

> There can be no such thing as judicial authority, unless it is conferred by a Government or sovereignty; and if the judges and courts of Wisconsin possess the jurisdiction they claim, they must derive it either from the United States or the State. It certainly has not been conferred on them by the United States; and it is equally clear it was not in the power of the State to confer it, even if it had attempted to do so; for no State can authorize one of its judges or courts to exercise judicial power, by *habeas corpus* or otherwise, within the jurisdiction of another and independent Government. And although the State of Wisconsin is sovereign within its territorial limits to a certain extent, yet that sovereignty is limited and restricted by the Constitution of the United States.

The statesmen who framed the Constitution and the people who adopted it were convinced, said Taney,

> that it was necessary that many of the rights of sovereignty which the States then possessed should be ceded to the General Government; and that, in the sphere of action assigned to it, it should be supreme, and strong enough to execute its own law by its own tribunals, without interruption from a State or from State authorities.[48]

Taney's argument for the judicial supremacy of the federal government was so sweeping, and his commitment to the idea of divided sovereignty so complete, that at first glance he would appear to have struck a fatal blow at the entire doctrine of state sovereignty. In the long run, so far as constitutional law was concerned, the decision in Ableman v. Booth did have precisely this effect. In any discussion of national supremacy the case is almost certain to figure among the important precedents. And, by the irony of history, it is cited in many recent decisions striking down measures adopted by various southern states (in the name of state sovereignty), as part of their campaign of resistance to racial desegregation by court order in the public schools.[49]

---

consin 1 (June 7, 1854); and (for a writ that was denied) Ex parte Sherman M. Booth, 3 Wisconsin 145 (July 21, 1854).

[48] Ableman v. Booth, 21 Howard 506, at 515, 517 (March 7, 1859).

[49] Notably in Cooper v. Aaron, 358 U. S. 1, at 18 (Sept. 29, 1958). See also the decision of the three-judge federal district court in New Orleans, Nov. 30, 1960, which examined at length the historic doctrine of interposition and rejected it with brusque finality as "an amorphous concept," which was clearly "not a *constitutional doctrine,*" but was, "if taken seriously," simply an "illegal defiance of constitutional authority." Bush v. Orleans Parish School Board, 188 Federal Supplement 916, at 922, 926 (Nov. 30, 1960); citing Ableman v. Booth at 925.

NATIONAL SUPREMACY AND STATE SOVEREIGNTY

In its immediate historical context—in 1859 and 1860—the decision in Ableman v. Booth did not, however, convey to the public mind the implication of unqualified national supremacy that it conveys today. The decision was welcomed, naturally enough, by the partisans of slavery. Furthermore, they were conscious of no inconsistency in hailing it as a triumph for their own position. They considered it not a repudiation of the doctrine of state sovereignty but a vindication of one of the most important corollaries of that doctrine—namely, its extraterritorial implications.

The paradox disappears if one pays close attention to the limits within which Taney was careful to confine his argument. It is an error to say, as is often loosely said, that the decision in Ableman v. Booth upheld federal supremacy in a comprehensive or inclusive sense. It upheld federal *judicial* supremacy only, the argument being closely confined to the power of that one branch of government. The limits to federal legislative power *might* have been examined had the constitutionality of the fugitive-slave act been discussed in detail. But Taney dismissed the latter question in a single sentence, devoid of argument or citation. Nothing whatever in the opinion could be taken to imply that the supremacy so sweepingly asserted on behalf of the federal judiciary *vis-à-vis* the judiciaries of the several states had any sort of counterpart in the legislative or executive realm. Quite the reverse. Taney included in his decision an explicit reminder that "it is the duty of the courts of the United States to declare . . . unconstitutional and void" any federal statute that transgressed the Constitution, and he pointed out that the courts, by doing so, would "guard the States from any encroachment upon their reserved rights by the General Government." [50]

Two years before, in the Dred Scott case, Taney had denied to Congress any legislative power whatever in a matter that had become of crucial importance—slavery in the territories. He was by no means reversing his earlier decision. On the contrary, he was buttressing it against attack. In the Dred Scott opinion, Taney had pitted the judicial power against the legislative; in Ableman v. Booth he was exalting the judicial power to new heights.

In legal form, the decision in Ableman v. Booth was a vindication of federal judicial supremacy. In the actual historical context, however, federal judicial supremacy did not mean the supremacy of national policy over local or sectional policy. It meant precisely the reverse. It meant the denial to the federal government of any discretionary, policy-making function whatever in the matter of slavery. Questions regarding slavery were to be

---

[50] Ableman v. Booth, 21 Howard 506, at 520.

settled by the states that recognized the institution. And the federal judiciary—acting under the Constitution (which likewise recognized slavery)—was bound to give effect, extraterritorially, to the legal principles developed by the slaveholding states in connection with the peculiar kind of property that they alone possessed and that they alone, accordingly, were competent to legislate about. Even within the boundaries of the free states, legal procedure was to follow strictly the pattern set by and within the slaveholding states, regardless of any concepts of due process of law that the free community might deem fundamental. The principle of extraterritoriality could hardly take a form more extreme.

The controversy that reached its climax in the Booth case is conventionally interpreted as a conflict between federal supremacy on the one hand and state rights or state sovereignty on the other. Much is naturally made of the irony of the situation, the two factions to the slavery dispute having apparently switched their constitutional positions abruptly, in flagrant pursuit of immediate advantage.[51] A much more subtle analysis is necessary. It was not federal supremacy in general that the court upheld, but federal *judicial* supremacy. And federal judicial supremacy simply provided the means of enforcing the extraterritorial principles deduced from state sovereignty. In this particular conflict—to assert a paradox—the doctrine of state sovereignty was pitted against the doctrine of state rights, and the doctrine of state sovereignty won.

To make this distinction intelligible, I must digress briefly and ask the reader to examine with care the exact terminology of the American Constitution.

"POWERS" AND "RIGHTS"

The written Constitution—with which, in the following discussion, the Bill of Rights is included—nowhere uses the words "sovereign" or "sovereignty." [52] Moreover, it knows nothing of "rights" belonging either to the

---

[51] Thus Carl Schurz, an actual participant, later described the contest as one "in which the Republican party, the natural opponent of the States' rights doctrine . . . , planted itself upon extreme States' rights ground and went to the very verge of actual nullification, while the Democratic party, the traditional champion of the States' rights doctrine, became an ardent defender of the Federal power as against any pretensions of States' rights." But, he continued, "only two years later, when the bulk of the Slave States . . . had carried the States' rights doctrine to the logical length of secession," their opponents "rushed to arms to maintain the supreme authority of the Federal Government and to put down the pretensions of States' rights which were made in favor of slavery." "It was one of those struggles," he observed (quoting a remark of Lincoln's), "which . . . become so mixed that, in the heat of the wrestle, the combatants worked themselves into one another's coats." Schurz, *Reminiscences* (New York, 1907), II: 114–15.

[52] The Articles of Confederation, agreed to by the Continental Congress on Nov. 15, 1777, and finally ratified on March 1, 1781, did include the following provision: "Each state retains its sovereignty, freedom, and independence, and every Power, Jurisdiction and right, which is not by this confederation expressly delegated to the United States, in

states or to the federal government. The foundation stone of the state-rights argument is the Tenth Amendment, but this amendment speaks not of the *rights* of the states but of their *powers:* "The powers not delegated to the United States, by the Constitution, nor prohibited by it to the States are reserved to the States respectively, or to the people." [53] The Constitution does, of course, speak frequently of "rights"—and occasionally of "privileges" or "immunities"—but in every instance the term refers to something possessed by an individual person, never something possessed, or capable of being possessed, by a government.[54] Frequently such an individual right is protected, not positively by specifying the right, but negatively by denying to government some corresponding power.[55]

A clear-cut distinction pervades the entire written document. On the one hand, there are *powers*, which are exercised by government, which can

---

Congress assembled." Art. II. Advocates of state sovereignty frequently argued that the Constitution of 1787 continued to embody the principle, though it conspicuously failed to include the clause.

[53] The amendment is often flagrantly misquoted. At the Democratic Convention in Los Angeles in 1960, the southern minority submitted a dissenting report on the platform, insisting on "strict adherence to the constitutional guarantee that all powers not delegated by the states to the Union are reserved to the states or to the people." *New York Times*, July 13, 1960. Though the majority was said to "ignore the Tenth Amendment," the accusatorial minority deliberately ignored its provision referring to "powers . . . prohibited by it [the Constitution] to the States"—which is, of course, the crux of the matter. The constitutional situation, often misrepresented, is simply as follows: By the Fourteenth Amendment, the Constitution prohibits to every state the power to "deny to any person within its jurisdiction the equal protection of the laws." The Supreme Court has ruled that "separate educational facilities are inherently unequal." Brown v. Board of Education of Topeka, 347 U. S. 483 (May 17, 1954). Accordingly, any state action to enforce segregation in the public schools constitutes the use by the state of a prohibited power to "deny to any person . . . the equal protection of the laws." Thus the Tenth Amendment, by specifically recognizing that there are "powers . . . prohibited . . . to the States," raises no barrier to, but in fact gives support to, desegregation. In simplest terms, the question is not about powers delegated to the federal government but about powers prohibited to the states.

[54] The body of the Constitution refers only once to a "right": it empowers Congress to secure "to Authors and Inventors the exclusive Right to their respective Writings and Discoveries." Art. I, sec. 8, clause 8. On the other hand, the word appears in six of the first ten amendments, thereby justifying the popular appellation, "Bill of Rights." The body of the Constitution speaks of "Privileges and Immunities of Citizens"; and it uses the term "privilege" in two other connections: members of Congress are "privileged from Arrest," and "the Privilege of the Writ of Habeas Corpus" is safeguarded. See, respectively, Art. IV, sec. 2, and Art. I, secs. 6 and 9. The Bill of Rights does not use the word "privilege," but the phrase "privileges or immunities of citizens" reappears in the Fourteenth Amendment (1868). The word "power" is used throughout the Constitution—so frequently as to require no illustration.

[55] One example will suffice to show the different modes by which a right is protected. The Seventh Amendment expressly *acknowledges* "the right of trial by jury," and the Sixth Amendment uses similar language. In the body of the Constitution, however, the same right is safeguarded by a positive *instruction:* "The Trial of all Crimes, except in Cases of Impeachment, shall be by Jury." Art. III, sec. 2. The Fifth Amendment uses a *prohibition* to protect a related right: "No person shall be held to answer for a capital, or otherwise infamous crime, unless on a presentment or indictment of a Grand Jury."

be apportioned among the various branches and levels of government, and which can be denied to the federal government or to the states or to both. On the other hand are *rights,* which are enjoyed by citizens or persons, which can be set forth in positive terms, and which can also be defined negatively, by denying to one or another government a corresponding power. No usage inconsistent with this distinction is to be found anywhere in the written Constitution.[56] The distinction is recognized with absolute clarity in the companion clause to the Tenth Amendment, namely the Ninth, which reads: "The enumeration in the Constitution, of certain rights, shall not be construed to deny or disparage others retained by the people." In summary, certain powers, but no rights, are delegated to the federal government. Certain other powers, but again no rights, are reserved to the states.[57] Other powers, ungranted to either type of government, remain in the hands of the people, thus creating for them a body of unalienated rights. Among these are certain rights that are considered not merely unalienated but (in the language of the Declaration of Independence) unalienable. The latter are guaranteed in specific, positive terms by various clauses of the Constitution. Moreover, the enumeration of these particular rights may "not be construed to deny or disparage others retained by the people."

Given this consistent terminology, the phrase "state rights" is, strictly speaking, a constitutional solecism. As a term denoting a specific constitutional principle, indeed, it does not appear to have been used until 1798, in the debates over the alien and sedition acts.[58] On this, its first appearance, however, the phrase was not so much a solecism as a bit of convenient shorthand. The question at issue—freedom of the press—involved a "right" in the strictest constitutional sense. The *power* of the state was thus being invoked to protect a *right.* Accordingly it is not a serious misuse of language to telescope the terms and describe the Kentucky and Virginia Resolutions

---

[56] The Declaration of Independence is equally consistent, notably in its most memorable passage. All men, it says, "are endowed by their Creator with certain unalienable *Rights.*" Governments, on the other hand, derive "their just *powers* from the consent of the governed." (Italics added.) There is much less consistency in the terminology of the Articles of Confederation, which often couples "right and power," as in granting to the United States in Congress assembled "the sole and exclusive right and power of determining on peace and war. . . ." Art. IX.

[57] As owners of property, of course, the states and the federal government do possess the ordinary rights associated with proprietorship. Moreover, they enjoy various immunities, both against one another (e.g., immunity from taxation) and against individual citizens (e.g., immunity from suit). These, however, are not the "rights" for which the state-rights argument contends.

[58] "The powers of our general Government are checked by State rights." Samuel Smith (Md.), H.R., June 21, 1798. *Annals,* 5 Cong., 2 Sess., 2022. Mitford M. Mathews, ed., *A Dictionary of Americanisms on Historical Principles* (Chicago, 1951), 1642, records no earlier use of the phrase in a technical constitutional sense. As a rhetorical expression, of course, it crops up earlier.

of 1798 as a defense of "state rights." Nor is the latter phrase inappropriate to describe state interposition against the fugitive-slave act in the 1850's.

STATE SOVEREIGNTY A DOCTRINE OF POWER

The doctrine of state rights, defined in this way, is a purely defensive doctrine. Arguments about sovereignty may be used to support it, but its spirit is essentially hostile to all the leading ideas associated with the concept of sovereignty—particularly with the concept of sovereignty as an indivisible and illimitable power, wielded by a definitive body, which must be the sole and final judge of its own authority. The latter conception, however, was central to the doctrine of state sovereignty. And its roots lay in a political tradition that the makers of the American Constitution had consciously rejected. In every form of government, Sir William Blackstone had written on the eve of the American Revolution, "there is and must be . . . a supreme, irresistible, absolute, uncontrolled authority, in which the *jura summi imperii,* or the rights of sovereignty, reside." [59] From such a postulate the British declaratory act of 1766 logically followed: that the King in Parliament "had, hath, and of right ought to have, full power and authority to make laws and statutes of sufficient force and validity to bind the colonies and people of *America,* subjects of the crown of *Great Britain,* in all cases whatsoever." [60]

The American Revolution involved a rejection not only of British sovereignty but also, in a profound and pervasive way, of the very concept of indivisible and uncontrollable sovereignty. The theory of divided sovereignty superseded it.[61] And the doctrine of state rights (as here defined) was perfectly compatible with the idea of divided sovereignty. By contrast, the doctrine of state sovereignty represented a return to the theory that sovereignty is, by its very nature, indivisible. Jefferson Davis, for example, dismissed the notion of divided sovereignty as "paradoxical." He insisted that "the only political community—the only independent corporate unit —through which the people can exercise their sovereignty, is the State." And he quoted with approval Burlamaqui's definition of sovereignty as "a right of commanding in the last resort in civil society." [62]

The doctrine of state sovereignty was not a doctrine of rights, but a doc-

---

[59] Blackstone, *Commentaries on the Laws of England* (1765–1769), Introduction, sec. 2, p. 49.

[60] 6 George III, chap. 12 (March 18, 1766). Accepted without question by Blackstone, Introduction, sec. 4, p. 109.

[61] The acceptance by the Constitutional Convention of 1787 of the principle of divided sovereignty will be discussed in the book from which the present paper is drawn. Space does not permit a recapitulation here. For the concept itself, however, see the quotations from Taney, n. 48 above.

[62] Jefferson Davis, *The Rise and Fall of the Confederate Government* (New York, 1881), I: 141–42.

trine of command and of power, imperious in its language, bristling with words like "supreme," "irresistible," "absolute," "uncontrolled," "paramount." Extraterritoriality, too, is an imperious principle, overriding local law and local custom and negating the idea of local self-government. These characteristics appeared in the conflict over fugitive slaves. The extraterritorial claims of the slaveholding states were to be enforced regardless of the views of the community within which the law was to be executed. Because this particular extraterritorial claim was recognized by the federal Constitution, state sovereignty could be made effective through the use of federal power. On the surface, therefore, the legal vindication of the proslavery position appeared to be simply a victory for federal supremacy. The legal form of the fugitive-slave decision, however, should not be allowed to obscure the fundamental role played by the doctrine of state sovereignty and its extraterritorial corollaries.

THE QUESTION OF SLAVERY IN THE TERRITORIES

The doctrine of state sovereignty played its most important role, however, in the conflict over slavery in the territories. In this conflict, moreover, it revealed itself even more clearly as a naked doctrine of power. Finally, the extraterritorial corollaries of state sovereignty constituted the indispensable foundation of the proslavery argument concerning the territories.

At this point a change of terminology becomes imperative, as the awkwardness of the last sentence indicates. The asserted right of a slaveowner to take his slaves into the territories and to hold and exploit them there is properly described as an extraterritorial right, for it was a right that was to be exercised and protected outside the territory of the state that created the right in the first place. Nevertheless, intolerable confusion results if one describes by the term *extra*territorial a right that was to be exercised *within* what was officially known as a "territory." To avoid this difficulty I propose, in the pages that follow, to employ as a synonym for "extraterritorial" a rather awkward neologism—namely, "extra-jurisdictional," meaning a right (or a power) exercised beyond the jurisdiction of the state in which it originated.[63]

Now the right to reclaim a fugitive slave was an extra-jurisdictional right explicitly recognized by the Constitution. But a right to carry slaves into the territories was nowhere mentioned in the written document. On the other hand, no power to prohibit the introduction of slaves was mentioned either. Every constitutional theory concerning the extension of slavery was thus a structure of pure inference—inference either from certain phrases of the written Constitution, or inference from past precedents, or inference

---

[63] Not to be confused, of course, with "extrajudicial," defined as "forming no part of the case before the court." *New English Dictionary on Historical Principles.*

from some abstract theory about the Constitution. The latter sort of inference predominated in the discussions—as, for example, when the antislavery forces invoked a "higher law," moral in content, or when the proponents of "squatter" sovereignty invoked the principle of local self-determination, or when (to return to our immediate subject) the defenders of slavery invoked the doctrine of state sovereignty.

It is a curious fact that though the American Constitution was designed for an expanding nation, the western territories have always been anomalies in the scheme. It is conventional to say that the Constitution created a dual system, composed of the federal government and the states. In reality the Union has always comprised three elements, the federal government, the states, *and* the territories. Only in recent years have the latter declined to a place of relative insignificance in the constitutional structure. All but nineteen of the existing fifty states have passed through a formal territorial stage. Almost three quarters of the continental area of the United States has been, at one time or another, under a territorial government established by federal statute.[64]

The anomalous position of the territories in the constitutional scheme is simply this: Within the parts of the Union fully organized into states, the Constitution recognizes the existence of two governments, state and federal, operating simultaneously but independently and acting directly upon individuals. To each government a sphere of authority is constitutionally assigned. International and interstate relations are the supposed province of federal action. Questions of domestic social policy—involving the exercise of "police powers," so-called—belong clearly to the sphere of action reserved to the states. In the territories, however, no state government, in a constitutional sense, exists. By whose authority, then, are local police powers to be exercised?

Before examining the possible answers, it will be well to take careful note of the practical importance of the question—one that seems, at first glance, to belong to the realm of metaphysical speculation. Under ordinary circumstances, a precise answer was clearly unnecessary. A territory was simply an area in transition from unsettled wilderness to complete state-

---

[64] The exceptions were: the thirteen original states; two states that were almost immediately admitted (Vermont in 1791 and Kentucky in 1792); and four others for which the circumstances were exceptional: Maine (admitted in 1820 by consent of Massachusetts, of which it had been a part), Texas (annexed as a full-fledged state in 1845), California (admitted in 1850 under a state constitution that had been adopted before territorial government was extended over the Mexican cession), and West Virginia (which seceded from Virginia and was admitted in 1863). The present boundaries of these nineteen states include a gross area of 856,122 square miles, compared with 3,022,387 for continental United States as a whole (excluding Alaska). U. S. Bureau of the Census, *Statistical Abstract: 1955* (76th ed., Washington, 1955), 9 (Table 4). Maps showing the boundaries of the territories at all periods are in Charles O. Paullin and John K. Wright, *Atlas of the Historical Geography of the United States* (Washington, 1932), Plates 61–67.

hood. Whatever government existed *de facto* within a territory was bound to wield a police power for the time being, simply because it was charged with maintaining order. A rough and ready practicality, untroubled by elaborate theories about political structure, sufficed for carrying on the everyday affairs of a territory and handling (or postponing) its relatively simple problems. Territorial status was a temporary one. In the end, statehood would operate as an act of oblivion, curing or obliterating any theoretical irregularities that might have belonged to the territorial period.

This was true in most circumstances, but not in all. Slavery created problems of precisely the kind to convert these abstract and apparently trivial questions of constitutional theory into practical and momentous issues of constitutional law. The police power was, among other things, the power to deal with slavery. It was through their police powers that the slaveholding states enacted slave codes, it was through theirs that the free states abolished slavery. Whether or not slavery expanded into the territories thus depended upon how (and by whom) the police power was exercised there.

In the nature of the case, moreover, a decision on slavery during the territorial period would have permanent, not temporary, effects. If the police power were employed at the outset to protect the property rights of slaveholders, then slavery was likely to become so entwined with the institutions of the locality as to be in practice ineradicable. On the other hand, if the police power were used in such a way as to discourage the bringing in of slaves, then the territory would almost certainly produce a free-state majority when the time came to write a permanent constitution and seek admission to the Union.

Both parties to the controversy understood perfectly these implications. Lincoln, in a speech at Peoria on October 16, 1854, presented the antislavery argument against vesting the power of decision in the first settlers:

> Another important objection to this application of the right of self-government, is that it enables the first FEW, to deprive the succeeding MANY, of a free exercise of the right of self-government. The first few may get slavery IN, and the subsequent many cannot easily get it OUT. How common is the remark now in the slave States—"If we were only clear of our slaves, how much better it would be for us." They are actually deprived of the privilege of governing themselves as they would, by the action of a very few, in the beginning.[65]

Proslavery spokesmen were equally opposed to allowing the settlers to decide. James S. Green of Missouri stated the reasons in a speech to the Senate in 1860. Unless slave property is protected in the territories from the beginning, he argued,

---

[65] *Collected Works*, II: 268.

nobody will go there except those who do not own slaves; and when they come to the determination of the question, there will not be an interest sufficient to justify the adoption of the law of holding slaves. The consequence, the inevitable consequence, will be—not another slave State, no expansion of the South, no outlet to the South; but cramped and confined within her present limits, she may prosper for a while, but she will ultimately languish for the want of the power of expansion.[66]

To opponents and defenders of slavery alike, it seemed clear that the first decisions made in the territories would be the determining ones. However significant in theory might be the sovereignty of the state when eventually admitted to the Union, in practice this power—plenary but deferred—might well prove meaningless so far as slavery was concerned. Long before a state attained full standing, its social system could have been irrevocably fixed by decisions already made. Control of the police power during the territorial stage was thus the crux of the entire issue.

THE WILMOT PROVISO

It was the Wilmot Proviso of 1846 that brought this issue to the forefront of American politics and thus began the fifteen-year crisis that finally swept the nation into civil war. Under debate was an amendment to a two-million-dollar appropriation bill requested by President James K. Polk, for the purpose, as he said, of paying "for any concessions which may be made by Mexico" in a future peace treaty. The principal object, the President hardly needed to explain, was "the adjustment of a boundary between the two republics"—in plain language, territorial cessions by Mexico to the United States.[67] During debate in the House of Representatives, in the evening of August 8, 1846, David Wilmot of Pennsylvania moved the following amendment:

> *Provided,* That, as an express and fundamental condition to the acquisition of any territory from the Republic of Mexico by the United States, by virtue of any treaty which may be negotiated between them, and to the use by the Executive of the moneys herein

---

[66] Jan. 11, 1860. *Globe,* 36 Cong., 1 Sess., App., 77. In a speech to the Mississippi legislature on Nov. 16, 1858, Jefferson Davis likewise emphatically denied the right "of the first in the race of migration who reach a territory . . . to enact laws for the exclusion of other joint owners of the territory, who may . . . choose to take with them property recognized by the Constitution, but not acceptable to the first emigrants." Dunbar Rowland, ed., *Jefferson Davis, Constitutionalist: His Letters, Papers and Speeches* (Jackson, Miss., 1923), III: 345. Writing long after the Civil War, Davis reiterated his objection to the doctrine of popular sovereignty, as involving "a power in the Territorial Legislatures permanently to determine the fundamental, social, and political institutions of the Territory, and thereby virtually to prescribe those of the future State." *Rise and Fall of the Confederate Government,* I: 40.

[67] Message of the President, Aug. 8, 1846. *Globe,* 29 Cong., 1 Sess., 1211.

appropriated, neither slavery nor involuntary servitude shall ever exist in any part of said territory, except for crime, whereof the party shall first be duly convicted.[68]

The House adopted the proviso almost immediately, by a vote of 83 to 64.[69] The Senate refused to accept it, then or later.[70] But the fat was in the fire.

What made the Wilmot Proviso controversial? The answer requires a careful discrimination among constitutional principles. The proviso was in complete accord with the *law* of the Constitution, as understood up to that time. In banning slavery, the proviso used language almost identical with that of the Northwest Ordinance of July 13, 1787, adopted by the Continental Congress while the Constitutional Convention of 1787 was still sitting.[71] After the adoption of the Constitution, Congress immediately re-enacted the ordinance[72] and thereafter included the same prohibition, in virtually the same language, in a series of five territorial acts, from 1800 to 1838,[73] and in the Missouri Compromise of 1820.[74] The *power* to

---

[68] *Globe*, 29 Cong., 1 Sess., 1217.

[69] This vote was in committee of the whole. *Ibid*. In the House itself, the bill (with the Wilmot Proviso included) passed by a vote of 87 to 64. *Ibid*., 1218 (Aug. 8, 1846).

[70] Congress adjourned two days later (Aug. 10, 1846) with the Senate bogged down in debate on the measure. *Ibid*., 1220–21. At the next session a new bill (increasing the appropriation to three million dollars) was introduced. The House of Representatives, in committee of the whole, amended the measure on Feb. 15, 1847, to include an even more sweeping version of the proviso: *"Provided, further,* That there shall be neither slavery nor involuntary servitude in any territory on the continent of America which shall hereafter be acquired by or annexed to the United States by virtue of this appropriation, or in any other manner whatever, except for crimes whereof the party shall have been duly convicted. . . ."* The proviso was moved by Hannibal Hamlin of Maine (later Vice-President under Lincoln) and adopted, in committee of the whole, by a vote of 110 to 89. When the committee rose, the House of Representatives itself adopted the Wilmot Proviso (as it continued to be called, regardless of its actual mover) by a vote of 115 to 106, and then passed the bill, 115 to 105. *Globe*, 29 Cong., 2 Sess., 424–25 (Feb. 15, 1847). The Senate rejected the Wilmot Proviso on March 1, 1847, by a vote of 21 to 31. *Ibid*., 555.

The Senate bill, without the proviso, came before the House of Representatives on the last day of the session, March 3, 1847. An attempt to reinsert the Wilmot Proviso was finally defeated, 97 to 102, and the bill without it then passed the House, 115 to 81. *Ibid*., 573.

[71] "There shall be neither Slavery nor involuntary Servitude in the said territory otherwise than in the punishment of crimes, whereof the Party shall have been duly convicted. . . ." In "An Ordinance for the government of the territory of the United States North west of the river Ohio," July 13, 1787, Articles of Compact, Art. 6. *Territorial Papers*, II: 49.

[72] Act of Aug. 7, 1789, chap. 8. *Stat. at L.*, I: 50. Also printed, from the original MS, in *Territorial Papers*, II: 203–4.

[73] Acts creating governments for the territories of Indiana (1800), Michigan (1805), Illinois (1809), Wisconsin (1836), and Iowa (1838). These are listed, with citations, in the dissenting opinion of Justice Benjamin R. Curtis in the Dred Scott case, 19 Howard 393, at 618 (March 6, 1857). An analysis of the entire series of territorial acts is provided in Max Farrand, *The Legislation of Congress for the Government of the Organized Territories . . . , 1789–1895* (Newark, N. J., 1896). Texts of the basic acts are reprinted in

act on the matter had not, prior to 1846, been seriously challenged.[75]

The principle that the Wilmot Proviso thrust aside was not a *law* of the Constitution, but a *custom* of the Constitution, which dated back to the First Congress. On December 22, 1789, North Carolina ceded its western lands to the Union, to be governed according to the principles of the already re-enacted Northwest Ordinance, *"Provided always* that no regulations made or to be made by Congress shall tend to emancipate Slaves." [76] Congress accepted the condition and set up a Southwest Territory (later the state of Tennessee), explicitly providing that the antislavery section of the earlier ordinance should not apply.[77] Thereafter, from 1798 to 1822, Congress organized various southern territories in like manner, such acts roughly balancing in number those in which it prohibited slavery.[78] Moreover, the Missouri Compromise of 1820 established the parallel of 36° 30′ north latitude as a dividing line through the territories that had been acquired by the Louisiana Purchase and that remained in territorial status after the admission of Missouri to statehood. North of this line slavery was prohibited; south of it there was no restriction.[79] The established *custom* of the Constitution, before 1846, was thus to apportion the territories in an equitable fashion, so as to permit slaveholding in the southerly portions and prohibit it in the northerly.

The conservative position on the Constitution, throughout the entire crisis, was that the *law* and the *custom* of the Constitution (as here defined) were equally binding—in other words, that Congress had an indubitable

---

Francis N. Thorpe, ed., *The Federal and State Constitutions . . . of the States, Territories, and Colonies Now or Heretofore Forming the United States of America* (Washington, 1909), 7 vols.; hereafter cited as Thorpe, ed., *Constitutions.*

[74] Act of March 6, 1820, chap. 22, sec. 8. *Stat. at L.,* III: 545, at 548. Reprinted in Thorpe, ed., *Constitutions,* IV: 2148.

[75] An exhaustive and invaluable treatise on the legal aspects of the territorial system is provided by Francis S. Philbrick in the 477-page introduction to his edition of *The Laws of Illinois Territory, 1809–1818* (Collections of the Illinois State Historical Library, XXV, Springfield, 1950), hereafter cited simply as Philbrick. On the question of power to legislate for the territories, see especially pp. xcviii-clvii.

[76] North Carolina, act of cession, Dec. 22, 1789, sec. 4. *Territorial Papers,* IV (Washington, 1936): 7. Repeated verbatim in the deed of cession, Feb. 25, 1790, and in the act of Congress accepting it, April 2, 1790. *Ibid.,* 12, 16.

[77] "An Act for the government of the territory . . . south of the river Ohio," May 26, 1790, chap. 14. *Stat. at L.,* I: 123. *Territorial Papers,* IV: 18–19.

[78] In the list that Justice Curtis included in his dissent to the Dred Scott decision, 19 Howard 393, at 618, five territorial acts of this character from 1798 to 1822 were cited. These neatly balance the five territorial acts from 1800 to 1838 in which slavery was prohibited. Such a balance, however, is somewhat artificial, for many acts permitted slavery simply by remaining silent. More significant is the fact that seven states had emerged from the territorial stage before the end of 1846 with slavery as an established institution, namely: Tennessee (admitted 1796), Louisiana (1812), Mississippi (1817), Alabama (1819), Missouri (1821), Arkansas (1836), and Florida (1845); whereas five had emerged as free states, namely: Ohio (1803), Indiana (1816), Illinois (1818), Michigan (1837), and Iowa (1846); and another was in close prospect: Wisconsin (admitted 1848).

[79] See n. 74 above.

power to prohibit or permit slavery in the territories, but that it had a corresponding *obligation* to consider the interests of the slaveholding states in legislating for the southern territories and the wishes of the free states in legislating for the northern.[80] In immediate reaction to the Wilmot Proviso, this position was asserted in several substitute amendments that would have extended the Missouri Compromise line across all territories subsequently acquired. Each of these proposals was promptly voted down in the House of Representatives.[81] It was this rejection of the traditional approach to the problem that led to an intensive reexamination of constitutional precedents and postulates by all concerned, and hence produced the great constitutional crisis of 1846–1860.

THE CONSTITUTIONAL STATUS OF TERRITORIES

The precedents went back to a period before there was a formal constitution. Indeed, a conflict over the western territories blocked, for almost four years, the ratification of the first written instrument of federal government, the Articles of Confederation, drafted in 1777. Certain states claimed sovereignty over extensive areas in the West; certain others possessed no

---

[80] One of the ablest statements of the conservative position is a little-known book by Sidney George Fisher, published anonymously in November, 1859, *The Law of the Territories* (Philadelphia, 1859); see especially pp. 78–83. The conservative position (as here defined) was the one taken by Justice Curtis in his dissent in the Dred Scott case, wherein he rejected three alternative constitutional views that had been presented at the bar of the court. These he succinctly summarized as follows: "One is, that though Congress can make a regulation prohibiting slavery in a Territory, they cannot make a regulation allowing it; another is, that it can neither be established nor prohibited by Congress, but that the people of a Territory, when organized by Congress, can establish or prohibit slavery; while the third is, that the Constitution itself secures to every citizen who holds slaves, under the laws of any State, the indefeasible right to carry them into any Territory, and there hold them as property." 19 Howard 393, at 620. Obviously these were the positions, respectively, of the Republicans, of the "territorial sovereignty" Democrats under Douglas, and of the extreme southern Democrats (whose senatorial spokesman was Jefferson Davis). The fourth position (that is, the conservative one, which Curtis by implication accepted) was presumably the position of the Constitutional Union Party in 1860, though its platform and the speeches of its candidates were frustratingly vague. It was clearly the position of Senator John J. Crittenden of Kentucky, whose famous compromise resolutions, proposed in the Senate on Dec. 18, 1860, represented essentially a return to the constitutional understandings of the period prior to 1846, which he sought to put beyond question by embodying them in formal constitutional amendments. The crucial first article would have restored the Missouri Compromise line for all territory "now held, or hereafter acquired." *Globe*, 36 Cong., 2 Sess., 114.

[81] Immediately after the introduction of the Wilmot Proviso, on Aug. 8, 1846, an amendment to substitute the Missouri Compromise line was voted down by the House of Representatives, sitting as committee of the whole, 54 to 89. *Globe*, 29 Cong., 1 Sess., 1217. When the proviso came up again, on Feb. 15, 1847, three distinct amendments to like effect (one of them offered by Stephen A. Douglas) were similarly voted down by the House, again in committee of the whole. The votes were 82 to 109 and 81 to 104; the third amendment was rejected without a division. *Globe*, 29 Cong., 2 Sess., 424–25.

such claims. The latter insisted that these great unsettled areas become the property of the Union, rather than of particular states, and be developed for the common benefit. The log jam was broken in 1780, when various states (commencing with New York) began to cede their western claims, and Congress adopted a resolution promising that these lands would "be settled and formed into distinct republican states, which shall become members of the federal union, and have the same rights of sovereignty, freedom and independence, as the other states." [82] The smaller states were satisfied. On March 1, 1781, the last state gave its assent to the Articles of Confederation, and the United States began to live under its first written federal constitution.

The obvious—indeed, the necessary—assumption was that Congress would provide governments for the new territories. In doing so, it was morally bound to accord to actual settlers some degree of participation in territorial government and to advance them as rapidly as possible toward the fully self-governing stage that statehood would represent. Throughout the 1780's there were sharp conflicts of opinion about the proper balance to be struck between federal authority and local autonomy in the territories. But there was not the slightest hint that the individual states should play a separate and independent role—apart from the constituted organs of the Union—in governing the territories they had already ceded, thereby surrendering (in the words of the Virginia deed of cession) "all right, title and claim as well of soil as of jurisdiction." [83]

The real territorial question of the early republic was the degree of local self-government to be granted the inhabitants of a territory. On one side was Thomas Jefferson, who drafted the first land ordinance in 1784, and who proposed to give the settlers, from the very beginning, almost complete control over their own affairs. On the other side were the more conservative groups who shaped the Northwest Ordinance of 1787. This enactment specified a virtually colonial type of government, by federally appointed authorities, during the first stage of territorial existence; during the second stage it permitted the inhabitants some direct participation in territorial government; but it withheld full powers of self-government until the time for statehood arrived. The latter pattern prevailed, for the Ordinance of 1787 superseded the Ordinance of 1784 and became the prototype of all later territorial acts.[84]

Divergent as were these two philosophies of territorial government, they reached an identical conclusion so far as slavery was concerned. Jefferson's

---

[82] Resolution of Oct. 10, 1780. *Journals of the Continental Congress, 1774–1789* (Washington, 1904–1937), XVIII: 915.

[83] March 1, 1784. *Territorial Papers*, II: 9. The New York cession, March 1, 1781, used the words: "All the Right, Title, Interest, Jurisdiction and Claim." *Ibid.*, 5.

[84] See the elaborate comparison of the two plans of territorial government by Philbrick, ccl–ccclxxxvi.

original draft of 1784 included a prohibition of slavery in *all* the western territories.[85] The Ordinance of 1787 applied a similar prohibition to the particular area with which it dealt, "the territory of the United States North west of the river Ohio." [86] Jefferson's prohibitory clause was eliminated from the Ordinance of 1784 before enactment by Congress,[87] but its subsequent inclusion in the Ordinance of 1787 showed that the dropping of the provision did not imply a lack of power to adopt it.

There was, it is true, a subtly different philosophical basis for the two abolitionary clauses. In the Northwest Ordinance, Congress was simply legislating for the territories. This legislative power might, without question, be exercised in an opposite way, to permit slavery, and it was so exercised in 1790 when Congress created the Southwest Territory.[88] In the Jeffersonian scheme, on the other hand, the prohibition of slavery did not represent an exercise of federal legislative power, for Jefferson assigned virtually all legislative power to the inhabitants of the territories themselves. Instead, the prohibition of slavery in the territories was, in Jefferson's mind, simply a vindication of the principle of natural and unalienable rights.[89]

---

[85] "That after the year 1800 of the Christian aera, there shall be neither slavery nor involuntary servitude in any of the said states, otherwise than in punishment of crimes, whereof the party shall have been duly convicted to have been personally guilty." Report to Congress of the committee to prepare a plan for the temporary government of the western territory, March 1, 1784 (original in Jefferson's handwriting). Julian P. Boyd, ed., *The Papers of Thomas Jefferson*, VI (Princeton, N. J., 1952): 604. The clause appeared in the revised report, March 22, 1784 (also in Jefferson's hand). *Ibid.*, 608. As discussed in n. 87 below, it was rejected by Congress and does not appear in the ordinance as enacted on April 23, 1784. *Ibid.*, 613–15.

[86] See n. 71 above.

[87] The matter came to a vote on April 19, 1784. The motion was put in such a way that an affirmative majority was needed to retain Jefferson's prohibition of slavery. The motion was to strike out the section, but the question was put as follows: "Shall the words moved to be struck out stand?" Six states voted in the affirmative, against only three in the negative, but the rules of Congress required an affirmative vote of seven states, and the provision was lost. Actually the seven states from Pennsylvania northward were unanimously in favor, fourteen of their delegates in all voting aye. One of these states (New Jersey), however, was represented by only a single delegate, insufficient for a quorum; hence the state could not be counted. Among the southern states, only two (Maryland and South Carolina) were unanimously against the provision. In North Carolina the delegation was evenly divided; hence the vote of the state could not affect the decision. Within the Virginia delegation, too, there was division, and, by a bitter irony, Jefferson's affirmative vote was overridden by the negative votes of his two colleagues. Delaware and Georgia were absent. Altogether, only seven individual delegates were opposed to the provision, against sixteen in favor, two of the latter from southern states. *Journals of the Continental Congress*, XXVI: 247. Few issues so momentous have ever been decided by so unsatisfactory a ballot.

[88] See n. 77 above.

[89] Cf. the exclamations in his *Notes on Virginia*, written at this very time: "With what execrations should the statesman be loaded, who [permits] one half the citizens thus to trample on the rights of the other. . . . And can the liberties of a nation be thought secure when we have removed their only firm basis, a conviction in the minds of the people that these liberties are of the gift of God?" The way, he hoped, was "preparing, under the auspices of heaven, for a total emancipation." Jefferson, *Notes on the State of*

Slavery denied the fundamental right to liberty. To eliminate this violation of natural rights in the older states would require time, but there was no reason why slavery should not be banned from the beginning in new territories that were to grow up "in republican forms." [90] The prohibition of slavery was to be part of what Jefferson labeled a "Charter of Compact" —in effect a primordial bill of rights, and, as such, "fundamental" and "unalterable." [91] Whether the abolition of slavery be regarded as a legislative measure or as a constitutional protection of fundamental rights, the fact was that by 1787 it had entered clearly into the system of law being evolved for the territories.

In terms of the American concept of constitutional law—which grants priority to the language of the written Constitution over any mere tradition of constitutional action—the basic question was whether the Constitution of 1787 validated the measures that had already been taken respecting the territories. If not—and especially if the Constitution could be construed as forbidding these measures—then the policy (no matter of how long standing) could be reversed on constitutional grounds. This was precisely the result at which the defenders of slavery aimed in the constitutional doctrine they developed after 1846. They built up, from state-sovereignty premises, a theory of the Constitution that denied the legality of every measure prohibiting slavery in the territories that had ever been enacted from the time the Union was perfected in 1787–1788.

They were aided in doing so by the undeniable vagueness and ambiguity of the single clause of the written Constitution that dealt with territorial matters:

> The Congress shall have Power to dispose of and make all needful Rules and Regulations respecting the Territory or other Property belonging to the United States. . . .[92]

Though legislative power can be described as the power to make rules and regulations,[93] nevertheless the language of this clause was obviously

---

Virginia (William Peden, ed., Chapel Hill, N. C., 1955), 162–163. He still hoped that Virginia would pass legislation he had earlier favored, which would "emancipate all slaves born after passing the act." *Ibid.*, 137; see also Boyd, ed., *Jefferson Papers*, II: 472 n.

[90] Phrases promising "a Republican Form of Government" echoed through all the documents of the founding period. See, for example, the resolution of Congress of Oct. 10, 1780, on the cession of western lands (cited in n. 82 above); Jefferson's draft ordinance of 1784 (from which the phrase in the text is quoted); and the Constitution itself, Art. IV, sec. 4. Such guarantees furnished one basis for the view that the federal government should exercise a general superintendence over the institutions that might develop in the territories—including the institution of slavery. Thus Timothy Fuller of Massachusetts declared in the House of Representatives on Feb. 15, 1819, that "the existence of slavery in any State is so far a departure from republican principles." *Annals*, 15 Cong., 2 Sess., 1180.

[91] Boyd, ed., *Jefferson Papers*, VI: 605. On the essential unreality of the supposed "compact," see Philbrick, clxxix, *et seq.*

[92] Constitution, Art. IV, sec. 3, clause 2.

[93] Certain of the most important powers of Congress were delegated to it in this lan-

weaker than that employed in giving Congress the power "to exercise exclusive Legislation in all Cases whatsoever" over the District of Columbia and over such federal sites as forts and dockyards.[94] Moreover, by referring to "Territory or *other Property*," and by emphasizing the power "to *dispose of*" both, the clause might be interpreted as referring to real-estate transactions rather than to territorial government.

By making the most of these ambiguities, proslavery theorists could argue either that this particular clause did not apply to the situation at all or that it delegated to Congress such limited authority over the territories that no legislative interference with slavery was permissible there. A different kind of power—a nonlegislative power, deriving from a different constitutional source—could then be assigned to Congress. And this power, being a creation of pure constitutional theorizing, could be so defined that it would be capable of protecting slavery in the territories without, at the same time, subjecting it to the hazard of hostile legislation.

If full legislative power over the territories had not been vested in Congress by the Constitution, then surely the power must belong to the inhabitants themselves. This had been the Jeffersonian alternative. And it was the alternative that Stephen A. Douglas supported with vigor and consistency under the name of territorial or popular sovereignty. To most supporters of slavery it seemed, for a decade after 1846, the best defense against the hated Wilmot Proviso. But as events in Kansas gradually pointed, in the later 1850's, toward an ultimate free-state victory there, proslavery forces turned venomously upon the author of the Kansas-Nebraska Bill and repudiated his doctrine and all his works. The theory of state sovereignty came to full fruition in the brief period that followed. And it showed its imperious quality by the peremptory way in which its supporters rejected every vestige of the idea that the people of a territory were sovereign or self-governing. Typical was a speech in the House of Representatives in 1859 by Otho R. Singleton of Mississippi:

> Sovereignty, as I understand it, and as it is defined by lexicographers, is the highest power—the supreme power in a State; and, if this definition be correct, (and I apprehend nobody will controvert it,) when Mr. Douglas and his followers undertake to put the Territorial Legislature upon the same footing with a State Legislature, in my judgment they are guilty of a most egregious blunder. Now, let me ask what sovereignty is there—call it squatter sovereignty, popular sovereignty, or whatever else you please—belonging to the people of a Territory? Can they organize a territorial government for themselves? . . . Can they elect their own officers without the special permission of the Congress of the United States? Every act that is passed

---

guage, including the power "to regulate Commerce." Constitution, Art. I, sec. 8, clause 3; see also clauses 4, 5, 11, 14. Philbrick discusses the question at length, cv–cxxx.

[94] Art. I, sec. 8, clause 17.

by the Territorial Legislature is subject to the revision of Congress, and liable to be annulled by that body, and there is not a single act a Territorial Legislature can perform showing it to be sovereign.

But the gentlemen claim that the Legislature of a Territory has the same powers as the Legislature of a State. Why, sir, never was a more erroneous proposition asserted. A State Legislature may perform a thousand acts of sovereignty, its power being controlled by no superior. . . . The people of a State select their own officers, establish their own judicial tribunals, alter or abolish their State government at will. And when gentlemen undertake to put a State and Territory upon the same footing in respect to sovereignty, they involve themselves in difficulties which they cannot meet successfully.[95]

The doctrine of state sovereignty was as hostile to local self-determination in the territories as to the exercise of federal legislative power there. But what other alternative could there be? It was in answering this question that the theorists of state sovereignty revealed their extraordinary ingenuity. And the foundation of their argument was the extra-jurisdictional (or extraterritorial) principle that has already shown itself to be the most significant corollary of state sovereignty.

In legal terms, as we have seen, the question at issue was the source of the police power in the territories—the power that might determine, among other things, the existence or nonexistence of slavery. The state-sovereignty argument began by pointing out that the exercise of a police power is the prerogative of a sovereign. The people of a territory had not attained sovereignty, and the federal government had not received, by delegation, those attributes of sovereignty that would enable it to wield a power of local police. The idea that the federal government might exercise such powers in the territories—by default as it were—was rejected as untenable. The federal government is a government of delegated powers, and local police powers are precisely the ones not delegated to it, but "reserved" by the Tenth Amendment. And they are reserved to the full-fledged sovereign states of the Union, and to them alone.

One finds it hard to imagine how the several states could exercise any power of police in territories beyond their boundaries and outside their jurisdictions. And if they attempted to do so, each projecting its sovereignty into the same area, what possible result could there be but conflict, commotion, and chaos? The answer of state-sovereignty theorists was to assign to the federal government a peculiar, extraconstitutional role in the territories. It was to act there not as the government of the *United* States, but as the agent of the united *States*.

This ingenious dualism solved, with the elegance of Euclid, the constitutional problem that confronted the defenders of slavery. In traditional federal matters, the government of the United States was a *government*, with a

---

[95] Dec. 19, 1859. *Globe,* 36 Cong., 1 Sess., App., 52.

legislature capable of determining federal policy, an executive capable of enforcing it, and a judiciary sworn to uphold federal statutes as part of the supreme law of the land. In territorial matters, on the other hand, the federal government was not to be deemed a government at all, but a *trustee*. It was a trustee for the sovereign states, responsible to them severally, charged with giving extraterritorial effect to their laws, and denied any deliberative or discretionary power of its own. It had duties to perform and it possessed the power to perform them. But the power to act did not imply the power to decide. The proslavery constitutional theory succeeded in preserving a centralized authority powerful enough to enforce the rights of slaveowners outside the jurisdictions of the slaveholding states. At the same time, it denied to this central authority any power to make policy with respect to slavery in any place or in any manner.

THE REAL SIGNIFICANCE OF STATE SOVEREIGNTY

It is time to examine the various—and extraordinary—features of this fully developed doctrine of state sovereignty. The first point to be noted is that the theory did *not* propose a lessening of federal authority in the territories. Federal powers were to be kept in being—even enhanced—in order to protect the exposed flank of slavery. But these powers were so defined as to be capable of employment in only one way. President Franklin Pierce stated the ultimate and desired conclusion in a message to Congress in 1855. "The General Government," he said, "was forbidden to touch this matter [slavery] in the sense of attack or offense" but was obliged to act upon it "in the sense of defense against either invasion or domestic violence." [96] Senator John M. Berrien of Georgia was even more explicit. "Congress," he asserted, "may legislate upon this subject in the Territories, *affirmatively*," that is to say, "to facilitate the exercise of a constitutional right" to own slaves, but it had no power to legislate in such a way as "to create obstructions to the enjoyment" of this right.[97] Speaking for the Supreme Court, Chief Justice Roger B. Taney reiterated the view: "The Government of the United States had no right to interfere for any other purpose but that of protecting the rights of the owner." [98]

These conclusions—which found expression in all three branches of the federal government—were the product of several subtle but exceedingly important transformations in the realm of constitutional theory.

---

[96] Third annual message, Dec. 31, 1855. James D. Richardson, ed., *A Compilation of the Messages and Papers of the Presidents* (Washington, 1897), V: 343.

[97] Quoted by Thomas Hardeman, Jr. (Ga.), H.R., April 12, 1860. *Globe*, 36 Cong., 1 Sess., App., 223. Hardeman himself went on to offer a new and revealing distinction, quite different from the orthodox distinction between powers granted to the federal government and powers reserved to the states. Instead, Hardeman spoke of "the distinction between their [i.e., Congress's] powers of protection—for it was for that our Government was created—and those negative powers which belong not to Congress." *Ibid.*

[98] Dred Scott v. Sandford, 19 Howard 393, at 426 (March 6, 1857).

In the first place, the traditional criterion of constitutionality had been replaced by another. The federal government being a government of delegated powers, the accepted test applied to any federal measure had always been whether or not the power employed was delegated by the Constitution to the federal government. In place of this, a new criterion of constitutionality was insisted upon—a criterion of *purpose*. If a power were used in such a way as to weaken slavery, then it was without constitutional justification, regardless of whether the power, considered as such, lay within the scope of delegated powers. In a speech to the Senate in 1856, Clement C. Clay, Jr., of Alabama, brusquely swept aside as irrelevant, so far as slavery was concerned, the distinction between action that intruded upon the reserved powers of the states and action that fell within the recognized sphere of federal competence. Outright abolitionism, he said, was "less odious and dangerous" than the policy of "those who concede that slavery in the States is beyond the reach of Congress under the Constitution . . . but yet avow their intention and their power to assail it in the Territories, this District [of Columbia], and wherever the national flag floats." Their ultimate goal, he argued, was to "overthrow slavery in the States." The goal itself was unconstitutional, regardless of the means employed. The fact that opponents of slavery approached this goal by a "circuitous" path rendered their conduct not scrupulously constitutional but "insidious and dastardly." "An army with banners," Clement Clay exclaimed, "is preferable to a Trojan horse." [99]

This theory rendered unconstitutional any use of federal power anywhere or at any time in a fashion inimical to slavery. Nevertheless, the theory was still a negative one. Something more was needed: a mandate from the Constitution itself requiring the positive use of federal power to safeguard slavery in the territories. The second great transformation of constitutional theory looked to this particular end. Proslavery theorists undertook to discover in the Constitution itself such a clear guarantee of the rights of slaveowners that Congress and the President would be obliged, whatever their inclinations, to protect the institution of slavery in the territories, without acquiring thereby any concomitant power to debate or decide questions of policy relating to it.

The starting point of this theory was the fact that the Constitution did recognize the existence of slavery. Furthermore, it gave extraterritorial effect to the laws of the slaveholding states in the matter of fugitive slaves. Antislavery leaders, of course, conceded all this, but they considered slavery a tolerated evil, and they regarded the specific provisions of the Constitution as setting the uttermost limits of such toleration. Beyond these limits, they insisted, every constitutional power of the federal government might legitimately be directed against slavery, to limit, weaken, and eventually destroy

---

[99] April 21, 1856. *Globe,* 34 Cong., 1 Sess., App., 487–88.

it. The question of whether federal power should be used in this way was a question of policy, not of constitutional law—a question to be decided by the recognized deliberative organs of the federal government.

Proslavery constitutionalists took a diametrically opposite view. The clauses of the Constitution that recognized slavery were to be construed not narrowly but broadly—not as limits on the protection that slavery might enjoy but as tokens of the full protection that the Constitution implicitly promised. By recognizing slavery, moreover, the Constitution necessarily recognized the laws of the slaveholding states and made their principles the controlling ones in every question that affected slavery. No power to legislate about slavery had, after all, been delegated to Congress. But slavery was an institution that must be defined and provided for by law. There was only one place where such law could be found or could be made—in the sovereign states that upheld and protected slavery. Whenever an issue involving slavery arose in the domain of federal responsibility, therefore, the laws of the slaveholding states must take on extra-jurisdictional force, filling the void created by the constitutional incapacity of Congress to legislate on the subject. On all matters affecting slavery, in other words, the slaveholding states, as sovereigns, were to make policy not for themselves alone, but for the country as a whole, except within the boundaries of such sovereign states as had chosen to abolish the institution.[100]

Senator Berrien of Georgia stated the matter succinctly: "Slavery exists

---

[100] Even there, of course, the laws of the slaveholding states were to operate extraterritorially upon fugitive slaves. Extraterritoriality, one should observe, was to work in one direction only. The freedom that a slave might have gained by being taken into a free state vanished if he was taken back into a slave state. In his concurring opinion in the Dred Scott case, Justice Nelson emphatically rejected the argument "that as Dred Scott was free while residing in the State of Illinois, by the laws of that State, on his return to the State of Missouri he carried with him the personal qualities of freedom, and that the same effect must be given to his status there as in the former State." On the contrary, he said, "No State . . . can enact laws to operate beyond its own dominions. . . . Such laws can have no inherent authority extra-territorially. . . . Now, it follows from these principles, that whatever force or effect the laws of one State or nation may have in the territories of another, must depend solely upon the laws and municipal regulations of the latter." Dred Scott v. Sandford, 19 Howard 393, at 462, 460 (March 6, 1857); cited hereafter simply as Dred Scott case (with page reference). Furthermore, Nelson went on to treat federal statutes on the same basis, despite the fact that they are, by constitutional definition, part of "the supreme Law of the Land," binding "the Judges in every State . . . , any Thing in the Constitution or Laws of any State to the Contrary notwithstanding." Art. VI, clause 2. Oblivious to the difference between a federal law operating within the jurisdiction of a member state and a state law operating within the jurisdiction of a fellow state, he rejected the idea that the federally enacted Missouri Compromise (assuming it to be valid) "possessed some superior virtue and effect, extra-territorially, and within the State of Missouri, beyond that of the laws of Illinois, or those of Ohio." Dred Scott case, 463. Nelson did not rule on the constitutionality of the Missouri Compromise; hence he did not involve himself in the flagrant one-sidedness of a majority of his brethren, who accepted his reasoning and then combined it with their own, which concluded that the laws of a slaveholding state followed the slaveowner and protected his property whenever he went out from his own state into the territories that were under federal jurisdiction.

in the State where the owner dwells; it exists out of the State where the owner dwells. Once existing, it exists everywhere, until it comes within limits of a sovereignty which inhibits it." [101] The theory of state sovereignty, in other words, made slavery a national institution. Senator James S. Green of Missouri used this very term when he asserted "that the prohibition of slavery in the United States is local, and that the right to hold slave property wherever there is no prohibition is national." [102]

The doctrine of state sovereignty, in the last analysis, was a nationalistic doctrine, not a localistic one. Despite appearances, its real tendency was toward consolidation, not decentralization. By exalting sovereignty, it destroyed the philosophical foundation for a genuinely pluralistic society, in which diversity would be cherished. There was one peculiarity: indivisible sovereignty was ascribed to the several states rather than to the nation. As a consequence, the doctrine exhibited to the world two seemingly contradictory faces. Within their borders, the slaveholding states were invoking a sovereign's immunity from all external control. Beyond their borders, however, they were demanding—as sovereigns—the strictest respect for whatever rights they chose to place beneath the protective mantle of their sovereignty.

Such a view of the Constitution wiped out every policy-making function of the federal government. Its powers were converted from legislative to ministerial ones. Congress was to provide ways and means, it was not to deliberate upon ends. The President was not to shape policy but simply to execute the laws. Federal coercive authority, nevertheless, would be kept in being, for the extraterritorial claims of the slaveholding states would collapse without it. But the only branch of the federal government whose powers were to be exalted was the judiciary. The courts were obliged to take their cue directly from the Constitution. They were free to disregard the directives of possible antislavery majorities in the other branches. They could thus be expected to enforce the sweeping mandate that proslavery leaders found in the Constitution—a mandate to safeguard, under all circumstances, the constitutionally recognized institution of slavery.

This reliance upon the judiciary—indeed, this almost exclusive reliance —was inevitable, and gave to proslavery constitutional theory its highly legalistic tone. Of the three branches of the federal government, the legislative was least to be trusted. Antislavery majorities could already be mustered in the House of Representatives, and sooner or later would be in the Senate. Therefore no discretionary power over slavery could safely be left in the hands of Congress; its every act must be predetermined, so far as aim or purpose was concerned, by the Constitution and by judicial decision. For

---

[101] Quoted by Thomas Hardeman, Jr. (Ga.), H.R., April 12, 1860. *Globe*, 36 Cong., 1 Sess., App., 223.

[102] Senate, Jan. 11, 1860. *Globe*, 36 Cong., 1 Sess., App., 78.

the moment, the situation in the executive branch was more favorable. Throughout the period of controversy—especially during the administrations of Polk, Pierce, and Buchanan (1845–1849 and 1853–1861)—the proslavery faction were generally successful in committing the President to the policies they demanded. Nevertheless, this control was jeopardized at every election—indeed, the loss of the executive branch to the Republicans in 1860 was obviously a major reason for secession. Executive discretion ultimately was no more to be tolerated than legislative. Only the federal judiciary could be trusted to defend slavery in an active way. The idea that the Supreme Court could not make—and was not, in fact, making—national policy about slavery was a transparent fiction. But it was a useful fiction, from the southern point of view, for it meant that the court was under no obligation to reflect the views of popular majorities. Policy would be made *for* the nation, but not *by* the nation. Power would be neatly divorced from accountability, action from deliberation.

THE DRED SCOTT DECISION

This reliance upon the judiciary paid off in the most important of all the decisions on slavery—that in the case of Dred Scott, decided on March 6, 1857. The ultimate doctrine of state sovereignty, with all its extra-jurisdictional corollaries fully developed and applied, received its most authoritative formulation at the hands of Chief Justice Roger B. Taney, who wrote the opinion of the court in the case. Space does not permit an examination of the many points of this complex and fateful decision. But the heart of Taney's opinion, from the constitutional point of view, was his delineation of the nature of the Union and the conclusions he drew therefrom respecting the power of Congress in the territories and particularly its power over slavery.

The case involved a slave, Dred Scott, who had been taken by his master for an extended sojourn or residence in areas where slavery was forbidden by statute—for two years in the free state of Illinois and for two in that portion of the old Louisiana Purchase which lay north of 36° 30′, and in which slavery had been prohibited by the federally enacted Missouri Compromise of 1820. Having been brought back to the slaveholding state of Missouri, Dred Scott was suing for his freedom in the federal courts. His suit was denied on several grounds. What concerns us here is the pronouncement that Congress lacked constitutional authority to prohibit slavery in the territories, as it had attempted to do in the Missouri Compromise. Each of the nine justices filed a separate opinion. Seven concurred in the final result: that Dred Scott was still a slave. Only six held that the Missouri Compromise was invalid. And only five accepted Taney's reasoning that the measure was actually unconstitutional. The five, nevertheless, constituted a majority of the entire court; hence the constitutional theory about to be discussed became authoritative.[103]

Turning to the written Constitution, Taney could find in it no delegation to the federal government of powers of local government, even over areas that formed no part of any existing state. He denied that such powers were conferred by the clause authorizing Congress to "make all needful Rules and Regulations respecting the Territory or other Property belonging to the United States." Instead of arguing (as most defenders of state sovereignty had done) that the words were inadequate to convey the powers in question, Taney took the curious position that the clause applied only to territory already in the possession of the United States at the time the Constitution was adopted.[104] The effect (and obviously the intent) of this interpretation was to deny the applicability to the territories generally of the antislavery precedent set in the Northwest Ordinance of 1787.

Having rejected as a basis for his argument the one clause in the Constitution that made any reference to territory, Taney furnished himself with the kind of provision he needed by a wholesale discovery of implied powers, reminiscent of the most spacious opinions of John Marshall. The United States had, of course, acquired vast territories without benefit of an explicit grant of power to do so. Since Jefferson himself had swallowed his constitutional scruples in the matter when he consummated the Louisiana Pur-

---

[103] Dred Scot case, 393. In the opinion of the court, Chief Justice Taney (Md.) denied the constitutionality of federal legislation prohibiting slavery in the territories (our present concern) in a lengthy discussion, 431–52. The two dissenting justices, John McLean (Ohio) and Benjamin R. Curtis (Mass.) controverted his views on this point, 538–50 and 604–33, respectively. Of the six justices who agreed with Taney that Dred Scott was still a slave, one, James M. Wayne (Ga.) gave his "unqualified assent" to all Taney's arguments, 454–56. Another, Robert C. Grier (Pa.) concurred specifically with Taney's reasoning on the unconstitutionality of the Missouri Compromise, 469. Two others, Peter V. Daniel (Va.) and John A. Campbell (Ala.) argued this particular point afresh, 487–92 and 500–517, respectively. Accordingly, five of the nine justices subscribed to the doctrines discussed in the text above. One other justice, John Catron (Tenn.), believed the Missouri Compromise invalid rather than unconstitutional, because incompatible with the treaty that ceded Louisiana, and he took emphatic exception to certain of Taney's assertions denying congressional power over the territories, 519–29. The remaining justice, Samuel Nelson (N. Y.), held Dred Scott to be a slave for reasons that did not call the Missouri Compromise in question, 457–69.

Aside from certain technical questions, two other major points were ruled on by the court. (i) Nelson, in an opinion originally prepared to serve as that of the court, rested the case on the principle that it was for the courts of Missouri to decide Dred Scott's status after his return to that state, and hence to determine the effect to be given to his residence on free soil. The precedent for this was the decision in Strader v. Graham, 10 Howard 82, (1850). Seven of the nine members of the court were in agreement on this point. (ii) Taney held that a Negro could not, under any circumstances, be a citizen of the United States and hence that Dred Scott could not sue in the federal courts even if he were free. Only Wayne and Daniel agreed. McLean and Curtis dissented. On this point—profound in its implications—the vote was therefore three to two.

The literature on the Dred Scott case is too enormous for discussion here. Mention should be made, however, of Vincent C. Hopkins, *Dred Scott's Case* (New York, 1951).

[104] Dred Scott case, 432.

case in 1803, no one thereafter was bothered by such scruples.[105] Nevertheless, the possessions so acquired had presumably been sold, as well as governed, by virtue of the clause that spoke of "Rules and Regulations respecting the Territory." Not so, said Taney. The clause in question could not be stretched to include possessions acquired after 1787. Accordingly, Congress had been selling the public land without any written authority from the Constitution. Its power to sell, as well as its power to govern, was inferred from its power to acquire, and this in turn was inferred from the fact that the United States was an independent nation, and, like other nations, an acquisitive one.[106] The Dred Scott decision was a masterpiece of broad construction before Taney changed his course and made it also a masterpiece of strict construction.

The power to govern the territories being an implied power, and not a power derived from the written clause respecting territory, Taney was free to define the power in any way he saw fit. And he saw fit to define it in terms of the dualism we have already examined. Until a territory is ready for statehood, Taney asserted, "it is undoubtedly necessary that some Government should be established, in order to organize society, and to protect the inhabitants in their persons and property." This statement was implicitly restrictive, describing as it did a government with the barest minimum of functions. In establishing this minimal government, moreover, Congress was not acting in its normal capacity as the federal legislature. It was acting simply as agent of the several states, charged with preserving their interests. Taney expressed the idea thus:

> As the people of the United States could act in this manner only through the Government which represented them, . . . it was not only within the scope of its powers, but it was its duty to pass such laws and establish such a Government as would enable those by whose authority they acted to reap the advantages anticipated from its acquisition.[107]

This was the concept of trusteeship. The term itself had already appeared in another crucial passage:

---

[105] See Andrew C. McLaughlin, *A Constitutional History of the United States* (New York, 1935), 294–98.

[106] In the Insular Cases following the Spanish-American War, the power to govern, implied from the implied power to acquire, became the basis for a ruling that (in the popular phrase of the time) the Constitution does not follow the flag. "We are also of opinion that the power to acquire territory by treaty implies, not only the power to govern such territory, but to prescribe upon what terms the United States will receive its inhabitants, and what their status shall be in what Chief Justice Marshall termed the 'American empire.'" In other words, "the Constitution is applicable to territories acquired by purchase or conquest only when and so far as Congress shall so direct." Downes v. Bidwell, 182 U. S. 244, at 279 (May 27, 1901).

[107] Dred Scott case, 448.

> Whatever it [the general government] acquires, it acquires for the
> benefit of the people of the several States who created it. It is their
> trustee acting for them, and charged with the duty of promoting the
> interests of the whole people of the Union.

The territory, he reiterated, "was acquired by the General Government, as
the representative and trustee of the people of the United States, and it
must therefore be held in that character for their common and equal
benefit." [108]

This distinction between legislative power and trusteeship was vital to
Taney's argument. If Congress were authorized to legislate (in the full
sense) for a territory, then it would stand in the same relation to the people
of the territory as a state legislature stands in relation to the people of the
state.[109] It could make policy with respect to the domestic and local institutions of the area. It would be empowered, as a state legislature was empowered, to decide upon the existence or nonexistence of slavery in the
territory. On the other hand, if Congress were acting simply as trustee for
the people of the several states, then it would enjoy no such freedom of decision on matters of policy. It could, of course, perform within the territories the ordinary federal functions that it performed within the states.
Beyond this, however, its powers and duties in the territories were those of
a temporary caretaker only. The normal legislative power bestowed upon
Congress extended only to purely federal matters. No powers of local government—no police powers—were included. Such powers as might be in-
dispensably necessary for the maintenance of order would have to be implied. But these had neither the character nor the scope of the constitutionally delegated powers of Congress. The implied power to provide government for a territory was drastically and peremptorily restricted by the concept of trusteeship.

From this premise, Taney's specific conclusions easily followed. In devising the mere machinery of government, Congress was relatively free to use
its judgment. In legislating on substantive matters, however, it was permitted no discretion and no power of decision of its own. "The power of
Congress over the person or property of a citizen can never be a mere dis-

---

[108] *Ibid.* See also Daniel's concurring opinion: "Congress was made simply the agent or
trustee for the United States, and could not, without a breach of trust and a fraud, appropriate the subject of the trust to any other beneficiary . . . than . . . the people of
the United States, upon equal grounds, legal or equitable" (italics in the original). *Ibid.*,
489.

[109] Marshall, indeed, had already held that in legislating for the territories, "Congress
exercises the combined powers of the general, and of a state government." American
Insurance Co. v. Canter, 1 Peters 511, at 546 (1828). Taney distinguished the case. Dred
Scott, 444. Marshall's position is unquestionably that of present-day constitutional law.
"In the territories, Congress has the entire dominion and sovereignty, national and local,
and has full legislative power over all subjects upon which a State legislature might act."
Corwin, ed., *Constitution . . . Analysis*, 703.

cretionary power under our Constitution and form of Government." [110] Therefore "citizens of the United States who migrate to a Territory belonging to the people of the United States, cannot be ruled as mere colonists, dependent upon the will of the General Government, and to be governed by any laws it may think proper to impose." [111]

The federal government, admittedly, was duty-bound to preserve order and protect property. But it was obliged to do so, Taney insisted, in such a way as not to infringe upon any property right enjoyed by an American citizen by virtue of the laws of his own state. Ordinary civil and criminal laws, if common to all the states of the Union, might presumably be enacted by Congress for the territories. But laws that infringed upon a property right recognized by any state would be *ultra vires*. The holding of slaves was obviously such a state-protected property right. No distinction between slave property and other property was authorized by the Constitution, Taney continued, and none could be made by Congress.[112] Accordingly, a federal statute abolishing slavery in a territory was, under any and every circumstance, unconstitutional. The Chief Justice drove the point home by citing—for almost the first time in constitutional adjudication, though not for the first time in the debates over slavery[113]—the Fifth Amendment (and especially its "due process" clause) in defense of vested property rights. "An act of Congress," he asserted, "which deprives a citizen of the United States of his liberty or property, merely because he came himself or brought his property into a particular Territory of the United States, and who had com-

---

[110] Dred Scott case, 449.   [111] Dred Scott case, 447.

[112] "If the Constitution recognises the right of property of the master in a slave, and makes no distinction between that description of property and other property owned by a citizen, no tribunal, acting under the authority of the United States, whether it be legislative, executive, or judicial, has a right to draw such a distinction." Dred Scott case, 451. In his concurring opinion, however, Daniel insisted that the Constitution did make a distinction, placing property in slaves *above* other property. "The only private property which the Constitution has *specifically recognised,* and has imposed it as a direct obligation both on the States and the Federal Government to protect and *enforce,* is the property of the master in his slave; no other right of property is placed by the Constitution upon the same high ground, nor shielded by a similar guaranty." *Ibid.,* 490.

[113] It was only a year earlier that the modern concept of "substantive due process" received clear formulation in a New York case, Wynehamer v. People, 13 N. Y. 378 (1856), involving a liquor law. The decision is characterized as "epoch-making" by Rodney L. Mott, *Due Process of Law* (Indianapolis, 1926), 317–18. Taney, who cited no precedents, is often assumed to have had the Wynehamer case in mind, and his application of the Fifth Amendment to vested property rights in slaves is usually regarded as a striking innovation. As early as 1832, however, in the debates that occurred in the Virginia General Assembly over a proposal for gradual emancipation, James H. Gholson argued that any measure taking slaves from their masters would violate property rights protected both by the Virginia Constitution and by the Fifth Amendment of the federal Constitution. He seems, it is true, to have emphasized the clause reading "nor shall private property be taken for public use, without just compensation," rather than the due process clause. See Theodore M. Whitfield, *Slavery Agitation in Virginia, 1829–1832* (Baltimore, 1930), 77.

mitted no offence against the laws, could hardly be dignified with the name of due process of law." [114]

PROSLAVERY DEMANDS IN 1860

Upheld in their constitutional views by the Dred Scott decision of 1857, defenders of slavery worked out with logical completeness the program which they insisted the federal government must carry out. The final formulation was in a set of resolutions that Jefferson Davis introduced in the Senate on February 2, 1860, and that he pushed through to adoption on May 24 and 25. The resolutions began by reciting the orthodox postulate of state sovereignty: "that in the adoption of the Federal Constitution, the States adopting the same acted severally as free and independent sovereignties." [115] But the document mounted quickly to a climax in the fourth resolution, which demanded that the powers of the central government be exerted to any extent necessary to safeguard slavery throughout all the territories. In Davis's original draft, the section read as follows:

> *Resolved,* That neither Congress nor a territorial legislature, whether by direct legislation or legislation of an indirect and unfriendly nature, possess the power to annul or impair the constitutional right of any citizen of the United States to take his slave property into the common territories, but it is the duty of the federal government there to afford, for that as for other species of property, the needful protection; and if experience should at any time prove that the judiciary does not possess power to insure adequate protection, it will then become the duty of Congress to supply such deficiency.[116]

Davis's resolutions, an election-year manifesto, were adopted in May, 1860. Six months later the election returns were in. The victory of Lincoln and the Republican Party destroyed every hope of achieving the proslavery program for the territories that Jefferson Davis had laid down in the spring. Even without control of Congress, the incoming Republican President would wield powers capable of blocking any measure for protecting slavery in the territories. His veto could strike down a federal slave code, should Congress seek to enact one, and his power to appoint and remove territorial

---

[114] Dred Scott case, 450.   [115] Senate, 36 Cong., 1 Sess., *Journal*, 112 (Feb. 2, 1860).

[116] *Ibid.*, 113. On March 1, 1860, Davis substituted a revised, but by no means weakened, text, which divided this resolution into two. *Ibid.*, 203. The revised resolutions were adopted by the Senate on May 24–25, 1860. *Ibid.*, 507–10, 513–18. Horace Greeley labeled them the "Democratic Platform, Adopted by the United States Senate." Horace Greeley and John F. Cleveland, eds., *A Political Text-Book for 1860* (New York, 1860), 194–97. The views, of course, were not those of the Democratic Party as a whole, but of its southern faction. When the latter nominated John C. Breckinridge for the presidency on June 28, 1860, the first two planks of its platform simply paraphrased Davis's crucial resolution, avoiding the contentious word "slave." Porter and Johnson, *National Party Platforms*, 31.

governors (each armed with a veto power) could forestall similar action by territorial legislatures. If Stephen A. Douglas was right when he said that slavery could not exist in a territory without positive legislation in its favor,[117] then slavery in the territories could hardly survive even the calculated *in*action of a Republican administration. Lincoln's election was hardly "an immediate menace to slavery in the states" (as some writers have argued [118] with scanty supporting evidence), but it was indubitably an immediate menace to slavery *in the territories*. And the throttling of slavery in the territories would mean—according to the professed beliefs of opponents and defenders of slavery alike—the ultimate extinction of the institution everywhere. When the election of 1860 ended the possibility of federal protection for slavery in the territories, the principal leaders of the proslavery party chose, or accepted, the long-discussed alternative of secession.

Secession, however, was not in itself a program for the positive protection of slavery. Secession could not be an end in itself. It made sense only as the means to an end. And the end, unconcealed, was to create a new constitutional system, with built-in protection for slavery. To see the character of that system we have only to look at the permanent Constitution of the Confederate States of America, adopted on March 11, 1861.

THE CONFEDERATE CONSTITUTION AND SLAVERY

It has been conventional to say, with Nathaniel Wright Stephenson, that the framers of the Confederate Constitution "left unstated their most distinctive views." [119] The new document, it is true, was largely a scissors-and-paste redaction of the original Constitution of the United States and its amendments.[120] The seceding states, ironically enough, said nothing whatever in their Constitution about the right of secession. Though the preamble included the phrase "each State acting in its sovereign and independent character," the actual restrictions placed upon the powers of the states were almost precisely what they had been in the old Constitution. The general government had slightly less power in certain respects and slightly more

---

[117] This was the essence of his "Freeport Doctrine": "It matters not what way the Supreme Court may hereafter decide as to the abstract question whether slavery may or may not go into a territory under the constitution, the people have the lawful means to introduce it or exclude it as they please, for the reason that slavery cannot exist a day or an hour anywhere, unless it is supported by local police regulations." Douglas, speech in debate at Freeport, Aug. 27, 1858, in Lincoln, *Collected Works*, III: 51.

[118] Notably J. G. de Roulhac Hamilton, cited in n. 20 above.

[119] Stephenson, *The Day of the Confederacy* (New Haven, 1919), 10 n.

[120] The texts of the Constitution of the United States and of the permanent Constitution of the Confederate States of America are conveniently printed in parallel columns, with differences indicated by italics, in App. K of Jefferson Davis, *Rise and Fall of the Confederate Government*, I: 648–75.

in others; on balance, the relative influence of the central government and the states was about the same as before.[121]

On one matter, however, the "distinctive views" of the framers were completely worked out. With respect to the extra-jurisdictional claims of slavery—particularly, its claim to protection throughout the territories—the Confederate Constitution left nothing to surmise or to chance. It spelled out every one of the crucial demands that proslavery leaders had made. But —and this is the most striking fact of all—once these demands were incorporated in the written Constitution, the state-sovereignty theory of the territories was quietly jettisoned. With respect to slavery, the Confederate Constitution created a much more "consolidated" union than any which antislavery leaders had been accused of desiring.

Partisans of slavery had denied that the old Constitution gave to Congress the power to legislate for the territories. Instead of clearing up the doubtful point by specifically denying Congress the disputed power and reserving it to the states, the framers of the Confederate Constitution did precisely the opposite. They *granted* their Congress the power in set terms. After revising the old clause about "all needful Rules and Regulations respecting the Territory or other Property belonging to the United States," so that it would refer clearly to real estate,[122] they went on to add a new paragraph, the first sentence of which reads as follows:

> The Confederate States may acquire new territory; and Congress shall have power to legislate and provide governments for the inhabitants of all territory belonging to the Confederate States, lying without the limits of the several States; and may permit them, at such times and in such manner as it may by law provide, to form States to be admitted into the Confederacy.[123]

This was a grant of precisely the power which Republicans had insisted, all along, that the federal government did and must possess. Abandoned completely was the state-sovereignty argument that the federal government was,

---

[121] For example, protective tariffs, bounties, and federal appropriations for internal improvements were prohibited (Art. I, sec. 8, clauses 1 and 3), but export duties were permitted by two-thirds vote of both houses (Art. I, sec. 9, clause 6) and amendments to the Constitution required ratification by two thirds instead of three fourths of the states (Art. V, sec. 1). The phrase about "general welfare" was omitted from the grant of financial powers, but the "necessary and proper" clause was retained intact (Art. I, sec. 8, clauses 1 and 18). On the one hand, a state legislature might impeach a federal officer "resident and acting solely within [its] limits" (Art. I, sec. 2, clause 5); on the other, the power of the federal executive was enhanced by giving the President the power to veto individual items in an appropriation bill (Art. I, sec. 7, clause 2), by requiring a two-thirds vote of both houses to appropriate money not asked by him (Art. I, sec. 9, clause 9), by giving him an explicit removal power (Art. II, sec. 2, clause 3), and by authorizing Congress to grant Cabinet members a seat on the floor (Art. I, sec. 6, clause 2).

[122] ". . . all needful rules and regulations concerning the property of the Confederate States, including the lands thereof." Art. IV, sec. 3, clause 2.

[123] Art. IV, sec. 3, clause 3, sentence 1.

with respect to the territories, merely the trustee of the several states. The Confederate Constitution wiped out, at a stroke, the theory of the Union on which the Dred Scott decision had rested.

The reason for abandoning the state-sovereignty theory of the Union becomes obvious when one reads the rest of the clause just quoted. The following sentence completes the paragraph:

> In all such territory, the institution of negro slavery, as it now exists in the Confederate States, shall be recognized and protected by Congress and by the territorial government; and the inhabitants of the several Confederate States and Territories shall have the right to take to such Territory any slaves lawfully held by them in any of the States or Territories of the Confederate States.[124]

The institution of slavery was now placed, firmly and unequivocally, under *national* protection. The state-sovereignty theory of the territories, so long the basis of proslavery demands, had served its purpose. It was now not only useless but potentially harmful. It might conceivably weaken the centralized safeguards for slavery newly provided.

Any danger to slavery from the policy of nationalization was effectually prevented by one new constitutional restriction on federal power. The Confederate Congress was forbidden to pass any "law denying or impairing the right of property in negro slaves."[125] Moreover, the new Constitution guaranteed to slave-owners extra-jurisdictional rights throughout the Confederacy—not only in the territories but within the member states as well. Citizens of each state were entitled to "the right of transit and sojourn in any State of this Confederacy, with their slaves and other property; and the right of property in said slaves shall not be thereby impaired."[126] Finally, the fugitive-slave clause was enlarged to cover slaves "lawfully carried into" another state, as well as those escaping to it.[127] No law of any state, according to the new provision, could work the emancipation of a foreign-owned slave found upon its soil, no matter how the slave had come there.

One element of state sovereignty theoretically remained. A state was not forbidden to abolish slavery. It is difficult to say, however, exactly what the abolition of slavery by a single state could have actually meant, in the

---

[124] *Ibid.*, sentence 2.   [125] Art. I, sec. 9, clause 4.   [126] Art. IV, sec. 2, clause 1.

[127] Art. IV, sec. 2, clause 3. Jefferson Davis embodied all these provisions in a proposal to amend the Constitution of the United States, which he presented to the Senate on Dec. 24, 1860: "*Resolved*, That it shall be declared, by amendment of the Constitution, that property in slaves, recognized as such by the local law of any of the States of the Union, shall stand on the same footing in all constitutional and Federal relations as any other species of property so recognized; and, like other property, shall not be subject to be divested or impaired by the local law of any other State, either in escape thereto, or of transit or sojourn of the owner therein; and in no case whatever shall such property be subject to be divested or impaired by any legislative act of the United States, or of any of the Territories thereof." *Globe*, 36 Cong., 2 Sess., 190. Less than a month later Davis vacated his seat after announcing the secession of his state, Mississippi. *Ibid.*, 487 (Jan. 21, 1861).

context of the Confederate Constitution. No time limit was specified in connection with the right of transit and sojourn. Any Confederate statute that prescribed the duration of a slaveowner's sojourn with his slaves in a state that had "abolished" slavery would undoubtedly run afoul of the provision forbidding any law "impairing the right of property in negro slaves." At the same time, a state statute that gave freedom to slaves who had been kept within its limits longer than a specified time would certainly violate the Constitution, which forbade a state to discharge from service or labor a slave "lawfully carried into" it. Presumably a state might forbid its own citizens to possess slaves, but it could do little else. The state could not constitutionally exclude slaves or compel foreign slaveowners to remove or emancipate them. And it could hardly regulate the use to which such imported slaves might be put without transgressing one or another of the injunctions of the Confederate Constitution.

Slavery was no longer a local institution, the Confederate Constitution made it a national one. With respect to slavery the Confederacy was a unitary, consolidated, national state, denying to each of its allegedly sovereign members any sort of local autonomy with respect to this particular one among its domestic institutions.

CONCLUDING REFLECTIONS

In the long aftermath of the Civil War, leaders of the former Confederacy built up an elaborate apologia explaining what they had been about. Central to their thesis was the assertion that the South had contended, single-mindedly and consistently, for one basic constitutional philosophy—the philosophy that opposed centralization and exalted local self-government. Writing in 1868, Alexander H. Stephens of Georgia, Vice-President of the Confederate States, declared that "this whole subject of Slavery, so-called, in any and every view of it, was, to the Seceding States, but a drop in the ocean compared with . . . other considerations." [128] These were, in the highest and purest sense, constitutional considerations. The war, he maintained, resulted from the prolonged resistance of the South to "the assumption on the part of the Federal authorities, that the people of the several States were . . . citizens of the United States, and owed allegiance to the Federal Government, as the absolute Sovereign power over the whole country, consolidated into one Nation." [129]

A Lost Cause must have its myths. But before myths became necessary—before the cause became a lost one—Alexander H. Stephens saw just as clearly, and stated just as openly, as any other southern leader, the question at issue. On March 21, 1861, six weeks after his election to the second

---

[128] Stephens, *Constitutional View of the Late War between the States,* I: 542.
[129] *Ibid.,* 29.

highest post in the new Confederate government, Stephens delivered at Savannah what was thereafter known as his "corner-stone speech." Eulogiz· ing the frame of government just erected, he said:

> The new constitution has put at rest, *forever,* all the agitating ques-
> tions relating to our peculiar institution—African slavery as it exists
> amongst us—the proper *status* of the negro in our form of civilization.
> This was the immediate cause of the late rupture and present revolu-
> tion.

Explicitly repudiating the antislavery sentiments of Thomas Jefferson, Stephens continued:

> The prevailing ideas entertained by him and most of the leading
> statesmen at the time of the formation of the old constitution, were
> that the enslavement of the African was . . . wrong in *principle,*
> socially, morally, and politically. . . . This was an error. . . .
>
> Our new government is founded upon exactly the opposite idea; its
> foundations are laid, its corner-stone rests upon the great truth, that
> the negro is not equal to the white man; that slavery—subordination
> to the superior race—is his natural and normal condition.
>
> This, our new government, is the first, in the history of the world,
> based upon this great physical, philosophical, and moral truth.[130]

Alexander H. Stephens was speaking, in 1861, with complete under-standing and complete accuracy. The drafters of the Confederate Consti-tution had added to the document they inherited only such provisions as they deemed essential for securing to themselves and their posterity the blessings they had given up hope of securing within the old Union. What these blessings were supposed to be, the Confederate Constitution made crystal clear. Its people were to enjoy the privilege of living—to use Stephen's carefully chosen words—under a government, the first in the history of the world, whose foundations were laid, whose cornerstone rested, upon the great philosophical and moral truth that the enslavement of one part of the human race is not a wrong but the opposite of a wrong —that slavery is the natural and normal condition of the colored races of the world. To build this principle into the very fabric of a new government was the purpose of the Confederate Constitution. To build it into the fabric of the old government had been the purpose of the constitutional theorists who elaborated the doctrine of state sovereignty before 1860.

State sovereignty, as I have already said, was a doctrine of power, not a doctrine of rights. Any contention that it operated to safeguard the *rights*

---

[130] Corner-Stone Speech, March 21, 1861, reprinted in Henry Cleveland, *Alexander H. Stephens, in Public and Private: With Letters and Speeches* (Philadelphia, 1866), 721. Stephens gave excerpts from this speech in his *Constitutional View,* II: 85–86, 521–24, but did not include the passages quoted here.

of minorities is utterly specious.[131] What the theory did attempt to safe-guard was the *power* of a regional elite, which happened to find itself a minority in the nation as a whole. And the power that was to be sustained included the power to domineer over all minorities within the ambit of authority and influence of this privileged group or class. By employing the high language of sovereignty, moreover, they were demanding a power that would be absolute, unquestioned, and uncontrolled.

State sovereignty was a theory designed not to protect but to override individual rights. This was the character of the doctrine during the crisis of 1846–1860, when its obvious purpose was to perpetuate a system that kept human beings in bondage, thus denying them the elementary right of freedom. This is the character of the refurbished doctrine today, when its obvious purpose is to perpetuate a system of racial segregation that denies to men and women of color the right to that "equal protection of the laws" which the Constitution of the United States explicitly guarantees.

---

[131] The most respectable statement of this curious, but widely accepted, interpretation is by Jesse T. Carpenter. Writing in 1930, he said: "No problem is more pressing in governments of the people and by the people than the problem of minorities. If in a democracy political power resides in numbers, what rights, if any, has a minority to im-pose restraints upon the will of a numerical majority?" No one can deny the profound importance of the question, but one can well doubt Carpenter's assumption that a relevant answer can be found by conceiving "of the Old South as a sectional minority consciously striving for seventy odd years to evolve an adequate philosophy of protection to its interests in the American Union." His conclusion can only be described as fantastic: "Here in the first great experiment in democracy is found the first thorough treatment of democracy's greatest problem: the relation of numerical majority rule to effective minority protection." Carpenter, *The South as a Conscious Minority, 1789–1861* (New York, 1930), 3.

XVII

The Civil War: Repressible or Irrepressible Conflict?

INTRODUCTION

The subject of our great Civil War has provoked and inspired and continues to provoke and inspire the most voluminous historical literature in America. A great part of this literature was highly controversial from its beginnings. It was most so among the generation which made and fought the War. Henry Wilson (The Rise and Fall of the Slave Power, *3 volumes, 1872–1877) saw slavery and the slavocracy as the primary cause of the war, and Alexander H. Stephens* (A Constitutional View of the Late War Between the States, *2 volumes, 1868–1870) saw the cause of the South as the cause of the Grecian against the Asiatic form of government, of liberty (states rights) against a leviathan centralism (a coercive union). At the end of the century, James Ford Rhodes, in his multivolume work covering the last half of the century, asserted firmly and confidently that it could be safely stated that the Civil War arose from a single cause—slavery.*

Twentieth-century historians have differed as much among themselves as nineteenth-century historians did. Charles Beard saw the Civil War as the "Second American Revolution," the contest between industrial, finance capitalism and cotton capitalism, and saw the victory of the North as the victory of the former, which wrote its program into legislation after the departure of the Southern members of Congress. Edward Channing entitled the sixth and last volume of his history of the United States The Struggle for Southern Nationality *(1925), in which he developed the idea that the Southern states by 1860 stood before the world with the attributes of nationhood and were struggling for independence.*

In the thirties there was a tendency on the part of some historians (notably Dwight Dumond and Gilbert Barnes) to redirect attention to slavery as the primary cause of the tensions that led up to secession and war. But at the same time there emerged a new and more numerous school of historians calling themselves "revisionists" or "realists," who reached the peak of their influence during the forties. The most prominent historians in this school are Avery Craven, Frank Owsley, and J. G. Randall, of whom, though this could be argued, the last attained the highest reputation. This group developed the idea of the "repressible conflict," the "needless war" as applied to the Civil War. "If one word or phrase were selected to account for the War," Randall stated, "that word would not be slavery, or states rights, or diverse civilization. It would have to be such a word as fanaticism (on both sides) or misunderstanding, or perhaps politics." A "blundering generation" under the impulse of fanaticism and passion, and driven forward by emotional catchwords (Bleeding Kansas, Black Republican, Bully Brooks) involved Americans of the 1860's in the most costly, though tragically "needless," civil war the world had yet known. The essay by Randall printed below develops these ideas, but they are best sought in his extensive writings in book form on the Civil War period.

There has been in the fifties a strong reaction against the revisionist school. Characteristic of this reaction, though it has its strong American partisans, is the essay by the Dutch historian, Pieter Geyl, reproduced below.

The Blundering Generation

J. G. Randall[1]

When one visits a moving picture, or reads Hergesheimer's *Swords and Roses,* which is much the same thing, he may gather the impression that the Civil War, fought in the days before mechanized divisions, aerial bombs, and tanks, was a kind of *chanson de geste* in real life. "The Civil War in America," writes Hergesheimer, "was the last of all wars fought in the grand manner. It was the last romantic war, when army corps fought as individuals and lines of assault . . . charged the visible enemy." "The war created a heroism . . . that clad fact in the splendor of battle flags."[2] Hergesheimer feeds his readers chunks of sombre beauty, winterless climate, air stirred with faint cool music, fine houses, Spanish moss and cypress, trumpet vine and bay blossom, live oaks and linden, bridal wreath, japonica, moonflower, and honeysuckle. In his foreword to "Dear Blanche" he writes: "Here is a book of swords . . . of old-fashioned dark roses . . . [of] the simpler loveliness of the past." His pages live up to the foreword. He gives dear Blanche "The Rose of Mississippi," "The Lonely Star," "Shadows on the Sea," and "Gold Spurs." Of "Jeb" Stuart he says:

> Ladies in Maryland gave him the spurs and ladies wherever he chanced to be gave him the rosebuds. . . . Naturally he was in the cavalry. He was different. . . . [He] wore a brown felt hat . . . with . . . sweeping black plume; . . . his boots in action were heavy, . . . afterwards he changed them for immaculate boots of patent leather worked with gold thread; but he danced as well as fought in his spurs.[3]

From *Mississippi Valley Historical Review,* XXVII (June 1940), 3–28. Reprinted by permission.

[1] Presidential address delivered before the Mississippi Valley Historical Association at Omaha on May 2, 1940.

[2] Joseph Hergesheimer, *Swords and Roses* (New York, 1929), 297, 299.　　[3] *Ibid.,* 267.

The picture is filled in with red-lined cape, French sabre, yellow sash and tassels, The Bugles Sang Truce, The Dew is on the Blossom, orders given when asleep, animal vitality dancing in brilliant eyes.

Escapists may put what they will between the covers of a book; unfortunately the historian must be a realist. Whatever may be the thrill, or the emotional spree, of treating the Civil War romantically, it may be assumed that this has not been neglected. This paper, therefore, will attempt a very different task, that of weighing some Civil War realities, examining some of the irrational ideas of war "causation," and pondering some aspects of the Civil War mind.

Without stressing that Zeebrugge or Westerplatte or the Karelian Isthmus matched any Civil War exploit, or that aviation is as smart as cavalry, it is sufficient to note a few comparisons. If the World War produced more deaths, the Civil War produced more American deaths. If weapons have become more brutal, at least medicine and sanitation have advanced. One seldom reads of the Civil War in terms of sick and wounded. Medical officers of the sixties repeated the experience of a British medical officer in the Burmese War who advised his commander how to avoid scurvy and was told: "Medical opinions are very good when called for." [4] A Union surgeon at Bull Run reported extreme difficulty in inducing field officers to listen to complaints of disease resulting from foul tents into which fresh air was "seldom if ever" [5] admitted. Because ambulances were on the wrong side of the road, this also at Bull Run, twelve thousand troops had to pass before some of the wounded could be taken to the emergency hospital.[6] Wounded men arriving from the field were thrust into freight cars where they lay on the bare floor without food for a day; numbers died on the road.[7] One of the officers refused hospital admittance to wounded soldiers not of his regiment.[8] Medical supplies were thrown away for want of transportation,[9] injured men were exposed to heavy rain,[10] gangrene resulted from minor wounds.[11]

Romance and glory suggest at least the memory of a name. This implies an identified grave, but after making calculations based upon the official medical history issued by the surgeon general, the student would have to inform dear Blanche, or perhaps Mr. Ripley, that if the surgeon general's figures are right the unknown dead for the Civil War exceeded the number killed in battle! In round numbers there were about 110,000 Union deaths from battle, but the surgeon general reported that in November, 1870, there were 315,555 soldier graves, of which only 172,109 had been identified by name,[12] leaving over 143,000 unidentified graves.

---

[4] Joseph K. Barnes, ed., *The Medical and Surgical History of the War of the Rebellion* (Washington, second issue, 1875), Pt. 1, Vol. I, Append., 2.

[5] *Ibid.*, Append., 1.   [6] *Ibid.*, Append., 2.   [7] *Ibid.*, Append., 7.   [8] *Ibid.*, Append., 3.

[9] *Ibid.*, Append., 99.   [10] *Ibid.*, Append., 146.   [11] *Ibid.*, Append., 137.

[12] *Ibid.*, Intro., xxxiii.

The number of soldiers known in the adjutant general's records to have died during the war is much greater than the number identified as to burial or reburial. It must be remembered that the soldier regularly carried no means of identification, that graves of men buried by comrades were marked by hasty devices, that Confederates appropriated Union arms and clothing, that teamsters, refugees, camp followers, or even fugitive slaves might have been buried with soldiers, and that the number reported as killed in action was inaccurate.[13] Yet after making all these allowances, the vast number of the nameless leaves the inquiring mind unsatisfied. It is no more satisfactory to realize that about half the Union army became human waste in one form or another, as dead, disabled, deserted, or imprisoned.[14]

"Jeb" Stuart may have worn gold spurs, but the common soldier was more familiar with fleas. Sashes may have adorned generals but privates were often in rags. It was reported that one of the army surgeons boarded for an entire winter on Sanitary Commission stores.[15] Camps were dirty, sanitation was faulty, cooking was shiftless. Reporting on one of the hospitals, an inspector referred to a leaky roof, broken glass, dirty stairs, insufficient sanitary facilities, and unclean disgusting beds.[16] The soldier who was brutally struck by a sentry of his own company or who contracted malaria would hardly think of his experience as a thing of romance. Without exposing all the euphemisms that obscure the truth of this subject, it may be noted that the great majority of Union deaths were from causes medically regarded as preventable, leaving aside the cynical assumption that war itself is not preventable. Pneumonia, typhus, cholera, miasmic

---

[13] *Ibid.*, Intro., xxxiv, xxxvi; Charles G. Souder, Medical Corps, U. S. Army, to the author, November 17, 1939.

[14] Of 360,000 Union deaths (round numbers), 110,000 resulted from battle, over 224,500 from disease, and nearly 25,000 from miscellaneous causes including suicide. United States Adjutant General's letter to the author, November 3, 1939. Suicides are mentioned by J. J. Woodward who writes the introduction to Barnes, *Medical and Surgical History*, Pt. 1, Vol. I, xxxvii. Woodward also (*loc. cit.*, intro., xlii), states that there were 285,545 men discharged from the Union army for disability. The adjutant general mentions 223,535 discharged for "physical disability" (letter to author, November 3, 1939). Union prisoners numbered nearly 195,000 and Union deserters, not counting draft dodgers, may be conservatively estimated at about 200,000. James G. Randall, *Civil War and Reconstruction* (Boston, 1937), 439, 432; Fred A. Shannon, *Organization and Administration of the Union Army, 1861–1865* (Cleveland, 1928), II, 179 n. It thus appears that over a million were among the dead, disabled, deserted, or imprisoned. A careful statistician has stated: "It is doubtful if there were 2,000,000 individuals actually in [Union] service during the [Civil] war." William F. Fox, *Regimental Losses in the American Civil War, 1861–65* (Albany, 1889), 527.

[15] Lewis H. Steiner, "Account of the Field Relief Corps of the U. S. Sanitary Commission of the Army of the Potomac," *Sanitary Commission, Pamphlet No. 72* (New York, 1863), 6.

[16] H. W. Bellows, "Notes of a Preliminary Sanitary Survey of the Forces of the United States in the Ohio and Mississippi Valleys near Midsummer, 1861," *Sanitary Commission, Pamphlet No. 26* (Washington, 1861), 15.

fever, and the like hardly find their way into the pages of war romance, but they wrought more havoc than bayonets and guns. Where there was danger of infection the rule-of-thumb principle of the Civil War surgeon was to amputate,[17] and from operating tables, such as they were, at Gettysburg, arms and legs were carried away in wagon loads. Marching was hatefully wearisome, desertion was rampant, corruption was rife. Individual injustices of the war were shocking. Some generals got credit that was undeserved, others were broken by false report or slandered by an investigating committee of Congress. The men who languished in prison were several times more numerous than those stopped by bullets. That there was heroism in the war is not doubted, but to thousands the war was as romantic as prison rats and as gallant as typhoid or syphilis.

One does not often speak or read of the war in reality, of its blood and filth, of mutilated flesh, and other revolting things.[18] This restraint is necessary, but it ought to be recognized that the war is not presented when one writes of debates in Congress, of flanking movements, of retreats and advances, of cavalry and infantry, of divisions doing this and brigades doing that. In the sense of full realism war cannot be discussed. The human mind will not stand for it. For the very word "war" the realist would have to substitute some such term as "organized murder" or "human slaughterhouse." In drama as distinguished from melodrama murder often occurs offstage. In most historical accounts, especially military narratives, the war is offstage in that its stench and hideousness do not appear.

With all the recent revisionist studies it is difficult to achieve a full realization of how Lincoln's generation stumbled into a ghastly war, how it blundered during four years of indecisive slaughter, and how the triumph of the Union was spoiled by the manner in which the victory was used. In the hateful results of the war over long decades one finds partisanship at its worst. To see the period as it was is to witness uninspired spectacles of prejudice, error, intolerance, and selfish grasping. The Union army was inefficiently raised, poorly administered, and often badly commanded. In government there was deadlock, cross purpose, and extravagance. One can say that Lincoln was honest, but not that the country was free from corruption during the Lincoln administration. There was cotton plundering, army-contract graft, and speculative greed. Where Lincoln was at his best, where he was moderate, temperate, and far-seeing, he did not carry his

---

[17] "In army practice, attempts to save a limb which might be perfectly successful in civil life, cannot be made . . . . Conservative surgery is here an error; in order to save life, the limb must be sacrificed." Frederick L. Olmsted, "Report of a Committee of the Associate Medical Members of the Sanitary Commission on the Subject of Amputations," *Sanitary Commission F* (Washington, 1861), 5.

[18] In postwar reminiscence the Union soldier might hold forth on the subject of the war as a purifying force and a builder of character where the same individual during the war recorded his feeling of disgust with what was around him, of degradation, and of the tearing down of character.

party with him. Even those matters dissociated from the war, such as home-steading and railroad extension, came to be marred by exploitation and crooked finance. The period of the Civil War and the era of Jim Fisk and Jay Gould were one and the same generation.

If it was a "needless war," a "repressible conflict," as scholars now believe, then indeed was the generation misled in its unctuous fury. To suppose that the Union could not have been continued or slavery outmoded without the war and without the corrupt concomitants of the war, is hardly an enlightened assumption. If one questions the term "blundering generation," let him inquire how many measures of the time he would wish copied or repeated if the period were to be approached with a clean slate and to be lived again. Most of the measures are held up as things to be avoided. Of course it is not suggested that the generation of the sixties had any copyright on blundering. It is not that democracy was at fault. After all, civil war has not become chronic on these shores, as it has in some nations where politics of force is the rule. One can at least say that the Civil War was exceptional; that may be the best thing that can be said about it. A fuller measure of democracy would probably have prevented the war or at least have mitigated its abuses. To overlook many decades of American democracy and take the Civil War period as its test, would be to give an unfair appraisal. Nor does this probing of blunders involve lack of respect for the human beings of that generation. As individuals we love and admire them, these men and women who look at us from the tintypes and Brady photographs of the sixties, though we may have "malice toward some." The distortions and errors of the time were rather a matter of mass thinking, of social solidification, and of politics.

In the present vogue of psychiatry, individual mental processes and behavior have been elaborately studied. Psychiatry for a nation, however, is still in embryo, though it is much the fashion to have discussions of mass behaviorism, public opinion, pressure groups, thought patterns, and propaganda. Scholars in the field of history tend more and more to speak in terms of culture; this often is represented as a matter of cultural conflict, as of German against Slav, of Japanese against Chinese, and the like. Such concepts were given overemphasis at the meeting of the American Historical Association last December. Historians are doing their age a disservice if these factors of culture are carried over, as they often are, whether by historians or others, into justifications or "explanations" of war. The note of caution here should be a note of honest inquiry. It may be seriously doubted whether war rises from fundamental motives of culture or economics so much as from the lack of cultural restraint or economic inhibition upon militaristic megalomania. Modern wars do not relieve population pressure. Whether wars are need for economic outlets or for obtaining raw materials is highly doubtful. International trade brings all that. Those who create war throttle the very flow of trade that would promote economic objectives. Where the economy of a nation hinges upon an export market, it may happen that plotters of war in that nation will stupidly kill that market by devices of economic autarchy and then claim that they have to go to war to have trade outlets. It is the same with incoming goods. Of such is the economic argument for war. War makers do not open up economic benefit so much as they stifle it. Their relation to culture is no better than their relation to economy.

There is the word astrology for bogus astronomy and alchemy for false chemistry. Ought there not to be some such word for the economic alchemists of this world? Perhaps it exists in the word autarchy. Is it not in the category of bogus economics, or *ersatz* economics, that one should put those who study war as a matter of trade, supply, resources, needs, and production? As for the Civil War the stretch and span of conscious economic motive was much smaller than the areas or classes of war involvement. Economic diversity offered as much motive for union, in order to have a well rounded nation, as for the kind of economic conflict suggested by secession. One fault of writers who associate war-making with economic advantage is false or defective economics; another is the historical fault. It is surprising how seldom the economic explanation of war has made its case historically, *i.e.* in terms of adequate historical evidence bearing upon those points and those minds where actually the plunge into war occurred. One hears war treated as a matter of culture, but cultural and racial consciousness are as strong in Scandinavia or the Netherlands or Switzerland as in militarist-ridden countries. To make conquest a matter of culture is poor history. It may be the vanquished whose culture survives. Culture is not easily transplanted if force be the method. When war comes by the violence of a few in control and by the stifling of economic and cultural processes, it ill becomes the scholar to add his piping to the cacophonous blare of militaristic propaganda.

War causation tends to be "explained" in terms of great forces. Something elemental is supposed to be at work, be it nationalism, race conflict, or quest for economic advantage. With these forces predicated, the move toward war is alleged to be understandable, to be explained, and therefore to be in some sense reasonable. Thought runs in biological channels and nations are conceived as organisms. Such thought is not confined to philosophers; it is the commonest of mental patterns. A cartoonist habitually draws a nation as a person. In this manner of thinking Germany does so and so; John Bull takes this or that course, and so on. When thought takes so homely a form it is hardly called a philosophical concept; for that purpose the very same thing would appear under a Greek derivative or Freudian label. However labeled, it may be questioned whether the concept is any better than a poor figure of speech, a defective metaphor which is misleading because it has a degree of truth.

Ruritania—to be no more specific—does so and so in the sense that it has a government, the government acts for the nation, and for political purposes there is no other way in which the country can act. The doubtful part is to infer that there is one directing mind for Ruritania which is the distillation of all the millions of minds. Where government has a bogus quality such an inference is more doubtful than if government has a well grounded or established quality. Given certain conditions of forced leadership and suppressed thought, the oneness of executive action in a nation may in fact represent nothing at all in terms of consolidated will and intent distilled from the whole mass. What passes for mass thought these days is not so much distilled as it is translated from golden plates handed down on some ideological Hill of Cumorah and read through the magic of authoritarian Urim and Thummim. The terrifying fact is that such bogus thought can be manufactured; it can be produced wholesale and distributed at top speed; it can control a nation; it is the shabby mental *ersatz* of an abnormal period.

War-making is too much dignified if it is told in terms of broad national urges, of great German motives, or of compelling Russian ambitions. When nations stumble into war, or when peoples rub their eyes and find they have been dragged into war, there is at some point a psychopathic case. Omit the element of abnormality, or of bogus leadership, or inordinate ambition for conquest, and diagnosis fails. In the modern scene it fails also if one omits manipulation, dummies, bogeys, false fronts, provocative agents, made-up incidents, frustration of elemental impulses, negation of culture, propaganda that is false in intent, criminal usurpation, and terrorist violence. These are reflections on the present bedeviled age, but their pertinence to the subject at hand is seen in the fact that scholarly discussions in explanation of war on the economic or cultural basis frequently include the Civil War as a supposedly convincing example. The writer doubts seriously whether a consensus of scholars who have competently studied the Civil War would accept either the cultural motive or the economic basis as the effective cause.

If one were to explain how this or that group or individual got into the Civil War, he could rely on no one formula. He would have to make up a series of elements or situations of which the following are only a few that might be mentioned: the despairing plunge, the unmotivated drift, the intruding dilemma, the blasted hope, the self-fulfilling prediction, the push-over, the twisted argument, the frustrated leader, the advocate of rule or ruin, and the reform-your-neighbor prophet. Robert Toombs said he would resist Stephen A. Douglas though he could see "nothing but . . . defeat in the future" [19]; there is your despairing plunge. Young Henry Watterson, a Tennessee antislavery Unionist who fought for the Confederacy,

---

[19] Ulrich B. Phillips, ed., *The Correspondence of Robert Toombs, Alexander H. Stephens, and Howell Cobb*, in *American Historical Association, Annual Report, 1911* (Washington, 1913), II, 469.

is an example of the unmotivated drift. To many an individual the problem was not to fight with the side whose policies he approved of, but to be associated with the right set. Such an individual motive could not by a process of multiplication become in any reasonable sense a large-group motive. Yet it would be understandable for the individual. Usually in war time individuals have no choice of side, though in the American Civil War they sometimes did, especially on the border. Even where such choice was possible, the going to war by the individual in the sixties was due less to any broad "cause" or motive than to the fact that war existed, so that fighting was the thing to do. The obtaining of soldiers is not a matter of genuine persuasion as to issues. War participation is not a proof of war attitude.

The intruding dilemma was found in the great border and the great upper South where one of two ugly courses had to be chosen, though neither choice made sense in terms of objectives and interests in those broad regions.[20] The self-fulfilling prediction is recognized in the case of those who, having said that war must come, worked powerfully to make it come. The blasted hope, *i.e.* the wish for adjustment instead of butchery, was the experience of most of the people, especially in the border and upper South. The frustrated leader is seen in the Unionist who came to support secession, or in such northerners as Thurlow Weed and William H. Seward who sought compromise and then supported war. The plea that "better terms" could be had out of the Union, which implied a short secession gesture though uttered by determined secessionists, was the crafty argument for secession to be used in addressing Unionists. This might be dubbed the twisted argument. The push-over is seen in the whole strategy of secession leaders by which anti-secession states and Union-loving men were to be dragged in by the accelerated march of events.

These are things which belong as much to the "explanation" of the Civil War as any broad economic or cultural or elemental factor. It should be remembered how few of the active promoters of secession became leaders of the Confederacy; their place in the drama was in the first act, in the starting of trouble. Nor should sectional preference cause one to forget how large a contribution to Union disaster, and how little to success, was given by northern radicals during the war. Clear thinking would require a distinction between causing the war and getting into the war. Discussion which overlooks this becomes foggy indeed. It was small minorities that caused the war; then the regions and sections got into it. No one seems to have thought of letting the minorities fight it out. Yet writers who descant upon the causation of the war write grandly of vast sections, as if the fact of a section being dragged into the slaughter was the same as the interests of

---

[20] "They say Virginia 'has no grievance.'" Entry of May 9, 1861, Mary B. Chesnut, *A Diary from Dixie* (New York, 1906), 50.

that section being consciously operative in its causation. Here lies one of the chief fallacies of them all.

In writing of human nature in politics Graham Wallas has shown the potent effect of irrational attitudes.[21] He might have found many a Civil War example. None of the "explanations" of the war make sense, if fully analyzed. The war has been "explained" by the choice of a Republican president, by grievances, by sectional economics, by the cultural wish for southern independence, by slavery, or by events at Sumter. But these explanations crack when carefully examined. The election of Lincoln fell so far short of swinging southern sentiment against the Union that secessionists were still unwilling to trust their case to an all-southern convention or to cooperation among southern states. In every election from 1840 to 1852 Lincoln voted for the same candidate for whom many thousands of southerners voted. Lincoln deplored the demise of the Whig party and would have been only too glad to have voted in 1856 for another Harrison, another Taylor, or another Fillmore. Alexander Stephens stated that secessionists did not desire redress of grievances and would obstruct such redress. Prophets of sectional economics left many a southerner unconvinced; it is doubtful how far their arguments extended beyond the sizzling pages of *De Bow's Review* and the agenda of southern commercial congresses. The tariff was a potential future annoyance rather than an acute grievance in 1860. What existed then was largely a southern tariff law. Practically all tariffs are one-sided. Sectional tariffs in other periods have existed without producing war. Southern independence on broad cultural lines is probably more of a modern thesis than a contemporary motive of sufficient force to have carried the South out of the Union on any cooperative, all-southern basis.

It was no part of the Republican program to smash slavery in the South, nor did the territorial aspect of slavery mean much politically beyond agitation. Southerners cared little about actually taking slaves into existing territories; Republicans care so little in the opposite sense that they avoided the prohibition of slavery in those territorial laws that were passed with Republican votes in February and March, 1861.[22] Things said of "the South" often failed to apply to southerners, or of "the North" to northerners. Thwarted "Southern rights" were more often a sublimation than a definite entity. "The North" in the militant pre-war sense was largely an abstraction. The Sumter affair was not a cause, but an incident resulting from pre-existing governmental deadlock; Sumter requires explanation, and that explanation carries one back into all the other alleged factors. In contemporary southern comments on Lincoln's course at Sumter one finds

---

[21] Graham Wallas, *Human Nature in Politics* (London, 1909, 1st ed.), *passim.*
[22] These matters are treated by the writer in a paper entitled "The Civil War Restudied," to be published in a forthcoming issue of the *Journal of Southern History.*

not harmony but a jangling of discordant voices. Virginia resented Lincoln's action at Sumter for a reason opposite to that of South Carolina; Virginia's resentment was in the antisecessionist sense. By no means did all the North agree with Lincoln's course as to Sumter. Had Lincoln evacuated Sumter without an expedition, he would have been supported by five and a half of seven cabinet members, Chase taking a halfway stand and Blair alone taking a positive stand for an expedition.[23] What Lincoln refused as to Sumter was what the United States government had permitted in general as to forts and arsenals in the South. Stronger action than at Sumter was taken by Lincoln at Pickens without southern fireworks. There is no North-versus-South pattern that covers the subject of the forts. Nor is the war itself to be glibly explained in rational North-versus-South terms.

Let one take all the factors—the Sumter maneuver, the election of Lincoln, abolitionism, slavery in Kansas, cultural and economic differences—and it will be seen that only by a kind of false display could any of these issues, or all of them together, be said to have caused the war if one omits the elements of emotional unreason and overbold leadership. If one word or phrase were selected to account for the war, that word would not be slavery, or state-rights, or diverse civilizations. It would have to be such a word as fanaticism (on both sides), or misunderstanding, or perhaps politics. To Graham Wallas misunderstanding and politics are the same thing.

The fundamental or the elemental is often no better than a philosophical will o' the wisp. Why do adventitious things, or glaringly abnormal things, have to be elementally or cosmically accounted for? If, without proving his point, the historian makes war a thing of "inevitable" economic conflict, or cultural expression, or *Lebensraum*,[24] his generalizations are caught up by others, for it would seem that those historians who do the most generalizing, if they combine effective writing with it, are the ones who are most often quoted. The historian's pronouncements are taken as the statement of laws whether he means them so or not; he is quoted by sociologists, psychologists, behaviorists, misbehaviorists, propagandists, and what not; he becomes a contributor to those "dynamic" masses of ideas, or ideologies, which are among the sorriest plagues of the present age. As to wars, the ones that have not happened are perhaps best to study. Much could be said about such wars. As much could be said in favor of them as

---

[23] The writer has treated Lincoln's relation to the Sumter question in "When War Came in 1861," *Abraham Lincoln Quarterly* (Springfield, Ill.), I, March, 1940, pp. 3–42. (Cabinet opinion on Sumter is here treated as of March 15, 1861; two weeks later there was a somewhat different cabinet alignment.)

[24] *Lebensraum* as a war motive is meaningless unless one links it with the following factors: the demand of an aggressive nation to own and rule where its nationals live, repudiation of the idea that Dutch can live with Swiss except under Dutch domination, denial of *lebensraum* to the dispossessed people even in their own country, and the ideological justification of such denial on the ground that the intruding race with the bigger guns is superior by nature and has superior rights.

of actual wars. Cultural and economic difficulties in wars that have not occurred are highly significant. The notion that you must have war when you have cultural variation, or economic competition, or sectional difference is an unhistorical misconception which it is stupid in historians to promote. Yet some of the misinterpretations of the Civil War have tended to promote it.

What was the mind of America in Lincoln's day? It was human, which means it was partly simian! It was occidental. It was New World. It was American, though one would have to be a Stephen Benét to state what that means.[25] It had somewhat of a sense of humor, though not enough. It was southern, or Yankee, or midwestern, or otherwise sectional. It was the mind of the McGuffey reader, by which a world of ready-made ideas is suggested. It was Victorian; it had inhibitions which today appear as droll as its unrepressed whiskers. It was less mechanized than today, being of the horse-and-buggy age. It was soul-searching. It was Christian and it was chiefly Protestant; yet the one most numerous faith was Catholic. Religiously it was fundamentalist. It was not profoundly philosophical and took with resentment the impact of Darwinism. Though polyglot it was far from cosmopolitan. The soapbox flavor or the backwoods tang was characteristic of its humorists. It was partly conditioned by racial backgrounds, such as the Dutch, German, Irish, Anglo-Saxon, or Scandinavian. It differed in the degrees of its Americanization; there was a staggering at variant distances from immigrant ancestors. Often the recent immigrant, such as the German or Scandinavian, took American democracy with more simple faith than the seasoned American. When disillusion came to such, it came hard.

The mind of the time was many things socially, being of the four hundred if one considers the De Peysters and Van Courtlands, or Boston Brahmin, or mountaineer, or of the numerous small farmer group, or of the unvocal laboring class. If one were to have searched for class consciousness in this age, it would have been found less among underprivileged masses than among the aristocrats, the planters, the capitalists; it was they who were indeed class-conscious. Such a matter as the southern gentleman's conventionalized code of honor, including the *code duello,* was a bulwark of exclusiveness and a deliberate social barrier.[26]

As to its war attitude, the mind of Lincoln's day was in part a mind during war, in part pro-war, in part anti-war, in part merely at war. Where it was pro-war it was not necessarily militaristic. Where it was German it was usually not Prussian, being spiritually closer to Weimar or Frankfort-

---

[25] Benét did it in the invocation of *John Brown's Body.* Of American historians, Turner has perhaps come as near it as any.

[26] Charles S. Sydnor, "The Southerner and the Laws," presidential address before the Southern Historical Association, Lexington, Kentucky, November 3, 1939, *Journal of Southern History* (University, Louisiana), VI, 1940, pp. 3–23.

on-Main. What is meant here are minds that were more or less genuine; this would rule out the politician whose mind was usually a synthetic affair made up for the vote-getting occasion. The mind of the time was often the product of intra-American migration. Thus it was Virginia or Kentucky in Illinois, Tennessee in Missouri, Vermont in Indiana, Massachusetts or upstate New York in Ohio. Rural areas had contributed more to these migrations than cities; not much relief of urban congestion had come by way of the westward movement. Perhaps predominantly the mind of America was rural. Yet hardly at all was it a peasant mind, much less proletarian. Never would its educated people have called themselves the intelligentsia. To refer to its middle class as bourgeois would be to use a non-American concept. The middle class did not function as a set social type or bloc.

It would be of interest to examine this mind in segments, but they would have to be complex segments. There would be the American-Victorian-New York-élite mind, the midwest-German-farmer mind, the Irish-Tammany-East-side mind, the immigrant-labor mind, the old American frontier mind, and so on. Quite generally it was three things: Victorian, restless, and habituated to politician-like thinking. The puritanical Victorianism of the age combined with financial imperatives when one of Jay Cooke's cashiers committed the astounding indiscretion of driving a four-in-hand in Central Park on a Sunday afternoon. Cooke warned him that if that were known "amongst financial People" it would bring "great discredit to the Bank." "Credit," he admonished, "is a tender plant." Its delicate growth would be affected by "such a stupid display as a four-in-hand." [27] Business men who did not walk the straight and narrow were "under suspicion." Wall Street was an uplifting factor. Sabbath observance had its Bradstreet rating.[28] Yet it may have been the appearance of evil that was detrimental, for corruption was rampant and social disapproval by no means always attached to methods of questionable financial dealing. Graft and special privilege were respectable. Many a fortune of Civil War origin belonged to the ill-gotten class. Defrauding the government did not make one a social pariah.

In spite of much nobility of sentiment, the Civil War mind seems a sorry *melange* of party bile, crisis melodrama, inflated eloquence, unreason, religious fury, self-righteousness, unctuous self-deception, and hate. Bad party feeling was evident when Seward appeared in the Senate on January 9, 1860, "& not a man from the democracy save Douglas . . . came to greet him." "D—n their impudence," was the comment of William P. Fessenden.[29] Yet this was more than a year before the war opened. It was a time of crisis psychosis. Men felt they were living in great days. The genera-

---

[27] Henrietta M. Larson, *Jay Cooke, Private Banker* (Cambridge, 1936), 189.
[28] It would now be called that; in Civil War days it was the R. G. Dun rating.
[29] William P. Fessenden to Hamilton Fish, Washington, January 10, 1860, Hamilton Fish MSS. (Library of Congress.)

tion had its self-consciousness of mission and destiny. Even the private soldier filled his letters with exalted talk. At the beginning of the war a Massachusetts soldier, telling of a rail journey from Boston to New York, wrote: "Refreshments were lavished upon us . . . cannon sent their boom over hill and dale and bells peeled [*sic*] their tocsin of warning . . . that our train was approaching bearing a Regiment of brave hearts to the defence of our country's capitol [*sic*]." Passing the "Constitution" he wrote: "May they the [colors] ever float over that notable ship . . . as she rides proudly upon the waters of the Union." This proudly riding epistle was but a soldier's letter to his brother.[30] Similar attitudes were characteristic of the South; Mrs. Chesnut referred to "the high-flown style which of late seems to have gotten into the very air." [31]

What the war did to the mind of Ralph Waldo Emerson deserves careful study, though here it can be only hinted. To the Emerson of the sixties New England was the custodian of sense and elegance, Boston superiority was axiomatic, the South was boorish as well as wicked, and John Brown, well-known in Concord, was a martyr. There are "crises which demand nations," he thought, and a generation might well perish to insure a better life for generations that follow.[32] "What a healthy tone exists!" he wrote in May, 1861.[33] To Emerson not merely *the war* but *war* was an elemental, purifying force. Ridiculing the sentimentalist, demanding that the North must conquer as a matter of culture, he wrote grandly of a strong wind, of "one energetic mind" where there had been "incapacity to move," of war as a searcher of character. War to Emerson was a "dynamometer," taking the fop in the street, the beau at the ball, and lifting them up by something "in the air." [34] "A civil war," he naively wrote, "sweeps away all the false issues." [35] "This revolution," he said, "is the work of no man, but the effervescence of Nature." [36] Reaching almost Nietzschean ecstasy, he burbled: "War is a realist, shatters everything flimsy and shifty, sets aside all false issues . . . breaks through all that is not real." "On with the war" might have been his slogan. "Let it search," he said, "let it grind, let it overturn, and . . . when it finds no more fuel, it burns out." [37]

To illustrate the benefit of war he looked for a simile and found it in the cholera! On this theme he wrote: "We watch its course [that of the war] as we did the cholera, which . . . took only the susceptible, set its seal on every putrid spot . . . followed the limestone, and left the gran-

---

[30] Lt. H. N. Holbrook, 5th Massachusetts Volunteer Militia, to "Dear Brother James," Washington, D. C., April 28, 1861. (For the use of this manuscript letter the writer is indebted to its owner, H. E. Pratt, executive secretary, Abraham Lincoln Association, Springfield, Illinois.)

[31] Chestnut, *Diary from Dixie*, 3.

[32] Ralph L. Rusk, ed., *The Letters of Ralph Waldo Emerson* (New York, 1939), V, 332.

[33] Edward W. Emerson and Waldo E. Forbes, eds., *Journals of Ralph Waldo Emerson* (Boston, 1909), IX, 325.   [34] *Ibid.*, IX, 411, 429.   [35] *Ibid.*, IX, 459.   [36] *Ibid.*, IX, 572.

[37] *Ibid.*, IX, 461, 462.

ite."[38] What to David Starr Jordan was an annihilator of the finest and of potential descendants of those best fit to reproduce,[39] was to Emerson a beneficial cosmic force finding its origin in the motion of the planets. Norman Angell's great illusion counted its mental victims among those who passed for philosophers.

When philosophers turned war mongers it was not to be expected that pacifists would have a hearing. The broad cause of peace was one of the casualties of war. In its antebellum background the peace crusade in America was a small affair of humanitarian groups with variant attitudes. It embraced men of intelligent idealism, but its efforts never bore fruit as did other crusades such as that of Dorothea Dix for the neglected insane or of Horace Mann for public elementary education. The Peace Society, launched with the impetus of Christian evangelism by William Ladd in 1828, and promoted by Elihu Burritt and other choice spirits, was thirty-three years old when the guns spoke at Sumter. In those years the society had not been idle. It had made use of the familiar techniques of agitation: lectures, local agents, local chapters, tracts, prize essays, magazines, books, national congresses, and petitions to the seat of government. A vigorous literature was produced, world peace congresses were held, arguments against war were marshalled, arbitration among nations urged, and disarmament advocated. Diverse elements were enlisted, such as Quakers, insurance men, free-traders, and merchants.[40]

Pacifism of the early nineteenth century differed from that of the twentieth chiefly in this, that it was economically and socially conservative. Peace agitation was a matter of Christian evangelism and of social stability. It drew more from the Gospel than from fundamental philosophy. Its swing was to the right rather than the left. It did not march with socialism. It contained sectional trouble-makers in its ranks. Christian and conservative as it was, it often met opposition or at least non-cooperation from ordained ministers. Taking a stand against war was difficult and complex. Questions arose touching the duty of fighting a defensive war or concerning the right of revolution. To favor peace in the sense of having governments avoid the outbreak of war was very different from avoiding individual participation once war had broken out. Organized peace men were chiefly northerners, rather northeasterners, and the movement was interlocked with collateral movements, especially antislavery. Peace advocacy might or might not mean nonresistance. Not all peace men could accept Garrison's formula of doing nothing to preserve the Union against armed secession.

When war came and as the struggle dragged on, demands for peace were regarded as a kind of defeatism, of surrender to forces which northern

<hr/>

[38] *Ibid.*, IX, 462.
[39] David S. Jordan and Harvey E. Jordan, *War's Aftermath: A Preliminary Study of the Eugenics of War* (Boston, 1914).
[40] Arthur C. F. Beales, *The History of Peace* (New York, 1931), 53 and *passim*.

idealists considered destructive and evil. Peace became a matter of politics, of anti-Lincoln agitation, of what was called Copperhead disloyalty. Forces that stood outwardly for Christianity denounced it the loudest. Though praising Seward's peace efforts before Sumter, the Peace Society formulated its war-time position after Sumter as follows: *"Peace is always loyal. . . . We cannot . . . tolerate rebellion. . . . The cause of Peace was never meant to meet such a crisis as is now upon us."* [41] The society was a negligible thing; indeed one could read many tomes of American history without seeing it mentioned. It did not associate itself with opposition to the war powers, with anti-Lincoln demands for civil rights, with Vallandigham partisanship, nor with obstruction of the draft. It never made enough of a stir to become notorious. It did not arouse the horrendous and vindictive ire of any Dies committee. Many of its members preferred war to the continuance of slavery; others preferred war to disunion; still others deemed human slaughter not too high a price for ascendancy of a favorite party.

Denunciation of war easily became denunciation of rebellion; this readily passed over into a demand to put down rebellion. The cause of peace as a crusade found a new orientation when war actually existed, for nonresistance could not stop the torrent. It was the dilemma of the pacificist. When peace men face an existing war begun by what they consider an aggressor, their attachment to peace becomes outraged indignation against those who, in their opinion, have broken the peace. Such a feeling is consistent with the motive of stopping the war maker. It is only the cynic who would laugh at the discomfiture of the pacifist when once war exists and when the choice of peace is no longer open. The self-contradiction belongs to those who would put the label of war monger upon peace-time efforts to implement international cooperation and to buttress war prevention. The inconsistency is in misapplying the term "peace bloc" to those isolationist groups which have worked to frustrate international security by way of peaceful organization among nations.

For the Civil War generation the problem of the advocate of peace was only in a limited sense the problem of the conscientious objector. Objectors in the Lincoln period were chiefly associated with established anti-war creeds of religious groups. General objectors on other than religious grounds were not much in evidence. In this the Civil War presented a contrast to the World War, wherein refusal to fight was associated not only with specific Quaker-like groups but with broad liberal attitudes. In both wars the mass effect of organized religion was the opposite of pacifist. In each war administrative authorities of the United States respected the idealism of the objector and gave them the alternative of noncombatant service. In the World War more objectors were relieved than imprisoned, though the

---

[41] *Advocate of Peace* (Boston and Washington), May-June, 1861, p. 258.

imprisoned received the most attention. Imprisonment of objectors as such was not a Civil War practice.

If the pacifist had a dilemma, so did the government. The sincere and serene Christianity of the Quakers could not but command respect, and those who stood their ground were, as a rule, honorably excused from fighting. In the Civil War this leniency was at first an administrative adjustment in a situation where the objector might have expected severe treatment; late in the war it was a matter of statutory amendment to the conscription act. As originally passed the Conscription Act of 1863 did not even exempt ministers. For the objector to stand his ground in early Civil War days meant defiance of the government; the government was demanding a service which the objector refused; leniency was an afterthought. Non-resistance was a Quaker tenet, but here the Quakers, or rather the strictest of them, would have to resist, as did Cyrus Pringle of Vermont, unless their government would make a concession which in such cases it did make. No government can be completely unbending. Government is, after all, an art, perhaps a compromise. If the objector remained obdurate, either the government had to withdraw somewhat from the principle of compulsory military service or a man would be punished for being a Christian. The government took an attitude toward Quakers which it could not take toward all, if conscription were its principle. The Quaker came through the dilemma with less compromise than the government.[42]

It is not of record that Lincoln's Cabinet contained a "minister of national enlightenment and propaganda"; yet propaganda itself was not lacking.[43] In the public "enlightenment" of that time there was boasting, there was rumor, there were atrocity tales, and there was falsehood. Atrocity stories were found not only in newspapers but in congressional reports. There were circumstantial accounts of Confederates bayoneting wounded captives, kicking heads about like footballs, insulting women, and engaging in gruesome tortures. William B. Hesseltine has shown that anti-southern horror tales were not without governmental inspiration in the North and that the secretary of war, the surgeon general, and the committee on the conduct of the war took pains to spread tales of the sufferings of northern prisoners in the South.[44] Motives were various: tales might be spread to carry forward the abolitionist's denunciation of southern cruelty, to satisfy the moral sense by besmirching the foe, or to discourage surrender into southern hands. When the backfire came and these atrocity stories led to

---

[42] Edward N. Wright, *Conscientious Objectors in the Civil War* (Philadelphia, 1931); Rufus M. Jones, *The Later Periods of Quakerism* (London, 1921), II, 728–753; Rufus M. Jones, ed., *The Record of a Quaker Conscience: Cyrus Pringle's Diary* (New York, 1918); Randall, *Civil War and Reconstruction*, 416–419.

[43] G. Winston Smith, Generative Forces of Union Propaganda: A Study in Civil War Pressure Groups (MS. doctoral dissertation, University of Wisconsin, 1939).

[44] William B. Hesseltine, "The Propaganda Literature of Confederate Prisons," *Journal of Southern History*, I, February, 1935, pp. 56–66.

questions as to why prisoners were not exchanged, it became necessary to invent the tale that exchange had been stopped by a vicious South intent upon destroying the lives of prisoners. Even the humanitarian motive promoted atrocity tales, and the report of the Sanitary Commission on this subject in no way fell short of governmental accounts.

Lincoln's attitude on such matters was expressed in a speech delivered at a Sanitary Fair in Baltimore in 1864. Referring to the rumored massacre of colored prisoners at Fort Pillow, Lincoln carefully avoided pointing up the reputed atrocity, declared that the event was not known to have occurred, and promised an investigation. He also promised retribution if needed, but, as in the case of similar threats by the Confederacy, the motive was humanitarian. The threat of retaliation was intended to make actual retaliation unnecessary, as well as to satisfy that type of vindictiveness at the North which was strangely bound up with humanitarianism. On this point Lincoln reached the height of caution when he said: "It will be a matter of grave consideration in what exact course to apply the retribution." [45] What seemed to worry Lincoln was not a vicious South, but the need to satisfy his own northern public, including the humanitarianly vindictive public. For the latter he gave a threat of retribution which in fact he never carried out, and probably never intended to.

In spite of its lack of modern techniques such as radio and the movies, Civil War propaganda found many devices. There were drawings in *Harper's*, *Leslie's*, and *Vanity Fair*, though not daily cartoons. There were popular songs such as "Father Abraham" which gave the chief a nickname and personified the cause in a benevolent President. There was recruiting propaganda by poster and otherwise, and there was partisanly patriotic propaganda in appeals for soldier votes. Generals of the political variety made flourishing speeches. The Loyal Publications Society sent out its material by the bushel, including stereotypes to local editors, tracts, broadsides, pamphlets, and in one case a forged speech attributed to Alexander H. Stephens, whose alleged language was startlingly similar to that of Helper's *Impending Crisis*.[46]

The word "propaganda" is an inexact expression which eludes definition. Every public appeal to support a cause could be loosely called propaganda. An advertisement might be propaganda in this broad sense, so also an editorial, a parade, a novel, a Sanitary Fair, a request for funds, a Thanksgiving proclamation, an anecdote, an envelope, a letter-head, a postage stamp, a dollar bill, a legislative preamble, a sermon, a petition, a sewing circle,

---

[45] John G. Nicolay and John Hay, eds., *Abraham Lincoln, Complete Works* (New York, 1920), 2 vol. ed., II, 514. (In later citations of the *Works* the reference is to this edition.)

[46] Randall, *Civil War and Reconstruction*, 638–639. See also, Frank Freidel, "The Loyal Publication Society: A Pro-Union Propaganda Agency," *Mississippi Valley Historical Review*, XXVI, 359–376.

or a school primer. One might use propaganda in christening a baby, naming a street, or addressing the Almighty. Motives in reaching the public were mixed. Propaganda in Lincoln's day was more often complex than simple, hybrid oftener than thoroughbred; it had one purpose grafted upon another. Publicity for the national cause was universal, but this broad appeal was often linked with an ulterior purpose which was in fact the main interest of the promoting agency. Thus a party rally would masquerade as a Union mass meeting, an appeal for peace in England might be an effort to withhold ironclads from the Confederacy, a volunteer fire brigade would be a unit of Tammany Hall, and the anniversary at Baltimore in 1862 of the anti-Union riot of April, 1861, was a boost for the newly elected mayor and council which had become Unionist. When Jay Cooke urged people to buy bonds he did not hesitate to blend self-interest with patriotism as he stressed the advantages of tax-free seven per cents. Even the name "Union" applied to the Republican party in Civil War days was an example of this tendency. Among themselves Republican leaders understood each other perfectly and continued to refer to their party as Republican, while for public consumption it was called "Union." [47]

Much could be said of party propaganda, but this was not peculiar to war time; party agitation is always with us. That the national cause was appropriated for a party purpose was seen in the Union League. It is unnecessary to comment on the league at large, with its expensive club buildings, its social impressiveness, its exploitation of the American propensity for joining, its masses of war literature, and its showy efforts toward recruiting and soldier relief; but there is need for further study of the league's campaign activities, especially the procedures of its local chapters. The minute-book of a local league in the nineteenth ward of New York City belongs to the type of sources that are seldom dug up.[48] The minutes here recorded are generally quite sterile as they creep along with routine matters till the approach of election time. Indeed it was not until September 19, 1864, that the nineteenth-ward leaguers "heartily approved" the early June nomination of Abraham Lincoln and Andrew Johnson at Baltimore. It was in October and the first days of November, 1864, that this local league suddenly came alive, sending loyal newspapers to soldiers, passing sizzling anti-Democratic resolutions, publishing campaign documents, and appointing poll-watchers to swing into action at sunrise on the eighth of November. Just after the election the minutes report "no quorum," and from that time this patriotic organization sank back into utter inactivity.

---

[47] Published tickets often carried the name "Union" or "National Union" party, but a printed circular in Massachusetts urging the formation "of a Union Club . . . in every town" is headed: "Headquarters Republican State Committee . . . Boston, Sep. 26, 1864." Supporting Lincoln and Johnson, this circular said "We should be put in . . . correspondence with working Republicans of every town in the State." Andrew MSS. (Massachusetts Historical Society, Boston), XXVIII, no. 90.

[48] MS. (New York Public Library.)

Repeatedly there was the "no quorum" record; in February, 1865, it was voted to adopt measures to increase interest in the meetings. On April 3, 1865, the minutes flicker out altogether. Similar accounts with different terms, including the names of Tammany and the Knights of the Golden Circle, would illuminate the history of the Democratic party.

Official propaganda took many forms, including governmentally inspired foreign missions of prominent Americans. Thurlow Weed promoted the Union cause in the British press, Archbishop John Hughes sought contact with Catholics in Europe, Bishop McIlwaine of the Episcopal Church made his appeal to the British clergy. In addition, the irrepressible Robert J. Walker appealed to British financial groups in opposition to southern bond sales, while John M. Forbes and William H. Aspinwall labored to halt naval building for the Confederacy in Britain.

President Lincoln, who once owned a newspaper, by no means neglected publicity. Naturally he addressed the people in occasional speeches, in his two inaugurals, his proclamations, and his messages to Congress. Beyond this there was the use of patronage for newspapers, an obscure subject yet to be explored, and there was the case of J. W. Forney whose Philadelphia *Chronicle* and Washington *Chronicle* were known as Lincoln organs. In March, 1862, the President asked Henry J. Raymond for an article in the *Times*.[49] So much of the writing on Lincoln has been of the sentimentally stereotyped variety that people have overlooked Lincoln's trenchant comments on his own times, on wartime profits,[50] on corruption, and on the manner in which every "foul bird" and "every dirty reptile" came forth in war time.[51] It is safe to say that Lincoln saw the war more clearly and faced it more squarely than Emerson. He faced it with an amazing lack of hatred and rancor.

The Civil War generation, not alone military and political events, but life and *mores,* social conditions and thought-patterns that accompanied the war as well as non-war aspects of the age, will receive further attention by inquisitive historians. In Arthur C. Cole's pages in the Fox-Schlesinger series one finds many a cue for further investigation and many a product of mature study.[52] Beyond the boundaries of even the newer books lie disappearing and forgotten stories. Where the stories are recoverable the present age of historiography, as shown in Cole's book, is more capable of accomplishing the recovery than previous ages. History has its vogues and its movements. Just as Americans beginning about 1935 executed something like an about-face in their interpretation of the World War, including American participation in it and attitudes preceding it, so the retelling of the Civil War is a matter of changed and changing viewpoints.

[49] Nicolay and Hay, *Works,* II, 132.
[50] "The . . . question of profit controls all." *Ibid.,* 358.   [51] *Ibid.,* 420.
[52] Arthur C. Cole, *The Irrespressible Conflict, 1850–1865,* Arthur M. Schlesinger and Dixon R. Fox, *A History of American Life* (New York, 1934), VII.

In the present troubled age it may be of more than academic interest to reexamine the human beings of that war generation with less thought of the "splendor of battle flags" and with more of the sophisticated and unsentimental searchlight of reality.[53]

---

[53] The author wishes to give acknowledgment to his students in the Harvard summer session of 1939, especially to Paul Driscoll on the "last romance," to Elizabeth Mohr on peace, and to Frederick S. Allis Jr. on Emerson.

The American Civil War and the Problem of Inevitability

Pieter Geyl

"The quarrel which broke up the Union in 1860–1861 was about slavery. It had been gathering strength for a long time and at last erupted with elemental violence. The North and the South, divided by a moral issue of the first magnitude, the one detesting slavery, the other glorifying it as the basis of its social system, were unable to understand each other and the Civil War came as an inevitable result."

This is a fair summary of what was once the view taken by most American historians of the origins of the great crisis of the sixties. The picture was presented in different colorings: all sorts of admissions or reservations were made and complications introduced. Nevertheless, this is in the main the impression that one will gather from Rhodes and Woodrow Wilson, from Channing and Morison, from Lord Charnwood, from James Truslow Adams, and from countless others.

For some time now this interpretation has been subjected to attack. First, the proposition that the quarrel was about slavery came under fire. Charles and Mary Beard, true to their system of economic interpretation, transposed the whole matter from the moral sphere to the sphere of the struggle of interests, and placed in opposition, instead of slavery and liberty, agrarian economy and capitalism, free trade and protection. Their view has had a profound influence, and rightly so, for they emphasized phenomena which had not, indeed, been completely overlooked, but which had not received

---

From *Debates with Historians*, Vol. I, © Copyright 1958 by Meridian Books, Inc. Reprinted by permission of Meridian Books, Inc.

the attention which they deserve. It is only when they attempt to sub-stitute the economic factor for the moral issue that one feels bound to part company with them. One notices, on looking critically at their argument, that they glide over the awkward fact that at the moment of decision the most powerful capitalistic interests in the North were all for compromise. One reflects that the hysterical excitement and self-glorification of the South can hardly be understood as a reaction to a merely economic menace, especially not as the country happened to be doing so well in a material sense. This mood cannot be explained except as the reply to a moral indictment. The accusation of the Abolitionists was such a painful hit because in it there spoke the spirit of the times. Behind that little group of fanatics there stood the silent condemnation of the free North, of Europe, of the world. By clinging to its "peculiar institution" the South cut itself adrift from the modern development of Western civilization, isolated itself in an obstinate and wilful self-righteousness, and fell under the spell of its wildest, blindest, and most reactionary elements.

A good deal more could be said about the economic thesis of the Beards, but the point that I propose to deal with in this essay is the other one on which for some time now the critics of the traditional interpretation of the origins of the Civil War have concentrated their energies, that of the inevitability of the conflict. Here the Beards did not depart from the tradi-tion. To them the economic forces seemed to be as ineluctable as had the moral issue to their predecessors. Yet I think that their view, and the despiritualization of the whole episode which resulted from it, contributed to bring about the state of mind in which others soon proceeded to question the traditional presentation of an "irrespressible conflict."

I shall not try to trace the emergence of the rival view that the Civil War was a mistake, which could have been, and ought to have been, avoided. I came across this new interpretation years ago in a little book that I picked up in the shilling box of a shop in the Charing Cross Road in London, a somewhat irresponsible little book, but one which I found very illuminating, and which is indeed not only amusing but written with ability. It is *The Secession of the Southern States* (1933) by Gerald W. Johnson. I have never found it mentioned in any bibliography, but it has played a part in my education. "The fatalistic theory," Mr. Johnson writes, "grows more and more unsatisfactory to modern writers." And he goes on to quote from the well-known book by Dwight L. Dumond, *The Secession Movement* (1931): "That idea implies that the American people were incapable of solving a difficult problem except by bloodletting, and confuses the designs of party politicians with the art of statesmanship."

Many books have appeared since in which the period preceding the out-break of war is studied, and in several this line of argument has been pursued. Prominent among them is, of course, the work of Avery Craven; but for the sake of clearness I shall concentrate on the writings of J. G.

Randall, in which the thesis of the avoidability of the conflict forms a central theme. I shall deal mainly with the first two volumes of his *Lincoln the President* (1945), but shall also glance occasionally at his earlier work, *Civil War and Reconstruction* (1937), and at his volume of essays, *Lincoln the Liberal Statesman* (1947).

I admire the work of Professor Randall, and I am conscious of my own status as an amateur in the field where he is an acknowledged master. If I venture upon a discussion of his view, it is because I feel that his argument springs from a philosophy of history—or of life, for it comes to the same thing—against which I am tempted to pitch my own; and the more so as I have to do with a man who not only places a wealth of historical documentation fairly before his reader, but who presents his case with a vigorous and practised historical dialectic.

Randall detests the thesis of the irrepressible conflict and his work is a sustained attempt to refute it. He argues that we cannot do justice to the pre-war years if we will see them only in the light of the war *we* know was coming. There were expressions of antagonism no doubt, but if we compose our account of the period preceding 1860–1861 by simply combining those, we subject the past to a mere literary device. One should not read back from the fact of war to the supposition that war-making tendencies were the nation's chief preoccupation in the fifties. "In those years ship-owners were interested in the merchant marine, writers in literature, captains of industry in economic enterprise; if any class was concerned chiefly with factors of sectional antagonism it would seem to have been certain groups of politicians and agitators."

The warning that a period can be torn out of focus by interpreting it too resolutely with the help of the familiar outcome is one after my own heart, but that does not mean that criticism will have to disarm when looking at the actual practice.

No, Randall says elsewhere, there was no irreconcilable contrast between North and South. The very concept of two sections was an oversimplification. A further trick was played: the politicians and the agitators, in their pamphlets, their speeches, and their newspaper articles, pictured the two sections as hopelessly antagonistic. Yet there were influences making for peace; only, they attracted insufficient attention. Alarms tending toward war, on the other hand, whose appeal was not to reason, were loud and vociferous. Their menace was in a kind of emotional unbalance. Their language was that of name-calling, shibboleths, tirades. In that way normal life could be upset, and a conflict precipitated, that no majority in any section would have deliberately willed. "One of the most colossal of misconceptions is the theory that fundamental motives produce war. The glaring and obvious fact is the artificiality of war-making agitation."

There we have the thesis, and to establish it, Randall marshals his evidence with inexhaustible energy and ingenuity. His material consists largely

596

of incontrovertible facts. It is the great advantage of a mental attitude like his that it is perceptive of the rich diversity of life. Randall discerns an infinity of shadings where most historians had been content with clear-cut contrasts. He is himself very much aware of this. He refers repeatedly to his historical revisionism, although he prefers the terms "realism" or "historical restoration." This latter word strikingly reveals his faith in the attainability of objectivity. He does not seem to realize that it is not *the* Civil War that emerges as a result of his revisions, but that, in spite of the undoubted finality of some of his fact-finding, it is still *his* Civil War and *his* Lincoln. His judgments of persons and of actions—and he works with judgments as well as with facts—are governed by a definite attitude of mind, the same in fact as that from which springs his thesis itself. Even incontrovertible facts can be used for arguments which are not equally acceptable to all of us.

It can readily be conceded that in no part of the country did there exist at any moment before the actual crisis a majority for extreme solutions. Lincoln's two-fifths share of the poll of 1860 no doubt comprised a majority of the votes cast in the North, but Lincoln, for all that the South pictured him as the secret ally of the Abolitionists, consistently did what he could to reduce the conflict to the smallest proportions. Of the Northern electors who cast their votes for him, the large majority therefore never meant a pronouncement in favor of war, either to liberate the slaves or to establish an economic domination.

As regards the South, Breckinridge, the candidate of the extreme state-rights party, remained in a minority there compared with the aggregate of votes cast for his rivals. But Breckinridge himself was comparatively moderate: he never mentioned secession as did Yancey and Rhett. No more than the North, therefore, did the South pronounce in favor of secession in November, 1860. And when now suddenly, starting from South Carolina, the secession snowball was set rolling, it was because people saw in Lincoln's election a victory of the spirit of John Brown and because they attributed to the new President the most evil designs against the South—because, in other words, people labored under grievous misconceptions.[1] At the same time, moreover, the opinion was propagated that the North would stand by inactively when the slaveholding states seceded. As a matter of fact, some Abolitionists had on occasion shouted for a separation from the immoral South, and there were moderates, too, who were prepared to say, with the old commander of the Union army, Winfield Scott: "Wayward sisters, depart in peace!" Yet it was an idea completely

---

[1] That the same might be said about the Northern people is brought out very clearly by David M. Potter in his *Lincoln and his Party in the Secession Crisis* (1942). Lincoln and the Republicans generally never took the secession talk in the South seriously; they looked upon it as blackmail. Not until the very last moment, well after the election at any rate, did they realize that the war danger was an awful reality.

divorced from reality to think that the North would allow the Union to be broken up without resistance. The prospect had the immediate effect of causing the Northwest to feel itself one with the Northeast. It was an intolerable thought for those new regions that the lower course of the Mississippi, their main outlet to the outside world while the overland connections with the East were still defective, would come to be situated in foreign territory. But in the entire North, Union sentiment, quite apart from the feelings about slavery, was strong.

So it was fear, and at the same time it was illusion, that dominated men's minds in the South. But even so the secession had to be forced through in a manner which was denounced as dictatorial by its opponents. The convention of South Carolina refused to have its decision subjected to a referendum. Yet, once proclaimed, the secession immediately created ambitions and a loyalty of its own. Jefferson Davis, who had lately had leanings towards unionism and who had tried to put on the brakes at the last moment, nevertheless accepted the dignity of the presidency of the Confederation. Alexander Stephens, who had grumbled bitterly at the excitability of the crowd when in state after state the conventions were passing the secession resolutions (several against considerable minorities), let himself be elected Vice-President as soon as the issue was determined. In the slave states on the border, which were still sitting on the fence, feverishly discussing schemes of compromise and negotiating with Lincoln, it was only the shots fired on Fort Sumter which brought about the decision.

How different a picture can be constructed out of all these complications and divisions from that of the inevitable war arising out of a clear-cut contrast. One seems to discern all sorts of sidepaths and ways out to a very different future from that of these four terrible years of war, followed by that miserable episode of Reconstruction. And the impression is strengthened when one looks more closely at the North after the rupture and observes how weak were the foundations of Lincoln's position, in his own section, now that as War President he admitted no other aim than that of the restoration of the Union, that is to say of a continuation of the struggle down to the complete subjugation of the states in revolt. It is true that not all the criticism, not all the opposition which he had to endure, came from the moderates or the doubters. There were, too, the violent, the impatient. The Abolitionists now felt themselves carried along by the tide of events and urged and pushed Lincoln on. But the moderates and the doubters were a powerful party for all that. The accusation of the South, describing Lincoln as the despot trying by brute force of arms to do violence to free American states, found echoes in the Northern press and in the Congress at Washington. "Negotiate!"—was a loud clamour, not merely an underground murmur. After the early death in 1861 of Douglas, who had supported Lincoln's view, the entire Democratic party in the North adopted that cry, and in 1864, when the presidential election came along, it looked for some time as if its candidate would win. In that case the fate of a country would have been entrusted to the man whose tenderness for the interests of the slave-holders had been a difficulty when Lincoln in 1862 contemplated his Eman-cipation Decree, the commander who had been suspected of not really wanting to beat Lee.

But why go on piling up instances and particulars? I am quite ready to concede the point. The American people had suddenly found themselves in the Civil War and the majority in none of the sections had deliberately willed it. But what does this prove? Does it prove that the war might there-fore have been avoided? Is it not rather one more proof of the general truth that the course of history is not governed by the conscious will of the ma-jority? Jefferson Davis was a believer in this truth. Is 1864 two Northerners came across the lines under a white flag and laid a proposal before the Presi-dent of the Confederation—which had not, however, Lincoln's sanction. They suggested that a truce should be concluded in order to hold a refer-endum, and that both North and South should promise to abide by the result. But Jefferson Davis was not interested. "Neither current events nor history," he said, "show that the majority rules, or ever did rule. The con-trary I think is true."

And is not this indeed what we can read on every page of the book of history? Did the majority of the Netherlands people will the complete rup-ture with Philip II and with the Roman Church, the independence and the change of religion? Did they will these things in 1566, in 1572, in 1579, in 1581? There can be only one reply—even though we cannot for the six-teenth century as for the nineteenth rely on election statistics—: no. Did the majority of the English people will the overthrow of the monarchy and the execution of Charles I, in 1642, in 1649?—no. Did the French people will the Republic and the execution of Louis XVI? In 1789, in 1790, even in 1791, those who had ever thought of these developments as within the sphere of possibility must have been a tiny minority; but in 1792 and 1793 as well: no. Did the majority of the Belgian people in 1830 will the break-up of the union with Holland? Till the very last moment the leaders themselves spoke only of an administrative separation, but even when it happened—did they will it?—no. Did the majority of the German people in 1933 want Hitler, did they will war?—no. When the English people in 1939 took up the challenge of the Third Reich they already found them-selves in a position of compulsion. Or if one wants to look at it from a different angle, one can say that the bulk of them had no notion yet of what they were letting themselves in for, and at any rate in 1940, when their eyes were opened, the position of compulsion was there beyond a doubt. But who does not remember the storm of cheers that greeted Neville Chamberlain and Munich in 1938, and not only in England, but in Ger-many, in France, in a country like Holland? The large majority wanted peace. "The ship-owner thought of his ships, the writer of his books, the manufacturer of his machines." Here, there and everywhere peace was what men wanted, "and the war came." [2] The instinctive aversion of the mass of people is no evidence that it might have been avoided. It is possible to believe—note that I am not saying, one can prove—that there were forces at work, stronger than individual desires or fears, or than their sum as resulting from the ballot box, which made it inevitable. How striking in this connection is the example of recent American history. I need hardly recall the way in which the United States entered both the First and the Second World Wars. This is a controversial subject, but to me it seems that in the light of his own country's experiences, Randall's postulate of a strict majority democracy as a fixed standard of historical judgment comes to wear a somewhat ghostly look of unreality.

"Forces? Indeed!" Randall will say: "Name calling, shibboleths, epithets, tirades." An appeal, not to reason or to true interest, but to the emotions. And who will deny that sentiment, passion, extra-rational conviction, supply a fertile soil to the monster growths of misunderstanding and exaggeration, misrepresentation, hatred and recklessness! The question remains whether one is justified in labelling these extra-rational factors with contemptuous terms and deny to them, as Randall does, a rightful rôle in the drama of history, relegating them without further ado to the category of "artificial agitation," which can on no condition be reckoned among "fundamental causes."

Two histories might be written—so says the Count de la Gorce in his striking little book on Louis XVIII—about the Restoration. One would be the sober and serious history of the good services rendered by that régime to France from day to day and in an unsensational manner. The other one is the history of violent incidents, the execution of Ney, the expulsion of Manuel, et cetera, which, pictured in colorful prints, struck the popular imagination. And it is this second history which culminates in the revolution of 1830. You will notice here, in the writing of the French royalist, the same idea—merely indicated in passing however—, that the historian's rational criticism, working after the events, can detach from the total of what happened the emotions which brought about the catastrophe and that in the other sequence he will retain the real, the proper history. The suggestion is at least that this ought to have been the real history.

Now this idea is the basic idea of Randall's work. He constantly comes back to it. The Americans of the fifties both surprise and irritate him. An essay in which he recapitulates his grievances against them bears the title *A Blundering Generation*. How was it possible for these people to work up such excitement over trifles! All problems are distorted by them. Look how they made mountains out of molehills and exaggerated matters which seen

---

[2] To quote the words used by Lincoln in his Second Inaugural.

in their true size would never have stood in the way of a peaceful settlement.

Take the Kansas-Nebraska Bill, with which Douglas in 1854 set going so fateful a controversy. Randall is much concerned to exculpate Douglas. Douglas is a man after his heart: a practical man, a man who wanted to do business, and with Northerners and Southerners alike. Can one wonder if Douglas was astonished at the hubbub? Was it such a crime that by his principle of popular sovereignty he created the possibility of slavery in those territories situated so far North? The very fact of the situation of Kansas and Nebraska made it most improbable that slavery would ever take root there. The raving in the North about a mere theoretical possibility was therefore, according to Randall, lacking in all sense of reality; it was an example of the hollowness of all that vehement quarreling.

But now let us try to picture to ourselves the state of affairs. Shortly before, in 1850, the new Compromise had been reached, intended to put an end to the dangerous tension that had been growing up over the disposal of the newly acquired Western lands. The Compromise was worthless if it did not confine the extension of slavery within limits accepted by both sides. But here in effect the demarcation line of 1820, which had been looked upon as fixed, was wiped out, among loud cheers from the South. Moreover, what dominated the situation was Southern fears of the rapid increase in power of the North, and Northern suspicions that the South, to ward off that danger, was trying by all means to fasten its grip on the Federal Government. Must one not wilfully blindfold one's historical imagination in order to avoid seeing that the excitement was natural?

Besides, what happened? Had it been possible to apply the principle of popular sovereignty honestly, as doubtless Douglass had intended, then indeed neither Kansas nor Nebraska would have thought of introducing slavery. But the slaveholders from the neighboring slave states sent settlers with slaves to Kansas. A race developed between supporters of the two systems: a civil war in miniature. At last an unrepresentative, tumultuous, armed assembly passed a constitution with slavery and sent it to Washington. Douglas shrank from an approval which must have definitely alienated the North. In fact, the proceedings in Kansas were a mockery of his proudly proclaimed principle. His opposition to recognition roused much ill-feeling against him among the Democrats in the South, with whom he had all along wanted to strengthen the ties. Meanwhile "Bleeding Kansas" had become a new slogan to arouse the North. But, Randall reflects, why is it that "squatter sovereignty" came to be a source of confusion? "Not so much because of genuine conflict of local interests, but because a minority of trouble makers, aided by outside agitators, made turbulence rather than reasonable pacification their business." And that is probably a fair statement of the case. But it does not in the least affect the fact that, in the circumstances, and with the public temper prevailing in the United States at that moment, the principle introduced by Douglas could not but be a new occasion for quarrel over the old point at issue, and that his policy was therefore a capital mistake. Douglas had wanted to do business, but he had underestimated the inflammable state of public opinion concerning that great point which he had thought he could safely use for a bargain. "Morally blind" is the way Morison describes him.[3]

In 1858, on the occasion of a senatorial election, the famous debates between Lincoln and Douglas were held up and down Illinois. Lincoln kept on, indefatigably, directing his attacks to the questions of Kansas, popular sovereignty, slavery in the Western territories. To Randall's mind it is but a foolish business. There might have been sense in it if the speakers had at least discussed slavery in general, but Lincoln, as everybody knows, was as little prepared to interfere in the internal affairs of the Southern States as was his opponent. So the debates ran on slaves in those regions where there were hardly any and where there were not likely ever to be many slaves. Was this really the only subject on which to claim the attention, for weeks at a stretch, of the electors of Illinois and of the newspaper readers of the United States? Would not the time of the speakers have been better employed if they had dealt with problems like immigration, tariff, international policy, promotion of education?

This is indeed a striking instance of Randall's somewhat masterful attitude towards his personages. In effect, he tells the speakers of 1858 what subjects they ought to have treated. Is it not the historian's more obvious line simply to conclude from their choice, and from the enormous impression they made, that the country's mood was strained to the utmost by the Kansas-Nebraska complication?

And this was indeed a great question. It did bring along, in spite of what Randall says, a discussion of the slavery question itself. Some of Lincoln's gravest, most profoundly moving utterances about the Negro's fate were

---

[3] Allan Nevins entitles the chapter of his *Ordeal of the Union* in which he introduces the story of the Kansas-Nebraska Bill "Disaster: 1854." His account throughout differs radically from that of Randall. He quotes with approval the utterance of an Abolitionist, Quincy, who had characterized the situation as early as 1852 by the biblical phrase which Lincoln was to use six years later: A house divided against itself cannot stand. In 1852, so shortly after the Compromise of 1850, peace might seem safe enough. But Nevins judges that "the Compromise had laid over the erupting lava of 1849–50" only a thin crust (II, 79). "The slavery question was in fact irrepressible." Indeed, the account in this work of 1947 does not differ in essence from the traditional view which I briefly summarized at the outset of my argument. It is full with the fulness of life, it does not try to skip over the complications or to slur the multiple shadings of reality, but it places the moral issue of slavery in the very centre. Randall had been led by his aversion to, or misunderstanding of, the passions aroused by the measure to attempt the whitewashing of Douglas. Nevins is severe on the man who tore "open all the wounds of 1848–50," (121) and if he admits that "circumstances" may have had their share in the "disaster," he does not try to dispose of the reactions as merely due to agitators or politicians.

made in those speeches. Douglas attacked him over his phrase, "A house divided cannot stand," in which he professed to read an incitement to civil war. Lincoln replied that he had only drawn attention to an undeniable danger. The generation of the Founding Fathers had believed that slavery was dying a natural death, so it had not been hard then to practice mutual forbearance and to compromise. Now, on the contrary, the slave power was full of self-confidence, or even of imperialistic ardor. Was not the recent verdict of the Supreme Court in the case of Dred Scott startling evidence of this? The Supreme Court, under its judicial mask, had always been a political body and it was now, after nominations by a succession of Southern Presidents, dominated by the Southerners. The split of the churches, too, was touched upon. It is as if Lincoln is polemicising with Randall when he says that here at least it is impossible to suspect the hand of "the politicians" or "the agitators." Furthermore he commented on the restraints on freedom of speech in the South, and on the Southern desire that the North should keep silent on slavery. But even silence was not enough. What they really wanted was express approval and admiration. The survival of democracy itself seemed concerned with the resistance to Southern arrogance; that is a point to which Lincoln frequently recurs. Does Randall in earnest want us to believe that the attention of Lincoln's audience was thrown away on questions like these?

Even the Fugitive Slave Law is, according to Randall, all things considered, but a small matter. And, indeed, one can say: were a few hundred fugitive slaves worth the risk of getting enmeshed in a destructive civil war? Answer: neither for the slave-holders, nor for the Northerners, who had to look on, on very rare occasions and in very few localities, when one was seized and forcibly carried back. Lincoln himself said that we must not act upon all our moral or theoretical preferences. "Ungodly," he exclaimed sadly, when once he came into contact with a case; "but it is the law of the land!" One can accept a personality in which were united deep moral feeling with caution, a sense of responsibility, and a capacity for weighing for and against in the scales of reason. But is it not just as understandable that a crowd assembled when a captured fugitive in Boston was taken to the harbor and that a battalion of soldiers and a war vessel had to be commandeered to see that the law was executed? The Southerners clung to the law because they desired to have from the North an acknowledgment of their right rather than because of the material advantage. A moral revulsion in the North[4] soon made the execution impracticable, and this in its turn created bad blood in the South. Seen in this way—and it seems a truer way than the merely statistical one—, this was a considerable matter. It carried grist to the mills of the Abolitionists.

But Randall thinks himself entitled to brush aside the whole of that

---

[4] Nevins connects this immediately with the Kansas-Nebraska Bill.

group as fundamentally insignificant—and here the Beards had set the example. Like the Beards he always points to their small numbers and to the fact that their extreme position excludes them from practical politics. Their only significance, and a baleful one, he sees in the exaggerated importance attached in the South to their periodicals and speeches. Misunderstanding once again. Later, when the war results in making them more influential and they finally help to decide the course taken by the North, he lays all stress on the disastrous effects of their intervention. Here again Randall is representative of a current in modern thought on these questions. The narrowness and cultivation of hatred of the puritan idealists during the Reconstruction period have given them a bad press with contemporary American historians. Nothing is more readily understandable. But should that lead us to overlook the dynamic strength which their ideas, in spite of their isolated position, showed in the prewar years?

Not more than a generation before the Civil War, slavery was accepted in the North itself and the black man was despised. There the first struggle had to be waged. In those years the tendency in the North was to reassure the South on the great question, to meet it more than half way. The first Abolitionists, Lovejoy and Birney, had to endure violent persecution in their own North. It was in those days that Tocqueville wrote his *Démocratie en Amérique,* in which he shows so much concern about majority tyranny. Not without due cause, yet he seems now to have been lacking in a perception of the moral forces which defied that trend, often at the risk of being thrown into a river or hanged on a tree. There was something heroic about that struggle of a few men of conviction against their entire environment. Their ultimate success[5] shows that it is not sufficient to count noses. It shows the incalculable influence which may be exerted by an idea, by conscience, by individual moral strength, by passion in the service of an ethical cause. It shows, too, that America formed a part of the great Western civilization which no longer tolerated slavery. The tremendous disturbance caused in American society by the question acquires a deeper meaning when this is clearly understood.

The spectacle of the dour fight put up by that small group of men, and even of the next generation who prepared for and lived through the Civil War, of Garrison, Wendell Phillips, Sumner, has a quality of greatness. I

---

[5] Although this success stands in need of qualification. Even when the tide seemed to be running with the Abolitionists, there was in the North more fervor for abolition of slavery in the abstract than willingness to accept the Negro as a citizen on an equal footing. Indeed the Free Soil agitation in the West was largely due to fear of the black man's low wage competition, and the lot of the free Negro was in most of the Northern states far from being a happy one. The Southerners were not entirely without justification when they railed at the element of hypocrisy in the attitude of their Northern critics, who moreover seemed to be forgetting the wretched conditions under which their own white factory workers had to labor. (A. Nevins, I, 518 ff.) The anti-Negro outbreak in New York at the height of the Civil War shows that actual contact between the races could still rouse ugly feelings in the North.

find encouragement in it. I know all about the unattractive characteristics of these men; the newer American books do not spare them.[6] I do not myself belong to their type and I have a keen perception, therefore, of the dangers which are inherent in it. Those heroes of the human conscience, who stand firm against the majority, and before whom the majority sometimes suddenly collapses, do not know half-measures. To expect of them that they should combine the championship of their idea with any conception of the relative advantages of what they attack, or only with a recognition of the innocence of those who defend the old order as their rightful heritage; to expect that they should be alive to the disastrous consequences of a sudden upheaval;—one may as well expect that the tiger will make his meal of grass.

Lincoln—yes. In Lincoln's case there is that rare combination of courage to stand alone with moderation; of detestation of the evil with understanding for the difficulties of the human agent or of the society in which the evil flourishes. But Lincoln was not an Abolitionist. He loathed slavery, but in abolitionism he perceived the defiance of the South and unconstitutionality. I admire that mentality and that temperament, but I wonder if with that alone, the spiritual revolution in the North, and the abolition of slavery in the South, could have been achieved. A foolish question, I admit, for how can abolitionism, even in the imagination, be eliminated from the situation?

Lincoln's relationship to the Abolitionists reminds a Dutch historian of that between William the Silent and the Calvinists. The Calvinists caused a great deal of trouble to William the Silent, and their activities had at times disastrous consequences. But how could anyone write a history of the revolt of the Netherlands, who saw in them nothing but eccentric enthusiasts, a minority, who did nothing but keep on foot an artificial agitation? One has to begin by accepting their conviction as a profound historic reality and their dynamic strength as an element in the situation, from which it cannot be eliminated even in the imagination. William the Silent, the master of expedients and of compromises, regarded them at first with disapproval and aversion. But when once the crisis had fairly set in, he could not do without their alliance. In fact, he was himself animated by so profound a sentiment that he was able to understand these men, and at times they were able to understand him. Nevertheless, he had every now and again to restrain them, mostly without result, and they paid him back with impatience, even with enmity. It was not until he was dead that his figure could

---

[6] Nevins discriminates admirably between those amongst them who while attacking the institution of slavery refrained from reviling the slave-holders and the bitter spirits, so wrapped up in their feeling of rectitude or warped by their detestation of the black man's wrong, that they seemed to take a pleasure in antagonizing Southern opinion. It was especially Garrison and Sumner who did a great deal of harm in that way, although again they were very dissimilar and Sumner at one time disapproved of Garrison's extremism. *Ordeal of the Union*, I, 144, 146; II, 438.

be harmoniously integrated into the Calvinistic legend, so that in 1618 the forceful action of Maurice could be undertaken under the auspices of the murdered martyr's name.

All this can be applied to Lincoln and the Abolitionists. As long as there was a chance of a peaceable solution, which he pursued without sacrificing his detestation of slavery, he kept them at arm's length. When war had once broken out, he could not possibly do without them any more, but even now he resisted their attempts to get hold of him, to push and to pester him beyond his purpose. So he never became the man after their hearts. The more violent spoke of the President with impatience, with scorn and contumely, with contempt and hatred. They worked against him, they tried to encompass his downfall. But once he was murdered, immediately after the conclusion of the great struggle, and at the moment when his moderation, self-restraint, and capacity for seeing both sides, might have proved a blessing in the work of healing and reconciliation, then the Abolitionists, even those who had been blind to his greatness, began glorifying Lincoln as a martyr. Yet in the same breath they advocated and forced through a policy of hatred and of revenge, of humiliation and destruction of the vanquished South, a policy which was in the most flagrant contradiction of his spirit.

Many years previously, Lincoln—who was then a member of the Legislature of Illinois—had cast a look of concern on the turbulent conditions in what was in many ways still a primitive pioneer community. "Reason," he said, "unimpassioned reason, must furnish all the materials for our future support and defence." A most characteristic utterance, and a noble utterance. As a directive for political action in a democratic community I know no proposition that is more worthy of being followed. But as a historian I know, too, that in its absolute form it lays down a rule which is beyond the capacity of man. Lincoln's own career furnishes striking proof that the fate of mankind is not from first to last governed by reason. Kindhearted as Lincoln was, lover of a rule of law, given to consultation and give and take, he had to school himself for the task of leadership in a civil war of unheard-of ferocity. And being a man of full human capacity, he did not fail to draw the lesson.

In his Second Inaugural he reminded his hearers of the circumstances in which, four years earlier, he had spoken as President for the first time. Then all thoughts were anxiously directed to an impending civil war. Both parties deprecated war, but, said Lincoln, the South tried to break the Union without war, while he himself had tried to save it without war. *"And the war came."* A peculiar and powerful interest had grown up in the South around slavery, an interest which strove after expansion. "All knew that this interest was, somehow, the cause of the war."—"Neither party expected for the war the magnitude or the duration which it has already attained. . . . Each looked for an easier triumph, and a result less fundamental and astounding." "The Almighty has his own purposes."

It is in this speech that Lincoln, a month before he was assassinated, announced his intentions with respect to the vanquished: "With malice toward none, with charity for all"—this is still the best-remembered part. But the leading idea, expressed in religious terms, is that events had taken their course independently of human control. To me this humility in the face of the mighty happenings seems to be a truer proof of wisdom than Randall's rationalism. The conception in which it is founded may have its tragic implications; it has not, to anyone who accepts life in its entirety, anything depressing. What seems depressing is rather that attempt to show, over and over again, that those people could have been spared all their misfortunes, if they had only been sensible. For do we not know at long last that man is not a sensible being? Moreover, the wisdom which Randall preaches to his fellow countrymen of three generations ago does not strike me as very convincing. Compromise; and when the seemingly final concessions have been made, for heaven's sake make short work of the remaining scruples. The denial of contrasts which do not appear to have to do with the interest of the majority. The ignoring of moral facts. And, in short, crying peace where there is no peace. Could the conflict have been—I do not say postponed, but —solved in that way? One can easily imagine that out of a new Compromise, fabricated in 1861, after those of 1820 and 1850, in those feverish peace talks at Washington, a new crisis would soon have sprung, and, who knows, an even worse war.

There is one solution which, if one holds the bloodshed and the distress of the war to be worse than anything, could perhaps be more easily tried out in the imagination—I mean that of a peaceable separation. But it seems as if for American writers the overriding importance of the maintenance of the Union allows of no discussion. Even Randall, argumentative as he is, and filled with loathing for the war, assumes that paramount necessity implicitly as an underlying axiom. It would throw this essay out of proportion if I tried, at the last moment, to deal thoroughly with that question, but I will not omit touching upon it. It is difficult for a European to suppress the reflection that the difference in civilization between the North and the South might have supplied a basis on which to establish two separate political entities, and that perhaps in that way a more natural and a more harmonious development would have been possible, without the ill feelings resulting from friction in too close a contact, and without the subjection of the weaker party which followed in actual fact.[7]

Union sentiment was no doubt strong in the North and once the conflict had broken out it created the sense of sacred obligation. Lincoln felt from the first that an appeal to this principle would have a rallying effect on Northern opinion, and it might even make an impression in the South, while the abolitionist cry as a war aim would divide. The Dutch historian

---

[7] Nevins ends his second volume with a chapter entitled "Contrast of Cultures."

cannot help thinking of William the Silent, who for identical reasons kept *haec religionis causa* in the background and insisted on *haec libertatis causa*. For naturally the proposition that the revolt was undertaken for the sake of the Protestant religion must have a chilling effect on the Catholic majority. It was ever his contention, therefore, that the fight was being waged for the sake of liberty, for political reasons, in other words. In Calvinistic ears this almost sounded as sacrilege, just as Lincoln's emphasis on the Union motif roused the scorn of the Abolitionists. But Lincoln was not, of course, in speaking as he did, guided by tactical considerations alone. His heart was set on the Union. The thought uppermost in his mind was the failure and loss of prestige of the democratic idea everywhere that must follow upon the disruption of the one big democratic republic which then existed. That is indeed a great thought, and one is almost tempted to believe that it was inspired by a prophetic vision of our own times. The world rôle played by the United States today, and the rôle which no doubt it will be called upon to play in the future, would be impossible if the split of the sixties had not been averted. Lincoln was not the only one whose mind ran on these lines. The German-American Schurz and the French-American Laboulaye both said that the Union must be preserved and must be strong in order to uphold the cause of democracy in the world. On the other hand, the conservatives in Europe hoped for the disruption, because a united American continent would in the long run mean a power which they feared would make itself a universal nuisance.[8] But if one asks, is the part in world affairs played by the United States today worth the sacrifices made by the generation of the Civil War; does it justify the subjection and permanent effacement of the South?—it is impossible to give an answer based on reason alone. Randall, therefore, convinced that he is proceeding critically and realistically all the time, constructs his argument from the bottom upward on a faith.

For the men of the sixties this too was a problem. A realization of that fact will intensify the feeling that the vision of "a blundering generation"

---

[8] The fear is not so surprising when one remembers the overbearing tone and spirit as well as the actual violence which had of late years characterized American foreign policy. When conservative Europeans wished that the Civil War might lead to a permanent break-up of the Union (striking utterances are for instance to be found in a leading article of the London *Dispatch,* quoted by Sandburg, *Abraham Lincoln, The War Years,* II, 68, or in *Aus dem Leben Th. von Bernhardis,* VI, 194), this does not necessarily denote sympathy with slavery or with an aristocratic slave-holding class. Gladstone's well-known utterance about Jefferson Davis having succeeded in creating a nation proceeded from a different line of thought altogether. I am inclined to regard it as meaning exactly what it said and as evidence of Gladstone's keen interest in national movements, however mistaken the application may have been in this case. See Paul, *A History of Modern England,* II, 340. When the Beards interpolate in connection with Gladstone's indiscretion the remark that his "family fortune contained profits from the slave trade," they only reveal the dangers inherent in a preconceived opinion that everything must be explained by economic factors or motives of self-interest.

does not do justice to the past. That vision belittles what had real greatness; it ignores the tragedy of that struggle with an overwhelming moral problem, slavery. For this was the struggle in which that generation engaged, after its fashion, that is to say after a human fashion. The problem was never posed in absolute purity, and it could not be so posed. The Southerners knew the practical difficulties of abolition; the Northerners had no constitutional right of interference. Union and state rights, and the whole concept of unity or of national diversity, were inextricably mixed up with the problem, and so were material interests on both sides. It is impossible, therefore, to say that in that painful crisis the South was wholly wrong and the North wholly right. This, too, Lincoln knew. In his Second Inaugural he represented the war as just retribution for the evil of slavery, but North and South shared the punishment, because the offence had come by both.

The two main points on which the conventional conceptions of the origins of the war have of recent times been criticized, as I said at the outset, are that of slavery as the central issue, and that of the inevitability of the conflict. As regards the first, I have clearly enough expressed my opinion that neither with the one-sided attention to economic aspects of the Beards nor with Randall's determination to reduce everything to exclusively practical and reasonable terms can the importance of the moral problem be done justice.

As regards the second, I want to guard myself against a possible misunderstanding. I have not been arguing that the war was inevitable, not even—for that is what the discussion is mostly about—in the ten years preceding the outbreak. I have been arguing that Randall's argument in favor of the opposite contention is unconvincing. The question of evitable or inevitable is one on which, it seems to me, the historian can never form any but an ambivalent opinion. He will now stress other possibilities, then again speak in terms of a coherent sequence of causes and effects. But if he is wise, he will in both cases remain conscious that he has not been able to establish a definite equilibrium between the factors, dissimilar and recalcitrant to exact valuation as they are, by which every crisis situation is dominated.

And here I return to a point on which I find it possible to speak more positively. Randall's way of distinguishing between fundamental and artificial causes seems to me inadmissible. With his impressive scholarship and keen intelligence, schooled in historical dialectic, he counts among artificial causes everything that does not agree with the wishes of the majority or with its true interests, defined by himself in accordance with the best rational standards. But in the sequence of cause and effect, of which the human mind will never have complete command, the category of the *imponderabilia,* passion and emotion, conviction, prejudice, misunderstanding, have their organic function. No doubt it is this very fact which makes that command unattainable for us, but we are not therefore entitled to ignore those non-rational factors or to argue them away with the help of wisdom after the event.

309

33760